P9-DTR-154

Reviewer Acclaim for *Debugging Applications for Microsoft .NET and Microsoft Windows*

"If you became a Bugslayer with John Robbins's *Debugging Applications*, you'll become a managed and native BugslayerEx with *Debugging Applications for Microsoft .NET and Microsoft Windows*."

Christophe Nasarre, Development Manager, Business Objects

"Although .NET does take care of some of the bugs we used to experience in Win32, you still have to debug. John's book taught me many things I didn't know about .NET and debugging. When I get stuck, John's the person I call."

Jeffrey Richter, Cofounder, Wintellect

"*Debugging Applications for Microsoft .NET and Microsoft Windows* is a fantastic book for developers writing software for Windows or .NET. Tracking down bugs can be time-consuming and expensive. Robbins gives countless tips and tools to make this process more efficient, not to mention more fun. He attacks debugging from several angles, including writing code that's easy to debug, learning which tools to use and how to use their hidden features, understanding what's going on inside a debugger, and creating cool Visual Studio extensions."

Brian Morearty, Staff Software Engineer and Code Champion, QuickBooks, Intuit

"One of the hallmarks of a great developer is the willingness to admit that there is always more to learn. Whatever your level of experience, from rank beginner to debugging guru, John's book has something to teach you."

Barry Tannenbaum, BoundsChecker Technical Lead, Compuware NuMega Lab

"The single quality that best separates the experienced developer from the novice is effective debugging. The first edition of this book captured that debugging experience and codified it; this version adds to that and includes debugging tips and tricks for managed code. Using the arsenal of tools introduced in this book along with John's simple debugging steps, developers can attack even the toughest bugs."

Joe Abbott, Software Design Engineer Lead, Developer Division Build and Release Team, Microsoft

"John has gathered together a truly wonderful collection of debugging knowledge within these pages. Whereas many books end their discussions with practices of avoidance and some amount of tracking methodology, John's book covers those items and continues on to discuss available tools as well as APIs that are poorly documented elsewhere. Add to that information the utility of having example code for the key items, and this book is a true gold mine that no .NET or Win32 programmer should be without."

Kelly Brock, Electronic Arts

"In his second book, John Robbins has surpassed the bar he set himself with *Debugging Applications*. If you want to transfer years of .NET or Win32 development experience to your work without putting in all the years, this book is for you. Even though some of the subjects are deep and complex, John Robbins transfers the knowledge so easily that it is amazing. In my opinion, this book sets the quality bar for all other development books. After 19 years of developing Windows software, if I were restricted to a single book on my bookshelf, this would be it."

Osiris Pedroso, Optimizer Consulting

"Visual Studio .NET is already a great development tool, and at first it appeared to me that everything that I would need was already there. However, John Robbins yet again came up with a book that explains things I didn't even know I needed to know! Thanks again, John, for a great resource that .NET developers can turn to!"

Peter Ierardi, Software Evolutions

"This is the most enjoyable, intense, detailed, real-world book that you will find to teach you the secrets of Windows debugging, written by a practicing veteran who has seen it all. Read this book to learn how to prevent and solve the hardest bugs. This book is simply humankind's best hope for higher quality software."

Spencer Low, Developer, Microsoft SQL Server Division

"If you've ever had a project miss its date due to bugs, John's book is a must! Not only does John teach you how to find those nasty bugs in your released code, he teaches you about tools and methodologies that will help you avoid introducing bugs into your code base in the first place."

James Naftel, Product Manager, XcelleNet

Microsoft®

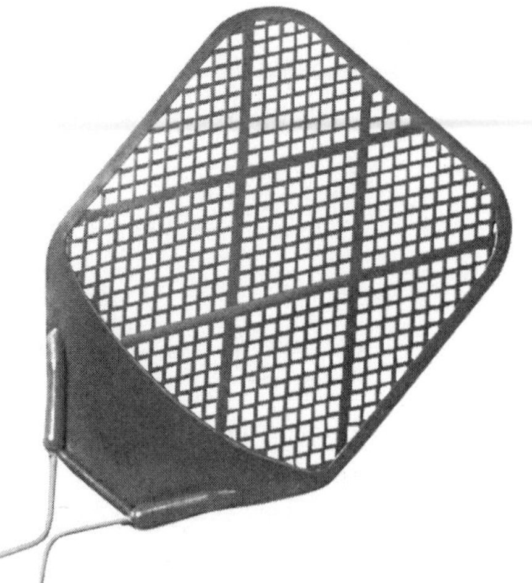

DEBUGGING APPLICATIONS

FOR MICROSOFT® .NET AND MICROSOFT WINDOWS®

John Robbins

Wintellect®
Know how.

Microsoft® .net™

PUBLISHED BY
Microsoft Press
A Division of Microsoft Corporation
One Microsoft Way
Redmond, Washington 98052-6399

Library of Congress Cataloging-in-Publication Data
Robbins, John, 1964-
Debugging Applications for Microsoft .NET and Microsoft Windows / John Robbins.--2nd ed.
p. cm.
Includes index.
Rev. ed. of Debugging Applications, c2000.
ISBN 0-7356-1536-5
1. Application software--Development. 2. Debugging in computer science. 3. Microsoft .NET. 4. Microsoft Windows (Computer file) I. Robbins, John, 1964- Debugging applications. II. Title.

QA76.76.A65R598 2003
005.4'469--dc21 2002045522

Printed and bound in the United States of America.

1 2 3 4 5 6 7 8 9 QWT 8 7 6 5 4 3

Distributed in Canada by H.B. Fenn and Company Ltd.

A CIP catalogue record for this book is available from the British Library.

Microsoft Press books are available through booksellers and distributors worldwide. For further information about international editions, contact your local Microsoft Corporation office or contact Microsoft Press International directly at fax (425) 936-7329. Visit our Web site at www.microsoft.com/mspress. Send comments to *mspinput@microsoft.com.*

Acquisitions Editor: Anne Hamilton
Project Editor: Sally Stickney
Technical Editor: Robert Lyon

Body Part No. X08-68737

To my wife, Pam.
Did I tell you how proud I am of you yet today?

In memory of Helen Robbins.
You always made the reunions the place to be. We miss you terribly.

Contents at a Glance

Table of Contents

List of Sidebars

Common Debugging Question

Debugging War Story

Acknowledgments

If you read the first edition of this book or any of my "Bugslayer" columns, or if you heard me speak at a conference or in a class, I can't thank you enough! Your interest in debugging and writing better code is what kept me slogging through the tough times of writing this second edition. I greatly appreciate the e-mail exchanges and discussions we've had. You've taught me a great deal. Thank you.

Five extraordinary people have made this book happen, and I can't sing their praises enough: Sally Stickney (project editor, twice in a row!), Robert Lyon (technical editor), Jean Ross (technical editor), Victoria Thulman (copy editor), and Rob Nance (artist). They took my incoherent ramblings and ugly drawings and made them into the book you have in your hands. The effort they put in was simply tremendous, and there's no way I can ever thank them enough.

As with the first edition, a great group of folks have my eternal gratitude—my "Review Crew." These hearty souls put up with my rough drafts and suggested many absolutely amazing debugging tricks. They represent the best in the business today, and I am humbled by the time they took to help. Here's the lineup: Joe Abbott (Microsoft), Scott Bilas (Gas Powered Games), Kelly Brock (Electronic Arts), Peter Ierardi (Software Evolutions), Spencer Low (Microsoft), Brian Morearty (Intuit), James Naftel (XcelleNet), Christophe Nassarre (Business Objects), Osiris Pedroso (Optimizer Consulting), Andy Pennell (Microsoft), Jeffrey Richter (Wintellect), and Barry Tannenbaum (Compuware). A special thanks to Christophe Nasarre for going way above the call of duty when reviewing!

I am also deeply humbled to be associated with my fellow Wintellectuals who contributed to this book in innumerable ways: Jim Bail, Francesco Balena, Roger Boissonneau, Jason Clark, Paula Daniels, Peter DeBetta, Dino Esposito, Gary Evinson, Dan Fergus, Lewis Frazer, John Lam, Berni McCoy, Jeff Prosise, Brent Rector, Jeffrey Richter, Kenn Scribner, and Chris Shelby.

Finally, the biggest thank you of all goes, as usual, to my wife, Pam. She sacrificed a lot of evenings and weekends while I was working on this book. Even when I was extremely frustrated, she still believed in it and got my spirits back in shape so that I could keep on. Honey, it's done. You can have your husband back.

Introduction

Bugs suck. Period. Bugs are the reason you're subjected to death-march projects with missed deadlines, late nights, and grouchy coworkers. Bugs can truly make your life miserable because if enough of them creep into your software, customers might stop using your product, and you could lose your job. Bugs are serious business.

Many times, people in our industry portray bugs simply as annoyances. Nothing could be further from the truth. All engineers can point to projects with runaway bug counts and even to companies that have folded because they released software so full of bugs that the product was unusable. As I was writing the first edition of this book, NASA lost a Mars space probe because of a bug that snuck in during the requirements and design phase. While I was writing this edition, a bomb was dropped on American Special Forces soldiers instead of the intended target because batteries were changed in GPS software, causing a programming error. With computers controlling more and more mission-critical systems, medical devices, and super expensive hardware, bugs can no longer be laughed at or viewed as something that just happens as a part of development.

My hope is that the information in this book will help you learn how to write your applications with fewer bugs in the first place—and that when you're required to debug, you can do it much faster. Without realizing it, most teams spend an average of 50 percent of their development cycle debugging. If you start debugging properly, you can drastically reduce that amount of time, which means you'll ship your products faster. You can't cut corners when it comes to requirements gathering and design, but you can certainly learn to debug much smarter. This book takes a holistic approach to debugging. I don't consider debugging as a separate step but as an integral part of the entire product cycle. I believe you need to start debugging in the requirements phase and continue through to the final release to manufacturing.

Two issues make debugging in the Microsoft .NET and Microsoft Windows environment difficult and time-consuming. The first issue is that debugging has always been a self-taught skill—you've basically been on your own to figure it out. Even if you have a computer science degree, I'm willing to bet that you never took a single college class dedicated to debugging. Other than some esoteric subjects, such as devising automatic program verification for languages that no one uses or developing debuggers for wildly optimistic, massively parallel-processing computers, the science of debugging as it applies to commercial software doesn't seem to be popular with the educational establishment. Some professors point out that you shouldn't be writing code with bugs in the first place. Although that's an excellent point and an ideal we should all strive for, reality is a little different. Learning systematic, proven techniques for debugging won't save you from ever writing another bug, but following the practices in this book will help you to limit the number of bugs you add to your code and to track down more quickly those inadvertent bugs that do occur.

The second issue is that though many excellent books on specific .NET and Windows technologies are available, none of them cover debugging those technologies in enough depth to be useful. To debug any technology effectively, you have to know far more than a book focused on a specific technology provides. It's one thing to know how to write an ASP.NET control that plugs into your ASP.NET page, but it's another thing entirely to be able to debug that ASP.NET control. To debug that ASP.NET control, you'll have to know the ins and outs of .NET and ASP.NET, how DLLs get put in the ASP.NET cache, and how ASP.NET goes about finding those controls in the first place. Some books make it look easy to implement sophisticated features, such as remote database connections, by using the hot technology du jour, but when "db.Connect ("Foo")" fails in your program—and it eventually will—you're on your own to find and mend the broken link in the technology chain. Moreover, although a few books on project management do discuss debugging, they tend to focus on managerial and administrative issues rather than on developers' concerns. Those books might include fine information about how to plan for debugging, but they don't help much when you're staring at a corrupted database or a crash returning from a callback function.

The idea for this book came out of my trials and tribulations as a developer and manager trying to ship high-quality products on time and as a consultant trying to help others ship on time. Over the years, I've learned skills and techniques that I use to deal with each of the two issues that help make developing Windows-based applications a challenge. To address the first issue, the lack of formal debugging training, I wrote the first part of this book to give you a crash course in debugging—with a decided slant toward commercial development. As for the second issue, the need for a book specifically on debugging .NET as well as the native Windows environment, I think I've provided a book that bridges the gap between specific technologies and nitty-gritty, real-world debugging techniques.

I've been extremely fortunate to have had the opportunity to focus on debugging almost exclusively for the last eight years. A few experiences have helped shape my unique perspective on the subject of debugging. The first experience was at NuMega Technologies (now Compuware), where I was one of the first engineers working on cool projects such as BoundsChecker, TrueTime, TrueCoverage, and SoftICE. While working at NuMega, I started writing the "Bugslayer" column in *MSDN Magazine*, and then I eventually left to write the first edition of this book. The fantastic e-mail exchanges and interaction I've had with engineers developing every type of application imaginable teaches me even more about the issues that engineers face today when shipping products.

Finally, the most important experience of all in shaping my view has been forming Wintellect, which gives me the chance to go out and help solve those amazing problems for companies all over the world. Imagine that you're sitting in some office at 2 a.m., you're out of ideas, and the client's going to go out of business if you don't solve the bug—this scenario can be scary, but it also gets your adrenaline flowing. Working with the best engineers at such companies as Microsoft, eBay, Intuit, and many others is the best way I know to learn all sorts of great tricks and techniques for solving bugs.

Who Should Read This Book?

I wrote this book for developers who are tired of spending late nights at work debugging and want to improve the quality of their code and their organizations. I also wrote this book for managers and team leaders who want to develop more efficient and effective teams.

From a technical perspective, the "ideal reader" is someone who has one to three years of experience developing on the .NET or Windows platform. I also expect the reader to have been a member of a real-world development team and to have shipped at least one product. Although I don't care for the term, the software industry labels developers with this level of experience "intermediate developers."

Advanced developers will probably learn a great deal as well. Many of the most enthusiastic e-mail messages I received about the first edition were from advanced developers who didn't expect to learn anything. I was thrilled that the book was able to give them tools they could add to their toolboxes. Again, as in the first edition, a wonderful group of friends named the "Review Crew" reviewed and critiqued the chapters before I submitted them to Microsoft Press. These engineers, who are listed in the Acknowledgments section of this book, are the crème de la crème of developers, and they made sure that everyone reading the book would learn something.

How to Read This Book and What's New in the Second Edition

The first edition focused on Microsoft Visual Studio 6 and Microsoft Win32 debugging. As we now have a brand new development environment, Microsoft Visual Studio .NET 2003, and a whole new programming paradigm, .NET, there's quite a bit more to cover. In fact, the first edition was 512 pages and this edition is around 850 pages, so you can see that the information I need to cover has grown considerably. As several of the reviewers commented: "I don't know why you're calling this a second edition because this is a whole new book!" To give you another idea of how much larger the second edition is, the first edition had 2.5 MB of text source code. This edition has 6.9 MB! Remember, that's just *text* and supporting files, not compiled binaries (compiling everything adds up to over 1 GB). What's even more astounding is that I didn't even include two chapters from the first edition in the second edition. As you can see, this is a whole new book.

I divided the book into four distinct parts. You should read the first two parts (Chapters 1 through 8) in order because I build the information in a logical progression.

In the first part of the book, "The Gestalt of Debugging" (Chapters 1 through 3), I define the different types of bugs and develop a process for debugging that all great developers follow. As requested by readers of the first edition, I expanded and deepened the discussion. I also discuss the infrastructure requirements necessary for proper team debugging. I strongly suggest you pay particular attention to the discussion on setting up symbol servers in Chapter 2. Finally, because you can (and should) do a tremendous amount of debugging during the coding phase, I cover how you can proactively debug as you're writing your code. The discussion on assertions in Chapter 3 should be the final word on the subject for both .NET and Win32.

In the second part of the book, "Power Debugging" (Chapters 4 through 8), I start with an explanation of operating-system debugging support and how Win32 debuggers work, because Win32 debugging has more magic going on behind the scenes than .NET. The more you understand your tools, the better able you are to use them. I also cover the Visual Studio .NET debugger in considerable depth so that you can learn to maximize its usage for both .NET and Win32. One thing I learned while working with developers from across the industry—from the inexperienced to the very experienced—was that they were using only a tiny fraction of the power of the Visual Studio .NET debugger. Although this sentiment might sound odd coming from an author of a book about debugging, I want to keep you out of the debugger as much as possible. As you read this book, you'll see that much of my goal for you isn't just to learn how to fix bugs and crashes but how to avoid them in the first place. I also want to teach you to use the debuggers to their maximum effectiveness because there will be times when you're forced to use them.

In the third part of the book, "Power Tools and Techniques for .NET" (Chapters 9 through 11), I offer up some excellent utilities for .NET development. Chapter 9 covers the outstanding extensibility mode offered with Visual Studio .NET. In that chapter, I build several great macros and add-ins that will help you speed up your development no matter whether you're working in .NET or Win32 exclusively. Chapter 10 and Chapter 11 cover the exciting .NET Profiling API and build two tools that will easily help you track exceptions and the flow through your .NET applications.

In the final part of the book, "Power Tools and Techniques for Native Code" (Chapters 12 through 19), offers solutions to common debugging problems you'll encounter when writing Windows-based applications. I cover topics ranging from finding the source file and line number with just a crash address to how to properly handle crashes in your application so that you can get the most information possible. Although Chapters 15 through 18 appeared in the first edition, I significantly updated the chapter text and completely rewrote some of the utilities (DeadlockDetection, Tester, and MemDumperValidator). Also, tools such as Tester work perfectly well with both native as well as .NET code. Finally, I added two new Windows debugging tools, FastTrace (Chapter 18) and Smooth Working Set (Chapter 19).

The final part of the book, "Appendixes" (Appendix A and Appendix B), provides additional information you'll find useful in your debugging adventures. In Appendix A, I explain how to read and interpret a Dr. Watson log. In Appendix B, you'll find annotated lists of resources—books, tools, and Web sites—that have helped me hone my skills as a developer/debugger.

In the first edition, I offered a few sidebars about various debugging war stories I'd seen. The response was so overwhelming that in this edition, I greatly expanded the number of war stories. I hope that by sharing with you some of the really "good" bugs I've helped solve (and some I've helped write!), you'll see the practical application of the approaches and techniques I recommend. I also want to help you avoid the mistakes that I've made.

I also kept a list of all the questions I was asked in the first edition and made sure to answer them in the Common Debugging Question sidebars. The war stories and Common Debugging Questions are listed on pages xix to xx.

System Requirements

To use this book, you'll need the following:

- Microsoft Windows 2000 SP3 or later, Microsoft Windows XP Professional, or Windows Server 2003
- Microsoft Visual Studio .NET Professional 2003, Microsoft Visual Studio .NET Enterprise Developer 2003, or Microsoft Visual Studio .NET Enterprise Architect 2003

What Comes with This Book's Sample Files?

As I've already mentioned, there's 6.9 MB of just source files. Considering that the source files alone are bigger than some commercial projects, I'm more than willing to bet that you're getting more source code with this book than any other .NET or Windows book ever published. There are over 20 utilities or libraries and over 35 example programs that show individual constructs. By the way, these numbers don't account for all the unit tests for the various utilities or libraries! Most of the code for the utility programs has been battle-tested in so many commercial applications that I lost count at over 800. I'm honored that so many companies have found my code good enough to use in their products and hope you use it as well.

Robert Lyon, the fantastic technical editor for this book, put together DEBUGNET.CHM, which serves as the README about how to build and use the code in your projects as well as describes every binary built from the source code.

Also with the sample files are the following Microsoft-supplied tools:

- Application Compatibility Toolkit (ACT) version 2.6
- Debugging Tools for Windows version 6.1.0017.2

I developed and tested all the projects with Microsoft Visual Studio .NET Enterprise Edition 2003. As for operating systems, I tested against Windows 2000 Service Pack 3, Windows XP Professional Service Pack 1, and Windows Server 2003 RC2 (previously named Windows .NET Server 2003).

READ THIS! Windows 98/Me and ANSI Code

Because Microsoft Windows Me is outdated and there's only one of me, I dropped all support for any operating systems prior to Windows 2000. I was supporting only Windows 2000 and later, so I made the extra effort and converted all my code to UNICODE as well. I used the TCHAR.H macros and ensured that I left interfaces on libraries that supported ANSI characters. However, I didn't compile any of the code as ANSI/multibyte, so you might run into compilation problems or run-time bugs if you do.

READ THIS! The DBGHELP.DLL Symbol Engine

In several of the native code utilities, I use the DBGHELP.DLL symbol engine distributed with Debugging Tools for Windows version 6.1.0017.2. As DBGHELP.DLL is now finally redistributable, I've included it in the Release and Output directories in the source code tree. As always, you should find out whether a newer version of Debugging Tools for Windows is available by checking *www.microsoft.com/ddk/debugging* so that you can get a newer version of DBGHELP.DLL. For compilation, DBGHELP.LIB is included with Visual Studio .NET.

If you're going to use any of my native code utilities, you'll need to move the included DBGHELP.DLL (or a later version) into the same directory as the utility. The versions of DBGHELP.DLL that come with Windows 2000 and Windows XP are earlier than version 6.1.0017.2.

Feedback

I'm very interested in knowing what you think of this book. If you have questions—or your own debugging war stories—I'd love to hear them! The best place to post questions about this book or debugging in general is in the "Debugging and Tuning" forum at *www.wintellect.com/forum*. The beauty of the forum is that you can search through the questions that other readers have already had and keep track of possible corrections and updates.

If you do have a question that you don't feel comfortable posting in a public forum, you can send e-mail to *john@wintellect.com*. Please keep in mind that I travel quite a bit and get a lot of e-mail, so you might not get an immediate response. But I will do my best to answer your e-mail.

Thanks for reading, and happy debugging!
John Robbins
February 2003
Hollis, New Hampshire
Bob in 2020

Microsoft Press Support Information

Every effort has been made to ensure the accuracy of the book and the contents of the companion CD. Microsoft Press provides corrections for books through the World Wide Web at:

http://www.microsoft.com/mspress/support/

To connect directly to the Microsoft Press Knowledge Base and enter a query regarding a question or issue that you may have, go to:

http://www.microsoft.com/mspress/support/search.asp

If you have comments, questions, or ideas regarding the book or the CD-ROM, or questions that are not answered by querying the Knowledge Base, please send them to Microsoft Press via e-mail to:

mspinput@microsoft.com

or via postal mail to:

Microsoft Press
Attn: Debugging Applications for Microsoft .NET and Microsoft Windows Editor
One Microsoft Way
Redmond, WA 98052-6399

Please note that product support is not offered through the above addresses.

Part I

The Gestalt of Debugging

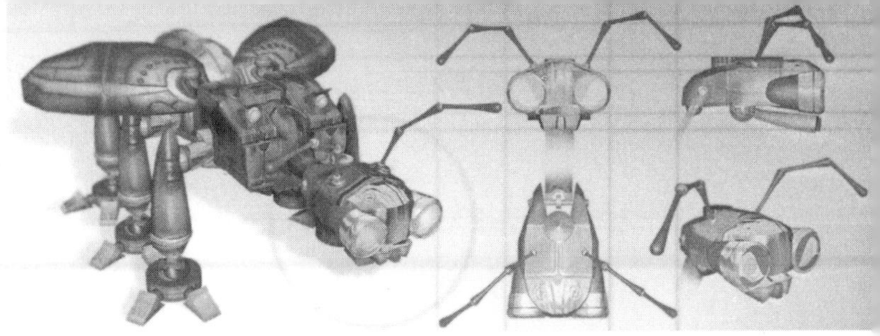

1

Bugs: Where They Come From and How You Solve Them

Debugging is a fascinating topic no matter what language or platform you're using. It's the only part of software development in which engineers kick, scream at, or even throw their computers. For a normally reticent, introverted group, this degree of emotion is extraordinary. Debugging is also the part of software development that's famous for causing you to pull all-nighters. I've yet to run into an engineer who has called his or her partner to say, "Honey, I can't come home because we're having so much fun doing our UML diagrams that we want to pull an all-nighter!" However, I've run into plenty of engineers who have called their partner with the lament, "Honey, I can't come home because we've run into a whopper of a bug."

Bugs and Debugging

Bugs are cool! They help you learn the most about how things work. We all got into this business because we like to learn, and tracking down bugs is the ultimate learning experience. I don't know how many times I've had nearly every programming book I own open and spread out across my office looking for a good bug. It feels just plain great to find and fix those bugs! Of course, the coolest bugs are those that you find before the customer sees your product. That means you have to do your job to find those bugs before your customers do. Having your customers find them is extremely uncool.

Compared with other engineering fields, software engineering is an anomaly in two ways. First, software engineering is a new and somewhat immature branch of engineering compared with other forms of engineering that have been around for a while, such as structural and electrical engineering. Second, users have come to accept bugs in our products, particularly in PC software. Although they grudgingly resign themselves to bugs on PCs, they're still not happy when they find them. Interestingly enough, those same customers would never tolerate a bug in a nuclear reactor design or a piece of medical hardware. With PC software becoming more a part of people's lives, the free ride that the software engineering field has enjoyed is nearly over. I don't doubt that the liability laws that apply to other engineering disciplines will eventually cover software engineering as well.

You need to care about bugs because ultimately they are costly to your business. In the short term, customers contact you for help, forcing you to spend your time and money sustaining the current product while your competitors work on their next versions. In the long term, the invisible hand of economics kicks in and customers just start buying alternatives to your buggy product. Software is now more of a service than a capital investment, so the pressure for higher quality software will increase. With many applications supporting Extensible Markup Language (XML) for input and output, your users are almost able to switch among software products from various vendors just by moving from one Web site to another. This boon for users will mean less job security for you and me if our products are buggy and more incentive to create high-quality products. Let me phrase this another way: the buggier your product, the more likely you are to have to look for a new job. If there's anything that engineers hate, it's going through the job-hunting process.

What Are Bugs?

Before you can start debugging, you need a definition of bugs. My definition of a bug is "anything that causes a user pain." I classify bugs into the following categories:

- Inconsistent user interfaces
- Unmet expectations
- Poor performance
- Crashes or data corruption

Inconsistent User Interfaces

Inconsistent user interfaces, though not the most serious type of bug, are annoying. One reason for the success of the Microsoft Windows operating system is that all Windows-based applications generally behave the same way. When an application deviates from the Windows standard, it becomes a burden for the user. An excellent example of this nonstandard, irksome behavior is the Find accelerators in Microsoft Outlook. In every other English-language Windows-based application on the planet, Ctrl+F brings up the Find dialog box so that you can find text in the current window. In Outlook, however, Ctrl+F forwards the open message, which I consider a bug. Even after many years of using Outlook, I can never remember to use the F4 key to find text in the currently open message.

With client applications, it's pretty easy to solve problems with inconsistent user interfaces by following the recommendations in the book *Microsoft Windows User Experience* (Microsoft Press, 1999), which is also available from MSDN Online at *http://msdn.microsoft.com/library/en-us/dnwue/html/welcome.asp*. If that book doesn't address a particular issue, look for another Microsoft application that does something similar to what you're trying to achieve and follow its model. Microsoft seems to have infinite resources and unlimited time; if you take advantage of their extensive research, solving consistency problems won't cost you an arm and a leg.

If you're working on Web front ends, life is much more difficult because there's no standard for user interface display. As we've all experienced from the user perspective, it's quite difficult to get a good user interface (UI) in a Web browser. For developing strong Web client UIs, I can recommend two books. The first is the standard bible on Web design, Jacob Nielsen's *Designing Web Usability: The Practice of Simplicity*. The second is an outstanding small book that you should give to any self-styled usability experts on your team who couldn't design their way out of a wet paper bag (such as any executive who wants to do the UI but has never used a computer): Steve Krug's *Don't Make Me Think! A Common Sense Approach to Web Usability*. Whatever you do for your Web UI, keep in mind that not all your users will have 100-MB-per-second pipes for their browsers, so keep your UI simple and avoid lots of fluff that takes forever to download. When doing research on great Web clients, User Interface Engineering (*www.uie.com*) found that approaches such as *CNN.com* worked best with all users. A simple set of clean links with information groups under clean sections let users find what they were looking better than anything else.

Unmet Expectations

Not meeting the user's expectations is one of the hardest bugs to solve. This bug usually occurs right at the beginning of a project, when the company doesn't do sufficient research on what the real customer needs. In both types of shops—shrink-wrap (those writing software for sale) and Information Technology (or IT, which are those writing in-house applications)—the cause of this bug comes down to communication problems.

In general, development teams don't communicate directly with their product's customers, so they aren't learning what the users need. Ideally, all members of the engineering team should be visiting customer sites so that they can see how the customers use their product. Watching over a customer's shoulder as your product is being used can be an eye-opening experience. Additionally, this experience will give you the insight you need to properly interpret what customers are asking your product to do. If you do get to talk to customers, make sure you speak with as many as possible so that you can get input from across a wide spectrum. In fact, I would strongly recommend that you stop reading right now and go schedule a customer meeting. I can't say it strongly enough: the more you talk with customers, the better an engineer you'll be.

In addition to customer visits, another good idea is to have the engineering team review the support call summaries and support e-mails. This feedback will allow the engineering team to see the problems that the users are having, without any filtering applied.

Another aspect of this kind of bug is the situation in which the user's level of expectation has been raised higher than the product can deliver. This inflation of user expectations is the classic result of too much hype, and you must resist misrepresenting your product's capabilities at all costs. When users don't get what they anticipated from a product, they tend to feel that the product is even buggier than it really is. The rule for avoiding this situation is to never promise what you can't deliver and to always deliver what you promise.

Poor Performance

Users are very frustrated by bugs that cause the application to slow down when it encounters real-world data. Invariably, improper testing is the root of all poor performance bugs—however great the application might have looked in development, the team failed to test it with anything approaching real-world volumes. One project I worked on, NuMega's BoundsChecker 3.0, had this bug with its original FinalCheck technology. That version of FinalCheck inserted additional debugging and contextual information directly into the source code so that BoundsChecker could better report errors. Unfortunately, we failed to sufficiently test the FinalCheck code on larger real-world applications before we released BoundsChecker 3.0. As a result, more users than we cared to admit couldn't use that feature. We completely rewrote the FinalCheck feature in subsequent releases, but because of the performance problems in the original version, many users never tried it again, even though it was one of the product's most powerful and useful features. Interestingly enough, we released BoundsChecker 3.0 in 1995 and I still had people seven years later—at least two eons in Internet time—telling me that they still hadn't used FinalCheck because of one bad experience!

You tackle poor performance bugs in two ways. First, make sure you determine your application's performance requirements up front. To know whether you have a performance problem, you need a goal to measure against. An important part of performance planning is keeping baseline performance numbers. If your application starts missing those numbers by 10 percent or more, you need to stop and determine why your performance dropped and take steps to correct the problem. Second, make sure you test your applications against scenarios that are as close to the real world as possible—and do this as early in the development cycle as you can.

Here's one common question I continually get from developers: "Where can I get those real-world data sets so that I can do performance testing?" The answer is to talk to your customers. It never hurts to ask whether you can get their data sets so that you can do your testing. If a customer is concerned about privacy issues, take a look at writing a program that will change sensitive information. You can let the customer run that program and ensure that the changes hide sufficient sensitive information so that the customer feels comfortable giving you the data. It also helps to offer free software when the customer needs some motivation to give you their data.

Crashes or Data Corruption

Crashes and data corruption are what most developers and users think of when they think of a bug. I also put memory leaks into this category. Users might be able to work around the types of bugs just described, but crashes stop them dead, which is why the majority of this book concentrates on solving these extreme problems. In addition, crashes and data corruption are the most common types of bugs. As we all know, some of these bugs are easy to solve, and others are almost impossible. The main point to remember about crashes and data corruption bugs is that you should never ship a product if you know it has one of these bugs in it.

Process Bugs and Solutions

Although shipping software without bugs is possible—provided you give enough attention to detail—I've shipped enough products to know that most teams haven't reached that level of software development maturity. Bugs are a fact of life in this business. However, you can minimize the number of bugs your applications have. That is what teams that ship high-quality products—and there are many out there—do. The reasons for bugs generally fall into the following process categories:

- Short or impossible deadlines
- The "Code First, Think Later" approach
- Misunderstood requirements
- Engineer ignorance or improper training
- Lack of commitment to quality

Short or Impossible Deadlines

We've all been part of development teams for which "management" has set a deadline that was determined by either a tarot card reader or, if that was too expensive, a Magic 8-Ball. Although we'd like to believe that managers are responsible for most unrealistic schedules, more often than not, they aren't to blame. Engineers' work estimates are usually the basis of the schedule, and sometimes engineers underestimate how long it will take them to develop a solid product. Engineers are funny people. They are introverted but almost always very positive thinkers. Given a task, they believe down to their bones that they can make the computer stand up and dance. If their manager comes to them and says that they have to add an XML transform to the application, the average engineer says "Sure, boss! It'll be three days." Of course, that engineer might not even know how to spell "XML," but he'll know it'll take three days. The big problem is that engineers and managers don't take into account the learning time necessary to make a feature happen. In the section "Scheduling Time for Building Debugging Systems" in Chapter 2, I'll cover some of the rules that you should take into account when scheduling. Whether an unrealistic ship date is the fault of management or engineering or both, the bottom line is that a schedule that's impossible to meet leads to cut corners and a lower quality product.

I've been fortunate enough to work on several teams that have shipped software on time. In each case, the development team truly owned the schedule, and we were good at determining realistic ship dates. To figure out realistic ship dates, we based our dates on a feature set. If the company found the proposed ship date unacceptable, we cut features to move up the date. In addition, everyone on the development team agreed to the schedule before we presented it to management. That way, the team's credibility was on the line to finish the product on time. Interestingly, besides shipping on time, these products were some of the highest quality products I've ever worked on.

The "Code First, Think Later" Approach

My friend Peter Ierardi coined the term "Code First, Think Later" to describe the all-too-common situation in which an engineering team starts programming before they start thinking. Every one of us is guilty of this approach to an extent. Playing with compilers, writing code, and debugging is the fun stuff; it's why we got interested in this business in the first place. Very few of us like to sit down and write documents that describe what we're going to do.

If you don't write these documents, however, you'll start to run into bugs. Instead of stopping and thinking about how to avoid bugs in the first place, you'll start tweaking the code as you go along to work around the bugs. As you might imagine, this tactic will compound the problem because you'll introduce more and more bugs into an already unstable code base. The company I work for goes around the world helping debug the nastiest problems that developers encounter. Unfortunately, many times we are brought in to help solve corruption or performance problems and there's nothing we can do because the problems are fundamentally architectural. When we bring the problems to the management who hired us and tell them it's going to take a partial rewrite to fix the problems, we sometimes hear, "We've got too big an investment in this code base to change it now." That's a sure sign of a company that has fallen into the "Code First, Think Later" problem. When reporting on a client, we simply report "CFTL" as the reason we were unsuccessful when helping them.

Fortunately, the solution to this problem is simple: plan your projects. Some very good books have been written about requirements gathering and project planning. I cite them in Appendix B, and I highly recommend that you read them. Although it isn't very sexy and is generally a little painful, up-front planning is vital to eliminating bugs.

One of the big complaints I got on the first version of this book was that I recommended that you plan your projects but didn't tell you how to do it. That complaint is perfectly valid, and I want to make sure I address the issue here in the second edition. The only problem is that I really don't know how! Now you're wondering if I'm doing the bad author thing and leaving it as an exercise to the reader. Read on, and I'll tell you what planning tactics have worked for me. I hope they'll provide you with some ideas as well.

If you read my bio at the end of the book, you'll notice that I didn't get started in the software business until I was in my late 20s and that it's really my second career. My first career was to jump out of airplanes and hunt down the enemy, as I was a paratrooper and Green Beret in the United States Army. If that's not preparation for the software business, I don't know what is! Of course, if you meet me now, you'll see just a short fat guy with a pasty green glow—a result of sitting in front of a monitor too much. However, I really did used to be a man. I really did!

Being a Green Beret taught me how to plan. When you're planning a special operations mission and the odds are fairly high that you could die, you are extremely motivated to do the best planning possible. When planning one of those operations, the Army puts the whole team in what's called "isolation." At Fort Bragg, North Carolina, the home of Special Forces, there are special areas where they actually lock the team away to plan the mission. The whole key during the planning was called "what if-ing yourself to death." We'd sit around and think about scenarios. What happens if we're supposed to parachute in and we pass the point of no return and the Air Force can't find the drop zone? What happens if we have casualties before we jump? What happens if we hit the ground and can't find the guerilla commander we're supposed to meet? What happens if the guerilla commander we're supposed to meet has more people with him than he's supposed to? What happens if we're ambushed? We'd spend forever thinking up questions and devising the answers to these questions before ever leaving isolation. The idea was to have every contingency planned out so that nothing was left to chance. Trust me: when there's a good chance you might die when doing your job, you want to know all the variables and account for them.

When I got into the software business, that's the kind of planning I was used to doing. The first time I sat in a meeting and said, "What if Bob dies before we get through the requirements phase?" everyone got quite nervous, so now I phrase questions with a less morbid spin, like "What if Bob wins the lottery and quits before we get through the requirements phase?" However, the idea is still the same. Find all the areas of doubt and confusion in your plans and address them. It's not easy to do and will drive weaker engineers crazy, but the key issues will always pop out if you drill down enough. For example, in the requirements phase, you'll be asking questions such as, "What if our requirements aren't what the user wants?" Such questions will prompt you to budget time and money to find out if those requirements are what you need to be addressing. In the design phase, you'll be asking questions like, "What if our performance isn't good enough?" Such questions will make you remember to sit down and define your performance goals and start planning how you're going to achieve those goals by testing against real-world scenarios. Planning is much easier if you can get all the issues on the table. Just be thankful that your life doesn't depend on shipping software on time!

Debugging War Story

Severe CFTL

The Battle

A client called us in because they had a big performance problem and the ship date was fast approaching. One of the first things we ask for when we start on these emergency problems is a 15-minute architectural overview so that we can get up to speed on the terminology as well as get an idea of how the project fits together. The client hustled in one of the architects and he started the explanation on the white board.

Normally, these circle and arrow sessions take 10 to 15 minutes. However, this architect was still going strong 45 minutes later, and I was getting confused because I needed more than a roadmap to keep up. I finally admitted that I was totally lost and asked again for the 10-minute system overview. I didn't need to know everything; I just needed to know the high points. The architect started again and in 15 minutes was only about 25 percent through the system!

The Outcome

This was a large COM system, and at about this point I started to figure out what the performance problem was. Evidently, some architect on the team had become enamored with COM. He didn't just sip from a glass of COM Kool-Aid; he immediately started guzzling from the 55-gallon drum of COM. In what I later guessed was a system that needed 8–10 main objects, this team had over 80! To give you an idea how ridiculous this was, it was like every character in a string was a COM object. This thing was over-engineered and completely under-thought. It was the classic case in which the architects had zero hands-on experience.

After about a half a day, I finally got the manager off to the side and said that there wasn't much we could do for performance because the overhead of COM itself was killing them. He was none too happy to hear this and immediately blurted out this infamous phrase: "We've got too big an investment in this code to change now!" Unfortunately, with their existing architecture, we couldn't do much to effect a performance boost.

(continued)

Debugging War Story *(continued)*

The Lesson

This project suffered from several major problems right from the beginning. First, team members handed over the complete design to nonimplementers. Second, they immediately started coding when the plan came down from on high. There was absolutely no thought other than to code this thing up and code it up now. It was the classic "Code First, Think Later" problem preceded by "No-Thought Design." I can't stress this enough: you have to get realistic technology assessments and plan your development before you ever turn on the computer.

Misunderstood Requirements

Proper planning also minimizes one of the biggest bug causers in development: feature creep. Feature creep—the tacking on of features not originally planned—is a symptom of poor planning and inadequate requirements gathering. Adding last-minute features, whether in response to competitive pressure, as a developer's pet feature, or on the whim of management, causes more bugs in software than almost anything else.

Software engineering is an extremely detail-oriented business. The more details you hash out and solve before you start coding, the fewer you leave to chance. The only way to achieve proper attention to detail is to plan your milestones and the implementation for your projects. Of course, this doesn't mean that you need to go completely overboard and generate thousands of pages of documentation describing what you're going to do.

One of the best design documents I ever created for a product was simply a series of paper drawings, or paper prototypes, of the user interface. Based on research and on the teachings of Jared Spool and his company, User Interface Engineering, my team drew the user interface and worked through each user scenario completely. In doing so, we had to focus on the requirements for the product and figure out exactly how the users were going to perform their tasks. In the end, we knew exactly what we were going to deliver, and more important, so did everyone else in the company. If a question about what was supposed to happen in a given scenario arose, we pulled out the paper prototypes and worked through the scenario again.

Even though you might do all the planning in the world, you have to really understand your product's requirements to implement them properly. At one company where I worked—mercifully, for less than a year—the requirements for the product seemed very simple and straightforward. As it turned out, however, most of the team members didn't understand the customers' needs well enough to figure out what the product was supposed to do. The company made the classic mistake of drastically increasing engineering head count but failing to train the new engineers sufficiently. Consequently, even though the team planned everything to extremes, the product shipped several years late and the market rejected it.

There were two large mistakes on this project. The first was that the company wasn't willing to take the time to thoroughly explain the customers' needs to the engineers who were new to the problem domain, even though some of us begged for the training. The second mistake was that many of the engineers, both old and new, didn't care to learn more about the problem domain. As a result, the team kept changing direction each time marketing and sales reexplained the requirements. The code base was so unstable that it took months to get even the simplest user scenarios to work without crashing.

Very few companies train their engineers in their problem domain at all. Although many of us have college degrees in engineering, we generally don't know much about how customers will use our products. If companies spent adequate time up front helping their engineers understand the problem domain, they could eliminate many bugs caused by misunderstood requirements.

The fault isn't just with the companies, though. Engineers must make the commitment to learn the problem domain as well. Some engineers like to think they're building tools that enable a solution so that they can maintain their separation from the problem domain. As engineers, we're responsible for solving the problem, not merely enabling a solution!

An example of enabling a solution is a situation in which you design a user interface that technically works but doesn't match the way the user works. Another example of enabling a solution is building your application in such a way that it solves the user's short-term problem but doesn't move forward to accommodate the user's changing business needs.

When solving the user's problem rather than just enabling a solution, you, as the engineer, become as knowledgeable as you can about the problem domain so that your software product becomes an extension of the user. The best engineers are not those who can twiddle bits but those who can solve a user's problem.

Engineer Ignorance or Improper Training

Another significant cause of bugs results from developers who don't understand the operating system, the language, or the technology their projects use. Unfortunately, few engineers are willing to admit this deficiency and seek training. Instead, they cover up their lack of knowledge and, unintentionally, introduce avoidable bugs.

In many cases, however, this ignorance isn't a personal failing so much as a fact of life in modern software development. So many layers and interdependencies are involved in developing software these days that no one person can be expected to know the ins and outs of every operating system, language, and technology. There's nothing wrong with admitting that you don't know something. It's not a sign of weakness, and it won't take you out of the running to be the office's alpha geek. In fact, if a team is healthy, acknowledging the strengths and limitations of each member works to the team's advantage. By cataloging the skills their developers have and don't have, the team can get the maximum advantage from their training dollars. By strengthening every developer's weaknesses, the team will better be able to adjust to unforeseen circumstances and, in turn, broaden the whole team's skill set. The team can also schedule development time more accurately when team members are willing to admit what they don't know. You can build in time for learning and create a much more realistic schedule if team members are candid about the gaps in their knowledge.

The best way to learn about a technology is to do something with that technology. Years ago, when NuMega sent me off to learn about Microsoft Visual Basic so that we could write products for Visual Basic developers, I laid out a schedule for what I was going to learn and my boss was thrilled. The idea was to develop an application that insulted you, appropriately called "The Insulter." Version 1 was a simple form with a single button that, when pressed, popped up a random insult from the list of hard-coded insults. The second version read insults from a database and allowed you to add new insults by using a form. The third version connected to the company Microsoft Exchange server and allowed you to e-mail insults to others in the company. My manager was very happy to see how and what I was going to do to learn the technology. All your manager really cares about is being able to tell his boss what you're doing day to day. If you give your manager that information, you'll be his favorite employee. When I had my first encounter with .NET, I simply dusted off the Insulter idea, and it became Insulter .NET!

I'll have more to say about what skills and knowledge are critical for developers to have in the section "Prerequisites to Debugging" later in this chapter.

Common Debugging Question

Should we do code reviews?

Absolutely! Unfortunately, many companies go about them in completely the wrong way. One company I worked for required formal code reviews that were straight out of one of those only-in-fantasyland software engineering textbooks I had in college. Everything was role-based: there was a Recorder for recording comments, a Secretary for keeping the meeting moving, a Door Keeper to open the door, a Leader to suck oxygen, and so on. All that you really had, however, were 40 people in a room, none of whom had read the code. It was a huge waste of time.

The kind of code reviews I like are the one-on-one informal kind. You simply sit down with a printout of the code and read it line by line with the developer. As you read it, you're keeping track of all the input and outputs so that you can see what's happening in the code. Think about what I just wrote. If that sounds perilously close to debugging the code, you're exactly right. Focus on what the code does—that's the purpose of a code review.

Another trick for ensuring that your code reviews are worthwhile is to have the junior developers review the senior developer's code. Not only does that teach the less experienced developers that their contribution is valuable, but it's also a fine way to teach them about the product and show them great programming tips and tricks.

Lack of Commitment to Quality

The final reason that bugs exist in projects is, in my opinion, the most serious. Every company and every engineer I've ever talked to has told me that they are committed to quality. Unfortunately, some companies and engineers lack the real commitment that quality requires. If you've ever worked at a company that was committed to quality or with an engineer who was, you certainly know it. They both feel a deep pride in what they are producing and are willing to spend the effort on all parts of development, not on just the sexy parts. For example, instead of getting all wrapped up in the minutia of an algorithm, they pick a simpler algorithm and spend their time working on how best to test that algorithm. The customer doesn't buy algorithms, after all; the customer buys high-quality products. Companies and individuals with a real commitment to quality exhibit many of the same characteristics: careful up-front planning, personal accountability, solid quality control, and excellent communication abilities. Many companies and individuals go through the motions of the big software development tasks (that is, scheduling, coding, and so on), but only those who pay attention to the details ship on time with high quality.

A good example of a commitment to quality is when I had my first monthly review at NuMega. First off, I was astounded that I was getting a review that quickly when normally you have to beg for any feedback from your managers. One of the key parts of the review was to record how many bugs I had logged against the product. I was stunned to discover that NuMega would evaluate this statistic as part of my performance review, however, because even though tracking bugs is a vital part of maintaining a product's quality, no other company I had worked at had ever checked something so obvious. The developers know where the bugs are, but they must be given an incentive to enter those bugs into the bug tracking system. NuMega found the trick. When I learned about the bug count entry part of my review, you'd better believe I logged everything I found, no matter how trivial. With all the technical writers, quality engineers, development engineers, and managers engaged in healthy competition to log the most bugs, few surprise bugs slipped through the cracks. More important, we had a realistic idea of where we stood on a project at any given time.

Another excellent example from the engineering side is the first edition of this book. On the book's companion CD was over 2.5 MB of source code (and that wasn't compiled code, it was just the source code!). That's quite a bit of code, and I'm happy to say many multiples more than what you get with most books. What many people don't realize is that I spent over 50 percent of the time on that book just testing the code. People get really excited when they find a bug in the Bugslayer code, and the last thing I want is one of those "Gotcha! I found a bug in the Bugslayer!" e-mails. While I can't say that I had zero bugs on that CD, I did have only five. My commitment to the readers was to give them the absolute best of my ability. My goal for this edition is fewer than five in the 6+ MB of source code for this edition.

When I was a development manager, I followed a ritual that I'm sure fostered a commitment to quality: each team member had to agree that the product was ready to go at every milestone. If any person on the team didn't feel that the product was ready, it didn't ship. I'd rather fix a minor bug and suffer through another complete day of testing than send out something the team wasn't proud of. Not only did this ritual ensure that everyone on the team thought the quality was there, but it also gave everyone on the team a stake in the outcome. An interesting phenomenon I noticed was that team members never got the chance to stop the release for someone else's bug; the bug's owner always beat them to it.

A company's commitment to quality sets the tone for the entire development effort. That commitment starts with the hiring process and extends through the final quality assurance on the release candidate. Every company says that it wants to hire the best people, but few companies are willing to offer salaries and benefits that will draw them. In addition, some companies aren't willing to provide the tools and equipment that engineers need to produce high-quality products. Unfortunately, too many companies resist spending $500 on a tool that will solve a nasty crash bug in minutes but are willing to blow many thousands of dollars to pay their developers to flounder around for weeks trying to solve that same bug.

A company also shows its commitment to quality when it does the hardest thing to do in business—fire people who are not living up to the standards the organization set. When building a great team full of people on the right-hand side of the bell curve, you have to work to keep them there. We've all seen the person whose chief job seems to be stealing oxygen but who keeps getting raises and bonuses like you even though you're killing yourself and working late nights and sometimes weekends to make the product happen. The result is good people quickly realizing that the effort isn't worth it. They start slacking off or, worse yet, looking for other jobs.

When I was a project manager, I dreaded doing it, but I fired someone two days before Christmas. I knew that people on the team were feeling that this one individual wasn't working up to standards. If they came back from the Christmas holiday with that person still there, I'd start losing the team we had worked so hard to build. I had been documenting the person's poor performance for quite a while, so I had the proper reasons for proceeding. Trust me, I would rather have been shot at again in the Army than fire that person. It would have been much easier to let it ride, but my commitment was to my team and to the company to do the quality job I had been hired to do. In all, I ended up firing a total of three people on my teams. It was better to go through that upheaval than to have anyone turn off and stop performing. I agonized over every firing, but I had to do it. A commitment to quality is extremely difficult and will mean that you'll have to do things that will keep you up at night, but that's what it takes to ship great software and take care of your people.

If you do find yourself in an organization that suffers from a lack of commitment to quality, you'll find that there's no easy way to turn a company into a quality-conscious organization overnight. If you're a manager, you can set the direction and tone for the engineers working for you and work with upper management to lobby for extending a commitment to quality across the organization. If you're an engineer, you can work to make your code the most robust and extensible on the project so that you set an example for others.

Planning for Debugging

Now that we've gone over the types and origins of bugs and you have some ideas about how to avoid or solve them, it's time to start thinking about the process of debugging. Although many people start thinking about debugging only when they crash during the coding phase, you should think about it right from the beginning, in the requirements phase. The more you plan your projects up front, the less time—and money—you'll spend debugging them later.

As I mentioned earlier in the chapter, feature creep can be a bane to your project. More often than not, unplanned features introduce bugs and wreak havoc on a product. This doesn't mean that your plans must be cast in stone, however. Sometimes you must change or add a feature to a product to be competitive or to better meet the user's needs. The key point to remember is that before you change your code, you need to determine—and plan for—exactly what will change. And keep in mind that adding a feature doesn't affect only the code; it also affects testing, documentation, and sometimes even marketing messages. When revising your production schedule, a general rule to follow is that the time it takes to add or remove a feature grows exponentially the further along the production cycle you are.

In Steve McConnell's excellent book *Code Complete* (Microsoft Press, 1993, pp. 25–26), he refers to the costs of fixing a bug. To fix a bug during the requirements and planning phases costs very little. As the product progresses, however, the cost of fixing a bug rises exponentially, as does the cost of debugging—much the same scenario as if you add or remove features along the way.

Planning for debugging goes together with planning for testing. As you plan, you need to look for different ways to speed up and improve both processes. One of the best precautions you can take is to write file data dumpers and validators for internal data structures as well as for binary files, if appropriate. If your project reads and writes data to a binary file, you should automatically schedule someone to write a testing program that dumps the data in a readable format to a text file. The dumper should also validate the data and check all interdependencies in the binary file. This step will make both your testing and your debugging easier.

By properly planning for debugging, you minimize the time spent in your debugger, and this is your goal. You might think such advice sounds strange coming from a book on debugging, but the idea is to try to avoid bugs in the first place. If you build sufficient debugging code into your applications, that code—not the debugger—should tell you where the bugs are. I'll cover the issues concerning debugging code more in Chapter 3.

Prerequisites to Debugging

Before we get into the meat of debugging, I want to cover what you must know to be a good debugger. The first quality that all expert debuggers have in common is being good developers too. You simply can't be a good debugger without being a good developer, and vice versa.

The Skill Set

Good debuggers and, conversely, good developers all have strong problem-solving skills that are particular to software. Fortunately, you can learn and hone those skills. What sets great debuggers/developers apart from good debuggers/developers is that in addition to having basic problem-solving skills, great debuggers/developers understand how all the parts of a project relate to the project as a whole.

The following list contains the areas in which you need to be proficient to become a great—or at least a better—debugger/developer:

- Your project
- Your language
- Your technology/tools
- Your operating system/environment
- Your CPU

Know Your Project

Knowing your project is the first line of defense for user interface, logic, and performance bugs. By knowing how and where features are implemented in the various source files, you can quickly narrow down who is doing what to whom.

Unfortunately, because each project is different, the only way to learn your project is to read the design documents (if they exist), and to walk through the code in the debugger. Modern development environments have class browser views that can show you the basics, but you might want to turn to a real browsing tool such Source Dynamics's Source Insight. Additionally, you can use real modeling tools such as Microsoft Visual Studio .NET Enterprise Architect with its Microsoft Visio integration, which can show you the relationship or Unified Modeling Language (UML) diagrams that describe the code. Even poorly documented source code is better than nothing if it saves you from having to interpret a disassembly listing.

Know Your Language

Knowing the language (or languages) your project uses is more difficult than it sounds. I'm referring to knowing what your language is doing behind the scenes as well as knowing how to program in it. For example, C++ developers sometimes forget that local variables that are classes or overloaded operators can create temporary items on the stack. Alternatively, an assignment operator might look innocent enough, but it can cause a great deal of code to execute. Many bugs, especially performance problems, are the result of language misuse, so it's well worth the effort to spend some time reading up on the idiosyncrasies of the programming languages you use.

Know Your Technology/Tools

Getting a handle on the technologies you're using is the first big step to tackling the harder bugs. For example, if you have an idea of what COM does to instantiate a COM object and return an interface, you'll have a much easier time tracking down why a specific interface request failed. The same goes for something like ISAPI filters. If you're having a problem with your filter being called correctly, you need to know where and when INETINFO.EXE should be loading your filter. I'm not saying that you need to quote files and lines from the source code or a book. Rather, I'm saying that you should have at least a general understanding of the technologies you're using and, more important, you should know exactly where you can find more detailed information if you need it.

In addition to knowing the technology, it's vital to know the tools you're using. A big portion of this book is spent discussing advanced usage of the debugger, but many other tools are out there, such as those distributed with the Platform SDK. Taking a day simply to explore and learn all the tools you have at your disposal is a very wise investment. This exploration includes downloading and evaluating commercial tools because those can make a huge difference in your development.

Know Your Operating System/Environment

Knowing the basics of how your operating system or operating environment goes about doing its work can make the biggest difference between solving a bug and just floundering around. If you're working on native code, you should be able to answer questions like the following: What is a dynamic-link library (DLL)? How does an image loader work? How does the registry work? For managed code, you should know things such as, How does ASP.NET find the components a page is using? When do finalizers get called? What's the difference between an application domain and an assembly? Many of the worst bugs appear when you misuse the operating system or environment. My friend Matt Pietrek, who taught me a great deal about debugging, maintains that knowing the operating system/environment and the CPU is what separates the debugging gods from mere mortals.

Know Your CPU

This brings me to the last thing you must know to be a debugging god for native code: the CPU. You must know a little about the CPU to solve most of the nastiest bugs you'll encounter. Although it would be nice if you always crashed where source code was available, the majority of your crashes drop you right into the Disassembly window. It always amazes me how many engineers don't know—and say they have no interest in knowing—assembly language. Assembly language isn't that hard, and three or four hours spent learning it can save countless hours in the debugger. Again, I'm not saying that you need to be able to write your whole program in assembly language. Even I don't think I could do that anymore. The point is that you need to be able to read it. All you need to know about assembly language is in Chapter 7.

Learning the Skill Set

With any job that regularly deals with technology, you have to study continually just to keep up, let alone get better and advance. Although I can't help you learn your specific projects, in Appendix B I list all the resources that have helped me—and can help you—become a better debugger.

Besides reading books and magazines on debugging, you should also write utilities, any kind of utilities. The ultimate way to learn is by doing, and in this business, coding and debugging are what you need to do. Not only will you enhance your hard skills, such as coding and debugging, but if you treat these utilities as real projects (that is, by completing them on time and with high quality), you'll also enhance your soft skills, such as project planning and schedule estimating.

To give you some impetus to complete your utilities, consider this: completed utilities are excellent show-and-tell items to bring to job interviews. Although very few engineers bring their own code to demonstrate their skills to interviewers, companies consider those candidates who do well before those candidates who don't. Bringing a portfolio of the work you did on your own time at home shows that you can complete work independently and that you have a passion for software engineering, and it will almost immediately put you in the top 20 percent of engineers.

Another practice that has helped me a great deal, especially when it comes to learning more about languages, technologies, and the operating system, is to look at other engineers' code. As you probably know, a great deal of code that you can look at is floating around on the Internet. By running different programs under the debugger, you can see how someone else tackles bugs. If you're having trouble coming up with a utility you'd like to write, you can simply add a feature to one of the utilities you find.

Another technique I would recommend to learn more about technologies, the operating system, and the virtual machine (CPU) is to do some reverse engineering. It will help get you up to speed with assembly language and the advanced features in the debugger. After reading Chapter 6 and Chapter 7, you should know enough about Microsoft Intermediate Language (MSIL) and IA32 assembly language, respectively, to get started. Although I wouldn't recommend you start out by completely reverse engineering the operating system loader, you might consider tackling some smaller tasks. For example, I found it very instructive to walk through the implementation of `CoInitializeEx` for native code and the `System.Diagnostics.TraceListener` class in managed code.

Reading books and magazines, writing utilities, reviewing other engineers' code, and doing reverse engineering are all great ways to improve your debugging skills. However, your greatest resources are your engineering friends and coworkers. Never be afraid to ask them how they did something or how something works; unless they are in the middle of a deadline crunch, they should be happy to help. I enjoy it when people ask me questions because I end up learning more than the individuals who ask the questions! Programming newsgroups are also excellent places to pose questions. I read them all the time because their responses are so good, especially from those folks Microsoft has designated MVPs (Most Valuable Professionals).

The Debugging Process

Finally, let's start talking about hands-on debugging by discussing the debugging process. Determining a process that works for all bugs, even "freak" bugs (bugs that come out of the blue and don't make any sense), was a bit challenging. But by drawing on my own experiences and by talking to my colleagues about their experiences, I eventually came up with a debugging approach that all great developers intuitively follow but that less experienced (or just poorer) developers often don't find obvious.

As you'll see, this debugging process doesn't take a rocket scientist to implement. The hard part is making sure you start with this process every time you debug. Here are the nine steps involved in the debugging approach that I recommend:

- Step 1: Duplicate the bug
- Step 2: Describe the bug
- Step 3: Always assume that the bug is yours
- Step 4: Divide and conquer
- Step 5: Think creatively

- Step 6: Leverage tools
- Step 7: Start heavy debugging
- Step 8: Verify that the bug is fixed
- Step 9: Learn and share

Depending on your bug, you can skip some steps entirely because the problem and the location of the problem are entirely obvious. You must always start with Step 1 and get through Step 2. At any point between Step 3 and Step 7, however, you might figure out the solution and be able to fix the bug. In those cases, after you fix the bug, skip to Step 8 to verify and test the fix. Figure 1-1 illustrates the steps of the debugging process.

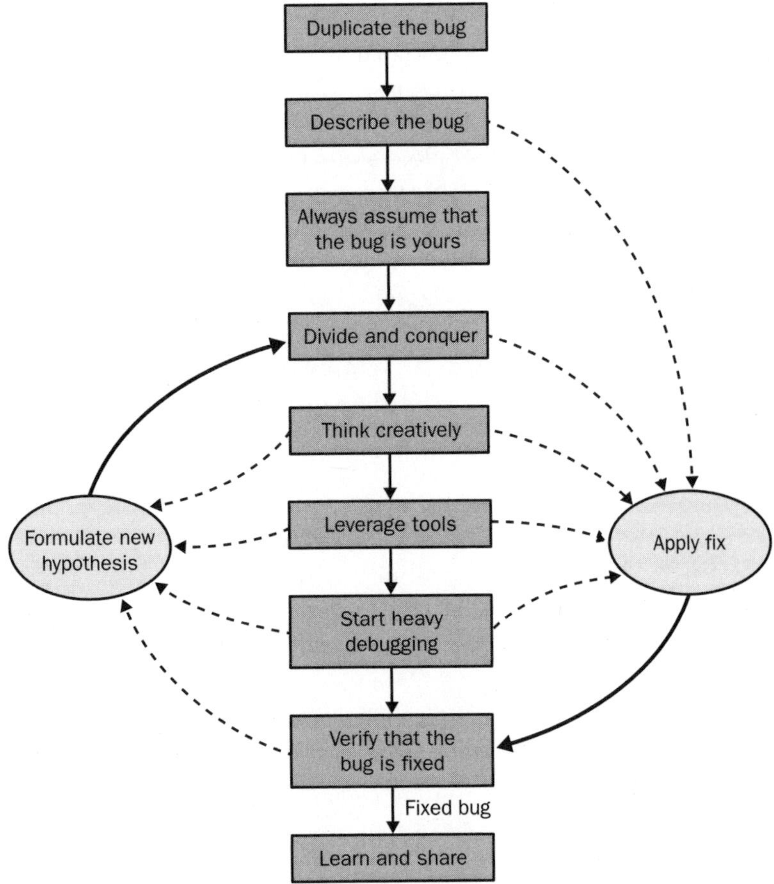

Figure 1-1 The debugging process

Step 1: Duplicate the Bug

The most critical step in the debugging process is the first one: duplicating the bug. This is sometimes difficult, or even impossible, but if you can't duplicate a bug, you probably can't eliminate it. When trying to duplicate a bug, you might need to go to extremes. I had one bug in my code that I couldn't duplicate just by running the program. I had an idea of the data conditions that might cause it, however, so I ran the program under the debugger and entered the data I needed to duplicate the bug directly into memory. It worked. If you're dealing with a synchronization problem, you might need to take steps such as loading the same tasks so that you can duplicate the state in which the bug occurred.

At this point you're probably thinking, "Well, duh! Of course the first thing you do is duplicate the bug. If I could duplicate it all the time, I wouldn't need your book!" It all depends on your definition of "duplicatability." My definition is duplicating the bug on a single machine once in a 24-hour period. That's sufficient for my company to come in to work on it. Why? Simple. If you can get it on one machine, you can throw 30 machines at it and get the bug duplicated 30 times. The big mistake people make with duplicating the bug is to not get as many machines as possible into the mix. If you have 30 people to manually punch keys for you, that's great. However, a valuable effort would be to automate the user interface to drive the bug out into the open. You can use either the Tester application from Chapter 17 or a commercial automated regression testing tool.

Once you've duplicated the bug by using one general set of steps, you should evaluate whether you can duplicate the bug through a different set of steps. You can get to some bugs via one code path only, but you can get to other bugs through multiple paths. The idea is to try to see the behavior from all possible angles. By duplicating the bug from multiple paths, you have a much better sense of the data and boundary conditions that are causing the problems. Additionally, as we all know, some bugs can mask other bugs. The more ways you can find to duplicate a bug, the better off you'll be.

Even if you can't duplicate the bug, you should still log it into your bug tracking system. If I have a bug that I can't duplicate, I always log it into the system anyway, but I leave a note that says I couldn't duplicate it. That way, if another engineer is responsible for that section of the code, she at least has an idea that something is amiss. When logging a bug that you can't duplicate, you need to be as descriptive as possible. If the description is good enough, it might be sufficient for you or another engineer to solve the problem eventually. A good description is especially important because you can correlate various non-reproducible bug reports, enabling you to start seeing patterns in the bug's behavior.

Step 2: Describe the Bug

If you were a typical engineering student in college, you probably concentrated on your math and engineering classes and barely passed your writing classes. In the real world, your writing skills are almost more important than your engineering skills because you need to be able to describe your bugs, both verbally and in writing. When faced with a tough bug, you should always stop right after you duplicate it and describe it. Ideally, you do this in your bug tracking system, even if it's your responsibility to debug the bug, but talking it out is also useful. The main reason for describing the bug is that doing so often helps you fix it. I can't remember how many times another engineer's description helped me look at a bug in a different way.

Step 3: Always Assume That the Bug Is Yours

In all the years I've been in software development, only a miniscule percentage of the bugs I've seen were the result of the compiler or the operating environment. If you have a bug, the odds are excellent that it's your fault, and you should always assume and hope that it is. If the bug is in your code, at least you can fix it; if it's in your compiler or the operating environment, you have bigger problems. You should eliminate any possibility that the bug is in your code before spending time looking for it elsewhere.

Step 4: Divide and Conquer

If you've duplicated your bug and described it well, you have started a hypothesis about the bug and have an idea of where it's hiding. In this step, you start firming and testing your hypothesis. The important thing to remember here is the paraphrased line from the movie *Star Wars*: "Use the source, Luke!" Read the source code, and desk-check what you think is happening with what the code really does. Reading the code will force you to take the extra time to look at the problem. Starting with the state of the machine at the time of the crash or problem, work through the various scenarios that could cause you to get to that section of code. If your hypothesis of what went wrong doesn't pan out, stop for a moment and reassess the situation. You've learned a little more about the bug, so now you can reevaluate your hypothesis and try again.

Debugging is like a binary search algorithm. You're trying to find the bug, and with each iteration through your different hypotheses, you are, hopefully, eliminating the sections of the programs where the bug is not. As you continue to look, you eliminate more and more of the program until you can box the bug into a section of code. As you continue to develop your hypothesis and learn more about the bug, you can update your bug description to reflect the new information. When I'm in this step, I generally try out three to five solid hypotheses before moving on to the next step. If you feel you're getting close, you can do a little "light" debugging in this step to do final verification of the hypothesis. By light, I mean double-checking states and variable values, not slogging through looking at everything.

Step 5: Think Creatively

If the bug you're trying to eliminate is one of those nasty ones that happens only on certain machines or is hard to duplicate, start looking at the bug from different perspectives. This is the step in which you should start thinking about version mismatches, operating system differences, problems with your program's binaries or its installation, and other external factors.

A technique that sometimes works wonders for me is to walk away from the problem for a day or two. You can sometimes focus so intensely on a problem that you lose sight of the forest for the trees and start missing obvious clues. By walking away from the bug, you give your subconscious a chance to work on the problem for a while. I'm sure everyone reading this book has solved a bug on the way home from work. Of course, walking away from that bug might be difficult if the bug is the one holding up shipment and your boss is breathing down your neck.

At several companies I've worked at, the highest priority interrupt has been something called "Bug Talk." That means you are totally stumped and need to talk the bug over with someone. The idea is that you can walk into a person's office and present the problem on a white board. I don't know how many times I've walked into someone's office, uncapped the marker, touched the marker on the board, and solved my problem without even saying a word. Just getting your mind prepared to present the problem helps you get past the individual tree you're staring at and lets you see the whole forest. When you pick a person to do a Bug Talk with, you should pick someone other than the colleagues you're working very closely with on the same section of the project. That way, you can ensure your Bug Talk partner isn't making the same assumptions you are about the problem.

What's interesting is the "someone" doesn't even have to be a human. My cats, as it turns out, are excellent debuggers, and they have helped me solve a number of really nasty bugs. After rounding them up, I draw the problem out on my white board and let them work their magic. Of course, the day I was doing this without having taken a shower and wearing nothing but shorts was a little difficult to explain to the UPS delivery guy standing at my door.

The one person you should always avoid doing Bug Talks with is your spouse or significant other. For some reason, the fact that you're having a relationship with that person means there's a built-in problem. Of course, you've probably already seen this when you try to describe that bug and the person's eyes glaze over and he or she nearly passes out.

Step 6: Leverage Tools

I've never understood why some companies let their engineers spend weeks searching for a bug when spending a thousand dollars for error detection, performance, and code-coverage tools would help them find the current bug—and bugs they will encounter in the future—in minutes.

Several companies, such as Compuware and Rational, make excellent tools for both managed and native code. I always run my code through their tools before I tackle the heavy debugging step. Since native code bugs are always harder to find than managed code bugs, the tools are much more important. From Compuware NuMega you have BoundsChecker (an error detection tool), TrueTime (a performance tool), and TrueCoverage (a code-coverage tool). Rational makes Purify (error detection), Quantify (performance), and PureCoverage (code coverage). The point is that if you're not using a third-party tool to help you debug your products, you're spending more time debugging than you need to.

For those of you who are unfamiliar with these types of tools, let me explain what each of them does. An error detection tool looks for invalid memory accesses, invalid parameters to system APIs and COM interfaces, memory leaks, and resource leaks, among other things. A performance tool helps you track down where your application is slow; that spot is invariably somewhere other than where you think it is. A code-coverage tool shows you the source lines not executed when you run your program. Code-coverage information is helpful because if you're looking for a bug, you want to look for it only in lines that are executing.

Step 7: Start Heavy Debugging

I differentiate heavy debugging from the light debugging I mentioned in Step 4 by what you're doing in the debugger. When you're doing light debugging, you're just looking at a few states and a couple of variables. In contrast, when you're doing heavy debugging, you're spending a good deal of time exploring your program's operation. It is during the heavy debugging stage that you want to use the debugger's advanced features. Your goal is to let the debugger do as much of the heavy lifting as possible. Chapters 6 through 8 discuss the various debuggers' advanced features.

Just as when you're doing light debugging, when you're doing heavy debugging, you should have an idea of where you think your bug is before you start using the debugger, and then use the debugger to prove or disprove your hypothesis. Never sit in the debugger and just poke around. In fact, I strongly encourage you to actually write out your hypothesis before you ever fire up the debugger. That will help you keep completely focused on exactly what you're trying to accomplish.

Also, when you're doing heavy debugging, remember to regularly review changes you made to fix the bug in the debugger. I like to have two machines set up side by side at this stage. That way I can work at fixing the bug on one machine and use the other machine to run the same code with normal condition cases. The idea is to always double-check and triple-check any changes so you're not destabilizing the normal operation of your product. I'll give you some career advice and let you know that your boss really hates it when you check in code to fix a bug and your product handles only weird boundary conditions and no longer handles the normal operation case.

If you set up your project correctly and follow the debugging steps in this chapter and the recommendations in Chapter 2, you hopefully won't have to spend much time doing heavy debugging.

Step 8: Verify That the Bug Is Fixed

When you think you've finally fixed the bug, the next step in the debugging process is to test, test, and retest the fix. Did I also mention that you need to test the fix? If the bug is in an isolated module on a line of code called once, testing the fix is easy. However, if the fix is in a core module, especially one that handles your data structures and the like, you need to be very careful that your fix doesn't cause problems or have side effects in other parts of the project.

When testing your fix, especially in critical code, you should verify that it works with all data conditions, good and bad. Nothing is worse than a fix for one bug that causes two other bugs. If you do make a change in a critical module, you should let the rest of the team know that you made the change. That way, they can be on the lookout for any ripple effects as well.

Debugging War Story

Where Did the Integration Go?

The Battle

One of the developers I worked with at NuMega thought he'd found a great bug in NuMega's Visual C++ Integrated Development Environment (VC IDE) integration because it didn't work on his machine. For those of you who are unfamiliar with NuMega's VC IDE integration, let me provide a little background information. NuMega's software products integrate with the VC IDE—and have for a number of years. This integration allows NuMega's windows, toolbars, and menus to appear seamlessly inside the VC IDE.

The Outcome

This developer spent a couple of hours using SoftICE, a kernel debugger, exploring the bug. After a while, he had set breakpoints all over the operating system. Finally, he found his "bug." He noticed that when he started the VC IDE, `CreateProcess` was being called with the \\R2D2\VSCommon\MSDev98\Bin\MSDEV.EXE path instead of the C:\VSCommon\MSDev98\Bin\MSDEV.EXE path he thought it should be called with. In other words, instead of running the VC IDE from his local machine (C:\VSCommon\MSDev98\Bin\MSDEV.EXE), he was running it from his old machine (\\R2D2\VSCommon\MSDev98\Bin\MSDEV.EXE). How did this happen?

The developer had just gotten a new machine and had installed the full NuMega VC IDE integration for the products. To get it set up faster, he copied his desktop shortcuts (LNK files) from his old machine, which were installed without VC IDE integration, to his new machine by dragging them with the mouse. When you drag shortcuts, the internal paths update to reflect the location of the original target. Since he was always starting the VC IDE from his desktop shortcut, which was pointing to his old machine, he'd been running the VC IDE on his old machine all along.

(continued)

Debugging War Story *(continued)*

The Lesson

The developer went about debugging the problem in the wrong way by just jumping right in with a kernel debugging instead of attempting to duplicate the problem in multiple ways. In Step 1 of the debugging process, "Duplicate the Bug," I recommended that you try to duplicate the bug in multiple ways so that you can be assured you're looking at the right bug, not just multiple bugs masking and compounding one another. If this developer had followed Step 5, "Think Creatively," he would have been better off because he would have thought about the problem first instead of plunging right in.

Step 9: Learn and Share

Each time you fix a "good" bug (that is, one that was challenging to find and fix), you should take the time to quickly summarize what you learned. I like to record my good bugs in a journal so that I can later see what I did right in finding and fixing the problem. More important, I also want to learn what I did wrong so that I can learn to avoid dead ends when debugging and solve bugs faster. You learn the most about development when you're debugging, so you should take every opportunity to learn from it.

One of the most important steps you can take after fixing a good bug is to share with your colleagues the information you learned while fixing the bug, especially if the bug is project-specific. This information will help your coworkers the next time they need to eliminate a similar bug.

Final Debugging Process Secret

I'd like to share one final debugging secret with you: the debugger can answer all your debugging questions as long as you ask it the right ones. Again, I'm suggesting that you need to have a hypothesis in mind—something you want to prove or disprove—before the debugger can help you. As I recommended earlier in Step 7 I write out my hypothesis before I ever touch the debugger to ensure that I have a purpose each time I use it.

Remember that the debugger is just a tool, like a screwdriver. It does only what you tell it to do. The real debugger is the software in your hardware cranium.

Summary

This chapter started out defining bugs and describing process problems that contribute to bugs. Then it discussed what you should know before you start debugging. Finally, it presented a debugging process that you should follow when you debug your code.

The best way to debug is to avoid bugs in the first place. If you plan your projects properly, have a real commitment to quality, and learn about how your products fit with their technologies, the operating environment, and the CPU, you can minimize the time you spend debugging.

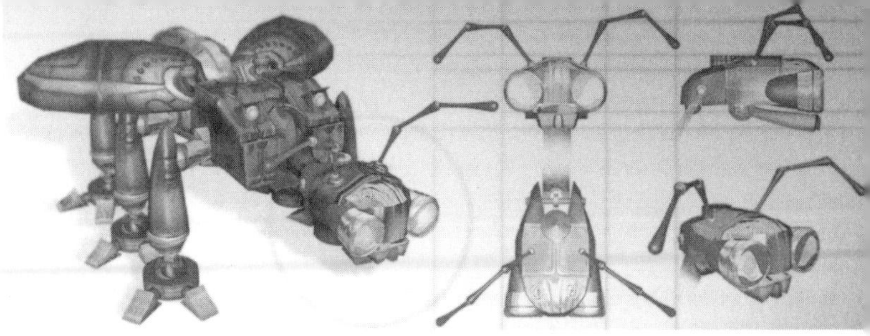

2 Getting Started Debugging

In this chapter, I'll introduce some important infrastructure tools and requirements that will contribute to your debugging success over the lifetime of your application. Some of the tools involve the engineering process, and others are software utilities. What they all have in common is that they allow you to see the progress of your project on a daily basis. I believe this daily monitoring is the key to getting your product out the door on time—with quality. Projects don't slip massively in one day; they slip a little each day along the way.

All the ideas presented here and in Chapter 3 come from my experience shipping real-world software products as well as my work as a consultant with some of the best development shops in the world. I can't imagine developing without these tools and techniques. I've learned some lessons the hard way and watched others learn the same lessons, and I hope to save you time and pain by sharing with you what these lessons have taught me. You might think that some of these ideas don't apply to you because you're on a two-person or three-person team. Don't worry, they do. Even when I'm on a team of one, I still approach a project in the same way. I've worked on projects of every size you can think of, so I know the recommendations I make scale from the tiniest to the largest teams.

Track Changes Until You Throw Away the Project

Version control and bug tracking systems are two of the most important infrastructure tools you have because they give you the history of your project. Although the developers might say they can keep everything in their heads, the company needs to have some record of what's been accomplished on the project in case the entire development team wins the lottery and everyone quits the next day. Because most teams don't adequately maintain their requirements and design documents throughout the life of a project, the only real documentation becomes the audit trail in the version control and bug tracking systems.

I hope I'm preaching to the converted. Unfortunately, I keep running into teams that haven't yet started using these tools, especially bug tracking systems. As someone interested in history, I feel you have to know where you've been to know where you're going. Putting these two tools to use is the only sure way to learn that lesson. By monitoring the outstanding bugs and bug fix rates in the bug tracking system, you can better predict when your product will be ready to ship. With the version control system, you'll get an idea of your "code churn," or the volume of changes, so that you can see how much additional testing needs to be done. Additionally, these tools are the only effective way to judge whether you're getting any results from changes you implement in your development cycle.

When you bring a new developer to your team, these tools can pay for themselves in a single day. When the new developer starts, have her sit down with the version control and bug tracking software and begin working her way through the changes. Good design documents are ideal, but if they aren't available, the version control and bug tracking systems at least provide a record of the code evolution and highlight any trouble areas.

I'm talking about these two tools in the same breath because they are inseparable. The bug tracking system captures all the events that might have driven changes to your master sources. The version control system captures every change. Ideally, you want to maintain the relationship between reported problems and actual changes in the master sources. By correlating the relationship, you can see your cause and effect for bug fixes. If you don't track the relationship, you're left wondering why certain changes to the code occurred. Invariably, in later versions of the product, you have to find the developer who made the change and hope he remembers the reason for the change.

Some products are integrated and automatically track the relationship of the master source change to the bug report, but if your current systems don't, you'll need to maintain the relationship manually. You can track the relationship by including the bug number in the comments that describe the fix. When you check the file back into version control, you'll need to identify the bug number you're fixing in the check-in comment for the file.

Version Control Systems

The version control system isn't just for your project's master sources. Anything and everything related to the project—including all test plans, automated tests, the help system, and design documents—needs to go into the version control system. Some companies even include the build tools (that is, the compiler, linker, include files, and libraries), which allow them to completely re-create the shipped version of their products. If you have any question about whether something should go in version control, ask yourself whether maintenance programmers could use the information in a couple of years. If you think they could, that information belongs in the version control system.

The Importance of Including Unit Tests

Even though I just said to check in everything that could be of use, one of the biggest problems I've seen in development shop after development shop is not including the unit tests in the version control system. In case you're not familiar with the term *unit test*, I'll briefly describe it here. A unit test is the piece of code that drives your main program code. (It's sometimes also referred to as *test apps* or *test harness*.) It's the testing code created by the developer that allows the developer to do "glass box," or "white box," testing to ensure the basic operations take place. For a complete definition of unit tests, see Chapter 25, "Unit Testing," of Steve McConnell's book *Code Complete* (Microsoft Press, 1993).

Including the unit tests in version control accomplishes two key objectives. First, you make the job of maintenance developers infinitely easier. So many times, the maintenance developer, who could easily turn out to be you, has to reinvent the wheel when upgrading or fixing the code. Doing so is not only a huge waste of effort but also a real morale killer. Second, you make general testing for QA teams trivial so that those teams can focus on the important testing areas, such as performance and scalability as well as fit and finish. One sign of a seasoned professional is that she always has her unit tests checked in.

Of course, checking in your unit tests means that you automatically have to keep them up to date with code changes. Yes, that's going to be additional work on your behalf. Nothing is worse than having a maintenance developer hunting you down and slapping you silly because the unit tests no longer work. Having outdated unit tests is worse than having no unit tests in the version control system.

If you look at the source code for this book, you'll notice that all my unit tests are included as part of the code. In fact, there's a separate build to automatically build all the unit tests for all the utilities or examples I include. I'm not about to recommend anything in this book that I don't do myself.

Some readers might be thinking that implementing the unit test discipline I advocate is going to take a lot more work. In reality, it's not going to take that much longer because most developers (I hope!) are already conducting unit tests. The big differences I'm suggesting are keeping those tests checked in and up to date as well as possibly generating a build script of some sort for them. The time you'll save by following the proper procedures will be huge. For example, for most of this book, I did my development on a machine with Microsoft Windows 2000 Server installed. To turn around and do immediate testing on my Microsoft Windows XP machines, I simply had to get the code from version control and do the build scripts. Many developers do a one-off unit test, so testing on other operating systems is difficult because they have no easy way to get the unit tests over and built. If everyone is making unit tests part of the code, you can shave many weeks off your schedules.

Controlling Changes

Tracking changes is vital; however, having a good bug tracking system in place doesn't mean that developers should be allowed to make wholesale changes to the master sources whenever they want. Such carte blanche would make all the tracking pointless. The idea is to control the changes during development, restricting certain types of changes to certain stages of the project so that you can have an idea of the state of the master sources on a day-to-day basis. The best scheme I've heard of for controlling changes comes from my friend Steve Munyan, and he calls it "Green, Yellow, and Red Times." In Green Time, anyone can check in anything to the master sources. The earliest parts of the project are usually fully in Green Time because at this point the team is working on new features.

Yellow Time is when the product is in a bug fix phase or nearing a code freeze. The only code changes allowed are for bug fixes—and *only* bug fixes. No new features or other changes are permitted. Before a developer can check in a bug fix, a technical lead or a development manager must approve it. The developer making the bug fix must describe the bug fix he's making and what it affects. In essence, this process is a mini code review for every single bug fix. The important item to remember when conducting that code review is to utilize the version control product's differencing utility to ensure exactly which changes occurred so that extraneous changes don't sneak in. On some teams I've been on, the product was in Yellow Time from day one because the team liked the code review aspects of this stage. We did loosen the approval requirements so that any other developer could approve changes. The interesting outcome was that because of the constant code reviews, the developers caught many bugs before they checked the code into the master sources.

Red Time occurs when you're in a code freeze or near a key milestone and all code changes require the product manager's approval. When I was a product manager (the person on the team responsible for the code as a whole), I even went to the extent of changing the permissions in the version control system so that the team had read-only access. I took this step mainly because I understood what the developers were thinking: "This is just a little change; it will fix this bug, and it won't hurt anything else." The developers' intentions were good, but that one little change could mean that the entire team would have to restart the test plan from the beginning.

The product manager must strictly enforce Red Time. If the product has a reproducible crash or data corruption, the decision to make the change is essentially automatic because you just do it. In most cases, however, deciding whether to fix a particular bug is less black and white. To help me decide how critical a bug fix was, I always asked the following questions with the company's needs in mind:

- How many people does this problem affect?
- Is the change in a core or a peripheral part of the product?
- If the change is made, what parts of the application will need to be retested?

The answers to these questions provided the criteria I needed to allow or to decide against the change. Let me put some concrete numbers behind this list and give you my general rules for the beta phases. If the is the bug is serious, which means that it's less than a crash or data corruption showstopper, and it's going to affect greater than 15 percent of our external testers, the bug is an automatic fix. If the bug will result in a change to a data file, I go ahead and fix it so that we don't have to change file formats later in the development process and so that beta testers can consequently get larger data sets for subsequent betas.

The Importance of Labeling

One of the most important commands that you can learn to use in your version control system is its label command. Microsoft Visual SourceSafe calls it a label, MKS Source Integrity calls it a checkpoint, and PVCS Version Manager calls it a version label. Different version control systems might refer to the label command in different ways, but whatever it's called, a label marks a particular set of master sources. A label allows you to retrieve a specific version of your master sources in the future. If you make a labeling mistake, you might never be able to retrieve the exact master sources used for a particular version. That could mean that you might not be able to discover why a particular version is crashing.

When deciding what to label, I've always followed these five hard-and-fast rules:

1. Label all internal milestones.
2. Label any transitions from Green, Yellow, or Red development times.
3. Label any build sent to someone outside the team.

4. Label any time you branch a development tree in the version control software.

5. Label after the daily build and smoke tests complete correctly. (Smoke tests are discussed in the "Smoke Tests" section later in this chapter.)

In all cases, I follow a scheme of "<Project Name> <Milestone/Reason> <Date>" so that the label names are descriptive.

The third labeling rule is one that many people forget. Your quality engineers are usually working with the milestone or daily build, so when they report a problem, they do so against a particular version of the master sources. Because developers can change code quickly, you want to make it simple for them to get back to the exact version of the files they need to reproduce the bug.

Common Debugging Question

What do we do if we're having trouble reproducing builds sent to others outside the team?

Every time you do a build for someone outside the team, you should make a complete copy of the project build directory to CD/DVD or tape. This copy will include all your source files, the intermediate files, the symbol files, and the final output. Also include the installation kit that you sent the customer. You might even want to consider copying the build tools. CD/DVDs and tapes are inexpensive insurance against future problems.

Even when I've done everything possible to preserve a particular build in version control, I've still experienced cases in which a rebuild produced a binary that differed from the original. By having the complete build tree archived, you can debug the user's problem with exactly the same binaries that you sent.

Bug Tracking Systems

In addition to tracking your bugs, the bug tracking system makes an excellent vehicle for jotting down reminders and keeping a to-do list, especially when you're in the process of developing code. Some developers like to keep notes and to-do lists in notebooks, but essential information often gets lost between random hexadecimal number streams from a debugging session and the pages on pages of doodling that you used to keep yourself awake in the last management status meeting. By putting these notes into the bug tracking system and assigning them to yourself, you consolidate them in one place, making them easier to find. Additionally, although you probably like to think that you "own" the code you work on, you really don't—it belongs to the team. With your to-do list in the bug tracking system, other team members who have to interface with your code can check your list to see what you have or haven't done. Another benefit of including to-do lists and notes in the bug tracking system is that fewer details fall through the cracks at the last minute as a result of you forgetting about a problem or another issue. I always find myself running the bug tracking system so that I can quickly jot down important notes and to-dos right when I think about them.

I like to reserve the lowest priority bug code in the system for notes and to-do lists. Flagging notes and to-do lists as lowest priority bugs makes it easier to keep them separate from the real bugs, but at the same time, you can quickly raise their priority if you need to. You should also structure your bug metrics reports so that they don't include the lowest priority bug code, because it will skew your results.

Don't be afraid to peruse the bug tracking data either. All the unvarnished truths about your products are there. When you're planning an update, run through the bug tracking system and find those modules or features that had the most bugs reported against them. Consider adding some time in your schedule to allow team members to go back and strengthen those sections.

When deploying your bug tracking system, make sure that everyone who needs it has it. At a minimum, everyone on the development team and the technical support team needs access to it. If your bug tracking system supports different levels of access, you might also want to think about allowing others, such as sales engineers (technical experts who are part of the sales organization and help the salespeople as needed when they're selling a complicated product) and marketing representatives, to have access as appropriate. For example, you might want to allow certain sales and marketing people to enter bugs and feature requests but not to view existing bugs. These two groups are generally out talking to customers more than your typical engineers are, and the customer feedback they can supply can be invaluable. Of course, this means you're going to have to give sales and marketing folks classes on how to fill out bug reports. They're more than happy to help, but you need to give them the guidance so that they can do it properly. Having these groups log their requests and problems in the same system that everyone else uses is efficient and practical. The idea is to have one central place where all problems and feature requests reside. If you store this information in multiple locations, such as in the product manager's e-mail inbox, in engineer paper notebooks, and in the bug tracking system, you're more likely to lose track of it.

Choosing the Right Systems for You

Numerous version control systems are available. Some might be easier to use than others or offer more features, but the real issue in choosing the best version control system comes down to your specific requirements. Obviously, if you're in a shop that has high-end requirements, such as multiple platform support, you're going to need to look at one of the more expensive systems or possibly an open source solution such as CVS. If you're a small team targeting just Microsoft Windows development, however, you can consider some of the less costly alternatives. Make sure you spend some time doing some hard evaluation of the system you're thinking about implementing, especially in trying to predict what you'll need in the future. You're going to be living with your version control system for a while, so make sure it will grow with you. And keep in mind that just as important as choosing the right version control system is using a version control system in the first place: any system is better than no system.

As for bug tracking systems, I've seen many people try to limp along with a homegrown system. Although doing a project with a homemade system is possible, I'd strongly recommend investing in a commercial product or utilizing an open source solution. The information in the bug tracking system is too vital to put into an application that you don't have the time to support and that can't grow to meet your needs six months or a year into the project. Additionally, developers avoid wasting time on internal tools and work instead on revenue-producing products.

The same criteria apply for choosing a bug tracking system as for choosing a version control system. Once, as a product manager, I decided on a bug tracking system without spending enough time looking at the most important part, reporting bugs. The product was easy enough to set up and use. Unfortunately, its reporting capabilities were so limited that we ended up transferring all our existing bugs over to another product right after we hit our first external code milestone. I was rather embarrassed for not having evaluated the product as thoroughly as I should have.

As I mentioned earlier in the chapter, you should definitely consider a bug tracking product that offers integration with a version control product. In the Windows marketplace, most version control systems support the Microsoft Source Code Control Interface (MSSCCI). If your bug tracking system supports MSSCCI as well, you can coordinate the bug fixes with particular file versions.

Some people have described code as the lifeblood of a development team. If that description is accurate, the version control and bug tracking systems are the arteries. They keep the lifeblood flowing and moving in the right direction. Don't develop without them.

Schedule Time for Building Debugging Systems

As you're doing the design and initial scheduling for your project, make sure to add in time for building your debugging systems. You need to decide up front how you're going to implement your crash handlers (a topic covered in Chapter 13), file data dumpers, and other tools you'll need to help you reproduce problems reported from the field. I've always liked to treat the error handling systems as if they were a product feature. That way, others in the company can see how you're going to handle bugs proactively when they come up.

As you're planning your debugging systems, you need to establish your preventive debugging policies. The first and most difficult parts of this process involve determining how you're going to return error conditions in the project. Whatever you do, make sure you pick only one way and stick with it. One project I encountered long ago (and fortunately wasn't a part of) had three different ways to return errors: return values, `setjmp/longjmp` exceptions, and through a global error variable similar to the C run-time library's `errno` variable. Those developers had a very difficult time tracking errors across subsystem boundaries.

When it comes to .NET development, choosing how to handle error conditions is fairly simple. You can either continue to rely on return values or use exceptions. The beauty of .NET is that, unlike native code, there's a standard exception class, `System.Exception`, which all other exceptions derive from. The one drawback to .NET exceptions is that you still have to rely on excellent documentation or code inspections to know exactly which exception is thrown by a method. As you'll see in my code, I still tend to use the return value approach for normal operation and expected errors, because it will always be a little faster than the overhead necessary to generate the `throw` and `catch` code. However, for any anomalous errors, I always `throw`.

With native code, on the other hand, you're basically forced to use only the return value approach. The problem is that C++ has no standard exception class that's automatically assumed to be thrown, and the implementation issues of technologies such as COM can't have exceptions crossing apartment or process boundaries. As you'll see in great detail in Chapter 13, C++ exceptions are one of the biggest performance and bug producing areas known to developerkind. Do yourself a great favor and forget that C++ exceptions exist. They are great from a theoretical standpoint, but you have to keep in mind that reality is a cruel master.

Build All Builds with Debugging Symbols

Some of the debugging system recommendations that I do make aren't that controversial. I've been harping on my first recommendation for years: build all builds, including release builds, with full debugging symbols. Debugging symbols are the data that let the debugger show you source and line information, variable names, and data type information for your program. All that information is stored in a .PDB (Program Database) file associated with your modules. If you're paid by the hour, spending forever at the assembly language level could do wonders for paying your mortgage. Unfortunately, the rest of us don't have the luxury of infinite time, so speedily finding those bugs is a priority.

Of course, debugging release builds with symbols has its drawbacks. For example, the optimized code that the just-in-time (JIT) compiler or native compiler produces won't always match the flow of execution in the source code, so you might find that stepping through release code is a little harder than stepping through debug code. Another problem to watch out for in native release builds is that sometimes the compiler optimizes the stack registers such that you can't see the complete call stack, as you would in a straight debug build. Also be aware that when you do add debugging symbols to the binary, it will grow a small amount to account for the debug section string that identifies the .PDB file. However, the few-byte size increase is negligible when compared to the ease of being able to solve bugs quickly.

Turning on debug symbols for a release build is quite easy, though it should have been turned on by default in the wizard-generated projects. For a C# project, open the project Property Pages dialog box and select the Configuration Properties folder. Select All Configurations or Release in the Configurations dropdown list, display the Configuration Properties folder, Build property page, and set the Generate Debugging Information field to True. This sets the `/debug:full` flag for CSC.EXE. Figure 2-1 shows the project Property Pages dialog box in which you turn on debugging information.

For reasons that I still can't quite fathom, the Microsoft Visual Basic .NET project Property Pages dialog box is different from the one for C# projects, but the compiler switch is still the same. Figure 2-2 shows setting a release build that produces full debug symbols. Open the project Property Pages dialog box and select the Configuration Properties folder. Select All Configurations or Release in the Configuration drop down list, display the Configuration Properties folder, Build property page, and check the Generate Debugging Information check box.

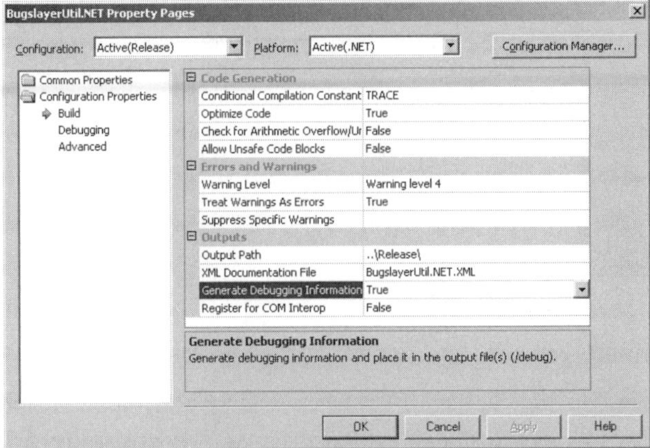

Figure 2-1 Generating debugging information for a C# project

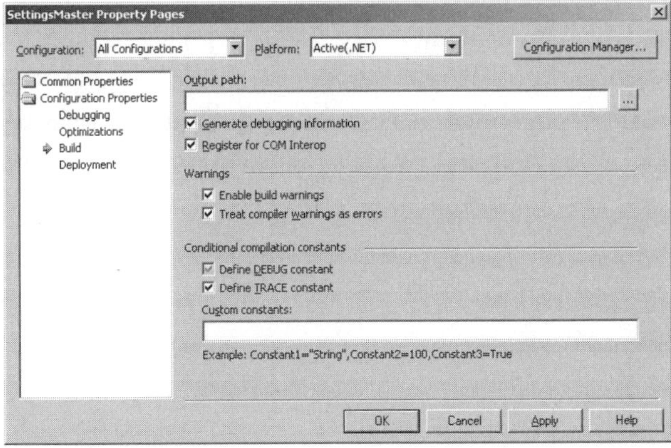

Figure 2-2 Generating debugging information for a Visual Basic .NET project

For native C++, the `/Zi` switch turns on the PDB file for the compiler. In the project Property Pages dialog box, display the C/C++ folder, General property page, and set Debug Information Format to Program Database (/Zi). Make sure you don't select Program Database For Edit & Continue or your release build will be built with all the extra padding bytes necessary for editing and continuing, and thus be quite fat and slow. Figure 2-3 shows the appropriate compiler settings. There are other settings for better builds set in Figure 2-3, and I'll discuss them in the Common Debugging Question, "What additional compiler and linker options will help me with my proactive debugging of native code?"

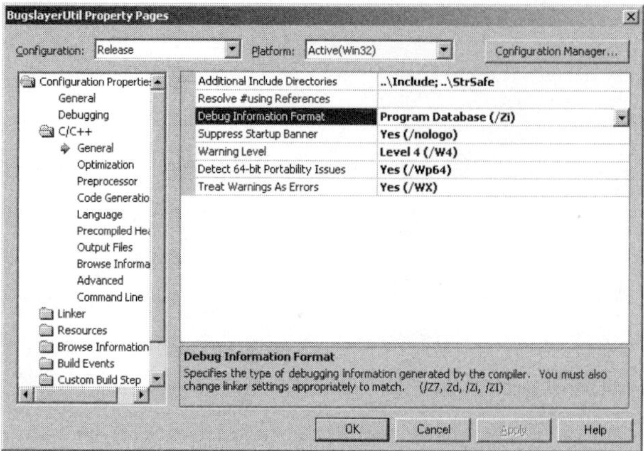

Figure 2-3 Setting the C++ compiler to generate debugging information

After setting the compiler switch, you'll need to set the appropriate linker switches: `/INCREMENTAL:NO`, `/DEBUG`, and `/PDB`. The incremental linking option resides in the project Property Pages dialog box, Linker folder, General property page, and Enable Incremental Linking field. Figure 2-4 shows the switch location.

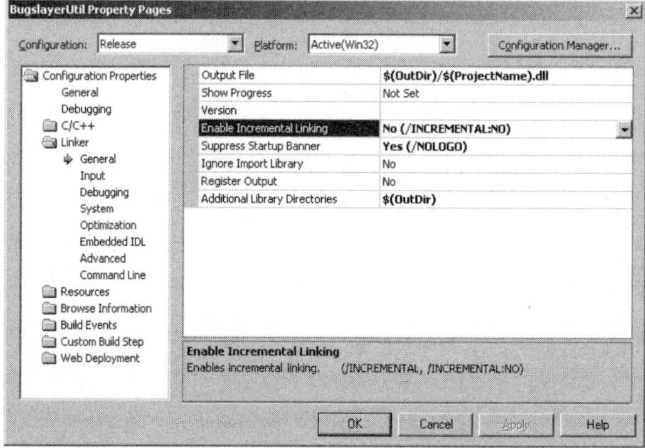

Figure 2-4 Turning off incremental linking in the C++ linker

In the project Property Pages dialog box, Linker folder, Debugging property page, set the Generate Debug Info option to Yes (/DEBUG). To set the `/PDB` option, place $(OutDir)/$(ProjectName).PDB in the Generate Program Database File option, which is directly below the Generate Debug Info field. In case you haven't noticed, the Microsoft Visual Studio .NET project system finally fixed some of the big problems prior versions had with generic build options. The values starting with $ and in parentheses are macro values. From their names, you can probably guess what they are. All the other macros are accessible by clicking in most editable options in the property page and then selecting <Edit...> from the drop-down list. The dialog box that pops up will show all the macros and what they'll expand to. Figure 2-5 demonstrates how to set the `/DEBUG` and `/PDB` switches. The rest of the settings in the figure are important for native C++ code. Later in the chapter, I'll discuss the Common Debugging Question, "What additional compiler and linker options will help me with my proactive debugging of native code?"

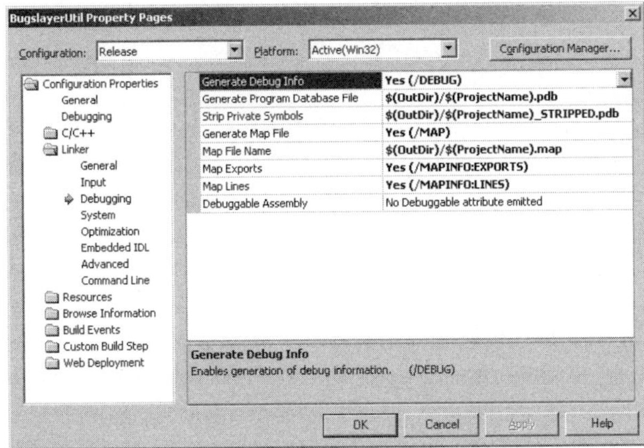

Figure 2-5 C++ linker debug node settings

To properly get debugging symbols for C++, two more settings are necessary: `/OPT:REF` and `/OPT:ICF`. Both switches are set in the Linker folder, Optimization property page, as shown in Figure 2-6. Set the References option to Eliminate Unreferenced Data (/OPT:REF). Set the Enable COMDAT Folding option to Remove Redundant COMDATs (/OPT:ICF). Using the `/DEBUG` switch with the linker automatically tells the switch to bring in all functions whether or not they are referenced, which is the default for debug builds. The `/OPT:REF` switch tells the linker to bring in only functions that your program calls directly. If you forget to add the `/OPT:REF` switch, your release application will also contain the functions that are never called, making the application much larger than it should be. The `/OPT:ICF` switch will combine identical data COMDAT records when necessary so that you'll have only one constant data variable for all references to that constant value.

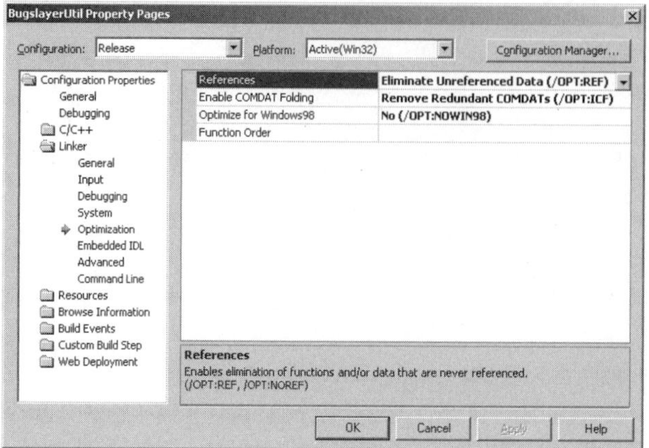

Figure 2-6 C++ optimization linker settings

After you build your release builds with full PDB files, you need to store the PDB files in a safe place along with any binary files you ship to customers. If you lose your PDB files, you'll be right back to debugging at the assembly-language level. Treat your PDB files as you would your distributed binaries.

If the thought of manually changing your project's settings to build with debug symbols, as well as the rest of the proper build switches, has you dreading the work, don't worry—there's hope. For Chapter 9, I wrote an extremely cool add-in, SettingsMaster, that takes all the work out of changing project settings. SettingsMaster's defaults are to set up your projects using the settings recommended in this chapter.

For Managed Code, Treat Warnings as Errors

If you've written anything more than "Hello World!" in managed code, you've certainly noticed that the compilers don't let much slide as far as compiler errors are concerned. For those of you coming from a C++ background and new to .NET, you are probably amazed at how much tighter everything feels—in C++, you could cast values to almost anything and the compiler would blindly go on its merry way. In addition to making sure data types are explicit, the managed code compilers can do much more to help you with errors if you let them. As usual, the trick to debugging smarter is not one big gesture, but taking advantage of lots of small steps along the way. Making your tools as smart as possible is one of those steps.

In the Visual Studio .NET documentation, if you browse the Contents pane and then go to Visual Studio .NET\Visual Basic and Visual C#\Reference\Visual C# Language\C# Compiler Options\Compiler Errors CS0001 Through CS9999, you'll see all the compiler errors for C#. (The Visual Basic .NET compiler errors are also included in the documentation, but amazingly the compiler errors aren't indexed in the Contents pane.) As you scroll down the list of errors, you'll notice that some say Compiler Warning and indicate a level, for example, Compiler Warning (level 4) CS0028. If you keep scrolling down the list, you'll find warning levels from 1 through 4. When you have a warning, the compiler indicates that the construct at that location in the source code is syntactically correct but might not be contextually correct. A perfect example is CS0183, shown in the following code. (The given expression is always of the provided ('type') type.)

```
// Generates warning CS0183 because a string (or any type in .NET for that
// matter) is ALWAYS derived from Object.
public static void Main ( )
{
    String StringOne = "Something pithy. . ." ;
    if ( StringOne is String )    // CS0183
    {
        Console.WriteLine ( StringOne ) ;
    }
}
```

Given that the compiler can tell you all sorts of wonderful contextual problems like this, doesn't it make sense to fix these problems? I don't like to call the problems warnings because they are really errors. If you've ever had the opportunity to learn about compiler construction, particularly parsing, you probably walked away with two thoughts: parsing is extremely hard, and people who write compilers are different from the rest of us. (Whether that's a good different or bad different, I'll let you decide.) If the compiler writers go to tremendous trouble to report a warning, they are telling you something they obviously feel is quite important and is probably a bug. When a client asks us to help with a bug, the first thing we do is verify with them that the code compiles with no warnings. If it doesn't, I tell them that I'll be glad to help, but not until their code compiles cleanly.

Fortunately, Visual Studio .NET generates projects with the appropriate warning levels by default, so you shouldn't have to set the warning levels manually. If you're building your C# project manually, you'll want to set the `/WARN` switch to `/WARN:4`. For Visual Basic .NET manual compiles, warnings are on by default, so you specifically have to turn them off.

Although the warning levels are appropriately set by Visual Studio .NET, the default for treating warnings as errors is not set correctly. Cleanly compiling code is next to godliness, so you'll want to get the `/WARNASERROR+` switch set for both the C# and Visual Basic .NET compilers. That way you can't even begin to start debugging until the code is perfect. For C# projects, in the project Property Pages dialog box, Configuration Properties, Build property page, under the Errors And Warnings column, set Treat Warnings As Errors to True. See Figure 2-1 for an illustration of that page. For Visual Basic .NET projects, in the project Property Pages dialog box, Configuration Properties, Build property page, check the Treat Compiler Warnings As Errors check box, as shown in Figure 2-2.

For C# projects in particular, treating warnings as errors will stop the build on all sorts of excellent problems such as CS0649 (Field 'field' is never assigned to, and will always have its default value 'value'), which indicates you have a class member that is uninitialized. However, other messages, such as CS1573 (Parameter 'parameter' has no matching param tag in XML comment (but other parameters do)), might seem so annoying that you'll be tempted to turn off treating warnings as errors. I strongly suggest you don't.

In the case of CS1573, you're using the phenomenal `/DOC` switch to generate the XML documentation for your assembly. (Personally, I think it's a huge crime that Visual Basic .NET and C++ don't support the `/DOC` switch and XML documentation.) This is a perfect error because if you're using XML documentation, someone else on your team is probably going to be reading that documentation, and if you aren't documenting everything you assume with parameters, or anything else for that matter, you're doing everyone on your team a disservice.

One warning that's improperly treated as an error is CS1596: (XML documentation not updated during this incremental rebuild; use /incremental- to update XML documentation.) Although creating the XML documentation is great, this error stops the build cold. Because there's no way to turn off this error, the only workaround is to turn off incremental building in either debug or release. Since fast compiles are nice, I turn off incremental building in the release build and produce only XML documentation in the release build. That way I can still benefit from the fast turnaround compiles but get my XML documentation when I need it.

For Native Code, Treat Warnings as Errors—Mostly

Compared to managed code, native C++ not only lets you shoot yourself in the foot when it comes to compilation issues, but it also hands you the loaded gun and cocks it for good measure. When you get a warning in C++ code, you're really being told that the compiler is taking a wild guess as to what you intended. A warning such as C4244 ('conversion' conversion from 'type1' to 'type2', possible loss of data), which is always reported on conversions between signed and unsigned types, is an excellent example. This is where the compiler has a fifty-fifty chance of reading your mind and picking what should happen with that upper bit.

In many cases, fixing the error is as trivial as applying a cast to a variable. The whole idea is to make the code as unambiguous as possible so that there is no guessing on the compiler's part. Some of the warnings are fantastic for clarifying your code, such as C4101 (*'identifier'* : unreferenced local variable), which tells you that a local variable is never referenced. Fixing the C4101 warning will make your code much more readable for code reviews and maintenance programmers, and no one will waste time wondering what that extra variable is for or where it's used. Other warnings, such as C4700 (local variable 'name' used without having been initialized), tell you exactly where you've got a bug in your code. For some of our clients, simply bumping the warning level up and fixing these warnings solved bugs they would otherwise have spent weeks trying to track down.

The default projects that the Visual C++ wizards create are at warning-level 3, which corresponds to the `/W3` switch in CL.EXE. The next step up is warning-level 4, `/W4`, and you should even have the compiler treat all warnings as errors with `/WX`. These levels are all easy to set in the project Property Pages dialog box, C/C++ folder, General property page. In the Warning Level field, select Level 4 (/W4). Two fields down is the Treat Warnings As Errors field, which you'll want to set to Yes (/WX). Figure 2-3 shows both fields properly filled out.

Although I can almost justify making the global statement "All builds should compile with warning-level 4, and you should treat all warnings as errors," reality intrudes to force me to temper this remark. The Standard Template Library (STL) that comes with Visual C++ has many warning-level 4 issues in it. The compiler also has a few problems with templates. Fortunately, you can work around most of these issues.

You might think that just setting the warning level to 4 and turning off treating warnings as errors would be fine; in fact, that scheme defeats the purpose. I've found that developers quickly become desensitized to warnings in the Build window. If you don't fix all the warnings as they happen, no matter how innocuous a warning seems, you'll start to lose more important warnings because they'll be hidden amid the output stream. The trick is to be more explicit about which warnings you want to handle. Although your goal should be to get rid of most warnings by writing better code, you can also turn off specific errors with the `#pragma warning` directive. Additionally, you can use the `#pragma warning` directive to control the error level around specific headers.

A good example of lowering the error level is when you're including headers that don't compile at warning-level 4. The extended `#pragma warning` directive, first offered in Visual C++ 6, can lower the warning level. In the following code snippet, I set the warning level before including the suspect header and reset it so that my code compiles with warning-level 4:

```
#pragma warning ( push , 3 )
#include "IDoNotCompileAtWarning4.h"
#pragma warning ( pop )
```

You can also disable individual warnings with the `#pragma warning` directive. This directive comes in handy when you're using a nameless structure or union and you get a C4201 error, "nonstandard extension used : nameless struct/union," with warning-level 4. To turn off that warning, you use the `#pragma warning` directive as in the following code. Notice that I commented what I was turning off and explained why I was turning it off. When disabling individual warnings, be sure to restrict the scope of the `#pragma warning` directive to specific sections of code. If you place the directive at too high a level, you can mask other problems in your code.

```
// Turning off "nonstandard extension used : nameless struct/union"
// because I'm not writing portable code
#pragma warning ( disable : 4201 )
struct S
{
    float y;
    struct
    {
        int a ;
        int b ;
        int c ;
    } ;
} *p_s ;
// Turn warning back on.
#pragma warning ( default : 4201 )
```

One warning, C4100, "'*identifier*' : unreferenced formal parameter," seems to cause confusion about how to fix it. If you have a parameter that's not being referenced, you should probably remove that parameter from the definition of the method. However, if you're doing object-oriented programming, you can derive from a method that no longer needs the parameter and then you can't change the base class. The following code snippet shows how to properly work around the C4100 error:

```
// This code will generate the C4100 error.
int ProblemMethod ( int i , int j )
{
    return ( 5 ) ;
}
// The following code properly avoids the C4100 error.
int GoodMethod ( int /* i */ , int /* j */ )
{
    return ( 22 ) ;
}
```

If you're not using STL, this scheme works well. If you're using STL, it might work, but it might not. Your best bet with STL is to include only the STL headers in your precompiled headers. It makes isolating the `#pragma warning ( push , 3 )` and `#pragma warning ( pop )` around the headers much easier. The other huge benefit is that your compiles will speed up dramatically. A precompiled header is essentially the parse tree, and because STL includes so much stuff, precompiling headers will save lots of time. Finally, to fully track memory leaks and corruptions in the C run-time library, you'll need to keep the STL headers together. The debug C run-time library is discussed in Chapter 17.

The bottom line is that you must compile at warning-level 4 and treat all warnings as errors from the start of your project. When you first boost the warning level for your project, you'll probably be surprised by the number of warnings you get. Go through and fix each one. You'll probably notice that just fixing the warnings will solve a bug or two. For those of you who think getting your program to compile with `/W4` and `/WX` is impossible, I have proof otherwise: all the native sample code on this book's companion CD compiles with both flags set for all configurations.

Common Debugging Question

The STL supplied with Visual Studio .NET is hard to read and debug. Is there anything to make it easier to understand?

I realize that people much smarter than I wrote the STL supplied with Visual Studio .NET, but even so, it's nearly impossible to understand. On one hand, the concept of STL is good because it has a consistent interface and is widely used. On the other hand, the reality of the STL supplied with Visual Studio .NET and with templates in general is that if you have any kind of problem, you have more difficulty figuring it out than you would debugging straight at the assembly-language level.

Better than the Visual Studio .NET–supplied STL is the free STL from STLport (*www.stlport.org*). Not only is STLport infinitely more readable, but it also has much better support for multithreading and excellent debugging support built in. Given these advantages and the fact that it has absolutely no restrictions on commercial use, I would highly recommend that you use it instead of the STL supplied with Visual Studio .NET if you have to use STL at all.

For Native Code, Know Where Your DLLs Load

If you've ever been hiking in the woods, you know that landmarks can be very important in keeping you from getting lost. When you don't have any landmarks, you can end up going around in circles. When your application crashes, you need a similar kind of landmark to help point you in the right direction so that you're not wandering around in the debugger.

The first big landmark for crashes is the base address of your dynamic-link libraries (DLLs) and ActiveX controls (OCXs), which indicates where they loaded into memory. When a customer gives you a crash address, you should be able to narrow down which DLL it came from quickly by the first two or three numbers. I don't expect you to have all the system DLLs memorized, but you should memorize at least the DLL base addresses for the DLLs in your project.

If all your DLLs load at unique addresses, you have some good landmarks to help guide your search for the crash. But what do you think would happen if all your DLLs had the same load address? Obviously, the operating system doesn't map them all into the same place in memory. It has to "relocate" any incoming DLL that wants to occupy memory that's already filled by putting the incoming DLL into a different place. The issue then becomes one of trying to figure out which DLL is loaded where. Unfortunately, you have no way of knowing what the operating system will do on different machines. This means you'll get a crash address and literally have no idea where that address came from. And that means your boss will be extremely upset because you can't tell him why the application died.

By default for wizard-created projects, Visual Basic 6 ActiveX DLLs load at 0x11000000, and Visual C++ DLLs load at 0x10000000. I'm willing to bet that at least half the DLLs in the world today try to load at one of those addresses. Changing the base address for your DLL is called *rebasing*, and it's a simple operation in which you specify a load address different from the default.

Before we jump into rebasing, let's look at two easy ways to find out whether you have load conflicts in your DLLs. The first way is to use the Visual Studio .NET debugger Modules window. Run your application in Visual Studio .NET and display the Modules window, which is accessible from the Debug menu, Windows submenu, or by pressing CTRL+ALT+U with the default keyboard mapping. If a module has been rebased, its icon displays a red ball with an exclamation point next to the name. Additionally, the load address for the module has an asterisk after the address range. Figure 2-7 shows where the SYMSRV.DLL was relocated in the debugging session.

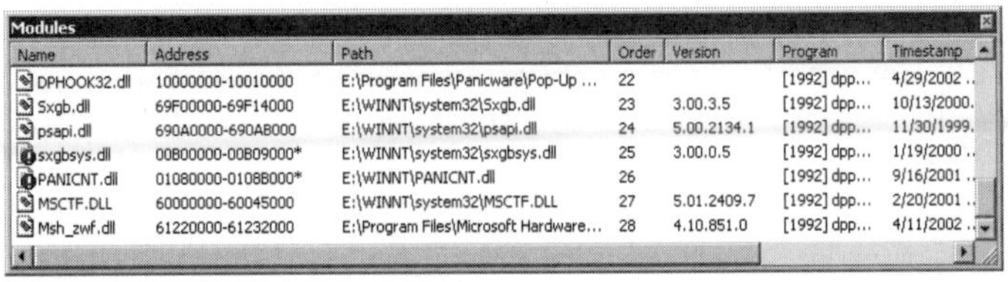

Figure 2-7 The Visual Studio .NET debugger Modules window with a relocated DLL

The second way is to download the free Process Explorer, written by my good friend and onetime neighbor, Mark Russinovich, from Sysinternals (*www.sysinternals.com*). Process Explorer, as its name implies, shows you all sorts of information about your processes, for example, loaded DLLs and all open handles. It's such a useful tool that if you don't have it on your machines right now, stop immediately and go download it! Also, make sure to read Chapter 14 for additional hints and tricks you can use to make your debugging life easier with Process Explorer.

Seeing whether you have relocated DLLs is very easy. Just follow the next set of steps. Figure 2-8 shows what it looks like to have relocated DLLs in a process.

1. Start Process Explorer as well as your process.
2. Select View DLLs from the View menu.
3. Select Highlight Relocated DLLs from the Options menu.
4. Select your process in the upper half of the main window.

If any DLLs show up highlighted in yellow, they have been relocated.

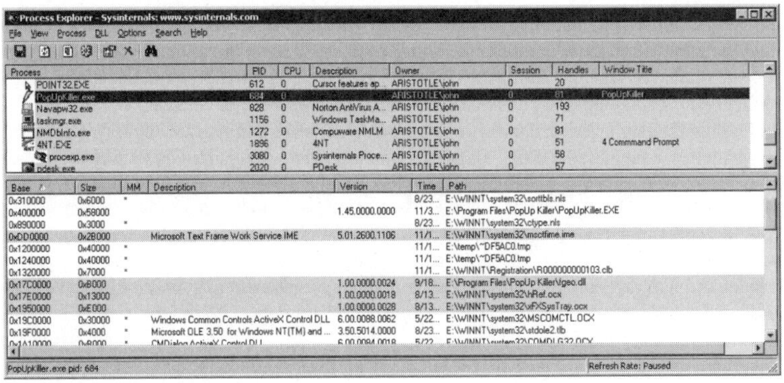

Figure 2-8 Process Explorer showing relocated DLLs

Another excellent tool that will show relocated DLLs with not only the relocated address but also the original address is ProcessSpy from Christophe Nasarre's excellent "Escape from DLL Hell with Custom Debugging and Instrumentation Tools and Utilities, Part 2" in the August 2002 edition of *MSDN Magazine*. Process Explorer and ProcessSpy are similar utilities, but ProcessSpy comes with source code so that you can see how all the magic happens.

In addition to making it difficult to find a crash, when the operating system has to relocate a DLL, your application slows down. When relocating, the operating system needs to read all the relocation information for the DLL, run through each place in the code that accesses an address within the DLL, and change the address because the DLL is no longer at its preferred place in memory. If you have a couple of load address conflicts in your application, startup can sometimes take more than twice as long!

The other big problem is that because of the relocation, the operating system can't completely swap out that module from memory if it needs the room for other code. If the module loads at its preferred load address, the operating system can read the module back in directly from disk if the module was swapped out. If a module is rebased, the problem is that the code memory for that module has been changed for that process. Therefore, the operating system must keep that memory around someplace—which happens to be the page file—even if the module is swapped out. As you can imagine, this can eat up large chunks of memory and cause the computer to slow down as it's moving this memory around.

There are two ways to rebase the DLLs in your application. The first method is to use the REBASE.EXE utility that comes with Visual Studio .NET. REBASE.EXE has many different options, but your best bet is to call it using the `/b` command-line switch with the starting base address and place the appropriate DLLs on the command line. The good news is that once you do the rebasing, you'll almost never have to touch those DLLs again. Also make sure to do any rebasing before you sign a DLL. If you rebase a DLL after it's been signed, that DLL won't load.

Table 2-1 shows a table from the Visual Studio .NET documentation for rebasing your DLLs. As you can see, the recommended format is to use an alphabetical scheme. I generally follow this scheme because it's simple. The operating system DLLs load from 0x70000000 to 0x78000000, so using the range in Table 2-1 will keep you from conflicting with the operating system. Of course, you should always look in your application's address space by using Process Explorer or ProcessSpy to see whether any DLLs are already loaded at the address you want to use.

Table 2-1 DLL Rebasing Scheme

DLL First Letter	Starting Address
A–C	0x60000000
D–F	0x61000000
G–I	0x62000000
J–L	0x63000000
M–O	0x64000000
P–R	0x65000000
S–U	0x66000000
V–X	0x67000000
Y–Z	0x68000000

If you have four DLLs in your application, APPLE.DLL, DUMPLING.DLL, GINGER.DLL, and GOOSEBERRIES.DLL, you run REBASE.EXE three times to get all the DLLs rebased appropriately. The following three commands show how to run REBASE.EXE with those DLLs:

```
REBASE /b 0x60000000 APPLE.DLL
REBASE /b 0x61000000 DUMPLING.DLL
REBASE /b 0x62000000 GINGER.DLL GOOSEBERRIES.DLL
```

If multiple DLLs are passed on the REBASE.EXE command line, as shown here with GINGER.DLL and GOOSEBERRIES.DLL, REBASE.EXE will rebase the DLLs so that they are loaded back to back starting at the specified starting address.

The other method of rebasing a DLL is to specify the load address when you link the DLL. In Visual C++, specify the address by selecting Linker folder, Advanced property page in the project Property Pages dialog box. The Base Address field is where you'll set the hexadecimal address. The address will be used with the `/BASE` switch passed to LINK.EXE. Figure 2-9 shows where you set the base address.

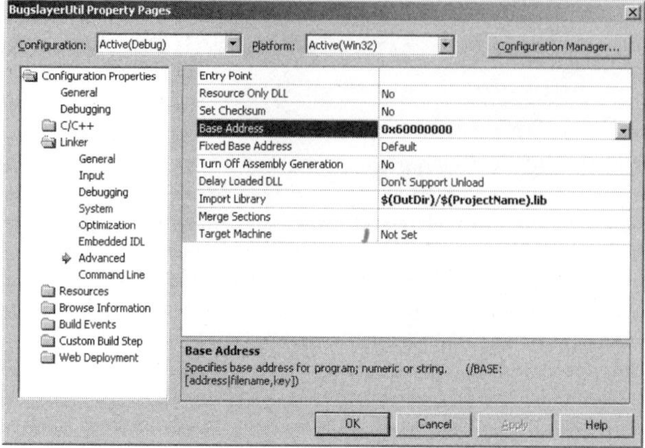

Figure 2-9 Setting the base address for a DLL

Although you can use REBASE.EXE to automatically handle setting multiple DLL load addresses at a time, you have to be a little more careful when setting the load address at link time. If you set the load addresses of multiple DLLs too close together, you'll see the relocated DLL in the debugger Module window. The trick is to set the load addresses far enough apart that you never have to worry about them after you set them.

Using the same DLLs from the REBASE.EXE example, I'd set their load address to the following:

```
APPLE.DLL           0x60000000
DUMPLING.DLL        0x61000000
GINGER.DLL          0x62000000
GOOSEBERRIES.DLL    0x62100000
```

The important two DLLs are GINGER.DLL and GOOSEBERRIES.DLL because they begin with the same character. When that happens, I use the third-highest digit to differentiate the load addresses. If I were to add another DLL that started with "G," its load address would be 0x62200000.

To see a project in which the load addresses are set manually, look at the WDBG project in Chapter 4. The `/BASE` switch also allows you to specify a text file that contains the load addresses for each DLL in your application. In the WDBG project, I use the text-file scheme.

Either method, using REBASE.EXE or rebasing the DLLs manually, will rebase your DLLs and OCXs, but it might be best to follow the second method and rebase your DLLs manually. I manually rebased all the sample DLLs on this book's companion CD. The main benefit of using this method is that your MAP file will contain the specific address you set. A MAP file is a text file that indicates where the linker put all the symbols and source lines in your program. You should always create MAP files with your release builds because they are the only straight text representation of your symbols that you can get. MAP files are especially handy in the future when you need to find a crash location and your current debugger doesn't read the old symbols. If you use REBASE.EXE to rebase a DLL instead of rebasing it manually, the MAP file created by the linker will contain the original base address, and you'll have to do some arithmetic to convert an address in the MAP file to a rebased address. In Chapter 12, I'll explain MAP files in more detail.

One of the big questions I get when I tell people to rebase their files is, "What files am I supposed to rebase?" The rule of thumb is simple: if you or someone on your team wrote the code, rebase it. Otherwise, leave it alone. If you're using third-party components, your binaries will have to fit around them.

What About Managed Modules and Base Addresses?

At this point you're probably thinking that since managed components are compiled to DLLs, you might want to rebase those as well. If you've explored the compiler switches for the C# and Visual Basic .NET compilers, you might have seen the `/BASEADDRESS` switch for setting the base address. Well, when it comes to managed code, things are quite a bit different. If you really look at a managed DLL with DUMPBIN.EXE, the Portable Executable (PE) dumper from Visual Studio .NET, or with Matt Pietrek's excellent PEDUMP (*MSDN Magazine*, February 2002), you'll notice a single imported function, `_CorDllMain` from MSCOREE.DLL, and a single relocation entry.

Thinking that there might be actual executable code in managed DLLs, I disassembled a few and everything in the module code section looked like data. I scratched my head a bit more and noticed something very interesting. The entry point of the module, which is the place where execution starts, happens to be the same address as the imported `_CorDllMain`. That helped confirm there's no native executable code.

In the end, rebasing isn't going to buy you a tremendous advantage in the same way it does for native code. Nonetheless, I do it anyway because it seems to me that the operating system loader is still involved, so in the end, loading a relocated managed DLL will be slightly slower. If you do choose to rebase your managed DLLs, you must do it at build time. If you use REBASE.EXE on a managed signed DLL, the security code will see that the DLL has been changed and refuse to load it.

Common Debugging Question

What additional C# compiler options will help me with my proactive debugging of managed code?

Although managed code eliminates many of the most common errors that plagued us with native code, certain errors can still affect your code. Fortunately, there are some fine command-line options to help find some of those errors. The good news about Visual Basic .NET is that it has all the appropriate defaults, so no additional compiler switches are necessary. If you don't want to set all of these manually, the SettingsMaster add-in from Chapter 9 will do the work for you.

`/checked+` (Check Integer Arithmetic)

You can specify the `checked` keyword around potential problem areas, but it's something you have to remember to do as you're typing the code. The `/checked+` command-line option will turn on integer underflow and overflow checking for the whole program. If a result is outside the range of the data type, the code will automatically throw a run-time exception. This switch will cause quite a bit of extra code generation, so I like to leave it on in debug builds and look for the places in code where I would need to use the `checked` keyword for explicit checking in release builds. You can turn this switch on in the project Property Pages dialog box, Configuration Properties folder, Build property page by setting the Check For Arithmetic Overflow/Underflow to True.

`/noconfig` (Ignore CSC.RSP)

Interestingly, you can't set this switch in Visual Studio .NET. However, it's worth knowing what the switch can allow you to do if you want to build from the command line. By default, the C# compiler reads in the CSC.RSP file to set default command-line options before it processes the command line. You can set any valid command-line options in that file to prime the pump. In fact, the default supplied CSC.RSP file includes a slew of `/REFERENCE` command-line options to common assemblies that we all use over and over. If you've ever wondered why you don't need to specifically reference something like System.XML.dll, it's because System.XML.dll is included in CSC.RSP with the `/r: System.XML.dll` switch. CSC.RSP is located in the .NET Framework version directory, <Windows Dir>\Microsoft.NET\Framework\<Framework Version>.

Common Debugging Question

What additional compiler and linker options will help me with my proactive debugging of native code?

A number of compiler and linker switches can help you control your application's performance and better debug your application. Additionally, I don't completely agree with the default compiler and linker settings that the Visual C++ project wizards give you, as I mentioned earlier in the chapter. Consequently, I always change some of the settings. If you don't want to set all of these manually, the SettingsMaster add-in from Chapter 9 will do the work for you.

Compiler Switches for CL.EXE

Although you can add these switches manually in the project Property Pages dialog box, C/C++ folder, Command Line property page, Additional Options text box, you're much better off setting them in their appropriate locations. Adding command-line switches in the Additional Options text box can lead to problems because developers aren't used to looking there for command-line options.

`/EP` `/P` (Preprocess to a File)

If you're having trouble with a macro, the `/EP` and `/P` switches will preprocess your source file, expanding all macros and including all include files, and send the output to a file with the same name but with an .I extension. You can look in the .I file to see how your macro expanded. Make sure that you have sufficient disk space because the .I files can be several megabytes apiece. You might also want to specify the `/C` (Don't strip comments) option as well to keep comments in the preprocessed file.

Set the `/EP` and `/P` switches in the project Property Pages dialog box, C/C++ folder, Preprocessor property page, and set Generate Preprocessed File to Without Line Numbers (/EP /P). The Keep Comments option on the same property page allows you to set the `/C` compiler option. Keep in mind that using these switches will not pass the .I file on to the compiler for compilation, so your build will report errors. Once you're finished determining the problem, turn off these switches. As I've learned from personal experience, checking in a project with these switches still on won't endear you to your teammates or manager.

(continued)

Common Debugging Question *(continued)*

/X (Ignore Standard Include Paths)

Getting a correct build can sometimes be a pain if you have multiple compilers and SDKs installed on your machine. If you don't use the `/X` switch, the compiler, when invoked by a MAK file, will use the `INCLUDE` environment variable. To control exactly which header files are included, the `/X` switch will cause the compiler to ignore the `INCLUDE` environment variable and look only for header files in the locations you explicitly specify with the `/I` switch. You can set this switch in the project Property Pages dialog box, C/C++ folder, Preprocessor property page, Ignore Standard Include Path property.

/Zp (Struct Member Alignment)

You should *not* use this flag. Instead of specifying on the command line how structure members should be aligned in memory, you should align structure members by using the `#pragma pack` directive inside specific headers. I've seen some huge bugs in code because the development team originally built by setting `/Zp`. When they moved to a new build or another team went to use their code, the `/Zp` switch was forgotten, and structures were slightly different because the default alignment was different. It took a long time to find those bugs. You can set this switch in the project Property Pages dialog box, C/C++ folder, Code Generation property page\Struct Member Alignment property.

If you do happen to be setting the `#pragma pack` directive, don't forget about the new `#pragma pack (show)` option, which will report the packing to the Build window when compiling. That option will help you keep track of what the current alignment across sections of code actually is.

/Wp64 (Detect 64-bit Portability Issues)

This excellent switch will save you lots of time getting your code 64-bit ready. You can turn it on in the project Property Pages dialog box, C/C++ folder, General property page by setting Detect 64-bit Portability Issues to Yes (/Wp64). It's best to start your new development with this switch. If you try it on a bunch of code for the first time, you can be overwhelmed by the number of problems reported since it's very picky. Additionally, some of the Microsoft-supplied macros that are supposed to help with Win64 portability, such as `SetWindowLongPtr`, have errors reported by the `/Wp64` switch.

/RTC (Run-Time Error Checks)

These are the greatest switches known to C++ kind! There are three run-time check switches. /RTCc enables checking for data loss when converting values to a smaller data type. /RTCu helps track down uninitialized variable references. /RTCs enables some excellent stack-frame checking by initializing all local variables to a known value (0xCC), detecting local variable underruns and overruns, and validating stack pointers for stack corruption. You can set these switches in the project Property Pages dialog box, C/C++ folder, Code Generation property page\Smaller Type Check and Basic Runtime Checks properties. These switches are so important that I discuss them in detail in Chapter 17.

/GS (Buffer Security Check)

One of the most common techniques of virus writers is to exploit buffer overruns so that they can redirect the return address to malicious code. Fortunately, the /GS switch inserts security checks to ensure that the return address isn't overwritten, which makes writing those kinds of viruses much more difficult. /GS is set by default in release builds, and I would encourage you to use it in your debug builds as well. The first time it tracks down that one wild write that just so happens to overwrite only the return address, you'll see how many weeks of horrific debugging this switch can save you. Turn on /GS in the project Property Pages dialog box, C/C++ folder, Code Generation property page by setting Buffer Security Check to Yes (/GS). I'll explain how to change the default notifications for errors caught by /GS in Chapter 17.

/O1 (Minimize Size)

By default, a C++ project created by wizards uses /O2 (Maximize Speed) for its release-build configurations. However, Microsoft builds all its commercial applications with /O1 (Minimize Size), and that's what you should be using. You can set this switch in the project Property Pages dialog box, C/C++ folder, Optimization property page and in the Optimization property. What Microsoft has found is that after picking the best algorithm and writing tight code, avoiding page faults can help speed up your application considerably. As I've heard it said, "Page faults can ruin your day!"

A page is the smallest block of code or data (4 KB for x86-based machines) that the memory manager can manipulate as a unit. A page fault occurs when a reference is made to an invalid page. A page fault can

(continued)

Common Debugging Question *(continued)*

occur for a variety reasons, such as trying to access a page that is on standby or on the modified list, or trying to access a page that is no longer in memory. To resolve a page fault, the operating system must stop executing your program and place the new page on the CPU. If the page fault is soft, meaning that the page is already in memory, the overhead isn't too terrible—but it's extra overhead nonetheless. If the page fault is hard, however, the operating system must go out to disk and bring the page into memory. As you can imagine, this little trip will cause hundreds of thousands of instructions to execute, slowing down your application. By minimizing the size of your binary, you decrease the total number of pages your application uses, thereby reducing the number of page faults. Granted, the operating system's loaders and cache management are quite good, but why take more page faults than you have to?

In addition to using `/O1`, you should look at using the Smooth Working Set (SWS) utility from Chapter 19. SWS will help you order your most commonly called functions to the front of your binary so that you minimize your working set, that is, the number of pages kept in memory. With your common functions up front, the operating system can swap out the unneeded pages. Thus, your application runs faster.

`/GL` (Whole Program Optimization)

Microsoft has spent a considerable effort to improve the code generators, and they have done a masterful job of generating very small and very fast code with Visual C++ .NET. The big change is that instead of doing optimizations in only a single file (also known as a compiland) at compile time, they can now do cross-file optimization when the program is linked. I'm sure the first time anyone compiles a C++ project under Visual C++ .NET, he will see a dramatic reduction in code size. Amazingly, default Visual C++ projects release builds don't have this wonderful switch on by default. Set it in your release builds in the project Property Pages dialog box, Configuration Properties folder, General property page by ensuring Whole Program Optimizations is set to Yes. This will also set the appropriate linker switch, `/LTCG`, as well.

`/showIncludes` (List Include Files)

This switch does exactly what the name says. As you compile a file, it lists all the include files in a hierarchical listing so you can see who is including what from where. Turn on this switch in the project Property Pages dialog box, C/C++ folder, Advanced property page, and set the Show Includes property to Yes (/showIncludes).

Linker Switches for LINK.EXE

Although you can add these switches manually in the project Property Pages dialog box, Linker folder, Command Line property page, Additional Options text box, you're much better off setting these in their appropriate locations. Adding command-line switches in the Additional Options text box can lead to problems because developers aren't used to looking there for command-line options.

`/MAP` (Generate MAP File)

`/MAPINFO:LINES` (Include Line Information in MAP File)

`/MAPINFO:EXPORTS` (Include Export Information in MAP File)

These switches build a MAP file for the linked image. (See Chapter 12 for instructions on how to read a MAP file.) You should always create a MAP file because it's the only way to get textual symbolic information. Use all three of these switches to ensure that the MAP file contains the most useful information. You can set these switches in the project Property Pages dialog box, Linker folder, Debug property page.

`/NODEFAULTLIB` (Ignore Libraries)

Many system header files include `#pragma comment ( lib#, XXX )` records to specify which library file to link with, where *XXX* is the name of the library. `/NODEFAULTLIB` tells the linker to ignore the pragmas. This switch lets you control which libraries to link with and in which order. You'll need to specify each necessary library on the linker command line so that your application will link, but at least you'll know exactly which libraries you're getting and in which order you're getting them. Controlling the order in which libraries are linked can be important any time the same symbol is included in more than one library, which can lead to very difficult-to-find bugs. You can set this switch in the project Property Pages dialog box, Linker folder, Input property page, Ignore All Default Libraries property.

`/OPT:NOWIN98`

If you aren't supporting Windows 9x and Windows Me, you can squeeze a little size out of your executables by not requiring sections to be aligned on 4 K boundaries by using this switch. You can set this switch in the project Property Pages dialog box, Linker folder, Optimization property page, Optimize For Windows98 property.

(continued)

Common Debugging Question *(continued)*

/ORDER (Put Functions in Order)

After you run Smooth Working Set (Chapter 19), the /ORDER switch allows you to specify the file that contains the order for the functions. /ORDER will turn off incremental linking, so use it only on release builds. You can set this switch in the project Property Pages dialog box, Linker folder, Optimization property page, Function Order property.

/VERBOSE (Print Progress Messages)

/VERBOSE:LIB (Print Libraries Searched Only Progress Messages)

If you're having trouble linking, these messages can show you what symbols the linker is looking for and where it finds them. The output can get voluminous, but it can show you where you're having a build problem. I've used /VERBOSE and /VERBOSE:LIB when I've had an odd crash because a function being called didn't look, at the assembly-language level, anything like I thought it should. It turned out that I had two functions with identical signatures, but different implementations, in two different libraries, and the linker was finding the wrong one. You can set these switches in the project Property Pages dialog box, Linker folder, General property page, Show Progress property.

/LTCG (Link-Time Code Generation)

The companion switch to /GL to perform the cross-compiland optimization. This switch is automatically set when the /GL switch is used.

/RELEASE (Set the Checksum)

Where the /DEBUG switch tells the linker to generate debug code, the misnamed /RELEASE switch does not do the opposite and tell the linker to do an optimized release build link. This switch should really be named /CHECKSUM. All this switch does is set the checksum value in the Portable Executable (PE) header. While required by device drivers in order to load, it's not required by your user-mode applications. However, it's not a bad idea to set it for your release builds because WinDBG, discussed in Chapter 8, will always report if the checksum isn't set for a binary. You shouldn't add /RELEASE to debug builds because it requires that incremental linking be turned off. To set /RELEASE for your release builds, go to the project Property Pages dialog box, Linker folder, Advanced property page, and set the Set Checksum property to Yes (/RELEASE).

/PDBSTRIPPED (Strip Private Symbols)

One of the biggest debugging problems you have at customer sites is getting a clean call stack. The reason you can't get good call stacks is that the stack walking code doesn't have the special frame pointer omission (FPO) data necessary for it to help decipher the current stack. Since the PDB files for your application are what contain the FPO data, you can just ship them to your customers. While that rightfully makes you and your manager nervous, up until Visual C++ .NET you were at a loss for getting those clean call stacks.

If you ever installed the operating system symbols from Microsoft (more on this later in the section "Install the Operating System Symbols and Set Up a Symbol Store"), you probably noticed that the Microsoft supplied symbols gave you the full call stacks without giving away any secrets. What they were doing was stripping the private information, such as variables and source and line information, and just leaving public functions as well as the all-important FPO data.

With the `/PDBSTRIPPED` switch, you can safely generate the same type of symbols for your application and not have to give away any secrets. Even better news is that the stripped PDB file is generated right alongside the full PDB file, so you'll want to turn on this switch in your release builds. In the project Property Pages dialog box, Linker folder, Debug property page, set the Strip Private Symbols property to the output location and name for the symbol. I always use the string `$(OutDir)/$(ProjectName)_STRIPPED.PDB` so that it's obvious which PDB file is the stripped version. If you do send your stripped PDB files out to a customer site, make sure to remove the "_STRIPPED" on the name so that tools such as Dr. Watson will load them.

Design a Lightweight Diagnostic System for Release Builds

The bugs I hate the most are those that happen only on the machines of one or two users. Every other user is merrily running your product, but one or two users have something unique going on with their machines—something that is almost impossible to figure out. Although you could always have the user ship the misbehaving machine to you, this strategy isn't always practical. If the customer is in the Caribbean, you could volunteer to travel there and debug the problem. For some reason, however, I haven't heard of too many companies that are that quality conscious. Nor have I heard of many developers who would volunteer to go to the Arctic Circle to fix a problem either.

When you do have a problem situation that occurs on only one or two machines, you need a way to see the program's flow of execution on those machines. Many developers already track the flow of execution through logging files and writing to the event log, but I want to stress how important that log is to solving problems. The problem-solving power of flow logging increases dramatically when the whole team approaches tracking the program's flow of execution in an organized fashion.

When logging your information, following a template is especially important. With the information in a consistent format, developers will find it much easier to parse the file and report the interesting highlights. If you log information correctly, you can record tons of information and have scripts written in Perl or another language pull out the significant items so that you don't need to spend 20 minutes reading a text file just to track down one detail.

What you need to log is mostly project-dependent, but at a minimum, you should definitely log failure and abnormal situations. You also want to try to capture a logical sense of the program operation. For example, if your program is performing file operations, you wouldn't want to log fine-grained details such as "Moving to offset 23 in the file," but you would want to log the opening and closing of the file so that if the last entry in the log is "Preparing to open D:\Foo\BAR.DAT," you know that BAR.DAT is probably corrupt.

The depth of the logging also depends on the performance hit associated with the logging. I generally log everything I could possibly want and keep an eye on the release-build performance when not logging. With today's performance tools, you can quickly see whether your logging code is getting in the way. If it is, you can start to back off on the logging a little bit until you strike enough of a balance that you get sufficient logging without slowing down the application too much. The "what" to log is the hard part. In Chapter 3 I discuss the code necessary to log in managed applications, and in Chapter 18 I show how to do high-speed tracing in native applications with minimal effort. Another technology you might want to look at is the very fast but misnamed Event Tracing system, which is built into Windows 2000 and later. You can find more information at *http://msdn.microsoft.com/library/default.asp?url=/library/en-us/perfmon/base/event_tracing.asp*.

Frequent Builds and Smoke Tests Are Mandatory

Two of the most important pieces of your infrastructure are your build system and your smoke test suite. The build system is what compiles and links your product, and the smoke test suite comprises tests that run your program and verify that it works. Jim McCarthy, in his book *Dynamics of Software Development* (Microsoft Press, 1995), called the daily build and smoke test the heartbeat of the product. If these processes aren't healthy, the project is dead.

Frequent Builds

Your project has to be built every day. That process is the heartbeat of the team, and if you're not building, you've got a dead project. Many people tell me that they have absolutely huge projects that can't be built every day. Does that mean that those people have projects that are even larger than the 40 million lines of code in the Windows XP or Windows Server 2003 source code tree? Given that it's the largest commercial software project in existence and it builds every day, I don't think those people do. So there's no excuse for not building every day. Not only must you build every day, but you must have a build that is completely automated.

When building your product, you should be building both release and debug versions at the same time. As you'll see later in the chapter, the debug builds are critical. Breaking the build must be treated as a sin. If developers check in code that doesn't compile, they need to pay some sort of penalty to right the wrong. A public flogging might be a little harsh (though not by much), but what has always worked on the teams I've been on is penance in the form of supplying donuts to the team and publicly acknowledging the crime. If you're on a team that doesn't have a full-time release engineer, you can punish the build breaker by making him or her responsible for taking care of the build until the next build breaker comes along.

One of the best daily-build practices I've used is to notify the team via e-mail when the build is finished. With an automated nightly build, the first message everyone can look for in the morning is the indication of whether the build failed; if it did, the team can take immediate action to correct it.

To avoid problems with the build, everyone must have the same versions of all build tools and parts. As I mentioned earlier, some teams like to keep the build system in version control to enforce this practice. If you have team members on different versions of the tools, including the service pack levels, you've got room for error in the build. Unless there is a compelling reason to have someone using a different version of the compiler, no developer should be upgrading on his or her own. Additionally, everybody must be using the same build script as the build machine to do their builds. That way there's a valid relationship between what developers are developing and what the testers are testing.

Your build system will be pulling the latest master sources from your version control system each time you do a build. Ideally, the developers should be pulling from version control every day as well. If it's a large project, developers should be able to get the daily compiled binaries easily to avoid big compilation times on their machines. Nothing is worse than spending time trying to fix a nasty problem only to find out that the problem is related to an older version of a file on a developer's machine. Another advantage of developers pulling frequently is that it helps enforce the mantra of "no build breaks." By pulling frequently, any problem with the master build automatically becomes a problem with every developer's local build. Whereas managers get annoyed when the daily build breaks, developers go ballistic when you break their local build. With the knowledge that breaking the master build means breaking the build for every individual developer, the pressure is on everyone to check only clean code into the master sources.

Common Debugging Question

When should I freeze upgrades to the compiler and other tools?

Once you've hit feature complete, also known as beta 1, you should definitely not upgrade any tools. You can't afford the risk of a new compiler optimization scheme, no matter how well thought out, changing your code. By the time you hit beta 1, you've already done some significant testing, and if you change the tools, you'll need to restart your testing from ground zero.

Smoke Tests

In case you're not familiar with the term, a smoke test is a test that checks your product's basic functionality. The term comes from the electronics industry. At some point in a product's life cycle, electronics engineers would plug in their product to see whether it smoked (literally). If it didn't smoke, or worse, catch fire, they were making progress. In most software situations, a smoke test is simply a run-through of the product to see whether it runs and is therefore good enough to start testing seriously. A smoke test is your gauge of the baseline health of the code.

Your smoke test is just a checklist of items that your program can handle. Initially, start out small: install the application, start it, and shut it down. As you progress through the development cycle, your smoke test needs to grow to exercise new features of the product. The best rule of thumb is that the smoke test should contain at least one test for every feature and major component of the product. If you are in a shrink-wrap company, that means testing each feature that appears in a bullet point for your ads. In an IT shop, that means testing each of the major features you promised the CIO and your client. Keep in mind that your smoke test doesn't need to exhaustively test every code path in your program, but you do want to use it to judge whether you can handle the basics. Once your program passes the smoke test, the quality engineers can start doing the hard work of trying to break the program in new and unique ways.

One vital component of your smoke test is some sort of performance benchmark. Many people forget to include these and pay the price later in the development cycle. If you have an established benchmark for an operation (for example, how long the last version of the product took to run), you can define failure as a current run that is 10 percent or more over or under your benchmark. I'm always amazed by how many times a small change in an innocuous place can have a detrimental impact on performance. By monitoring performance throughout the development cycle, you can fix performance problems before they get out of hand.

The ideal situation for a smoke test is one in which your program is automated so that it can run without requiring any user interaction. The tool you use to automate the input and operations on your application is called a regression-testing tool. Unfortunately, you can't always automate every feature, especially when the user interface is in a state of flux. A number of good regression-testing tools are on the market, and if you're working with a large, complicated application and can afford to have someone assigned to maintaining the smoke tests, you might want to consider purchasing such a tool. If you can't get your boss to pay for a commercial tool, you can use the Tester application from Chapter 16, which does a great job of recording your mouse and keyboard input into a JScript or VBScript file, which you can then play back.

Breaking the smoke test should be as serious a crime as breaking the build. It takes more effort to create a smoke test, and no developer should treat it lightly. Because the smoke test is what tells your QA team that they have a build that's good enough to work on, keeping the smoke test running is mandatory. If you have an automated smoke test, you should also consider having the smoke test available for the developers so that they can use it to help automate their testing as well. Additionally, with an automated smoke test, you should have the daily build kick it off so that you can immediately gauge the health of the build. As with the daily build, you should notify the team via e-mail to let them know whether the smoke test succeeded or failed.

Build the Installation Program Immediately

Begin developing the installation program immediately after you start developing your project. The installation program is the first part of your product that your users see. Too many products give a poor first impression, showing that the installation program was left to the last minute. By getting the installation program started as early as possible, you have sufficient time to test and debug it. If the installation program is done early, you can also incorporate it into your smoke test. This way, you're always testing it and your tests will be one step closer to simulating how the users will be running your program.

Earlier in the chapter, I recommended that you should build both release and debug versions of your product. You also need to have an installation program that allows you to install either version. Even though managed applications have the vaunted XCOPY installation, that's only for baby programs. Real-world managed applications are going to have to initialize databases, put assemblies in the global assembly cache, and handle other operations that just can't be done with a simple copy. Of course for native applications, don't forget that COM is still alive and kicking; COM needs so much stuff in the registry that it's almost impossible to properly use an application without running its installation program. By having a debug build installation program, developers can easily get a debug version on a machine so that they can quickly start debugging a problem.

One extra benefit of having the installation program done as early as possible is that others in your company can start testing your program that much sooner. With the installation program done, the technical support engineers can start using your program and providing you with feedback early enough in the cycle so that you can actually do something about the problems they find.

QA Must Test with Debug Builds

If you follow my recommendations in Chapter 3, you'll have some excellent diagnostics in your code base. The problem is that, generally, only the developers benefit from the diagnostics. To better help debug problems, the quality engineers need to be using the debug builds as well. You'll be amazed at how many problems you'll find and fix when the QA folks do their testing with debug builds.

One key point is that any assertions you add to the code can have their output disabled so that they do not mess up any automated tests the QA department runs. In the next chapter I discuss assertions for managed and native code. Both the managed code and my SUPERASSERT for native code have ways of turning off any popup message boxes or other interrupting output that cause automated tests to fail.

In the initial stages of the product cycle, the quality engineers should be alternating between debug and release builds. As the product progresses, they should gradually start concentrating more on the release builds. Until you reach the alpha release milestone, at which point you have enough of the features implemented to show customers the product, you should have the quality engineers use the debug build two to three days a week. As you approach beta 1, they should drop to two days a week. After beta 2, when all features and major bugs are fixed, they should drop to one day a week. After the release candidate milestone, they should be on the release build exclusively.

Install the Operating System Symbols and Set Up a Symbol Store

As anyone who has spent more than 5 minutes of development time on Windows knows, getting the correct symbols lined up is the secret to debugging faster. In managed code, if you don't have symbols, you might not be able to debug at all. In native code, without symbols, you probably won't get clean call stacks because to walk stacks, you need the frame pointer omission (FPO) data that's included as part of the PDB file.

If you think *you* have trouble getting everyone on your team and in the company to work with the correct symbols, think about how bad the operating system team at Microsoft has it. They have the largest commercial application in the world, with 40 plus million lines of code. They build every day and can have thousands of different builds of the operating system running at any time across the world. All of a sudden, your symbol challenges seem quite small—even if you think you're on a big project, your project can't even hold a candle to that much symbol pain!

In addition to the challenge of getting the symbols lined up, Microsoft was also facing the problem of getting the binaries lined up. One new technology that Microsoft introduced to help them debug crashes better is called a *minidump*, or a *crash dump*. These are files that contain the state of the application at the time of the crash. For some of you coming from other operating systems, you might refer to these as *core dumps*. The beauty of a minidump is that by having the state of the application, you can load it up into the debugger so it's almost as if you were sitting there at the time of the crash. I'll discuss the mechanics of creating your own minidumps, as well as how to read them in the debuggers, in subsequent chapters. The big issue with minidumps is getting the correct binaries loaded. While you might be developing on a post–Windows Server 2003 operating system, the customer's minidump could have been written on Windows 2000 with only Service Pack 1 applied. Like the case with the symbols, if you can't get the exact binaries loaded that were in the address space when the minidump was written, you're completely out of luck if you think you can solve the bug easily with the minidump.

The developers at Microsoft realized they had to do something to make their lives easier. We folks outside Microsoft also had been complaining for a long time that our debugging experiences were a few steps short of abysmal because of the lack of operating system symbols and binaries that matched the myriad of hot fixes on any machine. The concept of symbol servers is simple: store all the public builds symbols and binaries in a known location, and make the debuggers smarter so that they load the correct symbols and binaries for every module loaded into a process—regardless of whether that module is loaded from your code or from the operating system—without any user interaction at all. The beauty is that the reality is nearly this simple! There are a few small issues that I'll point out in this section, but with the symbol server properly set up, no one on your team or in your company should ever lack the correct symbols or binaries regardless of whether you're doing managed, native, or both styles of development, or you're using Visual Studio .NET or WinDBG as your debugger. Even better, I've supplied a couple of files that will take all the thinking work out of ensuring you have the perfect symbols and binaries for the operating system as well as for your products.

The Visual Studio .NET documentation mentions a technique for getting the symbol server set up for debugging, but you'll have to follow the same steps for every solution you load, which is a huge pain. Additionally, the documentation doesn't discuss the most important idea, which is getting *your* symbols and binaries into the symbol server. Since that's where the huge benefit to using the symbol server lies, you need to follow these steps to reach symbol server nirvana.

The steps for getting a server machine that everyone in your company who is executing your projects can access are quite simple. You'll probably want to name this server \\SYMBOLS to identify it easily. For the rest of this discussion, I'll assume that's the name of the server. This machine doesn't have to have much horsepower. It's simply going to act as a file server. One thing you'll definitely want is a good bit of disk space on that server. At least 40 to 80 GB should be a good start. Once the server software's installed, create two shared directories named OSSYMBOLS and PRODUCTSYMBOLS that everyone in development and QA has read and write access to. As you can tell by the share names, one directory is for the operating system symbols and binaries, and the other is for your product's symbols and binaries. You'll want to keep them separate for ease of management. Of course, it's quite easy for me to assume that you can get a server in your organization. I'll leave all the political battles of getting that server as an exercise for the reader.

The next step toward reaching developer machine symbol nirvana is to either download and install the latest version of Debugging Tools for Windows from *www.microsoft.com/ddk/debugging* or install Debugging Tools for Windows with this book's sample files, because the symbol server binaries are developed by the Windows team, not the Visual Studio .NET team. You'll want to check back for updated versions of Debugging Tools for Windows; the team seems to be updating the tools frequently. After installing Debugging Tools for Windows, add the installation directory to the master `PATH` environment variable. The four key binaries, SYMSRV.DLL, DBGHELP.DLL, SYMCHK.EXE, and SYMSTORE.EXE, must be able to read from and write to your symbol servers.

For those of you who are working behind proxy servers that require you to log in each time you access the Internet, you have my sympathies. Fortunately, the Windows team does feel your pain. New with Debugging Tools for Windows version 6.1.0017 is a version of SYMSRV.DLL that will work for companies that monitor your every Internet packet. You'll want to read the Debugging Tools for Windows documentation that discusses proxy and firewalls under the topic "Using Symbol Servers and Symbol Stores." In there, you'll see how to set up the `_NT_SYMBOL_PROXY` environment variable to download symbols without requiring you to enter your username and password with each request.You'll also want to keep an eye on *www.microsoft.com/ddk/debugging* for new versions of Debugging Tools for Windows. Since the Windows team is always looking for ways to make symbol servers better, you should keep an eye on new releases.

Once you have Debugging Tools for Windows installed, the final step is to set up the master environment for Visual Studio and WinDBG. It's best to set this environment variable in the master (machine-wide) settings. To access this area in Windows XP and Windows Server 2003, right-click on My Computer and select Properties from the shortcut menu. Click on the Advanced tab, and at the bottom of the property page click the Environment Variables button. Figure 2-10 shows the Environment Variables dialog box. You'll want to create a new

_NT_SYMBOL_PATH environment variable, if one doesn't exist, and set it to the following. (Note that the line below is all supposed to be entered on one line.)

```
SRV*\\Symbols\OSSymbols*http://msdl.microsoft.com/download/symbols;
     SRV*\\Symbols\ProductSymbols
```

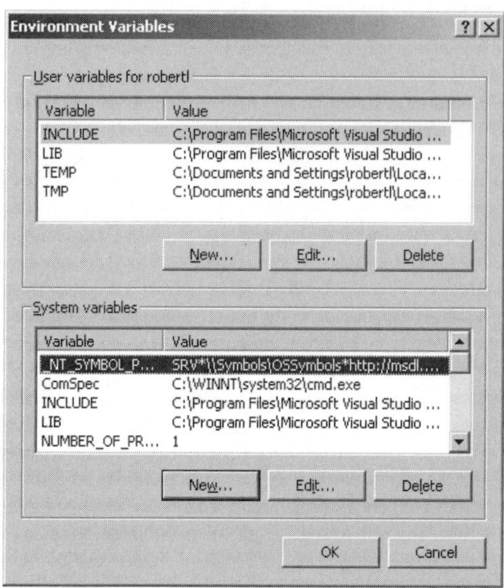

Figure 2-10 The Environment Variables dialog box

_NT_SYMBOL_PATH is where Visual Studio .NET and WinDBG will look to figure out where the symbol servers are. There are two distinct symbol servers being accessed in the above string separated by the semicolon. The first is for the operating system and the second is your product. The SRV in front of each tells the debuggers to load SYMSRV.DLL and to pass the values after the SRV string to SYMSRV.DLL. In the first symbol server, you are telling SYMSRV.DLL to access \\Symbols\OSSymbols as the symbol server; the second asterisk is the HTTP address where SYMSRV.DLL will look to download any symbols, but not binaries, not found in the existing symbol server. The first portion of the _NT_SYMBOL_PATH above is what will take care of getting your operating symbols completely up to date. The second portion of the _NT_SYMBOL_PATH string simply tells SYMSRV.DLL to only look in your \\Symbols\ProductSymbols share for your product specific symbols. If you want to search other paths, you can add those paths to the string _NT_SYMBOL_PATH by separating them with semicolons. For example, the following adds your system root System32 directory because that directory is where Visual Studio .NET puts the C run-time and MFC PDB files during installation:

```
SRV*\\Symbols\OSSymbols*http://msdl.microsoft.com/download/symbols;
    SRV*\\Symbols\ProductSymbols;c:\windows\system32
```

The absolute beauty of symbol server is revealed when you populate it with operating system symbols downloaded from Microsoft. If you've been a good bugslayer over the years, you're probably already installing the operating system symbols on your machine. However, those installations have always been a little frustrating because you probably have a few hot fixes on your machine, and certain operating system symbols never include the hot fix symbols. The great news with symbol servers is that you can be guaranteed of always getting the operating system symbols that are exactly right with no work whatsoever! This is a huge boon that will make your life easier. The magic here is that Microsoft has made the symbols available for downloading for all released operating systems from Microsoft Windows NT 4 through the latest release of Windows XP and Windows .NET Server 2003, including all operating system service packs and hot fixes.

The next time you start debugging, the debugger automatically sees that `_NT_SYMBOL_PATH` is set, starts downloading the operating symbols through HTTP from Microsoft, and then places them in your symbol store if the symbol file hasn't already been downloaded. Just to be clear: the symbol server will download only the symbols it needs, not every single operating system symbol. By having the symbol store in a shared directory, when one of your teammates has already downloaded the symbol, you don't have to go through the potentially long download.

The symbol store itself is nothing very exciting. It's simply a database that happens to use the file system to find the files. Figure 2-11 shows a partial listing from Windows Explorer of the tree for the symbol server on my symbol server computer. The root directory is OSSymbols, and each different symbol file, such as ADVAPI32.PDB, is listed at the first level. Under each symbol filename is a directory that corresponds to the date/time stamp, signature, and other information necessary to completely recognize a particular version of that symbol file. Keep in mind that if you have multiple versions of a file such as ADVAPI32.PDB for different operating system builds, you'll have multiple directories under ADVAPI32.PDB for each unique version you have accessed. In the signature directory, you'll most likely have the particular symbol file for that version. There are provisions for having special text files point to other locations in the symbol store, but using them the way I recommend, you'll have the actual symbol files.

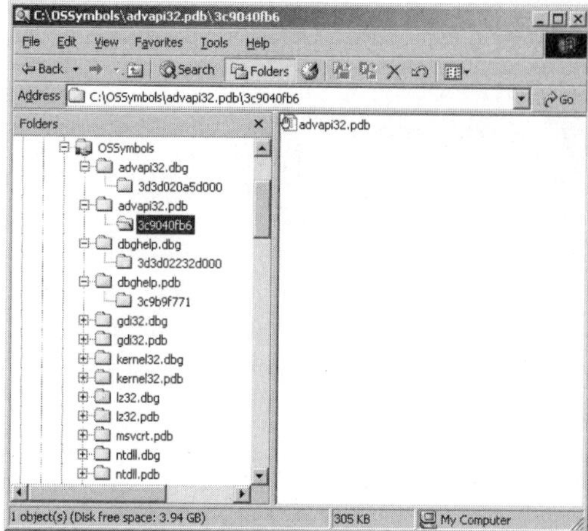

Figure 2-11 An example of the symbol server database

Although getting the symbols downloaded while you're debugging is great, it does nothing for getting the operating system binaries into your symbol server. Additionally, instead of relying on developers debugging applications to get the symbols, you might want to prepopulate your symbol servers with all the operating system binaries and symbols for all versions you are supporting. That way, you'll be able to handle any minidumps coming in from the field as well as any debugging challenges you'll encounter in your development shop.

The Debugging Tools for Windows (which includes WinDBG) includes two tools that do the heavy lifting. The first, Symbol Checker (SYMCHK.EXE), takes care of getting the symbols down from Microsoft and into your symbol server. The second, Symbol Store (SYMSTORE.EXE), takes care of getting the binaries into the symbol store. Since I realized I'd have to run both tools to get my operating system symbol server fully populated with symbols and binaries for all OS versions I wanted to support, I decided to automate the process. I wanted to quickly build up my operating system symbol server as well as keep it filled with the latest binaries and symbols with essentially no work at all.

When you're setting up your initial operating system symbol server, you'll install the first version of the operating system without any service packs or hot fixes. You'll install the Debugging Tools for Windows, and you'll probably want to add its installation directory to your path. To get the binaries and symbols for that operating system, you'll run my OSSYMS.JS file, which I'll discuss in a moment. After OSSYMS.JS finishes, you'll install the first service pack and reexecute OSSYMS.JS. After you've gotten all service packs loaded and their binaries and symbols copied, you'll finally apply any hot fixes recommended by the Windows Update feature of Windows 2000, Windows XP, and Windows .NET

Server 2003 and run OSSYMS.JS one last time. Once you run through this process for all operating systems you need to support, you'll just have to run OSSYMS.JS whenever you install a hot fix or a new service pack to keep your symbol server nice and spiffy. For planning purposes, I've found that it takes a little less than a gigabyte for each operating system and approximately the same for each service pack.

While you might think OSSYMS.JS (along with its support file WRITEHOTFIXES.VBS, which you'll need to copy to the same directory as OSSYMS.JS) is just a simple wrapper around calling SYMCHK.EXE and SYMSTORE.EXE, it's actually a pretty nice wrapper. If you look at the command-line options for both programs, you'll definitely want help automating them because it's very easy to mess up their usage. If you execute OSSYMS.JS without any command-line parameters, you'll see the following output showing you all the options:

```
OSsyms - Version 1.0 - Copyright 2002-2003 by John Robbins
  Debugging Applications for Microsoft .NET and Microsoft Windows

  Fills your symbol server with the OS binaries and symbols.
  Run this each time you apply a service pack/hot fix to get the perfect
  symbols while debugging and for mini dumps.
  SYMSTORE.EXE and SYMCHK.EXE must be in the path.

Usage : OSsyms <symbol server> [-e|-v|-b|-s|-d]

  <symbol server> - The symbol server in \\server\share format.
  -e              - Do EXEs as well as DLLs.
  -v              - Do verbose output.
  -d              - Debug the script. (Shows what would execute.)
  -b              - Don't add the binaries to the symbol store.
  -s              - Don't add the symbols to the symbol store.
                    (Not recommended)
```

The only required parameter is the symbol server in *\\server\share* format. When you execute OSSYMS.JS, it first figures out the operating system version and service pack level as well as all hot fixes that are applied. This is important for properly filling out the product, version, and comment information for SYMSTORE.EXE so that you can identify exactly what symbols and binaries you have in your symbol server. I'll discuss the specific SYMSTORE.EXE command-line options and how to see what's in your database in a few paragraphs. Getting the hot fix information is vital because that way if you get a minidump from the field, you can quickly determine if you've got that particular binary and symbols pair in your symbol server.

Once OSSYMS.JS has all the system information, it runs through and recursively adds all DLL binaries from the operating system directory (`%SYSTEMROOT%`). After the binary files are copied, OSSYMS.JS calls SYMCHK.EXE to automatically download all the symbols it can for those DLLs. If you would like to also add all EXE binaries and associated symbols, add the –e command-line option to OSSYMS.JS after the symbol server parameter.

To see what binaries and symbols were added or ignored (including the reasons why), check out the two text files, DllBinLog.TXT and DllSymLog.TXT, which show the binary add results and the symbol add results, respectively. For EXEs, the two files are ExeBinLog.TXT and ExeSymLog.TXT.

Keep in mind that OSSYMS.JS can take quite a while to run. Copying the binaries up to your symbol server will be very fast, but downloading the symbols can take a lot of time. If you download both DLL and EXE operating system symbols, you've probably got somewhere around 400 MB of data to download. One thing you'll want to avoid is having multiple computers adding binary to the symbol server at once. That's because the SYMSTORE.EXE program uses the file system and a text file as its database, so it has no sort of transactional capabilities. SYMCHK.EXE doesn't access the SYMSTORE.EXE text file database, so it's perfectly fine to have multiple developers adding symbols only.

Microsoft is putting more of its product's symbols on their public HTTP download area all the time. OSSYMS.JS is flexible enough that you can easily add different directories where you'd like to have binaries as well as symbols installed into your symbol server. To add your new binaries, search for the `g_AdditionalWork`, a global variable near the top of the file. The OSSYMS.JS file has `g_AdditionalWork` set to `null` so it's not processed in the `main` routine. To add a new set of files, allocate an `Array` and add a `SymbolsToProcess` class as the element. The following code snippet shows how to add processing to add all the DLLs that appear in the Program Files directory. Note that the first element doesn't always have to be an environment variable; it could have been a specific directory, such as "e:\ Program Files." However, by using a common system environment variable, you'll avoid hard-coded drives.

```
var g_AdditionalWork = new Array
(
    new SymbolsToProcess ( "%ProgramFiles%"    ,   // Start directory.
                           "*.dll"             ,   // Searching wildcard.
                           "PFDllBinLog.TXT"   ,   // Binary logging file.
                           "PFDllSymLog.TXT"   )   // Symbol logging file.
) ;
```

Now that you've seen how to get your operating system symbols and binaries, let's turn to getting *your* product symbols into the symbol store with SYMSTORE.EXE. SYMSTORE.EXE has a number of command-line switches. I show the important switches in Table 2-2.

Table 2-2 SYMSTORE Important Command-Line Options

Switch	Explanation
`add`	Adds files to a symbol store
`del`	Deletes the files added in a particular set
`/f` File	Adds a particular file or directory
`/r`	Adds files or directories recursively
`/s` Store	The root directory of the symbol store
`/t` Product	The name of the product
`/v` Version	The product version
`/c`	Additional comment
`/o`	Verbose output helpful for debugging
`/i` ID	The ID from history.txt to delete
`/?`	Help output

The best way to use SYMSTORE.EXE is to have it automatically add your build tree's EXEs, DLLs, and PDBs at the end of every daily build (after the smoke test verifies that the product works), after each milestone, and for any builds sent outside the engineering team. You probably don't want to have developers adding their local builds unless you're really into chewing up tons of disk space. For example, the following command stores all PDB and binary files into your symbol store for all directories found under D:\BUILD (inclusive).

```
symstore add /r /f d:\build\*.* /s \\Symbols\ProductSymbols
    /t "MyApp" /v "Build 632" /c "01/22/03 Daily Build"
```

Although the `/t` (Product) option is always required when adding files, unfortunately, `/v` (Version) and `/c` (Comment) are not. I strongly recommend that you always use `/v` and `/c` because you can never have too much information about what files are in your product symbol server. This gets extremely important as your product symbol server fills up. Even though the symbols placed in your operating system symbol server are smaller because they are stripped of all private symbols and types, your product's symbols are huge and can lead to quite a bit of wasted disk space on a six-month project.

You'll always want to leave milestone builds as well as builds sent outside the engineering team in your symbol server. I also like to keep no more than the last four weeks' daily build symbols and binaries in my symbol store. As you saw in Table 2-2, SYMSTORE.EXE does support deleting files.

To ensure that you're deleting the correct files, you'll need to look at a special directory, 000admin, under your shared symbol server directory. In there is the HISTORY.TXT file, which contains the history of all transactions that occurred in this symbol server and, if you've added files to the symbol server, a set of numbered files that contain the list of actual files added as part of a transaction.

HISTORY.TXT is a comma separated value (CSV) file whose fields are shown in Table 2-3 (for adding files) and Table 2-4 (for deleting files).

Table 2-3 HISTORY.TXT CSV Fields When Adding

Field	Explanation
`ID`	The transaction number. This is a 10-digit number, so you can have 9,999,999,999 total transactions in your symbol server.
`Add`	When adding files, this field will always say `add`.
`File or Ptr`	Indicates whether a file (`file`) or a pointer to a file in another location (`ptr`) was added
`Date`	The date of the transaction
`Time`	The time the transaction started
`Product`	The product text from the `/t` switch
`Version`	The version text from the `/v` switch (optional)
`Comment`	The comment text from the `/c` switch (optional)
`Unused`	An unused field for future use

Table 2-4 HISTORY.TXT CSV Fields When Deleting

Field	Explanation
`ID`	The transaction number
`Del`	When deleting files, this field will always say `del`.
`Deleted Transaction`	The 10-digit number of the deleted transaction

Once you've located the transaction ID you want to delete, it's a simple matter to tell SYMSTORE.EXE to do the work.

```
symstore del /i 0000000009 /s \\Symbols\ProductSymbols
```

One thing I've noticed that's a little odd about deleting from your symbol server is that you don't get any output telling you if the deletion succeeded. In fact, if you forget a vital command-line option, such as the symbol server itself, you're not warned at all and you might mistakenly think that the deletion happened. After doing a deletion, I always check the HISTORY.TXT file to ensure that the deletion actually took place.

Your Source and Symbol Servers

After getting all the symbols and binaries lined up for debugging, the next piece of the puzzle is to line up your source code. Having perfect call stacks is nice, but single-stepping through comments in the source code is not fun. Unfortunately, until Microsoft integrates the compilers with the version control system so that the compilers pull and label the source as you build, you're going to have to do some manual work.

You might not have noticed it, but the compilers that come with Visual Studio .NET all now embed the complete path to the source file as part of the PDB files. Prior versions of the compilers didn't, so it was nearly impossible to get your source straight. With the complete path there, you now have a fighting chance to get the source lined up when debugging prior versions of your product or looking at a minidump.

On your build machine, use the `SUBST` command to set the top level of your development tree to be the S: drive. Now when you build, the S: drive will be at the root of the embedded source information for all PDB files you'll add to your symbol engine. When a developer needs to debug a prior version's source code, he can pull that version out of the version control system and use the `SUBST` command to map an S: drive to that pulled version of the source code. When the debuggers go to show the source code, they'll get the correct version of the symbol files with a minimum of fuss.

I've covered quite a bit about symbol servers, but I strongly encourage you to read the "Symbols" section completely in the Debugging Tools for Windows documentation. The symbol server technology is so critical to debugging better that it's in your best interest to know as much about it as possible. I hope I was able to show you the value and ways to apply it better. In fact, if you haven't already set up a symbol server, you are ordered to stop reading immediately and go set one up.

Summary

This chapter covered vital infrastructure requirements necessary to help you minimize your debugging time. They run the gamut from version control and bug tracking systems, to the compiler and linker settings you need, to the benefits of daily builds and smoke tests, to the importance of symbols.

Although you might need additional infrastructure requirements for your unique environment, you'll find the ones covered in this chapter are generic across all environments. And, they are the ones that I've seen make a great deal of difference in real-world development. If you don't have one or more of these infrastructure tools or techniques set up at your development shop, I strongly encourage you to implement them immediately. They will save you literally hundreds of hours of debugging time.

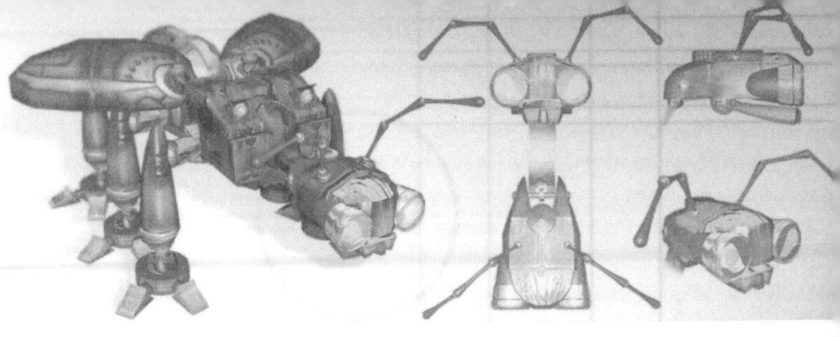

3

Debugging During Coding

In Chapter 2, I laid the groundwork for the project-wide infrastructure needed to enable engineers to work more efficiently. In this chapter, we'll turn to what you need to do to make debugging easier while you're heavy in the coding battles. Most people refer to this process as defensive programming, but I like to think of it as something broader and deeper: proactive programming, or debugging during coding. To me, defensive programming is the error handling code that tells you an error occurred. Proactive programming tells you why the error occurred.

Coding defensively is only part of the battle of fixing and solving bugs. Engineers generally attempt to make the obvious defensive maneuvers—for example, verifying that a C++ pointer to a string isn't `NULL`—but they often don't take the extra step that proactive programming would require: checking that same parameter to see whether the memory is sufficient to hold the maximum string allowed. Proactive programming means doing everything possible to avoid ever having to use the debugger and instead making the code tell you where the problems are. The debugger can be one of the biggest time drains in the world, and the way to avoid it is to have the code tell you exactly when something isn't perfect. Whenever you type a line of code, you need to stop and look at what you're assuming is the good-case scenario and determine how you're going to verify that the case in question is exactly what the state will be every time you execute that line of code.

It's a simple fact: bugs don't just magically appear in code. The "secret" is that you and I put them in as we're writing the code, and those pesky bugs can come from myriad sources. They can be the result of a problem as critical as a design flaw in your application or as simple as a typographical error. Although some bugs are easy to fix, others are nearly impossible to solve without major rewrites. It would be nice to blame the bugs in your code on gremlins, but you need to accept the fact that you and your coworkers are the ones putting the bugs in the code. (If you're reading this book, it has to be mainly your coworkers putting the bugs in.)

Because you and the other developers are responsible for any bugs in the code, the issue becomes one of finding ways to create a system of checks and balances that lets you catch bugs as you go. I've always referred to this approach as "trust, but verify," which is Ronald Reagan's famous quote about how the United States was going to enforce one of the nuclear arms limitation treaties with the former Soviet Union. I trust that my colleagues and I will use my code correctly. To avoid bugs, however, I verify everything. I verify the data that others pass into my code, I verify my code's internal manipulations, I verify every assumption I make in my code, I verify data my code passes to others, and I verify data coming back from calls my code makes. If there's something to verify, I verify it. This obsessive verification is nothing personal against my coworkers, and I don't have any psychological problems (to speak of). It's just that I know where the bugs come from; I also know that you can't let anything by without checking it if you want to catch your bugs as early as you can.

Before we go any further, I need to stress one key tenet of my development philosophy: code quality is the sole responsibility of the development engineers, not the test engineers, technical writers, or managers. You and I are the ones writing, implementing, and fixing the code, so we're the only ones who can take meaningful measures to ensure the code we write is as bug free as possible.

As a consultant, one of the most surprising attitudes I encounter in many organizations is that developers should only develop and testers only test. The prevailing problem with this approach is that developers write a bunch of code and ever-so-briefly decide whether it executes the good condition before throwing it over the wall to the testers. It goes without saying that you're asking for schedule slippage as well as a poor quality product when developers don't take responsibility for testing their code.

In my opinion, a developer is a tester is a developer. I can't stress this enough: *if a developer isn't spending at least 40 to 50 percent of his development time testing his code, he is not developing*. A tester's job is to focus on issues such as fit and finish, stress testing, and performance testing. Finding a crash should be an extremely rare occurrence for a tester. If the code does crash, it reflects directly on the development engineer's competence. The key to developer testing is the unit test. Your goal is to execute as much of your code as possible to ensure that it doesn't crash and properly meets established specifications and requirements. Armed with solid unit test results, the test engineers can look for integration issues and systemwide test issues. We'll go over unit testing in detail in the section "Trust Yourself, but Verify (Unit Testing)" later in this chapter.

Assert, Assert, Assert, and Assert

I hope most of you already know what an assertion is, because it's the most important proactive programming tool in your debugging arsenal. For those who are unfamiliar with the term, here's a brief definition: an assertion declares that a certain condition must be true at a specific point in a program. The assertion is said to *fail* if the condition is false. You use assertions in addition to normal error checking. Traditionally, assertions are functions or macros that execute only in debug builds and bring up a message box telling you what condition failed. I extend the definition of assertions to include conditionally compiled code that checks conditions and assumptions that are too complex for a general assertion function or macro to handle. Assertions are a key component of proactive programming because they help developers and test engineers determine not just that bugs are present but also why the errors are happening.

Even if you've heard of assertions and drop them in your code occasionally, you might not be familiar enough with them to use them effectively. Development engineers can never be too rich or too thin—or use too many assertions. The rule of thumb I've always followed to judge whether I've used enough assertions is simple: I have enough assertions when my junior coworkers complain that they get multiple message boxes reporting assertion failures whenever they call into my code with invalid information or assumptions.

If used sufficiently, assertions will tell you most of the information you need to diagnose a problem at the first sign of trouble. Without assertions, you'll spend considerable time in the debugger working backward from the crash searching for where things started to go wrong. A good assertion will tell you where and why a condition was invalid. A good assertion will also let you get into the debugger after a condition fails so that you can see the complete state of the program at the point of failure. A bad assertion tells you something's wrong, but not what, why, or where.

A side benefit of using plenty of assertions is that they serve as outstanding additional documentation in your code. What assertions capture is your intent. I'm sure you go well out of your way to keep your design documents perfectly up to date, but I'm just as sure that a few random projects let their design documents slip through the cracks. By having good assertions throughout your code, the maintenance developer can see exactly what value ranges you expected for a parameter or what you anticipated would fail in a normal course of operation versus a major failure condition. Assertions will never replace proper comments, but by using them to capture the elusive "here's what I meant, which is not what the docs say," you can save a great deal of time later in the project.

How and What to Assert

My stock answer when asked what to assert is to assert everything. I would love to say that for every line of code you should have an assertion, but it's an unrealistic albeit admirable goal. You should assert any condition because it might be the one you need to solve a nasty bug in the future. Don't worry that putting in too many assertions will hamper your program's performance—assertions usually are active only in debug builds, and the bug-finding opportunities created more than outweigh the small performance hit.

Assertions should never change any variables or states of a program. Treat all data you check in assertions as read-only. Because assertions are active only in debug builds, if you do change data by using an assertion, you'll have different behavior between debug and release builds, and tracking down the differences will be extremely difficult.

In this section, I want to concentrate on how to use assertions and what to assert. I'll do this by showing code examples. I need to mention that in these examples, `Debug.Assert` is the .NET assertion from the `System.Diagnostic` namespace, and `ASSERT` is the native C++ method, which I'll introduce later in this chapter.

Debugging War Story

A Career-Limiting Move

The Battle

A long, long time ago, I worked at a company whose software product had serious stability problems. As the senior Windows engineer on this behemoth project, I found that many of the issues affecting the project resulted from a lack of understanding about why calls made to others' modules failed. I wrote a memo advising the same practices I promote in this chapter, telling project members why and when they were supposed to use assertions. I had a little bit of power, so I also made it part of the code review criteria to look for proper assertion usage.

After sending out the memo, I answered a few questions people had about assertions and thought everything was fine. Three days later, my boss came into my office and started screaming at me about how I screwed everyone up, and he ordered me to rescind my assertion memo. I was stunned, and we proceeded to get into an extremely heated argument about my assertion recommendations. I couldn't quite understand what my boss was arguing about, but it had something to do with making the product much more unstable. After five minutes of yelling at each other, I finally challenged my boss to prove that people were using assertions incorrectly. He handed me a code printout that looked like the following:

```
BOOL DoSomeWork ( HMODULE * pModArray , int iCount , LPCTSTR szBuff )
{
    ASSERT ( if ( ( pModArray == NULL ) &&
                ( IsBadWritePtr ( pModArray ,
                                ( sizeof ( HMODULE ) * iCount ) ) &&
                ( iCount != 0 ) &&
            ( szBuff != NULL ) ) )
            {
                return ( FALSE ) ;
            }
           ) ;
     for ( int i = 0 ; i < iCount ; i++ )
     {
          pModArray[ i ] = m_pDataMods[ i ] ;
     }
    ⋮
}
```

The Outcome

I should also mention here that my boss and I generally didn't get along. He thought I was a young whippersnapper who hadn't paid his dues and didn't know a thing, and I thought he was a completely clueless mouth-breathing moron who couldn't engineer his way out of a wet paper bag. As I read over the code, my eyes popped completely out of my head! The person who had coded this example had completely misunderstood the purpose of assertions and was simply going through and wrapping all the normal error handling in an assertion macro. Since assertions disappear in release builds, the person who wrote the code was removing *all* error checking in release builds!

By this point, I was livid and screamed at the top of my lungs, "Whoever wrote this needs to be fired! I can't believe we have an engineer on our staff who is this incredibly and completely @#!&*&$ stupid!" My boss got very quiet, grabbed the paper out of my hands, and quietly said, "That's my code." My career-limiting move was to start laughing hysterically as my boss walked away.

The Lesson

I can't stress this enough: use assertions *in addition* to normal error handling, never as a replacement for it. If you have an assertion, you need to have some sort of error handling near it in the code. As for my boss, when I went into his office a few weeks later to resign because I had accepted a job at a better company, I was treated to a grown person dancing on his desk and singing that it was the best day of his life.

How to Assert

The first rule when using assertions is to check a single item at a time. If you check multiple conditions with just one assertion, you have no way of knowing which condition caused the failure. In the following example, I show the same function with two assertion checks. Although the assertion in the first function will catch a bad parameter, the assertion won't tell you which condition failed or even which of the three parameters is the offending one.

```
// The wrong way to write an assertion. Which parameter was bad?
BOOL GetPathItem ( int i , LPTSTR szItem , int iLen )
{
    ASSERT ( ( i > 0                                        ) &&
             ( NULL != szItem                               ) &&
             ( ( iLen > 0 ) && ( iLen < MAX_PATH )          ) &&
             ( FALSE == IsBadStringPtr ( szItem , iLen ) ) ) ;
    ⋮
}

// The proper way. Each parameter is checked individually so that you
// can see which one failed.
BOOL GetPathItem ( int i , LPTSTR szItem , int iLen )
{
    ASSERT ( i > 0 ) ;
    ASSERT ( NULL != szItem ) ;
    ASSERT ( ( iLen > 0 ) && ( iLen < MAX_PATH ) ) ;
    ASSERT ( FALSE == IsBadStringPtr ( szItem , iLen ) ) ;
    ⋮
}
```

When you assert a condition, you need to strive to check the condition completely. For example, if your .NET method takes a string as a parameter and you expect the string to have something in it, checking against `null` checks only part of the error condition.

```
// An example of checking only a part of the error condition
bool LookupCustomerName ( string CustomerName )
{
    Debug.Assert ( null != CustomerName , "null != CustomerName" ) ;
    ⋮
}
```

You can check the full condition by also checking to see whether the string is empty.

```
// An example of completely checking the error condition
bool LookupCustomerName ( string CustomerName )
{
    Debug.Assert ( null != CustomerName , "null != CustomerName" ) ;
    Debug.Assert ( 0 != CustomerName.Length ,"\"\" != CustomerName.Length" ) ;
    ⋮
```

Another step I always take is to ensure that I'm asserting against specific values. The following example shows first how to check for a positive value incorrectly and then how to check for it correctly:

```
// Example of a poorly written assertion:  nCount should be positive,
// but the assertion doesn't fail when nCount is negative.
void UpdateListEntries ( int nCount )
{
    ASSERT ( nCount ) ;
    ⋮
}

// A proper assertion that explicitly checks against what the value
// is supposed to be
void UpdateListEntries ( int nCount )
{
    ASSERT ( nCount > 0 ) ;
    ⋮
}
```

The incorrect sample essentially checks only whether `nCount` isn't 0, which is just half of the information that needs to be asserted. By explicitly checking the acceptable values, you guarantee that your assertion is self-documenting, and you also ensure that your assertion catches corrupted data.

What to Assert

Now that you're armed with an idea of how to assert, we can turn to exactly what you need to be asserting throughout your code. If you haven't guessed from the examples I've presented so far, let me clarify that the first mandatory items to assert are the parameters coming into the method. Asserting parameters is especially critical with module interfaces and class methods that others on your team call. Because those gateway functions are the entry points into your code, you want to make sure that each parameter and assumption is valid. As I pointed out in the debugging war story earlier in this chapter, "A Career-Limiting Move," assertions never take the place of normal error handling.

As you move inside your module, the parameters of the module's private methods might not require as much checking, depending mainly on where the parameters originated. Much of the decision about which parameters to validate comes down to a judgment call. It doesn't hurt to assert every parameter of every method, but if a parameter comes from outside the module, and if you fully asserted it once, you might not need to again. By asserting each parameter on every function, however, you might catch some errors internal to your module.

I sit right in the middle of the two extremes. Deciding how many parameter assertions are right for you just takes some experience. As you get a feel for where you typically encounter problems in your code, you'll figure out where and when you need to assert parameters internal to your module. One safeguard I've learned to use is to add parameter assertions whenever a bad parameter blows up my code. That way, the mistake won't get repeated because the assertion will catch it.

Another area that's mandatory for assertions is method return values because the return values tell you whether methods succeeded or failed. One of the biggest problems I see in debugging other developers' code is that they simply call methods without ever checking the return value. I have seen so many cases in which I've looked for a bug, only to find out that some method early on in the code failed but no one bothered to check its return value. Of course, by the time you realize the culprit, the bug is manifested, so the program dies or corrupts data some 20 minutes later. By asserting return values appropriately, you at least know about a problem when it happens.

Keep in mind that I'm not advocating asserting on every single possible failure. Some failures are expected in code, and you should handle them appropriately. Having an assertion fire each time a lookup in the database fails will likely drive everyone to disabling assertions in the project. Be smart about it, and assert on return values when it's something serious. Handling good data throughout your program should never cause an assertion to trigger.

Finally, I recommend that you use assertions when you need to check an assumption. For example, if the specifications for a class require 3 MB of disk space, you should check this assumption with a conditional compilation assertion inside that class to ensure the callers are upholding their end of the deal. Here's another example: if your code is supposed to access a database, you should have a check to see whether the required tables actually exist in the database. That way you'll know immediately what's wrong instead of wondering why you're getting weird return values from other methods in the class.

In both of the preceding examples, as with most assumption assertions, you can't check the assumptions in a general assertion method or macro. In these situations, the conditional compilation technique that I indicated in the last paragraph should be part of your assertion toolkit. Because the code executed in the conditional compilation works on live data, you must take extra precautions to ensure that you don't change the state of the program. To avoid the serious problems that can be created by introducing code with side effects, I prefer to implement these types of assertions in separate methods, if possible. By doing so, you avoid changing any local variables inside the original method. Additionally, the conditionally compiled assertion methods can come in handy in the Watch window, as you'll see in Chapter 5 when we talk about the Microsoft Visual Studio .NET debugger. Listing 3-1 shows a conditionally compiled method that checks whether a table exists so that you'll get the assertion before you start any heavy access. Note that this test method assumes that you've already validated the connection string and can fully access the database. `AssertTableExists` ensures the table exists so that you can validate this assumption instead of looking at an odd failure message from deep inside the bowels of your code.

```
 [Conditional("DEBUG")]
static public void AssertTableExists ( string ConnStr ,
                                       string TableName )
{
    SqlConnection Conn = new SqlConnection ( ConnStr ) ;

    StringBuilder sBuildCmd = new StringBuilder ( ) ;

    sBuildCmd.Append ( "select * from dbo.sysobjects where " ) ;
    sBuildCmd.Append ( "id = object_id('" ) ;
    sBuildCmd.Append ( TableName ) ;
    sBuildCmd.Append ( "')" ) ;

    // Make the command.
    SqlCommand Cmd = new SqlCommand ( sBuildCmd.ToString ( ) , Conn ) ;

    try
    {
        // Open the database.
        Conn.Open ( ) ;

        // Create a dataset to fill.
        DataSet TableSet = new DataSet ( ) ;

        // Create the data adapter.
        SqlDataAdapter TableDataAdapter = new SqlDataAdapter ( ) ;

        // Set the command to do the select.
        TableDataAdapter.SelectCommand = Cmd ;

        // Fill the dataset from the adapter.
        TableDataAdapter.Fill ( TableSet ) ;

        // If anything showed up, the table exists.
        if ( 0 == TableSet.Tables[0].Rows.Count )
        {
            String sMsg = "Table : '" + TableName +
                                "' does not exist!\r\n" ;
```

Listing 3-1 `AssertTableExists` checks whether a table exists

```
            Debug.Assert ( false , sMsg ) ;
        }
    }
    catch ( Exception e )
    {
        Debug.Assert ( false , e.Message ) ;
    }
    finally
    {
        Conn.Close ( ) ;
    }
}
```

Before I describe issues unique to the various assertions for .NET and native code, I want to show an example of how I handle assertions. Listing 3-2 shows the `StartDebugging` function from the native code debugger in Chapter 4. This code is an entry point from one module to another, so it shows all the appropriate assertions I covered in this section. I chose a C++ method because so many more problems can surface in native C++ and thus there are more conditions to assert. I'll go over some of the issues you'll see in this example later in the section "Assertions in Native C++ Applications."

```
HANDLE DEBUGINTERFACE_DLLINTERFACE __stdcall
    StartDebugging ( LPCTSTR          szDebuggee        ,
                     LPCTSTR          szCmdLine         ,
                     LPDWORD          lpPID             ,
                     CDebugBaseUser * pUserClass        ,
                     LPHANDLE         lpDebugSyncEvents  )
{
    // Assert the parameters.
    ASSERT ( FALSE == IsBadStringPtr ( szDebuggee , MAX_PATH ) ) ;
    ASSERT ( FALSE == IsBadStringPtr ( szCmdLine , MAX_PATH ) ) ;
    ASSERT ( FALSE == IsBadWritePtr ( lpPID , sizeof ( DWORD ) ) ) ;
    ASSERT ( FALSE == IsBadReadPtr ( pUserClass ,
                                     sizeof ( CDebugBaseUser * ) ) ) ;
    ASSERT ( FALSE == IsBadWritePtr ( lpDebugSyncEvents ,
                                      sizeof ( HANDLE ) *
                                            NUM_DEBUGEVENTS ) ) ;
    // Check them all for real.
    if ( ( TRUE == IsBadStringPtr ( szDebuggee , MAX_PATH )       ) ||
         ( TRUE == IsBadStringPtr ( szCmdLine , MAX_PATH )        ) ||
         ( TRUE == IsBadWritePtr ( lpPID , sizeof ( DWORD )     ) ) ||
         ( TRUE == IsBadReadPtr ( pUserClass ,
                                  sizeof ( CDebugBaseUser * ) ) ) ||
         ( TRUE == IsBadWritePtr ( lpDebugSyncEvents ,
                                   sizeof ( HANDLE ) *
                                        NUM_DEBUGEVENTS )     )       )
```

Listing 3-2 Full assertion example

```
    {
        SetLastError ( ERROR_INVALID_PARAMETER ) ;
        return ( INVALID_HANDLE_VALUE ) ;
    }

    // The string used for the startup acknowledgment event
    TCHAR szStartAck [ MAX_PATH ] = _T ( "\0" ) ;

    // Load up the string for startup acknowledgment.
    if ( 0 == LoadString ( GetDllHandle ( )       ,
                           IDS_DBGEVENTINIT       ,
                           szStartAck             ,
                           MAX_PATH                ) )
    {
        ASSERT ( !"LoadString IDS_DBGEVENTINIT failed!" ) ;
        return ( INVALID_HANDLE_VALUE ) ;
    }

    // The handle of the startup acknowledgment that this function
    // will wait on until the debug thread gets started
    HANDLE hStartAck = NULL ;

     // Create the startup acknowledgment event.
    hStartAck = CreateEvent ( NULL   ,     // Default security
                              TRUE   ,     // Manual-reset event
                              FALSE  ,     // Initial state=Not signaled
                              szStartAck ) ; // Event name
    ASSERT ( NULL != hStartAck ) ;
    if ( NULL == hStartAck )
    {
        return ( INVALID_HANDLE_VALUE ) ;
    }

    // Bundle up the parameters.
    THREADPARAMS stParams ;
    stParams.lpPID = lpPID ;
    stParams.pUserClass = pUserClass ;
    stParams.szDebuggee = szDebuggee ;
    stParams.szCmdLine  = szCmdLine  ;

    // The handle to the debug thread
    HANDLE hDbgThread = INVALID_HANDLE_VALUE ;

    // Try to create the thread.
    UINT dwTID = 0 ;
    hDbgThread = (HANDLE)_beginthreadex ( NULL        ,
                                          0           ,
                                          DebugThread ,
                                          &stParams   ,
                                          0           ,
                                          &dwTID       ) ;
```

(continued)

```
ASSERT ( INVALID_HANDLE_VALUE != hDbgThread ) ;
if (INVALID_HANDLE_VALUE == hDbgThread )
{
    VERIFY ( CloseHandle ( hStartAck ) ) ;
    return ( INVALID_HANDLE_VALUE ) ;
}

// Wait until the debug thread gets good and cranking.
DWORD dwRet = ::WaitForSingleObject ( hStartAck , INFINITE ) ;
ASSERT (WAIT_OBJECT_0 == dwRet ) ;
if (WAIT_OBJECT_0 != dwRet )
{
    VERIFY ( CloseHandle ( hStartAck ) ) ;
    VERIFY ( CloseHandle ( hDbgThread ) ) ;
    return ( INVALID_HANDLE_VALUE ) ;
}

// Get rid of the acknowledgment handle.
VERIFY ( CloseHandle ( hStartAck ) ) ;

// Check that the debug thread is still running. If it isn't,
// the debuggee probably couldn't get started.
DWORD dwExitCode = ~STILL_ACTIVE ;
if ( FALSE == GetExitCodeThread ( hDbgThread , &dwExitCode ) )
{
    ASSERT ( !"GetExitCodeThread failed!" ) ;
    VERIFY ( CloseHandle ( hDbgThread ) ) ;
    return ( INVALID_HANDLE_VALUE ) ;
}
 ASSERT ( STILL_ACTIVE == dwExitCode ) ;
if ( STILL_ACTIVE != dwExitCode )
{
    VERIFY ( CloseHandle ( hDbgThread ) ) ;
    return ( INVALID_HANDLE_VALUE ) ;
}

// Create the synchronization events so that the main thread can
// tell the debug loop what to do.
BOOL bCreateDbgSyncEvts =
              CreateDebugSyncEvents ( lpDebugSyncEvents , *lpPID ) ;
ASSERT ( TRUE == bCreateDbgSyncEvts ) ;
if ( FALSE == bCreateDbgSyncEvts )
{
    // This is a serious problem. I got the debug thread going, but
    // I was unable to create the synchronization events that the
    // user interface thread needs to control the debug thread. My
    // only option here is to punt. I'll kill the
    // debug thread and just return. I can't do much else.
    TRACE ( "StartDebugging : CreateDebugSyncEvents failed\n" ) ;
    VERIFY ( TerminateThread ( hDbgThread , (DWORD)-1 ) ) ;
    VERIFY ( CloseHandle ( hDbgThread ) ) ;
    return ( INVALID_HANDLE_VALUE ) ;
}
```

```
    // Just in case someone modifies the function and fails to properly
    // initialize the returned value.
    ASSERT ( INVALID_HANDLE_VALUE != hDbgThread ) ;

    // Life is good!
    return ( hDbgThread ) ;
}
```

Assertions in .NET Windows Forms or Console Applications

Before I get into the gritty details of .NET assertions, I want to mention one key mistake I've seen in almost all .NET code written, especially in many of the samples from which developers are lifting code to build their applications. Everyone forgets that it's entirely possible to have an object parameter passed as `null`. Even when developers are using assertions, the code looks like the following:

```
void DoSomeWork ( string TheName )
{
    Debug.Assert ( TheName.Length > 0 ) ;
⋮
```

Instead of triggering the assertion, if `TheName` is `null`, calling the `Length` property causes a `System.NullReferenceException` exception in your application, effectively crashing it. This is the horrible case where the assertion is causing a nasty side effect, thus breaking the cardinal rule of assertions. Of course, it logically follows that if developers aren't checking for `null` objects in their assertions, they aren't checking for them in their normal parameter checking. Do yourself a huge favor and start checking objects for `null`.

The fact that .NET applications don't have to worry about pointers and memory blocks means that at least 60 percent of the assertions we were used to handling in the C++ days just went away. On the assertion front, the .NET team added as part of the `System.Diagnostic` namespace two objects, `Debug` and `Trace`, which are active only if you defined `DEBUG` or `TRACE`, respectively, when compiling your application. Both of these defines can be specified as part of the project Property Pages dialog box. As you've seen, the `Assert` method is the method handling assertions in .NET. Interestingly enough, both `Debug` and `Trace` have identical methods, including an `Assert` method. I find it a little confusing to have two possible assertions that are conditionally compiled differently. Consequently, since assertions should be active only in debug builds, I use only `Debug.Assert` for assertions. Doing so avoids surprises from end users calling me up and asking about a weird dialog box or message telling them something went bad. I strongly suggest you do the same so that you contribute to some consistency in the world of assertions.

There are three overloaded Assert methods. All three take a Boolean value as their first or only parameter, and if the value is false, the assertion is triggered. As shown in the preceding examples in which I used Debug.Assert, one of the methods takes a second parameter of type string, which is shown as a message in the output. The final overloaded Assert method takes a third parameter of type string, which provides even more information when the assertion triggers. In my experience, the two-parameter approach is the easiest to use because I simply copy the condition checked in the first parameter and paste it in as a string. Of course, now that the assertion requiring the conditional expression is in quotes, make it part of your code reviews to verify that the string value always matches the real condition. The following code shows all three Assert methods in action:

```
Debug.Assert ( i > 3 )
Debug.Assert ( i > 3 , "i > 3" )
Debug.Assert ( i > 3 , "i > 3" , "This means I got a bad parameter")
```

The .NET Debug object is intriguing because you can see the output in multiple ways. The output for the Debug object—and the Trace object for that matter—goes through another object, named a TraceListener. Classes derived from TraceListener are added to the Debug object's Listener collection property. The beauty of the TraceListener approach is that each time an assertion fails, the Debug object runs through the Listener collection and calls each TraceListener object in turn. This convenient functionality means that even when new and improved ways of reporting assertions surface, you won't have to make major code changes to benefit from them. Even better, in the next section, I'll show you how you can add new TraceListener objects without changing your code at all, which makes for ultimate extensibility!

The default TraceListener object, appropriately named DefaultTraceListener, sends the output to two different places, the most visible of which is the assertion message box shown in Figure 3-1. As you can see in the figure, the bulk of the message box is taken up with the stack walk and parameter types as well as the source and line for each item. The top lines of the message box report the string values you passed to Debug.Assert. In the case of Figure 3-1, I just passed "Debug.Assert assertion" as the second parameter to Debug.Assert.

The result of pressing each button is described in the title bar for the message box. The only interesting button is Retry. If you're running under a debugger, you simply drop into the debugger at the line directly after the assertion. If you're not running under a debugger, clicking Retry triggers a special exception and then launches the Just In Time debugger selector to allow you to pick which registered debugger you'd like to use to debug the assertion.

In addition to the message box output, `Debug.Assert` also sends all the output through `OutputDebugString` so the attached debugger will get the output. The output has a nearly identical format, shown in the following code. Since the `DefaultTraceListener` does the `OutputDebugString` output, you can always use Mark Russinovich's excellent DebugView (*www.sysinternals.com*) to view the output even when you're not running under a debugger. I'll discuss this in more detail later in the chapter.

```
---- DEBUG ASSERTION FAILED ----
---- Assert Short Message ----
Debug.Assert assertion
---- Assert Long Message ----


    at HappyAppy.Fum()  d:\asserterexample\asserter.cs(15)
    at HappyAppy.Fo(StringBuilder sb)  d:\asserterexample\asserter.cs(20)
    at HappyAppy.Fi(IntPtr p)  d:\asserterexample\asserter.cs(24)
    at HappyAppy.Fee(String Blah)  d:\asserterexample\asserter.cs(29)
    at HappyAppy.Baz(Double d)  d:\asserterexample\asserter.cs(34)
    at HappyAppy.Bar(Object o)  d:\asserterexample\asserter.cs(39)
    at HappyAppy.Foo(Int32 i)  d:\asserterexample\asserter.cs(46)
    at HappyAppy.Main()  d:\\asserterexample\asserter.cs(76)
```

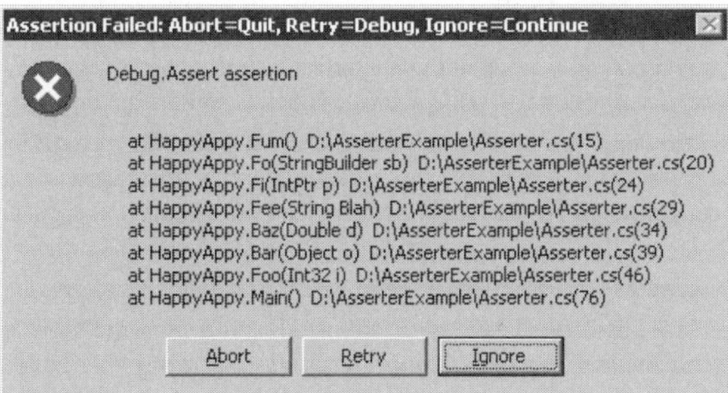

Figure 3-1 The `DefaultTraceListener` message box

Armed with the information supplied by `Debug.Assert`, you should never again have to wonder how you got into the assertion condition! The .NET Framework also supplies two other `TraceListener` objects. To write the output to a text file, use the `TextWriterTraceListener` class. To write the output to the event log, use the `EventLogTraceListener` class. Unfortunately, the `TextWriterTraceListener` and `EventLogTraceListener` classes are essentially worthless because they log only the message fields to your assertions and not the stack trace at all. The good news is that implementing your own `TraceListener` objects is fairly trivial, so as part of BugslayerUtil.NET.DLL, I went ahead and wrote the correct versions for `TextWriterTraceListener` and `Event-`

`LogTraceListener` for you: `BugslayerTextWriterTraceListener` and `BugslayerEventLogTraceListener`, respectively.

Neither `BugslayerTextWriterTraceListener` nor `BugslayerEventLogTraceListener` are very exciting classes. `BugslayerTextWriterTraceListener` is derived directly from `TextWriterTraceListener`, so all it does is override the `Fail` method, which is what `Debug.Assert` calls to do the output. Keep in mind that when using `BugslayerTextWriterTraceListener` or `TextWriterTraceListener`, the associated text file for the output isn't flushed unless you set the `trace` element `autoflush` attribute to `true` in the application configuration file, explicitly call `Close` on the stream or file, or set `Debug.AutoFlush` to `true` so that each write causes a flush to disk. For some bizarre reason, the `EventLogTraceListener` class is sealed, so I couldn't derive directly from it and had to derive from the abstract `TraceListener` class directly. However, I did retrieve the stack trace in an interesting way. The default `StackTrace` class provided by .NET makes it easy to get the current stack trace at any point, as the following snippet shows:

```
StackTrace StkTrc = new StackTrace ( ) ;
```

Compared with the gyrations you have to go through with native code to get a stack trace, the .NET way is a fine example of how .NET can make your life easier. `StackTrace` returns the collection of `StackFrame` objects that comprise the stack. Looking through the documentation for `StackFrame`, you'll see that it has all sorts of interesting methods for getting the source line and number. The `StackTrace` object has a `ToString` method that I thought for sure would have some sort of option for adding the source and line to the resulting stack trace. Alas, I was wrong. Therefore, I had to spend 30 minutes coding up and testing a class that `BugslayerStackTrace` derived from `StackTrace`, which overrides `ToString`, to add the source and line information beside each method. The two methods from `BugslayerStackTrace` that do the work are shown in Listing 3-3.

```
/// <summary>
/// Builds a readable representation of the stack trace
/// </summary>
/// <returns>
/// A readable representation of the stack trace
/// </returns>
public override string ToString ( )
{
    // New up the StringBuilder to hold all the stuff.
    StringBuilder StrBld = new StringBuilder ( ) ;

    // First thing on is a line feed.
    StrBld.Append ( DefaultLineEnd ) ;
```

Listing 3-3 `BugslayerStackTrace` building a full stack trace with source and line information

```
    // Loop'em and do'em!  You can't use foreach here as StackTrace
    // is not derived from IEnumerable.
    for ( int i = 0 ; i < FrameCount ; i++ )
    {
        StackFrame StkFrame = GetFrame ( i ) ;
        if ( null != StkFrame )
        {
            BuildFrameInfo ( StrBld , StkFrame ) ;
        }
    }
    return ( StrBld.ToString ( ) ) ;
}

/*//////////////////////////////////////////////////////////////////
// Private methods.
//////////////////////////////////////////////////////////////////*/

/// <summary>
/// Takes care of the scut work to convert a frame into a string
/// and to plop it into a string builder
/// </summary>
/// <param name="StrBld">
/// The StringBuilder to append the results to
/// </param>
/// <param name="StkFrame">
/// The stack frame to convert
/// </param>
private void BuildFrameInfo ( StringBuilder StrBld   ,
                              StackFrame    StkFrame  )
{
    // Get the method from all the cool reflection stuff.
    MethodBase Meth = StkFrame.GetMethod ( ) ;

    // If nothing is returned, get out now.
    if ( null == Meth )
    {
        return ;
    }

    // Grab the method.
    String StrMethName = Meth.ReflectedType.Name ;

    // Slap in the function indent if one is there.
    if ( null != FunctionIndent )
    {
        StrBld.Append ( FunctionIndent ) ;
    }

    // Get the class type and name on there.
    StrBld.Append ( StrMethName ) ;
    StrBld.Append ( "." ) ;
    StrBld.Append ( Meth.Name ) ;
```

```
    StrBld.Append ( "(" ) ;

    // Slap the parameters on, including all param names.
    ParameterInfo[] Params = Meth.GetParameters ( ) ;
    for ( int i = 0 ; i < Params.Length ; i++ )
    {
        ParameterInfo CurrParam = Params[ i ] ;
        StrBld.Append ( CurrParam.ParameterType.Name ) ;
        StrBld.Append ( " " ) ;
        StrBld.Append ( CurrParam.Name ) ;
        if ( i != ( Params.Length - 1 ) )
        {
            StrBld.Append ( ", " ) ;
        }
    }

    // Close the param list.
    StrBld.Append ( ")" ) ;

    // Get the source and line on only if there is one.
    if ( null != StkFrame.GetFileName ( ) )
    {
        // Am I supposed to indent the source?  If so, I need to put
        // a line break on the end followed by the indent.
        if ( null != SourceIndentString )
        {
            StrBld.Append ( LineEnd ) ;
            StrBld.Append ( SourceIndentString ) ;
        }
        else
        {
            // Just add a space.
            StrBld.Append ( ' ' ) ;
        }

        // Get the file and line of the problem on here.
        StrBld.Append ( StkFrame.GetFileName ( ) ) ;
        StrBld.Append ( "(" ) ;
        StrBld.Append ( StkFrame.GetFileLineNumber().ToString());
        StrBld.Append ( ")" ) ;
    }
    // Always stick a line feed on.
    StrBld.Append ( LineEnd ) ;
}
```

Now that you have other `TraceListener` classes that are worth adding to the `Listeners` collection, we can add and remove `TraceListener` objects in code. As with any .NET collection, call the `Add` method to add an object and the `Remove` method to get rid of one. Note that the default trace listener is named "Default." The following code example shows adding `BugslayerTextWriter-TraceListener` and removing `DefaultTraceListener`:

```
Stream AssertFile = File.Create ( "BSUNBTWTLTest.txt" ) ;

BugslayerTextWriterTraceListener tListener =
            new BugslayerTextWriterTraceListener ( AssertFile ) ;

Debug.Listeners.Add ( tListener ) ;

Debug.Listeners.Remove ( "Default" ) ;
```

Controlling the `TraceListener` Object with Configuration Files

If you develop console and Windows Forms applications, for the most part, `DefaultTraceListener` should serve most of your needs. However, having a message box that pops up every once in a while can wreak havoc on any automated test scripts you might have. Alternatively, you use a third-party component in a Win32 service and the debug build of that component is properly using `Debug.Assert`. In both of these cases, you want to be able to shut off the message box generated by `DefaultTraceListener`. You could add code to remove the `DefaultTraceListener` object, but you can also remove it without touching the code.

Any .NET binary can have an external XML configuration file associated with it. This file resides in the same directory as the binary and is the name of the binary with .CONFIG appended to the end. For example, the configuration file for FOO.EXE is FOO.EXE.CONFIG. You can easily add a configuration file to your project by adding a new XML file named APP.CONFIG. That file will automatically be copied to the output directory and named to match the binary.

In the XML configuration file, the `assert` element under `system.diagnostics` has two attributes. If you set the first attribute, `assertuienabled`, to `false`, .NET doesn't display message boxes and the output still goes through `OutputDebugString`. The second attribute, `logfilename`, allows you to specify a file you want any assertion output written to. Interestingly, when you specify a file in the `logfilename` attribute, any trace statements, which I'll discuss later in the chapter, will also appear in the file. A minimal configuration file is shown in the next code snippet, and you can see how easy it is to shut off the assertion message boxes. Don't forget that the master configuration file MACHINE.CONFIG has the same settings as the EXE configuration file, so you can optionally turn off message boxes on the whole machine using the same settings.

```
<?xml version="1.0" encoding="UTF-8" ?>
<configuration>
    <system.diagnostics>
        <assert assertuienabled="false"
                logfilename="tracelog.txt" />
    </system.diagnostics>
</configuration>
```

As I mentioned earlier, you can add and remove listeners without touching the code, and as you probably guessed, the configuration file has something to do with it. This file looks straightforward in the documentation, but the documentation at the time I am writing this book is not correct. After a little experimentation, I figured out all the gyrations necessary to control your listeners correctly without changing the code.

All the action happens under the `trace` element of the configuration. The `trace` element happens to have one very important optional attribute you should always set to `true` in your configuration files: `autoflush`. By setting `autoflush` to `true`, you force the output buffer to be flushed each time a write operation occurs. If you don't set `autoflush`, you'll have to add calls to your code to get the output.

Underneath `trace` is the `listener` element, where `TraceListener` objects are added or removed. Removing a `TraceListener` object is very simple. Specify the `remove` element, and set the `name` attribute to the string name of the desired `TraceListener` object. Below is the complete configuration file necessary to remove `DefaultTraceListener`.

```
<?xml version="1.0" encoding="UTF-8" ?>
<configuration>
    <system.diagnostics>
      <trace autoflush="true" indentsize="0">
        <listeners>
          <remove name="Default" />
        </listeners>
      </trace>
    </system.diagnostics>
</configuration>
```

The `add` element has two required attributes. The `name` attribute is a string that specifies the name of the `TraceListener` object as it is placed into the `TraceListener.Name` property. The second attribute, `type`, is the one that's confusing, and I'll explain why. The documentation shows only adding a type that is in the global assembly cache (GAC) and hints that adding your own trace listeners is much harder than it needs to be. The one optional attribute, `initializeData`, is the string passed to the constructor of the `TraceListener` object.

To add a `TraceListener` object that's in the GAC, the `type` element specifies only the complete class of the `TraceListener` object. The documentation indicates that to add a `TraceListener` object that's not in the GAC, you'll have to plug in a whole bunch of stuff like culture and public key tokens. Fortunately, all you need to do is simply specify the complete class, a comma, and the name of the assembly. That's what causes the `System.Configuration.ConfigurationException` to be thrown, so don't include the comma and class name. The following shows the proper way of adding the global `TextWriterTraceListener` class:

```
<?xml version="1.0" encoding="UTF-8" ?>
<configuration>
    <system.diagnostics>
      <trace autoflush="true" indentsize="0">
         <listeners>
            <add name="CorrectWay"
                 type="System.Diagnostics.TextWriterTraceListener"
                 initializeData="TextLog.log"/>
         </listeners>
      </trace>
    </system.diagnostics>
</configuration>
```

To add those TraceListener objects that don't reside in the GAC, the assembly containing the TraceListener derived class must reside in the same directory as the binary. I tried every possible path combination and configuration setting option, and I found that there's no way to force the configuration file to include an assembly from a different directory. When adding the derived TraceListener object, you do add the comma followed by the name of the assembly. The following shows how to add BugslayerTextWriterTraceListener from BugslayerUtil.NET.DLL:

```
<?xml version="1.0" encoding="UTF-8" ?>
<configuration>
    <system.diagnostics>
      <trace autoflush="true" indentsize="0">
         <listeners>
            <add name="AGoodListener"
                 type=
"Wintellect.BugslayerTextWriterTraceListener,BugslayerUtil.NET"
                 initializeData="BSUTWTL.log"/>
         </listeners>
      </trace>
    </system.diagnostics>
</configuration>
```

Assertions in ASP.NET Applications and XML Web Services

I'm really glad to see a development platform that has ideas for handling assertions built in. We have a whole namespace in System.Diagnostics that contains all these helpful classes, culminating in the Debug object. Like most of you, I started learning .NET by creating console and Windows Forms applications because they were a lot easier to fit in my head at the time. When I turned to ASP.NET, I was already using Debug.Assert, and I figured that Microsoft had done the right thing by getting rid of the message box automatically. Surely they realized that when running under ASP.NET, I'd be able to break into the debugger when encountering an assertion. Imagine my surprise when I triggered an assertion and nothing stopped! I did see the normal assertion output written to the debugger Output window, but I didn't see any OutputDebugString calls showing the assertion. Because XML Web services in .NET are essentially ASP.NET applications without a user interface, I tried the same experiments with an XML Web service and had the same results. (For the rest of this section, I'll use the term ASP.NET to include ASP.NET and XML Web services.) Amazingly, this meant that no real assertions existed in ASP.NET! Without assertions you might as well not program! The only good news is that `DefaultTraceListener` doesn't pop up the normal message box in ASP.NET applications.

Without assertions, I felt like I was programming naked, and I knew I had to do something about it. After thinking about whether to introduce a new assertion object, I decided the best solution was to stick with `Debug.Assert` as the one and only way of handling assertions. Doing so enabled me to deal with several key issues. The first was having one consistent way of doing assertions across all of .NET—I didn't ever want to wonder whether code would run in Windows Forms or ASP.NET and possibly use the wrong assertion. The second issue concerned using a third-party library that does use `Debug.Assert` and ensuring that those assertions appeared in the same place as all the other assertions.

A third issue was to make using the assertion library as painless as possible. After writing lots of utility code, I realized the importance of integrating the assertion library easily into an application. The final issue I wanted to deal with was having a server-side control that enabled you to see the assertions easily on the page. All the code is in BugslayerUtil.NET.DLL, so you might want to open that project as well as the test harness application, BSUNAssertTest, which is located in the Test directory below BugslayerUtil.NET. Make sure you create a virtual directory in Microsoft Internet Information Services (IIS) that points to the BSUNAssertTest directory before you open the project.

The issues I wanted to address made it blindingly obvious that I was looking at creating a special class derived from `TraceListener`. I'll talk about that code in a moment, but no matter how cool I made `TraceListener`, I had to find a way to hook up my `TraceListener` object as well as remove `DefaultTraceListener`. No matter what, that was going to require a code change on your part because I had to get some code executed. To make using assertions simple and to ensure the assertion library would be called as early as possible, I used a class derived from `System.Web.HttpApplication` because the constructor and `Init` method are the very first things called in an ASP.NET application. The first step to assertion nirvana is to derive your `Global` class in Global.ASAX.cs (or Global.ASAX.vb) by using my `AssertHttpApplication` class. That will get my `ASPTraceListener` properly hooked up as well as put a reference to it in the application state bag under "ASPTraceListener" so that you can change output options on the fly. If all you want in your application is the option to stop when an assertion triggers, this is all you have to do.

To see assertions on the page, I wrote a very simple control named, appropriately enough, AssertControl. You can add AssertControl to your Toolbox by right-clicking on the Web Forms tab and selecting Add/Remove Items from the shortcut menu. In the Customize Toolbox dialog box, select the .NET tab, click the Browse button, and browse over to BugslayerUtil.NET.DLL in the File Open dialog box. Now you can simply drag AssertControl to any page for which you need assertions. You don't need to touch the control in your code because the `ASPTraceListener` class will hunt it down on the page and produce the appropriate output. Even if AssertControl is nested in another control, it will still be found. If no assertions occur when processing the page on the server, AssertControl produces no output at all. If you do have an assertion, the same assertion messages and stack trace displayed in a Windows-based or console application are displayed by AssertControl. Since multiple assertions can appear on the page, AssertControl shows all of them. Figure 3-2 shows the BSUNAssertTest page after an assertion is triggered. The text at the bottom of the page is the AssertControl output.

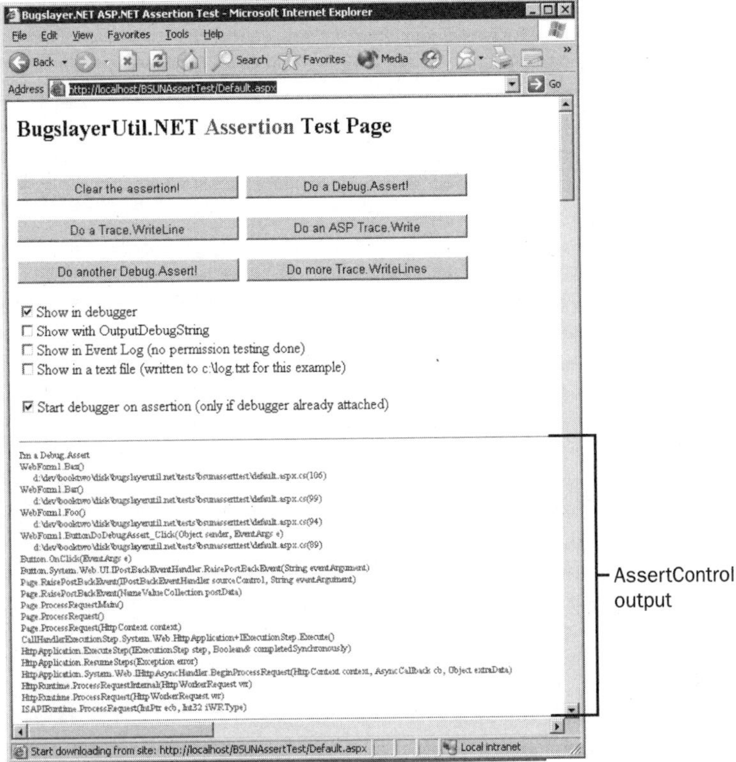

Figure 3-2 An ASP.NET application displaying an assertion using AssertControl

All the real work takes place in the `ASPTraceListener` class, the bulk of which is shown in Listing 3-4. To be your one-stop-shop `TraceListener`, `ASPTraceListener` has several properties that allow you to redirect as well as change output on the fly. Table 3-1 describes those properties and lists their default values.

Table 3-1 `ASPTraceListener` Output and Control Properties

Property	Default Value	Description
`ShowDebugLog`	`true`	Shows output in any attached debugger
`ShowOutputDebugString`	`false`	Shows output through `OutputDebugString`
`EventSource`	`null/Nothing`	The name of the event source for writing output to the event log. No permissions or security checking for access to the event log is done inside BugslayerUtil.NET.DLL. You'll need to request permissions before setting the `EventSource`.
`Writer`	`null/Nothing`	The `TextWriter` object for writing output to a file
`LaunchDebuggerOnAssert`	`true`	If a debugger is attached, the debugger stops immediately when an assertion triggers.

All the main work for doing the assertion output, which includes finding the assertion controls on the page, is done by the `ASPTraceListener.HandleOutput` method, shown in Listing 3-4. My first attempt at writing the `HandleOutput` method was much more involved. Although I could get the current `IHttpHandler` for the current HTTP request from the static `HttpContext.Current.Handler` property, I couldn't find a way to determine whether the handler was an actual `System.Web.UI.Page`. If I could figure out that it was a page, I could easily grind through and find any assertion controls on the page. My original attempt was to write quite a bit of code by using the very cool reflection interfaces so that I could walk the derivation chains myself. As I was getting close to finishing around 500 lines of code, Jeff Prosise innocently asked if I had seen the `is` operator, which determines whether a run-time type of an object is compatible with a given type. Developing my own `is` operator functionality was an interesting exercise, but it wasn't something I needed to do.

Once I had the `Page` object, I started looking for an AssertControl on the page. I knew it could be embedded inside another control, so I used a little recursion to walk through everything. Of course, when doing recursion, I needed to ensure I had a degenerative case or I could have easily ended up in an infinite recursion case. For `ASPTraceListener.FindAssertControl`, I chose to take advantage of the very interesting `out` keyword, which allows you to pass a method parameter by reference but doesn't require you to initialize it. It's more logical to treat the condition not found as `null`, and the `out` keyword lets me do that.

The final work I do with an assertion in the `ASPTraceListener.HandleOutput` method is determine whether I'm supposed to pop into the debugger when an assertion is triggered. The wonderful `System.Diagnostics.Debugger` object allows you to communicate with a debugger from inside your code. If a debugger is currently debugging the code, the `Debugger.IsAttached` property will be `true` and you can simply call `Debugger.Break` to force a breakpoint stop in the debugger. This solution assumes, of course, that you're actively debugging that particular Web site. I still need to handle the case of getting a debugger cranked up when you're not debugging.

If you look at the `Debugger` class, you'll see it has a very cool method named `Launch` that allows you to start a debugger to attach to your process. However, if the user account the process is running under isn't in the Debugger Users group, `Debugger.Launch` doesn't work. If you want to attach the debugger from the assertion code when you're not running under a debugger, you're going to have to get the account ASP.NET runs under in the Debugger Users group. Before I go on, I need to say that by allowing ASP.NET to spawn the debugger, you are potentially opening security holes, so you'll want to enable this only on development machines that aren't directly connected to the Internet.

On Windows 2000 and Windows XP, ASP.NET runs under the ASPNET account, so that's what you'll add to the Debugger Users group. Once you've added the account, you'll need to restart IIS so that `Debugger.Launch` will bring up the Just-In-Time (JIT) Debugging dialog. For Windows Server 2003, ASP.NET runs under the NETWORK SERVICE account. After you add NETWORK SERVICE to Debugger Users, you'll need to restart the machine.

Once I got `Debugger.Launch` working by getting the security correct, I had to ensure that I wasn't going to be calling `Debugger.Launch` only under the right conditions. If I called `Debugger.Launch` when no one was logged in on the server, I was going to cause lots of problems because the JIT debugger could be waiting for a key press on a window station no one could get to! In the `ASPTraceListener` class, I need to make sure the HTTP request is from the local machine because that indicates someone is logged in and there to debug the assertion. The `ASPTraceListener.IsRequestFromLocalMachine` method checks to see whether either the host address is 127.0.0.1 or the `LOCAL_ADDR` server variable is equal to the user's host address.

One final comment I have to make about bringing up the debugger involves Terminal Services. If you have a Remote Desktop Connection window open to a server, the Web address for any requests to the server will resolve as an IP address on the server, as you would expect. My assertion code's default property, if the requesting address comes from the same machine as the server, is to call Debugger.Launch. As I was testing an ASP.NET application by using Remote Desktop and running the browser on the server, I was in for a rude shock when an assertion triggered. (Keep in mind that I was not debugging the process on any machine.)

While I expected to see either the security warning message box or the JIT Debugger dialog box, all I saw was a hung browser. I was quite perplexed until I walked over to the server and moved the mouse. There on the server's logon screen was my security message box! It dawned on me that although it looked like a bug, it was explainable. As it is the ASPNET/NETWORK SERVICE account that brings up the message box or JIT Debugger dialog box, ASP.NET has no knowledge that it was a Terminal Services session that had the connection. There's no way for those accounts to keep track of exactly which session called Debugger.Launch. Consequently, the output goes to the only real window station on the machine.

The good news is that if you have a debugger attached, either inside the Remote Desktop Connection window or on another machine, the call to Debugger.Launch works exactly how you'd expect and stops in the debugger. Additionally, if you make the call into the server from a browser on another machine, the call to Debugger.Launch will not stop. The moral of the story is that if you're going to use Remote Desktop Connection to connect to the server and if you are going to run a browser inside that Remote Desktop Connection window (for example, on the server), you need to have a debugger attached to that server's ASP.NET process.

Although it's inexcusable that Microsoft made no provisions for assertions inside ASP.NET, at least armed with AssertControl, you can start programming. If you're looking for a control to learn how to extend, AssertControl is pretty bare bones. An interesting extension to AssertControl would be to use JavaScript in the code to bring up a better UI, like a Web dialog box, to tell the user there was a problem.

```
public class ASPTraceListener : TraceListener
{
    /* CODE REMOVED FOR CLARITY * /

    // The method that's called when an assertion failed.
    public override void Fail ( String Message       ,
                                String DetailMessage  )
    {
        // For reasons beyond me, it's nearly impossible to
        // consistently be able to get the number of items on the
        // stack up to the Debug.Assert. Sometimes it's 4 other
        // times it's 5. Unfortunately, the only way I can see
        // to handle this is to manually figure it out. Bummer.
        StackTrace StkSheez = new StackTrace ( ) ;
```

Listing 3-4 Important methods of ASPTraceListener

```
        int i = 0 ;
        for ( ; i < StkSheez.FrameCount ; i++ )
        {
            MethodBase Meth = StkSheez.GetFrame(i).GetMethod ( ) ;

            // If nothing is returned, get out now.
            if ( null != Meth )
            {
                if ( "Debug" == Meth.ReflectedType.Name )
                {
                    i++ ;
                    break ;
                }
            }
        }
        BugslayerStackTrace Stk = new BugslayerStackTrace ( i ) ;
        HandleOutput ( Message , DetailMessage , Stk ) ;
    }

    /* CODE REMOVED FOR CLARITY * /

    /// <summary>
    /// Private assertion title message.
    /// </summary>
    private const String AssertionMsg = "ASSERTION FAILURE!\r\n" ;
    /// <summary>
    /// Private hard coded carriage return line feed string.
    /// </summary>
    private const String CrLf = "\r\n" ;
    /// <summary>
    /// The private assertion string boarder.
    /// </summary>
    private const String Border =
        "----------------------------------------\r\n" ;

    /// <summary>
    /// Output the assertion or trace message.
    /// </summary>
    /// <remarks>
    /// Takes care of all the output for the trace or assertion.
    /// </remarks>
    /// <param name="Message">
    /// The message to display.
    /// </param>
    /// <param name="DetailMessage">
    /// The detailed message to display.
    /// </param>
    /// <param name="Stk">
    /// The  value
    /// containing stack walk information for the assertion. If this is
    /// not null, this function is called from an assertion. Trace
    /// output sets this to null.
    /// </param>
    protected void HandleOutput ( String              Message       ,
                                  String              DetailMessage ,
                                  BugslayerStackTrace Stk           )
```

(continued)

```
{
    // Create the StringBuilder to help me build the text
    // string for the output here.
    StringBuilder StrOut = new StringBuilder ( ) ;

    // If the StackArray is not null, it's an assertion.
    if ( null != Stk )
    {
        StrOut.Append ( Border ) ;
        StrOut.Append ( AssertionMsg ) ;
        StrOut.Append ( Border ) ;
    }

    // Pop on the message.
    StrOut.Append ( Message ) ;
    StrOut.Append ( CrLf ) ;

    // Poke on the detail message if it's there.
    if ( null != DetailMessage )
    {
        StrOut.Append ( DetailMessage ) ;
        StrOut.Append ( CrLf ) ;
    }

    // If an assertion, show the stack below a border.
    if ( null != Stk )
    {
        StrOut.Append ( Border ) ;
    }

    // Go through and poke on all the stack information
    // if it's present.
    if ( null != Stk )
    {
        Stk.SourceIndentString = "      " ;
        Stk.FunctionIndent = "   " ;
        StrOut.Append ( Stk.ToString ( ) ) ;
    }

    // Since I use the string multiple places, get it once here.
    String FinalString = StrOut.ToString ( ) ;

    if ( ( true == m_ShowDebugLog          ) &&
         ( true == Debugger.IsLogging ( ) )    )
    {
        Debugger.Log ( 0 , null , FinalString ) ;
    }
    if ( true == m_ShowOutputDebugString )
    {
        OutputDebugStringA ( FinalString ) ;
    }
    if ( null != m_EvtLog )
    {
        m_EvtLog.WriteEntry ( FinalString ,
            System.Diagnostics.EventLogEntryType.Error ) ;
    }
```

```
        if ( null != m_Writer )
        {
            m_Writer.WriteLine ( FinalString ) ;
            // Add a CRLF just in case.
            m_Writer.WriteLine ( "" ) ;
            m_Writer.Flush ( ) ;
        }

        // Always do the page level output!
        if ( null != Stk )
        {
            // Do the warning output to the current TraceContext.
            HttpContext.Current.Trace.Warn ( FinalString ) ;

            // Hunt down the AssertionControl on the page.

            // First, make sure the handler is a page!
            if ( HttpContext.Current.Handler is System.Web.UI.Page )
            {
                System.Web.UI.Page CurrPage =
                    (System.Web.UI.Page)HttpContext.Current.Handler ;

                // Take the easy way out if there are no
                // controls (which I doubt!)
                if ( true == CurrPage.HasControls( ) )
                {
                    // Hunt down the control.
                    AssertControl AssertCtl = null ;
                    FindAssertControl ( CurrPage.Controls ,
                                        out AssertCtl      ) ;

                    // If there was one, add the happy assertion!
                    if ( null != AssertCtl )
                    {
                        AssertCtl.AddAssertion ( Message       ,
                                                 DetailMessage ,
                                                 Stk           ) ;
                    }
                }
            }

            // Finally, launch the debugger if I'm supposed to.
            if ( true == m_LaunchDebuggerOnAssert )
            {
                // If a debugger is already attached, I can just use
                // Debugger.Break on it. It doesn't matter where the
                // debugger is running, as long as it's running on this
                // process.
                if ( true == Debugger.IsAttached )
                {
                    Debugger.Break ( ) ;
                }
                else
                {
                    // With the changes to the security model for the
                    // RTM release of .NET, the ASPNET account that
```

(continued)

```
                    // ASPNET_WP.EXE uses is set to User instead of
                    // running as the System account. In order to
                    // allow Debugger.Launch to work, you need to add
                    // ASPNET to the Debugger Users group. While this
                    // is safe for development systems, you may want
                    // to be careful on production systems.
                    bool bRet = IsRequestFromLocalMachine ( ) ;
                    if ( true == bRet )
                    {
                        Debugger.Launch ( ) ;
                    }
                }
            }
        }
        else
        {
            // The TraceContext is accessible right off the
            // HttpContext.
            HttpContext.Current.Trace.Write ( FinalString ) ;
        }
    }

    /// <summary>
    /// Determines if the request came from a local machine.
    /// </summary>
    /// <remarks>
    /// Checks if the IP address is 127.0.0.1 or the server variable
    /// LOCAL_ADDR matches the current machine.
    /// </remarks>
    /// <returns>
    /// Returns true if the request came from the local machine,
    /// false otherwise.
    /// </returns>
    private bool IsRequestFromLocalMachine ( )
    {
        // Get the request object.
        HttpRequest Req = HttpContext.Current.Request ;

        // Is the user sitting on the loopback node?
        bool bRet = Req.UserHostAddress.Equals ( "127.0.0.1" ) ;
        if ( false == bRet )
        {
            // Get the local IP address out of the server
            // variables.
            String LocalStr =
                Req.ServerVariables.Get ( "LOCAL_ADDR" ) ;
            // Compare the local IP with the IP address that
            // accompanied the request.
            bRet = Req.UserHostAddress.Equals ( LocalStr ) ;
        }
        return ( bRet ) ;

    }

    /// <summary>
    /// Finds any assertion controls on the page.
    /// </summary>
    /// <remarks>
```

```
    /// All assertion controls have the name "AssertControl" so this
    /// method simply loops through the page's control collection
    /// looking for them. It also looks through children of children
    /// recursively.
    /// </remarks>
    /// <param name="CtlCol">
    /// The collection control to look through.
    /// </param>
    /// <param name="AssertCtrl">
    /// The output parameter that contains the assertion control found.
    /// </param>
    private void FindAssertControl ( ControlCollection CtlCol       ,
                                     out AssertControl AssertCtrl )

    {
        // Loop through all the controls in the control array.
        foreach ( Control Ctl in CtlCol )
        {
            // Is this one the assertion control?
            if ( "AssertControl" == Ctl.GetType().Name )
            {
                // Yep!  Stop now.
                AssertCtrl = (AssertControl)Ctl ;
                return ;
            }
            else
            {
                // If this control has children do them too.
                if ( true == Ctl.HasControls ( ) )
                {
                    FindAssertControl ( Ctl.Controls ,
                                        out AssertCtrl ) ;
                    // If one of the children had the assertion,
                    // I can stop now.
                    if ( null != AssertCtrl )
                    {
                        return ;
                    }
                }
            }
        }
        // Didn't find it in this chain.
        AssertCtrl = null ;
        return  ;
    }
}
```

Assertions in Native C++ Applications

For years an old computer joke describing all the different computer languages as different cars has always described C++ as a Formula One racer, fast but dangerous to drive. Another joke says that C++ gives you a gun to shoot yourself in the foot and has the trigger nearly pulled when you get past "Hello World!" I think it's safe to say native C++ is a Formula One car that has two shotguns so that you can shoot yourself in the foot at the same time you crash. Even with the smallest mistake capable of crashing your application, using assertions heavily with C++ is the only way you stand a chance of debugging your native applications.

C and C++ also have all sorts of functions that can help make your assertions as descriptive as possible. Table 3-2 shows the helper functions you can use to check which condition you need.

Table 3-2 Helper Functions for Descriptive C and C++ Assertions

Function	Description
`GetObjectType`	A graphics device interface (GDI) subsystem function that returns the type for a GDI handle
`IsBadCodePtr`	Checks that the memory pointer can be executed
`IsBadReadPtr`	Checks that the memory pointer is readable for the specified number of bytes
`IsBadStringPtr`	Checks that the string pointer is readable up to the string's `NULL` terminator or the maximum number of characters specified
`IsBadWritePtr`	Checks that the memory pointer is writable for the specified number of bytes
`IsWindow`	Checks whether the `HWND` parameter is a valid window

The `IsBad*` functions are not thread-safe. Whereas one thread calls `IsBadWritePtr` to check the access permissions on a piece of memory, another thread could be changing the memory the pointer points to. What these functions give you is a snapshot of a moment in time. Some readers of this book's first edition argued that since the `IsBad*` functions aren't multithread-safe, you should never use them because they can lead you into a false sense of security. I couldn't disagree more. There's no practical way of guaranteeing truly thread-safe memory checks unless you wrap every byte access inside structured exception handling (SEH). Doing this is possible, but the code would be so slow that you couldn't use the machine. The one problem, which a few people have blown well out of proportion, is that the `IsBad*` functions can eat `EXCEPTION_GUARD_PAGE` exceptions in very rare cases. In all my years of Windows development, I've never run into this problem. I'm more than willing to live with these two limitations of the `IsBad*` functions for all the wonderful benefits of knowing that a pointer is bad.

The following code shows one of the mistakes I used to make with my C++ assertions:

```
// Poor assertion usage
BOOL CheckDriveFreeSpace ( LPCTSTR szDrive )
{
    ULARGE_INTEGER ulgAvail ;
    ULARGE_INTEGER ulgNumBytes ;
```

```
    ULARGE_INTEGER ulgFree ;
    if ( FALSE == GetDiskFreeSpaceEx ( szDrive       ,
                                       &ulgAvail     ,
                                       &ulgNumBytes ,
                                       &ulgFree      ) )
    {
        ASSERT ( FALSE ) ;
        return ( FALSE ) ;
    }
    :
}
```

Although I was using ASSERT, which is good, I wasn't showing the condition that failed. The assertion message box showed only the expression "FALSE," which isn't that helpful. When using an assertion, you want to try to get as much information about the assertion failure in the message box as possible.

My friend Dave Angel pointed out to me that in C and C++, you can just use the logical NOT operator (!) and use a string as its operand. This combination gives you a much better expression in the assertion message box so that you at least have an idea of what failed without looking at the source code. The following example shows the proper way to assert a false condition:

```
// Proper assertion usage
BOOL CheckDriveFreeSpace ( LPCTSTR szDrive )
{
    ULARGE_INTEGER ulgAvail ;
    ULARGE_INTEGER ulgNumBytes ;
    ULARGE_INTEGER ulgFree ;
    if ( FALSE == GetDiskFreeSpaceEx ( szDrive       ,
                                       &ulgAvail     ,
                                       &ulgNumBytes ,
                                       &ulgFree      ) )
    {
        ASSERT ( !"GetDiskFreeSpaceEx failed!" ) ;
        return ( FALSE ) ;
    }
    :
}
```

You can also extend Dave's assertion trick by using the logical AND conditional operator (&&) to perform a normal assertion and still get the message text. The following example shows how. Note that when using the logical AND trick, you do *not* use the "!" in front of the string.

```
BOOL AddToDataTree ( PTREENODE pNode )
{
    ASSERT ( ( FALSE == IsBadReadPtr ( pNode , sizeof ( TREENODE) ) ) &&
             "Invalid parameter!"                                  ) ;
    :
}
```

The VERIFY Macro

Before we get into the various assertion macros and functions you'll encounter in Windows development as well as some of the problems with them, I want to talk about the `VERIFY` macro that's used quite a bit in Microsoft Foundation Class (MFC) library development. In a debug build, the `VERIFY` macro behaves the same way as a normal assertion because it's defined to be `ASSERT`. If the condition evaluates to 0, the `VERIFY` macro triggers the normal assertion message box to warn you. In a release build, the `VERIFY` macro does not display a message box, however, the parameter to the `VERIFY` macro stays in the source code and is evaluated as a normal part of processing.

In essence, the `VERIFY` macro allows you to have normal assertions with side effects, and those side effects stay in release builds. Ideally, you should never use conditions for any type of assertion that causes side effects. However, in one situation the `VERIFY` macro is useful—when you have a function that returns an error value that you wouldn't check otherwise. For example, when you call `ResetEvent` to clear a signaled event handle and the call fails, there's not much you can do other than terminate the application, which is why most engineers call `ResetEvent` and never check the return value in either debug or release builds. If you wrap the call with the `VERIFY` macro, at least you'll be notified in your debug builds that something went wrong. Of course, I could achieve the same results by using `ASSERT`, but `VERIFY` saves me the trouble of creating a new variable just to store and verify the return value of the `ResetEvent` call—a variable that would probably be used only in debug builds anyway.

I think most MFC programmers use the `VERIFY` macro for convenience, but you should try to break yourself of the habit. In most cases, when programmers use the `VERIFY` macro, they should be checking the return value instead. A good example of where everyone seems to use `VERIFY` is around the `CString::LoadString` member function, which loads resource strings. Using `VERIFY` this way is fine in a debug build because if `LoadString` fails, the `VERIFY` macro warns you. In a release build, however, if `LoadString` fails, you end up using an uninitialized variable. If you're lucky, you'll just have a blank string, but most of the time, you'll crash in your release build. The moral of this story is to check your return values. If you're about to use a `VERIFY` macro, you need to ask whether ignoring the return value will cause you any problems in release builds.

Debugging War Story

Disappearing Files and Threads

The Battle

While working on a version of NuMega's BoundsChecker, we had incredible difficulty with random crashes that were almost impossible to duplicate. The only clues we had were that file handles and thread handles occasionally became invalid, which meant that files were randomly closing and thread synchronization was sometimes breaking. The user interface developers were also experiencing occasional crashes, but only when running under the debugger. These problems plagued us throughout development, finally escalating to the point where all developers on the team stopped what they were doing and started trying to solve these bugs.

The Outcome

The team nearly tarred and feathered me because the problem turned out to be my fault. I was responsible for the debug loop in BoundsChecker. In the debug loop, you use the Windows debugging API to start and control another process, the debuggee, and to respond to debug events the debugger generates. Being a conscientious programmer, I saw that the `WaitForDebugEvent` function was returning handle values for some of the debugging event notifications. For example, when a process started under a debugger, the debugger would get a structure that contained a handle to the process and the initial thread for that process.

Because I'm so careful, I knew that if an API gave you a handle to some object and you no longer needed the object, you called `CloseHandle` to free the underlying memory for that object. Therefore, whenever the debugging API gave me a handle, I closed that handle as soon as I finished using it. That seemed like the reasonable thing to do.

However, much to my chagrin, I hadn't read the fine print in the debugging API documentation, which says that the debugging API itself closes any process and thread handles it generates. What was happening was that I was holding some of the handles returned by the debugging API until I needed them, but I was closing those same handles after I finished using them—after the debugging API had already closed them.

To understand how this situation led to our problem, you need to know that when you close a handle, the operating system marks that handle value as available. Microsoft Windows NT 4, the operating system we were using at the time, is particularly aggressive about recycling handle

(continued)

Debugging War Story *(continued)*

values. (Microsoft Windows 2000 and Microsoft Windows XP exhibit the same aggressive behavior toward handle values.) Our UI portions, which were heavily multithreaded and opened many files, were creating and using new handles all the time. Because the debugging API was closing my handles and the operating system was recycling them, sometimes the UI portions would get one of the handles that I was saving. As I closed my copies of the handles later, I was actually closing the UI's threads and file handles!

I was barely able to avoid the tar and feathers because I showed that this bug was also in the debug loop of previous versions of Bounds-Checker. We'd just gotten lucky before. What had changed was that the version we were working on had a new and improved UI that was doing much more with files and threads, so the conditions were ripe for my bug to do more damage.

The Lesson

I could have avoided this problem if I'd read the fine print in the debugging API documentation. Additionally—and this is the big lesson—I learned that you always check the return values to `CloseHandle`. Although you can't do much when you close an invalid handle, the operating system does tell you when you're doing something wrong, and you should pay attention.

As a side note, I want to mention that if you attempt to double-close a handle or pass a bad value to `CloseHandle` and you're running under a debugger, Windows operating systems will report an "Invalid Handle" exception (0xC0000008). When you see that exception value, you can stop and explore why it occurred.

I also learned that it really helps to be able to out-sprint your coworkers when they're chasing you with a pot of tar and bags of feathers.

Different Types of Visual C++ Assertions

Even though I define all my C++ assertion macros and functions to just plain `ASSERT`, which I'll talk about in a moment, I want to quickly go over the different types of assertions available in Visual C++ and provide a little information about their implementation. That way, if you see one of them in someone else's code, you can recognize it. I also want to alert you to the problems with some of the implementations.

assert, _ASSERT, and _ASSERTE

The first type of assertion is from the C run-time library, the ANSI C standard assert macro. This version is portable across all C compilers and platforms and is defined by including ASSERT.H. In the Windows world, if you're working with a console application and it fails an assertion, assert will send the output to stderr. If your application is a Windows graphical user interface (GUI) application, assert will show the assertion failure as a message box.

The second type of assertion in the C run-time library is specific to Windows. These assertions are _ASSERT and _ASSERTE, which are defined in CRTDBG.H. The only difference between the two is that the _ASSERTE version also prints the expression passed as its parameter. Because the expression is so important to have, especially when your test engineers are testing, if you're using the C run-time library, you should always use _ASSERTE. Both macros are part of the extremely useful debug run-time library code, and the assertions are only one of its many features.

Although assert, _ASSERT, and _ASSERTE are convenient to use and free of charge, they do have a few drawbacks. The assert macro has two problems that can cause you some grief. The first problem is that the filename display truncates to 60 characters, so sometimes you don't have any idea which file triggered the assertion. The second problem with assert occurs if you're working on a project that doesn't have a UI, such as a Windows service or a COM out-of-process server. Because assert sends its output to stderr or to a message box, you can miss the assertion. In the case of the message box, your application will hang because you can't dismiss the message box when you can't display your UI.

The C run-time implementation macros, on the other hand, address the issue with defaulting to a message box by allowing you to redirect the assertion to a file or to the OutputDebugString API function by calling the _CrtSetReportMode function. All the Microsoft-supplied assertions suffer from one fatal flaw, however: they change the state of the system, which is the cardinal rule assertions can't break. Having your assertion calls suffer from side effects is almost worse than not using assertions at all. The following code shows an example of how the supplied assertions can change your state between debug and release builds. Can you spot the problem?

```
// Send the message over to the window. If it times out, the other
// thread is hung, so I need to abort the thread. As a reminder, the
// only way to check whether SendMessageTimeout failed is to check
// GetLastError. If the function returned 0 and the last error is
// 0, SendMessageTimeout timed out.
_ASSERTE ( NULL != pDataPacket ) ;
if ( NULL == pDataPacket )
{
    return ( ERR_INVALID_DATA ) ;
}
```

```
LRESULT lRes = SendMessageTimeout ( hUIWnd                  ,
                                    WM_USER_NEEDNEXTPACKET  ,
                                    0                       ,
                                    (LPARAM)pDataPacket     ,
                                    SMTO_BLOCK              ,
                                    10000                   ,
                                    &pdwRes                  ) ;
_ASSERTE ( FALSE != lRes ) ;
if ( FALSE == lRes )
{
    // Get the last error value.
    DWORD dwLastErr = GetLastError ( ) ;
    if ( 0 == dwLastErr )
    {
        // The UI is hung or not processing data fast enough.
        return ( ERR_UI_IS_HUNG ) ;
    }
    // If the error is anything else, there was a problem
    // with the data sent as a parameter.
    return ( ERR_INVALID_DATA ) ;
}
return ( ERR_SUCCESS ) ;
    ⋮
```

The problem, which is insidious, is that the supplied assertions destroy the last error value. In the preceding case, the "_ASSERTE (FALSE != lRes)" executes, shows the message box, and changes the last error value to 0. Thus in debug builds, the UI thread always appears to hang, whereas in the release build, you see the cases in which the parameters passed to SendMessageTimeout are bad.

The fact that the last error value is destroyed with the system-supplied assertions might never be an issue in the code you write, but my own experience has been different—two bugs that took a great deal of time to track down turned out to be related to this problem. Fortunately, if you use the assertion presented later in this chapter in the section "SUPERASSERT," I'll take care of this problem for you as well as give you some information that the system-supplied version doesn't.

ASSERT_KINDOF and ASSERT_VALID

If you're programming with MFC, you'll run into two additional assertion macros that are specific to MFC and are fantastic examples of proactive debugging. If you've declared your classes with DECLARE_DYNAMIC or DECLARE_SERIAL, you can use the ASSERT_KINDOF macro to check whether a pointer to a CObject-derived class is a specific class or is derived from a specific class. The ASSERT_KINDOF assertion is just a wrapper around the CObject::IsKindOf method. The following code snippet first checks the parameter in the ASSERT_KINDOF assertion and then does the real parameter error checking.

```
BOOL DoSomeMFCStuffToAFrame ( CWnd * pWnd )
{
    ASSERT ( NULL != pWnd ) ;
    ASSERT_KINDOF ( CFrameWnd , pWnd ) ;
    if ( ( NULL  == pWnd ) ||
         ( FALSE == pWnd->IsKindOf ( RUNTIME_CLASS ( CFrameWnd ) ) ) )
    {
        return ( FALSE ) ;
    }
    :
    // Do some MFC stuff; pWnd is guaranteed to be a CFrameWnd or
    // to be derived from a CFrameWnd.
    :
}
```

The second MFC-specific assertion macro is ASSERT_VALID. This assertion resolves down to AfxAssertValidObject, which completely validates that the pointer is a proper pointer to a CObject-derived class. After validating the pointer, ASSERT_VALID calls the object's AssertValid method. AssertValid is a method that you can override in your derived classes so that you can check each of the internal data structures in your class. This method is a great way to do a deep validation on your classes. You should override AssertValid for all your key classes.

SUPERASSERT

Having told you what the problems are with the supplied assertions, now I want to show you how I was able to fix and extend the assertions to really make them tell you how and why you had a problem, plus much more. Figures 3-3 and 3-4 show examples of a SUPERASSERT error dialog box. In the first edition of this book, the SUPERASSERT output was a message box that showed the location of the failed assertion, the last error value translated into text, and the call stack. As you can see in Figures 3-3 and 3-4, SUPERASSERT has certainly grown up! (However, I have resisted calling it SUPERDUPERASSERT!)

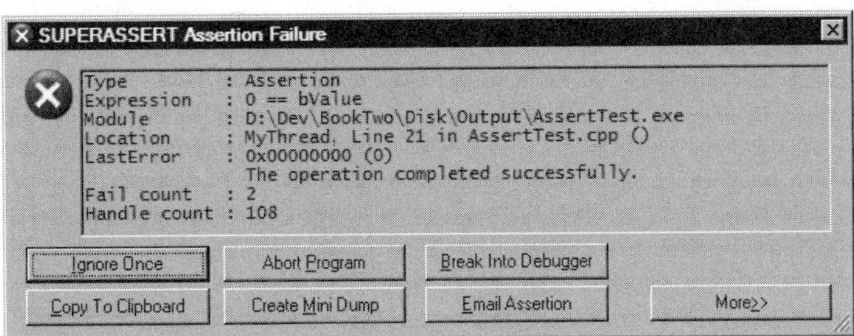

Figure 3-3 Example of a folded SUPERASSERT dialog box

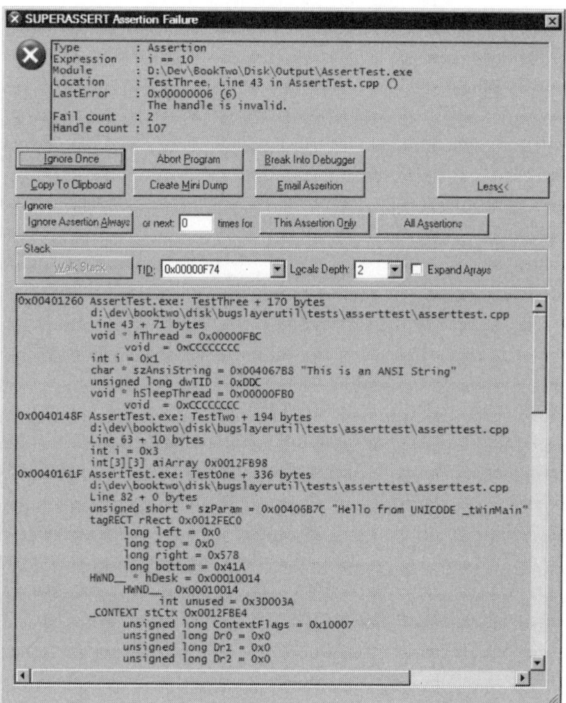

Figure 3-4 Example of an unfolded SUPERASSERT dialog box

The most amazing part about writing books and articles is the incredible conversations I've had with readers through e-mail and in person. I feel so lucky to learn from such amazingly smart folks! Soon after the first edition came out, Scott Bilas and I had a great e-mail exchange about his theories on what assertion messages should do and how they should be used. I originally used a message box because I wanted to be as lightweight as possible. However, after swapping lots of interesting thoughts with Scott, I was convinced that assertion messages should offer more features, such as assertion suppression. As we chatted, Scott even provided some code to accomplish dialog box folding as well as his ASSERT macros for keeping track of ignore counts and such. After being inspired by Scott's ideas, I worked up the new version of SUPERASSERT. I did this right after the first version came out and have been using the new code in all my development since, so it's been sufficiently thrashed.

Figure 3-3 shows the parts of the dialog box that are always visible. The failure edit control contains the reason for the failure, either assertion or verify, the expression that failed, the location of the failure, the decoded last error value, and how many times this particular assertion has failed. If the assertion is running on Windows XP, Windows Server 2003 or higher, it will also display the total kernel handle count in the process. In SUPERASSERT, I translate the last error values into their textual representations. Seeing the error messages written out as text is extremely helpful when an API function fails: you can see why it failed and can start debugging faster. For example, if `GetModuleFileName` fails because the input buffer isn't large enough, `SUPERASSERT` will set the last error value to 122, which is `ERROR_INSUFFICIENT_BUFFER` from WINERROR.H. By immediately seeing the text "The data area passed to a system call is too small," you know exactly what the problem is and how to fix it. Figure 3-3 shows a standard Windows error message, but you can add your own message resource to the `SUPERASSERT` last error message translation. For more information about using your own message resources, look up the "Message Compiler" topic in MSDN. An added incentive for using message resources is that they make internationalizing your application much easier.

The Ignore Once button, located below the failure edit control, simply continues execution. It is the default button, so you can press Enter or the spacebar to immediately move past an assertion after analyzing its cause. Abort Program calls `ExitProcess` to attempt to do a clean shutdown of the application. The Break Into Debugger button causes a `DebugBreak` call so that you can start debugging the failure by either popping into the debugger or starting the JIT debugger. The Copy To Clipboard button on the second row copies to the clipboard all the text from the failure edit control as well as the information from all threads you have done stack walks for. The last button, More>> or Less<<, toggles the dialog box folding.

The Create Mini Dump and Email Assertion buttons need a little explanation. If the version of DBGHELP.DLL loaded in the process space has the minidump functions exported, the Create Mini Dump button is enabled. If the minidump functions are not accessible, the button is disabled. To best preserve the state of the application, `SUPERASSERT` suspends all other threads in the application. This means that `SUPERASSERT` can't use the common file dialog because that dialog cranks up some background threads that stick around after it goes away. When `SUPERASSERT` suspends all the threads, the common file dialog code hangs because it's waiting on a suspended thread. Consequently, I can't use the common file dialog. The dialog that pops up after clicking Create Mini Dump, then, is a simple prompt dialog box with an edit box that asks you for the full path and name of the minidump.

The Email Assertion button is active only if you've put a special define in your source file that indicates the e-mail address you want the assertion information mailed to. This is a fantastic feature for testers to use to send the appropriate assertion to the correct developer. All the information, including all stack walks, is part of the e-mail message, so developers should be able to get exactly why the assertion triggered. At the top of each source file, you'll want to include code like the following to automatically get the e-mail capabilities. It's not required to use `SUPERASSERT` to define `SUPERASSERT_EMAIL`, but I strongly suggest you do.

```
#ifdef SUPERASSERT_EMAIL
#undef SUPERASSERT_EMAIL
// Please put your own email address in!
#define SUPERASSERT_EMAIL "john@wintellect.com"
#endif
```

The unfolded SUPERASSERT dialog box in Figure 3-4 has all sorts of helpful options in it. The Ignore section allows you to control how you want to ignore the assertion. The first button, Ignore Assertion Always, marks the particular assertion as ignored for the life of the program. You can also specify a specific ignore count by typing it into the edit box. To set the ignore specific count to the desired assertion, click This Assertion Only. To ignore subsequent assertions no matter where they come from, click All Assertions. Originally, I didn't think you should ever ignore an assertion, but after having had the option to skip an assertion that's triggered in every iteration through a loop, I don't know how I lived without it.

The final part of the dialog box is dedicated to the call stack. Even though I had the call stack in the first version of SUPERASSERT, if you look closely at the call stack in the edit box, you'll see all the local variables and their current values under each function! The SymbolEngine library, which is part of BugslayerUtil.DLL, can decode all basic types, structures, classes, and arrays. It's also smart enough to decode important values such as character pointers and character arrays. In Figure 3-4 you can see that it's showing both ANSI and Unicode strings as well as decoding a RECT structure. Building the proper symbol decoding was one of the toughest pieces of code I've written! If you're interested in the dirty details, you can read more about the SymbolEngine library in Chapter 4. The good news for you is that I did all the hard work, so you don't even have to think about it if you don't want to!

The first button in the Stack section, Walk Stack, allows you to walk the stack. Walk Stack is disabled in Figure 3-4 because the stack has already been walked. The Thread ID drop-down list allows you to pick the thread you want to take a look at. If the application has only a single thread, the Thread ID drop-down list doesn't appear in the dialog box. The Locals Depth drop-down list allows you choose how deep local variables will be expanded. This drop-down list is akin to the plus arrows next to expandable items in the debugger watch window. The higher the number, the more will be displayed about appropriate local variables. For example, if you had a local of type int**, you'd have to set the locals depth to 3 to see the value of the integer pointed to by that variable. The Expand Arrays check box tells SUPERASSERT to expand all array types encountered. Calculating deeply nested types or pointers as well as large arrays is quite expensive, so you probably don't want to expand arrays unless you need to. Of course, SUPERASSERT does the right thing by reevaluating all the local variables on the fly when you change the locals depth or request, so you can see the information you need when you need it.

SUPERASSERT has some global options you can change on the fly as well. The Global SUPERASSERT Options dialog box is shown in Figure 3-5 and can be opened by selecting Options from the system menu.

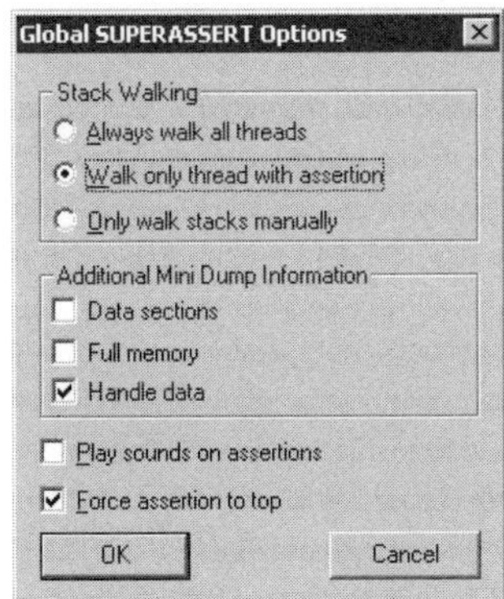

Figure 3-5 The Global SUPERASSERT Options dialog box

The Stack Walking section determines how much stack walking will be done when the SUPERASSERT dialog box appears. The default is to walk only the thread that had the assertion, but if you want to have the fastest popup possible, you might want to set it to only walk stacks manually. The Additional Mini Dump Information section specifies how much information you want written out to any minidumps. (For more information, see the MINIDUMP_TYPE enumeration documentation.) Checking Play Sounds On Assertions plays the default message beep when the SUPERASSERT dialog box pops up. Checking Force Assertion To Top sets the SUPERASSERT dialog box as the topmost window. If the process is being debugged, the topmost window setting is not applied because SUPERASSERT can block the debugger. All SUPERASSERT global settings are stored in the registry under HKCU\Software\Bugslayer\SUPERASSERT. Also stored in the registry are the last location and fold state so that SUPERASSERT returns to the same position you expect every time.

I want to mention a few other details about SUPERASSERT. The first is that, as you see in Figures 3-3 and 3-4, SUPERASSERT has a grippy area in the lower right corner so that you can resize the dialog box. SUPERASSERT is also multiple-monitor-aware, so on the system menu is an option allowing you to center the dialog box on the current monitor so that you can get SUPERASSERT back to a desired location. What you can't see from the figures is that you don't have to display SUPERASSERT at all. At first, you might think that option is counterproductive, but I assure you it isn't! If you followed my recommendations in Chapter 2 and started testing your debug builds with a regression-testing tool, you know that handling random assertion messages is almost impossible. Because of the problems in handling assertion messages, your test engineers are much less likely to use the debug build. With my assertion code, you can specify that you want the output to go to OutputDebugString, a file handle, the event log, or any combination of the three. This flexibility allows you to run the code and get all the great assertion information but still automate your debug builds. Finally, SUPERASSERT is super smart about when it pops up. It always checks whether an interactive user is logged into the process windows station. If no one is interactively logged into that window station, SUPERASSERT won't pop up and hang your application.

Because of all the information SUPERASSERT gives me, I'm using the debugger less than ever before, which is a huge win for debugging speed. When I hit an assertion, I position the SUPERASSERT dialog box to pop up on my second monitor. I look through the local variable information and start reading source code on my primary monitor. I've found that I'm able to solve about 20 percent more bugs without starting the debugger. Although the first edition was very helpful, the second edition really rocks!

Using SUPERASSERT

Integrating SUPERASSERT into your applications is quite easy. You simply need to include BUGSLAYERUTIL.H, which is probably best included in your precompiled header, and link against BUGSLAYERUTIL.LIB so that you bring BUGSLAYERUTIL.DLL into the address space. That gives you the ASSERT macro and automatically redirects any existing ASSERT and assert calls to my functions. My code does not redirect the _ASSERT and _ASSERTE macros because you might be doing some advanced work or specific output with the debug run-time library and I don't want to break your existing solutions. My code leaves ASSERT_KINDOF and ASSERT_VALID alone as well.

If you'd like to change where output goes, such as to the event log or a text file, use the SETDIAGASSERTOPTIONS macro, which takes several self-explanatory bit field macros that determine the location of the output. These bit field macros are all defined in DIAGASSERT.H.

A Word About Ignoring Assertions

It's always a bad moment when another developer or tester drags you over to his machine to blame your code for a crash. It's even worse when you start diagnosing the problem by asking him if he clicked the Ignore button on an assertion that popped up. Many times he'll swear to you that he didn't, but you know that there's no way that crash could have occurred without a particular assertion trigger. When you finally pin him down and force him to admit that he did click that Ignore button, you're on the verge of ripping his head off. If he had reported that assertion, you could have easily solved the problem!

The Ignore button, if you haven't already guessed, is potentially a very dangerous option because people are so tempted to press it! Although it might have been a little draconian, I seriously considered not putting an Ignore button on SUPERASSERT to force you to deal with the assertion and its underlying cause. In some companies, the developers add an easy way to check whether any assertions have been ignored in the current run. This allows them to check whether the Ignore button has been clicked before they waste their time looking at the crash.

If you're using SUPERASSERT, and you want to see how many assertions have been triggered overall, you can look at the global variable, g_iTotalAssertions, in SUPERASSERT.CPP. Of course, this presumes that either you have a debugger attached to the crashed program or you have a memory dump of the crashed program. If you'd like to get the total assertion counts programmatically, call GetSuperAssertionCount, which is exported from BUGSLAYERUTIL.DLL.

What you might want to consider adding to SUPERASSERT is complete logging of all assertions that are triggered. That way you'd automatically have a running total of the number of Ignore values clicked by users, allowing you to validate what user actions led to the crash. Some companies automatically log assertions to a central database so that they can keep track of assertion frequencies and determine whether developers and testers are improperly using the Ignore button.

Since I've talked about protecting yourself against the user's knee-jerk reaction of pressing the Ignore button, it's only fair that I mention that you might be doing it too. Assertions should never pop up in normal operation—only when something is amiss. Here's a perfect example of an improperly used assertion that I encountered while helping debug an application. When I choose an item on the most recently used menu that didn't have a target item, an assertion fired before the normal error handling. In such a case, the normal error handling was more than sufficient. If you're getting complaints that assertions are firing too much, you need to carefully analyze whether those assertions really need to be there.

SUPERASSERT Implementation Highlights

If you start looking at the code for SUPERASSERT, you might think it looks a little convoluted because it's spread across two separate sets of assertion code, SUPERASSERT.CPP and DIAGASSERT.CPP. The DIAGASSERT.CPP portion is actually the first version of SUPERASSERT. I left that code in place because quite a bit of UI code was involved with building the new SUPERASSERT, and since I couldn't use SUPERASSERT on itself, I needed a second set of assertions to make the SUPERASSERT development cleaner and more robust. Lastly, because

SUPERASSERT requires more supporting code, the old assertion code is what you'll need to use in the one case in which SUPERASSERT can't be used, that is, when doing assertions in RawDllMain before anything in your module has been initialized.

The first interesting part of SUPERASSERT is the macro that eventually resolves down to the call to the SuperAssertion function, as shown in Listing 3-5. Since SUPERASSERT needs to keep track of local assertion ignore counts, the macro creates a new scope each time it's used. Inside the scope, it declares the two static integers to keep track of the number of times the particular assertion failed as well as the number of times the user wants to ignore the assertion. After checking the result of the expression, the rest of the macro is getting the current stack pointer and the frame pointer, and it is calling the actual SuperAssertion function.

```
#ifdef _M_IX86
#define NEWASSERT_REALMACRO( exp , type )                                   \
{                                                                            \
    /* The local instance of the ignore count and the total hits. */        \
    static int sIgnoreCount = 0 ;                                            \
    static int sFailCount   = 0 ;                                            \
    /* The local stack and frame at the assertion's location. */            \
    DWORD dwStack ;                                                          \
    DWORD dwStackFrame ;                                                     \
    /* Check the expression. */                                              \
    if ( ! ( exp ) )                                                         \
    {                                                                        \
        /* Houston, we have a problem. */                                    \
        _asm { MOV dwStack , ESP }                                           \
        _asm { MOV dwStackFrame , EBP }                                      \
        if ( TRUE == SuperAssertion ( TEXT ( type )          ,               \
                                      TEXT ( #exp )          ,               \
                                      TEXT ( __FUNCTION__ )  ,               \
                                      TEXT ( __FILE__ )      ,               \
                                      __LINE__               ,               \
                                      SUPERASSERT_EMAIL      ,               \
                                      (DWORD64)dwStack       ,               \
                                      (DWORD64)dwStackFrame  ,               \
                                      &sFailCount            ,               \
                                      &sIgnoreCount            ) )           \
        {                                                                    \
            __asm INT 3                                                      \
        }                                                                    \
    }                                                                        \
}
#endif  // _M_IX86
```

Listing 3-5 The main ASSERT macro

Most processing of the assertion is handled in SUPERASSERT.CPP, shown in Listing 3-6. The majority of the work is done in two functions, `RealSuperAssertion` and `PopTheFancyAssertion`. `RealSuperAssertion` determines whether the assertion is ignored, builds the actual assertion message, and figures out where the output needs to go. `PopTheFancyAssertion` has more interesting functionality. To minimize the impact on the application, I suspend all the other threads in the application when the `SUPERASSERT` dialog box is up. That way I can cleanly get the call stacks as well. To suspend all the threads and stop everything, I boost the asserting thread to time-critical priority. I found that some tricky issues come up when you suspend all other threads in an application! The biggest problem was not being able to allocate memory right before I was going to suspend the threads. It's entirely possible for another thread to be holding onto the C run-time heap critical section, and if I suspend it and then need memory, I can't acquire the critical section. Although I can run through and count the threads before boosting the priority, that's even more time the other threads are running while the asserting thread is grinding through lots of stuff. Consequently, I decided that it was best to just set a fixed array of the maximum number of threads I'm willing to handle. If you have more than 100 threads in your application, you'll need to update the `k_MAXTHREADS` value at the top of SUPERASSERT.CPP.

```
/*----------------------------------------------------------------------
Debugging Applications for Microsoft .NET and Microsoft Windows
Copyright (c) 1997-2003 John Robbins -- All rights reserved.
----------------------------------------------------------------------*/
#include "PCH.h"
#include "BugslayerUtil.h"
#include "SuperAssert.h"
#include "AssertDlg.h"
#include "CriticalSection.h"
#include "resource.h"
#include "Internal.h"

/*//////////////////////////////////////////////////////////////////////
// File Scope Typedefs, Constants, & Defines
//////////////////////////////////////////////////////////////////////*/
// The maximum number of threads I can handle at once.
const int k_MAXTHREADS = 100 ;

// The GetProcessHandleCount typedef.
typedef BOOL (__stdcall *GETPROCESSHANDLECOUNT)(HANDLE , PDWORD) ;
```

Listing 3-6 SUPERASSERT.CPP *(continued)*

```
/*//////////////////////////////////////////////////////////////////////
// File Scope Prototypes
//////////////////////////////////////////////////////////////////////*/
// Does the actual work to pop the assertion dialog.
static INT_PTR PopTheFancyAssertion ( TCHAR * szBuffer      ,
                                      LPCSTR  szEmail       ,
                                      DWORD64 dwStack       ,
                                      DWORD64 dwStackFrame  ,
                                      DWORD64 dwIP          ,
                                      int *   piIgnoreCount  ) ;

// Tries to get the module causing the assertion.
static SIZE_T GetModuleWithAssert ( DWORD64 dwIP   ,
                                    TCHAR * szMod  ,
                                    DWORD   dwSize  ) ;

// Yes, this is the compiler intrinsic, but you have to prototype it in
// order to use it.
extern "C" void * _ReturnAddress ( void ) ;
#pragma intrinsic ( _ReturnAddress )

// A function to hide the machinations to get the open handles in the
// process.
static BOOL SafelyGetProcessHandleCount ( PDWORD pdwHandleCount ) ;

/*//////////////////////////////////////////////////////////////////////
// File Scope Globals
//////////////////////////////////////////////////////////////////////*/
// The number of assertions to ignore on a global basis.
int g_iGlobalIgnoreCount = 0 ;
// The total number of assertions.
static int g_iTotalAssertions = 0 ;
// The critical section that protects everything.
static CCriticalSection g_cCS ;
// The pointer to the GetProcessHandleCount function.
static GETPROCESSHANDLECOUNT g_pfnGPH = NULL ;

/*//////////////////////////////////////////////////////////////////////
// Implementation!
//////////////////////////////////////////////////////////////////////*/
// Turn off "unreachable code" error from this function calling
// ExitProcess.
#pragma warning ( disable : 4702 )
BOOL RealSuperAssertion ( LPCWSTR  szType        ,
                          LPCWSTR  szExpression  ,
                          LPCWSTR  szFunction    ,
                          LPCWSTR  szFile        ,
                          int      iLine         ,
                          LPCSTR   szEmail       ,
                          DWORD64  dwStack       ,
                          DWORD64  dwStackFrame  ,
                          DWORD64  dwIP          ,
```

```
                          int *    piFailCount   ,
                          int *    piIgnoreCount  )
{
    // Always start by bumping up the total number of assertions seen
    // so far.
    g_iTotalAssertions++ ;

    // Bump up this particular instance failure count.
    if ( NULL != piFailCount )
    {
        *piFailCount = *piFailCount + 1 ;
    }

    // See if there is any way to short circuit doing the whole dialog.
    // A "-1" means ignore everything.
    if ( ( g_iGlobalIgnoreCount < 0                          ) ||
         ( ( NULL != piIgnoreCount ) && *piIgnoreCount < 0 )    )
    {
        return ( FALSE ) ;
    }

    // If I am in the middle of ignoring all assertions for a bit, I can
    // skip out early!
    if ( g_iGlobalIgnoreCount > 0 )
    {
        g_iGlobalIgnoreCount-- ;
        return ( FALSE ) ;
    }

    // Am I supposed to skip this local assertion?
    if ( ( NULL != piIgnoreCount ) && ( *piIgnoreCount > 0 ) )
    {
        *piIgnoreCount = *piIgnoreCount - 1 ;
        return ( FALSE ) ;
    }

    // Holds the return value of the string (STRSAFE) manipulation
    // functions.
    HRESULT hr = S_OK ;

    // Save off the last error value so I don't whack it doing the
    // assertion dialog.
    DWORD dwLastError = GetLastError ( ) ;

    TCHAR szFmtMsg[ MAX_PATH ] ;
    DWORD dwMsgRes = ConvertErrorToMessage ( dwLastError ,
                                             szFmtMsg    ,
                                             sizeof ( szFmtMsg ) /
                                                    sizeof ( TCHAR ) ) ;
    if ( 0 == dwMsgRes )
```

(continued)

```
    {
        hr = StringCchCopy ( szFmtMsg                                   ,
                             sizeof ( szFmtMsg ) / sizeof ( TCHAR ) ,
                  _T ( "Last error message text not available\r\n" ) ) ;
        ASSERT ( SUCCEEDED ( hr ) ) ;
    }

    // Get the module information.
    TCHAR szModuleName[ MAX_PATH ] ;
    if ( 0 == GetModuleWithAssert ( dwIP , szModuleName , MAX_PATH ))
    {
        hr = StringCchCopy ( szModuleName                               ,
                             sizeof ( szModuleName ) / sizeof (TCHAR) ,
                             _T ( "<unknown application>" )            );
        ASSERT ( SUCCEEDED ( hr ) ) ;
    }

    // Grab the synchronization object to block other threads from
    // getting to this point.
    EnterCriticalSection ( &g_cCS.m_CritSec ) ;

    // The buffer to hold the expression message.
    TCHAR szBuffer[ 2048 ] ;
#define BUFF_CHAR_SIZE ( sizeof ( szBuffer ) / sizeof ( TCHAR ) )

    if ( ( NULL != szFile ) && ( NULL != szFunction ) )
    {
        // Split out the base name from the whole filename.
        TCHAR szTempName[ MAX_PATH ] ;
        LPTSTR szFileName ;
        LPTSTR szDir = szTempName ;

        hr = StringCchCopy ( szDir                                      ,
                             sizeof ( szTempName ) / sizeof ( TCHAR ) ,
                             szFile                                     );
        ASSERT ( SUCCEEDED ( hr ) ) ;
        szFileName = _tcsrchr ( szDir , _T ( '\\' ) ) ;
        if ( NULL == szFileName )
        {
            szFileName = szTempName ;
            szDir = _T ( "" ) ;
        }
        else
        {
            *szFileName = _T ( '\0' ) ;
            szFileName++ ;
        }
        DWORD dwHandleCount = 0 ;
        if ( TRUE == SafelyGetProcessHandleCount ( &dwHandleCount ) )
        {
            // Use the new STRSAFE functions to ensure I don't run off
            // the end of the buffer.
```

```
            hr = StringCchPrintf (
                        szBuffer                                      ,
                        BUFF_CHAR_SIZE                                ,
                       _T ( "Type           : %s\r\n"                )\
                       _T ( "Expression     : %s\r\n"                )\
                       _T ( "Module         : %s\r\n"                )\
                       _T ( "Location       : %s, Line %d in %s (%s)\r\n")\
                       _T ( "LastError      : 0x%08X (%d)\r\n"       )\
                       _T ( "                 %s"                    )\
                       _T ( "Fail count     : %d\r\n"                )\
                       _T ( "Handle count : %d"                      ),
                        szType                                        ,
                        szExpression                                  ,
                        szModuleName                                  ,
                        szFunction                                    ,
                        iLine                                         ,
                        szFileName                                    ,
                        szDir                                         ,
                        dwLastError                                   ,
                        dwLastError                                   ,
                        szFmtMsg                                      ,
                        *piFailCount                                  ,
                        dwHandleCount                                 );
            ASSERT ( SUCCEEDED ( hr ) ) ;
        }
        else
        {
            hr = StringCchPrintf (
                        szBuffer                                      ,
                        BUFF_CHAR_SIZE                                ,
                        _T ( "Type       : %s\r\n"                   ) \
                        _T ( "Expression : %s\r\n"                   ) \
                        _T ( "Module     : %s\r\n"                   ) \
                        _T ( "Location   : %s, Line %d in %s (%s)\r\n")\
                        _T ( "LastError  : 0x%08X (%d)\r\n"          ) \
                        _T ( "             %s"                       ) \
                        _T ( "Fail count : %d\r\n"                   ) ,
                        szType                                        ,
                        szExpression                                  ,
                        szModuleName                                  ,
                        szFunction                                    ,
                        iLine                                         ,
                        szFileName                                    ,
                        szDir                                         ,
                        dwLastError                                   ,
                        dwLastError                                   ,
                        szFmtMsg                                      ,
                        *piFailCount                                  );
            ASSERT ( SUCCEEDED ( hr ) ) ;
        }
    }
    else
```

(continued)

```
    {
        if ( NULL == szFunction )
        {
            szFunction = _T ( "Unknown function" ) ;
        }
        hr = StringCchPrintf ( szBuffer                              ,
                               BUFF_CHAR_SIZE                        ,
                               _T ( "Type       : %s\r\n"            ) \
                               _T ( "Expression : %s\r\n"            ) \
                               _T ( "Function   : %s\r\n"            ) \
                               _T ( "Module     : %s\r\n"            ) \
                               _T ( "LastError  : 0x%08X (%d)\r\n"   )
                               _T ( "             %s"                ) ,
                               szType                                ,
                               szExpression                          ,
                               szFunction                            ,
                               szModuleName                          ,
                               dwLastError                           ,
                               dwLastError                           ,
                               szFmtMsg                               ) ;
        ASSERT ( SUCCEEDED ( hr ) ) ;
    }

    if ( DA_SHOWODS == ( DA_SHOWODS & GetDiagAssertOptions ( ) ) )
    {
        OutputDebugString ( szBuffer ) ;
        OutputDebugString ( _T ( "\n" ) ) ;
    }

    if ( DA_SHOWEVENTLOG ==
                    ( DA_SHOWEVENTLOG & GetDiagAssertOptions ( ) ) )
    {
        // Only write to the event log if everything is really kosher.
        static BOOL bEventSuccessful = TRUE ;
        if ( TRUE == bEventSuccessful )
        {
            bEventSuccessful = OutputToEventLog ( szBuffer ) ;
        }
    }

    if ( INVALID_HANDLE_VALUE != GetDiagAssertFile ( ) )
    {
        static BOOL bWriteSuccessful = TRUE ;

        if ( TRUE == bWriteSuccessful )
        {
            DWORD dwWritten ;
            int   iLen = lstrlen ( szBuffer ) ;
            char * pToWrite = NULL ;

#ifdef UNICODE
            pToWrite = (char*)_alloca ( iLen + 1 ) ;
```

```
            BSUWide2Ansi ( szBuffer , pToWrite , iLen + 1 ) ;
#else
            pToWrite = szBuffer ;
#endif
            bWriteSuccessful = WriteFile ( GetDiagAssertFile ( )  ,
                                           pToWrite               ,
                                           iLen                   ,
                                           &dwWritten             ,
                                           NULL                    ) ;
            if ( FALSE == bWriteSuccessful )
            {
                OutputDebugString (
                  _T ( "\n\nWriting assertion to file failed.\n\n" ) ) ;
            }
        }
    }

    // By default, treat the return as an IGNORE. This works best in
    // the case the user does not want the MessageBox.
    INT_PTR iRet = IDIGNORE ;

    // Only show the dialog if the process is running interactively and
    // the user wants to see it.
    if ( ( DA_SHOWMSGBOX == ( DA_SHOWMSGBOX & GetDiagAssertOptions()))&&
         ( TRUE == BSUIsInteractiveUser ( )                          )  )
    {
        iRet = PopTheFancyAssertion ( szBuffer       ,
                                      szEmail        ,
                                      dwStack        ,
                                      dwStackFrame   ,
                                      dwIP           ,
                                      piIgnoreCount   ) ;
    }

    // I'm done with the critical section!
    LeaveCriticalSection ( &g_cCS.m_CritSec ) ;

    SetLastError ( dwLastError ) ;

    // Does the user want to break into the debugger?
    if ( IDRETRY == iRet )
    {
        return ( TRUE ) ;
    }

    // Does the user want to abort the program?
    if ( IDABORT == iRet )
    {
        ExitProcess ( (UINT)-1 ) ;
        return ( TRUE ) ;
    }
```

(continued)

```
    // The only option left is to ignore the assertion.
    return ( FALSE ) ;
}

// Takes care of the grunge to get the assertion dialog shown.
static INT_PTR PopTheFancyAssertion ( TCHAR * szBuffer        ,
                                      LPCSTR  szEmail         ,
                                      DWORD64 dwStack         ,
                                      DWORD64 dwStackFrame    ,
                                      DWORD64 dwIP            ,
                                      int *   piIgnoreCount   )
{
    // I don't do any memory allocation in this routine because I can
    // get into some weird problems. I am about to boost this threads
    // priority pretty high, in an attempt to starve the other
    // threads so I can suspend them. If I try to allocate memory at
    // that point, I can end up in a situation where a lower priority
    // thread has the CRT or OS heap synch object and this thread needs
    // it. Consequently, you are looking at one fat, happy deadlock.
    // (Yes, I originally did this to myself, that's how I know about
    // it!)
    THREADINFO aThreadInfo [ k_MAXTHREADS ] ;
    DWORD aThreadIds [ k_MAXTHREADS ] ;

    // The first thread in the thread info array is ALWAYS the current
    // thread. It's a zero based array, so the dialog code can treat
    // all threads as equals. However, for this function, the array
    // is treated as a one-based array so I don't suspend the current
    // thread and such.
    UINT uiThreadHandleCount = 1 ;

    aThreadInfo[ 0 ].dwTID = GetCurrentThreadId ( ) ;
    aThreadInfo[ 0 ].hThread = GetCurrentThread ( ) ;
    aThreadInfo[ 0 ].szStackWalk = NULL ;

    // The first thing is to blast the priority for this thread up to
    // real time. I don't want to have a thread created while I'm
    // preparing to suspend them.
    int iOldPriority = GetThreadPriority ( GetCurrentThread ( ) ) ;
    VERIFY ( SetThreadPriority ( GetCurrentThread ( )           ,
                                 THREAD_PRIORITY_TIME_CRITICAL  ) ) ;

    DWORD dwPID = GetCurrentProcessId ( ) ;

    DWORD dwIDCount = 0 ;
    if ( TRUE == GetProcessThreadIds ( dwPID                    ,
                                       k_MAXTHREADS             ,
                                       (LPDWORD)&aThreadIds     ,
                                        &dwIDCount              ) )
    {
        // There has to be at least one thread!!
```

```
        ASSERT ( 0 != dwIDCount ) ;
        ASSERT ( dwIDCount < k_MAXTHREADS ) ;

        // Calculate the number of handles.
        uiThreadHandleCount = dwIDCount ;
        // If the number of handles is 1, it's a single threaded app,
        // and I don't need to do anything!
        if ( ( uiThreadHandleCount > 1             ) &&
             ( uiThreadHandleCount < k_MAXTHREADS )    )
        {
            // Open each handle, suspend it, and store the
            // handle so I can resume them later.
            int iCurrHandle = 1 ;
            for ( DWORD i = 0 ; i < dwIDCount ; i++ )
            {
                // Of course, don't suspend this thread!!
                if ( GetCurrentThreadId ( ) != aThreadIds[ i ] )
                {
                    HANDLE hThread =
                            OpenThread ( THREAD_ALL_ACCESS ,
                                         FALSE             ,
                                         aThreadIds [ i ]    ) ;
                    if ( ( NULL != hThread                 ) &&
                         ( INVALID_HANDLE_VALUE != hThread )    )
                    {
                        // If SuspendThread returns -1, there no point
                        // and keeping that thread value around.
                        if ( (DWORD)-1 != SuspendThread ( hThread ) )
                        {
                            aThreadInfo[iCurrHandle].hThread = hThread ;
                            aThreadInfo[iCurrHandle].dwTID =
                                                    aThreadIds[ i ] ;
                            aThreadInfo[iCurrHandle].szStackWalk = NULL;
                            iCurrHandle++ ;
                        }
                        else
                        {
                            VERIFY ( CloseHandle ( hThread ) ) ;
                            uiThreadHandleCount-- ;
                        }
                    }
                    else
                    {
                        // Either this thread has some security set on
                        // it or it happened to end right after I
                        // collected the threads.  Consequently, I need
                        // to decrement the total thread handles or I
                        // will be one off.
                        TRACE( "Can't open thread: %08X\n" ,
                               aThreadIds [ i ]            ) ;
                        uiThreadHandleCount-- ;
                    }
```

(continued)

```
                }
            }
        }
    }

    // Drop the thread priority back down!
    SetThreadPriority ( GetCurrentThread ( ) , iOldPriority ) ;

    // Ensure the application resources are set up.
    JfxGetApp()->m_hInstResources = GetBSUInstanceHandle ( ) ;

    // The assertion dialog its self.
    JAssertionDlg cAssertDlg ( szBuffer                      ,
                               szEmail                       ,
                               dwStack                       ,
                               dwStackFrame                  ,
                               dwIP                          ,
                               piIgnoreCount                 ,
                               (LPTHREADINFO)&aThreadInfo    ,
                               uiThreadHandleCount            ) ;

    INT_PTR iRet = cAssertDlg.DoModal ( ) ;

    if ( ( 1 != uiThreadHandleCount            ) &&
         ( uiThreadHandleCount < k_MAXTHREADS )    )
    {
        // Crank up the thread priority again!
        int iOldPriority = GetThreadPriority ( GetCurrentThread ( ) ) ;
        VERIFY ( SetThreadPriority ( GetCurrentThread ( )          ,
                                     THREAD_PRIORITY_TIME_CRITICAL  ) );

        // If I've suspended the other threads in the process, I need to
        // resume them, close the handles and delete the array.
        for ( UINT i = 1 ; i < uiThreadHandleCount ; i++ )
        {
            VERIFY ( (DWORD)-1 !=
                        ResumeThread ( aThreadInfo[ i ].hThread ) ) ;
            VERIFY ( CloseHandle ( aThreadInfo[ i ].hThread ) ) ;
        }
        // Drop the thread priority back to what it was.
        VERIFY ( SetThreadPriority ( GetCurrentThread ( ) ,
                                     iOldPriority           ) ) ;
    }
    return ( iRet ) ;
}

BOOL BUGSUTIL_DLLINTERFACE
    SuperAssertionA ( LPCSTR  szType        ,
                      LPCSTR  szExpression  ,
                      LPCSTR  szFunction    ,
                      LPCSTR  szFile        ,
```

```
                    int      iLine          ,
                    LPCSTR   szEmail        ,
                    DWORD64 dwStack         ,
                    DWORD64 dwStackFrame    ,
                    int *    piFailCount    ,
                    int *    piIgnoreCount   )
{
    int iLenType = lstrlenA ( szType ) ;
    int iLenExp = lstrlenA ( szExpression ) ;
    int iLenFile = lstrlenA ( szFile ) ;
    int iLenFunc = lstrlenA ( szFunction ) ;

    wchar_t * pWideType = (wchar_t*)
                        HeapAlloc ( GetProcessHeap ( )          ,
                                    HEAP_GENERATE_EXCEPTIONS ,
                                    ( iLenType + 1 ) *
                                      sizeof ( wchar_t )        ) ;
    wchar_t * pWideExp = (wchar_t*)
                       HeapAlloc ( GetProcessHeap ( )          ,
                                   HEAP_GENERATE_EXCEPTIONS ,
                                   ( iLenExp + 1 ) *
                                     sizeof ( wchar_t )        ) ;
    wchar_t * pWideFile = (wchar_t*)
                        HeapAlloc ( GetProcessHeap ( )          ,
                                    HEAP_GENERATE_EXCEPTIONS ,
                                    ( iLenFile + 1 ) *
                                        sizeof ( wchar_t )    );
    wchar_t * pWideFunc = (wchar_t*)
                        HeapAlloc ( GetProcessHeap ( )          ,
                                    HEAP_GENERATE_EXCEPTIONS ,
                                    ( iLenFunc + 1 ) *
                                        sizeof ( wchar_t )    ) ;

    BSUAnsi2Wide ( szType , pWideType , iLenType + 1 ) ;
    BSUAnsi2Wide ( szExpression , pWideExp , iLenExp + 1 ) ;
    BSUAnsi2Wide ( szFile , pWideFile , iLenFile + 1 ) ;
    BSUAnsi2Wide ( szFunction , pWideFunc , iLenFunc + 1 ) ;

    BOOL bRet ;
    bRet = RealSuperAssertion ( pWideType                    ,
                                pWideExp                     ,
                                pWideFunc                    ,
                                pWideFile                    ,
                                iLine                        ,
                                szEmail                      ,
                                dwStack                      ,
                                dwStackFrame                 ,
                                (DWORD64)_ReturnAddress ( )  ,
                                piFailCount                  ,
                                piIgnoreCount                 ) ;

    VERIFY ( HeapFree ( GetProcessHeap ( ) , 0 , pWideType ) ) ;
```

(continued)

```
    VERIFY ( HeapFree ( GetProcessHeap ( ) , 0 , pWideExp ) ) ;
    VERIFY ( HeapFree ( GetProcessHeap ( ) , 0 , pWideFile ) ) ;

    return ( bRet ) ;
}

BOOL BUGSUTIL_DLLINTERFACE
    SuperAssertionW ( LPCWSTR szType         ,
                      LPCWSTR szExpression   ,
                      LPCWSTR szFunction     ,
                      LPCWSTR szFile         ,
                      int     iLine          ,
                      LPCSTR  szEmail        ,
                      DWORD64 dwStack        ,
                      DWORD64 dwStackFrame   ,
                      int *   piFailCount    ,
                      int *   piIgnoreCount   )
{
    return ( RealSuperAssertion ( szType                      ,
                                  szExpression                ,
                                  szFunction                  ,
                                  szFile                      ,
                                  iLine                       ,
                                  szEmail                     ,
                                  dwStack                     ,
                                  dwStackFrame                ,
                                  (DWORD64)_ReturnAddress ( ) ,
                                  piFailCount                 ,
                                  piIgnoreCount                ) ) ;
}

// Returns the number of times an assertion has been triggered in an
// application. This number takes into account any way the assertion
// was ignored.
int BUGSUTIL_DLLINTERFACE GetSuperAssertionCount ( void )
{
    return ( g_iTotalAssertions ) ;
}

static BOOL SafelyGetProcessHandleCount ( PDWORD pdwHandleCount )
{
    static BOOL bAlreadyLooked = FALSE ;
    if ( FALSE == bAlreadyLooked )
    {
        HMODULE hKernel32 = ::LoadLibrary ( _T ( "kernel32.dll" ) ) ;
        g_pfnGPH = (GETPROCESSHANDLECOUNT)
                   ::GetProcAddress ( hKernel32                  ,
                                      "GetProcessHandleCount"  ) ;
        FreeLibrary ( hKernel32 ) ;
        bAlreadyLooked = TRUE ;
    }
    if ( NULL != g_pfnGPH )
```

```
    {
        return ( g_pfnGPH ( GetCurrentProcess ( ) , pdwHandleCount ) );
    }
    else
    {
        return ( FALSE ) ;
    }
}

static SIZE_T GetModuleWithAssert ( DWORD64 dwIP   ,
                                    TCHAR * szMod  ,
                                    DWORD   dwSize  )
{
    // Attempt to get the memory base address for the value on the
    // stack. From the base address, I'll try to get the module.
    MEMORY_BASIC_INFORMATION stMBI ;
    ZeroMemory ( &stMBI , sizeof ( MEMORY_BASIC_INFORMATION ) ) ;
    SIZE_T dwRet = VirtualQuery ( (LPCVOID)dwIP                       ,
                                  &stMBI                              ,
                                  sizeof ( MEMORY_BASIC_INFORMATION ) );
    if ( 0 != dwRet )
    {
        dwRet = GetModuleFileName ( (HMODULE)stMBI.AllocationBase ,
                                    szMod                         ,
                                    dwSize                        ) ;
        if ( 0 == dwRet )
        {
            // Punt and simply return the EXE.
            dwRet = GetModuleFileName ( NULL , szMod , dwSize ) ;
        }
    }
    return ( dwRet ) ;
}
```

The actual dialog code in ASSERTDLG.CPP is pretty uneventful, so it's not worth printing in the book. When Scott Bilas and I discussed what the dialog box should be written in, we realized it needed to be written in a lightweight language that didn't require any extra binaries other than the DLL containing the dialog box—pretty much ruling out MFC. At the time I wrote the dialog box, the Windows Template Library (WTL) hadn't been released. But I probably wouldn't have chosen to use it anyway, because I find templates problematic. Very few developers actually understand the ramifications of templates, and most of the bugs my company is involved in fixing are a direct result of templates, so I am hesitant to use them. Several years ago, Jeffrey Richter and I were involved in a project that needed an extremely lightweight UI, and we developed a straightforward UI class library named JFX. Jeffrey will tell you JFX stands for "Jeffrey's Framework," but it really stands for "John's Framework" no matter what he says. Regardless of the name, I used JFX to handle the UI. The complete source code is included with this book's sample files. There are a couple of test programs under the JFX directory that show you how to use JFX as well as the `SUPERASSERT` dialog code. The good news is that JFX is extremely small and compact—the release version of BugslayerUtil.DLL, which does a whole lot more than just `SUPERASSERT`, is less than 70 KB.

Common Debugging Question

Why do you always put the constants on the left-hand side of conditional statements?

As you look through my code, you'll notice that I always use statements such as "`if ( INVALID_HANDLE_VALUE == hFile )`" instead of "`if ( hFile == INVALID_HANDLE_VALUE )`." The reason I use this style is to avoid bugs. You can easily forget one of the equal signs, and using the former version will yield a compiler error if you do forget. The latter version might not issue a warning (whether or not it does depends on the warning level), and you'll change the variable's value. In compilers, trying to assign a value to a constant will produce a compiler error. If you've ever had to track down a bug involving an accidental assignment, you know just how difficult this type of bug is to find.

If you pay close attention, you'll notice that I also use constant variables on the left side of the equalities. As with the constant values case, the compilers will report errors when you try to assign a value to a constant variable. I've found that it's a lot easier to fix compiler errors than to fix bugs in the debugger.

Some developers have complained, sometimes vociferously, that the way I write conditional statements makes the code more confusing to read. I don't agree. My conditional statements take only a second longer to read and translate. I'm willing to give up that second to avoid wasting huge amounts of time later.

Trace, Trace, Trace, and Trace

Assertions might be the best proactive programming trick you can learn, but trace statements, if used correctly with assertions, will truly allow you to debug your application without the debugger. For some of you old hands out there, trace statements are essentially `printf`-style debugging. You should never underestimate the power of `printf`-style debugging because that's how most applications were debugged before interactive debuggers were invented. Tracing in the .NET world is intriguing because when Microsoft first mentioned .NET publicly, the key benefits were not for developers but rather for network administrators and IT workers responsible for deploying the applications developers write. One of the critical new benefits Microsoft listed was the ability of IT workers to easily turn on tracing to help find problems in applications! I was quite stunned when I read that because it showed Microsoft responding to the pain our end users experience when dealing with buggy software.

The trick to tracing is analyzing how much information you need for solving problems on machines that don't have the development environment installed. If you log too much, you get large files that are a real pain to slog through. If you log too little, you can't solve your problem. The balancing act requires having just enough logged to avoid a last-minute, 5,000-mile plane trip to a customer who just duplicated that one nasty bug—a plane trip in which you have to sit in the middle seat next to a crying baby and a sick person. In general, that means you need two levels of tracing: one level to give you the basic flow through the software so that you can see what's being called when and another level to add key data to the file so that you can look for data-stream–dependent problems.

Unfortunately, each application is different, so I can't give you an exact number of trace statements or other data marks that would be sufficient for your log. One of the better approaches I've seen is giving some of the newer folks on the team a sample log and asking whether they can get enough of a clue from it to start tracking down the problem. If they give up in disgust after an hour or two, you probably don't have enough information. If after an hour or two they can get a general idea of where the application was at the time of the corruption or crash, you've got a good sign that your log is contains the right amount of information.

As I mentioned in Chapter 2, you must have a team-wide logging system. Part of that logging system design has to consider the format of the tracing, especially so that debug build tracing is easier to deal with. Without that format, tracing effectiveness quickly vanishes because no one will want to wade through a ton of text that has no rhyme or reason to it. The good news for .NET applications is that Microsoft did quite a bit of work to make controlling the output easier. For native applications, you will have to come up with your own systems, but I'll give you some hints to get you going later in this chapter in the section "Tracing in Native C++ Applications."

Before I jump into the different platform-specific issues, I want to mention one extremely cool tool you always need to have on your development machines: DebugView. My former neighbor Mark Russinovich wrote DebugView and many other outstanding tools you can download from Sysinternals (*www.sysinternals.com*). The price is right (free!), many of the tools come with source code, and Mark's tools solve some very difficult problems, so you should visit Sysinternals at least once a month. DebugView monitors any calls to the user mode `OutputDebugString` or the kernel mode `DbgPrint`, so you can see any debug output when your application isn't running under a debugger. What makes DebugView even more useful is that it can burrow its way across machines, so you can monitor from a single machine all the machines that are part of a distributed system.

Tracing in Windows Forms and Console .NET Applications

As I mentioned earlier, Microsoft made some marketing noise about tracing in .NET applications. In general, they did a good job creating a clean architecture that better controls tracing in real-world development. I already mentioned the `Trace` object during the assertion discussion, because you should use it for your tracing. Like the `Debug` object, the `Trace` object uses the concept of `TraceListeners` to handle the output. This is why my ASP.NET assertion code changed the listeners for both objects: so all output would go to the same place. In your development, you'll want your assertion code to do the same thing. The `Trace` object's method calls are active only if `TRACE` is defined. The default for both debug and release build projects created by Visual Studio .NET is to have `TRACE` defined, so the methods are probably already active.

The `Trace` object has four methods to output trace information: `Write`, `WriteIf`, `WriteLine`, and `WriteLineIf`. You can probably guess the difference between `Write` and `WriteLine`, but understanding the `*If` methods is a little more challenging: they allow for conditional tracing. If the first parameter to the `*If` method evaluates to `true`, the trace happens; evaluating to `false` means it doesn't. That's quite convenient, but it possibly could lead to some big performance problems if you're not careful. For example, if you write code like that shown in the first portion of the next snippet, you will incur the overhead of the string concatenation every time the line executes because the determination for doing the actual tracing occurs inside the `Trace.WriteLineIf` call. You're much better off following the second method in the next snippet, where you use an `if` statement to make the call to `Trace.WriteLine` only when you need to, minimizing how often you must incur the string concatenation overhead.

```
// Paying the overhead every time
Trace.WriteLineIf ( bShowTrace , "Parameters: x=" + x + " y =" + y ) ;

// Causing the concatenation only when necessary
if ( true == bShowTrace )
{
    Trace.WriteLine ("Parameters: x=" + x + " y =" + y ) ;
}
```

I think the .NET designers did us all a favor when they added the TraceSwitch class. With the *If methods for the Trace object allowing for conditional compilation, it took only a small step to define a class that provided for multiple levels of tracing and a consistent way to set them. The most important part of TraceSwitch is the name it's given in the first parameter of the constructor. (The second parameter is a descriptive name.) The name enables you to control the switch from outside the application, which I'll talk about in a moment. TraceSwitch objects wrap a tracing level. The levels are shown in Table 3-3. To check whether TraceSwitch matches a particular level, you use a set of properties, such as TraceError, that returns true if the switch condition is met. Combined with the *If methods, using TraceSwitch objects is quite straightforward.

```
public static void Main ( )
{
    TraceSwitch TheSwitch = new TraceSwitch ( "SwitchyTheSwitch",
                                              "Example Switch"  );
    TheSwitch.Level = TraceLevel.Info ;
    Trace.WriteLineIf ( TheSwitch.TraceError ,
                        "Error tracing is on!" ) ;
    Trace.WriteLineIf ( TheSwitch.TraceWarning ,
                        "Warning tracing is on!" ) ;
    Trace.WriteLineIf ( TheSwitch.TraceInfo ,
                       "Info tracing is on!" ) ;
    Trace.WriteLineIf ( TheSwitch.TraceVerbose ,
                        "VerboseSwitching is on!" ) ;
}
```

Table 3-3 TraceSwitch Levels

Trace Level	Value
Off	0
Error	1
Warnings (and errors)	2
Info (warnings and errors)	3
Verbose (everything)	4

The real magic of TraceSwitch objects is that they allow you to easily set them from outside the application in the ubiquitous CONFIG file. The switches element under the system.diagnostic element is where you specify the add elements to add and set the name and level. Listing 3-7 shows a complete configuration file for an application. Ideally you have a separate TraceSwitch object for each assembly in your application. Keep in mind that the TraceSwitch settings can also be applied to the global MACHINE.CONFIG.

```
<?xml version="1.0" encoding="UTF-8" ?>
<configuration>
    <system.diagnostics>
        <switches>
            <add name="Wintellect.ScheduleJob" value="4" />
            <add name="Wintellect.DataAccess" value="0" />
        </switches>
    </system.diagnostics>
</configuration>
```

Listing 3-7 Setting `TraceSwitch` flags in a configuration file

Tracing in ASP.NET Applications and XML Web Services

In spite of the very well designed `Trace` and `TraceSwitch` objects, ASP.NET, and by extension, XML Web services, have a completely different tracing system. Based on the location of ASP.NET tracing output, I can see why their systems are different, but I still find these differences confusing. The `System.Web.UI.Page` class has its own `Trace` object derived from `System.Web.TraceContext`. To help keep the different traces straight, I'll refer to the ASP.NET version as `TraceContext.Trace`. The two key methods for `TraceContext.Trace` are `Write` and `Warn`. Both handle tracing output, but the `Warn` method writes the output in red. Each method has three overloads, and both take the same parameters: the usual message and category with message versions, but also a version that takes the category, message, and `System.Exception`. That last version writes out the exception string as well as the source and line where the exception was thrown. To avoid extra overhead processing when tracing isn't enabled, check whether the `IsEnabled` property is `true`.

The easiest way to turn on tracing is to set the `Trace` attribute to `true` inside the `@Page` directive at the top of your ASPX files.

```
<%@ Page Trace="true" %>
```

That magic little directive turns on a ton of tracing information that appears directly at the bottom of the page, which is convenient, but it will be seen by both you and the users. In fact, there's so much tracing information that I really wish it were divided into several levels. Although seeing the Cookies and Headers Collections as well as the Server Variables is nice, most of the time you don't need them. All sections are self-explanatory, but I want to point out the Trace Information section because any calls you make to `TraceContext.Trace` appear here. Even if you don't call `TraceContext.Trace.Warn/Write`, you'll still see output in the Trace Information section because ASP.NET reports when several of its methods have been called. This section is also where the red text appears when you call `TraceContext.Trace.Warn`.

Setting the `Trace` attribute at the top of each page in your application is tedious, so the ASP.NET designers put a section in WEB.CONFIG that allows you to control tracing. This tracing section, named, appropriately enough, `trace` element, is shown here:

```
<?xml version="1.0" encoding="utf-8" ?>
<configuration>
    <system.web>
        <trace
            enabled="false"
            requestLimit="10"
            pageOutput="false"
            traceMode="SortByTime"
            localOnly="true"
        />
    </system.web>
</configuration>
```

The `enabled` attribute dictates whether tracing is turned on for this application. The `requestLimit` attribute indicates how many trace requests to cache in memory on a per-application basis. (In just a moment, I'll discuss how to view these cached traces.) The `pageOutput` element tells ASP.NET where to show the trace output. If `pageOutput` is set to `true`, the output appears on the page just as it would if you set the `Trace` attribute in the `Page` directive. You probably won't want to change the `traceMode` element so that the Trace Information section in the trace is sorted by time. If you do want to see the sort by category, you can set `traceMode` to `SortByCategory`. The final attribute, `localOnly`, tells ASP.NET whether the output should be visible only on the local machine or visible to any client applications.

To see cached traces when `pageOutput` is `false`, append the HTTP handler, trace.axd, to the application directory, which will show a page that allows you to choose the stored trace you'd like to see. For example, if your directory is *http://www.wintellect.com/schedules*, to see the stored traces, the path would be *http://www.wintellect.com/schedules/trace.axd*. As soon as the `requestLimit` is reached, ASP.NET stops recording traces. You can restart the traces by viewing the trace.axd page and clicking the Clear Current Trace link at the top of the page.

As you can see, if you're not careful with tracing, your end users will be looking at them, which is always a little scary since developers are notorious for trace statements that could be career limiting if the output fell into the wrong hands. Luckily, setting `localOnly` to `true` keeps the trace viewing only on the local server, even when accessing the trace log through the trace.axd HTTP handler. To view your application trace logs, you'll simply have to use the greatest piece of software known to humankind, Terminal Services, so that you can access the server directly from your office and don't even have to get up from your desk. You'll want to update the `customErrors` section of WEB.CONFIG so that you have a `defaultRedirect` page, preventing your end users from seeing the ASP.NET "Server Error in '`AppName`' Application" error if they try to access trace.axd from a remote machine. You'll also want to log that someone tried to access trace.axd, especially because an attempted access is probably an indication of a hacker.

At this point, some of you might be wondering about a particular problem with tracing in ASP.NET: ASP.NET has `TraceContext.Trace` send its output to one place, and `DefaultTraceListener` for the `System.Diagnostic.Trace` object sends its output someplace else. With straight ASP.NET, this is a huge problem, but if you use the BugslayerUtil.NET assertion code described earlier in the chapter, the `ASPTraceListener` is also used as the sole `TraceListener` for the `System.Diagnostic.Trace` object, so I redirect all traces to the `TraceContext.Trace` so that they show up in the same place.

Tracing in Native C++ Applications

Nearly all native tracing is done with a C++ macro traditionally named `TRACE` and is active only in debug builds. Eventually, the function called by the `TRACE` macro will call the Windows API `OutputDebugString` so that you can see the trace either in the debugger or in DebugView. Keep in mind that calling `OutputDebugString` causes a kernel mode transition. That's no big deal in debug builds, but it can have a negative impact on performance in a release build, so be aware of any calls you might have floating around in your release builds. In fact, when the Windows team was looking for ways to speed up the performance of Windows as a whole, they removed numerous traces we all used to rely on, such as the DLL load conflict message that occurred on a DLL load, and it contributed to a very nice performance boost.

If you don't have a `TRACE` macro, you can use the one I provide as part of BugslayerUtil.DLL. All the actual work takes place in the `DiagOutputA/W` functions in DIAGASSERT.CPP. The advantage to my code is that you can call `SetDiagOutputFile` and pass in a file handle as the parameter and record all tracing to a file.

In addition to providing the `TRACE` macro, Chapter 18 covers my FastTrace tool for native server applications. The last thing you want to do when it comes to heavily multithreaded applications is force all those threads to block on a synchronization object when you turn on tracing. The FastTrace tool gives you the highest possible tracing performance without losing the all-important flow of information.

Comment, Comment, Comment, and Comment

One day, my friend François Poulin, who was working full-time on maintaining some code that someone else wrote, came in wearing a button that said, "Code as if whoever maintains your code is a violent psychopath who knows where you live." François is by no means a psychopath, but he did have a very good point. Although you might think your code is the model of clarity and completely obvious, without descriptive comments it is as bad as raw assembly language to the maintenance developers. The irony is that the maintenance developer for your code can easily turn out to be you! Not too long before I started writing the second edition of this book, I received an e-mail message from a company I had worked for nearly 10 years ago asking me whether I could update a project I had written for them. It was an amazing experience to look at code I wrote that long ago! I was also amazed at how bad my commenting was. Remember François's button every time you write a line of code.

Our job as engineers is twofold: develop a solution for the user, and make that solution maintainable for the future. The only way to make your code maintainable is to comment it. By "comment it," I don't mean simply writing comments that duplicate what the code is doing; I mean documenting your assumptions, your approach, and your reasons for choosing the approach you did. You also need to keep your comments coordinated with the code. Normally mild-mannered maintenance programmers can turn into raving lunatics when they're trying to update code that does something different from what the comments say it's supposed to do.

I use the following approach to commenting:

- Each function or method needs a sentence or two that clarifies the following information:
  - What the routine does
  - What assumptions the routine makes
  - What each input parameter is expected to contain
  - What each output parameter is expected to contain on success and failure
  - Each possible return value
  - Each exception directly thrown by the function
- Each part of the function that isn't completely obvious from the code needs a sentence or two that explains what it's doing.
- Any interesting algorithm deserves a complete description.

- Any nontrivial bugs you've fixed in the code need to be commented with the bug number and a description of what you fixed.
- Well-placed trace statements, assertions, and good naming conventions can also serve as good comments and provide excellent context to the code.
- Comment as if you were going to be the one maintaining the code in five years.
- Avoid keeping dead code commented out in source modules whenever possible. It's never really clear to other developers whether the commented-out code was meant to be removed permanently or removed only temporarily for testing. Your version control system is there to help you revert to areas of code that no longer exist in current versions.
- If you find yourself saying, "This is a big hack" or "This is really tricky stuff," you probably need to rewrite the function instead of commenting it.

Proper and complete documentation in the code marks the difference between a serious, professional developer and someone who is playing at it. Donald Knuth once observed that you should be able to read a well-written program just as you read a well-written book. Although I don't see myself curling up by the fire with a copy of the TeX source code, I strongly agree with Dr. Knuth's sentiment.

I recommend that you study "Self-Documenting Code," Chapter 19 of Steve McConnell's phenomenal book *Code Complete (Microsoft Press, 1993)*. Reading this chapter is how I learned to write comments. If you comment correctly, even if your maintenance programmer turns out to be a psychopath, you know you'll be safe.

Since I'm discussing comments, I need to mention how much I love the XML documentation comments added to C# and how it's criminal that they aren't supported by all the other languages produced by Microsoft. Hopefully, in the future all languages will get the first-class XML documentation comments. By having a clean commenting format that can be extracted during the build, you can start building solid documentation for your project. In fact, I like the XML documentation comments so much, I built a moderately complicated macro, `CommenTater`, in Chapter 9, that takes care of adding and keeping your XML documentation comments current as well as ensuring that you're adding them.

Trust Yourself, but Verify (Unit Testing)

I always thought Andy Grove, former CEO of Intel, had it right when he titled his book *Only the Paranoid Survive*. This notion is especially true for software engineers. I have many good friends who are excellent engineers, but when it comes to having them interface with my code, I verify their data down to the last bit. In fact, I even have a healthy skepticism about myself. Assertions, tracing, and commenting are how I start verifying my fellow developers who are calling my code. Unit testing is how I verify myself. Unit tests are the scaffolding that you put in place to call your code outside the normal program as a whole to verify that the code performs as expected.

The first way I verify myself is to start writing my unit tests as soon as I start writing my code, developing them in parallel. Once I figure out the interface for a module, I write the stub functions for that module and immediately write a test program, or harness, to call those interfaces. As I add a piece of functionality, I add new test cases to the test harness. Using this approach, I can test each incremental change in isolation and spread out the test harness development over the development cycle. If you do all the regular development after you've implemented the main code, you generally don't have enough time to do a good job on the harness and therefore do a less thorough job implementing an effective test.

The second way I verify myself is to think about how I'm going to test my code before I write it. Try not to fall into the trap of thinking that your entire application has to be written before you can test your code. If you discover that you're a victim of this pitfall, you need to step back and break down your testing. I realize that sometimes you must rely on important functionality from another developer to compile your code. In those cases, your test code should consist of stubs for the interfaces that you can compile against. At a minimum, have the interfaces hard-coded to return appropriate data so that you can compile and run your code.

One side benefit of ensuring that your design is testable is that you quickly find problems that you can fix to make your code more reusable and extensible. Because reusability is the Holy Grail of software, whatever steps you can take to make your code more reusable are worth the effort. A good example of this windfall is the `BugslayerStackTrace` from BugslayerUtil.NET.DLL. When I first implemented the ASP.NET tracing code, I embedded the code for walking the stack inside the `ASPTraceListener` class. As I was testing the code, I quickly realized that I might need that stack trace in other places as well. I pulled the stack walking code out of `ASPTraceListener` and put it in its own class named `BugslayerStackTrace`. When I eventually needed to write the `BugslayerTextWriterTraceListener` and `BugslayerEventLogTraceListener` classes, I already had the core code written and completely tested.

While you're coding, you should be running your unit tests all the time. I seem to think in an isolated functionality unit of about 50 lines of code. Each time I add or change a feature, I rerun the unit test to see whether I broke anything. I don't like surprises, so I try to keep them to a minimum. I definitely recommend that you run your unit tests before you check in your code to the master sources. Some organizations have specific tests, called check-in tests, that need to be run before code can be checked in. I've seen these check-in tests drastically reduce the number of build and smoke test breakages.

The key to the most effective unit tests comes down to two words: *code coverage*. If you take nothing else away from this chapter except those two words, I'll consider the chapter a success. Code coverage is simply the percentage of lines you've executed in your module. If 100 lines are in your module and you execute 85, you have 85 percent code coverage. The simple fact is that a line not executed is a line waiting to crash.

In my consulting work, I'm constantly asked whether there is a single key to great code. I'm to the point now where I enter "religion mode" because I believe in code coverage so much. If you were standing in front of me right now, I'd be jumping up and down and extolling the virtues of code coverage with evangelical fervor. Many developers tell me that taking my advice and trying to get good code coverage has paid off with huge improvements in code quality. It works and is the only secret there is.

You can get code-coverage statistics in two ways. The first way is the hard way and involves using the debugger and setting a breakpoint on every single line in your module. As your module executes a line, clear the breakpoint. Continue running your code until you've cleared all the breakpoints and you have 100 percent coverage. The easy way to get coverage is to use a third-party code-coverage tool such as Compuware NuMega's TrueCoverage, Rational's Visual PureCoverage, or Bullseye's C-Cover. Personally, I don't check in any code to the master sources until I've executed at least 85 to 90 percent of the lines in my code. I know some of you are groaning right now. Yes, getting good code coverage can be time consuming. Sometimes you need to do far more testing than you ever considered, and it can take a while. Getting the best coverage means that you need to run your application in the debugger and change data variables to execute code paths that are hard to hit otherwise. Your job is to write solid code, however, and in my opinion, code coverage is about the only way you'll get it during the unit test phase.

Nothing is worse than having your QA staff sitting on their hands while they're stuck with builds that crash. If you get 90 percent code coverage in the unit test, your QA people can spend their time testing your application on different platforms and ensuring that the interfaces between subsystems work. QA's job is to test the product as a whole and to sign off on the quality as a whole. Your job is to test a unit and to sign off on the quality of that unit. When both sides do their jobs, the result is a high-quality product.

Granted, I don't expect developers to test on every Microsoft Win32–based operating system that customers might be using. However, if engineers can get 90 percent coverage on at least one operating system, the team wins 66 percent of the battle for quality. If you're not using one of the third-party code-coverage tools, you're cheating yourself on quality.

In addition to the code coverage, I frequently run third-party error detection and performance tools, as discussed in Chapter 1, on my unit test projects. Those tools help me catch bugs much earlier in the development cycle so that I spend less time debugging overall. However, of all the error detection and performance tools I own, I use the code coverage products many orders of magnitude more than anything else. By the time I've gotten my code coverage numbers high enough, I've already solved nearly all the bugs and performance problems in the code.

If you follow the recommendations presented in this section, you'll have some effective unit tests at the end of your development—but the work doesn't stop there. If you look at the code included with this book's sample files, you'll see a directory named Tests under the main source code directory for each tool. That directory holds my unit tests for that tool. I keep my unit tests as part of the code base so that others can find them easily. In addition, when I make a change to the source code, I can easily test to see whether I broke anything. I highly recommend that you check your tests into your version control system. Finally, although most unit tests are self-explanatory, make sure that you document any key assumptions so that others don't waste their time wrestling with your tests.

Summary

This chapter presented the best proactive programming techniques you can use to debug during coding. The best technique is to use assertions everywhere so that you gain control whenever a problem occurs. The .NET assertion code in BugslayerUtil.NET.DLL and the native SUPERASSERT code presented avoid all the problems associated with the assertions supplied by the Microsoft compilers. In addition to assertions, proper tracing and comments can make maintaining and debugging your code much easier for you and others. Finally, the most important quality gauges for engineers are unit tests. If you can properly test your code before you check it in, you can eliminate many of the bugs and problems that frustrate maintenance engineers later.

The only way to unit test properly is to run a code-coverage tool while you're doing your tests. You need to strive to get at least 85 to 90 percent coverage on your code before you ever check it in to the master sources. The more time you spend debugging your code during development, the less time you'll have to spend debugging it later.

Part II

Power Debugging

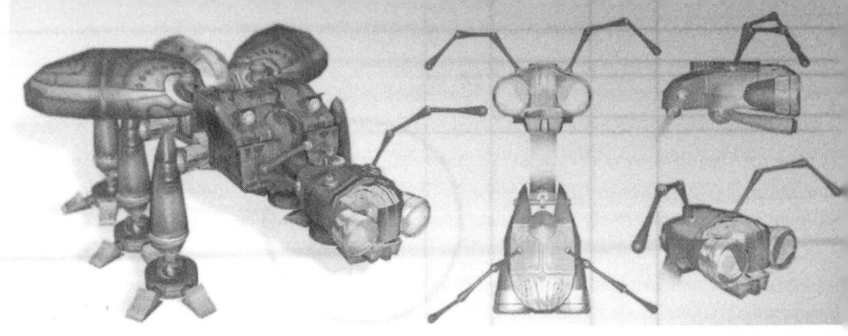

4

Operating System Debugging Support and How Win32 Debuggers Work

Learning how your tools operate is a crucial part of this business. If you understand the capabilities and limitations of your tools, you can maximize their return and thus spend less time debugging. Most of the time, debuggers help you out tremendously, but sometimes they can cause subtle problems that baffle you. What makes native code debugging even more interesting is that the operating systems jump in and change the behavior of your processes because they are running under a debugger. Additionally, there's some extremely interesting support inside the operating system to assist you in certain difficult debugging situations. In this chapter, I'll explain what a debugger is, demonstrate how various debuggers operate in Microsoft Win32 operating systems, and discuss the tricks necessary to master the Win32 debugging environment.

After providing a brief overview of the Win32 debuggers at your disposal, I'll go over in detail the special features available when your process is running under a debugger. To show you how debuggers actually work, I'll present two debuggers, the source code of which is with this book's sample files. The first debugger, MinDBG, does just enough to call itself a debugger. The second, WDBG, is a real Win32 debugger sample that does everything a real debugger is supposed to, including manipulating symbol tables to show locals and structures, handling breakpoints, generating disassembly, and coordinating with a graphical user interface (GUI). In discussing WDBG, I'll also cover topics such as how breakpoints work and what all the different symbol files types are and what they mean. Finally, I'll talk about the extra cool symbol engine wrapper I wrote, which makes manipulating locals and arguments simple. The symbol engine was some of the hardest code I wrote for this book, and I'm sure you'll find it very useful!

Why Isn't There a Chapter on .NET Debuggers?

You might be wondering why there isn't a corresponding chapter in this book on how Microsoft .NET debuggers work. Originally, I had intended to write that chapter, but as I was researching the .NET Debugging API, I realized that unlike Win32 debuggers, which are nearly undocumented, the .NET run-time team did a tremendous job documenting the .NET debugging interface. Additionally, the debugger sample provided shows how to do everything a .NET debugger is supposed to do. The sample is about 98 percent of the source code console debugger, CORDBG. (The only part that's missing is the native code disassembler commands.) I spent a couple of weeks working on a .NET debugger, and I quickly realized that I was going to be doing nothing more than rehashing the excellent .NET documentation and that I wouldn't be showing anything that wasn't already shown in the CORDBG sample. The Microsoft Word files, Debug.doc and DebugRef.doc, that describe the .NET Debugging API are already installed on your computer as part of the Visual Studio .NET installation and are in the <Visual Studio .NET Installation Directory>\SDK\v1.1\Tool Developers Guide\Docs directory.

Finally, before jumping into the chapter, I want to make sure I define two standard terms that I'll be using throughout this book: debugger and debuggee. Simply put, a *debugger* is a process that can control another process in a debugging relationship, and a *debuggee* is a process started under a debugger. Some operating systems refer to the debugger as the *parent process* and the debuggee as the *child process*.

Types of Windows Debuggers

If you've been programming Win32 for any length of time, you've probably heard about several different types of debuggers that you can use. Two types of debuggers are available in the Microsoft Windows world: *user-mode debuggers* and *kernel-mode debuggers*.

User-mode debuggers are much more familiar to most developers. Not surprisingly, user-mode debuggers are for debugging user-mode applications. The Microsoft Visual Studio .NET debugger is a prime example of a user-mode debugger. Kernel-mode debuggers, as the names implies, let you debug the operating system kernel. These debuggers are used mostly by device driver writers when they're debugging their device drivers.

User-Mode Debuggers

As I just mentioned, user-mode debuggers are used to debug any application that runs in user mode, which includes any GUI programs as well as applications you wouldn't expect, such as Windows services. Generally, user-mode debuggers use GUIs. The main hallmark of user-mode debuggers is that they use the Win32 Debugging API. Because the operating system marks the debuggee as running in a special mode, you can use the `IsDebuggerPresent` API function to find out whether your process is running under a debugger. Checking whether you're running under a debugger can be useful when you want to turn on more diagnostic information only when a debugger is attached to your process.

On Microsoft Windows 2000 and earlier operating systems, the problem with the Win32 Debugging API was that once a process was running under the Debugging API, if the debugger terminated, the debuggee terminated as well. In other words, the debuggee was permanently debugged. This limitation was fine when everyone was working on client applications, but it was the bane of server application development, especially when programmers were trying to debug production servers. With Microsoft Windows XP, Windows Server 2003, and later, you can attach and detach all you want from running processes without any special steps. With Visual Studio .NET, you can detach from a process by selecting it in the Processes dialog and selecting Detach.

Interestingly, Visual Studio .NET now offers the Visual Studio Debugger Proxy (DbgProxy) service on Windows 2000, which allows you to debug processes that you can detach from. DbgProxy serves as the debugger, so your application is still running under a debugger. Now, however, you can detach and re-attach all you want under Windows 2000. One problem I keep seeing with developers—regardless of whether we're using Windows XP, Windows Server 2003, or DbgProxy on Windows 2000—is that because we're so used to the old "debugger forever" problem, we forget to take advantage of the new ability to detach.

For interpreted languages and run times that use a virtual machine approach, the virtual machines themselves provide the complete debugging environment and don't use the Win32 Debugging API. Some examples of those types of environments are the Microsoft or Sun Java Virtual Machines (VMs), the Microsoft scripting environment for Web applications, and, of course, the Microsoft .NET common language runtime (CLR).

As I mentioned earlier, .NET CLR debugging is fully covered by the documents in the Tool Developers Guide directory. I also won't go into the Java and scripting debugging interfaces, subjects beyond the scope of this book. For information on writing a script debugger, search MSDN for the "Microsoft Windows Script Interfaces-Introduction" topic. Like .NET CLR debugging, the script debugger objects provide a rich interface for accessing scripts and document-hosted scripts.

A surprising number of programs use the Win32 Debugging API. These include the Visual Studio .NET debugger when debugging native code, which I cover in depth in Chapter 5 and Chapter 7; the Windows Debugger (WinDBG), which I discuss in Chapter 8; Compuware NuMega's BoundsChecker; the Platform SDK Depends program (which you can install as part of Visual Studio .NET); the Borland Delphi and C++ Builder debuggers; and the NT Symbolic Debugger (NTSD). I'm sure there are many more.

Common Debugging Question

How can I protect my Win32 program from being debugged?

One of the most common requests I get from developers working on vertical market applications with proprietary algorithms is how can they protect those algorithms and keep their competitors from taking a peek at them with a debugger. Although you can call `IsDebuggerPresent`, which tells you whether a user-mode debugger is running, if someone has half a brain, the first thing she'll do when reverse engineering is patch `IsDebuggerPresent` to return 0 so that it appears as though no debugger is running.

Although there's no perfect way to protect against a very determined hacker who has physical access to your binaries, you can at least make life a little more different for him at run time. Interestingly enough, the check that `IsDebuggerPresent` does to see whether a debugger is running on the process has been the same check in all Microsoft operating systems up to the time of this writing. There's no guarantee that it won't change, but the odds are good that it will stay the same for the future.

The next bit of code is a function you can add to your code that does the same thing as `IsDebuggerPresent`. Of course, just adding that function won't make it impossible to debug your application. To make debugging tougher, you might want to look at interspersing innocuous instructions between the main instructions so that hackers can't simply search for the byte pattern of the `IsDebuggerPresent` code. A whole book can be written about anti-hacking techniques. However, if you can pass the "two-hour test," which is that it should take longer than two hours for an average developer to try to hack your application, your application is probably safe from all but the most determined and talented hackers.

```
BOOL AntiHackIsDebuggerPresent ( void )
{
    BOOL bRet = TRUE ;
    __asm
    {
        // Get the Thread Information block (TIB).
        MOV       EAX , FS:[00000018H]
        // 0x30 bytes into the TIB is a pointer field that
        // points to a structure related to debugging.
        MOV       EAX , DWORD PTR [EAX+030H]
        // The second WORD in that debugging structure indicates
        // the process is being debugged.
        MOVZX     EAX , BYTE PTR [EAX+002H]
        // Return the result.
        MOV       bRet , EAX
    }
    return ( bRet ) ;
}
```

Kernel-Mode Debuggers

Kernel-mode debuggers sit between the CPU and the operating system. That means that when you stop in a kernel-mode debugger, the operating system also stops completely. As you can imagine, bringing the operating system to an abrupt halt is helpful when you're working on timing and synchronization problems.

There are three kernel-mode debuggers: the kernel debugger (KD), WinDBG, and SoftICE. I'll briefly describe each of these debuggers in the following sections.

Kernel Debugger (KD)

Windows 2000, Windows XP, and Windows Server 2003 are interesting in that the actual kernel-mode debugger portion is part of NTOSKRNL.EXE, the main kernel file of the operating system. This debugger is available in both the free (release) and checked (debug) builds of the operating system. To turn on kernel-mode debugging for x86-based systems, set the `/DEBUG` boot option in BOOT.INI and, additionally, the `/DEBUGPORT` boot option when you need to set the communications port for the kernel-mode debugger to a port other than the default (COM1). KD runs on its own machine, called the *host*, and communicates with the target machine either through a null modem cable or, optionally, a 1394 (FireWire) cable on Windows XP or Windows Server 2003.

The NTOSKRNL.EXE kernel-mode debugger does just enough to control the CPU so that the operating system can be debugged. The bulk of the debugging work—handling symbols, advanced breakpoints, and disassembly—happens on the KD side. At one time, the Microsoft Windows NT 4 Device Driver Kit (DDK) documented the protocol used across the null modem cable. However, Microsoft no longer documents this protocol.

KD is included in the Debugging Tools for Windows, which is downloadable from *http://www.microsoft.com/ddk/debugging*. (The current version at the time I wrote this book is also available with this book's sample files.) The power of KD is apparent when you see all the commands it offers for accessing the internal operating system state. If you've ever wanted to see what happens in the operating system, these commands will show you. Having a working knowledge of how Windows device drivers operate will help you follow much of the command's output. Interestingly enough, for all its power, KD is almost never used outside of Microsoft because it's a console application, which makes it tedious to use with source-level debugging. However, for the operating system teams at Microsoft, it's the kernel debugger of choice.

WinDBG

WinDBG is included in the Debugging Tools for Windows. It's a hybrid debugger in that it can be a kernel-mode debugger as well as a user-mode debugger and, with a bit of work, WinDBG lets you debug both kernel-mode and user-mode programs at the same time. For kernel-mode debugging, WinDBG offers all the same power of KD because it shares the same debugging engine as KD. However, WinDBG offers a GUI front end that isn't nearly as easy to use as the Visual Studio .NET debugger, although it is easier to use than KD. With WinDBG, you can debug your device drivers nearly as easily as you would your user-mode applications.

As a user-mode debugger, WinDBG is good, and I strongly recommend that you install it if you haven't already. WinDBG offers more power than the Visual Studio .NET debugger in that WinDBG shows you much more information about your process. However, that power does come at a cost: WinDBG is harder to use than the Visual Studio .NET debugger. Still, I'd advise you to spend some time and effort learning about WinDBG, and I'll show you key highlights and tricks in Chapter 8. The investment might pay off by helping you solve a bug much faster than you could with the Visual Studio .NET debugger alone. On average, I find that I spend about 95 percent of my debugging time in the Visual Studio .NET debugger and the rest in WinDBG.

SoftICE

SoftICE is a commercial kernel-mode debugger from Compuware NuMega and is the only commercial kernel-mode debugger (that I know of) on the market. It's also the only kernel-mode debugger that can operate on a single machine. Unlike the other kernel-mode debuggers, however, SoftICE does an excellent job debugging user-mode programs. As I mentioned earlier, kernel-mode debuggers sit between the CPU and the operating system; SoftICE also sits between the CPU and the operating system when debugging a user-mode program, thereby stopping the entire operating system dead.

At first glance, you might not be impressed by the fact that SoftICE can bring the operating system to a halt. But consider this question: What happens if you have some timing-dependent code you need to debug? If you're using an API function such as `SendMessageTimeout`, you can easily time out as you step through another thread with a typical GUI debugger. With SoftICE, you can step all you want because the timer that `SendMessageTimeout` relies on won't be executing while you're running under SoftICE. SoftICE is the only debugger that allows you to effectively debug multithreaded applications. The fact that SoftICE stops the entire operating system when it's active means that solving timing problems is far easier.

Another benefit of SoftICE sitting between the CPU and the operating system is that debugging cross-process interactions becomes very easy. If you're doing COM programming with multiple out-of-process servers, you can easily set breakpoints in all the processes and step between them. Finally, if you do need to step from user mode to kernel mode and back, SoftICE makes such shifting trivial.

The other major advantage that SoftICE has over all other debuggers is that it has a phenomenal collection of informational commands that let you see virtually everything that's happening in the operating system. Although KD and WinDBG have a substantial number of these commands, SoftICE has many more. You can view almost anything in SoftICE, from the state of all synchronization events, to complete `HWND` information, to extended information about any thread in the system. SoftICE can tell you anything that's happening on your system.

As you might expect, all this wonderful raw power has a price tag. SoftICE, like any kernel-mode debugger, has a steep learning curve because it's essentially its own operating system when it's running. However, your return on investment makes learning how to use SoftICE worth the effort.

Windows Operating System Support for Debuggees

In addition to defining the API that a debugger must call in order to be a debugger, Windows provides a few other features that help you find problems with your applications. Some of these features aren't that well known and can be confusing the first time you encounter them.

Just-In-Time (JIT) Debugging

Although some of the Visual Studio .NET marketing materials make it sound like Visual Studio is performing the magic behind JIT debugging, the magic is really occurring in the operating system. When an application crashes, Windows looks in the registry key `HKEY_LOCAL_MACHINE\SOFTWARE\Microsoft\Windows NT\CurrentVersion\AeDebug` to determine what debugger it should call to debug the application. If no values are in the key, Windows XP reports the standard crash dialog box, and Windows 2000 shows a message box and the address of the crash. If the key is present and the appropriate values are filled, under Windows XP, the Debug button in the lower left corner is active so that you can debug the application. Under Windows 2000, the Cancel button is available so that you can start debugging the crash.

The three important values used by JIT debugging in the `AeDebug` key are the following:

- `Auto`
- `UserDebuggerHotKey`
- `Debugger`

If `Auto` is set to 0 (zero), the operating system generates the standard crash dialog box and enables the Cancel button so that you can attach the debugger. If `Auto` is set to 1 (one), the debugger is automatically started. If you want to drive your coworkers crazy, sneak onto their systems and set `Auto` to 1—they'll have no idea why the debugger is starting each time an application crashes. The `UserDebuggerHotKey` value identifies the key that is used to break into the debugger. (I'll discuss its usage momentarily.) Finally, the most important key, the `Debugger` value, specifies the debugger that the operating system will start on the crashed application. The only requirement for the debugger is that it supports attaching to a process. After I discuss the `UserDebuggerHotKey` value, I'll explain more about the `Debugger` value and its format.

Quick Break Keys with the `UserDebuggerHotKey`

At times, you need a way to get into the debugger as fast as possible. If you're debugging a console-based application, pressing Ctrl+C or Ctrl+Break will cause a special exception, `DBG_CONTROL_C`. The `DBG_CONTROL_C` exception will pop you right into the debugger and allow you to start debugging.

A nice feature of Windows operating systems is that you can also pop into the debugger at any time for your GUI-based applications. When running under a debugger, by default, pressing the F12 key forces a call to `DebugBreak` nearly the instant the key is pressed. An interesting aspect of the F12 key processing is that even if you're using F12 as an accelerator or otherwise processing the keyboard messages for F12, you'll still break into the debugger.

The quick break key defaults to F12 but, if you like, you can specify which key to use. The `UserDebuggerHotKey` value is the numeric `VK_*` value you use to make the key the debugger hot key. For example, if you want to use the Scroll Lock key to break into the debugger, set the `UserDebuggerHotKey` value to 0x91. After you set a new value, you must reboot the computer for the change to take effect. A wonderful joke to play on your coworkers is to change the `UserDebuggerHotKey` to 0x45 (the letter *E*) so that every time they press the E key, the key breaks into the debugger. However, I take no responsibility if your coworkers gang up on you and make your life miserable.

The Debugger Value

Under the `AeDebug` key is the `Debugger` value, where the main action takes place. If you look at the value that's entered for `Debugger` for a freshly installed operating system, it looks like a string passed to the `wsprintf` API function: `drwtsn32 -p %ld -e %ld -g`. That's exactly what it is. The `-p` is the process ID for the crashing process, and the `-e` is an event handle value that the debugger needs to signal when its debug loop gets the first thread exit debug event. Signaling the event handle tells the operating system that the debugger attached cleanly. The `–g` tells Dr. Watson to continue executing the program after attaching.

At any time, you can change the `Debugger` value to invoke a different debugger. To set Visual Studio .NET as the native debugger, open Visual Studio .NET and select Options from the Tools menu. In the Options dialog box, Debugging folder, select the Just-In-Time property page and ensure that a check mark is next to the Native entry in the list box. You can set WinDBG or Dr. Watson as your debugger of choice by executing `WinDBG -I` (note that the switch is case sensitive) or `DRWTSN32 -I` from any command prompt. After you change the `Debugger` value, make sure to shut down Task Manager if it's running. Task Manager caches the `AeDebug` key when it starts, so if you attempt to debug a process from the Task Manager Processes page, the debugging might not work if the prior debugger was Visual Studio .NET.

Choosing the Debugger at Crash Time

It's great to have JIT debugging bring up the debugger when your application crashes, but the big limitation is that you can have only a single debugger at a time in the `Debugger` value. As we'll see in later chapters, the various debuggers you have at your disposal have strengths and weaknesses depending on particular debugging situations. Nothing is worse than having the wrong debugger pop up when you really want the one you know will simplify solving that bug you've spent weeks trying to duplicate.

This was a problem begging to be solved, so I set out to do so. However, because of what look like bugs in the way JIT debugging starts under Visual Studio .NET, I had to work through a lot of trial and error to get my approach working. Before I can discuss the problems, I need to show you how Debugger Chooser, or DBGCHOOSER for short, works.

The idea behind DBGCHOOSER is that it acts as a shim program that gets called when the debuggee crashes and passes on to the real debugger the information necessary to debug the application. To set up DBGCHOOSER, first copy it to a directory on your computer where it won't be accidentally deleted. The operating system tries to start the debugger executable specified in the `Debugger` value of the `AeDebug` key, so if the debugger isn't available, you won't get any chance to debug the crash. To initialize DBGCHOOSER, simply run it. Figure 4-1 shows the configuration dialog box in which you set the appropriate commands for each of the various debuggers supported by DBGCHOOSER. The initial run of DBGCHOOSER is set with the appropriate defaults for most developer machines. If you don't have the various debuggers in the path, you can specify the appropriate paths. Pay special attention to the Visual Studio .NET debugger path because the JIT shell used by Visual Studio .NET isn't in the path by default. After you click OK in the configuration dialog box, DBGCHOOSER writes your debugger setting to an INI file stored in your Windows directory and sets itself as the default debugger in the `AeDebug` key of the registry.

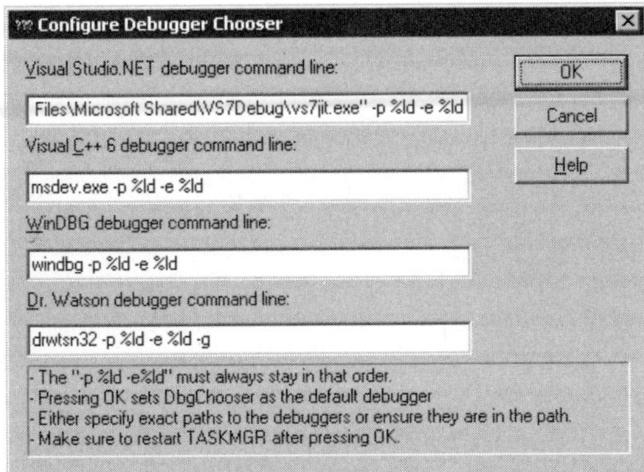

Figure 4-1 The DBGCHOOSER configuration dialog box

After you experience what I hope is one of your rare crashes, you'll see the actual chooser dialog box pop up when you click Debug in the crash dialog boxes, as shown in Figure 4-2. Simply select the debugger you want to use and start debugging.

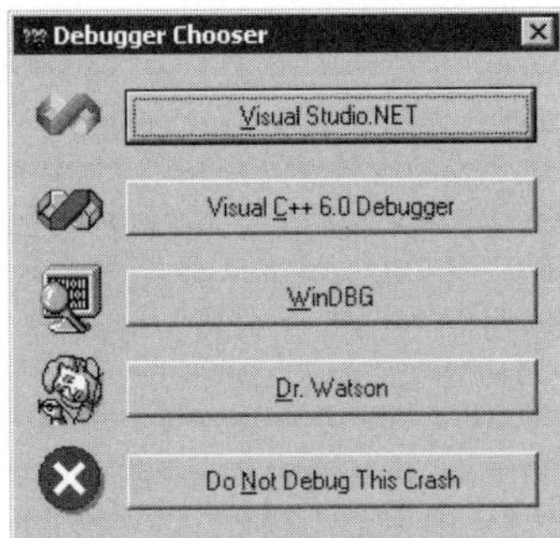

Figure 4-2 The DBGCHOOSER debugger chooser dialog box

The implementation of DBGCHOOSER is nothing exciting. The first point of interest is that when I called `CreateProcess` on the debugger the user chose, I had to ensure that I set the inherit handles flag to `TRUE`. To ensure everything is copacetic with the handles, I have DBGCHOOSER wait on the spawned debugger until it ends. That way I know any necessary inherited handles are still there for the debugger. Although it was more of a pain to figure out than interesting to implement, getting Visual Studio .NET to work properly from DBGCHOOSER took some doing. Everything worked like a champ with WinDBG, Microsoft Visual C++ 6, and Dr. Watson. However, when I'd start Visual Studio .NET (actually VS7JIT.EXE, which in turn spawns the Visual Studio .NET debugger), a message box would pop up indicating that JIT debugging was disabled and wouldn't start debugging.

At first I was a little stumped about what was going on, but a quick check with the wonderful registry monitor program (Regmon), from Mark Russinovich and Bryce Cogswell at *www.sysinternals.com*, showed me that VS7JIT.EXE was checking the `AeDebug` key's `Debugger` value to see whether it was set as the JIT debugger. If it wasn't, up popped the JIT debugging disabled message box. I was able to verify that this was the case by stopping DBGCHOOSER in the debugger while DBGCHOOSER was active because of a crash, and changing the `Debugger` key back so that it pointed to VS7JIT.EXE. I have no idea why VS7JIT.EXE feels it's so important that it won't debug unless the debugger is the JIT debugger. I did a little quick coding in DBGCHOOSER to fake out VS7JIT.EXE by changing the `Debugger` value to VS7JIT.EXE before I spawned it, and all was good with the world. To get DBGCHOOSER.EXE reset as the JIT debugger, I spawned a thread that waits for 5 seconds and resets the `Debugger` value.

As I mentioned when I first started talking about DBGCHOOSER, my solution isn't perfect because of problems with JIT debugging in Visual Studio .NET. On Windows XP, I was testing all permutations of starting and running Visual Studio .NET and found that VS7JIT.EXE stopped running. After playing with it a bit, I found that two instances of VS7JIT.EXE actually run when starting Visual Studio .NET as the JIT debugger. One instance spawns the Visual Studio .NET IDE, and the other instance runs under the RPCSS DCOM server. On rare occasions, only during testing with the supplied implementation, I got the system into states where attempting to spawn VS7JIT.EXE would fail because the DCOM instance wouldn't start. I mainly ran into this problem when I worked on the code to reset the `Debugger` value in the `AeDebug` key. Once I settled on the current way of implementing DBGCHOOSER, I've run into the problem just once or twice and only when I set up test cases in which multiple process crashes were happening all at once. I wasn't able to track down the exact cause, but I've never seen this problem in normal work.

Automatically Starting in a Debugger (Image File Execution Options)

Some of the hardest types of applications to debug are those started by another process. Windows services and COM out-of-process servers fall into this category. In many cases, you can use the `DebugBreak` API function to force a debugger to attach to your process. In two instances, however, using `DebugBreak` won't work. First, in some cases, `DebugBreak` won't work with Windows services. If you need to debug the service startup, calling `DebugBreak` will get the debugger to attach, but by the time the debugger gets started, the service timeout limit might be reached and Windows will stop your service. Second, `DebugBreak` won't work when you need to debug a COM out-of-process server. If you call `DebugBreak`, the COM error handling will catch the breakpoint exception and terminate your COM out-of-process server. Fortunately, Windows lets you specify that your application should start in a debugger. This feature allows you to start debugging right from the first instruction. Before you enable this feature for a Windows service, however, make sure to configure your service to allow interaction with the desktop.

The best way to set up automatic debugging is to manually set the option with the registry editor. In the `HKEY_LOCAL_MACHINE\SOFTWARE\Microsoft\Windows NT\CurrentVersion\Image File Execution Options` key, create a key that is the same as your application's filename. For example, if your application is FOO.EXE, your registry key is `FOO.EXE`. In your application's registry key, create a new string value named `Debugger`. In the `Debugger` value, type the complete path and filename to your debugger of choice.

Now when you start your application, the debugger automatically starts with your application loaded. If you want to specify any command-line options to the debugger, you can specify them as well in the `Debugger` value. For example, if you want to use WinDBG and automatically initiate debugging as soon as WinDBG starts, you can fill your `Debugger` value with "`d:\windbg\windbg.exe -g`".

To use Visual Studio .NET as your debugger of choice, you'll have to do a bit more work. The first problem is that Visual Studio .NET cannot debug an executable without a solution file. If you're developing the executable (in other words, you have a solution with source code), you can use that solution. However, the last build open will be the build run. Therefore, if you want to debug the release build or a binary you don't have source code to, open the project, set the active solution configuration to Release, and close the solution. If you don't have a solution file for the executable, click the File, Open Solution menu option and open the executable as the solution. Start debugging the solution and save the solution file when prompted.

Once you have the solution you'll use worked out, the command line you'll set in the `Debugger` value would look like the following. Unless you've manually added the Visual Studio .NET directory, <VS.NET Installation Dir>\Common7\IDE, to the system `PATH` environment variable, you'll need to specify the complete drive and directory with DEVENV.EXE. The `/run` command-line option to DEVENV.EXE tells it to start debugging the solution passed on the command line.

```
g:\vsnet\common7\ide\devenv /run d:\disk\output\wdbg.sln
```

The second problem you'll get to deal with is that the `Debugger` string value can be only 65 characters long. If you've installed Visual Studio .NET into the default paths, the path will almost certainly be too long to use. What you'll need to do is get creative with the `SUBST` command and assign the paths to DEVENV.EXE and your solution to drive letters.

Some of you old-timers out there might remember that you can set the `Debugger` key from GFLAGS.EXE, a small utility that comes with WinDBG. Unfortunately, GFLAGS.EXE is broken and will accept only a command-line string of 25 characters for the `Debugger` value. Consequently, it's still best to create the process key and `Debugger` value manually.

Common Debugging Question

My boss is sending me so much e-mail that I can't get anything done. Is there any way I can slow down the dreaded PHB e-mail?

Although many of your bosses mean well, their incessant e-mail messages can become distracting and keep you from the real work you need to do. Fortunately, there's a simple solution that works quite well and will give you a week or so of wonderful peace so that you can work at hitting your deadlines. The less technically proficient your boss and network administrators are, the more time you'll get.

In the previous section, I talked about the `Image File Execution Options` section of the registry and the fact that whenever you set a process's `Debugger` value, that process automatically starts under that debugger. The trick to ending the PHB (pointy haired boss) mail is the following:

1. Walk into your boss's office.
2. Open REGEDIT.EXE. If your boss is currently in the office, explain that you need to run a utility on his machine so that he can access the XML Web services you're building. (It doesn't really matter whether you're creating XML Web services—the buzzwords alone will cause your boss to readily let you mess with his machine.)
3. In the `Image File Execution Options` section, create a key **OUTLOOK.EXE**. (Substitute the executable name of your e-mail program if you don't use Microsoft Outlook.) Tell your boss that you're doing this to allow him to have e-mail access to XML Web services.
4. Create the `Debugger` value and set the string to **SOL.EXE**. Indicate to your boss that SOL is to allow your XML Web services to access Sun Solaris machines, so it's necessary you use it.
5. Close REGEDIT.EXE.

6. Tell your boss that he's all set and can now start accessing XML Web services. The real trick at this point is to keep a straight face while walking out of your boss's office.

Avoiding laughter during this experiment is much more difficult than it sounds, so you might want to practice these steps with a few coworkers first.

What you've just set up is a situation in which every time your boss starts Outlook, Solitaire runs instead. (Since most bosses spend their days playing Solitaire anyway, your boss will be sidetracked for a couple of games before he realizes that he meant to start Outlook.) Eventually, he'll continue to click the Outlook icon until so many copies of Solitaire are running that he'll run out of virtual memory and have to reboot his machine. After a couple of days of this click-a-million-times-and-reboot cycle, your boss will eventually have a network administrator come in and look at his machine.

The admin will get all excited because she has a problem that is a little more interesting than helping the folks in accounts receivable reset their passwords. The admin will play with the machine for at least a day in your boss's office, thus keeping your boss from even being close to a machine. If anyone asks your opinion, the stock answer is, "I've heard of strange interaction problems between EJB and NTFS across the DCOM substrata architecture necessary to access the MFT using the binary least squares sort algorithm." The admin will take your boss's machine back to her office and continue to play with it for a couple of days. Eventually, the admin will repave the hard disk and reinstall everything on the machine, taking another day or so. By the time your boss gets his machine back, he'll have four days of e-mail to get through, so it will be at least a day before he gets out from under all that mail, and you can safely ignore those messages for another day or two. If the PHB-mail starts getting thick again, simply repeat the steps.

Important note: Use this technique at your own risk.

MinDBG: A Simple Win32 Debugger

From a distance, a Win32 debugger is a simple program, with only a couple requirements. The first requirement is that the debugger must pass a special flag in the `dwCreationFlags` parameter to `CreateProcess`: `DEBUG_ONLY_THIS_PROCESS`. This flag tells the operating system that the calling thread will enter a debug loop to control the process it's starting. If the debugger can handle multiple processes spawned by the initial debuggee, it will pass `DEBUG_PROCESS` as the creation flag.

As you can see, since the debugger uses `CreateProcess`, the debugger and debuggee are in separate processes, making the Win32 operating systems much more robust when debugging. Even if the debuggee has wild memory writes, the debuggee won't crash the debugger. (Debuggers in the 16-bit Windows and pre–OS X Macintosh operating systems are susceptible to debuggee mischief because the debugger and the debuggee run in the same process context.)

The second requirement is that after the debuggee starts, the debugger must enter into a loop calling the `WaitForDebugEvent` API function to receive debugging notifications. When it has finished processing a particular debugging event, it calls `ContinueDebugEvent`. Be aware that only the thread that called `CreateProcess` with the special debug creation flags can call the Debugging API functions. The following pseudocode shows just how little code is required to create a Win32 debugger:

```
void main ( void )
{
    CreateProcess ( ..., DEBUG_ONLY_THIS_PROCESS ,... ) ;

    while ( 1 == WaitForDebugEvent ( ... ) )
    {
        if ( EXIT_PROCESS )
        {
            break ;
        }
        ContinueDebugEvent ( ... ) ;
    }
}
```

As you can see, a minimal Win32 debugger doesn't require multithreading, a user interface, or much of anything else. Nevertheless, as with most applications in Windows, the difference between minimal and reasonable is considerable. In reality, the Win32 Debugging API almost dictates that the actual debug loop needs to sit in a separate thread. As the name implies, `WaitForDebugEvent` blocks on an internal operating system event until the debuggee performs some operation that makes the operating system stop the debuggee so that it can tell the debugger about the event. If your debugger had a single thread, your user interface would totally hang until the debuggee triggered a debug event.

During the time a debugger sits in the debug loop, it receives various notifications that certain events took place in the debuggee. The following `DEBUG_EVENT` structure, which is filled in by the `WaitForDebugEvent` function, contains all the interesting information about a debug event. Table 4-1 describes each of the individual events.

```
typedef struct _DEBUG_EVENT {
    DWORD dwDebugEventCode;
    DWORD dwProcessId;
    DWORD dwThreadId;
    union {
        EXCEPTION_DEBUG_INFO Exception;
        CREATE_THREAD_DEBUG_INFO CreateThread;
        CREATE_PROCESS_DEBUG_INFO CreateProcessInfo;
        EXIT_THREAD_DEBUG_INFO ExitThread;
        EXIT_PROCESS_DEBUG_INFO ExitProcess;
        LOAD_DLL_DEBUG_INFO LoadDll;
        UNLOAD_DLL_DEBUG_INFO UnloadDll;
        OUTPUT_DEBUG_STRING_INFO DebugString;
        RIP_INFO RipInfo;
    } u;
} DEBUG_EVENT
```

Table 4-1 Debugging Events

Debugging Event	Description
CREATE_PROCESS_DEBUG_EVENT	This debugging event is generated whenever a new process is created in a process being debugged or whenever the debugger begins debugging an already active process. The kernel generates this debugging event before the process begins to execute in user mode and before the kernel generates any other debugging events for the new process. The DEBUG_EVENT structure contains a CREATE_PROCESS_DEBUG_INFO structure. This structure includes a handle to the new process, a handle to the process's image file, a handle to the process's initial thread, and other information that describes the new process. The handle to the process has PROCESS_VM_READ and PROCESS_VM_WRITE access. If a debugger has these types of access to a process handle, it can read and write to the process's memory by using the ReadProcessMemory and WriteProcessMemory functions. The handle to the process's image file has GENERIC_READ access and is opened for read-sharing. The handle to the process's initial thread has THREAD_GET_CONTEXT, THREAD_SET_CONTEXT, and THREAD_SUSPEND_RESUME access to the thread. If a debugger has these types of access to a thread, it can read from and write to the thread's registers by using the GetThreadContext and SetThreadContext functions and can suspend and resume the thread by using the SuspendThread and ResumeThread functions.

(continued)

Table 4-1 Debugging Events *(continued)*

Debugging Event	Description
CREATE_THREAD_DEBUG_EVENT	This debugging event is generated whenever a new thread is created in a process being debugged or whenever the debugger begins debugging an already active process. This debugging event is generated before the new thread begins to execute in user mode. The DEBUG_EVENT structure contains a CREATE_THREAD_DEBUG_INFO structure. This structure includes a handle to the new thread and the thread's starting address. The handle has THREAD_GET_CONTEXT, THREAD_SET_CONTEXT, and THREAD_SUSPEND_RESUME access to the thread. If a debugger has these types of access to a thread, it can read from and write to the thread's registers by using the GetThreadContext and SetThreadContext functions and can suspend and resume the thread by using the SuspendThread and ResumeThread functions.
EXCEPTION_DEBUG_EVENT	This debugging event is generated whenever an exception occurs in the process being debugged. Possible exceptions include attempting to access inaccessible memory, executing breakpoint instructions, attempting to divide by 0, or any other exception noted in the MSDN documentation, "Structured Exception Handling." The DEBUG_EVENT structure contains an EXCEPTION_DEBUG_INFO structure. This structure describes the exception that caused the debugging event. Besides the standard exception conditions, an additional exception code can occur during console process debugging. The kernel generates a DBG_CONTROL_C exception code when Ctrl+C is input to a console process that handles Ctrl+C signals and is being debugged. This exception code isn't meant to be handled by applications. An application should never use an exception handler to deal with it. It is raised only for the benefit of the debugger and is used only when a debugger is attached to the console process. When a process isn't being debugged or when the debugger passes on the DBG_CONTROL_C exception unhandled, the application's list of handler functions is searched. (For more information about console process handler functions, see the MSDN documentation for the SetConsoleCtrlHandler function.)

Table 4-1 Debugging Events *(continued)*

Debugging Event	Description
EXIT_PROCESS_DEBUG_EVENT	This debugging event is generated whenever the last thread in a process being debugged exits or calls ExitProcess. It occurs immediately after the kernel unloads the process's DLLs and updates the process's exit code. The DEBUG_EVENT structure contains an EXIT_PROCESS_DEBUG_INFO structure that specifies the exit code. The debugger deallocates any internal structures associated with the process on receipt of this debugging event. The kernel closes the debugger's handle to the exiting process and all the process's threads. The debugger should not close these handles.
EXIT_THREAD_DEBUG_EVENT	This debugging event is generated whenever a thread that is part of a process being debugged exits. The kernel generates this debugging event immediately after it updates the thread's exit code. The DEBUG_EVENT structure contains an EXIT_THREAD_DEBUG_INFO structure that specifies the exit code. The debugger deallocates any internal structures associated with the thread on receipt of this debugging event. The system closes the debugger's handle to the exiting thread. The debugger should not close these handles. This debugging event doesn't occur if the exiting thread is the last thread of a process. In this case, the EXIT_PROCESS_DEBUG_EVENT debugging event occurs instead.
LOAD_DLL_DEBUG_EVENT	This debugging event is generated whenever a process being debugged loads a DLL. This debugging event occurs when the system loader resolves links to a DLL or when the debugged process uses the LoadLibrary function. This debugging event is called each time the DLL loads into the address space. If the DLL's reference count falls to 0, the DLL is unloaded. The next time the DLL is loaded, this event will be generated again. The DEBUG_EVENT structure contains a LOAD_DLL_DEBUG_INFO structure. This structure includes a file handle to the newly loaded DLL, the base address of the DLL, and other information that describes the DLL. Typically, a debugger loads a symbol table associated with the DLL on receipt of this debugging event.

(continued)

Table 4-1 Debugging Events *(continued)*

Debugging Event	Description
OUTPUT_DEBUG_STRING_EVENT	This debugging event is generated when a process being debugged uses the OutputDebugString function. The DEBUG_EVENT structure contains an OUTPUT_DEBUG_STRING_INFO structure. This structure specifies the address, length, and format of the debugging string.
UNLOAD_DLL_DEBUG_EVENT	This debugging event is generated whenever a process being debugged unloads a DLL by using the FreeLibrary function. This debugging event occurs only the last time a DLL is unloaded from a process's address space (that is, when the DLL's usage count is 0). The DEBUG_EVENT structure contains an UNLOAD_DLL_DEBUG_INFO structure. This structure specifies the base address of the DLL in the address space of the process that unloads the DLL. Typically, a debugger unloads a symbol table associated with the DLL upon receiving this debugging event. When a process exits, the kernel automatically unloads the process's DLLs but doesn't generate an UNLOAD_DLL_DEBUG_EVENT debugging event.

When the debugger is processing the debug events returned by WaitForDebugEvent, it has full control over the debuggee because the operating system stops all the threads in the debuggee and won't reschedule them until ContinueDebugEvent is called. If the debugger needs to read from or write to the debuggee's address space, it can use ReadProcessMemory and WriteProcessMemory. If the memory is marked as read-only, you can use the VirtualProtect function to reset the protection levels if you need to write to that memory. If the debugger patches the debuggee's code via a call to WriteProcessMemory, it must call FlushInstructionCache to clear out the instruction cache for the memory. If you forget to call FlushInstructionCache, your changes might work when the memory is not in the CPU cache. If the memory is already in the CPU cache, the changes won't be applied until the memory is re-read into the CPU cache. Calling FlushInstructionCache is especially important on multiprocessor machines. If the debugger needs to get or set the debuggee's current context or CPU registers, it can call GetThreadContext or SetThreadContext.

The only Win32 debug event that needs special handling is the loader breakpoint, which is also referred to as the initial breakpoint. After the operating system sends initial CREATE_PROCESS_DEBUG_EVENT and LOAD_DLL_DEBUG_EVENT notifications for the implicitly loaded modules, the debugger receives an EXCEPTION_DEBUG_EVENT. This debug event is the loader breakpoint. The debuggee executes this breakpoint because the CREATE_PROCESS_DEBUG_EVENT indicates only that the process was loaded, not that it was executed. The loader breakpoint, which the operating system forces each debuggee to execute, is the first time the debugger knows when the debuggee is truly running. In real-world debuggers, the main data structure initialization, such as for symbol tables, is handled during process creation, and the debugger starts showing code disassembly or doing necessary debuggee patching in the loader breakpoint.

When the loader breakpoint occurs, the debugger should record that it saw the breakpoint so that the debugger can handle subsequent breakpoints accordingly. The only other processing needed for the first breakpoint (and for all breakpoints in general) depends on the CPU. For the Intel Pentium family, the debugger has to continue processing by calling ContinueDebugEvent and passing it the DBG_CONTINUE flag so that the debuggee resumes execution. Other CPUs might need to increment the instruction pointer past the breakpoint.

Listing 4-1 shows MinDBG, a minimal debugger that is available with this book's sample files. MinDBG processes all the debug events and properly runs a debuggee process. Additionally, it shows how to attach to an existing process as well as how to detach from a process being debugged. To start a process under MinDBG, pass the process to run on the command line along with any debuggee parameters. To attach and debug an existing process, pass the decimal process ID of the process on the command line prefixed with a hyphen (-). For example, if the process ID is 3245, you'd pass -3245 on the command line to affect the debugger attach. If you're running Windows XP or Windows Server 2003 and later, you can detach from debugging the process by pressing Ctrl+Break. If you run MinDBG, notice that the debug event handlers don't really do much other than show some basic information. Taking a minimal debugger and turning it into a real debugger involves quite a bit of work.

```
/*----------------------------------------------------------------------
Debugging Applications for Microsoft .NET and Microsoft Windows
Copyright (c) 1997-2003 John Robbins -- All rights reserved.

The world's simplest debugger for Win32 programs
----------------------------------------------------------------------*/

/*//////////////////////////////////////////////////////////////////////
// The Usual Includes
//////////////////////////////////////////////////////////////////////*/
#include "stdafx.h"

/*//////////////////////////////////////////////////////////////////////
// Prototypes and Types.
//////////////////////////////////////////////////////////////////////*/
// Shows the minimal help.
void ShowHelp ( void ) ;

// The break handler.
BOOL WINAPI CtrlBreakHandler ( DWORD dwCtrlType ) ;

// Display functions
void DisplayCreateProcessEvent ( CREATE_PROCESS_DEBUG_INFO & stCPDI ) ;
void DisplayCreateThreadEvent ( DWORD                      dwTID  ,
                                CREATE_THREAD_DEBUG_INFO & stCTDI  ) ;
void DisplayExitThreadEvent ( DWORD                    dwTID  ,
                              EXIT_THREAD_DEBUG_INFO & stETDI  ) ;
void DisplayExitProcessEvent ( EXIT_PROCESS_DEBUG_INFO & stEPDI ) ;
void DisplayDllLoadEvent ( HANDLE                hProcess ,
                           LOAD_DLL_DEBUG_INFO & stLDDI    ) ;
void DisplayDllUnLoadEvent ( UNLOAD_DLL_DEBUG_INFO & stULDDI ) ;
void DisplayODSEvent ( HANDLE                         hProcess ,
                       OUTPUT_DEBUG_STRING_INFO & stODSI     ) ;
void DisplayExceptionEvent ( EXCEPTION_DEBUG_INFO & stEDI ) ;

// The typedef for DebugActiveProcessStop.
typedef BOOL (WINAPI *PFNDEBUGACTIVEPROCESSSTOP)(DWORD) ;

/*//////////////////////////////////////////////////////////////////////
// File Scope Globals
//////////////////////////////////////////////////////////////////////*/
// The flag that indicates I'm supposed to detach.
static BOOL g_bDoTheDetach = FALSE ;

/*//////////////////////////////////////////////////////////////////////
// The Entry Point.
//////////////////////////////////////////////////////////////////////*/
void _tmain ( int argc , TCHAR * argv[ ] )
{
```

Listing 4-1 MINDBG.CPP

```
    // Check that there is a command-line argument.
    if ( 1 == argc )
    {
        ShowHelp ( ) ;
        return ;
    }

    // Have a buffer big enough for the command and command line
    // parameters.
    TCHAR szCmdLine[ MAX_PATH + MAX_PATH ] ;
    // The possible PID if attaching.
    DWORD dwPID = 0 ;

    szCmdLine[ 0 ] = _T ( '\0' ) ;

    // Check if the command line starts with "-" as that indicates a
    // process ID I will attach to.
    if ( _T ( '-' ) == argv[1][0] )
    {
        // Attempt to strip off the PID from the command line option.

        // Move past the '-' in the string.
        TCHAR * pPID = argv[1] + 1 ;
        dwPID = _tstol ( pPID ) ;
        if ( 0 == dwPID )
        {
            _tprintf ( _T ( "Invalid PID value : %s\n" ) , pPID ) ;
            return ;
        }
    }
    else
    {
        dwPID = 0 ;

        // I'm going to start up the process.
        for ( int i = 1 ; i < argc ; i++ )
        {
            _tcscat ( szCmdLine , argv[ i ] ) ;
            if ( i < argc )
            {
                _tcscat ( szCmdLine , _T ( " " ) ) ;
            }
        }
    }

    // The return value holder.
    BOOL bRet = FALSE ;

    // Set the CTRL+BREAK handler.
    bRet = SetConsoleCtrlHandler ( CtrlBreakHandler , TRUE ) ;
    if ( FALSE == bRet )
    {
```

(continued)

```
        _tprintf ( _T ( "Unable to set CTRL+BREAK handler!\n" ) ) ;
        return ;
    }

    // If the PID is zero, I'm starting the process.
    if ( 0 == dwPID )
    {
        // Try to start the debuggee process. The function call looks
        // like a normal CreateProcess call except for the special start
        // option flag DEBUG_ONLY_THIS_PROCESS.
        STARTUPINFO         stStartInfo     ;
        PROCESS_INFORMATION stProcessInfo   ;

        memset ( &stStartInfo   , NULL , sizeof ( STARTUPINFO         ));
        memset ( &stProcessInfo , NULL , sizeof ( PROCESS_INFORMATION));

        stStartInfo.cb = sizeof ( STARTUPINFO ) ;

        bRet = CreateProcess ( NULL                    ,
                               szCmdLine               ,
                               NULL                    ,
                               NULL                    ,
                               FALSE                   ,
                               CREATE_NEW_CONSOLE |
                               DEBUG_ONLY_THIS_PROCESS ,
                               NULL                    ,
                               NULL                    ,
                               &stStartInfo            ,
                               &stProcessInfo           ) ;

        // Don't forget to close process and thread handles returned
        // from CreateOricess.
        VERIFY ( CloseHandle ( stProcessInfo.hProcess ) ) ;
        VERIFY ( CloseHandle ( stProcessInfo.hThread ) ) ;

        // See whether the debuggee process started.
        if ( FALSE == bRet )
        {
            _tprintf ( _T ( "Unable to start %s\n" ) , szCmdLine ) ;
            return ;
        }

        // Save the process ID in case there's a detach.
        dwPID = stProcessInfo.dwProcessId ;
    }
    else
    {
        bRet = DebugActiveProcess ( dwPID ) ;
        if ( FALSE == bRet )
        {
            _tprintf ( _T ( "Unable to attach to %u\n" ) , dwPID ) ;
            return ;
        }
```

```
    }

    // The debuggee started, so let's enter the debug loop.
    DEBUG_EVENT stDE                                  ;
    BOOL        bSeenInitialBP    = FALSE  ;
    BOOL        bContinue         = TRUE   ;
    HANDLE      hProcess          = INVALID_HANDLE_VALUE ;
    DWORD       dwContinueStatus                  ;

    // Loop until told to stop.
    while ( TRUE == bContinue )
    {
        // Pause until a debug event notification happens.
        BOOL bProcessDbgEvent = WaitForDebugEvent ( &stDE , 100 ) ;

        if ( TRUE == bProcessDbgEvent )
        {
            // Handle the particular debug events. Because MinDBG is
            // only a minimal debugger, it handles only a few events.
            switch ( stDE.dwDebugEventCode )
            {
                case CREATE_PROCESS_DEBUG_EVENT    :
                {
                    DisplayCreateProcessEvent(stDE.u.CreateProcessInfo);
                    // Save the handle information needed for later.
                    // Note that you can't close this handle. If you
                    // do, CloseHandle fails.
                    hProcess = stDE.u.CreateProcessInfo.hProcess ;

                    // You can safely close the file handle. If you
                    // close the thread, CloseHandle fails deep in
                    // ContinueDebugEvent when you end the application.
                    VERIFY(CloseHandle(stDE.u.CreateProcessInfo.hFile));

                    dwContinueStatus = DBG_CONTINUE ;
                }
                break ;
                case EXIT_PROCESS_DEBUG_EVENT    :
                {
                    DisplayExitProcessEvent ( stDE.u.ExitProcess ) ;
                    bContinue = FALSE ;
                    dwContinueStatus = DBG_CONTINUE ;
                }
                break ;

                case LOAD_DLL_DEBUG_EVENT     :
                {
                    DisplayDllLoadEvent ( hProcess , stDE.u.LoadDll ) ;

                    // Don't forget to close the corresponding file
                    // handle.
                    VERIFY ( CloseHandle( stDE.u.LoadDll.hFile ) ) ;
```

(continued)

```
                dwContinueStatus = DBG_CONTINUE ;
            }
            break ;
            case UNLOAD_DLL_DEBUG_EVENT  :
            {
                DisplayDllUnLoadEvent ( stDE.u.UnloadDll ) ;
                dwContinueStatus = DBG_CONTINUE ;
            }
            break ;

            case CREATE_THREAD_DEBUG_EVENT  :
            {
                DisplayCreateThreadEvent ( stDE.dwThreadId      ,
                                           stDE.u.CreateThread  ) ;
                // Note that you can't close the thread handle. If
                // you do, CloseHandle fails deep inside
                // ContinueDebugEvent.

                dwContinueStatus = DBG_CONTINUE ;
            }
            break ;
            case EXIT_THREAD_DEBUG_EVENT    :
            {
                DisplayExitThreadEvent ( stDE.dwThreadId   ,
                                         stDE.u.ExitThread  ) ;
                dwContinueStatus = DBG_CONTINUE ;
            }
            break ;

            case OUTPUT_DEBUG_STRING_EVENT  :
            {
                DisplayODSEvent ( hProcess , stDE.u.DebugString ) ;
                dwContinueStatus = DBG_CONTINUE ;
            }
            break ;

            case EXCEPTION_DEBUG_EVENT      :
            {
                DisplayExceptionEvent ( stDE.u.Exception ) ;

                // The only exception that I have to treat specially
                // is the initial breakpoint the loader provides.
                switch(stDE.u.Exception.ExceptionRecord.ExceptionCode)
                {
                    case EXCEPTION_BREAKPOINT :
                    {
                        // If a breakpoint exception occurs and it's
                        // the first seen, I continue on my merry
                        // way; otherwise, I pass the exception on
                        // to the debuggee.
                        if ( FALSE == bSeenInitialBP )
                        {
                            bSeenInitialBP = TRUE ;
```

```
                        dwContinueStatus = DBG_CONTINUE ;
                    }
                    else
                    {
                        // Houston, we have a problem!
                        dwContinueStatus =
                                     DBG_EXCEPTION_NOT_HANDLED ;
                    }
                }
                break ;

                // Just pass on any other exceptions to the
                // debuggee.
                default                         :
                {
                    dwContinueStatus =
                                     DBG_EXCEPTION_NOT_HANDLED ;
                }
                break ;
            }
        }
        break ;

        // For any other events, just continue on.
        default                         :
        {
            dwContinueStatus = DBG_CONTINUE ;
        }
        break ;
    }

    // Pass on to the operating system.
#ifdef _DEBUG
    BOOL bCntDbg =
#endif
    ContinueDebugEvent ( stDE.dwProcessId ,
                         stDE.dwThreadId  ,
                         dwContinueStatus   ) ;

    ASSERT ( TRUE == bCntDbg ) ;
}
// Check to see if the detach is supposed to happen.
if ( TRUE == g_bDoTheDetach )
{
    // Detaching only works on XP and higher so I'll have to
    // do the GetProcAddress to look up the
    // DebugActiveProcessStop.
    bContinue = FALSE ;

    HINSTANCE hKernel32 =
                  GetModuleHandle ( _T ( "KERNEL32.DLL" ) ) ;
    if ( 0 != hKernel32 )
    {
```

(continued)

```
                    PFNDEBUGACTIVEPROCESSSTOP pfnDAPS =
                              (PFNDEBUGACTIVEPROCESSSTOP)
                           GetProcAddress ( hKernel32                ,
                                            "DebugActiveProcessStop"  ) ;
                    if ( NULL != pfnDAPS )
                    {
#ifdef _DEBUG
                        BOOL bTemp =
#endif
                        pfnDAPS ( dwPID ) ;

                        ASSERT ( TRUE == bTemp ) ;
                    }
                }
            }
        }
}

/*//////////////////////////////////////////////////////////////////////
// Monitors CTRL+BREAK processing.
//////////////////////////////////////////////////////////////////////*/
BOOL WINAPI CtrlBreakHandler ( DWORD dwCtrlType )
{
    // I'll only handle CTRL+BREAK. Anything else kills the debuggee.
    if ( CTRL_BREAK_EVENT == dwCtrlType )
    {
        g_bDoTheDetach = TRUE ;
        return ( TRUE ) ;
    }
    return ( FALSE ) ;
}

/*//////////////////////////////////////////////////////////////////////
// Display's program help.
//////////////////////////////////////////////////////////////////////*/
void ShowHelp ( void )
{
    _tprintf ( _T ( "Start a program to debug:\n" )
               _T ( "   MinDBG <program to debug> " )
               _T ( "<program's command-line options>\n" )
               _T ( "Attach to an existing program:\n" )
               _T ( "   MinDBG -PID\n" )
               _T ( "       PID is the decimal process ID\n" ) ) ;
}


/*//////////////////////////////////////////////////////////////////////
// Display's create process events.
//////////////////////////////////////////////////////////////////////*/
void DisplayCreateProcessEvent ( CREATE_PROCESS_DEBUG_INFO & stCPDI )
{
    _tprintf ( _T ( "Create Process Event      :\n" ) ) ;
    _tprintf ( _T ( "   hFile                  : 0x%08X\n" ) ,
```

```
                stCPDI.hFile                                    ) ;
    _tprintf ( _T ( "   hProcess                    : 0x%08X\n" ) ,
                stCPDI.hProcess                                 ) ;
    _tprintf ( _T ( "   hThread                     : 0x%08X\n" ) ,
                stCPDI.hThread                                  ) ;
    _tprintf ( _T ( "   lpBaseOfImage               : 0x%08X\n" ) ,
                stCPDI.lpBaseOfImage                            ) ;
    _tprintf ( _T ( "   dwDebugInfoFileOffset       : 0x%08X\n" ) ,
                stCPDI.dwDebugInfoFileOffset                    ) ;
    _tprintf ( _T ( "   nDebugInfoSize              : 0x%08X\n" ) ,
                stCPDI.nDebugInfoSize                           ) ;
    _tprintf ( _T ( "   lpThreadLocalBase           : 0x%08X\n" ) ,
                stCPDI.lpThreadLocalBase                        ) ;
    _tprintf ( _T ( "   lpStartAddress              : 0x%08X\n" ) ,
                stCPDI.lpStartAddress                           ) ;
    _tprintf ( _T ( "   lpImageName                 : 0x%08X\n" ) ,
                stCPDI.lpImageName                              ) ;
    _tprintf ( _T ( "   fUnicode                    : 0x%08X\n" ) ,
                stCPDI.fUnicode                                 ) ;
}

/*//////////////////////////////////////////////////////////////////////
// Display's create thread events.
//////////////////////////////////////////////////////////////////////*/
void DisplayCreateThreadEvent ( DWORD                         dwTID   ,
                                CREATE_THREAD_DEBUG_INFO & stCTDI   )
{
    _tprintf ( _T ( "Create Thread Event           :\n" ) ) ;
    _tprintf ( _T ( "   TID                         : 0x%08X\n" ) ,
                dwTID                                           ) ;
    _tprintf ( _T ( "   hThread                     : 0x%08X\n" ) ,
                stCTDI.hThread                                  ) ;
    _tprintf ( _T ( "   lpThreadLocalBase           : 0x%08X\n" ) ,
              stCTDI.lpThreadLocalBase                          ) ;
    _tprintf ( _T ( "   lpStartAddress              : 0x%08X\n" ) ,
                stCTDI.lpStartAddress                           ) ;
}

/*//////////////////////////////////////////////////////////////////////
// Display's exit thread events.
//////////////////////////////////////////////////////////////////////*/
void DisplayExitThreadEvent ( DWORD                       dwTID   ,
                              EXIT_THREAD_DEBUG_INFO & stETDI   )
{
    _tprintf ( _T ( "Exit Thread Event             :\n" ) ) ;
    _tprintf ( _T ( "   TID                         : 0x%08X\n" ) ,
                dwTID                                           ) ;
    _tprintf ( _T ( "   dwExitCode                  : 0x%08X\n" ) ,
                stETDI.dwExitCode                               ) ;
}

/*//////////////////////////////////////////////////////////////////////
// Display's exit process events.
```

(continued)

```
///////////////////////////////////////////////////////////////////////*/
void DisplayExitProcessEvent ( EXIT_PROCESS_DEBUG_INFO & stEPDI )
{
    _tprintf ( _T ( "Exit Process Event         :\n" ) ) ;
    _tprintf ( _T ( "   dwExitCode              : 0x%08X\n" ) ,
               stEPDI.dwExitCode                             ) ;
}

/*//////////////////////////////////////////////////////////////////////
// Display's DLL load events.
///////////////////////////////////////////////////////////////////////*/
void DisplayDllLoadEvent ( HANDLE                   hProcess ,
                           LOAD_DLL_DEBUG_INFO & stLDDI     )
{
    _tprintf ( _T ( "DLL Load Event             :\n" ) ) ;
    _tprintf ( _T ( "   hFile                   : 0x%08X\n" ) ,
               stLDDI.hFile                                  ) ;
    _tprintf ( _T ( "   lpBaseOfDll             : 0x%08X\n" ) ,
               stLDDI.lpBaseOfDll                            ) ;
    _tprintf ( _T ( "   dwDebugInfoFileOffset   : 0x%08X\n" ) ,
               stLDDI.dwDebugInfoFileOffset                  ) ;
    _tprintf ( _T ( "   nDebugInfoSize          : 0x%08X\n" ) ,
               stLDDI.nDebugInfoSize                         ) ;
    _tprintf ( _T ( "   lpImageName             : 0x%08X\n" ) ,
               stLDDI.lpImageName                            ) ;
    _tprintf ( _T ( "   fUnicode                : 0x%08X\n" ) ,
               stLDDI.fUnicode                               ) ;

    static bool bSeenNTDLL = false ;
    TCHAR szDLLName[ MAX_PATH ] ;

    // NTDLL.DLL is special. On W2K, the lpImageName is NULL and
    // on XP, the name just points to 'ntdll.dll' so I will fake the
    // load information.
    if ( false == bSeenNTDLL )
    {
        bSeenNTDLL = true ;
        UINT uiLen = GetWindowsDirectory ( szDLLName , MAX_PATH ) ;
        ASSERT ( uiLen > 0 ) ;
        if ( uiLen > 0 )
        {
            _tcscpy ( szDLLName + uiLen , _T ( "\\NTDLL.DLL" ) ) ;
        }
        else
        {
            _tcscpy ( szDLLName , _T ( "GetWindowsDirectory FAILED!" ));
        }
    }
    else
    {
        szDLLName[ 0 ] = _T ( '\0' ) ;

        // The value in lpImageName is a pointer to the full path
```

```
    // and name of the DLL being loaded. The address is in the
    // debuggee address space.
    LPCVOID lpPtr = 0 ;
    DWORD dwBytesRead = 0 ;
    BOOL bRet = FALSE ;

    bRet = ReadProcessMemory ( hProcess          ,
                               stLDDI.lpImageName ,
                               &lpPtr            ,
                               sizeof ( LPCVOID ) ,
                               &dwBytesRead       ) ;
    if ( TRUE == bRet )
    {
        // If the name in the debuggee is UNICODE, I can read it
        // directly into the szDLLName variable as all this code
        // is UNICODE.
        if ( TRUE == stLDDI.fUnicode )
        {
            // Occasionally, you can't read the whole buffer that
            // contains the name so I need to step down until
            // I can be sure there's no name at all.
            DWORD dwSize = MAX_PATH  * sizeof ( TCHAR ) ;
            do
            {

                bRet = ReadProcessMemory ( hProcess       ,
                                           lpPtr          ,
                                           szDLLName      ,
                                           dwSize         ,
                                           &dwBytesRead    ) ;
                dwSize = dwSize - 20 ;
            }
            while ( ( FALSE == bRet ) && ( dwSize > 20 ) ) ;
        }
        else
        {
            // Read the ANSI string and convert it to UNICODE.
            char szAnsiName[ MAX_PATH ] ;
            DWORD dwAnsiSize = MAX_PATH ;

            do
            {
                bRet = ReadProcessMemory ( hProcess       ,
                                           lpPtr          ,
                                           szAnsiName     ,
                                           dwAnsiSize     ,
                                           &dwBytesRead    ) ;
                dwAnsiSize = dwAnsiSize - 20 ;
            } while ( ( FALSE == bRet ) && ( dwAnsiSize > 20 ) ) ;
            if ( TRUE == bRet )
            {
                MultiByteToWideChar ( CP_THREAD_ACP    ,
                                      0                ,
```

(continued)

```
                                            szAnsiName          ,
                                            -1                  ,
                                            szDLLName           ,
                                            MAX_PATH            ) ;
                }
            }
        }
    }
    if ( _T ( '\0' ) == szDLLName[ 0 ] )
    {
        // This DLL has some issues. Try to read it with
        // GetModuleHandleEx. While you'd think this would work for all
        // it only seems to work if the module can't be retrieved by
        // the above means. If you can't retrieve the DLL name with the
        // code above, you're actually looking at a rebased DLL.
        DWORD dwRet = GetModuleFileNameEx ( hProcess                    ,
                                            (HMODULE)stLDDI.
                                                        lpBaseOfDll     ,
                                            szDLLName                   ,
                                            MAX_PATH                    );
        ASSERT ( dwRet > 0 ) ;
        if ( 0 == dwRet )
        {
            szDLLName[ 0 ] = _T ( '\0' ) ;
        }
    }

    if ( _T ( '\0' ) != szDLLName[ 0 ] )
    {
        _tcsupr ( szDLLName ) ;
        _tprintf ( _T ( "   DLL name                  : %s\n" ) ,
                   szDLLName                                  ) ;
    }
    else
    {
        _tprintf ( _T ( "UNABLE TO READ DLL NAME!!\n" ) ) ;
    }
}

/*//////////////////////////////////////////////////////////////////////
// Display's DLL unload events.
//////////////////////////////////////////////////////////////////////*/
void DisplayDllUnLoadEvent ( UNLOAD_DLL_DEBUG_INFO & stULDDI )
{
    _tprintf ( _T ( "DLL Unload Event             :\n" ) ) ;
    _tprintf ( _T ( "   lpBaseOfDll               : 0x%08X\n" ) ,
               stULDDI.lpBaseOfDll                            ) ;
}

/*//////////////////////////////////////////////////////////////////////
// Display's OutputDebugString events.
//////////////////////////////////////////////////////////////////////*/
void DisplayODSEvent ( HANDLE                    hProcess ,
```

```
                        OUTPUT_DEBUG_STRING_INFO & stODSI     )
{
    _tprintf ( _T ( "OutputDebugString Event   :\n" ) ) ;
    _tprintf ( _T ( "    lpDebugStringData      : 0x%08X\n" ) ,
               stODSI.lpDebugStringData                      ) ;
    _tprintf ( _T ( "    fUnicode               : 0x%08X\n" ) ,
               stODSI.fUnicode                               ) ;
    _tprintf ( _T ( "    nDebugStringLength     : %d\n"     ) ,
               stODSI.nDebugStringLength                     ) ;
    _tprintf ( _T ( "    String                 : " ) ) ;

    TCHAR szFinalBuff[ 512 ] ;
    if ( stODSI.nDebugStringLength > 512 )
    {
        _tprintf ( _T ( "String to large!!\n" ) ) ;
        return ;
    }

    DWORD dwRead ;
    BOOL bRet ;

    // Interestingly enough, all OutputDebugString calls, no matter if
    // the application is full UNICODE or not always come in as ANSI
    // strings.
    if ( false == stODSI.fUnicode )
    {
        // Read the ANSI string.
        char szAnsiBuff[ 512 ] ;
        bRet = ReadProcessMemory ( hProcess                   ,
                                   stODSI.lpDebugStringData   ,
                                   szAnsiBuff                 ,
                                   stODSI.nDebugStringLength  ,
                                   &dwRead                    ) ;
        if ( TRUE == bRet )
        {
            MultiByteToWideChar ( CP_THREAD_ACP ,
                                  0             ,
                                  szAnsiBuff    ,
                                  -1            ,
                                  szFinalBuff   ,
                                  512           ) ;
        }
        else
        {
            szFinalBuff[ 0 ] = _T ( '\0' ) ;
        }
    }
    else
    {
        // Read the UNICODE string.
        bRet = ReadProcessMemory ( hProcess                       ,
                                   stODSI.lpDebugStringData       ,
                                   szFinalBuff                    ,
```

(continued)

```
                                    stODSI.nDebugStringLength *
                                              sizeof ( TCHAR )   ,
                                    &dwRead                        ) ;
        if ( FALSE == bRet )
        {
            szFinalBuff[ 0 ] = _T ( '\0' ) ;
        }
    }

    if ( _T ( '\0' ) != szFinalBuff[ 0 ] )
    {
        _tprintf ( _T ( "%s\n" ) , szFinalBuff ) ;
    }
    else
    {
        _tprintf ( _T ( "UNABLE TO READ ODS STRING!!\n" ) ) ;
    }
}

/*//////////////////////////////////////////////////////////////////////
// Display's exception events.
//////////////////////////////////////////////////////////////////////*/
void DisplayExceptionEvent ( EXCEPTION_DEBUG_INFO & stEDI )
{
    _tprintf ( _T ( "Exception Event              :\n" ) ) ;
    _tprintf ( _T ( "   dwFirstChance             : 0x%08X\n" ) ,
               stEDI.dwFirstChance                              ) ;
    _tprintf ( _T ( "   ExceptionCode             : 0x%08X\n" ) ,
               stEDI.ExceptionRecord.ExceptionCode              ) ;
    _tprintf ( _T ( "   ExceptionFlags            : 0x%08X\n" ) ,
               stEDI.ExceptionRecord.ExceptionFlags             ) ;
    _tprintf ( _T ( "   ExceptionRecord           : 0x%08X\n" ) ,
               stEDI.ExceptionRecord.ExceptionRecord            ) ;
    _tprintf ( _T ( "   ExceptionAddress          : 0x%08X\n" ) ,
               stEDI.ExceptionRecord.ExceptionAddress           ) ;
    _tprintf ( _T ( "   NumberParameters          : 0x%08X\n" ) ,
               stEDI.ExceptionRecord.NumberParameters           ) ;
}
```

WDBG: A Real Debugger

I thought the best way to show you how a debugger worked was to write one, so I did. Although WDBG might not replace the Visual Studio .NET or WinDBG debuggers any time soon, it certainly does nearly everything a debugger is supposed to do. WDBG is available with this book's sample files. If you look at Figure 4-3, you'll see WDBG debugging the CrashFinder program from Chapter 12. In the figure, CrashFinder is stopped at the third instance of a breakpoint I set on `GetProcAddress` in KERNEL32.DLL. The Memory window, in the upper right-hand corner, is showing the second parameter that CrashFinder passed to this particular instance of `GetProcAddress`, the string `InitializeCriticalSectionAndSpinCount`. As you look around Figure 4-3, you'll see that WDBG takes care of the business you'd expect a debugger to tend to, including showing registers, disassembling code, and showing the currently loaded modules and the currently running threads. The exciting window is the Call Stack window, which is shown in the middle-right section of Figure 4-3. Not only does WDBG show the call stack as you would expect, but it also fully supports all locals and structure expansion. What you don't see in the picture but what will become apparent when you first run WDBG is that WDBG also supports breakpoints, symbol enumeration and display in the Symbols window, and breaking the application to stop in the debugger.

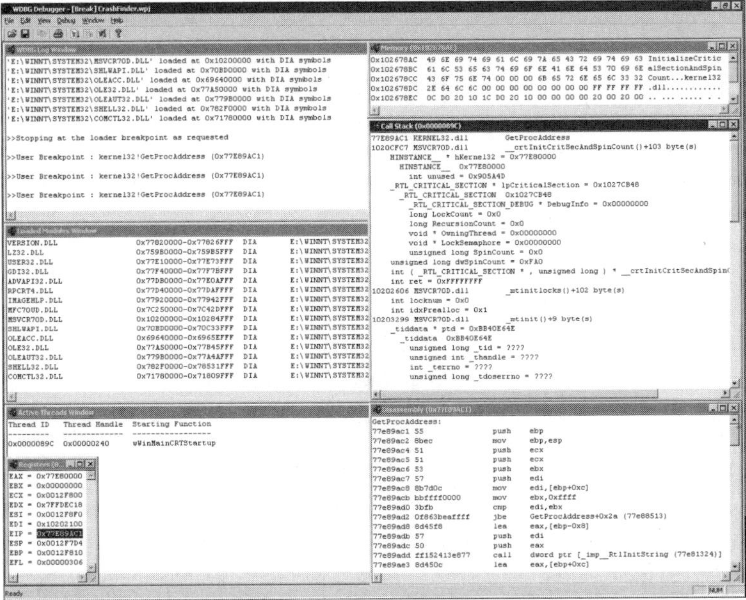

Figure 4-3 WDBG in action

Overall, I'm happy with WDBG because it's an excellent sample, and I'm proud that WDBG shows all the internals techniques that a debugger uses. Looking at the WDBG user interface (UI), however, you can see that I didn't spend a great deal of time fiddling with the UI portions. In fact, all the multiple-document interface (MDI) windows in WDBG are edit controls. That was intentional—I kept the UI simple because I didn't want UI details to distract you from the essential debugger code. I wrote the WDBG UI using the Microsoft Foundation Class (MFC) library, so if you're so inclined, you shouldn't have any trouble designing a spiffier UI.

Before moving into the specifics of debugging, let's take a closer look at WDBG. Table 4-2 lists all the main subsystems of WDBG and describes what they do. One of my intentions in creating WDBG was to define a neutral interface between the UI and the debug loop. With a neutral interface, if I wanted to make WDBG.EXE support remote debugging over a network, I'd just have to replace the local debugging DLLs.

Table 4-2 WDBG Main Subsystems

Subsystem	Description
WDBG.EXE	This module contains all the UI code. Additionally, all the breakpoint processing is taken care of here. Most of this debugger's work occurs in WDBGPROJDOC.CPP.
LOCALDEBUG.DLL	This module contains the debug loop. Because I wanted to be able to reuse this debug loop, the user code, WDBG.EXE in this case, passes a C++ class derived from `CDebugBaseUser` (defined in DEBUGINTERFACE.H) to the debug loop. The debug loop will call into that class when any of the debugging events occurs. The user's class is responsible for all synchronization. For WDBG.EXE, WDBGUSER.H and WDBGUSER.CPP contain the coordinating class. WDBG.EXE uses simple `SendMessage` synchronization. In other words, the debug thread sends a message to the UI thread and blocks until the UI thread returns. If the debugging event is one that required user input, the debug thread blocks after the send message on a synchronization event. Once the UI thread processes the Go command, it sets the synchronization event and the debug thread starts running again.
LOCALASSIST.DLL	This simple module is just a wrapper around the API functions for manipulating the debuggee's memory and registers. By using the interface defined in this module, WDBG.EXE and I386CPUHELP.DLL can instantly handle remote debugging just by replacing this module.
I386CPUHELP.DLL	This module is the IA32 (Pentium) helper module. Although this module is specific to Pentium processors, its interface, defined in CPUHELP.H, is CPU-independent. If you wanted to port WDBG to a different processor, this module is the only one you should have to replace. The disassembler in this module came from the Dr. Watson sample code that used to ship in the Platform SDK. Although the disassembler works, it appears to need updating to support the later Pentium CPU variants.

Reading and Writing Memory

Reading from a debuggee's memory is simple. `ReadProcessMemory` takes care of it for you. A debugger has full access to the debuggee if the debugger started it because the handle to the process returned by the `CREATE_PROCESS_DEBUG_EVENT` debug event has PROCESS_VM_READ and PROCESS_VM_WRITE access. If your debugger attaches to the process with DebugActiveProcess, you must have SeDebugPrivileges for the process you're attaching to get read and write access.

Before I can talk about writing to the debuggee's memory, I need to briefly explain an important concept: copy-on-write. When Windows loads an executable file, Windows shares as many mapped memory pages of that binary as possible with the different processes using it. If one of those processes is running under a debugger and one of those pages has a breakpoint written to it, the breakpoint obviously can't be present in all the processes sharing that page. As soon as any process running outside the debugger executed that code, it would crash with a breakpoint exception. To avoid that situation, the operating system sees that the page changed for a particular process and makes a copy of that page that is private to the process that had the breakpoint written to it. Thus, as soon as a process writes to a page, the operating system copies the page.

Writing to the debuggee memory is almost as straightforward as reading from it. Because the memory pages you want to write to might be marked as read-only, however, you first need to call VirtualQueryEx to get the current page protections. Once you have the protections, you can use the VirtualProtectEx API function to set the page to PAGE_EXECUTE_READWRITE so that you can write to it and Windows is prepared to do the copy-on-write. After you do the memory write, you'll need to set the page protection back to what it originally was. If you don't, the debuggee might accidentally write to the page and succeed when it should fail. If the original page protections were read-only, the debuggee's accidental write would lead to an access violation. By forgetting to set the page protection back, the accidental write wouldn't generate the exception and you'd have a case in which running under the debugger is different from running outside the debugger.

An interesting detail about the Win32 Debugging API is that the debugger is responsible for getting the string to output when an OUTPUT_DEBUG_STRING_EVENT comes through. The information passed to the debugger includes the location and the length of the string. When it receives this message, the debugger goes and reads the memory out of the debuggee. Since calls to OutputDebugString come through the Win32 Debugging API, which suspends all threads each time a debug event triggers, trace statements can easily change your application's behavior when running under a debugger. If your multithreading is correctly programmed, you can call OutputDebugString all you want without affecting your application. However, if you have bugs in your multithreading code, you can occasionally run into deadlocks from the subtle timing changes related to calling OutputDebugString.

Listing 4-2 shows how WDBG handles the OUTPUT_DEBUG_STRING_EVENT. Notice that the DBG_ReadProcessMemory function is the wrapper function around ReadProcessMemory from LOCALASSIST.DLL. Even though the Win32 Debugging API implies that you can receive both Unicode and ANSI strings as part of your OUTPUT_DEBUG_STRING_EVENT processing, up through Windows XP and Windows Server 2003, pass in only ANSI strings, even if the call comes from OutputDebugStringW.

```
static
DWORD OutputDebugStringEvent ( CDebugBaseUser *           pUserClass  ,
                               LPDEBUGGEEINFO             pData       ,
                               DWORD                      dwProcessId ,
                               DWORD                      dwThreadId  ,
                               OUTPUT_DEBUG_STRING_INFO & stODSI       )
{
    // OutputDebugString can dump huge numbers of characters so I'll
    // just allocate each time.
    DWORD dwTotalBuffSize = stODSI.nDebugStringLength ;

    if ( TRUE == stODSI.fUnicode )
    {
        dwTotalBuffSize *= 2 ;
    }

    PBYTE pODSData = new BYTE [ dwTotalBuffSize ] ;

    DWORD dwRead ;
    // Read the memory.
    BOOL bRet = DBG_ReadProcessMemory( pData->GetProcessHandle ( ) ,
                                       stODSI.lpDebugStringData    ,
                                       pODSData                    ,
                                       dwTotalBuffSize             ,
                                       &dwRead                      ) ;
    ASSERT ( TRUE == bRet ) ;
    if ( TRUE == bRet )
    {
        TCHAR * szUnicode = NULL ;
        TCHAR * szSelected = NULL ;
        if ( TRUE == stODSI.fUnicode )
        {
            szSelected = (TCHAR*)pODSData ;
        }
        else
        {
            szUnicode = new TCHAR [ stODSI.nDebugStringLength ] ;
            BSUAnsi2Wide ( (const char*)pODSData      ,
                           szUnicode                  ,
                           stODSI.nDebugStringLength  ) ;
```

Listing 4-2 OutputDebugStringEvent from PROCESSDEBUG-EVENTS.CPP

```
            int iLen = (int)strlen ( (const char*)pODSData ) ;
            iLen = MultiByteToWideChar ( CP_THREAD_ACP          ,
                                         0                      ,
                                         (LPCSTR)pODSData       ,
                                         iLen                   ,
                                         szUnicode              ,
                                         stODSI.nDebugStringLength ) ;

            szSelected = szUnicode ;
        }

        LPCTSTR szTemp =
                pUserClass->ConvertCRLF ( szSelected                ,
                                          stODSI.nDebugStringLength  );
        if ( NULL != szUnicode )
        {
            delete [] szUnicode ;
        }

        // Send the converted string on to the user class.
        pUserClass->OutputDebugStringEvent ( dwProcessId ,
                                             dwThreadId  ,
                                             szTemp       ) ;
        delete [] szTemp ;
    }
    delete [] pODSData ;
    return ( DBG_CONTINUE ) ;
}
```

Breakpoints and Single Stepping

Most engineers don't realize that debuggers use breakpoints extensively behind the scenes to allow the debugger to control the debuggee. Although you might not directly set any breakpoints, the debugger will set many to allow you to handle tasks such as stepping over a function call. The debugger also uses breakpoints when you choose to run to a specific source file line and stop. Finally, the debugger uses breakpoints to break into the debuggee on command (via the Debug Break menu option in WDBG, for example).

The concept of setting a breakpoint is simple. All you need to do is have a memory address where you want to set a breakpoint, save the opcode (the value) at that location, and write the breakpoint instruction into the address. On the Intel Pentium family, the breakpoint instruction mnemonic is `INT 3` or an opcode of `0xCC`, so you need to save only a single byte at the address you're setting the breakpoint. Other CPUs, such as the Intel Itanium, have different opcode sizes, so you would need to save more data at the address.

Listing 4-3 shows the code for the `SetBreakpoint` function. As you read through this code, keep in mind that the `DBG_*` functions are those that come out of LOCALASSIST.DLL and help isolate the various process manipulation routines, making it easier to add remote debugging to WDBG. The `SetBreakpoint` function illustrates the processing (described earlier in the chapter) necessary for changing memory protection when you're writing to it.

```
int CPUHELP_DLLINTERFACE __stdcall
    SetBreakpoint ( PDEBUGPACKET dp         ,
                    LPCVOID      ulAddr     ,
                    OPCODE *     pOpCode    )
{
    DWORD dwReadWrite = 0 ;
    BYTE bTempOp = BREAK_OPCODE ;
    BOOL bReadMem ;
    BOOL bWriteMem ;
    BOOL bFlush ;
    MEMORY_BASIC_INFORMATION mbi ;
    DWORD dwOldProtect ;

    ASSERT ( FALSE == IsBadReadPtr ( dp , sizeof ( DEBUGPACKET ) ) )  ;
    ASSERT ( FALSE == IsBadWritePtr ( pOpCode , sizeof ( OPCODE ) ) ) ;
    if ( ( TRUE == IsBadReadPtr ( dp , sizeof ( DEBUGPACKET ) ) ) ||
         ( TRUE == IsBadWritePtr ( pOpCode , sizeof ( OPCODE ) ) )    )
    {
        TRACE0 ( "SetBreakpoint : invalid parameters\n!" ) ;
        return ( FALSE ) ;
    }

    // Read the opcode at the location.
    bReadMem = DBG_ReadProcessMemory ( dp->hProcess    ,
                                       (LPCVOID)ulAddr ,
                                       &bTempOp        ,
                                       sizeof ( BYTE ) ,
                                       &dwReadWrite     ) ;
    ASSERT ( FALSE != bReadMem ) ;
    ASSERT ( sizeof ( BYTE ) == dwReadWrite ) ;
    if ( ( FALSE == bReadMem                  ) ||
         ( sizeof ( BYTE ) != dwReadWrite ) )
    {
        return ( FALSE ) ;
    }

    // Is this new breakpoint about to overwrite an existing
    // breakpoint opcode?
    if ( BREAK_OPCODE == bTempOp )
    {
        return ( -1 ) ;
    }
```

Listing 4-3 `SetBreakpoint` from I386CPUHELP.C

```
    // Get the page attributes for the debuggee.
    DBG_VirtualQueryEx ( dp->hProcess                          ,
                         (LPCVOID)ulAddr                       ,
                         &mbi                                  ,
                         sizeof ( MEMORY_BASIC_INFORMATION )  ) ;

    // Force the page to copy-on-write in the debuggee.
    if ( FALSE == DBG_VirtualProtectEx ( dp->hProcess           ,
                                         mbi.BaseAddress        ,
                                         mbi.RegionSize         ,
                                         PAGE_EXECUTE_READWRITE ,
                                         &mbi.Protect          ) )
    {
        ASSERT ( !"VirtualProtectEx failed!!" ) ;
        return ( FALSE ) ;
    }
     // Save the opcode I'm about to whack.
    *pOpCode = (void*)bTempOp ;

    bTempOp = BREAK_OPCODE ;
    dwReadWrite = 0 ;
    // The opcode was saved, so now set the breakpoint.
    bWriteMem = DBG_WriteProcessMemory ( dp->hProcess      ,
                                         (LPVOID)ulAddr    ,
                                         (LPVOID)&bTempOp  ,
                                         sizeof ( BYTE )   ,
                                         &dwReadWrite      ) ;
    ASSERT ( FALSE != bWriteMem ) ;
    ASSERT ( sizeof ( BYTE ) == dwReadWrite ) ;


    if ( ( FALSE == bWriteMem                  ) ||
         ( sizeof ( BYTE ) != dwReadWrite ) )
    {
        return ( FALSE ) ;
    }

    // Change the protection back to what it was before I blasted the
    // breakpoint in.
    VERIFY ( DBG_VirtualProtectEx ( dp->hProcess    ,
                                    mbi.BaseAddress ,
                                    mbi.RegionSize  ,
                                    mbi.Protect     ,
                                    &dwOldProtect    ) ) ;

    // Flush the instruction cache in case this memory was in the CPU
    // cache.
    bFlush = DBG_FlushInstructionCache ( dp->hProcess    ,
                                         (LPCVOID)ulAddr ,
                                         sizeof ( BYTE )  ) ;
    ASSERT ( TRUE == bFlush ) ;

    return ( TRUE ) ;
}
```

After you set the breakpoint, the CPU will execute it and will tell the debugger that an EXCEPTION_BREAKPOINT (0x80000003) occurred—that's where the fun begins. If it's a regular breakpoint, the debugger will locate and display the breakpoint location to the user. After the user decides to continue execution, the debugger has to do some work to restore the state of the program. Because the breakpoint overwrote a portion of memory, if you, as the debugger writer, were to just let the process continue, you would be executing code out of sequence and the debuggee would probably crash. What you need to do is move the current instruction pointer back to the breakpoint address and replace the breakpoint with the opcode you saved when you set the breakpoint. After restoring the opcode, you can continue executing.

There's only one small problem: How do you reset the breakpoint so that you can stop at that location again? If the CPU you're working on supports single-step execution, resetting the breakpoint is trivial. In single-step execution, the CPU executes a single instruction and generates another type of exception, EXCEPTION_SINGLE_STEP (0x80000004). Fortunately, all CPUs that Win32 runs on support single-step execution. For the Intel Pentium family, setting single-step execution requires that you set bit 8 on the flags register. The Intel reference manual calls this bit the TF, or Trap Flag. The following code shows the SetSingleStep function and the work needed to set the TF. After replacing the breakpoint with the original opcode, the debugger marks its internal state to reflect that it's expecting a single-step exception, sets the CPU into single-step execution, and then continues the process.

```
// SetSingleStep from i386CPUHelp.C
BOOL CPUHELP_DLLINTERFACE __stdcall
    SetSingleStep ( PDEBUGPACKET dp )
{
    BOOL bSetContext ;
    ASSERT ( FALSE == IsBadReadPtr ( dp , sizeof ( DEBUGPACKET ) ) )  ;
    if ( TRUE == IsBadReadPtr ( dp , sizeof ( DEBUGPACKET ) ) )
    {
        TRACE0 ( "SetSingleStep : invalid parameters\n!" ) ;
        return ( FALSE ) ;
    }

    // For the i386, just set the TF bit.
    dp->context.EFlags |= TF_BIT ;
    bSetContext = DBG_SetThreadContext ( dp->hThread , &dp->context ) ;
    ASSERT ( FALSE != bSetContext ) ;
    return ( bSetContext ) ;
}
```

After the debugger releases the process by calling ContinueDebugEvent, the process immediately generates a single-step exception after the single instruction executes. The debugger checks its internal state to verify that it was expecting a single-step exception. Because the debugger was expecting a single-step exception, it knows that a breakpoint needs to be reset. The single step caused the instruction pointer to move past the original breakpoint location. Therefore, the debugger can set the breakpoint opcode back at the original breakpoint location. The operating system automatically clears the TF each time the `EXCEPTION_SINGLE_STEP` exception occurs, so there's no need for the debugger to clear it. After setting the breakpoint, the debugger releases the debuggee to continue running.

If you want to see all the breakpoint processing in action, look for the `CWDBGProjDoc::HandleBreakpoint` method in the WDBGPROJDOC.CPP file with this book's sample files. I defined the breakpoints themselves in BREAKPOINT.H and BREAKPOINT.CPP, and those files contain a couple of classes that handle different styles of breakpoints. I set up the WDBG Breakpoints dialog box so that you could set breakpoints as the debuggee is running, just as you do in the Visual Studio .NET debugger. Being able to set breakpoints on the fly means that you need to keep careful track of the debuggee state and the breakpoint states. See the `CBreakpointsDlg::OnOK` method in BREAKPOINTSDLG.CPP, which is with this book's sample files, for details on how I handle enabling and disabling breakpoints, depending on what the debuggee state is.

One of the neater features I implemented in WDBG was the Debug Break menu option. This option means that you can break into the debugger at any time while the debuggee is running. In the first edition of this book, I went through a huge explanation of a technique in which I suspended all the debuggee threads, set a one-shot breakpoint in each thread, and to ensure the breakpoints executed, posted `WM_NULL` messages to the threads. (To find out more about one-shot breakpoints, see the section "Step Into, Step Over, and Step Out" later in this chapter.) It took quite a bit of code to get it working, and it generally worked fairly well. However, in the one case in which it didn't work, all the debuggee's threads were deadlocked on kernel-mode objects. Since the threads were suspended in kernel mode, there was no way I could bump them back down to user mode. I had to do all this work and live with the limitation of my implementation because WDBG needed to run on Windows 98 and Microsoft Windows Me as well as on Windows NT–based operating systems.

Since I dropped support for Windows 98 and Windows Me, implementing the Debug Break menu became absolutely trivial and always works. The magic is the wonderful function `CreateRemoteThread`, which isn't available on Windows 98 or Windows Me but is available on Windows 2000 and later. Another function that achieves the same effect as `CreateRemoteThread` but is available only on Windows XP and later is `DebugBreakProcess`. As you can see from the following code, the implementation of the function that does the work is simple. When the remote thread executes the `DebugBreak` call, I just treat the resulting breakpoint exception as if it were a user-defined breakpoint in the exception handling code.

```
HANDLE LOCALASSIST_DLLINTERFACE __stdcall
    DBG_CreateRemoteBreakpointThread ( HANDLE   hProcess   ,
                                       LPDWORD  lpThreadId  )
{
    HANDLE hRet = CreateRemoteThread ( hProcess              ,
                                       NULL                  ,
                                       0                     ,
                    (LPTHREAD_START_ROUTINE)DebugBreak       ,
                                       0                     ,
                                       0                     ,
                                       lpThreadId             ) ;
    return ( hRet ) ;
}
```

Although it might appear risky to pop a thread into a debuggee, I felt it was safe enough, especially because this is the exact same technique that WinDBG uses to affect its Debug Break menu. However, I do want to mention that there are side effects from calling CreateRemoteThread. When a thread starts in a process, the contract it has with the operating system is that it will call each DllMain for all loaded DLLs that haven't called DisableThreadLibraryCalls. Correspondingly, when the thread ends, all those DllMain functions that were called with the DLL_THREAD_ATTACH notification will be called with the DLL_THREAD_DETACH notification as well. This all means that if you have a bug in one of your DllMain functions, the CreateRemoteThread approach of stopping the debuggee could exacerbate the trouble. The odds are slim, but it's something to keep in mind.

Symbol Tables, Symbol Engines, and Stack Walking

The real black art to writing a debugger involves symbol engines, the code that manipulates symbol tables. Debugging at the straight assembly-language level is interesting for the first couple of minutes you have to do it, but it gets old quickly. Symbol tables, also called debugging symbols, are what turn hexadecimal numbers into source file lines, function names, and variable names. Symbol tables also contain the type information your program uses. This type information allows the debugger to take raw data and display it as the structures and variables you defined in your program.

Dealing with modern symbol tables is difficult. The most commonly used symbol table format, Program Database (PDB), finally has a documented interface, but the interface is quite challenging to work with and doesn't yet support extremely useful functionality such as stack walking. Fortunately, DBGHELP.DLL supplies enough of a wrapper to make things easier, as I'll discuss in a moment.

The Different Symbol Formats

Before diving into a discussion of accessing symbol tables, I need to go over the various symbol formats available. I've found that people are a little confused about what the different formats are and what they offer, so I want to set the record straight.

Common Object File Format (COFF) was one of the original symbol table formats and was introduced with Windows NT 3.1, the first version of Windows NT. The Windows NT team was experienced with operating system development and wanted to bootstrap Windows NT with some existing tools. The COFF format is part of a larger specification that different UNIX vendors followed to try to make common binary file formats. Visual C++ 6 was the last version of the Microsoft compilers to support COFF.

The C7, or CodeView, format first appeared as part of Microsoft C/C++ version 7 back in the MS-DOS days. If you're an old-timer, you might have heard the name CodeView before—CodeView was the name of the old Microsoft debugger. The C7 format has been updated to support the Win32 operating systems, and Visual C++ 6 is the last compiler to support this symbol format. The C7 format was self-contained in the executable module because the linker appends the symbolic information to the binary after it links. Attaching the symbol information to your binary means that your debugging binaries can be quite large; symbol information can easily be larger than your binary file.

The PDB (Program Database) format is the most common symbol format used today, and Visual C++, Visual C#, and Visual Basic .NET support it. As everyone with more than five minutes of experience has seen, PDB files store the symbol information separately from the binary. To see whether a binary contains PDB symbol information, run the DUMPBIN program that comes with Visual Studio .NET against the binary. Specifying the `/HEADERS` command-line option to DUMPBIN will dump out the Portable Executable (PE) file header information. Part of the header information contains the Debug Directories. If the information listed says the format is `cv` with the format as `RSDS`, it's a Visual Studio .NET–compiled binary with PDB files.

DBG files are unique because, unlike the other symbol formats, the linker doesn't create them. A DBG file is basically just a file that holds other types of debug symbols, such as COFF or C7. DBG files use some of the same structures defined by the PE file format—the format used by Win32 executables. REBASE.EXE produces DBG files by stripping the COFF or C7 debugging information out of a module. There's no need to run REBASE.EXE on a module that was built using PDB files because the symbols are already separate from the module. Microsoft distributes DBG files with the operating system debugging symbols because, for debuggers prior to Visual Studio .NET and the latest WinDBG, they're needed to find the appropriate PDB file for operating system binaries.

Accessing Symbol Information

The traditional way of handling symbols has been through the DBGHELP.DLL supplied by Microsoft. Previously, DBGHELP.DLL supported only public information, which basically amounts to function names and rudimentary global variables. However, that's more than enough information to write some excellent utilities. In the first edition of this book, I spent a few pages talking about how to get DBGHELP.DLL to load your symbols, but with the latest releases, DBGHELP.DLL has improved dramatically and it just works. There's no need for me to discuss what's already in the documentation about how to use the DBGHELP.DLL symbol functions, so I'll just refer you to the MSDN documentation. An updated DBGHELP.DLL is always distributed with Debugging Tools for Windows, so you should check *www.microsoft.com/ddk/debugging* occasionally to get the latest and greatest version.

When the first Visual Studio .NET betas came out, I was excited because Microsoft was supposed to provide an interface to PDB files. At first glance, I thought the Debug Interface Access (DIA) SDK was going to be quite a help to us folks who were interested in developing tools that could access local variables and parameters as well as provide a means for expanding structures and arrays—in short, a complete solution to our symbol needs.

When I first started the second edition of this book, I set out to write a symbol engine using DIA that came with Visual Studio .NET 2002. The first issue I encountered was that the DIA symbol engine is essentially nothing more than a PDB reader. That's no big deal, but it meant I was going to have to handle a good deal of the higher-level management functions myself. DIA does what it's supposed to do; I was just assuming that it might do more. I sat down and started to work and noticed that there didn't seem to be any support for walking the stack with DIA. The `StackWalk64` API, which I discuss later, expects some special functions to help it access various symbol information necessary to walk the stack. Unfortunately, it appears that DIA at the time didn't expose all the necessary information. For example, one piece of information the `StackWalk64` function needs is the frame pointer omission (FPO).

It looks the like the Visual Studio .NET 2003 release of DIA does support interfaces that have to do with stack walking, but it was given interfaces only in the IDL and there is very little documentation on how to actually use the new code. With this new support for stack walking, I thought I should still go on using DIA because it seemed to be the wave of the future even though DIA looked quite daunting. As I continued designing and developing, I ran into the biggest problem of all: the DIA interface is pseudo COM-based in that it looks like COM but is quite unwieldy, so you get all the extreme pain of COM with none of the benefits.

As I started working on some of the basic code, I ran into the interface that best demonstrates why good COM design is critical. The symbol interface, `IDiaSymbol`, has 95 documented methods. Unfortunately, nearly everything in DIA is a symbol. In fact, there are 31 unique symbol types in the `SymTagEnum` enumeration. What DIA calls symbols are things like array types or labels, not actual values. The huge problem with the `IDiaSymbol` interface is that all the types support only a few of the 95 interfaces. For example, a base type, the most rudimentary type for a symbol that describes items like integers, supports only two interfaces—one to get the basic type enumeration itself and one to get the length of the type. The rest of the interfaces simply return `E_NOTIMPLEMENTED`. Having a super-flat hierarchy in which a single interface does multiple duty is fine when the shared items are relatively small, but with the number of different types in DIA, it just leads to a ton of coding and gyrations that are, in my opinion, unnecessary. The types DIA uses are hierarchical, and the interface should have been designed as such. Instead of using a single interface for everything, the types should have been defined as their own interfaces, because they would be much easier to work with. As I started designing my wrapper on top of DIA, I quickly realized that I was going to be writing tons of code to put a hierarchy on top of DIA that should already have been in the interface.

I started to realize that I was about to reinvent the wheel while working on my DIA-based symbol engine, and I knew I was in trouble. The wheel I was looking at designing in this case was the DBGHELP.DLL symbol engine. I'd already looked at the DBGHELP.H header and figured out that DBGHELP.DLL from the latest release of WinDBG was supporting some form of local and parameter enumeration along with structure and array expansion. The only problem was that large portions of the local and parameter enumeration appeared to be undocumented. Fortunately, as I continued grinding through the DIA header files, I started to see some patterns in the return values in the DBGHELP.DLL code and, sure enough, they matched values I'd been seeing in one of the DIA SDK header files, CVCONST.H. That was a big breakthrough because it allowed me to get started using the DBGHELP.DLL local symbol information. It looks like DBGHELP.DLL is a wrapper on top of DIA and is quite a bit easier to deal with than raw DIA, so I decided to build on top of DBGHELP.DLL instead of completely rewriting it on my own.

The code I ended up writing is all in the SymbolEngine project, which is with this book's sample files. That code provides the local symbols for WDBG as well as for the SUPERASSERT dialog box. In general, the SymbolEngine project is a wrapper around the DBGHELP.DLL symbol engine functions to make it easier to use and extend the symbol handling. To avoid problems with exporting classes out of DLLs, I made SymbolEngine a static library. As you look at the SymbolEngine implementation, you might notice several builds that end in _BSU. Those are special builds of SymbolEngine for BUGSLAYERUTIL.DLL, because BUGSLAYERUTIL.DLL is used as part of SUPERASSERT. I didn't want it to use SUPERASSERT for its assertions, which would cause grief with reentrant code, so don't link against those versions. You might also notice in my use of the DBGHELP.DLL symbol engine that I always used the versions of the functions that end in 64. Although the documentation says that the non-64-bit functions are supposed to be just wrappers around the 64-bit functions, I found in a few cases that calling the 64-bit versions directly worked better than the wrappers. Consequently, that's why I always use them. You might want to pull up the SymbolEngine project because there's way too much code involved to print it here in the book and follow along with this discussion. I want to explain how to use my symbol enumeration as well as touch on a few of the implementation high points. Here is one last point about my SymbolEngine project: the DBGHELP.DLL symbol engine supports only ANSI characters. My SymbolEngine project is partially Unicode aware, so I didn't have to constantly convert every DBGHELP.DLL string into Unicode when using SymbolEngine. As I was working with it, I widened ANSI parameters to Unicode parameters as I needed them. Not everything has been converted over, but enough has to handle most uses.

The basic algorithm for enumerating the locals is shown in the following code. As you can see, it's rather simple. In the pseudocode, I used actual DBGHELP.DLL function names.

```
STACKFRAME64 stFrame ;
CONTEXT      stCtx   ;

Fill out stFrame

GetThreadContext ( hThread , &stCtx ) ;

while ( TRUE == StackWalk ( . . . &stFrame . . . ) )
{
    // Set the context information to indicate which locals you want to
    // enumerate.
    SymSetContext ( hProcess , &stFrame , &stCtx ) ;

    // Enumerate the locals.
    SymEnumSymbols ( hProcess , // Value passed to SymInitialize.
                     0        , // DLL base, set to zero to look across DLLs.
                     NULL     , // RegExp mask to search for, NULL==all.
                     EnumFunc , // The callback function.
                     NULL      ); // User context passed to callback.
}
```

The callback function passed to `SymEnumSymbols` gets a `SYMBOL_INFO` structure, as shown in the following code. If all you want is basic information for the symbol, such as the address and its name, the `SYMBOL_INFO` structure is all you need. Additionally, the `Flags` field will tell you whether the symbol is a local or a parameter.

```
typedef struct _SYMBOL_INFO {
    ULONG       SizeOfStruct;
    ULONG       TypeIndex;
    ULONG64     Reserved[2];
    ULONG       Reserved2;
    ULONG       Size;
    ULONG64     ModBase;
    ULONG       Flags;
    ULONG64     Value;
    ULONG64     Address;
    ULONG       Register;
    ULONG       Scope;
    ULONG       Tag;
    ULONG       NameLen;
    ULONG       MaxNameLen;
    CHAR        Name[1];
} SYMBOL_INFO, *PSYMBOL_INFO;
```

As with most things in computers, the difference between the minimal and what you want is pretty large, which is why there's so much code in my SymbolEngine project. I wanted functionality that would enumerate the locals but show me the types and values in the same way Visual Studio .NET does. As you can see from Figure 4-3 and the SUPERASSERT screen shots in Chapter 3, I was able to accomplish that.

Using my symbol enumeration code is quite simple. First define a function with the prototype shown in the next bit of code. This function is called back on each variable decoding. The string parameters are the completely expanded type, the variable name (if appropriate), and the value for the particular variable. The indent parameter tells you how far indented the value is compared with previous values. For example, if you have a local structure on the stack with two member fields and you told my enumeration code to expand up to three levels, your callback function would be called three times for the structure. The first call would be for the structure variable name and address with an indent level of zero. Each member variable would get its own callback with an indent level of one. And there you have your three callbacks.

```
typedef BOOL (CALLBACK *PENUM_LOCAL_VARS_CALLBACK)
                                    ( DWORD64  dwAddr       ,
                                      LPCTSTR  szType       ,
                                      LPCTSTR  szName       ,
                                      LPCTSTR  szValue      ,
                                      int      iIndentLevel ,
                                      PVOID    pContext      ) ;
```

To enumerate the locals in the middle of your stack walk, you simply call the EnumLocalVariables method; it takes care of setting the appropriate context and doing the symbol enumeration for you. The EnumLocalVariables prototype is shown in the following code. The first parameter is to your callback function. The second and third parameters tell the local enumeration code how much to expand and whether you want arrays to be expanded. As you can imagine, the more you expand, the slower the code executes. Additionally, expanding arrays can be very expensive because there's no way of telling how many elements appear in an array. The good news is that my expansion code does the right thing when it sees char * or wchar_t * arrays and doesn't expand each character, but expands the string directly. The fourth parameter is the memory read function that you pass to StackWalk. If you pass NULL, my enumeration code will use ReadProcessMemory. The rest of the parameters are self-explanatory.

```
BOOL EnumLocalVariables
              ( PENUM_LOCAL_VARS_CALLBACK        pCallback      ,
                int                              iExpandLevel   ,
                BOOL                             bExpandArrays  ,
                PREAD_PROCESS_MEMORY_ROUTINE64 pReadMem         ,
                LPSTACKFRAME64                   pFrame         ,
                CONTEXT *                        pContext       ,
                PVOID                            pUserContext    ) ;
```

To see the local enumeration code in action, your best bet is to start with the SymLookup test program in the SymbolEngine\Tests\SymLookup directory, which is with this book's sample files. SymLookup is small enough to enable you to see what's going on. It also shows every possible type of variable generated by the C++ compiler so that you can see how the different variables expand.

The implementation for all the local expansion is in three source files. SYMBOLENGINE.CPP contains the higher-level functions for decoding variables and expanding arrays. All the type decoding takes place in TYPEDECODING.CPP, and all the value decoding is in VALUEDECODING.CPP. When you read over the code, keep in mind *Captain Recursion*! (When I was in college, the professor teaching Computer Science 101 came into class dressed as Captain Recursion, wearing tights and a cape, to teach us all about recursion. It was a fairly scary sight, but I certainly learned all about recursion in one easy lesson.) The way symbols are decoded is much like they are stored in memory. Figure 4-4 shows an example of what gyrations the symbol expansion goes through when expanding a pointer to a structure. The SymTag* values are those types defined as the tag values according to CVCONST.H. The SymTagData value is the type that indicates that the subsequent recursion will be a data type.

The basic rules are that you continue to recurse down until you hit a type of some kind. Various types such as user-defined types (UDTs) and classes have child classes, so you always need to check for children.

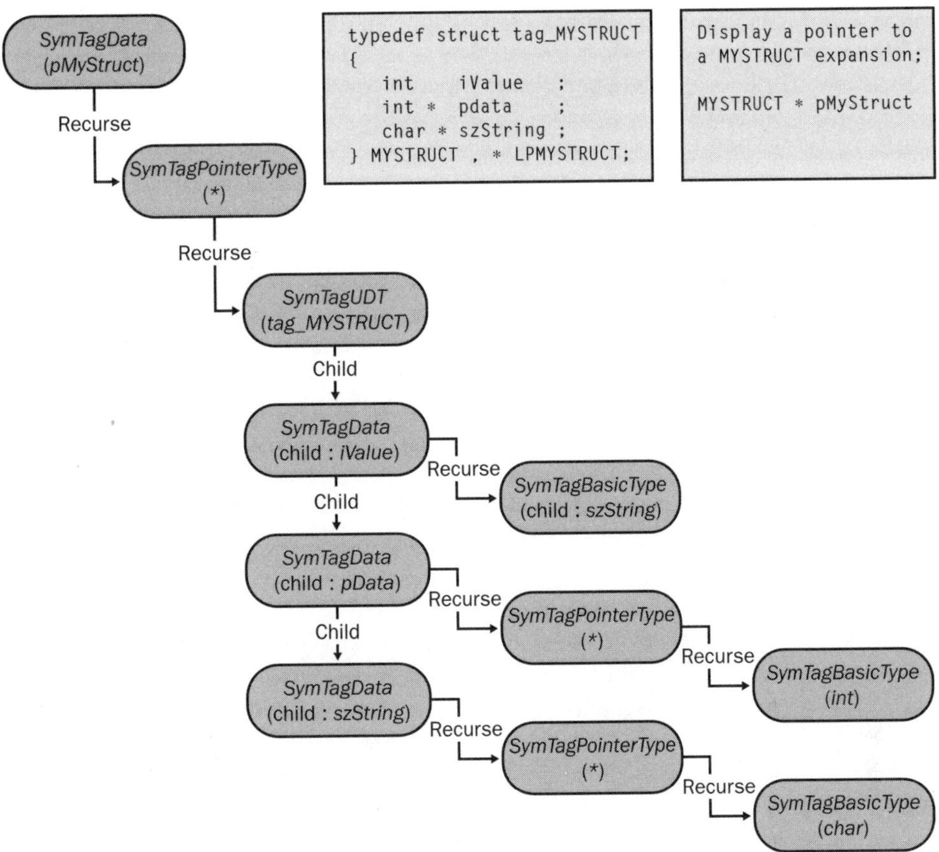

Figure 4-4 An example symbol expansion

Although I went into the development of the DBGHELP.DLL symbol engine thinking it was going to be relatively straightforward, I found Robert Burns was right: "The best laid plans of mice and men oft gang agley." Of all the code in this book, implementing SymbolEngine and getting it working correctly took far longer than anything else. As I had no clear picture of what symbol types derive down to, it took quite a bit of trial and error to eventually get everything working. The biggest lesson I learned is that even when you think you completely understand something, the proof is in the implementation.

Walking the Stack

Earlier I alluded to the fact that DBGHELP.DLL has the StackWalk64 API function, so we don't have to write our own stack walking code. StackWalk64 is straightforward and takes care of all your stack walking needs. WDBG uses the StackWalk64 API function, just as the WinDBG debugger does. The only snag you might encounter is that the documentation isn't explicit about what needs to be set in the STACKFRAME64 structure. The code here shows you the exact fields that need to be filled out in the STACKFRAME64 structure.

```
// InitializeStackFrameWithContext from i368CPUHelp.C.
BOOL CPUHELP_DLLINTERFACE __stdcall
    InitializeStackFrameWithContext ( STACKFRAME64 * pStack ,
                                      CONTEXT *      pCtx    )
{
    ASSERT ( FALSE == IsBadReadPtr ( pCtx , sizeof ( CONTEXT ) ) ) ;
    ASSERT ( FALSE == IsBadWritePtr ( pStack , sizeof ( STACKFRAME64) ));
    if ( ( TRUE == IsBadReadPtr ( pCtx , sizeof ( CONTEXT ) )      ) ||
         ( TRUE == IsBadWritePtr ( pStack , sizeof ( STACKFRAME ) ) )  )
    {
        return ( FALSE ) ;
    }

    pStack->AddrPC.Offset       = pCtx->Eip ;
    pStack->AddrPC.Mode         = AddrModeFlat    ;
    pStack->AddrStack.Offset    = pCtx->Esp ;
    pStack->AddrStack.Mode      = AddrModeFlat    ;
    pStack->AddrFrame.Offset    = pCtx->Ebp ;
    pStack->AddrFrame.Mode      = AddrModeFlat    ;

    return ( TRUE ) ;
}
```

StackWalk64 does such a good job of taking care of the details that you might not be aware that stack walking can be difficult with optimized code. The reason for the difficulty is that the compiler can optimize away the stack frame, the place where the code pushes stack entries, for some functions. The Visual C++ compiler is aggressive when it does the optimization, and if it can use the stack frame register as a scratch register, it will. To facilitate walking the stack in such situations, the compiler generates FPO data. The FPO data is a table of information that StackWalk64 uses to figure out how to handle those functions missing a normal stack frame. I wanted to mention FPO because occasionally you'll see references to it on MSDN and in various debuggers. If you're curious, WINNT.H contains the FPO data structures.

Step Into, Step Over, and Step Out

Now that I've described breakpoints and the symbol engine, I want to explain how debuggers implement the excellent Step Into, Step Over, and Step Out functionality. I didn't implement these features in WDBG because I wanted to concentrate on the core portions of the debugger. Step Into, Step Over, and Step Out require source and disassembly views that allow you to keep track of the current executing line or instruction. After you read the discussion in this section, you'll see that the core architecture of WDBG has the infrastructure you need to wire these features in and that adding these features is mostly an exercise in UI programming. Step Into, Step Over, and Step Out all work with one-shot breakpoints, which are breakpoints that the debugger discards after the breakpoints trigger.

Step Into works differently depending on whether you're debugging at the source level or the disassembly level. When debugging at the source level, the debugger must rely on one-shot breakpoints because a single high-level language line translates into one or more assembly language lines. If you set the CPU into single-step mode, you would be single-stepping individual instructions, not the source lines.

At the source level, the debugger knows the source line you're on. When you execute the debugger's Step Into command, the debugger uses the symbol engine to look up the address of the next line to execute. The debugger will do a partial disassembly at the next line address to see whether the line is a call instruction. If the line is a call instruction, the debugger will set a one-shot breakpoint on the first address of the function the debuggee is about to call. If the next line address isn't a call instruction, the debugger sets a one-shot breakpoint there. After setting the one-shot breakpoint, the debugger will release the debuggee so that it runs to the freshly set one-shot breakpoint. When the one-shot breakpoint triggers, the debugger will replace the opcode at the one-shot location and free any memory associated with the one-shot breakpoint. If the user is working at the disassembly level, Step Into is much easier to implement because the debugger will just force the CPU into single-step execution.

Step Over is similar to Step Into in that the debugger must look up the next line in the symbol engine and does the partial disassembly at the line address. The difference is that in Step Over, the debugger will set a one-shot breakpoint after the call instruction if the line is a call.

The Step Out operation is in some ways the simplest of the three. When the user selects the Step Out command, the debugger walks the stack to find the return address for the current function and sets a one-shot breakpoint on that address.

The processing for Step Into, Step Over, and Step Out seems straightforward, but there's one small twist that you need to consider. If you write your debugger to handle Step Into, Step Over, and Step Out, what are you going to do if you've set the one-shot breakpoint for those cases and a regular breakpoint triggers before the one-shot breakpoint? As a debugger writer, you have two choices. The first is to leave your one-shot breakpoints alone so that they trigger. The other option is to remove your one-shot breakpoint when the debugger notifies you that a regular breakpoint triggered. The latter option is what the Visual Studio .NET debugger does.

Either way of handling this case is correct, but by removing the one-shot breakpoint for Step Into, Step Over, and Step Out, you avoid user confusion. If you allow the one-shot breakpoint to trigger after the normal breakpoint, the user can easily be left wondering why the debugger stopped at an odd location.

So You Want to Write Your Own Debugger

Over the years, I've been amazed at the number of engineers who are interested in writing debuggers. I'm not amazed at why they want to do it since I've lived the debugger writer's life. We got interested in computers and software in the first place because we wanted to know how they worked, and debuggers are the magic looking glass that lets you see anything and everything about them. Consequently, I've received quite a bit of mail asking me what it takes to write a debugger and for advice on how to proceed. Part of my motivation for writing WDBG was to finally get a full example out for engineers to see how debuggers work.

The first step you need to take, after examining WDBG, is to get Jonathan Rosenberg's excellent book *How Debuggers Work* (Wiley, 1996). Although Jonathan's book doesn't present the code for a debugger, it's a wonderful introduction to and discussion about the real-world issues that you'll have to deal with when writing a debugger. Very few engineers have ever written a debugger, so it really helps to get a handle on the issues first.

You'll need to become intimately familiar with the PE file format and the particular CPU you're working on. You need to read Matt Pietrek's definitive articles on the PE file format in the February and March 2002 editions of *MSDN Magazine*. You can learn more about the CPU from the Intel CPU manuals available at *www.intel.com*.

Before you tackle a full debugger, you should probably write a disassembler. Writing a disassembler will not only teach you a great deal about the CPU, but it will also result in code you can use in the debugger. The disassembler in WDBG is read-only code. In other words, only the developer who wrote it can read it. Strive to make your disassembler maintainable and extensible. I've done a decent amount of assembly-language programming in the past, but it wasn't until I wrote my own disassembler that I really learned assembly language inside and out.

If you do want to write your own disassembler, the first place to start is with the Intel reference manuals, which you can download from Intel directly. They have all the information you need about the instructions and their opcodes. Additionally, in the back of Volume 2 is the complete opcode map, which is what you need to know to turn a number into an instruction. The source code to a few disassemblers is floating around the Internet. Before you embark on your writing, you might want to look at some of those disassemblers to get an idea of how others have handled problems.

What's Next for WDBG?

As it stands, WDBG does what it's supposed to do. However, you could improve it in plenty of ways. The following list should give you some ideas about what you can do to enhance WDBG if you're interested. If you do extend WDBG, I'd like to hear about it. In addition, as I mentioned in Chapter 1, examples of your own code are wonderful props to bring to a job interview. If you do add a significant feature to WDBG, you should show it off!

- The WDBG UI is just enough to get by. The first improvement you could undertake is to implement a better one. All the information is there; you just need to design better ways of displaying it.
- WDBG supports only simple location breakpoints. BREAKPOINT.H and BREAKPOINT.CPP are ready for you to add interesting kinds of breakpoints, such as skip count breakpoints (execute the breakpoint a specific number of times before stopping) or expression breakpoints (break only if an expression is true). Make sure you derive your new breakpoints from `CLocationBP` so that you get the serialization code and you don't have to change anything in WDBG.
- Add the ability to detach from processes when running under Windows XP, Windows Server 2003, and later versions of operating systems.
- With a little work, you should be able to extend WDBG to support multiple process debugging. Most of the interfaces are set up to work on a process identification scheme, so you would just need to track which process you're working on during a debug notification.

- The WDBG interface is set up to allow you to drop in remote debugging and different CPUs and still have the main UI work the same. Write the remote debugging DLLs and extend WDBG to allow the user to choose whether to debug on the local machine or on a remote machine.
- You could always write a better disassembler.
- The SymbolEngine code simply dumps the decoded symbols to a callback, and you have to set the amount of expansion when you first call `EnumLocalVariables`. If you want to mimic something like the Visual Studio .NET Watch window, you'll need to extend the local enumeration to return memory blobs that you can expand on the fly. You won't need to change anything in the SymbolEngine internals, just the higher-level code in SYMBOLENGINE.CPP that controls the enumeration. If you get this written, you might want to look at extending SUPERASSERT so that you can expand symbols on the fly.
- Right now SymbolEngine concentrates on expanding locals based on a context scope. Take a look at expanding SymbolEngine to allow you to enumerate global variables as well. The work is nearly all done; all you'll need to do is write a method that does everything `EnumLocalVariables` does except call `SymSetContext` with a `NULL` stack.

Summary

This chapter was an overview of what debuggers do and how they do it. By learning about your tools, you're better able to maximize their usage. The core Win32 Debugging API was presented, and some of the supporting systems that debuggers use, such as the symbol engine, were covered. You also learned about some of the other debuggers—besides the Visual Studio .NET debugger—that are available. Finally, the WDBG example provided a complete debugger sample that illustrates exactly how debuggers work.

If you had never seen how debuggers operate at this level before, you might have thought that they were magical pieces of code. However, as you look through the code for WDBG, I think you'll agree that debuggers go through the same data grunt work that any software goes through. Previously, the biggest deficiency to overcome when writing a Win32 debugger was finding some way to handle local variables, parameters, and types. Fortunately, with the help of the DBGHELP.DLL symbol engine (and also the SymbolEngine library), we now have an excellent resource for writing debuggers or interesting diagnostic code that wasn't possible before.

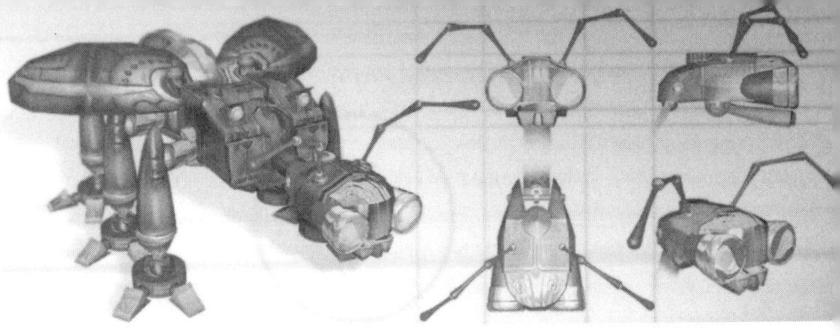

5

Advanced Debugger Usage with Visual Studio .NET

No matter how much great diagnostics code you use and how much planning you do, occasionally you need to run the debugger. As I've mentioned multiple times in this book, the whole key to debugging effectively is to avoid the debugger as much as possible because that's where you waste all your time. Now I know that most of you will be in the debugger to fix your coworkers' code, not your own (since the code you write is undoubtedly perfect). I want to make sure that when you must resort to the debugger, you're able to get the most out of it and fix problems as quickly as possible. This means you'll want to be able to get the most out of the debugger so that you can find and fix problems as fast as possible. In this chapter, I'll talk about how to take advantage of the wonderful Microsoft Visual Studio .NET debugger. If you've been developing for Microsoft platforms for a long time like I have, you can certainly see a marked progression of debugger improvements over the years. In my opinion, Visual Studio .NET is a huge jump in progress and is the state-of-the-art debugging tool. The team has done an outstanding job of combining an extremely easy-to-use user interface (UI) with power to spare for the really hard problems. The fact that Windows developers now have one debugger that handles script, Microsoft Active Server Pages (ASP), Microsoft ASP.NET, .NET, XML Web Services, native code, and SQL debugging in a single debugger UI is amazing.

This is the first of three chapters on the Visual Studio .NET debugger. In this chapter, I'll cover the common advanced ground of .NET and native debugging because so much is similar between the two environments. These features, which include advanced breakpoints, will assist you in solving your coding problems. I'll also provide a slew of tips to help you make the most out of the time you spend in the debugger. In Chapter 6, I'll cover specific issues related to .NET development. In Chapter 7, I'll discuss issues more specific to native code debugging. No matter what type of code you're debugging, you'll find many relevant tips in this chapter.

If you're new to the Visual Studio .NET debugger, I suggest that you read the documentation before continuing. I won't be covering the basics of the debugger in this chapter; I'll assume that you'll study the documentation if you need to. The debugger is discussed in the Visual Studio .NET documentation under Visual Studio .NET\Developing with Visual Studio .NET\Building, Debugging, and Testing or in the MSDN Online documentation under .NET Development\Visual Studio .NET\Product Documentation\Developing with Visual Studio .NET\Building, Debugging, and Testing (*http://msdn.microsoft.com/library/en-us/vsintro7/html/vxoriBuildingDebuggingandTesting.asp*).

Before you read any further, take note: if you haven't read about your symbol server and set it up as discussed in Chapter 2, you're missing one of the best capabilities of Visual Studio .NET. No matter whether you're developing .NET or native applications, getting perfect symbols automatically loaded means you'll always have a leg up solving your debugging problems.

Advanced Breakpoints and How to Use Them

Setting a breakpoint on a source line in the Visual Studio .NET debugger with Debug or project configuration is simple. Just load the source file, put the cursor on the line you want to stop on, and press the default breakpoint key, F9. Alternatively, you can click in the left margin next to the line. Although the folks coming from Microsoft Visual Basic 6 might not find the setting of margin breakpoints exciting (because Visual Basic has had them for years), C# and C++ developers will see them as a huge improvement. Setting a breakpoint on a source line this way is called *setting a location breakpoint*. When the code for such a line executes, the debugger will stop at that location. The ease of setting a location breakpoint belies its importance: the location breakpoint on a specific source code line is what separates the modern age of debugging from the debugging dark ages.

In the early days of computing, breakpoints simply didn't exist. Your only "strategy" for finding a bug was to run your program until it crashed and then look for the problem by wading through page after page of hexadecimal core-dump printouts of the state of memory. The only debuggers in the debugging dark ages were trace statements and faith. In the renaissance age of debugging, made possible by the introduction of higher-level languages, developers could set breakpoints but had to debug only at the assembly-language level. The higher-level languages still had no provisions for viewing local variables or seeing a program in source form. As the languages evolved into more sophisticated tools, the debugging modern age began, and developers were able to set a breakpoint on a line of source code and see their variables in a display that interpreted the variables' values into the exact types they specified. This simple location breakpoint is still extremely powerful, and with just it alone, my guess is that you can solve 99.46 percent of your debugging problems.

However wonderful, though, location breakpoints can get tedious very quickly. What would happen if you set the breakpoint on a line inside a `for` loop that executed from 1 through 10,000, and the bug turned up on the 10,000th iteration? Not only would you wear your index finger down to a nub from pressing the key assigned to the Go command, but you would also spend hours waiting to get to the iteration that produced the bug. Wouldn't it be nice if there were some way to tell the debugger that you want the breakpoint to execute 9,999 times before stopping?

Fortunately, there is a way: welcome to the realm of advanced breakpoints. In essence, advanced breakpoints allow you to program some smarts into breakpoints, letting the debugger handle the menial chores involved in tracking down bugs and minimizing the time and effort you have to spend in the debugger. A couple of conditions you can add with advanced breakpoints are having the breakpoint skip for a certain count and breaking when an expression is true. The advanced breakpoint capabilities have finally moved debuggers solidly into the modern age, allowing developers to do in minutes what used to take hours with simple location breakpoints.

Breakpoint Tips

Before we jump into advanced breakpoints, I just want to quickly mention four things you might not have been aware of when setting breakpoints. The first is that when setting advanced breakpoints, before you set them, it's always best if you start debugging with a single-step command. When you aren't debugging, the debugger uses IntelliSense to set the breakpoints. However, when you start debugging, you also get the actual Program Database (PDB) debugging symbols in addition to the IntelliSense to help set your breakpoints. For all the examples in this and the next two chapters, I started debugging before attempting to set any breakpoints.

One recommendation I have is that you should ensure your Breakpoints window—the view that shows which breakpoints are set—isn't a docked window. Sometimes when you're setting breakpoints, Visual Studio .NET will set them, and you'll wonder why they aren't triggered. By having the Breakpoints window as a full-fledged window, you'll be able to find it among all the other thousands of dockable windows in the Visual Studio .NET IDE. I don't know about you, but running Visual Studio .NET makes me long for a dual 35-inch monitor setup. To view the Breakpoints window, press Ctrl+Alt+B with the default keyboard mappings. Right-click on the Breakpoints window title bar, or tab and uncheck Dockable on the shortcut menu. You'll need to do this for both the normal editing mode as well as the debugging mode. Once you've got the Breakpoint window set as a full-fledged window, click and drag its tab over to the first position so that you can always find it.

The Breakpoints window shows various glyphs that indicate whether the breakpoint was set or not. Table 5-1 shows all the codes you'll see. The Warning glyph, the red dot with a white question mark in it, needs some extra explanation. In your normal debugging, you'll see the Warning glyph when you set a location breakpoint in a source file whose module has not been loaded yet, so the breakpoint is in essence an unresolved breakpoint. For those of you coming from the Microsoft Visual C++ 6 camp, the Additional DLLs dialog box is a thing of the past. Since I recommend that you start debugging before you set advanced breakpoints, if you see the Warning glyph in the Breakpoints window, you have a sign that the breakpoint wasn't set correctly.

Table 5-1 Breakpoint Window Codes

Glyph	State	Meaning
●	Enabled	Normal and active breakpoint
○	Disabled	Breakpoint is ignored by the debugger until re-enabled.
!	Error	Breakpoint could not be set.
?	Warning	Breakpoint could not be set because location is not loaded. If the debugger has to guess at the breakpoint, it shows the warning glyph.
◆	Mapped	A breakpoint set in ASP code on an HTML page

Although you might never have realized it, you can set breakpoints in the Call Stack window, except when doing SQL debugging. This capability is extremely helpful when trying to get stopped on recursion or deeply nested stacks. All you need to do is highlight the call you want to stop on and either press F9 or right-click on the line and select Insert Breakpoint from the shortcut menu. Even nicer, just as with margin breakpoints, you can right-click on any breakpoint in the Call Stack window to enable, disable, or set the properties of that breakpoint.

Another much underused feature for setting breakpoints is the Run To Cursor option for setting one-shot breakpoints. You can set them in source edit windows by right-clicking on the line and selecting the Run To Cursor option from the menu, which is available both when debugging and editing, and which will start debugging. For the default keyboard layout, pressing Ctrl+F10 will do the same thing. As with breakpoints, right-clicking in the magical Call Stack window pops up the shortcut menu, which also has a Run To Cursor option. If you hit a breakpoint before execution takes place on the Run To Cursor line, the debugger stops on that breakpoint and discards your Run To Cursor one-shot breakpoint.

Finally, in managed code, you can now set subexpression breakpoints. For example, if you have the following expression when debugging and you click in the margin next to the line, the red highlight extends only on the `i = 0 , m = 0` or on the initializer's portion of the expression. If you wanted to stop on the iterator's subexpression (in which the increment and decrement take place), place the cursor anywhere in the `i++ , m--` portion of the statement and press F9. In the following statement, you can have up to three breakpoints on the line. You can differentiate them in the Breakpoints window because each will indicate the line and character position. There will be only a single red dot in the margin indicating the breakpoints. To clear all breakpoints at once, click the red dot in the left margin.

```
for ( i = 0 , m = 0 ; i < 10 ; i++ , m-- )
{
}
```

Quickly Breaking on Any Function

The starting point for any advanced breakpoint is the Breakpoint dialog box, which is accessible by pressing Ctrl+B in the default keyboard mapping. This dialog box serves double duty as the New Breakpoint dialog box as well as the Breakpoint Properties dialog box. In many ways, the Breakpoint dialog box is simply a front end to the IntelliSense system. IntelliSense is extremely helpful for writing your code, but it's also used to help set breakpoints. There's an option for turning off IntelliSense to help verify breakpoints in the Options dialog box, Debugging folder, General property page, which can speed up mixed mode debugging, but I would highly recommend that you always leave the option Use IntelliSense To Verify Breakpoints checked on your systems. Also, you'll get IntelliSense breakpoints only when you have a project with source code open.

By using IntelliSense, you get a very powerful breakpoint-setting feature that can save you a tremendous amount of time. In the midst of my debugging battles, if I know the name of the class and method I want to break on, I can type it directly into the Breakpoint dialog box, Function tab's Function edit control. I've looked over the shoulder of countless developers who know the name of the method but spend 20 minutes wandering all over the project opening files just so they can move the cursor to the line and press F9. Setting breakpoints like this has some limitations, but they aren't too onerous. The first is that the name is case sensitive if the language is case sensitive, as you would expect. (This is where Visual Basic .NET is especially nice!) Second, in native C++, it's sometimes not possible to set the breakpoint because the actual method name is hidden by a define. Finally, the language selected in the Language drop-down list in the Breakpoint dialog box must be the correct language for the code.

Numerous things can happen when you try to set a breakpoint on a function using the Breakpoint dialog box. I want to go through the possible outcomes you'll see and explain how to work around any problems you might encounter. What you might want to do so that you can see the outcomes yourself is open up one of your projects or a project with this book's sample files and try to set a few breakpoints with the Breakpoint dialog box as I go through this discussion.

The first case of quickly setting a breakpoint that I'll discuss is when you want to set the breakpoint on a class and method that exists. For example, I have a Visual Basic .NET class named `MyThreadClass` with a method named `ThreadFunc`. When I pop up the Breakpoint dialog box with Ctrl+B, all I have to type in is `mythreadclass.threadfunc` (remember Visual Basic .NET is a case-insensitive language) and click OK. For Visual Basic .NET, J#, and C#, you separate the class and the method name with a period. For native C++, you separate the class and the method name with the language-specific double colons (`::`). Interestingly, for managed C++, you have to prefix the expression with `MC::` to get the expression parse correctly. Assuming the same class and method name from the Visual Basic .NET example were in managed C++, you'd have to enter `MC::MyThreadClass::ThreadFunc`. Figure 5-1 shows the filled-out Breakpoint dialog box using the Visual Basic .NET example. If you aren't currently debugging when you set the breakpoint, the breakpoint dot appears in the margin, but the red highlight doesn't appear on the `Public Sub ThreadFunc` because the breakpoint still has to be resolved. Once you start debugging, `Public Sub ThreadFunc` is highlighted in red. If you're debugging native C++, the instruction isn't highlighted. If you're currently debugging, the breakpoint will be fully resolved by showing a filled-in red dot in the Breakpoints window and you'll see that the `Public Sub ThreadFunc` is highlighted in red. (In C# or native C++, the breakpoint appears inside the function, but it's still the first instruction after the function prolog. Also, just a breakpoint dot appears in the margin.)

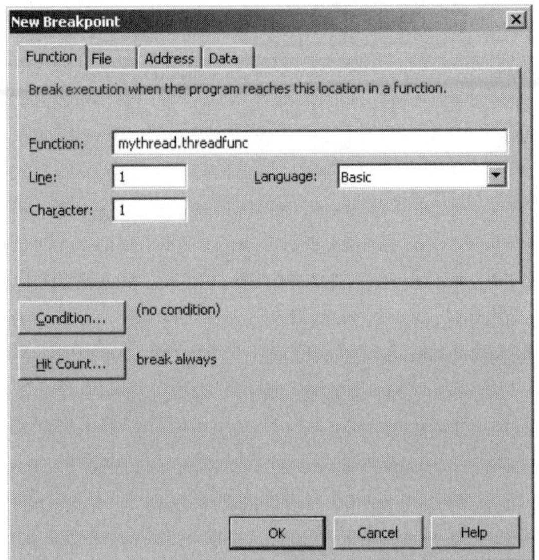

Figure 5-1 Breakpoint dialog box about to set a quick breakpoint on a function

If the class and method name you specify in the Breakpoint dialog is incorrect, you'll see a message box that says this: "IntelliSense could not find the specified location. Do you still want to set the breakpoint?" If you go ahead and set the breakpoint on the nonexistent method and you're doing managed code, you can be pretty certain that when you're debugging, the breakpoint will always have a question mark glyph next to it in the Breakpoints window because the breakpoint can't be resolved. As you'll see in Chapter 7, when we talk about native code debugging, you still have a chance to set the breakpoint correctly.

Because setting a breakpoint by specifying the class and method works well, I had to experiment with attempting to set a breakpoint in the Breakpoint dialog box by just specifying the method name. For C#, J#, Visual Basic .NET, and native C++, if the method name is unique in the application, the Breakpoint dialog box simply sets the breakpoint as if you typed in the complete class and method. Unfortunately, managed C++ doesn't seem to support setting breakpoints with just the method name.

Since setting a breakpoint with just the method name works quite well and will save you time debugging, you might be wondering what would happen if you had a large project and you wanted to set a breakpoint on a common method or an overloaded method. For example, suppose you have the WDBG MFC project from Chapter 4 open and you want to set a breakpoint on the `OnOK` method, which is the default method for handling the OK button click. If you enter `OnOK` in the Breakpoint dialog box and click OK, something wonderfully interesting happens and is shown in Figure 5-2.

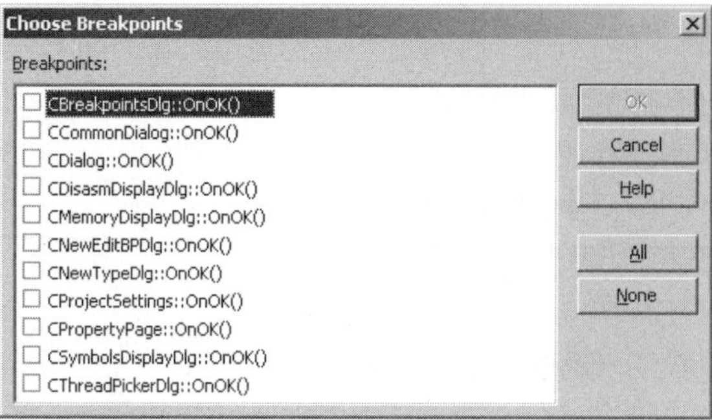

Figure 5-2 The Choose Breakpoints dialog box

What you see in Figure 5-2 is the IntelliSense listing from all classes in the WDBG project that have `OnOK` as a method. I don't know about you, but I think this is an outstanding feature—especially because you can see that clicking the All button allows you to set breakpoints on all those methods in one fell swoop, and it works for all languages supported by Visual Studio .NET except managed C++! The Choose Breakpoints dialog box also displays for overloaded methods in the same class. I don't know how many times I've gone to set a breakpoint and the Choose Breakpoints dialog box reminded me that I should consider stopping on other methods as well.

Another of my favorite things to do in C++ code is to type just the class name in the Breakpoint dialog box. The wonderful Choose Breakpoints dialog box pops up and offers every method in the class! Sadly, this killer feature works only on C++ code (and amazingly in managed C++ as well) and not on C#, J#, or Visual Basic .NET. But for C++, this incredible feature is a boon for testing. If you want to ensure your test cases are hitting every method in a class, simply type the class name in the Breakpoint dialog box and click All in the resulting Choose Breakpoints dialog box. This instantly sets breakpoints on every method so that you can start seeing whether your test cases are calling every method. This feature is also great for looking for dead code because if you set all the breakpoints and clear them as you hit them, any remaining breakpoints are code that's never executed.

At the time I wrote this book, I was using Visual Studio .NET 2003 RC2. When I was trying to figure out if C# and J# could set class breakpoints like native C++, I ran into a huge bug that will crash Visual Studio .NET. I hope this bug will be fixed in the final release; but if it's not, I want to make sure you know about it. For C# or J# projects, if you type in the class name followed by a period in the Breakpoint dialog box, for example, `Form1.` and click the OK button, you'll get a Visual C++ run time error message box telling you the application has attempted to terminate in an unusual way. When you click the OK button, the IDE will simply disappear. Attempting the same type of breakpoint in a Visual Basic .NET application does not close the IDE. Although this is a very nasty bug, at least only a few of you should run into it.

I'm simply amazed that the ability to select from multiple methods in your application when setting a breakpoint in the debugger isn't pointed out in big, bold type as a killer feature of Visual Studio .NET. In fact, there's only a passing reference to the Choose Breakpoints dialog box in the MSDN documentation. However, I'm very happy to toot the debugger team's horn for them.

As you can probably guess by this point, you don't have to go through the Choose Breakpoints dialog box if you know the class and method because you can type them directly in. Of course, you have to use the appropriate class and method separator based on the language. If you want to be extremely specific, you can even specify the parameter types to the overloaded method for Visual Basic .NET and C++, keeping in mind the particular syntactic requirements of the languages. Interestingly, C# and J# don't look at parameters and always pop up the Choose Breakpoints dialog box, which is probably a bug.

If you're debugging when you want to set a quick breakpoint, things get a little more interesting, especially in managed code. For native code, I'll save the discussion for Chapter 7 because when you're debugging, there's quite a bit more you have to manually check when setting breakpoints. For managed code, I noticed some very interesting power in the Breakpoint dialog box. During a brain cramp one day while debugging, I typed in the name of a class and method in the Microsoft .NET Framework class library instead of the class and method from my project, and a whole bunch of really weird-looking breakpoints popped up in the Breakpoints window. Let's say I have a console-managed application that calls `Console.WriteLine`, and while debugging, you type `Console.WriteLine` into the Breakpoint dialog box. You'll get the usual message about IntelliSense not knowing what to do. If you click Yes and go to your Breakpoints window, you'll see something that looks like Figure 5-3. (You might have to expand the top tree node.)

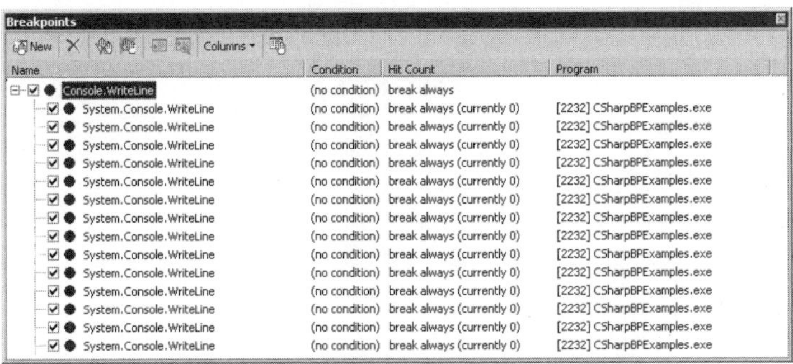

Figure 5-3 Child breakpoints in the Breakpoints window

What you're looking at in Figure 5-3 are child breakpoints. Basically, the Visual Studio .NET documentation says that they exist and that's it. For example, the documentation says child breakpoints occur when you set breakpoints on overloaded functions, but the Breakpoints window always shows them as top-level breakpoints. You can see child breakpoints when you're debugging multiple executables and both programs load the same control into their AppDomain/address spaces, and you set breakpoints in the same spot in that control in both programs. What's wild is that the Breakpoints window in Figure 5-3 is showing you a single program that's currently running in which I set a breakpoint on `Console.WriteLine`.

If you right-click on a child breakpoint while debugging and select Go To Disassembly, the Disassembly window displays the disassembly code. However, you'll get a clue as to what's happening if you right-click on a child breakpoint, select Properties from the shortcut menu, and in the resulting Breakpoint dialog box, click on the Address tab, shown in Figure 5-4. You'll see that the debugger reports that the breakpoint is set on `System.Console.WriteLine` at the very start of the function.

If that's not clear enough, you can always execute your program and notice that you stop deep down in the x86 assembly language soup. If you pull up the Call Stack window, you'll see that you're stopped inside a call to `Console.WriteLine` and you'll even see the parameter(s) passed. The beauty of this undocumented means of handling a breakpoint is that you'll always be able to get your applications stopped at a known point of execution.

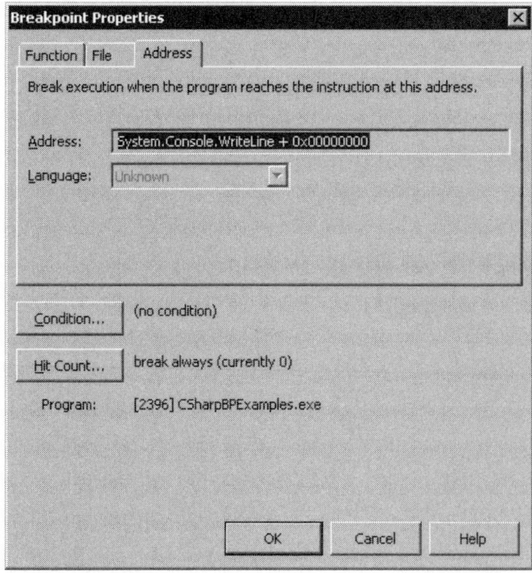

Figure 5-4 Breakpoint on any call to `Console.WriteLine`

Although I made only a single call to `Console.WriteLine` in my program, the Breakpoints window shows 19 child breakpoints, as shown in Figure 5-3. Based on some trial and error, I discovered that the child breakpoints count is related to the number of overloaded methods. In other words, setting breakpoints by typing in the .NET Framework class and method name, or typing where you don't have source code, will set a breakpoint on all overloaded methods. In case you check the documentation and see that `Console.WriteLine` only has 18 overloaded methods, let me tell you that if you look at the `System.Console` class with ILDASM, you'll see that there are really 19 overloaded methods.

The ability to stop on a method that's called anywhere in my AppDomain is amazingly cool. I've learned quite a bit about how the .NET Framework class library fits together by choosing to stop at specific .NET Framework class library methods. Although I've been using a static method as an example, this technique works perfectly well on instance methods as well as properties as long as those methods or properties are called in your AppDomain. Keep in mind that to set breakpoints on a property, you'll need to prefix the property with `get_` or `set_`, depending on what you want to break on. For example, to set a breakpoint on the `Console.In` property, you'd specify `Console.get_In`. Also, the language selected in the Breakpoint dialog box is still important. When setting these AppDomain-wide breakpoints in places where you don't have source code, I like to use Basic so that if I mess up the case, the breakpoint is still set.

There are two issues you need to be aware of when setting these AppDomain-wide breakpoints. The first is that breakpoints set this way aren't saved across executions. Consider the example in which we added a breakpoint while debugging on `Console.WriteLine`. The Breakpoints window will show "`Console.WriteLine`" when you re-execute the program, but the breakpoint changes to a question mark glyph and the breakpoint changes to unresolved and will never be set. Second, you can set these AppDomain-wide breakpoints only when the instruction pointer is sitting in code in which you have a PDB file. If you try to set the breakpoint in the Disassembly window with no source code available, the breakpoint will be set only as unresolved and never activated.

Although you might think I've beaten the topic of setting quick location breakpoints to death, there's still one completely non-obvious but extremely powerful place to set location breakpoints. Figure 5-5 shows the Find combo box on the toolbar. If you type the name of the class and method you want to break on in that combo box and press F9, a breakpoint on that method is set if that method exists. If you specify an overloaded method, the system will automatically set breakpoints on all the overloaded methods. The Find combo box is a little more discriminating in that if it can't set the breakpoint, it won't. Additionally, like the Breakpoint dialog box, if you're working on a C++ project, specifying the class name in the Find combo box and pressing F9 will set a breakpoint on each method in that class.

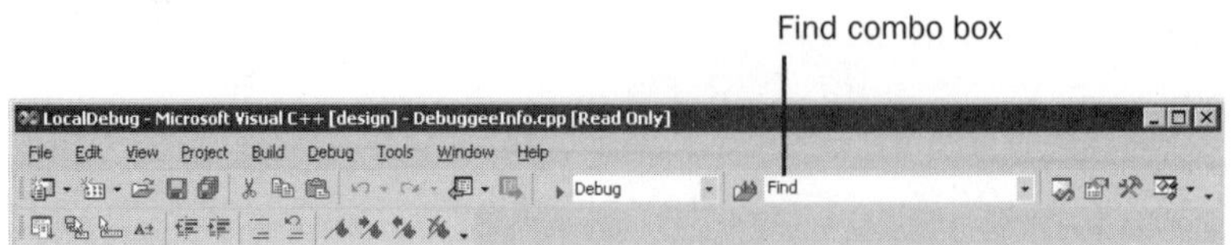

Figure 5-5 The Find combo box

That little Find combo box has two other hidden secrets as well. For the default keyboard layout, if you type in the name of a project file or an include file in the `INCLUDE` environment variable and press Ctrl+Shift+G, the Find combo box opens the file ready for editing. Finally, if you like the Command window in Visual Studio .NET, try this: in the Find combo box, enter the right arrow key symbol (>), and see the window turn into a mini Command window with its own IntelliSense. With all this undocumented magic in the Find combo box, I often wonder if I could type in "Fix my bugs!" and with a magic keystroke have it do just that.

Location Breakpoint Modifiers

Now that you know how to set location breakpoints anywhere with aplomb, I can turn to some of the scenarios discussed in the opening section on breakpoints. The whole idea is to add some real smarts to breakpoints so that you can use the debugger even more efficiently. The vehicles for these smarts are hit counts and conditional expressions.

Hit Counts

The simplest modifier applicable to location breakpoints is a *hit count*, also sometimes referred to as a *skip count*. A hit count tells the debugger that it should put the breakpoint in but not stop on it until the line of code executes a specific number of times. With this modifier, breaking inside loops at the appropriate time is trivial.

Adding a hit count to a location breakpoint is easy. First, set a regular location breakpoint either on a line or a subexpression of the line. For managed code, right-click on the red area of the line for the location breakpoint, and select Breakpoint Properties from the shortcut menu. For native code, right-click on the red dot in the left margin. Alternatively, you could also select the breakpoint in the Breakpoints window and click the Properties button, or right-click it in the window and select Properties. No matter how you do it, you'll end up in the Breakpoint dialog box, where you click the Hit Count button.

In the resulting Breakpoint Hit Count dialog box, you'll see that Microsoft improved the hit-count options from previous debuggers. In the When The Breakpoint Is Hit drop-down list, you can choose how you want the hit count calculated four different ways, as shown in Table 5-2. After choosing the evaluation you want, type the hit-count number in the edit box next to the drop-down list.

Table 5-2 Hit-Count Evaluations

Hit-Count Evaluation	Description
Break always	Stop every time this location is executed.
Break when the hit count is equal to	Only stop when the exact number of executions of this location has occurred. Note that the count is a 1-based count.
Break when the hit count is a multiple of	Break every x number of executions.
Break when the hit count is greater than or equal to	Skip all executions of this location until the hit count is reached and break every execution thereafter. This was the only hit count in previous editions of Microsoft debuggers.

What makes hit counts so useful is that when you're stopped in the debugger, the debugger tells you how many times the breakpoint has executed. If you have a loop that's crashing or corrupting data but you don't know which iteration is causing the problem, add a location breakpoint to a line in the loop and add a hit-count modifier that is larger than the total number of loop iterations. When your program crashes or the corruption occurs, bring up the Breakpoints window and, in the Hit Count column for that breakpoint, you'll see the number times that loop executed in parentheses. The Breakpoints window shown in Figure 5-6 displays the remaining hit count after a data corruption. For native code, keep in mind that the remaining count works only when your program is running at full speed. Single-stepping over a breakpoint doesn't update the hit count.

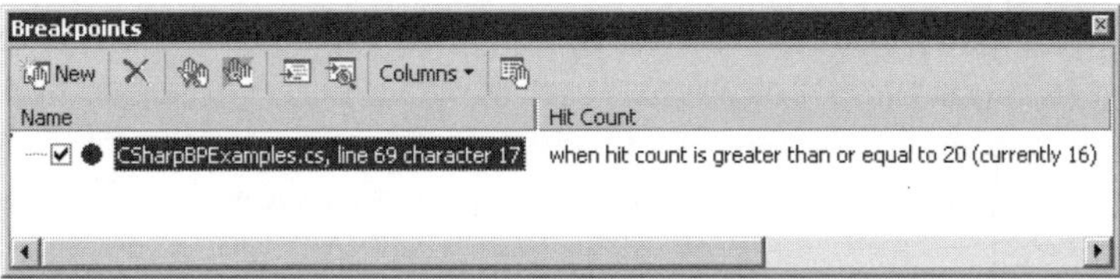

Figure 5-6 An example of remaining hit count breakpoint expressions

A new feature of hit counts is that you can reset the count back to zero at any time. Jump back into the Breakpoint dialog box, click the Hit Count button, and click the Reset Hit Count button in the Breakpoint Hit Count dialog box. One additional nice feature is that you can change the hit-count evaluation at any time or the hit-count number without changing the current hit count.

Conditional Expressions

The second modifier for location breakpoints—and the one that if used correctly saves you more time than any other type of breakpoint—is a *conditional expression*. A location breakpoint that has a conditional expression triggers only if its expression evaluates to true or changes from the last time it was evaluated. A conditional expression is a powerful weapon for gaining control exactly when you need it. The debugger can handle just about any expression you throw at it. To add a conditional expression to your breakpoint, open the Breakpoint dialog box for a location breakpoint and click the Condition button, which brings up the Breakpoint Condition dialog box.

In the Condition edit box, enter the condition you want to check and click OK. Both managed and native code have sufficiently varying support for conditions, each with their own set of "gotchas" that I'll have to discuss in their respective upcoming chapters. In a nutshell, the differences are that in managed code, you can call methods and functions from the conditional expressions (be very, very careful!) and have no support for pseudo registers/values (the special codes that begin with the `@` or $ symbol). For native code, you can't call functions from your conditional expressions, but you do have access to the pseudo registers/values.

However, both environments support general expressions that you can think of like this: "What's in the parentheses of an `if` statement that I'd enter on the breakpoint line?" You have full access to local and global variables because they are evaluated in the context of the currently executing scope. The conditional expression breakpoint modifier is extremely powerful because it allows you to directly test the specific hypothesis that you're out to prove or disprove. The important point to remember is that the expression syntax must follow the same rules as the language in which the breakpoint is set, so remember to mind your `And`'s and `||`'s as appropriate.

The default condition handling breaks into the debugger if the conditional expression you enter evaluates to true. However, if you want to break when the condition changes value, you can change the option button selection from Is True to Has Changed. One thing that can be confusing, but makes sense after some thought, is that the expression isn't evaluated when you enter the condition. The first time it's evaluated is when the associated location breakpoint is hit. Since the condition has never been evaluated, the debugger sees no value stored in the internal expression result field, so it saves off the value and continues execution. Thus it can possibly take two executions of that location before the debugger stops.

What's extra nice about the Has Changed evaluation is that the condition you enter doesn't have to be an actual condition. You can also enter a variable that is accessible from the scope of the location breakpoint, and the debugger evaluates and stores the result of that variable so that you can stop when it changes. Make sure to read the breakpoint discussions in both Chapter 6 and Chapter 7 to learn about the managed and native code twists on conditional breakpoint modifiers. Additionally, native debugging offers other types of breakpoints to make debugging easier. I do want to answer the question on the tip of your tongue (thus ruining the suspense): managed debugging does not support global breakpoints.

Multiple Breakpoints on a Single Line

One of the most common questions I'm asked when it comes to setting breakpoints is about setting multiple breakpoints on a single line. Prior to Visual Studio .NET, it wasn't possible, but now you can. However, you won't use multiple breakpoints on a line every day because they're not that easy to set. You'll also be using only conditional expression location breakpoint modifiers on each of the breakpoints. As you can imagine, setting two regular stop-always location breakpoints on a line isn't going to buy you very much!

After setting the first breakpoint using normal methods, the trick to setting the second one is to use the Breakpoint dialog box to do the magic. The easiest way to show you how to set multiple breakpoints is through an example. The following code snippet shows the line number in comments before each line.

```
/* Source file: CSharpBPExamples.cs. */
/*84*/    for ( i = 0 , m = 0 ; i < 10 ; i++ , m-- )
/*85*/    {
/*86*/        Console.WriteLine ( "i = {0} m = {0}" , i , m ) ;
/*87*/    }
```

I set the first breakpoint on line 86 by right-clicking in the margin and setting the conditional expression to `i==3`. To set the second breakpoint, shift to the Breakpoints window so that you can see the line number for the original breakpoint and bring up the Breakpoint dialog box by pressing Ctrl+B. Click the File tab in the Breakpoint dialog box because that's where you need to set the breakpoint. Type the file name into the File edit box, enter the line number in the Line edit box, and leave the Character edit box set to 1. Using this example, I use CSharpBPExamples.CS as the file and 86 for the line. Finally, click the Condition button and enter the condition you want for the second breakpoint. In my case, I'll enter `m==-1`.

The Breakpoints window shows two breakpoints set on the same line, and the icon glyph on the left-hand side shows full red circles, indicating that they are both active. When you start debugging, you'll see that the program stops on both breakpoints when the appropriate conditions are met. To check which condition is causing the breakpoint, look at the Breakpoints window to see which one is bold. Interestingly, right-clicking on the breakpoint in the source window and selecting Breakpoint Properties from the shortcut menu always displays the properties of the first breakpoint set for the line. Additionally, if you click on the margin dot, both breakpoints are cleared. While the example I showed you here was a little contrived—I would have combined both conditions with an or (||) operator—multiple breakpoints on a line come in very handy when you need to look at two different complicated expressions.

The Watch Window

If I had to give an Oscar for technical achievement and overall usefulness in Visual Studio .NET, the Watch window would win hands down. One idea that companies creating development tools for other environments and operating systems haven't figured out at all is that if developers can easily develop and debug their applications, they'll more likely flock to that environment or platform. The incredible power offered by the Watch window and its related cousins, the QuickWatch dialog box, Autos window, Locals window, and This/Me window, are what make the difference between floundering all day looking for an answer and quickly solving a bug.

I want to make sure to point out that you can use any of the related Watch windows to change a variable's value. Unfortunately, many developers coming over from other environments, and a few who have been doing Windows development for many years, aren't aware of the capabilities. Let's take the Autos window as an example. You just select the variable or the child variable you want to change, and click once on the value field for that variable. Simply type in the new value and you've changed the variable.

Many developers treat the Watch window as a read-only place in which they drop their variables and watch. What makes the Watch window exciting is that it has a complete expression evaluator built in. If you want to see something as an integer that's not an integer, simply cast or convert it in the same way you would if you were programming in the currently active programming language. Here's a simple example: Suppose CurrVal is declared as an integer and you want to see what it evaluates to as a Boolean. In the Name column of the Watch window, in C# and C++, enter (bool)CurrVal, or for Visual Basic .NET, enter CBool(CurrVal). The value is displayed as true or false as appropriate.

Changing an integer to a Boolean might not be that exciting, but the ability of the Watch window to evaluate expressions gives you the ultimate code-testing trick. As I've said several times in this book, code coverage is one of the goals you need to strive for when doing your unit testing. If, for example, you have a conditional expression inside a function and it's difficult to see at a glance what it evaluates to so that you can step into the true or false branch as appropriate, the Watch window becomes your savior. Since there's a full expression evaluator built in, you can simply drag the expression in question down to the Watch window and see what it evaluates to. Granted, there are some restrictions. If your expression calls all sorts of functions instead of using variables, you could be in trouble. If you look at my code, I follow the rule in which if I have three or more subexpressions in a conditional, I use only variables just so that I can see the result of the expression in the Watch window. Some of you might be truth table savants and be able to see how those expressions evaluate off the top of your heads, but I certainly am not one.

To make this clearer, let's use the next expression as an example. You can highlight everything inside the outer parentheses and drag it to the Watch window. However, since it's on three lines, the Watch window interprets it as three separate lines in its display. I still do that so that I can copy and paste the two lines into the first one and thus build my final expression without too much typing. Once the expression is entered on one line in the Watch window, the value column is either true or false, depending on the values in the variables.

```
if ( ( eRunning == m_eState     ) ||
     ( eException == m_eState   ) &&
     ( TRUE == m_bSeenLoaderBP )     )
```

The next step is to put each of the variables that make up a part of the expression in their own entries in the Watch window. The really cool part is that you can start changing the values of the individual variables and see that the full expression on the first line automatically changes based on the changing subexpressions. I absolutely love this feature because it not only helps with code coverage, but it also helps you see the data coverage you need to generate.

Calling Methods in the Watch Window

Something I've found relatively amusing about some developers who have moved to Windows development from those UNIX operating systems is that they insist UNIX is better. When I ask why, they indignantly respond in their suspender-wearing glory, "In GDB you can call a function in the debuggee from the debugger!" I was amazed to learn that operating system evaluations revolved around an arcane debugger feature. Of course, those suspenders snap pretty quickly when I tell them that we've been able to call functions from Microsoft debuggers for years. You might wonder what's so desirable about that. If you think like a debugging guru, however, you'll realize that being able to execute a function within the debugger allows you to fully customize your debugging environment. For example, instead of spending 10 minutes looking at 10 different data structures to ensure data coherency, you can write a function that verifies the data and then call it when you need it most—when your application is stopped in the debugger.

Let me give you two examples of places I've written methods that I called only from the Watch window. The first example is when I had a data structure that was expandable in the Watch window, but to see all of it I would have been expanding the little pluses all the way past the Canadian border and up into the North Pole area. By having the debugger-only method, I could more easily see the complete data structure. The second example was when I inherited some code that (don't laugh) had nodes that were shared between a linked list and a binary tree. The code was fragile, and I had to be doubly sure I didn't screw up anything. By having the debugger-only method, I was in essence able to have an assertion function I could use at will.

What's interesting in managed applications is that any time you view an object property in the Watch window, the getter accessor is called. You can easily verify this by putting the following property in a class, starting to debug, switching to the This/Me window, and expanding the `this/Me` value for the object. You'll see that the name returned is the name of the AppDomain the property is part of.

```
Public ReadOnly Property WhereAmICalled() As String
    Get
        Return AppDomain.CurrentDomain.FriendlyName
    End Get
End Property
```

Of course, if you have an object property that copies a 3-gigabyte database, the automatic property evaluation could be a problem. Fortunately, Visual Studio .NET allows you to turn off the property evaluation in the Options dialog box, Debugging folder, General property page, Allow Property Evaluation In Variables Windows check box. What's even better is that you can turn this property evaluation on and off on the fly and the debugger immediately responds to the change. You can instantly tell when property evaluation is disabled because the Watch window family says this in the Value field: "Function evaluation is disabled in debugger windows. Check your settings in Tools.Options.Debugging.General."

Native code is a bit different in that you have to tell the Watch window to call the method. Please note that I'm using the generic term "method" here. In actuality, for native code, you can reliably call only C functions or static C++ methods. As regular native C++ methods need the `this` pointer, which you might or might not have depending on the context. Managed methods are a little more `this` pointer friendly. If you're stopped in the class that contains the method to call, the Watch window automatically assumes the active `this` pointer is the one to use.

As you've seen, calling managed code properties is trivial. Calling methods in managed or native code is just like calling them from your code. If the method doesn't take any parameters, simply type the method name and add the open and close parameters. For example, if your debugging method is `MyDataCheck ( )`, you'd call it in the Watch window with `MyDataCheck ( )`. If your debugging method takes parameters, just pass them as if you're calling the function normally. If your debugging method returns a value, the Value column in the Watch window displays the return value.

A common problem when calling native functions from the Watch window is ensuring that they are valid. To check a function, type the function name into the Watch window and don't add any quotes or parameters. The Watch window will report the type and address of the function in the Value column if it can be found. Additionally, if you'd like to specify advanced breakpoint syntax (which I'll discuss in detail in Chapter 7) to the function, to narrow down scope, you can do that as well.

A few rules apply to both managed and native code when calling methods from the Watch window. The first rule is that the method should execute in less than 20 seconds because the debugger UI stops responding until the method finishes. After 20 seconds, managed code shows "Evaluation of expression or statement stopped," "error: function '<*method name*>' evaluation timed out," or "Error: cannot obtain value," and native code shows "CXX001: Error: error attempting to execute user function." The good news is that your threads will continue to execute. That's wonderful news because for calling native methods in Visual Studio 6 that timed out, the debugger just killed the currently executing thread. The other good news compared to previous editions of Visual Studio is that if you want to, you can leave called methods in the Watch window in multithreaded programs. Previous versions killed any thread that happened to become active in the place you originally executed your debug method in another thread. The final rule is common sense: only read memory to do data validations. If you think debugging a program that changes behavior because of a side effect in an assertion is tough, wait until you mess with something on the fly in the Watch window. Additionally, if you do some sort of output, make sure to stick with just the trace method of choice for the environment.

What I've covered here about the Watch window is what .NET and native debugging have in common. You can also expand your own types automatically in the Watch window, but there's quite a difference between how it's done in managed vs. native code. Additionally, native debugging offers all sorts of other options for data formatting and control. To learn more, make sure to read in Chapter 6 and Chapter 7 the individual discussions of the Watch window.

The Set Next Statement Command

One of the coolest hidden features in the Visual Studio .NET debugger is the Set Next Statement command. It is accessible in both source windows and the Disassembly window on the shortcut menu, but only when you're debugging. What the Set Next Statement command lets you do is change the instruction pointer to a different place in the program. Changing what the program executes is a fantastic debugging technique when you're trying to track down a bug or when you're unit testing and want to test your error handlers.

A perfect example of when to use Set Next Statement is manually filling a data structure. You single-step over the method that does the data insertion, change any values passed to the function, and use Set Next Statement to force the execution of that call again. Thus, you fill the data structure by changing the execution code.

I guess I should mention that changing the instruction pointer can easily crash your program if you're not extremely careful. If you're running in a debug build, you can use Set Next Statement without much trouble in the source windows. For native optimized builds in particular, your safest bet is to use Set Next Statement only in the Disassembly window. The compiler will move code around so that source lines might not execute linearly. In addition, you need to be aware if your code is creating temporary variables on the stack when you use Set Next Statement. In Chapter 7, I'll cover this last situation in more detail.

If I'm looking for a bug and my hypothesis is that said bug might be in a certain code path, I set a breakpoint in the debugger before the offending function or functions. I check the data and the parameters going into the functions, and I single-step over the functions. If the problem isn't duplicated, I use the Set Next Statement command to set the execution point back to the breakpoint and change the data going into the functions. This tactic allows me to test several hypotheses in one debugging session, thus saving time in the end. As you can imagine, you can't use this technique in all cases because once you execute some code in your program, executing it again can destroy the state. Set Next Statement works best on code that doesn't change the state too much.

As I mentioned earlier, the Set Next Statement command comes in handy during unit testing. For example, Set Next Statement is useful when you want to test error handlers. Say that you have an `if` statement and you want to test what happens when the condition fails. All you need to do is let the condition execute and use Set Next Statement to move the execution point down to the failure case. In addition to Set Next Statement, the Run To Cursor menu option, also available on the right-click shortcut menu in a source code window when debugging, allows you to set a one-shot breakpoint. I also use Run To Cursor quite a bit in testing.

Filling data structures, especially lists and arrays, is another excellent use of Set Next Statement when you're testing or debugging. If you have some code that fills a data structure and adds the data structure to a linked list, you can use Set Next Statement to add some additional items to the linked list so that you can see how your code handles those cases. This use of Set Next Statement is especially handy when you need to set up hard-to-duplicate data conditions when you're debugging.

Common Debugging Question

Can Visual Studio .NET also debug regular ASP Web applications?

It sure can, but not out of the box because you have to add some registry keys and set up DCOM permissions on the Web server. It's hard to find the steps because they're buried way down deep in the documentation. Search for the topic "ASP Remote Debugging Setup" to see the necessary steps.

Summary

Visual Studio .NET debugging is the state-of-the-art debugger on the market today. Microsoft listened to developers and produced a debugger that makes some extremely difficult debugging problems much easier to debug. This chapter introduced the common breakpoint features across managed and native code. As you've seen, the debugger can do a considerable amount of work for you if you know how to utilize it effectively. You should strive to make the most of the Visual Studio .NET debugger so that you can minimize the time you spend in it.

Advanced breakpoints help you avoid tedious debugging sessions by allowing you to specify the exact conditions under which a breakpoint triggers. While both managed and native code have special breakpoint features, the location breakpoint modifiers, hit counts, and condition expressions are your best friends, mainly because the breakpoint modifiers will save you a huge amount of time since they'll allow you to use the debugger more efficiently. I strongly encourage you to play with them a bit so that you can see what you can and can't do, thus avoiding having to learn their idiosyncrasies under extreme pressure.

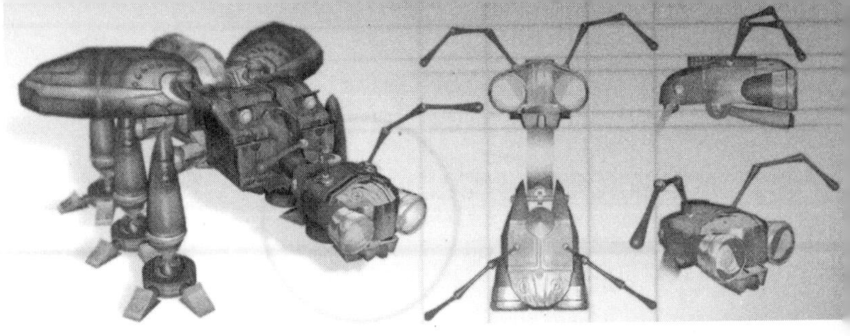

6

Advanced .NET Debugging with Visual Studio .NET

Although the Microsoft .NET Framework takes us past the age-old problem of memory corruptions and leaks, it still hasn't moved us into the realm of "the code does exactly what I mean, not what I type," which means that we still have all the fun of debugging and wondering where the bug lies. In this chapter, I want to cover specific strategies to help make your .NET debugging experiences less painful. I already mentioned some .NET debugging techniques using Visual Studio .NET in the last chapter, but in this chapter I'll go into more depth. We'll start by looking at a few things that are specific to debugging .NET applications of all stripes with Visual Studio .NET specifically, and then we'll move into various tricks and techniques related to .NET debugging in general. Finally, we'll finish up by learning how to use the Microsoft Intermediate Language Disassembler (ILDASM) and how to read Microsoft intermediate language (MSIL).

One new feature that's mentioned in conjunction with Visual Studio .NET 2003 that I won't talk about in this chapter (but will discuss later in the book) is the SOS (Son of Strike) debugger extension support. SOS extension support allows you to get .NET code information out of memory dumps and native debugging. I'll talk about SOS in Chapter 8 because I've found the SOS integration and usage to be much easier when used with WinDBG (strange, but true!) than when used with Visual Studio .NET. I strongly suggest you read the section on SOS if you have any possibility of getting memory dumps from your .NET applications.

Advanced Breakpoints for .NET Programs

In Chapter 5, you saw that the Visual Studio .NET debugger offers a fantastic amount of help for breaking exactly where you want. As for .NET code, there are some aspects of location breakpoint conditional expression modifiers I want to cover so that you fully understand the ramifications of using them.

Conditional Expressions

One of the most common questions I've been asked about conditional breakpoints over the years is this: "Can I call functions from the location breakpoint conditional expression modifier?" With native code debugging, you can't, but with .NET you certainly can. Calling functions or methods from conditional expressions opens up all sorts of excellent debugging capabilities, but as you can imagine, the side effects can make debugging almost impossible if you don't pay careful attention.

When I first started learning .NET, I didn't realize this extra power in conditional expressions existed because the functionality seemed natural. For example, I was using expressions such as `MyString.Length == 7`, thinking the debugger was reaching into the debuggee and getting the length value by reading memory directly just as it does in Win32 native debugging. After using an expression that called a more interesting property get accessor that did more work, I started experimenting to see everything I could do. Essentially, I figured out I could make any valid calls I wanted except to Web methods.

Probably the best way to show you the process of calling methods from conditional expressions is through an example. Listing 6-1 is a simple program, ConditionalBP (included with this book's sample code), which has a class, `TestO`, which keeps track of the number of times a method is called. If you set a conditional breakpoint on `Console.WriteLine` in `Main` with the expression `(x.Toggle() == true) || (x.CondTest() == 0)`, you'll see that you'll only break when the `m_bToggle` field is `true`, and the `m_CallCount` field is an odd value. When the loop stops, you can inspect the value of the `TestO` instance in `x` and see that its fields are being changed, indicating the code is being called.

```
using System ;
namespace ConditionalBP
{

class TestO
{
    public TestO ( )
```

Listing 6-1 Conditional breakpoint modifier example

```
    {
        m_CallCount = 0 ;
        m_bToggle = false ;
    }

    private Int32 m_CallCount ;

    public Int32 CondTest ( )
    {
        m_CallCount++ ;
        return ( m_CallCount ) ;
    }

    private Boolean m_bToggle ;

    public Boolean Toggle ( )
    {
        m_bToggle = !m_bToggle ;
        return ( m_bToggle ) ;
    }
}

class App
{
    static void Main(string[] args)
    {
        Test0 x = new Test0 ( ) ;

        for ( Int32 i = 0 ; i < 10 ; i++ )
        {
            // Set BP: (x.Toggle() == true) || (x.CondTest() == 0 )
            Console.WriteLine ( "{0}" , i ) ;
        }

        x = null ;
    }
}
}
```

Before you start slinging any property or method calls in your location breakpoint conditional expression modifiers, you should probably take a good look at what the property or method does. If it happens to copy a 3-GB database or otherwise changes state, you probably don't want to call it. What's also interesting about how the debugger evaluates the methods and properties you call is that the 20-second timeout that applies to the Watch window doesn't apply to calling methods from a conditional expression. If you have a method that happens to take days to evaluate, the debugger will merrily wait on the expression to finish. Fortunately, the Visual Studio .NET user interface (UI) isn't frozen, so pressing Ctrl+Alt+Break or selecting Break All from the Debug menu will immediately stop the debuggee.

This wonderful ability to call methods and properties from conditional breakpoints has one flaw in the Visual Studio .NET environment that I need to discuss. If you set a condition before you start debugging, the debugger will report that it can't evaluate the expression and will stop. However, if you set the condition incorrectly *after* you start debugging and the condition you set can't be evaluated or causes an exception to be thrown, the debugger won't stop. Once you've started debugging, if you set the condition incorrectly, you're completely out of luck.

With an invalid condition, the debugger will report that it couldn't set the breakpoint, as shown in Figure 6-1, but will continue to let the debuggee execute instead of stopping like you would expect. Nothing could be more frustrating than finally reproducing that one almost-impossible bug, only to have the debugger skip right over it. This was a bug in Visual Studio .NET 2002 and unfortunately is still a bug in Visual Studio .NET 2003. I certainly hope Microsoft fixes this problem in future versions of Visual Studio .NET so that when encountering the invalid condition, the debugger stops and lets you fix the problem condition.

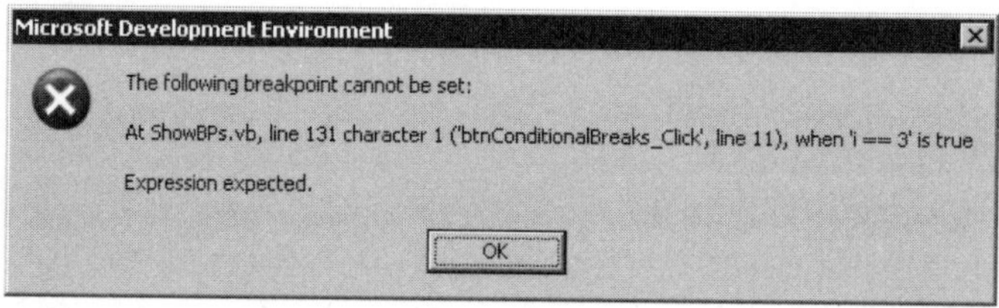

Figure 6-1 Visual Studio .NET indicating that it can't set a breakpoint

Because the breakpoint conditional expression modifier problem is so insidious, I want to show you a couple of examples where you can run into it. The first example shows how you have to be very careful of side effects from conditional expressions. In the following C# code, if you set a conditional breakpoint on the line that calls `Console.WriteLine` and you enter the condition as `i = 3` (notice there's only one equal sign in the condition), what do you think happens? If you guessed that the condition changes the value of `i` and causes an infinite loop, you're correct. I can't emphasize enough that you need to be extremely careful when entering your expressions so that they are correct.

```
for ( Int32 i = 0 ; i < 10 ; i++ )
{
    Console.WriteLine ( "{0}" , i ) ;
}
```

In the second example, I have a Windows Forms application written in Microsoft Visual Basic .NET with the following simple method:

```
Private Sub btnSkipBreaks_Click(ByVal sender As System.Object, _
                                ByVal e As System.EventArgs) _
                                Handles btnSkipBreaks.Click

    Dim i As Integer

    ' Clear the output edit control.
    edtOutput.Clear()

    m_TotalSkipPresses += 1

    edtOutput.Text = "Total presses: " + _
                     m_TotalSkipPresses.ToString() + _
                     vbCrLf

    For i = 1 To 10
        ' Append each character to the output edit box.
        edtOutput.Text += i.ToString() + vbCrLf
        ' Force the output edit box to update on each iteration.
        edtOutput.Update()
    Next
End Sub
```

If you happen to be thinking C# when entering a breakpoint inside the `For` loop and set the breakpoint conditional expression modifier to `i==3` (the correct Visual Basic .NET expression would be `i=3`) because the program is running, you'll see a fine message box similar to the one in Figure 6-1. What's sad is that you'll see the edit control fill with all the text, indicating that the code continues to execute. For Windows Forms and console applications, you should always set conditional expressions before starting the debugger. That way, if any of the expressions are ill-formed, Visual Studio .NET will notify you and stop on the first line of the program, thus giving you a fighting chance to correct the problem. For Microsoft ASP.NET applications and XML Web services, there's nothing you can do to get an early chance to rectify breakpoint conditional expression modifier problems, so you have to take extra care when setting the expressions.

The third example of where you'll run into problems with conditional expression breakpoints is when the expression happens to cause an exception for any reason. You'll see the same basic message box as shown in Figure 6-1. The good news is that the exception won't bring the program down because the exception is never passed to your application, but you still won't be able to stop and fix the expression. When using variables in an expression, take extra care to ensure that the expression is correct.

On a final note about conditional breakpoints, remember that in C# and J#, you can use `null`, `true`, and `false` as part of the expression. Oddly, `null` didn't work in Visual Studio .NET 2002. In Visual Basic .NET, you can use `True` and `False` for Boolean comparisons. To compare a variable to `Nothing`, the `Is` operator works just fine (`MyObject Is Nothing`).

Common Debugging Question

How can I break only when a specific thread calls a method?

To set a per-thread breakpoint, you need a way to uniquely identify the thread. Fortunately for us, the Microsoft .NET Framework team was thinking ahead and provided the `Name` property on the `System.Threading.Thread` class to make identifying a thread a trivial task, so you can simply set a conditional expression breakpoint with something like `"ThreadIWantToStopOn" == Thread.CurrentThread.Name`. Of course, this is assuming you always set the `Name` property inside your code whenever you start a thread.

The first way to obtain a unique thread identifier is to manually set the thread name by changing the value of the `Name` property in the Watch window. If you have the `MyThread` instance variable, you can enter `MyThread.Name` and enter the new thread name in the Value column. If you don't have a thread variable, you can use `Thread.CurrentThread.Name` to set the current thread's name. Setting the thread name from the debugger assumes that you're not also setting it from your code. The `Name` property can be set only once, and if you attempt to set it again, you'll cause an `InvalidOperationException`. If you're working with your own code without many third-party controls, it's fairly safe to set the thread name from the debugger because the .NET Framework class library doesn't access the `Name` property.

However, if you're working with lots of-third party controls or with code you suspect might access the `Name` property, there's another technique for getting a unique thread identifier that, although not as readily identifiable at a glance like a thread name, still yields a unique value. Buried deep in the `Thread` class is a private integer variable, `DONT_USE_InternalThread`, that is unique to each thread. (Yes, you can access private variables inside conditional expressions.) To stop on a specific thread, you'll need to use the Threads window to maneuver to the thread you want to stop on. In the Watch window, enter `Thread.CurrentThread.DONT_USE_InternalThread` to see the value of `DONT_USE_InternalThread` so that you can create the appropriate conditional breakpoint expression. Keep in mind that any variable named `DONT_USE_xxx` might disappear in the future.

The Watch Window

As I mentioned in the Chapter 5, the Watch window is one of the most exciting features in Visual Studio .NET debugging. Since I already discussed calling methods and setting properties, there's only one thing left to talk about concerning managed code in the Watch window and that's how to set up the Watch window to help you debug even faster.

Expanding Your Own Types Automatically

If you've done any amount of managed code debugging, you've probably seen that certain types seem to display more information in the Watch window than other types. For example, an exception type such as `System.ArgumentException` always displays the message associated with the exception in the Watch window Value column, whereas a type such as `System.Threading.Thread` displays only the type. In the former case, you can quickly see the important information about the class at a glance whereas in the latter you need to expand the class and hunt through a huge list of member fields to find more specific information such as the name. To me, it's not very useful when you have an entry in the Watch window, and the Value column and the Type column both show the same value. Figure 6-2 shows an example of a type that desperately needs some autoexpand help.

Figure 6-2 Desperately seeking autoexpand help

By adding your own types to the Watch window as well as key .NET Framework class library classes not already added, you can trim a great deal of time off debugging because the key information you need is always there at a glance. The best part of this expansion is that it also applies to the data tips that pop up when you hover your mouse over a variable in the Source windows as well as when showing parameters in the Call Stack window.

Although autoexpands is extremely cool, it's not perfect. The most serious shortcoming is that autoexpands work only for C#, J#, and Managed Extensions for C++. Like the unfortunate absence of XML documentation comments in Visual Basic .NET, the lack of autoexpands is quite sad because it makes debugging Visual Basic .NET code harder than it should be. Additionally, the rules file is read-only when you start Visual Studio .NET, so when adding autoexpand rules you'll be doing a lot of startup and shut down as you test your rules. Interestingly, with native code autoexpands, which I'll discuss in Chapter 7, the rules file is read each time you start debugging. A minor issue is that the file containing the expansion rules isn't stored with your project but rather must reside in the directory where Visual Studio .NET is installed. This means that when you put the team copy of the autoexpands file in your version control, you'll have to make sure you set the working directory to the hard-coded location, which is described in the next paragraph, so that the debugger can find it.

The first step to autoexpand bliss is finding the appropriate rules files. The files, MCEE_CS.DAT for C#, VJSEE.DAT for J#, and MCEE_MC.DAT for Managed Extensions for C++, are in your <Visual Studio .NET installation directory>\COMMON7\PACKAGES\DEBUGGER directory. As you peruse the three files, you'll notice that the C# version has quite a few more expansions in it than the Managed Extensions for C++ version. (The J# version has more Java-specific expansions.) If you're doing Managed Extensions for C++ development, you might want to copy the rules in MCEE_CS.DAT to MCEE_MC.DAT so that you'll get the additional rules.

The comments, delimited by semicolon characters, at the tops of both files describe the gyrations necessary for expanding C# and Managed Extensions for C++ types. Although the documentation implies through omission that only the actual field values can be used in the autoexpand rules, you can call property get accessors as well as methods in the rules. Obviously, you'll want to ensure that the method or property you access returns something that makes sense to return, such as a string or numeric value. Returning classes or complex value types show only the type, not any useful information. As usual, here's where I need to warn you about making sure you use only properties and methods that won't cause side effects.

As an example, I'll add the C# autoexpand for `System.Threading.Thread` class types so that you'll see the thread name in the Value column if the name is set. Looking at the examples Microsoft provides in MCEE_CS.DAT, you'll notice that most of the types are specified with complete namespace delimiters.

Since the tiny bit of documentation at the top of the MCEE_CS.DAT file doesn't indicate what the minimum level is, I always use the complete intrinsic type name to avoid any problems.

The MCEE_CS.DAT file documentation is shown in Bakus-Naur (BNR) form, which isn't always the easiest thing to read. To simplify the descriptions, I thought I'd show a cleaner and more common-sense formation: "<type>=[text]<member/method,format>..." Table 6-1 explains the meaning of each field. The angle brackets are mandatory on both the type element and around the member/method,format sections. Also note that the autoexpand rule can show multiple member values for a type.

Table 6-1 MCEE_CS.DAT and MCEE_MC.DAT Autoexpand Entries

Field	Description
type	The type name, which should be the complete type.
text	Any literal text. This field is generally the member name or a shorthand version of it.
member/method	The actual data member to display or method to call. This field can be an expression when you want to show a calculated value. The casting operators also work.
format	Additional format specifiers for the member variables to force numeric base display. Permissible values here are d (decimal), o (octal), and h (hexadecimal).

In the System.Threading.Thread autoexpand, I'm just interested in the Name property, so I place this value in the file:

```
<System.Threading.Thread>=Name=<Name>
```

Figure 6-3 shows the result of adding the expansion in the Watch window. The icing on the cake is shown in Figure 6-4, in which you can see that the tool tip shows the autoexpand as well. Included with this book's sample files is my MCEE_CS.DAT file, in which I added common autoexpands I thought Microsoft forgot, such as the StringBuilder class. You can use it as a base for starting your own expansion files.

Figure 6-3 The joy of autoexpands

```
t1.Start ( ) ;
t2 (local variable) System.Threading.Thread t1 = {Name="Bob" }
```

Figure 6-4 The ecstasy of autoexpands

Common Debugging Question

Is there any way I can see the flow of operation in a managed application in the debugger?

Sometimes, the best way to learn how something fits together is to see in a hierarchical manner who is calling what. Although the Visual Studio .NET debugger doesn't offer any such options (without someone possibly writing an add-in), CORDBG.EXE, the debugger that comes with the .NET Framework, does. (For a solution to viewing the flow without a debugger, see Chapter 11.) If you want to experience all the joys of PC debugging circa 1985, CORDBG.EXE's console-based debugging is all for you.

CORDBG.EXE has the `wt` command, which mimics WinDBG's `Watch` and `Trace` commands. In addition to showing the complete hierarchy of calls, `wt` also shows how many native instructions executed as a result of each method called. To best utilize the `wt` command, set a breakpoint on the first line of the method you want to start tracing from. The `wt` command will execute until it hits the return address of the starting scope.

The following shows the output of the `wt` command for an application (WT.CS, available with this book's sample files) that calls three empty functions. As you can imagine, calling items in the .NET Framework class library will generate volumes of output.

```
(cordbg) wt
       1         App::Main
       3          App::Foo
       3           App::Bar
       5          App::Baz
       3         App::Bar
       3        App::Foo
       3        App::Main
      21 instructions total
```

If you're just starting out with CORDBG.EXE, the most important command is `?` because that will get you the command help. A `?` followed by a command will show you more information about that command as well as provide example usages.

Tips and Tricks

Before I turn to ILDASM and the fun of Microsoft intermediate language (MSIL), I want to cover a few tips and tricks for managed code.

`DebuggerStepThroughAttribute` and `DebuggerHiddenAttribute`

Two very interesting attributes show the real power of attributed programming in .NET: `DebuggerStepThroughAttribute` and `DebuggerHiddenAttribute`. They can be specified on properties, methods, and constructors, but the common language runtime (CLR) never looks at or uses them. However, the Visual Studio .NET debugger uses them at run time to control how stepping occurs. Before I describe how to use `DebuggerStepThroughAttribute` and `DebuggerHiddenAttribute`, I must warn you that if you're not careful, these attributes can make debugging your code extremely difficult (if not impossible), so use them at your own risk. You've been warned!

The more useful of the two attributes is `DebuggerStepThroughAttribute`. When this attribute is applied to classes, structures, constructors, or methods, the Visual Studio .NET debugger automatically steps over those items even when you use the Step Into command. You can still set breakpoints in the items if you do want to debug them. This attribute is best used on items that have only a single line of code in them, such as get and set accessors. You'll also see this attribute used with the `InitializeComponent` method, added automatically by the Visual Basic .NET Windows Forms Designer–generated code. You might want to add it to your C#, J#, or Managed Extensions for C++ Windows Forms `InitializeComponent` method.

Whereas `DebuggerStepThroughAttribute` at least lets you set breakpoints, `DebuggerHiddenAttribute` both hides the method or property it is applied to and doesn't allow any breakpoints to be set within that method or property. I would strongly discourage you from using this attribute because using it means that you can't debug that part of the code. However, it might come in handy to completely hide internal methods. `DebuggerHiddenAttribute` won't be a foolproof antidebugging technique because it's up to the debugger implementers to read the metadata for the attribute. As of the time of this writing, Visual Studio .NET and the .NET Framework SDK debugger, DBGCLR.EXE, respect the attribute, but CORDBG.EXE does not.

Mixed Mode Debugging

Debugging a native code DLL at the source level when it's brought into a managed application is called *mixed mode debugging*. The first step to starting mixed mode debugging is figuring out how to turn it on. Figure 6-5 shows the setting for C# applications, and Figure 6-6 shows the setting for Visual Basic .NET applications. For the life of me, I still can't figure out why two completely different property page settings for C# and Visual Basic .NET are necessary when all the command-line options to the compilers, as well as most of the settings, are essentially identical.

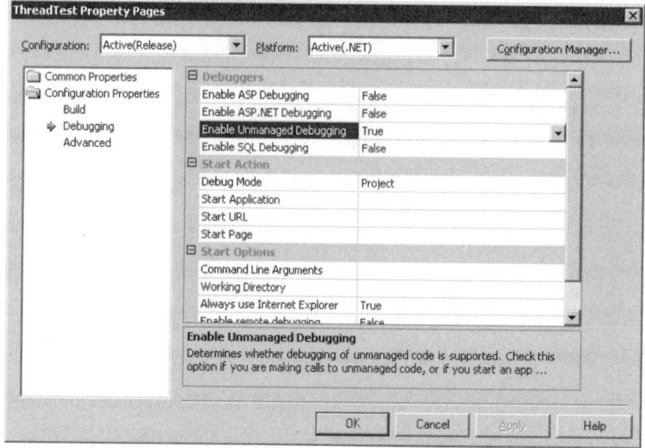

Figure 6-5 Turning on mixed mode debugging in a C# project

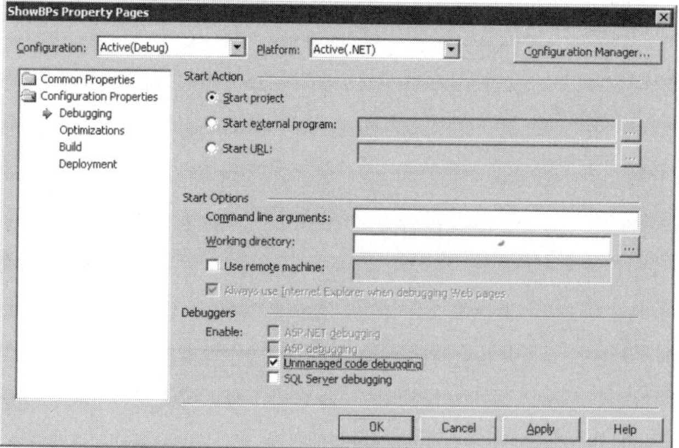

Figure 6-6 Turning on mixed mode debugging in a Visual Basic .NET project

The biggest drawback to mixed mode debugging is that it can be very slow. Your best bet is to take care of your managed and native debugging separately if possible. If you have to do mixed mode debugging, you should first turn off property evaluation, as shown in Figure 6-7, because most of the slowing down is related to the work necessary to evaluate items in the Watch window family. After turning off the property evaluation, mixed mode debugging is still slower than straight managed or native debugging, but it is faster than if you leave it turned on. One big difference between straight managed debugging and mixed mode debugging is that if you have mixed mode debugging on, you can right-click in the Modules window and select Show Modules For All Programs, which allows you to see all the modules loaded by your managed process.

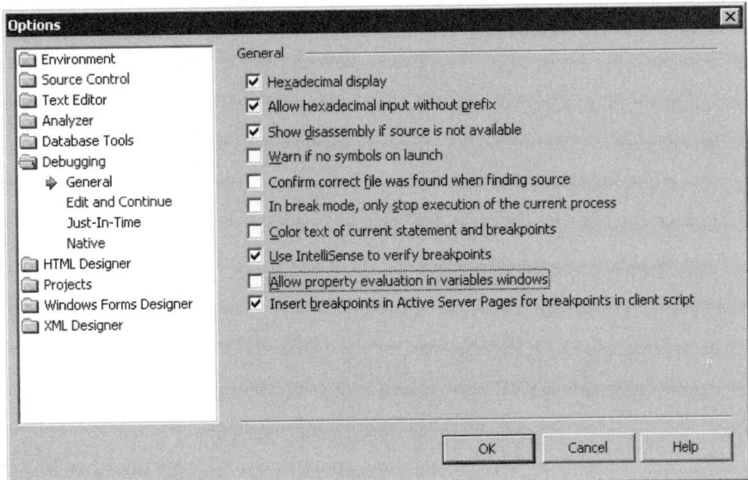

Figure 6-7 Turning off property evaluation

There are also a few smaller drawbacks to mixed mode debugging. The first is that even though you are doing native mode debugging on the process, you can't use any data breakpoints, which I'll discuss in the next chapter. Additionally, you cannot create mini dumps of the process, unless the debugger is sitting in a native function call.

Remote Debugging

Microsoft deserves a Nobel Peace Prize for helping to bring peace between two of the most contentious groups in history, developers and network administrators. Prior to managed applications, developers had to be part of the Administrators group on any machine they were going to use for debugging applications. However, when developers needed to debug on a production server, network administrators were very reluctant to give them that much power over the system—especially because developers occasionally abused that power and changed system settings that would, for example, force administrators to change their passwords for every login and require that password be 65 characters long. Not that I have done that, but I have heard tales about others who have done it.

The process that brought peace to all is remote debugging. I don't want to rehash the documentation here, but I do want to clear up a few issues I consistently hear developers ask about in regard to setting up and using remote debugging. The first is that you don't have to install a full copy of Visual Studio .NET on the remote machine for remote debugging to work; you need only the remote debugging components of Visual Studio .NET. Install the remote debugging pieces by clicking the "Remote Components Setup" link at the bottom of the Visual Studio .NET Setup application, as shown in Figure 6-8. In the screen that pops up, follow the directions under Full Remote Debugging Support and install the .NET Framework on the machine *before* clicking the Install Full button. It's very easy to forget to install the .NET Framework SDK, and if you do forget, you'll be scratching your head wondering why you can't debug or run any managed applications. Keep in mind that even though you don't have to be a part of the Administrators group to do remote debugging, you must be a member of the Administrators group to install the remote debugging components.

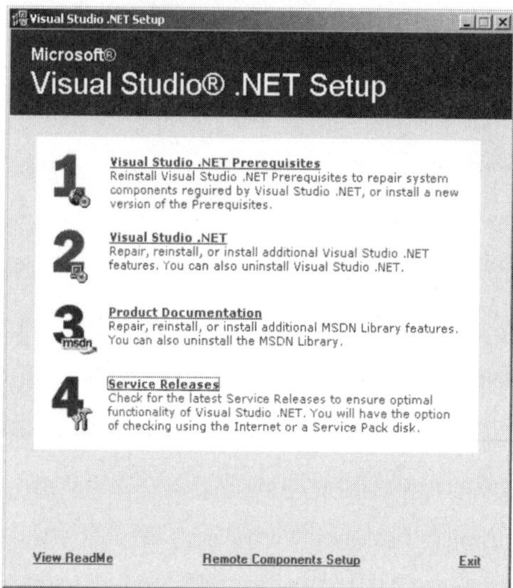

Figure 6-8 Installing just the remote debugging portion of Visual Studio .NET

The whole key to remote debugging is ensuring your account is in the Debugger Users group on the remote machine. Of course, to be able to add users to the Debugger Users group, you must be a member of the Administrators group on that machine. The most common problem I've seen with setting up remote debugging is forgetting to add your account to the Debugger Users group on the remote machine.

Common Debugging Question

When debugging XML Web services, I get exceptions indicating the operation has timed out. What can I do?

This can be a very common error when debugging XML Web services. Either in your code or in the Watch window, set the `TimeOut` property on the XML Web service object to `-1` to indicate infinite timeout.

ILDASM and Microsoft Intermediate Language

When I first started playing with .NET several years ago, I wrote the usual "Hello World!" program and immediately wanted to see how it all worked under the covers. I had quite the shock when I realized that .NET was essentially a whole new development environment! When learning a new environment, I like to get down to the simplest operation and start working my way up so that I can see how it all fits together.

For example, when I was making my transition from MS-DOS to Microsoft Windows 3.0 (wow, am I getting old!), whenever I got a little confused about what was going on, I took a peek at the assembly language the CPU was executing so that I could get a clue. The beautiful thing about assembly language (also known as unambiguous mode) is that it never lies. I was able to continue using this technique until I started moving to .NET, at which point my world became a little topsy-turvy. I lost my assembly-language crutch! I could look at the Intel assembly language in the debuggers, but it didn't help much. I was seeing quite a bit more assembly language that called through allocated addresses and other complicated techniques—the one-to-one mapping present in Microsoft C/C++ Win32 development no longer existed.

However, immediately after writing that first "Hello World!" program, I found the coolest feature in .NET: the Microsoft Intermediate Language Disassembler (ILDASM). Armed with a killer disassembler, I felt I could start tackling this elephant-sized mound of stuff known as .NET a single bite at a time. ILDASM allows you to see the pseudo-assembly language for .NET, called Microsoft intermediate language (MSIL). You or I might never write anything in MSIL, but knowing our way around the assembly language for an environment is the difference between merely using that environment and really learning it. Additionally, although the .NET documentation is excellent, nothing beats seeing exactly how an application is implemented.

Before we jump into ILDASM usage and MSIL, I want to address one common issue that always comes up with .NET and is a source of confusion. Many people have told me that they won't really consider .NET because it's so easy to reverse engineer, or decompile, so there's no protection for their intellectual property. That's a completely accurate assessment of .NET. In exchange for the power of true distributed objects, garbage collection, and ease of development, a .NET binary has to be self-describing. However, the argument is a complete red herring.

The same complaints were made about Java when it first burst on the scene. Lots of folks were aghast that it was so easy to decompile. In fact, a third-party company produced an excellent decompiler for Java binaries that was simply amazing. I remember talking with some of their customers who liked the results produced by this tool so much that they compiled their coworkers code and decompiled it with the tool because the tool produced better and more readable code than their coworkers! Even though all those people were extremely worried about protecting their intellectual property in the beginning, that worry sure didn't slow down Java's acceptance by enterprise developers.

For those of you doing Web applications or XML Web services, be aware that customers and users don't have physical access to the binaries and therefore you don't have to be concerned about reverse engineering. However, many of you are doing Windows Forms or console applications and might be a little worried. Starting with Visual Studio .NET 2003, Microsoft is distributing a "community edition" of PreEmptive Solutions, Dotfuscator. This version does nothing more than what looks to me like renaming your classes and methods, which might be good enough. Be prepared to spend some time with Dotfuscator because its graphical user interface (GUI) is in need of some serious user interface research.

If you're concerned about intellectual property issues in your Windows Forms or console applications, Wise Owl (also known as fellow Wintellectual Brent Rector) has written an outstanding obfuscator, Demeanor for .NET. Demeanor will completely protect your intellectual property. I strongly recommend it because it will eliminate any worries you might have about deploying .NET applications in cases where someone might have physical access to the binaries. You can learn more about Demeanor for .NET by surfing to *http://www.wiseowl.com*.

Of course, if you are going to us an obfuscator on your .NET code, make sure you have completely debugged and tested the code before obfuscating. As of now, there's no way to match the obfuscated code back to your source so you're left debugging at the x86 assembly language level.

Getting Started with ILDASM

ILDASM is located in your <Visual Studio .NET Install Directory>\SDK\v1.1\Bin directory, which might not be in your PATH environment variable by default. If you execute the VSVARS.BAT file from <Visual Studio .NET Installation Directory>\Common7\Tools, you'll get the appropriate .NET environment variables set up so that you can access any of the .NET utilities from the command line. When you start ILDASM and choose a file to disassemble, the initial view looks similar to Figure 6-9. What you're seeing is the metadata expansion for the module. Figure 6-9 shows all possible icons displayed for the types, but it's not very clear from the figure what all the icons are for and what their textual values are when you save the tree display to a file. I created Table 6-2 to make everything simple to understand.

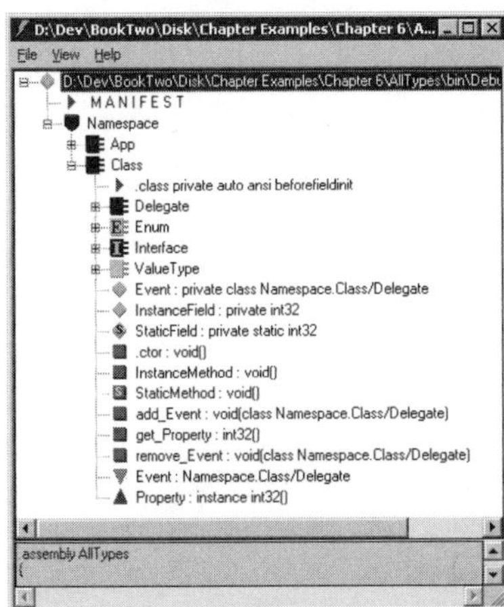

Figure 6-9 Main ILDASM display

Table 6-2 ILDASM Tree Output Descriptions

Glyph	Text Output	Description
	[MOD] for module heading	Informational directives, class declarations, and manifest information
	[NSP]	Namespace
	[CLS]	Class
	[INT]	Interface
	[ENU]	Enumeration
	[VCL]	Value class
	[MET]	Instance method (private, public, or protected)
	[STM]	Static method
	[FLD]	Instance field (private, public, or protected); also assembly
	[STF]	Static field
	[EVT]	Event
	[PTY]	Property (get and/or set)

If you'd like to see more information and statistics about files you're opening, start ILDASM with the `/ADV` command line option. This turns on advanced display information and appends three new items to the View menu:

- COR Header lets you view the file header information.
- Statistics lets you see various statistics concerning size percentages and a breakdown of all metadata in the system.
- MetaInfo contains a submenu that lets you select specific information to view. Choose the Show! submenu item (or press Ctrl+M) to see that information, which is displayed in a separate MetaInfo window. If you don't select any of the specific information, when you select Show!, you'll see a raw dump of the metadata.

If you have source code available for a particular module, you'll certainly want to turn on Show Source Lines on the View menu. Alternatively, you can specify the `/SOURCE` command line option. When you specify source line display, the disassembly shows the source lines as comments above the MSIL generated for them. To see all the command-line options, specify `/?` on the command line. I use a batch file that contains the following to start instances of ILDASM with the options I want:

```
ildasm /adv /source %1
```

To see the actual MSIL for a particular item, simply double-click on that item and another window will pop up. Depending on what you double-clicked, you'll see the disassembly, declaration information, or general information for the item. If the window looks like the one in Figure 6-10, you're ready to start learning MSIL. One nice little feature of ILDASM is that it supports drag-and-drop functionality, so you can easily jump between modules.

The final trick I want to share about ILDASM is how you can see your C#, J#, Managed Extensions for C++, or Visual Basic .NET code and the MSIL all at the same time. If you've looked at the debugger's Disassembly window when debugging a managed application, you've probably seen the .NET language code and only the Intel assembly language. The reason is that the MSIL is just-in-time (JIT) compiled, so you're only executing the native assembly language, never the MSIL. What makes ILDASM really interesting is that it achieves the Holy Grail of disassemblers: it's a true "round-trip" disassembler!

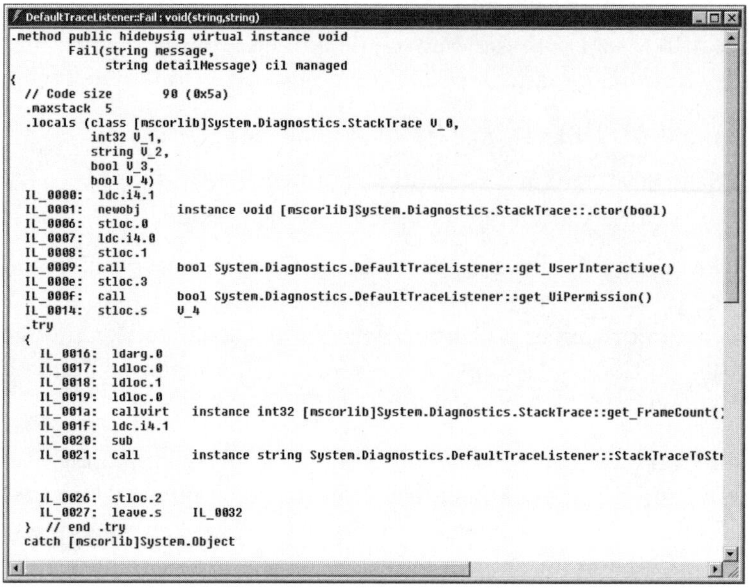

```
DefaultTraceListener::Fail : void(string,string)
.method public hidebysig virtual instance void
        Fail(string message,
             string detailMessage) cil managed
{
  // Code size       90 (0x5a)
  .maxstack  5
  .locals (class [mscorlib]System.Diagnostics.StackTrace V_0,
           int32 V_1,
           string V_2,
           bool V_3,
           bool V_4)
  IL_0000:  ldc.i4.1
  IL_0001:  newobj     instance void [mscorlib]System.Diagnostics.StackTrace::.ctor(bool)
  IL_0006:  stloc.0
  IL_0007:  ldc.i4.0
  IL_0008:  stloc.1
  IL_0009:  call       bool System.Diagnostics.DefaultTraceListener::get_UserInteractive()
  IL_000e:  stloc.3
  IL_000f:  call       bool System.Diagnostics.DefaultTraceListener::get_UiPermission()
  IL_0014:  stloc.s    V_4
  .try
  {
    IL_0016:  ldarg.0
    IL_0017:  ldloc.0
    IL_0018:  ldloc.1
    IL_0019:  ldloc.0
    IL_001a:  callvirt   instance int32 [mscorlib]System.Diagnostics.StackTrace::get_FrameCount()
    IL_001f:  ldc.i4.1
    IL_0020:  sub
    IL_0021:  call       instance string System.Diagnostics.DefaultTraceListener::StackTraceToSt


    IL_0026:  stloc.2
    IL_0027:  leave.s    IL_0032
  }  // end .try
  catch [mscorlib]System.Object
```

Figure 6-10 MSIL for a method

With a round-trip disassembler, you can disassemble a binary and immediately run it through an assembler to rebuild the application. Since .NET comes with ILASM, the Microsoft Intermediate Language Assembler, you've got everything you need to see your C#/J#/Managed Extensions for C++/Visual Basic .NET code and MSIL all at the same time. This view allows you to see how things fit together. Disassemble the file with the `/SOURCE` and `/OUT=` command-line options to ILDASM, specifying an output file name that ends in .IL. Compile the file with ILASM using the `/DEBUG` option. Now you'll step through the MSIL with Visual Studio .NET's debugger and see the corresponding C#/J#/Managed Extensions for C++/Visual Basic .NET code as comments. If you want to see it all, simply look at the Disassembly window and you'll see how the high-level language is compiled to MSIL, and how the MSIL is JIT compiled to Intel assembly language. Listing 6-2 shows a method disassembled with the original source embedded as comments from the ShowBPs program, included with this book's sample files.

```
.method private instance void
         btnConditionalBreaks_Click(object sender,
                                    class [mscorlib]System.EventArgs e)
                                    cil managed
{
  // Code size       139 (0x8b)
  .maxstack  4
  .locals init ([0] int32 i,
           [1] int32 j,
           [2] string[] _Vb_t_array_0,
           [3] class [System.Windows.Forms]
                          System.Windows.Forms.TextBox _Vb_t_ref_0)
//000120:
//000121: Private Sub btnConditionalBreaks_Click _
//                      ( ByVal sender As System.Object, _
//                        ByVal e As System.EventArgs) _
//                              Handles btnConditionalBreaks.Click
  IL_0000:  nop
//000122:         Dim i As Integer = 0
  IL_0001:  ldc.i4.0
  IL_0002:  stloc.0
//000123:         Dim j As Integer = 0
  IL_0003:  ldc.i4.0
  IL_0004:  stloc.1
//000124:
//000125: ' Clearn the output edit control.
//000126: edtOutput.Clear()
  IL_0005:  ldarg.0
  IL_0006:  callvirt   instance class
                [System.Windows.Forms]System.Windows.Forms.TextBox
                                  ShowBPs.ShowBPsForm::get_edtOutput()
  IL_000b:  callvirt   instance void
              [System.Windows.Forms]System.Windows.Forms.TextBoxBase::Clear(
)
  IL_0010:  nop
//000127:
//000128: ' Both are on one line to show how BPs can apply to part of a line.
//000129: For i = 1 To 5 : For j = 1 To 5
  IL_0011:  ldc.i4.1
  IL_0012:  stloc.0
  IL_0013:  ldc.i4.1
  IL_0014:  stloc.1
//000130: ' Do the output
//000131: edtOutput.Text += "i = " + i.ToString() + " j = " + _
//               j.ToString() + vbCrLf
  IL_0015:  ldarg.0
  IL_0016:  callvirt   instance class
```

Listing 6-2 Mixed source and MSIL *(continued)*

```
                 [System.Windows.Forms]System.Windows.Forms.TextBox
                        ShowBPs.ShowBPsForm::get_edtOutput()
  IL_001b:  stloc.3
  IL_001c:  ldloc.3
  IL_001d:  ldc.i4.6
  IL_001e:  newarr     [mscorlib]System.String
  IL_0023:  stloc.2
  IL_0024:  ldloc.2
  IL_0025:  ldc.i4.0
  IL_0026:  ldloc.3
  IL_0027:  callvirt   instance string
                [System.Windows.Forms]System.Windows.Forms.TextBox::get_Text()
  IL_002c:  stelem.ref
  IL_002d:  nop
  IL_002e:  ldloc.2
  IL_002f:  ldc.i4.1
  IL_0030:  ldstr      "i = "
  IL_0035:  stelem.ref
  IL_0036:  nop
  IL_0037:  ldloc.2
  IL_0038:  ldc.i4.2
  IL_0039:  ldloca.s   i
  IL_003b:  call       instance string [mscorlib]System.Int32::ToString()
  IL_0040:  stelem.ref
  IL_0041:  nop
  IL_0042:  ldloc.2
  IL_0043:  ldc.i4.3
  IL_0044:  ldstr      " j = "
  IL_0049:  stelem.ref
  IL_004a:  nop
  IL_004b:  ldloc.2
  IL_004c:  ldc.i4.4
  IL_004d:  ldloca.s   j
  IL_004f:  call       instance string [mscorlib]System.Int32::ToString()
  IL_0054:  stelem.ref
  IL_0055:  nop
  IL_0056:  ldloc.2
  IL_0057:  ldc.i4.5
  IL_0058:  ldstr      "\r\n"
  IL_005d:  stelem.ref
  IL_005e:  nop
  IL_005f:  ldloc.2
  IL_0060:  call       string [mscorlib]System.String::Concat(string[])
  IL_0065:  callvirt   instance void
          [System.Windows.Forms]System.Windows.Forms.TextBox::set_Text(string)
  IL_006a:  nop
//000132: ' For the output to show up.
//000133: edtOutput.Update()
  IL_006b:  ldarg.0
  IL_006c:  callvirt   instance class
```

```
                [System.Windows.Forms]System.Windows.Forms.TextBox
                       ShowBPs.ShowBPsForm::get_edtOutput()
  IL_0071:  callvirt   instance void
               [System.Windows.Forms]System.Windows.Forms.Control::Update()
  IL_0076:  nop
//000134: Next j
  IL_0077:  nop
  IL_0078:  ldloc.1
  IL_0079:  ldc.i4.1
  IL_007a:  add.ovf
  IL_007b:  stloc.1
  IL_007c:  ldloc.1
  IL_007d:  ldc.i4.5
  IL_007e:  ble.s      IL_0015

//000135: Next i
  IL_0080:  nop
  IL_0081:  ldloc.0
  IL_0082:  ldc.i4.1
  IL_0083:  add.ovf
  IL_0084:  stloc.0
  IL_0085:  ldloc.0
  IL_0086:  ldc.i4.5
  IL_0087:  ble.s      IL_0013

//000136:     End Sub
  IL_0089:  nop
  IL_008a:  ret
} // end of method ShowBPsForm::btnConditionalBreaks_Click
```

CLR Basics

Before you start grinding through MSIL instructions, I need to explain a little bit about how the CLR works. The CLR is essentially the CPU for MSIL instructions. Whereas traditional CPUs rely on registers and stacks to do everything, the CLR uses only a stack. This means that to add two numbers, the CLR loads both numbers onto the stack and calls an instruction to add them. The instruction removes the two numbers from the stack and puts the result on top of the stack. If you're like me, it sometimes helps to see the actual implementation. To see a system similar to the CLR that's small enough to digest, see Brian Kernighan and Rob Pike's book, *The Unix Programming Environment* (Prentice Hall, 1984). In it they implement a higher order calculator (hoc), a nontrivial C example of a stack-based machine. If you'd like to see a real CLR implementation, download the Shared Source Common Language Infrastructure (CLI)—that is, "Rotor"—which is the ECMA standard implementation of a cross-platform CLR. It's a ton of code, but you'll see how it all works. You can download the Shared Source CLI from *http://msdn.microsoft.com/netframework*.

The CLR evaluation stack can hold any type of value in the stack slots. Copying values from memory to the stack is referred to as *loading*, whereas copying items from the stack to memory is referred to as *storing*. Unlike the Intel CPU, the CLR stack doesn't hold the locals, but the locals are in memory. The stacks are local to the method doing the work, and the CLR saves them across method invocations. Finally, the stack is also where method return values are placed. Now that I've covered just enough about how the CLR works, I'll move on to the instructions.

MSIL, Locals, and Parameter

Before I jump into the heavy gyrations, I thought I'd start out with the simplest program possible, "Hello World!" written in MSIL. That way you can see a proper MSIL program in action so I can start pointing out the various items you'll see as part of ILDASM's output. Listing 6-3 shows the complete "Hello World!" program and is included with this book's sample files as HelloWorld.IL. Even if this is the first time you've seen MSIL, you can easily see what's going on. Anything that starts with a period is a directive for the assembler, ILASM.EXE, and comments are delimited with the standard C# double slashes.

```
// You need the .assembly for the program to run.
.assembly hello {}

// Declare a "C" like main.
.method static public void main() il managed
{
    // This tells the execution engine (EE) where to start executing.
    // You need one per program. This directive can apply to methods as
    // well.
    .entrypoint

    // This is not needed for ILASM, but ILDASM will always show it so
    // I included it.
    .maxstack 1

    // Push a string onto the stack.
    ldstr  "Hello World from IL!"

    // Call the System.Console.Writeline class.
    call   void [mscorlib]System.Console::WriteLine(class System.String)

    // Return to the caller. The file will compile if you forget this,
    // but you will cause an exception in the EE.
    ret
}
```

Listing 6-3 HelloWorld.IL

The important parts of the code in Listing 6-3 are the last three lines. The `ldstr` instruction takes care of getting the string onto the stack. Putting items on the stack is loading, so all instructions that start with "ld" are getting items from memory and putting them on the stack. Even though I didn't use storing in the "Hello World!" program, getting items from the stack and putting them into memory is storing, and all those instructions begin with "st." Armed with those two little facts and the help ILDASM gives you by placing the hard-coded strings inline with the disassembly, you can perform a good portion of your reverse engineering.

Now that I've shown you a little bit of MSIL assembly language, it's time to turn to what ILDASM shows you so that you can start seeing how the various constructs fit together.

Getting the parameters and return types in ILDASM is trivial because the disassembly gives them to you when you double-click on a method to view it. The best part is that the disassembly shows the actual parameter names. Class values are shown as `[`*module*`]`*namespace*`.`*class* format. The core primitive types, `int`, `char`, and so on, are shown as their specific class type. For example, `int` is shown as `Int32`.

Local variable display is very easy to decipher as well. If you have debugging symbols available, the locals display will show the actual names. However, disassembling the system classes will look like the following:

```
.locals (class [mscorlib]Microsoft.Win32.RegistryKey V_0,
         class System.Object V_1,
         int32 V_2,
         int32 V_3)
```

The `.locals` and the parentheses delineate the complete list of parameters, separated by commas. The type is given followed by a `V_#` format, where the # indicates each parameter number. As you'll see later, the number is used in quite a few instructions. In the previous snippet, `[mscorlib]` indicates the particular DLL the class comes from.

The Important Instructions

Instead of providing a huge table of instructions, I want to show the most important instructions you'll run into and examples of their use. I'll start with the loading instructions and explain all their options. As I get to the other types of instructions, I'll skip parts that are in common with the load instructions and just show their usage. The instructions I don't cover are quite easy to figure out based on their names.

ldc Load number constant

This instruction pushes a hard-coded number on the stack. The instruction format is `ldc.`*size*`[.`*num*`]`, where *size* is the byte size of the value and *num* is a special short encoding for a 4-byte integer from -128 through 127 (when size is `i4`). The size is either `i4` (4-byte integer), `i8` (8-byte integer), `r4` (4-byte floating point), or `r8` (floating point). There are numerous forms to this instruction to keep the number of opcodes down.

```
ldc.i4.0                    // Load 0 onto the stack using the
                            // special form.
ldc.r8  2.1000000000000001 // Load 2.1000000000000001.
ldc.i4.m1                   // Load -1 onto the stack. This
                            // is the special form.
ldc.i4.s -9                 // Load -9 onto the stack
                            // using the short form.
```

ldarg Load argument
ldarga Load argument address

The argument numbers start at 0. For instance methods, argument 0 is the `this` pointer, and the first argument starts at 1 rather than 0.

```
ldarg.2               // Load argument 2 onto the stack. 3 is the
                      // highest number using this form.
ldarg.s 6             // Load argument 6 onto the stack. All argument
                      // numbers past 4 (inclusive) use this form.
ldarga.s newSample    // Load newSample's address
```

ldloc Load local variable
ldloca Load local variable address

These instructions load the specified local variable onto the stack. All local variables are specified by the order in which they appear in the `locals` declaration. The instruction `ldloca` loads the local variable's address.

```
ldloc.0         // Load local 0 onto the stack. 3 is the
                // highest number using this form.
ldloc.s V_6     // Load local variable 6 onto the stack. All
                // variables past number 4 (inclusive) use this form.
ldloca.s V_5    // Load local variable 5's address onto the stack.
```

ldfld Load object field of a class
ldsfld Load static field of a class

These instructions load the normal or static field from an object onto the stack. MSIL disassembly of an object is very easy because the complete field value is specified. The instruction `ldflda` loads the field's address.

```
// Load the _Originator field from System.Reflection.AssemblyName.
// Notice the type of the field is given as well.
ldfld    unsigned int8[] System.Reflection.AssemblyName::_Originator
// Load the empty string from System.String.
ldsfld   class System.String [mscorlib]System.String::Empty
```

ldelem Load an element of an array

This instruction loads the specified element onto the stack for single-dimensional, zero-based arrays. The previous two instructions put the array item and the index onto the stack (in that order). The `ldelem` instruction removes the array and the index from the stack and puts the specified element on the top of the stack. A type field follows the `ldelem` instruction. The most common type field in the compiled base class library is `ldelem.ref`, which gets the element as an object. Other common types are `ldelem.i4` for getting the element as a signed 4-byte integer, and `ldelem.i8` to get a 8-byte integer.

```
.locals (System.String[] V_0, // The [] indicate an array declaration.
         int32 V_1 )          // The index.
...                           // Do work to fill V_0.
ldloc.0                       // Load the array.
ldc.i4.0                      // Load the zero index.
ldelem.ref                    // Get the object at index zero.
```

ldlen Load the **lLength** of an array

This instruction removes the zero-based, single-dimensional array from the stack and pushes the length of the array onto the stack.

```
// Load the attribute field, which is an array.
ldfld class System.ComponentModel.MemberAttribute[]
   System.ComponentModel.MemberDescriptor::attributes
stloc.1                    // Store the value into the first
                           // local (an array).
ldloc.1                    // Load the first local onto the stack.
ldlen                      // Get the array length.
```

starg Store a value in an argument slot

Takes the value off the top of the stack and places it into the specified argument.

```
starg.s categoryHelp             // Store the top of the stack into
                                 // categoryHelp. All starg
                                 // instructions use the .s form.
```

stelem Store an element of an array

Whereas the previous three instructions place the zero-based, single-dimensional array; the index; and the value onto the stack (in that order), the `stelem` instruction casts the value into the appropriate array type before moving the value into the array. The `stelem` instruction removes all three items from the stack. Like the `ldelem` instruction, the type field specifies the conversion. The most common conversion is `stelem.ref` to convert a value type to an object.

```
.method public hidebysig specialname
instance void  set_MachineName(class System.String 'value') il managed
{
  .maxstack  4
  .locals (class System.String[] V_0)
```

```
:
   ldloc.0                      // Load the array on the stack.
   ldc.i4.1                     // Load the index, the constant 1.
   ldarg.1                      // Load the argument, the string.
   stelem.ref                   // Store the element.
:
```

stfld Store into a field of an object

This instruction takes the value off the top of the stack and places it into the object field. As when loading a field, the complete reference is given.

```
stfld  int32[] System.Diagnostics.CategoryEntry::HelpIndexes
```

ceq Compare equal

This instruction compares the top two values on the stack. The two items are removed from the stack, and if the values are equal, a 1 is pushed onto the stack; otherwise, a 0 is pushed onto the stack.

```
ldloc.1                      // Load the first local.
ldc.i4.0                     // Load the constant zero.
ceq                          // Compare the items for equality.
```

cgt Compare greater than

This instruction also compares the top two values on the stack. The two items are removed, and if the first value pushed is greater than the second value, a 1 is pushed on the stack; otherwise, a 0 is pushed. The `cgt` instruction can also have the `.un` modifier applied to indicate the comparison is unsigned or unordered.

```
// Get the collection count.
call instance int32 System.Diagnostics.
  CounterCreationDataCollection::get_Count()
ldc.i4.0                      // Load the constant zero.
cgt                           // Compare if the count is
                              // greater than zero.
```

clt Compare less than

This instruction performs identically to `cgt` except that 1 is pushed when the first value is less than the second value.

```
// Get the trace switch level.
call instance value class System.Diagnostics.TraceLevel
       System.Diagnostics.TraceSwitch::get_Level()
ldc.i4.1                      // Load the constant 1.
clt                           // Compare if the trace level is
                              // less than one.
```

br Unconditional branch

This instruction is the goto of MSIL.

```
br.s IL_008d                    // Goto offset into the method.
```

brfalse Branch on false

brtrue Branch on true

Both instructions look at the value on the top of the stack and branch accordingly. The brtrue instruction branches only when the value is 1, whereas brfalse branches only when it is 0. Both instructions remove the value from the top of the stack.

```
ldloc.1                         // Load the first local.
brfalse.s   IL_006a             // If zero, branch.
ldloc.2                         // Load the second local.
brtrue.s    IL_006c             // Branch if one.
```

beq Branch on equal

bgt Branch on greater than or equal

ble Branch on less than or equal

blt Branch on less than

bne Branch on not equal

In each general branching case, the instruction takes the two values at the top of the stack and compares the top value with the next value. In all cases, the branch takes the place of a comparison followed by one of the Boolean branches. For example, bgt is equivalent to a cgt instruction followed by a brtrue instruction.

conv Data conversion

This instruction converts the data on the top of the stack to a new type and leaves the converted value on the top of the stack. The final conversion type follows the conv instruction. For example, conv.u4 converts to an unsigned 4-byte integer. The conv instruction with just the type doesn't throw any exceptions if there is any sort of overflow. If the instruction has .ovf between the conv and the type (for example, conv.ovf.u8), an overflow generates an exception.

```
ldloc.0                         // Load local zero (an array).
ldlen                           // Get the array length.
conv.i4                         // Convert the array length to a
                                // four byte value.
```

newarr Create a zero-based, one-dimensional array

This instruction creates a new array of the specified type with the number of elements indicated by the value on the top of the stack. The number of elements count is removed from the stack, and the new array is placed on the top of the stack.

```
ldc.i4.5                    // Set the number of elements to
                            // create to five.
                            // Create a new array.
newarr System.ComponentModel.MemberAttribute
```

newobj Create a new object

Creates a new object and calls the object's constructor. All constructor arguments are passed on the stack. If the creation succeeds, the arguments are removed from the stack and the object reference is left on the stack.

```
.method public hidebysig specialname rtspecialname
     instance void  .ctor(class [mscorlib]System.IO.Stream 'stream',
                          class System.String name) il managed
{
:
   ldarg.1                    // Load the stream argument.
                              // Create the new class.
   newobj instance void [mscorlib]
          System.IO.StreamWriter::.ctor(class
                                  [mscorlib]System.IO.Stream)
```

box Convert value type to object reference

This instruction forces a value into an object and leaves the object on the stack when the conversion is done. When boxing, this instruction does the work. You will see the following code a lot when passing parameters:

```
// Notice the value type INT32 is passed to this method.
.method public hidebysig specialname
        instance void  set_Indent(int32 'value') il managed
{
:
ldstr      "Indent"                  // Push the method name.
ldarga.s   'value'                   // Load the argument address of the
                                     // first parameter.
box        [mscorlib]System.Int32    // Convert the address into an
                                     // object.
                                     // Load the message.
ldstr      "The Indent property must be non-negative."
           // Create a new ArgumentOutOfRangeException
newobj     instance void [mscorlib]System.ArgumentOutOfRangeException::
.ctor(class System.String,
      class System.Object,
      class System.String)
```

unbox Convert boxed value type to its raw form

This instruction returns a managed reference to the value type in the boxed form. The returned reference isn't a copy but rather the actual object state. With C# and Visual Basic .NET compiled code, after an unbox instruction comes the ldind instruction (load value indirect onto the stack) or ldobj (copy value type to the stack).

```
// Convert the value into a System.Reflection.Emit.LocalToken
unbox System.Reflection.Emit.LocalToken
// Get the value onto the stack
ldobj System.Reflection.Emit.LocalToken
unbox [mscorlib]System.Int16        // Convert the value to an Int16
// object
ldind.i2                            // Put the object's value onto the
                                    // stack.
```

call Call a method

callvirt Call a method associated at run time with an object

The call instruction calls static and nonvirtual normal methods. Virtual methods and interface methods use the callvirt instruction. Arguments are placed in left-to-right order. Note that this order is the opposite of most calling conventions in the IA32 world. Here is an example of using callvirt:

```
// Load the parameter.
ldfld class System.String
 System.CodeDOM.Compiler.CompilerResults::pathToAssembly
// Call the virtual method set_CodeBase.
callvirt   instance void [mscorlib]
System.Reflection.AssemblyName::set_CodeBase
(class System.String)
⋮
ldarg.0                    // Load the this pointer, which is
                           // always the first parameter.
ldarg.1                    // Load argument one.
ldnull                     // Load a null value
                           // Call the virtual function
callvirt instance void
  System.Diagnostics.TraceListener::Fail(class System.String
                                         class System.String)
ret                        // Return to caller.
```

Other Reverse Engineering Tools

ILDASM is an excellent tool, but I want to mention two other tools that I find invaluable. For both of these tools, the price is right—they are free! The first is Lutz Roeder's .NET Reflector (*http://www.aisto.com/roeder/dotnet/*), which does everything that ILDASM does and much more. One of .NET Reflector's key features is that you can easily search for types in an assembly. You'd hope everyone would properly document all the custom exceptions they throw, but they don't always do so. With .NET Reflector, select Type Search and, in the Type Search window, above the Type field, type in *except*. All types that have *exception* in the name are shown.

At times, it's extremely valuable to see at a glance which methods a particular method calls. In .NET Reflector, in the tree control, highlight the particular method you're interested in and select Call Tree from the View menu. In the Call Tree window, expand any subcalls to see exactly what calls what from that method. It's an outstanding way to see how things fit together.

Finally, .NET Reflector's disassembly view is superior to ILDASM's. After selecting the method you want to view, press the Enter key to make the Disassembler window pop right up. If you're curious about what an instruction does, simply move the cursor over the instruction to make a tool tip pop up with an explanation. Parameter and local types as well as methods called by `call` instructions are underlined. Simply click on the item, and the main .NET Reflector window will jump to the type or method so that you can examine it.

The second tool I want to mention is called Anakrino, which is a Greek word meaning "to examine" or "judge." Anakrino is a decompiler for .NET that shows the C# or Managed Extensions for C++ code for an assembly. Anakrino was written by Jay Freeman and is downloadable from *http://www.saurik.com/net/exemplar/*. Unlike .NET Reflector, Anakrino has source code available. Although Anakrino isn't perfect, it's a fantastic way to learn about how the .NET Framework code all fits together. Using Anakrino is self-explanatory, so I won't bother to go into it. One caveat I will mention is that the source code is quite "original" with a huge amount of template usage, so you'll need to make a serious commitment if you want to extend it. A few commercial decompilers that produce better output have been released at the time of this writing, but they're prohibitively expensive, so Anakrino's foibles are perfectly acceptable.

Summary

Although managed code is terrific because we no longer have to mess with memory corruptions and leaks, we still have to know how to use the debugging features. In this chapter, I concentrated on the unique issues associated with Visual Studio .NET and debugging managed applications.

I started by discussing the issues particular to advanced breakpoints. It's absolutely wonderful that Visual Studio .NET can call methods and properties from conditional breakpoints, but it means you must be extra careful to avoid causing side effects in your breakpoints. Also remember that if you mess up the condition, the debugger won't stop if it can't properly evaluate the condition.

The exciting Watch window offers all sorts of extra power for managed applications. With its full expression evaluator, you can easily call methods and properties so that you can influence debugging behavior to help your testing efforts. Additionally, for C# and Managed Extensions for C++ applications, you can add your custom types to the autoexpand rules to make debugging even faster.

Finally, although you might never program in MSIL, it's simple to learn and can help you truly see what the .NET Framework class library is doing behind the scenes. If you'd like more information about MSIL, make sure to check out Partition III CIL.DOC, which you can find in <Visual Studio .NET installation directory>\SDK\v1.1\Tools Developers Guide\docs. In that information, you'll find the lowdown on every instruction and what each does.

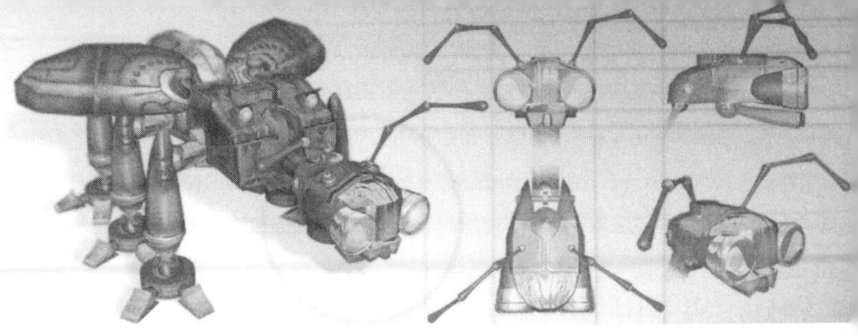

7

Advanced Native Code Techniques with Visual Studio .NET

Although managed development does a great job of protecting you from all sorts of potential problems, native code development gives you every opportunity not only to shoot yourself in the foot, but also to wound the person in the next cubicle over. Doing native development is more work, but on the positive side, you get the ultimate in control and speed. Additionally, even though some marketing folks might make it sound like you need to drop everything and shift to .NET, such an immediate changeover isn't going to happen any time soon.

In this chapter, I'll cover the advanced techniques Microsoft Visual Studio .NET gives you for debugging your native applications. I'll start with discussing breakpoints, because with native code, you have even more options for stopping a process. We'll move on to more details about the Watch window as well as remote debugging. Finally, I'll cover Intel IA32 (Pentium) assembly language so that you can always figure out what happened, even when you have no source code around and are left in the bowels of third-party or operating system code.

Advanced Breakpoints for Native Applications

Chapter 5 introduced the common breakpoints between native and managed applications. In this chapter, I'll turn to the unique issues related to native applications and some of the problems you'll run into. Additionally, I'll discuss the magical data breakpoints offered for native applications.

Advanced Breakpoint Syntax

Unlike managed debugging, native debugging has additional capabilities to control exactly when and where breakpoints occur. Because of the nature of native symbol generation, many times you need to provide the debugger with additional help so that it properly places the breakpoint where you want it. When it comes to debugging symbols, the rules are much looser than the strict C++ scoping rules. For example, it's perfectly reasonable to have multiple top-level symbols for `LoadLibrary`. Each module that imports `LoadLibrary` has a symbol for it (to indicate importing) and the module that exports it has a symbol as well (to indicate exporting). The advanced breakpoint syntax helps set the scope to the exact symbol you mean.

What's interesting about the advanced breakpoint syntax is that you used to see it all the time in Microsoft Visual C++ 6 and prior versions because that's how the old Breakpoint dialog box displayed the breakpoints you set. In Visual Studio .NET, you no longer see any advanced breakpoint syntax displayed, but you still need to know what that syntax is to truly control the debugger.

The advanced breakpoint syntax is composed of two parts. The first part is the context portion, and the second part is the location, expression, or variable. You can think of the context portion just as you do the scope of a variable when programming. The context simply provides the debugger with an unambiguous location for your breakpoint.

In debugger terms, the function, the source file, and the binary module specify the context, and the context is delineated in advanced breakpoint syntax as "{[function],[source file],[binary module]}." You need to specify only enough context information to get the breakpoint set, so the context portion can contain a single field or as many as all three. In your run-of-the-mill location breakpoint, all the information the debugger needs is the name of the source file. For example, in Visual C++ 6, you saw a standard location breakpoint on line 20 of TEST.CPP displayed in the Breakpoint dialog box as `{,TEST.CPP,}.20`. In fact, if you want to set that same breakpoint in Visual Studio .NET the really hard way, you can enter `{,TEST.CPP,}@20` in the Function edit control on the Function tab of the New Breakpoint dialog box. After you click OK, the "IntelliSense could not find the specified location. Do you still want to set the breakpoint?" message box pops up because IntelliSense doesn't know the advanced breakpoint syntax. Click Yes in the message box, and you'll see when you run the program that your breakpoint gets set. If you're already debugging, you'll see the red dot appear on the line.

The ability to specify the context for a location breakpoint allows you to solve a particularly nasty type of debugging problem. Consider the case in which you have a source file with a diagnostic function, `CheckMyMem`, used by two DLLs, A.DLL and B.DLL, and the function appears in both DLLs by static linking. Because you're doing lots of proactive programming, you're calling the function a great deal from both DLLs. However, you're experiencing a random crash only in B.DLL. If you set a standard location breakpoint in the `CheckMyMem` source code on line 27, the breakpoint will trigger in both DLLs even though you just want to see the calls made in B.DLL. To specify that you want the location breakpoint to trigger only in B.DLL, you would need to manually enter the breakpoint context `{,CHECKMYMEM.CPP,B.DLL}@27`. Although you're probably thinking this is a contrived example and you'd never share source code between modules like this, you probably never thought about what happens when you use inline functions in your C++ classes!

The second part of the advanced breakpoint syntax is where the location, expression, or variable is specified. However, in Visual Studio .NET, other than setting the source line and function name, as you'll see in a moment, you can't set any other values. That's not a problem because setting advanced breakpoints in Visual Studio .NET is much easier than setting them in Visual C++ 6 was.

Breakpoints on System or Exported Functions

In Chapter 5, I talked about all sorts of cool ways you could simply type in the name of a function or method and automatically get a breakpoint set. However, I didn't talk about setting a breakpoint on a function your program imports from a DLL. By setting a breakpoint on those DLL exported functions, you can solve some extremely hard problems. For example, you can gain control of the processing at a known point so that you can track down subsequent memory corruptions. Another good example is when you want to peek at what sort of information is being passed in various parameters. Interestingly, if you try to set the exported function breakpoint, you'll be disappointed. It doesn't work. There's nothing wrong with the debugger—you just need to give it some context information about where it can find the function. Additionally, one other small detail is important: the function name depends on whether symbols for the DLL are loaded. Before I get into this discussion, you first have to set the Visual Studio .NET debugger to load exports as symbols. In the Options dialog box\Debugging folder\Native property page, check Load DLL Exports. The reason for setting this option is that even if you don't have symbols, at least the exported symbols for the module will have a "pseudosymbol" table built out of the exported functions from the DLL. This way you'll see names for those exported functions instead of hexadecimal numbers.

To illustrate how to set a breakpoint on a system DLL, I'll set a breakpoint on the KERNEL32.DLL `LoadLibrary` function. You might want to follow along so that you can see the steps in action. As all real programs call `LoadLibrary`, you can pick any application to debug. Start by stepping into the program to get the debugger running and to initialize all symbol tables. If you just try specifying `LoadLibrary` in the New Breakpoint dialog box, you'll see that when you click the OK button, the breakpoint looks like it's accepted. However, as you should know by now, always check the Breakpoints window to see whether the breakpoint has a question mark or an exclamation point icon next to it, which indicates the breakpoint isn't set. In the application I'm using to set the breakpoints, WDBG from Chapter 4, the Breakpoint window shows the question mark icon next to text that shows this type `LoadLibrary(const unsigned short *)`.

The first step to setting an exported function breakpoint is to determine whether you have symbols loaded for the module that contains the export. Since you all should have stopped reading at the end of Chapter 2 and immediately created a symbol server so that you could always get all operating system symbols, you should have symbols loaded. There are two ways to check symbol loading. First, in the Debug Output window, if you see the text "'*<Program>*' : Loaded '*<DLL>*', Symbols loaded.", you have symbols loaded. The second way is with the Modules windows, accessible from the Windows submenu of the Debug menu or by pressing Ctrl+Alt+U using the default keyboard. The far-right column of the Module window, titled Information, tells you whether symbols are loaded. Highlight the module you're interested in and scroll all the way over to the right. If the Information column for your module displays Symbols Loaded, you have symbols. If it says anything else, and you know you have the correct PDB file for the DLL, right-click on the item in the Modules window and select Reload Symbols from the context menu. The Reload Symbols: *filename*.pdb dialog box that comes up allows you to browse for the correct PDB file. Since the symbol server will make setting up symbols trivial, I strongly suggest you go that route. If either the Debug Output window or the Modules window says anything else, you don't have symbols loaded.

If symbols aren't loaded, the location string you'll use is the name exported from the DLL. You can check the name by running the DUMPBIN utility, which comes with Visual Studio .NET, on the DLL: `DUMPBIN /EXPORTS` *DLL Name*. If you run DUMPBIN on KERNEL32.DLL, you won't see a `LoadLibrary` function but rather two similarly named functions, `LoadLibraryA` and `LoadLibraryW`. (`LoadLibraryExA` and `LoadLibraryExW` are different APIs.) Suffixes indicate the character set used by the function: the *A* suffix stands for ANSI and the *W* stands for Wide, or Unicode. Microsoft Windows operating systems other than Microsoft Windows 98/Me use Unicode internally for internationalization. If you compiled your program with `UNICODE` defined, you'll want to use the `LoadLibraryW` version. If you didn't, you can use `LoadLibraryA`. However, `LoadLibraryA` is just a wrapper that allocates memory to convert the ANSI string to Unicode and calls `LoadLibraryW`, so technically you could use `LoadLibraryW` as well. If you know for sure that your program is going to call only one of these functions, you can just set the breakpoint on that function. If you're not sure, set breakpoints on both functions.

If your application is targeting only Microsoft Windows 2000, Microsoft Windows XP, or.NET Server 2003, you should use Unicode throughout. You can get a nice performance boost. Matt Pietrek, in his December 1997 "Under the Hood" column in *Microsoft Systems Journal*, reported that the ANSI wrappers had a sizeable performance hit associated with them. In addition to having a faster program, you'll be several steps closer to full internationalization by using Unicode.

If symbols aren't loaded, the breakpoint syntax for breaking on `LoadLibrary` is `{,,KERNEL32.DLL}LoadLibraryA` or `{,,KERNEL32.DLL}LoadLibraryW`. If symbols are loaded, you need to do some calculations because you'll need to match the decorated symbol name. What you need to know is the calling convention of the exported function and the function prototype. I'll get into much more detail about calling conventions later in this chapter. For the `LoadLibrary` function, the prototype from WINBASE.H (with some macros expanded for clarity) is as follows:

```
__declspec (dllimport)
HMODULE
__stdcall
LoadLibraryA(
    LPCSTR lpLibFileName
    );
```

The `WINBASEAPI` macro expands into the standard call calling convention, `__stdcall`, which, by the way, is the calling convention for all system API functions. Standard call functions are decorated with an underscore prefix and suffixed with an "@" sign followed by the number of bytes pushed on the stack. Fortunately, calculating the number is easy; it's the sum of the parameter byte count. With the Intel Pentium family of CPUs, you can just count the number of parameters and multiply by 4. In the case of `LoadLibrary`, which takes one parameter, the final name is `_LoadLibraryW@4`. Here are some examples that will give you an idea of what final names look like: `CreateProcess`, which has 10 parameters, is `_CreateProcessW@40`; and `TlsAlloc`, which has no parameters, is `_TlsAlloc@0`. Even if a function doesn't have any parameters, you must keep the "@#" format. As is the case when symbols aren't loaded, the ANSI and

Unicode conditions still apply. If symbols are loaded, the breakpoint syntax for breaking on `LoadLibrary` is `{,,KERNEL32.DLL}_LoadLibraryA@4` or `{,,KERNEL32.DLL}_LoadLibraryW@4`.

After you've figured out the advanced breakpoint syntax for setting the breakpoint, bring up the New Breakpoint dialog box by pressing Ctrl+B. On the Function tab/Function edit control, enter the appropriate advanced breakpoint syntax. After clicking OK, you'll get the usual warning about IntelliSense not finding the breakpoint. Click OK so that the debugger will set the breakpoint. Look in the Breakpoints window and you'll see that a full red dot is next to the breakpoint and the Name column lists the breakpoint in full syntax glory. You can also right-click the breakpoint and select Go To Disassembly from the context menu to see where the exported function resides in memory.

Conditional Expressions

Although managed code allows you to call methods and properties from conditional expression breakpoint modifiers, native code doesn't. Additionally, conditional expressions can't evaluate C++ macro values, so if you want to compare a value against `TRUE`, you'd have to use 1 instead (though `true` and `false` are evaluated correctly evaluated). With C++ code, as with the particular languages in managed code, any conditional expressions must use the C++ values. Even with these small limitations, location breakpoint conditional expression modifiers are extremely powerful because in addition to the ability to evaluate variables values, you have access to a special set of values named pseudoregisters.

For the most part, pseudoregisters are register values that appear on the CPU. Visual Studio .NET greatly improved the register types you can use and display. In addition to the regular CPU registers, Visual Studio now supports advanced registers such as MMX, SSE, SSE2, and 3DNow! Some examples of pseudoregisters are shown in Table 7-1. Notice that actual CPU registers have the `@` delimiter and that the two special values start with `$`. You can find the complete list of register values by consulting the CPU documentation for both Intel and AMD (Advanced Micro Devices). Remember that in Visual C++ 6, you could also specify `@` in front of pseudoregisters. For backward compatibility, you can still do the same with Visual Studio .NET 2003, but future versions will support only `$` on pseudoregisters, so you should get used to setting it now. Additionally, to view the value, some of you are used to entering the register values without the `@` in front of the register name. However, I'll always show registers with the `@` prefix.

Table 7-1 Example Pseudoregisters

Pseudoregister	Description
@EAX	The return value register (32-bit value)
@BL	Low word of EBX register (16-bit value)
@MM0	MMX register 0
@XMM1	Streaming SIMD Extensions (SSE) register 1
$ERR	Last error value (special value)
$TIB	Thread information block (special value)

The last two values in Table 7-1 offer extra power with conditional breakpoints. With `$ERR`, you can look at the thread's last error value (the value returned by calling the `GetLastError` API), so you'd stop only when that last error condition was met. For example, if you wanted to stop only when the last error value returned by an API function was `ERROR_INSUFFICIENT_BUFFER`, indicating a data buffer was too small, you'd first look up `ERROR_INSUFFICIENT_BUFFER` in WINERROR.H and see the value is 122. Your breakpoint conditional expression would be `$ERR==122`.

The `$TIB` special pseudoregister opens up a solution to a vexing problem in Visual Studio .NET. Unfortunately, there's no built-in way to explicitly set a location breakpoint that fires only in a specific thread. (As you'll see in the next chapter, WinDBG does have this capability built in). When working on big server applications such as ISAPI filters, it's very common to have a few methods that are called by lots of threads, but you don't want to wear out your index finger pressing GO a million times because the debugger stops at each occurrence in each thread. The first step to getting around this problem is to be stopped in the debugger and bring up the Threads window so that you can see all the thread IDs. Determine which thread you want to stop in and remember the thread ID. The second step is to set a location breakpoint on the common routine and bring up the New Breakpoint dialog box by right-clicking on the breakpoint and selecting Properties. Click the Condition button and type in the following expression: `*(long*)($TIB+0x24) == <thread id>`. The thread ID is at offset 0x24 in the thread information block. (You can find this by reverse engineering `GetCurrentThreadId`, which we'll do later in the chapter.)

Finally, because you can't call functions in your expressions, breaking on a string with a specific value is difficult. In that case, just set up an expression that checks each character, such as this:

```
(szBuff[0]=='P')&&(szBuff[1]=='a')&&(szBuff[2]=='m')
```

Common Debugging Question

Is there a way to set the thread name in native code?

If you read the previous chapter, you know that it's easy to set the thread name appearing in the Threads window. Microsoft has documented a way to do the same thing in native applications. By default, native applications show the name of the function where the thread started. To show the actual name, you can use a special exception value to pass in a new name to use, and the debugger writer must read the memory address passed as part of the exception. I wrapped up the necessary code into a set of functions in BUGSLAYERUTIL.DLL: `BSUSetThreadName` and `BSUSetCurrentThreadName`. The code for `BSUSetThreadNameA` is shown here. After calling this function, the Threads window will show whatever you specified as the name. Unlike in managed code, in native code, you can change the thread name all you want. Finally, only the first 31 characters of the name are shown in the debugger.

```
typedef struct tagTHREADNAME_INFO
{
   DWORD  dwType     ; // Must be 0x1000
   LPCSTR szName     ; // Pointer to name (in user addr space)
   DWORD  dwThreadID ; // Thread ID (-1=caller thread)
   DWORD  dwFlags    ; // Reserved for future use, must be zero
} THREADNAME_INFO ;

void BUGSUTIL_DLLINTERFACE __stdcall
                            BSUSetThreadNameA ( DWORD   dwThreadID   ,
                                                LPCSTR  szThreadName  )
{
    THREADNAME_INFO stInfo ;
    stInfo.dwType       = 0x1000 ;
    stInfo.szName       = szThreadName ;
    stInfo.dwThreadID   = dwThreadID ;
    stInfo.dwFlags      = 0 ;

    __try
    {
        RaiseException ( 0x406D1388                           ,
                         0                                    ,
                         sizeof ( THREADNAME_INFO ) /
                                    sizeof ( DWORD )          ,
                         (DWORD*)&stInfo                      ) ;
    }
    __except ( EXCEPTION_CONTINUE_EXECUTION )
    {
    }
}
```

Data Breakpoints

Data breakpoints, also called global memory breakpoints, are one of the most powerful tools you have at your disposal. With a data breakpoint, whenever anything changes a particular piece of memory, the debugger stops immediately at the point right after the memory was changed. Data breakpoints are global in scope and are not related to any location except the one doing the memory change. As you can imagine, data breakpoints are just the thing for tracking down all sorts of problems like memory corruptions or overwrites.

In Visual C++ 6, getting data breakpoints set was a little tricky, but now they're pretty easy to use. The big problem was that with Visual C++ 6, if you didn't get the breakpoint set correctly, the debugger simply single-stepped every assembly instruction in your application and checked the memory location after each execution. Needless to say, having an exception and a few cross-process transitions on each exception was excruciatingly slow. If you did fall into this trap, the only thing you could do was kill the debugger. Fortunately, with Visual Studio .NET, you now get a warning message when you set the data breakpoints wrong.

What's neat about data breakpoints is that the heavy lifting behind them comes from the CPU instead of the debugger. Intel CPUs have four special registers, named the *debug registers* (DR0–DR3), that the CPU can use to set a hardware breakpoint on memory accesses. These debug registers are limited to monitoring an address and 1 byte, 2 bytes, or 4 bytes at that address. That means you can monitor a maximum of 16 bytes in your program at any given time.

The trick to setting data breakpoints is to use the address of the memory you want to watch. The New Breakpoint dialog box implies you can enter the variable name, but many times using the variable name will bring up a message box similar to Figure 7-1. When you see that message, always click No, because if you click Yes, the debugger will set the breakpoint by single-stepping every assembly language instruction in order to determine when the memory changes.

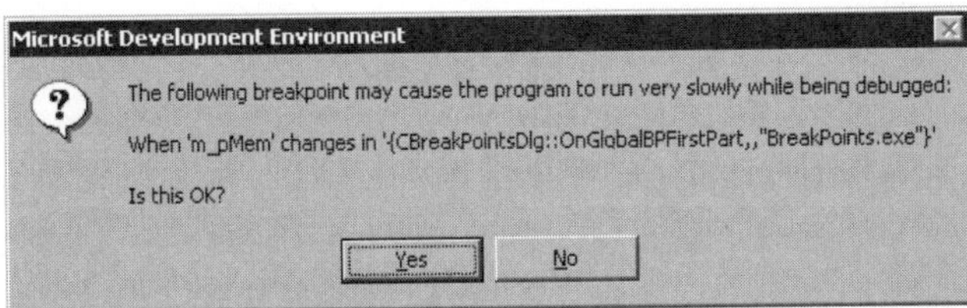

Figure 7-1 Data breakpoint about to cause single stepping

After you get the address of the memory you want to watch, setting a data breakpoint is pretty easy. Bring up the New Breakpoint dialog box and make the Data tab active, as shown in Figure 7-2. In the Variable edit control, enter the address you'd like to watch. It's critical you keep data alignment in mind when entering the address. The Items field indicates how many bytes you want to watch at that address. If you want to watch 4 bytes (a double word) the address you enter must end in 0, 4, 8, or C to maintain alignment. Likewise, if you want to watch only 2 bytes (a word), the address must end in 0, 2, 4, 6, 8, A, C, or E. If you try to set a data breakpoint where the alignment is off, such as setting a memory address that ends in 7 and setting the Items field to 4, the data breakpoint will appear to be set, but the debugger won't actually stop when the breakpoint is accessed. Interestingly, if you attempt to set a 4-byte data breakpoint on an address that ends in A, for example, the debugger will shift the breakpoint back to the natural alignment 2 bytes in front.

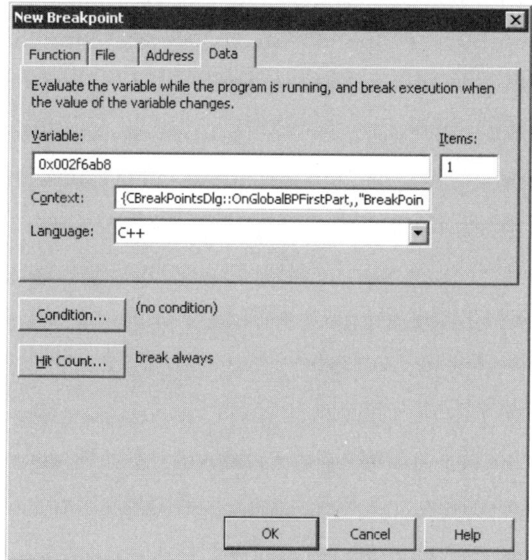

Figure 7-2 Setting a data breakpoint

As you can see in Figure 7-2, there are two additional fields available for setting data breakpoints. The Context field is used when you specify a variable name in the Variable field in case the variable is at a different scope from the current location. Since it's much better to use addresses, you can safely ignore the Context field. The same goes for the Language field because when using addresses, the language is ignored as well.

One incredibly great improvement to data breakpoints in Visual Studio .NET as compared with Visual C++ 6 is that you can now associate them with hit counts as well as conditions. This allows you to completely fine-tune the exact state you'll stop in the debugger.

Once you've entered your data breakpoint and checked the Breakpoints window to make sure the data breakpoint is fully validated, you can start running your application. When the data at the specified address changes, something interesting happens in the debugger, as shown in Figure 7-3. A message box appears indicating that your data breakpoint was hit. Many developers have questioned me as to why data breakpoints get this special treatment. The reason has to do with a really difficult user interface problem. Since data breakpoints can be triggered anywhere, having the debugger stop only at a point where no red dots in the margin indicate a breakpoint would be a little disconcerting. By popping up the message box, you at least know why the debugger stopped.

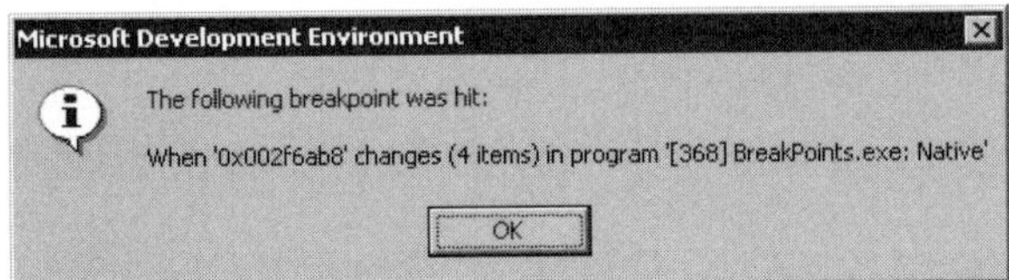

Figure 7-3 Hitting a data breakpoint

When using data breakpoints, after you stop a debugging session, you probably want to clear any data breakpoints you've set. Since I recommend using addresses for the data breakpoints, it's very probable that the memory location you want to watch will move around in subsequent runs. This is especially true with the stack memory you're watching.

Better Data Breakpoints

The new and improved data breakpoints are a wonderful improvement to Visual Studio .NET native debugging. However, if you've ever looked at the Intel Architecture Software Developer's Manuals, the documentation on the debug registers indicates that the registers can be set such that every read and read/write to the memory at the address specified can cause the hardware breakpoint to trigger. The behavior of the Visual Studio .NET data breakpoints is that they trigger only when the data changes in the address specified. So if the value you're writing to a location doesn't change the data at that location, you'll never stop.

Occasionally, you do want to see who is writing or reading from a memory location no matter what. I don't know how many times I've tracked down performance problems by counting how many times memory was touched.

Visual Studio .NET hides part of the power of the hardware debug registers, but I figured there had to be a way to get the full power in the debugger.

As I was pondering the solution, I got an e-mail message from Mike Morearty indicating that he wanted the same thing and had set out to solve the problem. Mike subsequently developed code that did exactly what I wanted, so there was no need for me even to think about the problem any more. All you have to do is visit *http://www.morearty.com/code/breakpoint* and read all about it. Mike's solution, which is really the only way to expose this functionality, is to add a small C++ class to your project that you use to set the better data breakpoint in your own code. Mike's Web page does a great job of describing how to use his `CBreakpoint` class, so I won't bother duplicating that information here. I will mention that since you need to create the breakpoint by manually adding code to your project, be very careful when checking code back in. If you leave the `CBreakpoint` class active, your daily builds won't run and you'll instantly learn the meaning of "career-limiting move"!

The Watch Window

As you've seen through the last two chapters, I really like the Watch window. For native code debugging, the Watch window offers even more power than ever before. One of the improvements you might have already noticed with native debugging in Visual Studio .NET is that the Watch window now automatically knows about `HRESULTS`, `wchar_t` (UNICODE characters), and `bool` types. Additionally, you also might have noticed that the data tips that pop up in the source windows seem to have gotten an extreme dose of steroids.

Formatting Data and Expression Evaluation

The first "trick" you'll need to master on your way to becoming proficient at manipulating the Watch window is memorizing the formatting symbols in Table 7-2 and Table 7-3, which derive from the Visual Studio .NET documentation. The Watch window is wonderfully flexible in how it displays data, and the way you bring out its flexibility is by using the format codes in these tables. As you can see from the tables, the formats are easy to use: follow your variable with a comma and then the format you want to use. The most useful format specifier for COM programming is `,hr`. If you keep the expression `@EAX,hr` in your Watch window, as you step over a COM method call, you can see the results of the call in a form you can understand. (`EAX` is the Intel CPU register at which return values are stored.) Using the format specifiers allows you to easily control how you see your data so that you can save huge amounts of time interpreting it.

Table 7-2 Formatting Symbols for Watch Window Variables

Symbol	Format Description	Sample	Display
d, i	Signed decimal integer	(int)0xF000F065,d	–268373915
u	Unsigned decimal integer	0x0065,u	101
o	Unsigned octal integer	0xF065,o	0170145
x, X	Hexadecimal integer	61541,X	0x0000F065
l, h	Long or short prefix for d, i, u, o, x, X	0x00406042,hx	0x0c22
f	Signed floating-point	3./2.,f	1.500000
e	Signed scientific notation	3./2,e	1.500000e+000
g	Signed floating-point or signed scientific notation, whichever is shorter	3./2,g	1.5
c	Single character	0x0065,c	'e'
s	ANSI String	szHiWorld,s	"Hello world"
su	Unicode string	szWHiWorld,su	"Hello world"
hr	`HRESULT` or Win32 error code	0x00000000,hr	`S_OK`
wc	Windows class flag	0x00000040,wc	`WC_DEFAULTCHAR` (Note that although documented, this format doesn't work in Visual Studio .NET.)
wm	Windows message numbers	0x0010,wm	`WM_CLOSE`

Table 7-3 Formatting Symbols for Watch Window Memory Dumps

Symbol	Format Description	Sample	Display
ma	64 ASCII characters	0x0012ffac,ma	0x0012ffac .4...0...".0W&.......1W&.0.:W.. 1....".1.JO&.1.2..".1...0y....1
m	16 bytes in hexadecimal format followed by 16 ASCII characters	0x0012ffac,m	0x0012ffac b3 34 cb 00 84 30 94 80 ff 22 8a 30 57 26 00 00 .4...0...".0W&..
mb	16 bytes in hexadecimal format followed by 16 ASCII characters	0x0012ffac,mb	0x0012ffac b3 34 cb 00 84 30 94 80 ff 22 8a 30 57 26 00 00 .4...0...".0W&..

(continued)

Table 7-3 Formatting Symbols for Watch Window Memory Dumps *(continued)*

Symbol	Format Description	Sample	Display
mw	8 words	0x0012ffac,mw	0x0012ffac 34b3 00cb 3084 8094 22ff 308a 2657 0000
md	4 double words	0x0012ffac,md	0x0012ffac 00cb34b3 80943084 308a22ff 00002657
mq	4 quadwords	0x0012ffac,mq	0x0012ffac 8094308400cb34b3 00002657308a22ff
mu	2-byte characters (Unicode)	0x0012ffac,mu	0x0012ffac 34b3 00cb 3084 8094 22ff 308a 2657 0000 ?.?????.
#	Expands a pointer to a memory location to the specified number of values	pCharArray,10	Expanded array of 10 characters using +/- expanders

The number format specifier `,#` allows you to expand a pointer to a memory location to a specified number of values. If you have a pointer to an array of 10 longs, the Watch window will show only the first value. To see the entire array, follow the variable with the number of values you'd like to see. For example, `pLong,10` would show an expandable array of your 10 items. If you have a large array, you can point to the middle of it and expand just the values you want with, for example, `(pBigArray+100),20`, to show the 20 elements starting at offset 99. You'll notice that when you enter a value such as this, the index values always begin at 0, regardless of the position of the first displayed element. In the `pBigArray` example, the first index will be shown as 0 even though it's the 100th array element. The second index, the 101st array element, will be shown as 1, and so on.

In addition to allowing you to format the data as you'd like it, the Watch window allows you to cast and cajole your data variables so that you can see exactly what you need to see. For example, you can use the `BY`, `WO`, and `DW` expressions to get at pointer offsets. To see the current thread ID in the Watch window, you could use `DW($TIB+0x24)`. The address-of operator (`&`) and the pointer operator (`*`) are also allowed, and both allow you to get the values at memory addresses and to see the results of casts in your code.

One great trick I like to use in my native debugging is watching variable values up the stack. Sometimes you have a local variable you'd like to keep an eye on as you're stepping through other functions. With the advanced breakpoint syntax context portion, which I discussed in the "Advanced Breakpoint Syntax" section earlier in this chapter, you can explicitly watch a value. For example, if you have a variable `szBuff` declared in the function `CopyDatabaseValue`, located in source file FOO.CPP in module DB.DLL, you'd specify the exact value of `szBuff` as `{CopyDatabaseValue,FOO.CPP,DB.DLL}szBuff`. Now, no matter where you are inside functions called by `CopyDatabaseValue`, you can easily keep an eye on `szBuff`.

Timing Code in the Watch Window

Here's another neat trick—using the Watch window to time code. The `$CLK` pseudoregister can serve as a rudimentary timer. In many cases, you want just a rough idea of the time between two points, such as how long a call to the database took. `$CLK` makes it easy to find out how long the call took. Keep in mind that this time includes the debugger overhead. The trick is to enter two `$CLK` watches, the first being just `$CLK` and the second `$CLK=0`. The second watch zeros out the timer after you start running again. Although not a perfect timer, `$CLK` is good enough for some ballpark guesses.

The Undocumented Pseudoregisters

Two new pseudoregisters have shown up in Visual Studio .NET. Since the word *undocumented* is in the title of this section, I have to warn you that these values might disappear in future versions of the debugger. The first pseudoregister is `$HANDLES`. This shows the number of open handles in the current process. This is a killer idea that allows you to keep an eye on handle leaks as you're debugging. If you see the number reported by `$HANDLES` creeping up, you know you have a leak. `$HANDLES,d` has a permanent place in my Watch window because it's so amazingly useful.

The second undocumented pseudohandle is `$VFRAME`, a great feature for helping track down the stack in release builds. `$VFRAME` is short for virtual frame pointer. On IA32 machines, `$VFRAME` points to the next stack frame so that you can use it to help walk the stack back manually. If you're using standard stack frame, `$VFRAME` points to the previous item's EBP value.

Expanding Your Own Types Automatically

Although managed C++ and C# debugging allows you to expand your own types in the Watch window, the autoexpansion offered by native debugging takes this ability to new heights. In fact, starting with Visual Studio .NET 2003, the Watch window and data tips now attempt to show you the first few members of structures and classes automatically. However, you've probably seen a few common types, such as `CObject`, `RECT`, and some of the STL types, expand in the Watch window with even more information, which all happens to be provided by the autoexpand rules. The magic happens in the AUTOEXP.DAT text file located in the <Visual Studio .NET installation directory>\COMMON7\PACKAGES\DEBUGGER subdirectory. You can add your own types to the autoexpand list by entering them into the AUTOEXP.DAT file. (Unfortunately, the AUTOEXP.DAT file must reside in that directory, so you'll have to set your version control software's working directory to pull AUTOEXPAND.DAT to that directory.)

As an example, I'll add an autoexpand entry for the `PROCESS_INFORMATION` structure that is passed to the `CreateProcess` API function. The first step is to check what the Visual Studio .NET debugger recognizes as the type. In a sample program, I put a `PROCESS_INFORMATION` variable in the Watch window and looked at the Type column on the right side of the Watch window. The type was `_PROCESS_INFORMATION`, which if you look at the following structure definition, matches the structure tag.

```
typedef struct _PROCESS_INFORMATION {
    HANDLE hProcess;
    HANDLE hThread;
    DWORD dwProcessId;
    DWORD dwThreadId;
} PROCESS_INFORMATION
```

The documentation in AUTOEXP.DAT says that the format for an autoexpand entry is `type=[text]<member[,format]>....` Table 7-4 shows the meanings for each field. Note that more than one member can be displayed as part of the autoexpand.

Table 7-4 AUTOEXP.DAT Autoexpand Entries

Field	Description
Type	The type name. For template types, this field can be followed by <*> to encompass all derived types.
Text	Any literal text. This field is generally the member name or a shorthand version of it.
member	The actual data member to display. This field can be an expression, so if you need to add some offsets to various pointers, you can include the offsets in the calculation. The casting operators also work.
format	Additional format specifiers for the member variables. These specifiers are the same as the formatting symbols shown in Table 7-2.

With the `PROCESS_INFORMATION` structure, I'm interested in looking at the `hProcess` and `hThread` values, so my autoexpand rule would be `_PROCESS_INFORMATION =hProcess=<hProcess,X> hThread=<hThread,X>`. I use the `,X` format specifiers because I always want to see the values as hexadecimal values. Figure 7-4 shows the autoexpand rule for `_PROCESS_INFORMATION` showing up in a data tip in the source window.

```
memset ( &pi , NULL , sizeof ( PROCESS_INFORMATION ) ) ;
            pi = {hProcess=0x00000000 hThread=0x00000000}
```

Figure 7-4 Autoexpand in a data tip

When entering my new autoexpand rule, I must place it after the section of the AUTOEXP.DAT file delineated by `[AutoExpand]`. Your best bet is to place your values right after `[AutoExpand]` so that you can find them easily and not mess up the techniques I'll discuss in the next section. The good news is that unlike the managed debugging autoexpands that are read only when you start Visual Studio .NET, the AUTOEXP.DAT file is read in each time you debug, so developing native autoexpand rules is much easier.

One special formatting code you'll see in the file is `<,t>`. This code tells the debugger to put in the type name of the most derived type. For example, if you have a base class *A* with a derived class *B* and only *A* has an autoexpand rule, the autoexpand for a variable of type *B* will be the class name *B* followed by the autoexpand rule for class *A*. The `<,t>` format is very helpful for keeping your classes straight.

Adding Your Own `HRESULT` Values

In addition to expanding your types, the Visual Studio .NET Watch window now has provisions to show your custom `HRESULT` values as text instead of as some hard-to-decipher number. The magical AUTOEXP.DAT also holds these values. At the end of the AUTOEXP.DAT file, add a new section named `[hresult]` and add each custom `HRESULT` using the following pattern: "<unsigned decimal value>=<HRESULT text>." The code that follows is an example that includes some of the values not handled automatically by the debugger. If you'd like to see the actual `HRESULT` value for one of the built-in conversions or one you've added to the `[hresult]` section, take the `HRESULT` variable and append `,u` or `,x` to the variable. That will force the variable to be displayed as an unsigned integer or a hexadecimal value, respectively.

```
[hresult]
2147500051=CO_E_CANT_REMOTE
2147500056=CO_E_CREATEPROCESS_FAILURE
2147500059=CO_E_LAUNCH_PERMSSION_DENIED
```

Adding Super Customized Display to the Watch Window

A major enhancement to the Watch window that's shown up for native debugging is the Expression Evaluator Add-In (EEAddIn). What EEAddIn allows you to do is to have the debugger call one of your DLLs when the Watch window is evaluating a specific type. This gives you an excellent opportunity to provide calculations that will display data in a more relevant way. For example, the Watch window will display a `SYSTEMTIME` structure (which represents the Win32 date and time) as a bunch of hexadecimal numbers, making it impossible for you to determine the time. When you use an EEAddIn, the Watch window displays a readable string such as `{5/13/2002 12:51 AM}` instead.

To tell the Watch window you have an EEAddIn DLL you'd like to load, you place an entry for each type you want to evaluate in the ubiquitous AUTOEXP.DAT file. Under the `[AutoExpand]` section, you'll indicate the expansion for a type using the following syntax:

```
type name=$ADDIN(dll name,exported function)
```

The type name is, as with the autoexpand rules, the name for the type the Watch window displays in the Type column for the variable. The DLL name is the name of the DLL. The documentation for the EEAddIn, which is just sample Visual Studio .NET project named, appropriately, EEAddIn, indicates that the DLL name just needs to be the name of the DLL because you're supposed to put your EEAddIns in the same directory as AUTOEXP.DAT. However, I've found that you should indicate the complete path to the DLL as part of the DLL name to ensure proper loading. The exported function is the function you want called to process your custom display for the given type.

Since your EEAddIns run in the address space of the debugger, you need to ensure that you properly handle any possible exceptions because you'll crash the debugger if you don't. The individual exported functions must match the `CUSTOMVIEWER` prototype, as shown in Listing 7-1. When your function is called, it will receive as parameters the address of the type; a pointer to a helper structure, `DEBUGHELPER`; the numeric base currently selected (decimal or hexadecimal); a Boolean value indicating whether the debugger is expecting UNICODE strings (which in Visual Studio .NET is ignored as it always expects ANSI characters returned); the string buffer to write the result to; and the maximum length of the string buffer. The helper structure, also shown in Listing 7-1, has a few pointers to functions you can call to get information about the values at the address for the type. The most important are `GetRealAddress` and `ReadDebuggeeMemoryEx`. You'll pass the address handed to your exported function, stored in `GetRealAddress`, to get the real address for the variable. You'll pass that value on to `ReadDebuggeeMemoryEx` in order to get the bytes for the type.

The beauty of the helper class is that it completely hides the magic necessary to get the data out of local and remote debuggee processes.

```
/*----------------------------------------------------------------------
        The only definition of the Expression Evaluator AddIns
                 Lifted from The EEAddIn Sample Project
----------------------------------------------------------------------*/

typedef struct tagDEBUGHELPER
{
    DWORD dwVersion ;
    BOOL (WINAPI *ReadDebuggeeMemory)( struct tagDEBUGHELPER * pThis  ,
                                       DWORD                   dwAddr ,
                                       DWORD                   nWant  ,
                                       VOID *                  pWhere ,
                                       DWORD *                 nGot   );
    // from here only when dwVersion >= 0x20000
    DWORDLONG (WINAPI *GetRealAddress)( struct tagDEBUGHELPER *pThis ) ;
    BOOL (WINAPI *ReadDebuggeeMemoryEx)( struct tagDEBUGHELPER *pThis  ,
                                         DWORDLONG              qwAddr ,
                                         DWORD                  nWant  ,
                                         VOID*                  pWhere ,
                                         DWORD *                nGot   );
    int (WINAPI *GetProcessorType)( struct tagDEBUGHELPER *pThis ) ;
} DEBUGHELPER ;

// The prototype each of your functions must be.
typedef HRESULT (WINAPI *CUSTOMVIEWER)( DWORD          dwAddress   ,
                                        DEBUGHELPER *  pHelper     ,
                                        int            nBase       ,
                                        BOOL           bUniStrings ,
                                        char *         pResult     ,
                                        size_t         max         ,
                                        DWORD          reserved    ) ;
```

Listing 7-1 EEAddIn export prototype and helper structure

Your exported function's job is to convert those bytes read in from the debuggee into something displayable in the Watch window. Since you can easily read the memory out of the debuggee, you'll be working with a copy of the information. When I first got a glimpse of the EEAddIn architecture, I immediately thought of a million cool displays I would love to have. The first was one that would take an HINSTANCE or HMODULE and show the value followed by the name of the DLL at that location. Of course, reality then intruded. Converting an HINSTANCE or HMODULE into a DLL name required a handle to the process. The DEBUGHELPER structure in Listing 7-1 gives you a way to read memory but not get the process handle. Of course, that's when I realized that if my EEAddIn function was working on a process being debugged remotely, even having the process handle wouldn't help because I couldn't do anything with that handle on the machine the debugger was running on. Maybe a future version of Visual Studio .NET will offer a means of querying information from the process that needs handle values.

Even with the restriction that you can read only the debuggee's memory, plenty of excellent opportunities to put better displays in the Watch window are still open to you so that you can debug faster. Included with this book's sample code is my current EEAddIn, BSU_ExpEval_AddIn. At the time I wrote this paragraph, I incorporated the `_SYSTEMTIME` and `_FILETIME` displays from the sample provided by Visual Studio, but I put error handling around them as well as the following structure expansions: `_OSVERSIONINFOA`, `_OSVERSIONINFOW`, `_OSVERSIONINFOEXA`, and `_OSVERSIONINFOEXW`. Now when you have one of the structures handled by `GetVersionEx`, you can see them displayed as shown in Figure 7-5, which shows some of the output of the test program for BSU_ExpEval_AddIn. Listing 7-2 shows the work necessary to expand the `_OSVERSIONINFOA` structure.

One debugging tip with EEAddIn DLLs is that if you return `E_FAIL` from your function, the Watch window will display "???", so you might want to return `S_OK` and set the result text to "..." so that your output matches the normal Watch window display. This can help you debug the DLL as well. Another tip is to consider putting failure results in the result text of your debug versions to make your debugger extensions easier to debug. Finally, if enough of us start sharing our EEAddIns, we can get much better debugging information than ever before from the IDE. I'd encourage you to look at any structures or classes you can from Win32, MFC, and ATL and see whether you can provide better output.

Watch 1

Name	Value	Type
⊞ stOSExA	{Windows .NET Datacenter Server (100) Service Pack 2}	_OSVERSIONINFOEXA
⊞ stOSA	{Windows NT 4.0 (100) Service Pack 2}	_OSVERSIONINFOA

Figure 7-5 EEAddIns at work

```
// This touches only the first 5 DWORDS in the structs, so you can pass
// both the ANSI and UNICODE versions in.
static int ConvertBaseOSV ( LPOSVERSIONINFOA pOSVA , char * szStr )
{
    int iCurrPos = 0 ;

    if ( ( pOSVA->dwMajorVersion == 4 ) && ( pOSVA->dwMinorVersion ==0))
    {
        if ( pOSVA->dwPlatformId == VER_PLATFORM_WIN32_NT )
```

Listing 7-2 EEAddIn example for `_OSVERSIONINFOA`

```
        {
            iCurrPos = wsprintf ( szStr , _T ( "Windows NT 4.0 " ) ) ;
        }
        else
        {
            iCurrPos = wsprintf ( szStr , _T ( "Windows 95 " ) ) ;
        }
    }
    else if ( ( pOSVA->dwMajorVersion == 4  ) &&
              ( pOSVA->dwMinorVersion == 10 )    )
    {
        iCurrPos = wsprintf ( szStr , _T ( "Windows 98 " ) ) ;
    }
    else if ( ( pOSVA->dwMajorVersion == 4  ) &&
              ( pOSVA->dwMinorVersion == 90 )    )
    {
        iCurrPos = wsprintf ( szStr , _T ( "Windows Me " ) ) ;
    }
    else if ( ( pOSVA->dwMajorVersion == 5  ) &&
              ( pOSVA->dwMinorVersion == 0  )    )
    {
        iCurrPos = wsprintf ( szStr , _T ( "Windows 2000 " ) ) ;
    }
    else if ( ( pOSVA->dwMajorVersion == 5  ) &&
              ( pOSVA->dwMinorVersion == 1  )    )
    {
        iCurrPos = wsprintf ( szStr , _T ( "Windows XP " ) ) ;
    }
    else if ( ( pOSVA->dwMajorVersion == 5  ) &&
              ( pOSVA->dwMinorVersion == 2  )    )
    {
        iCurrPos = wsprintf ( szStr , _T ( "Windows Server 2003 " ) ) ;
    }
    else
    {
        // Beats me!
        iCurrPos = 0 ;
    }
    return ( iCurrPos ) ;
}

// Again, this function uses the shared field between the A and W
// versions, so you can use it for both.
static int ConvertBuildNumber ( LPOSVERSIONINFOA pOSVA , char * szStr )
{
    int iCurrPos = 0 ;
    if ( VER_PLATFORM_WIN32_NT == pOSVA->dwPlatformId )
    {
        iCurrPos = wsprintf ( szStr                ,
                              _T ( "(%d) " )       ,
                              pOSVA->dwBuildNumber  ) ;
    }
```

(continued)

```
    else if ( VER_PLATFORM_WIN32_WINDOWS == pOSVA->dwPlatformId )
    {
        WORD wBuild = LOWORD ( pOSVA->dwBuildNumber ) ;
        iCurrPos = wsprintf ( szStr , _T ( "(%d) " ) , wBuild ) ;
    }
    return ( iCurrPos ) ;
}

ADDIN_API HRESULT WINAPI
        AddIn_OSVERSIONINFOA ( DWORD         /*dwAddress*/    ,
                               DEBUGHELPER* pHelper          ,
                               int           /*nBase*/        ,
                               BOOL          /*bUniStrings*/ ,
                               char *        pResult          ,
                               size_t        /*max*/          ,
                               DWORD         /*reserved*/      )
{
    if ( pHelper->dwVersion < 0x20000 )
    {
        // I'm not touching less than VS.NET.
        return ( E_FAIL ) ;
    }

    HRESULT hRet = E_FAIL ;

    __try
    {

        DWORDLONG      dwRealAddr = pHelper->GetRealAddress ( pHelper );
        DWORD          nGot       = 0 ;
        OSVERSIONINFOA stOSA ;

        // Try and read in the structure.
        if ( S_OK ==
                pHelper->
                    ReadDebuggeeMemoryEx ( pHelper                    ,
                                           dwRealAddr                 ,
                                           sizeof ( OSVERSIONINFOA ) ,
                                           &stOSA                     ,
                                           &nGot                       ))
        {

            // Make sure I got all of it.
            if ( nGot == sizeof ( OSVERSIONINFOA ) )
            {

                // Do the dance...
                char * pCurr = pResult ;
                int iCurr = ConvertBaseOSV ( &stOSA , pCurr ) ;
                if ( 0 != iCurr )
                {
                    pCurr += iCurr ;
```

```
                    iCurr = ConvertBuildNumber ( &stOSA , pCurr ) ;

                    pCurr += iCurr ;
                    if ( '\0' != stOSA.szCSDVersion[0] )
                    {
                        wsprintf ( pCurr                  ,
                                   _T ( "%s" )            ,
                                   stOSA.szCSDVersion     ) ;
                    }
                }
                else
                {
                    _tcscpy ( pResult , _T ( "..." ) ) ;
                }
            }
            hRet = S_OK ;
        }
    }
    __except ( EXCEPTION_EXECUTE_HANDLER )
    {
        hRet = E_FAIL ;
    }
    return ( hRet ) ;
}
```

Common Debugging Question

Has the 255-character debug limit problem been fixed?

YES! In versions of Visual Studio prior to Visual Studio .NET, the native debugging information was limited to a maximum of 255 characters. This wasn't a problem in the C days, but the advent of templates completely blew past 255 characters for even the simplest types. Visual Studio .NET can have arbitrary length debug symbols, so you should see complete expansion. This also means that the old C4786 informational message (debug information greater than 255 characters), which stopped compiles when treating warnings as errors, has finally been buried once and for all! We've been blessed!

Remote Debugging

Remote debugging of native applications works almost as seamlessly as remote debugging of managed applications. Simply install the remote debugging components as described in Chapter 6, ensure your account is set up as a member of the remote machine's Administrators group as well as the Debugger Users group, and you can connect and debug all you want through the new DCOM transport layer. This is the perfect way to attach and detach from those long-running server processes.

In addition to the DCOM transport layer, Visual Studio .NET 2003 offers two remote debugging options: Pipes and TCP/IP. The TCP/IP option has been around since Visual C++ 6, but it's not as secure as Pipes. Where TCP/IP remote debugging allows anyone to connect to the machine, the new Pipes allows you to specify exactly which user(s) you'll allow to connect and debug. Pipe debugging is now the default, though it is slower than TCP/IP.

Although not as convenient as DCOM, the Pipes and TCP/IP debugging can be a great tool for certain debugging challenges. One particularly nice new feature is that you can start processes with Pipes and TCP/IP debugging. Additionally, you can set up your Visual Studio .NET solutions to always start the process for remote debugging. This is especially helpful for heavy client-side applications such as DirectX games. A much-needed new feature is the ability to allow multiple connections to the remote machine so that you can debug multiple processes if necessary. Another fine feature is that if you're going to be doing only native debugging, you don't have to go through the complete Remote Components Setup to install just the Pipes and TCP/IP debugging. To get Pipes and TCP/IP debugging set up, you can copy the necessary binaries from a machine that has Visual Studio .NET installed to a directory on the remote machine. Table 7-5 lists the binaries and where you can find them on the Visual Studio .NET machine. Also keep in mind that the Visual C++ 6 version of MSVCMON.EXE cannot be used with Visual Studio .NET.

Table 7-5 Pipe and TCP/IP Remote Debugging Components

File	Copy From Location
MSVCR71.DLL	%SYSTEMROOT%\SYSTEM32
MSVCI71.DLL	%SYSTEMROOT%\SYSTEM32
MSVCP71.DLL	%SYSTEMROOT%\SYSTEM32
MSVCMON.EXE	<Visual Studio .NET Installation Dir>\COMMON7\PACKAGES\DEBUGGER
NATDBGDM.DLL	<Visual Studio .NET Installation Dir>\COMMON7\PACKAGES\DEBUGGER
NATDBGTLNET.DLL	<Visual Studio .NET Installation Dir>\COMMON7\PACKAGES\DEBUGGER

Before you start remote debugging, it's a very good idea to do a little planning to ensure that your remote debugging session will be successful. The Pipe and TCP/IP version of remote debugging with Visual Studio .NET is much less temperamental than the Visual C++ 6 version. The main trick is ensuring your symbols are locatable by Visual Studio .NET on the local machine, which is where the symbols are loaded. For the operating system symbols, your best bet is to have your symbol server set up as I described in Chapter 2. If you're working on a local build of your product, it's best to have the program you're going to debug installed in the same directories on both the remote and local machines. That way there's no confusion as to where things are supposed to be. Finally, it's an excellent idea to ensure that you can start your program on the remote machine, because nothing's worse than finding out that a DLL is missing right as you start remote debugging.

To start remote debugging with Pipe connections, you'll need to log in on the remote machine and run MSVCMON.EXE. By default, starting MSVCMON.EXE means that you must connect to the remote machine from the machine you're running the Visual Studio .NET IDE on, using the same account that you logged on to on the remote machine. If you're willing to open the remote machine up a little more, you can start MSVCMON.EXE with the `-u <domain\group or user>` command-line switch to specify which users and groups you're willing to let to the machine to start and debug processes.

Setting up the machine the Visual Studio .NET IDE runs on is pretty simple. It just entails setting a few items in the Debugging property page of the project properties. In the Action section, the Command and Working Directory fields must be filled out with the locations on the *remote* machine. Optionally, you can specify that you want to attach to the remote process by setting Attach to Yes. The last thing you might want to set in the Action section is the Symbol Path field if you don't have the binaries installed in the same places on both machines.

In the Remote Settings section, set Connection to Remote Via Pipe (Native Only). In the Remote Machine field, enter the name or the IP address of the machine hosting MSVCMON.EXE. You can also try to enter the machine name, but the IP address will always work. It's a good idea to test the connection to the remote machine by using PING.EXE to determine whether you can reach it. If you can reach it through the name of the remote machine, you can use that name, but the IP address will always work. Finally, the Remote Command field must contain the same complete path and name as specified in the Command field in the Action section. Figure 7-6 shows an example project with all the fields filled out.

Once the fields are filled in, you know fairly quickly whether you made a good connection. The console window in which MSVCMON.EXE is running will show you the name of the user making the connection, and you'll start debugging as you normally would. If there's a problem, you'll know what you need to do to fix it because Visual Studio .NET error messages are much better than messages in prior releases.

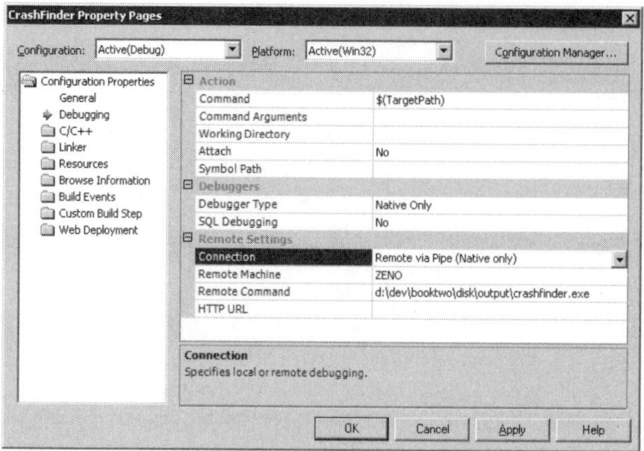

Figure 7-6 A project set up for Pipe debugging

If you're debugging into a machine running terminal server and multiple users could be doing remote Pipes debugging, the MSVCMON.EXE `–s <suffix>` switch allows you to specify a unique suffix onto the named pipe. Since the first user that starts doing remote Pipe debugging gets the default pipe name, subsequent users debugging into the same machine will need to uniquely identify the instance of MSVCMON.EXE they want to connect to. Once you've started MSVCMON.EXE with the `–s` option, you'll specify the suffix in the Remote Machine field of the Debugging property page of the project properties dialog, by appending the suffix to the machine name separated with an octothorpe (#). For example, if you run `MSVCMON -s pam` on the machine ZENO, you'd specify the machine name as `ZENO#pam`.

As I mentioned earlier, Pipe debugging is slower than TCP/IP debugging, though more secure. If you need the speed, you can turn on TCP/IP debugging with `-tcpip` command line switch. To tell the solution that you want to use TCP/IP, in the Debugging property page of the project properties dialog, you'll select Remote Via TCP/IP (Native Only) from the Remote Settings Section.

There are a few TCP/IP specific command-line options to MSVCMON.EXE you might be interested in. The first is `anyuser`, which allows you to let anyone connect to the machine with no security. The second is `–maxsessions`, which specifies the maximum number of debugging sessions you'll allow at any time. The third option is `–timeout`, which you can use to tell MSVCMON.EXE how long you're willing to let it wait for a connection before timing out.

Tips and Tricks

In this section I want to cover a few tips and tricks necessary to make the most of your native debugging.

Debugging Injected Code

One of the interesting new features in Visual C++ .NET is the new attributed programming model. This new model can make COM development much easier because it allows you to combine IDL attributes with your source file so that you must have only a single file to make a COM object. If you'd like to see a real example of attributed COM programming, check out the Tester object from Chapter 16. Additionally, attributed programming offers a consistent way to provide unified message handling for your applications. All the attributes work by injecting source code into your source file.

You've got several ways of debugging this injected code. When in the debugger, to see the source code, move to the Disassembly window and right-click to select Show Source Code from the context menu. However, an easier way to see what's happening with the injected source code is to compile with the `/Fx` switch for CL.EXE. You can turn this switch on within the Visual Studio environment by opening the Property Pages dialog box, expanding the C/C++ folder, selecting the Output Files property page, and setting Expand Attributed Source to Yes. This will create a file named *sourcename*.MRG.CPP in the same directory as the CPP file. You can open the file and look at the injected (merged) source code. If you'd like, you can also compile the merged file so that you can see how everything works in the source window when debugging.

The Memory Window and Auto Memory Evaluation

One huge improvement in native debugging is the Memory windows. For one thing, there's more than one, but more importantly, the Memory window no longer has the weird built-in Artificial Intelligence that made it monitor your eye movements to determine which address you were looking at and then move that address the next time you looked at the Memory window. It's also gained all sorts of additional memory display formats, so you should not have any issues seeing memory how you'd like it. Right-click in the Memory window to choose the display format. The new ability to evaluate Unicode text was a long time in coming.

Finally, the Memory window makes it much easier to automatically reevaluate changes to the memory block you're watching. In the Memory window, click the button to the right of the address field, and the debugger will keep the Memory window updated to the latest values. This functionality is especially valuable when you enter ESP (the stack pointer) so that you can monitor the stack as it changes. Later in the chapter, I'll discuss watching the stack.

Exception Monitoring

One of the biggest performance drains in native applications is the unnecessary exception. Since a native exception involves a trip to kernel mode every time it's triggered, you want to avoid it at all costs. Although the transition from user mode to kernel mode is relatively quick, all the extra work that occurs to process the exception in kernel mode eats tons of time. To help narrow down those performance bottlenecks, the Visual Studio .NET debugger's Exception dialog box allows you to control exactly how the debugger will process any exceptions. By properly understanding how to use this dialog box, you can more quickly track down your unnecessary exceptions.

Before I jump into discussing the Exception dialog box, I need to clarify what happens when an exception is encountered by a native code debugger. The instant an exception occurs, the operating system suspends the process (which means all threads stop), points at the spot where the exception occurred, and notifies the debugger that an exception occurred. This is called the *first chance exception* because it's the first time the debugger has an opportunity to handle it. The debugger has two choices: it can handle the exception so that the debuggee never sees the exception, or it can pass the exception on to the debuggee. The idea that the debugger can handle, or eat, the exception might strike you as odd. However, as you saw in Chapter 4, setting a breakpoint in native code entails setting the instruction at the location to `INT 3`, the breakpoint opcode. In the breakpoint case, the debugger is causing the exception in the debuggee, so the debugger must handle those exceptions. If the exception wasn't caused by the debugger, the debugger tells the operating system that it doesn't want to handle the exception, and the exception is passed back to the debuggee. The debugger also emits a message to the Output window indicating that a first chance exception occurred. The debuggee restarts and, if the debuggee has exception handling set up, the exception is processed and the debuggee continues on its merry way. If the debuggee doesn't have exception handling set up, the exception will propagate up to the final exception handlers inside NTDLL.DLL. At that point, the operating system will suspend the debuggee again and tell the debugger the second chance exception occurred for the exception. This means that the process is going to die from an unhandled exception.

The important issue to note about native exception handling is that when you see the first chance exception message in the Output window, an exception has occurred in your process. As I pointed out, exceptions are a performance bottleneck, so if you're seeing lots of "First-chance exception at..."

messages when you run your process, you have performance issues. The insidious problem here is that C++ exception handling is implemented with structured exception handling (SEH) behind the scenes, so using C++ exceptions can kill your performance. Exceptions are for exceptional conditions. Avoid C++ exceptions in native applications for general development.

To track down performance problems related to exceptions, you can always look for exceptions in code reviews. However, that can sometimes be a daunting task on a large code base. The Exceptions dialog box in Visual Studio .NET can make stopping immediately where exceptions occur and finding where they are handled a complete piece of cake. Figure 7-7 shows the Exceptions dialog box that's accessible from the Debug menu or by pressing Ctrl+Alt+E with the default keyboard mappings.

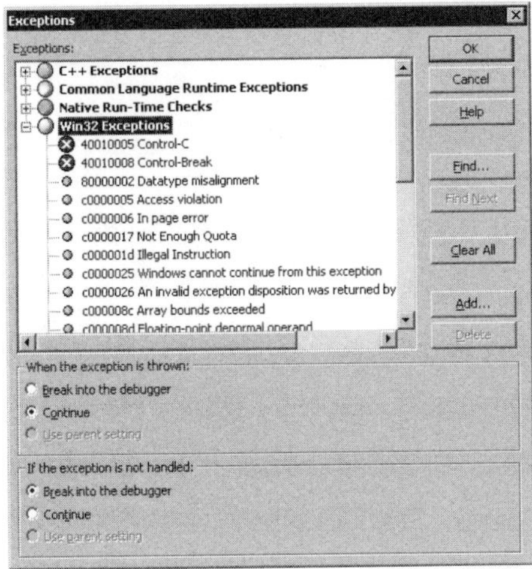

Figure 7-7 Exceptions dialog box

The Exceptions dialog box is a little confusing in that the native exceptions are split between two top level nodes, C++ Exceptions and Win32 Exceptions. The default settings are that the debugger will stop only on Control-C (0x40010005) and Control-Break (0x40010008) exceptions when debugging console applications. To tell the debugger to stop whenever any particular exception occurs, select the exception in the tree and, in the When The Exception Is Thrown (that is, on the first chance exception) group, select Break Into The Debugger. The glyph on the selected item will change to a large red ball with an X in it. In the dialog box, smaller grey balls denote exceptions that inherit their settings from the parent. A larger gray ball indicates the option is to continue on first chance exceptions. Finally, a small red ball says the parent node breaks on first chance exceptions and the child node inherits from the parent. The exception settings are stored on a per-solution basis.

What I like to do is set the Win32 Exceptions and C++ Exceptions nodes to Break Into The Debugger for both the When The Exception Is Thrown and If The Exception Is Not Handled options. That way, whenever any native exception of any kind occurs, the process will stop and allow me to determine whether the exception is legitimate. When you have either all exceptions or a single exception type set to stop, you'll see the dialog box in Figure 7-8, which shows a first chance C++ exception. If you click the Break button, you'll be dropped to the first function on the stack that has source code, which is generally directly in your code where the exception occurred. If you click Step Over or Step Into at this point, the debugger will prompt you with a message box asking whether you want to pass the exception on to the debuggee. Click Yes, and you'll immediately stop in the exception handler for the exception. This is fantastic for determining who's handling your exceptions. There are plenty of bugs for which the wrong exception handlers are handling exceptions.

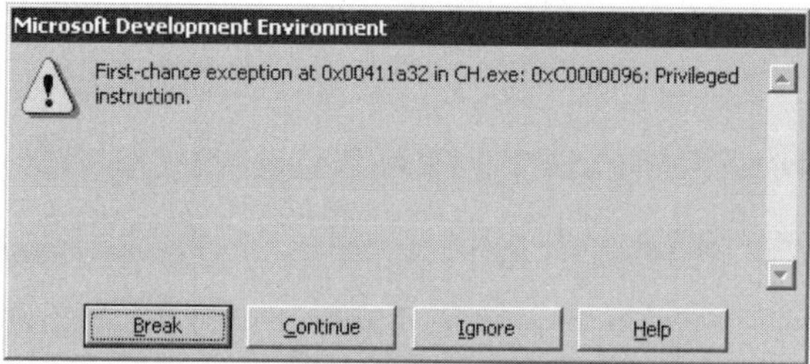

Figure 7-8 First chance exception dialog box

Clicking Continue in the first chance exception dialog box will pass the exception on to the debuggee and continue execution. The Ignore button is a little different and depends on the type of exception and whether the exception is listed in the Exceptions dialog box. If the exception is a hard exception generated by the CPU (such as an access violation), clicking the Ignore button will attempt to reexecute the offending instruction, which will pop up the first chance exception dialog box all over again. If the exception is generated by calling `RaiseException` (such as "0xC0000008, Invalid HANDLE was specified"), execution will continue as if the exception never occurred. Since C++ exceptions are generated through a call to `RaiseException`, your execution will perform as though the `throw` never occurred.

More Symbol Handling Tips

As I described in Chapter 2, Visual Studio .NET advanced symbol handling with the new symbol server and symbol store technology is absolutely out of this world. For native debugging, you can also set additional symbol paths inside the project, so you can have per-project symbol locations outside your normal symbol server.

In the project Property Pages dialog box\Configurations Properties\Debugging property page is a Symbol Path field. Here you can enter the specific symbol path for the project. The good news is that this is appended to any settings you have in the _NT_SYMBOL_PATH environment variable and thus doesn't overwrite them.

Detaching from Windows 2000 Processes

As you should know by now, you can detach from processes when you're debugging under Windows XP as well as Windows Server 2003. However, if you're still supporting Windows 2000, you're stuck—once you start debugging, you're debugging that process for life, which is especially irksome when debugging production server applications. Fortunately, Microsoft realized that not everyone was going to upgrade to the latest and greatest operating systems all at once and came up with a good solution for detaching from Windows 2000 processes.

Installed as part of Visual Studio .NET and the Remote Components Setup is a Win32 service named DBGPROXY, which stands for debugger proxy. This proxy service will run as the debugger on Windows 2000. This means you can easily attach and detach all you want on Windows 2000! In fact, once you execute DBGPROXY with the command `NET START DBGPROXY`, you don't need to do anything else. Visual Studio .NET automatically performs the magic for you, so you're simply debugging, and the detach options are available. Of course, if DBGPROXY does stop for some reason, all processes it was debugging are terminated. I'd highly recommend setting the DBGPROXY service to automatic start-up so that you can start benefiting from it!

Handling Dump Files

Back in Chapter 3 I discussed the SUPERASSERT dialog box and its Create Mini Dump button, which allows you to snap to disk the current state of the process so that you can load it up in the debugger later. Visual Studio .NET makes it easy to read any dump files you create. Opening a dump file in Visual Studio .NET is as simple as opening a regular solution.

After starting Visual Studio .NET, select Open Solution from the File menu. In the Open Solution dialog box, navigate to the directory where your dump file is stored. Dump files traditionally have the extension DMP, which is already in the Files Of Type combo box, so you can either choose it or enter `*.DMP` in the File Name edit control. Select your DMP file, and click the Open button. As always, Visual Studio .NET will create the ubiquitous solution file necessary to do anything in the environment. Press any of the debug keys—Step Into, Step, or Debug—to receive the prompt for saving the solution and to load the dump file.

If you're working on the machine where the dump file was created and your binaries were compiled, Visual Studio .NET will *automagically* find the source and symbols to match up with the dump file. To get the operating symbols lined up, either set the _NT_SYMBOL_PATH to include the symbol store for your location, or after starting debugging, open the Modules window, right-click on the modules without symbols, and browse over to the correct symbols.

To help the debugger specify where to find the modules, you've got two ways of telling the debugger where to look. The easiest way is to specify the module directories in the `MODPATH` environment variable. Simply add each directory separated by semicolons to the `MODPATH` environment variable as you would for the `PATH` environment variable. If you'd like to set the module look up path globally, you can specify them to the `SZ_REG` value `GlobalModPath` in either of the following two registry keys. Use the HKEY_LOCAL_MACHINE if you want the path available to all users on the machine.

```
HKEY_CURRENT_USER\Software\Microsoft\VisualStudio\7.1\NativeDE\Dumps\
HKEY_LOCAL_MACHINE\Software\Microsoft\VisualStudio\7.1\NativeDE\Dumps\
```

Unfortunately, the Visual Studio .NET debugger won't read binaries out of your symbol server directly, where WinDBG can. Therefore, if you're working with dump files from customer sites, you're probably better off using WinDBG, discussed in the next chapter, to handle those dump files.

In addition to opening dump files, Visual Studio .NET can also create them. At first that might not sound very exciting, but from a Bugslayer debugging standpoint, we now have another great technique for solving problems. By creating dump files at various stages during a hard-core debugging session, you instantly have a post mortem trail you can follow that leads up to the problem. This opens up excellent opportunities to grab program states to show others on the team as well as to verify behavior over time. I end up doing so many snapshots during hard debugging sessions that I can quickly fill up whole hard disks. However, hard disks are dirt cheap compared to the costs that can be incurred as a result of not fixing a bug.

Writing dump files is easy when you're in the middle of a debugging session. Select the Save Dump As menu option from the bottom of the Debug menu. That brings up a File Save dialog box in which you can specify exactly where the dump file should be created. Visual Studio .NET lets you write two types of dump files. Visual Studio .NET calls the first type simply *minidump*. This file contains the operating system version information, the stack walk of all threads, and the file version information of each module loaded in the process. The regular minidump files are quite small. I have a debugger attached to Word

2002 as I write this chapter and the minidump file is only 38 K when the working set is over 16 MB.

The second type of dump file you can write is a *minidump with heap*. This file writes out the same information as a minidump along with all allocated memory in the process. With this dump file format you can now follow pointer values through the entire address space. Of course, that extra information comes at a much bigger cost. The minidump with heap for Microsoft Word 2002 with this entire chapter loaded is 96 MB! In general, I mostly stick with the straight minidump version because I've rarely needed to wind through multiple pointer layers. However, it's nice to know it's there.

Unfortunately, Visual Studio .NET doesn't offer an option to write out the most useful dump format, the *minidump with handles*. The argument could be made that since Visual Studio .NET does not offer a means for viewing handle information, there's no need to write that information out. However, WinDBG does allow you to view handle information, as you'll see in the next chapter. Having the handle information is the difference between tracking down a multithreaded deadlock and not solving it. Since the handle information is so important, the SUPERASSERT dialog box does write it out.

Finally, make sure you read about WinDBG's dump file handling. Although WinDBG is harder to use, the debugger is better suited to reading the dump files you get from customers primarily because it can load the binaries out of your symbol store. With its better symbol handling and extra informational commands, you can determine the cause of those customer problems more easily.

Common Debugging Question

How do I set breakpoints in DLLs that aren't loaded yet?

One big problem with Visual Studio 6 was that trying to get breakpoints set in a DLL that was dynamically loaded in the Additional DLL dialog box was, to say it charitably, a disaster. Remote debugging was especially problematic. However, you might not have even noticed the change with Visual Studio .NET because Microsoft fixed the breakpoints so that they automatically rearm themselves when the module containing the source file comes into the address space. In the Breakpoint window, disarmed breakpoints have a white question mark in the red dot. The Additional DLL dialog box is gone, and good riddance!

x86 Assembly Language

In many cases, when your native application crashes, the real difference between solving the bug and screaming in frustration comes down to how well you can read a little assembly language. Although we'd all prefer our crashes to occur in a module with source code and a complete call stack, many crashes just don't happen that way. When you do crash, you're generally left looking at the Disassembly window in the Visual Studio .NET debugger and wondering how you're going to figure out where you are in the program, let alone why you crashed.

By no means am I saying that you need to know assembly language well enough to write all your programs using Microsoft Macro Assembler (MASM). The key is to learn enough assembly language to be comfortable reading it. My goal for this section is to present the information you need to have a working knowledge of assembly language. By the time you finish reading this section and practice for a couple of hours, you'll know more than enough assembly language to get by. This small investment of time can be the difference between flailing around in the debugger practicing your primal scream therapy and fixing your bugs. For those of you who have done assembly language programming in the past, keep in mind that everything I'm going to discuss here is in relation to what you'll see in the Disassembly window. You might remember more concise ways of doing some of these operations, but the important issue is getting familiar with how Visual Studio .NET displays assembly language.

Developers are sometimes wary of learning assembly language because they think some sort of black magic is involved. There's really nothing mysterious about assembly language, though; a single assembly language instruction does one thing and one thing only. Once you see the pattern and understand how the CPU carries out instructions, you'll realize that assembly language is actually quite elegant. If you want to look at black magic, take a look at any program that uses STL heavily. Those magical STL inline expansions can result in a call to 30 or 40 different functions and make an incredible number of assumptions. To me, STL is sometimes far more mystifying than assembly language.

After introducing you to assembly language, I'll turn back to the Visual Studio .NET debugger and show you how to survive in the Disassembly window. For example, I'll show you how to look up parameters on the stack and navigate within the Disassembly window. I'll also explain the relationship between the Memory window and the Disassembly window as well as supply you with tips and tricks that will help you debug at the assembly-language level.

Before we jump into assembly language, I need to issue one warning. Some of you are really going to get into assembly language. That's great, but it can lead to a problem for your career. Your bosses have already spoken with me and have asked that you not start jumping into assembly language every chance you get. It's not portable and can make maintenance much harder.

The Basics of the CPU

The Intel instruction set has been around for quite a while and has its roots in the 8086 CPU that Intel first released in 1978. In the days of MS-DOS and 16-bit Microsoft Windows, assembly language used to be a little quirky and hard to use because of the way the CPU handled memory, which was through 64 KB blocks of memory called segments. Fortunately, today on Windows operating systems, the CPU has direct access to the entire address space, which means that assembly language is much easier to deal with.

The assembly language that I'll be introducing here will be the basic 32-bit instruction set that is compatible across all x86 architecture CPUs from both Intel and AMD and is also referred to as IA32. The advanced features on the Intel Pentiums, such as MMX, aren't generally an issue because Windows uses relatively few such features. I won't get into the real grungy parts of assembly-language instruction formats such as the ModR/M and SIB bytes, which both indicate ways to access memory. For the purposes of this chapter, memory access is memory access. I also won't be covering floating-point instructions. Operations on the Intel CPU floating-point unit (FPU) are similar to normal instructions. The main differences are that the FPU has its own set of registers and the floating-point instructions use a register stack–based architecture. If this chapter inspires you to learn more about the Intel family of CPUs—and I hope it does—you should download the three-volume *Intel Architecture Software Developer's Manual* Adobe PDF files from *www.intel.com*. The most important manual is Volume 2, the *Instruction Set Reference*. Volumes 1 and 3 are for basic CPU architecture information and operating systems developers, respectively. For the price of a phone call, you can even get the actual Intel CPU reference manuals from Intel free. Although you don't really need the actual manuals, they sure do make you look smart when they're sitting on your bookshelf!

One key point to remember is that the x86 CPUs are very flexible and provide you with many ways to carry out similar operations. Fortunately for us, the Microsoft compilers do a good job of picking the fastest way to do an operation and reusing that construct wherever applicable, so recognizing what a section of code is doing is easier. In the following sections, I'll cover the most commonly used instructions you'll see in assembly language. If you're interested in all the assembly-language instructions, you can consult the Intel manuals.

Registers

The first topic I want to cover is the registers. Because every bit of data that your application handles passes through the registers at one time or another, knowing the purpose of each register can help you recognize code gone awry. x86 CPUs have eight general-purpose registers (`EAX`, `EBX`, `ECX`, `EDX`, `ESI`, `EDI`, `ESP`, and `EBP`), six segment registers (`CS`, `DS`, `ES`, `SS`, `FS`, and `GS`), an instruction pointer (`EIP`), and a flags register (`EFLAGS`). The CPU has other registers as well, such as the debug and machine control registers, but they're special-purpose registers and you won't encounter them in normal user-mode debugging. Figure 7-9 shows the layout of a general-purpose register. The thing to remember is that some of the registers allow mnemonics to access different portions of the complete 32-bit register. The complete breakdown of all general-purpose registers is listed in Table 7-6. The only segment register of interest for this discussion is the `FS` register, which holds the thread information block (TIB) that describes the currently executing thread. The other segment registers are used, but the operating system configures them in such a way that they're transparent to normal operation. The instruction pointer holds the address of the currently executing instruction.

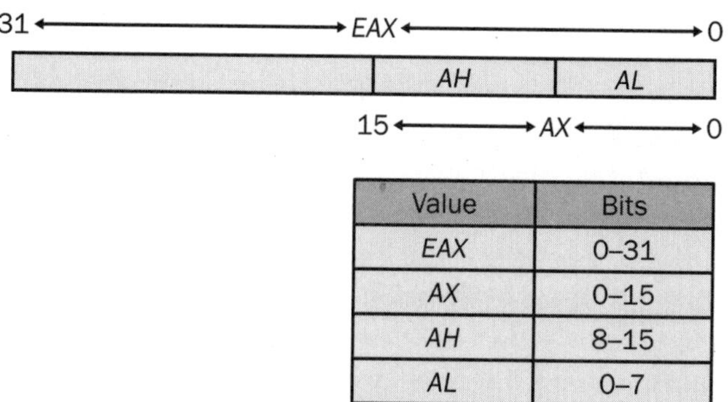

Value	Bits
EAX	0–31
AX	0–15
AH	8–15
AL	0–7

Figure 7-9 General-purpose register layout

The flags register, `EFLAGS`, contains the status flags and the control flags. Various instructions set bits in `EFLAGS` to indicate the result of those instructions. For example, the `ZF` (Zero Flag) bit is set to 1 when the result of an instruction is 0. In Chapter 4, I described setting the CPU to single-step mode, which involved setting the `TF` (Trap Flag) in the `EFLAGS` register. Figure 7-10 shows the Registers window from the Visual Studio .NET debugger. The Registers window displays the `EFLAGS` register as `EFL`. Notice that I'm not showing floating-point registers or any of the other special registers such as MMX or 3DNow! in the Registers window. You can choose the registers you want to see by right-clicking in the Registers window and selecting the registers you're interested in from the context menu.

Table 7-6 General-Purpose Registers

32-Bit Register	16-Bit Access	Low-Byte Access (Bits 0–7)	High-Byte Access (Bits 8–15)	Special Uses
EAX	AX	AL	AH	Integer function return values are stored here.
EBX	BX	BL	BH	
ECX	CX	CL	CH	Loop instruction counters use this register for counting.
EDX	DX	DL	DH	The high 32 bits of 64-bit values are stored here.
ESI	SI			In memory move or compare instructions, the source address is stored here.
EDI	DI			In memory move or compare instructions, the destination address is stored here.
ESP	SP			The stack pointer. This register is changed implicitly when calling functions, returning from functions, making room on the stack for local variables, and cleaning up the stack.
EBP	BP			Base/frame pointer. This register holds the stack frame for a procedure.

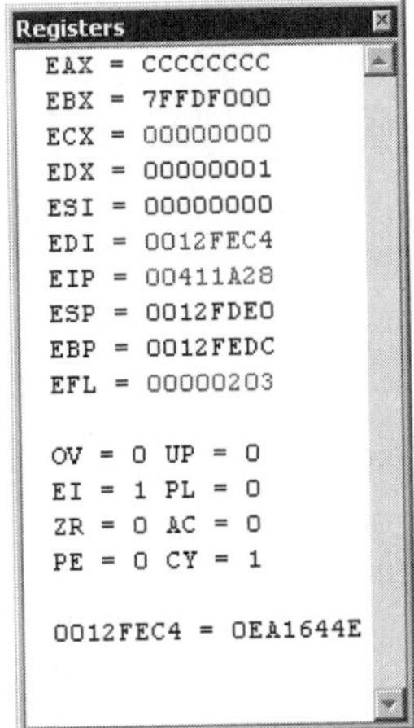

Figure 7-10 The Visual Studio .NET Registers window

Table 7-7 lists the flag values shown in the Registers window. The Visual Studio .NET documentation doesn't mention what the flag values in the Registers window mean, so you might never have seen these values before. Unfortunately, the mnemonics Visual Studio .NET uses for these flags don't correspond to the Intel mnemonics, so you'll have to translate when referring to the Intel documentation. However, one nice change to the Registers window with Visual Studio .NET is that the actual flag values change to red when they change. Previous editions of Visual Studio never highlighted the changed flag fields in any way, so it was very hard to determine what had changed. Fortunately, for essentially 100 percent of your native debugging, you'll never need to watch the flags.

Table 7-7 Registers Window Flag Values

Registers Window Flag	Meaning	Intel Manual Mnemonic	Notes
`OV`	Overflow flag	OF	Set to 1 if the operation resulted in an integer overflow or underflow.
`UP`	Direction flag	DF	Set to 1 if string instructions are processed from highest address to lowest address (autodecrement). 0 means that string instructions are processed from lowest address to highest address (autoincrement), which is always the case in C/C++ code generation.
`EI`	Interrupt Enable flag	IF	Set to 1 if interrupts are enabled. This flag will always be 1 in a user-mode debugger because if interrupts are off, you won't be able to use the keyboard or see any screen updating.
`PL`	Sign flag	SF	Reflects the most significant bit of an instruction result. Set to 0 for positive values, 1 for negative values.
`ZR`	Zero flag	ZF	Set to 1 if the instruction result is 0. This flag is important for compare instructions.
`AC`	Auxiliary Carry flag	AF	Set to 1 if a binary-coded decimal (BCD) operation generated a carry or a borrow.

Table 7-7 Registers Window Flag Values *(continued)*

Registers Window Flag	Meaning	Intel Manual Mnemonic	Notes
PE	Parity flag	PF	Set to 1 if the least significant byte of the result contains an even number of bits set to 1.
CY	Carry flag	CF	Set to 1 if an arithmetic operation generates a carry or a borrow out of the most significant bit of the result. Also set to 1 on an overflow condition for unsigned integer arithmetic.

One important feature of the Registers window is that you can edit the values in it. Although the Registers window looks like a standard text window, such as the Output window, you can change the values in it. Simply put the cursor anywhere within the number to the right of the equal sign for the register you want to change, and type in your revision. The place you put your cursor within the value is where you'll start overtyping the current value. Undo is also supported in the Register window.

Instruction Format and Memory Addressing

The basic instruction format .for the Intel CPUs is follows. All instructions follow the same pattern.

```
[prefix] instruction [operands]
```

For the most part, you see prefixes only on some string functions. (I'll cover the common situations in which string functions use prefixes in the "String Manipulation" section later in the chapter.) The operands format, shown here, indicates the direction of the operation. The source goes into the destination, so read the operands from right to left.

```
Single-instruction operands : XXX source
Two-instruction operands: XXX destination, source
```

In fact, the biggest trick to reading assembly language I can give you is to hold your index finger straight at the second (source) operand and make a little hop with your finger to the left until it's pointing at the destination operand. When you do the finger movement, say "source to destination" each time. That's exactly what I do when I read assembly language. The biggest mistake everyone makes with Intel assembly language is getting the source and destination backwards, so the little finger hop really helps. Some people have told me they help keep it straight by thinking of the comma between the source and destination as an equal sign. No matter what, the operation still feels backwards, unless, of course, you read Arabic or Hebrew.

The source operand can be a register, a memory reference, or an immediate value—that is, a hard-coded value. The destination operand can be a register or a memory reference. The Intel CPUs don't allow both a source and a destination to be memory references.

Memory references are those operands that appear within brackets. For example, the memory reference `[0040129Ah]` means "get the value at memory location 0x0040129A." The *h* is the assembly-language way of specifying a hexadecimal number. Using `[0040129Ah]` is the same as accessing a pointer to an integer in C with `*pIVal`. Memory references can be through registers, as in `[EAX]`, which means "get the memory at the address in `EAX`." Another common memory reference specifies an address by adding an offset to a register value. `[EAX+0Ch]` means "add 0xC to the value in `EAX` and get that memory." Some memory references, such as `[EAX+EBX*2]`, which indicates that the memory reference is from a calculation involving several registers, become fairly complicated.

To differentiate the sizes of memory references, you'll often see a memory reference preceded by a pointer size. The pointer sizes are shown as `BYTE PTR`, `WORD PTR`, and `DWORD PTR` for byte, word, and double-word references, respectively. You can think of these just as you think of a C++ cast. If the disassembly doesn't specify a pointer size, the size is a double word.

Sometimes an instruction's memory reference is straightforward and you can easily see the address for that memory. For example, a reference to `[EBX]` is just a reference to the memory held in the `EBX` register, so you can simply pull up the Memory window and type in `EBX` to look at it. Other times, however, it isn't possible to figure out the memory reference without performing some complicated hexadecimal multiplication. Fortunately, the Registers window will show you what memory the instruction is about to reference.

Notice the line `0012FEC4 = 0EA1644E` at the bottom of Figure 7-10. That line is the *effective address* display. The current instruction, in this case at 0x00411A28, is referencing the address 0x0012FEC4, the left-hand side of the line. The right-hand side of the line is the value at the 0x0012FEC4 memory location, 0x0EA1644E. Only those instructions that access memory will show the effective address in the Registers window. Because x86 CPUs allow only one of the operands to be a memory reference, just keeping an eye on the effective address display can show you what memory you're about to access and what the value is at that memory location.

If the memory access isn't valid, the CPU generates either a General Protection Fault (GPF) or a page fault. A GPF indicates that you're trying to access memory that you don't have access to. A page fault indicates that you're trying to access a memory location that doesn't exist. If you're looking at a line of assembly-language code that crashes, the part to look at is the memory reference. That will tell you which values were invalid. For example, if the memory reference is `[EAX]`, you need to look at the value in `EAX`. If `EAX` holds an invalid address, you need to start scanning backward in the assembly-language listing to see what instruction set `EAX` to the invalid value. Keep in mind that you might need to go back several calls to find the instruction. I'll show you how to walk the stack manually later in the chapter.

A Word About the Visual C++ .NET Inline Assembler

Before I jump into the assembly-language instructions, I want to talk for a bit about the inline assembler in Visual C++. Like most professional C++ compilers, the Visual C++ compiler allows you to embed assembly-language instructions directly in line with your C and C++ code. Although using inline assembly language isn't generally recommended because it restricts your code's portability, it's sometimes the only way to accomplish a task. In Chapter 15, I'll show you how to hook imported functions by using inline assembly language.

Earlier in this chapter, I said that you don't need to know how to write your programs in assembly language, and I'm not contradicting myself. Learning to use the inline assembler isn't the same as learning to write an entire program in MASM—your C/C++ program still provides the application infrastructure. You can think of the inline assembler as the programming equivalent of a Zoom feature. When you create a bitmap, for example, you start out by painting with broad strokes; when it comes time to put on the finishing touches, you zoom in so that you can control the individual pixels. In the same way, the inline assembler lets you "paint" your program in broad C/C++ strokes but allows you to zoom in when you need to control the individual assembly-language instructions. I want to show you how to use the inline assembler because just getting everyone to understand the odd MASM syntax for where directives are supposed to go would take about 100 pages, and inline assembly language is much easier to understand. Additionally, you can use the inline assembler to play around with the instructions I show you in this chapter so that you can see how they behave.

To show you the format for inline assembly language, I'll need to introduce your first instruction:

NOP No operation

NOP is the instruction that does nothing. The compiler sometimes uses NOP for padding inside functions to keep those functions aligned on proper memory reference boundaries.

The inline assembler keyword is __asm. After __asm, you enter the assembly-language instruction you want to execute. If you're not into carpal tunnel syndrome, to enter multiple instructions, you use __asm and enclose within braces as many assembly-language instructions as you'd like. The following two routines show you the format of inline assembly-language instructions. These routines are functionally equivalent.

```
void NOPFuncOne ( void )
{
    __asm NOP
    __asm NOP
}

void NOPFuncTwo ( void )
{
    __asm
    {
        NOP
        NOP
    }
}
```

Throughout the chapter, I'll use the inline assembler to illustrate assembly-language operations such as parameter and variable access. If you want to see how each instruction operates, open the ASMer program included with this book's sample files. This sample program contains all the assembly-language examples that follow.

Instructions You Need to Know

There are many different instructions on Intel CPUs; the Intel Instruction Set Reference chapter for the Pentium Xeon is 854 pages. That doesn't mean there are 854 instructions; it means that it takes 854 pages to describe what the instructions do. Fortunately, many of the instructions aren't used in user-mode programs, so you don't need to be concerned with them. I'll cover only the instructions that are frequently used by the Microsoft code generator and the situations in which you'll commonly need them. The format I'll use is to describe a couple of instructions and then demonstrate scenarios in which they apply. Additionally, all the actual assembly language will be displayed as you'd see it in the Visual Studio .NET Disassembly window. That way, you'll get used to the real-world assembly language you'll be reading.

Stack Manipulation

PUSH Push a word or a double word onto the stack

POP Pop a value from the stack

Intel CPUs use the stack extensively. Other CPUs, which have many more registers, might pass parameters to functions in the registers, but the Intel CPUs pass most parameters on the stack. The stack starts in high memory and grows downward. Both these instructions implicitly change the ESP register, which reflects the current top of the stack. After a PUSH, the value in the ESP register decreases. After a POP, ESP increases.

You can push registers, memory locations, or hard-coded numbers. Popping an item from the stack usually moves the item into a register. The key characteristic of the CPU stack is that it's a last in, first out (LIFO) data structure; if you push three registers to save their values, you must pop them off in reverse order, as shown here:

```
void PushPop ( void )
{
    __asm
    {
        // Save the values in EAX, ECX, and EDX.
        PUSH EAX
        PUSH ECX
        PUSH EDX

        // Do some operation here that might destroy the values in each
        // of those registers.

        // Restore the previously saved registers. Notice that they are
        // removed from the stack in LIFO order.
        POP EDX
        POP ECX
        POP EAX
    }
}
```

Even though there are far more efficient ways of exchanging values, the PUSH and POP instructions allow you to swap register values. The swap happens when you reverse the order of the POP instructions.

```
void SwapRegistersWithPushAndPop ( void )
{
    __asm
    {
        // Swap the EAX and EBX values using the stack. The sequence gives
        // you an idea of how to make this swap.
```

(continued)

```
        PUSH EAX
        PUSH EBX

        POP EAX
        POP EBX
    }
}
```

PUSHAD Push all general-purpose registers

POPAD Pop all general-purpose registers

Occasionally when you're debugging through system code, you'll run into these two instructions. Instead of having long chains of PUSH instructions to save all general registers followed later by an equally long set of POP instructions to retrieve all general registers, the Intel CPU offers these two instructions to save and retrieve the registers for you.

Very Common Simple Instructions

MOV Move

The MOV instruction is the most common instruction used on the CPU because it's the way to move values from one place to another. I just showed you how to swap two registers by using only PUSH and POP; now I'll show you how to make the same swap with the MOV command.

```
void SwapRegisters ( void )
{
    __asm
    {
        // The EAX register is a temporary holder, so I put it on the
        // stack so I don't destroy its value.
        // Swap the ECX and EBX values.
        PUSH EAX
        MOV  EAX , ECX
        MOV  ECX , EBX
        MOV  EBX , EAX
        POP  EAX
    }
}
```

SUB Subtract

The SUB instruction is the subtract operation. It subtracts the source operand from the destination operand and stores the result in the destination operand.

```
void SubtractExample ( void )
{
    __asm
    {
        // Set the registers and do a subtraction. The formula for
        // this subtract example is EAX = Value(EAX) - Value(EBX).
```

```
        MOV EAX , 5
        MOV EBX , 2
        SUB EAX , EBX
    }
}
```

After running this code, EAX will contain a value of 3 and EBX will contain a value of 2.

ADD Add

The ADD instruction adds the source operand to the destination operand and stores the result in the destination operand.

INT 3 Breakpoint

INT 3 is the breakpoint instruction for Intel CPUs. Microsoft compilers use this instruction as padding between functions in a file. The padding keeps portable executable (PE) sections aligned based on the linker's /ALIGN switch, which defaults to 4 KB. The opcode, the hexadecimal number that corresponds to INT 3, is 0xCC, which is why it's used for padding as well as initializing stack variables with the /RTCs switch.

LEAVE High-level procedure exit

The LEAVE instruction restores the CPU state when leaving a function. I'll go into more detail about LEAVE in the following section.

Common Sequence: Function Entry and Exit

The majority of the functions in Windows and in your program set up and leave functions in the same manner. The setup is called the *prolog*, and the leaving is called the *epilog*; the compiler generates both automatically. When setting up the prolog, the code is setting up to access the function's local variables and parameters. The access is called a *stack frame*. Although the x86 CPU doesn't explicitly specify any stack frame scheme, the design of the CPU and some instructions make it easiest for operating systems to use the EBP register to hold the pointer to the stack frame.

```
__asm
{
    // Standard prolog setup
    PUSH EBP            // Save the stack frame register.
    MOV  EBP , ESP      // Set the local function stack frame to ESP.
    SUB  ESP , 20h      // Make room on the stack for 0x20 bytes of
                        // local variables. The SUB instruction appears
                        // only if the function has local variables.
}
```

This sequence is common in both debug and release builds. In some release build functions, however, you might see some instructions interspersed between PUSH and MOV. CPUs with multiple pipelines, such as those in the Pentium family, can decode multiple instructions at a time, so the optimizer will try to set up the instruction stream to take advantage of this capability.

Depending on the optimizations you chose when compiling your code, you can also have functions that don't use EBP as the frame pointer. Those procedures have what is called frame pointer omission (FPO) data. When you look at the disassembly for functions with FPO data, the code in the function looks as if it just starts manipulating data. You'll find out how to identify one of these functions in the next section.

The following common epilog undoes the operations of the prolog and is the one you'll see the most in debug builds. This epilog matches the preceding prolog.

```
__asm
{
    // Standard epilog teardown
    MOV ESP , EBP    // Restore the stack value.
    POP EBP          // Restore the saved stack frame register.
}
```

In release builds, using the LEAVE instruction introduced earlier is faster than using the MOV/POP sequence, so you might see that the epilog will be just a LEAVE instruction. The LEAVE instruction is identical to the MOV/POP sequence. In debug builds, the compilers default to MOV/POP. Interestingly, the x86 CPU has a corresponding ENTER instruction to set up the prolog, but it's slower than the PUSH/MOV/ADD sequence, so the compilers don't use it.

How compilers choose to generate code depends a great deal on whether your program is optimized for speed or for size. If you optimize for size, as I strongly recommended in Chapter 2, many of your functions will use more standard stack frames. Optimizing for speed leads to the more convoluted FPO generation.

Pointer Manipulation

LEA Load effective address

LEA loads the destination register with the address of the source operand and is nearly always indicative of a local variable access. The following code snippet shows two examples of the LEA instruction. The first example shows how to assign an address to an integer pointer. The second shows how to retrieve the address of a local character array with the LEA instruction and pass the address as a parameter to the GetWindowsDirectory API function.

```
void LEAExamples ( void )
{
    int * pInt ;
    int iVal ;

    // The following instruction sequence is identical to the C code
    // pInt = &iVal ;.
    __asm
    {
        LEA EAX , iVal
        MOV [pInt] , EAX
    }

    ////////////////////////////////////////////////////////////////////

    char szBuff [ MAX_PATH ] ;

    // Another example of accessing a pointer through LEA. This
    // instruction sequence is identical to the C code
    // GetWindowsDirectory ( szBuff , MAX_PATH ) ;.
    __asm
    {
        PUSH 104h           // Push MAX_PATH as the second parameter.
        LEA  ECX , szBuff   // Get the address of szBuff.
        PUSH ECX            // Push the address of szBuff as the first
                            // parameter.
        CALL DWORD PTR [GetWindowsDirectory]
    }
}
```

Calling Procedures and Returning

`CALL` Call a procedure

`RET` Return from a procedure

Before I can start discussing where and how to access parameters and locals, I need to discuss how to call and return from functions. The `CALL` instruction is straightforward. When a `CALL` executes, the `CALL` implicitly pushes the return address on the stack, so if you stop at the first instruction of the called procedure and look at `ESP`, the address at the top of the stack is the return address.

The operand to the `CALL` instruction can be almost anything, and if you browse through the Disassembly window, you'll see calls that go through registers, memory references, parameters, and global offsets. You can use the effective address field of the Registers window to see the exact procedure you're about to call if the `CALL` is going through a pointer memory reference.

If you're calling a local function, your call will be a direct call to an address. However, many times you'll see calls that are through pointers, which are generally calls through your import address table (IAT) to imported functions or virtual function calls. If the symbols are loaded for the binary you're stepping through, you'll see something like the first CALL instruction shown in the CallSomeFunctions example that follows. This code indicates that you're calling through the IAT. The __imp__ is a dead giveaway. The CallSomeFunctions example also shows how to call a local function. In comments that follow the code, I note what the Disassembly window can show for the operation, depending on whether symbols are loaded.

```
void CallSomeFunctions ( void )
{
    __asm
    {
        // Call the imported function, GetLastError, which takes no
        // parameters. EAX will hold the return value. This is a
        // call through the IAT, so it is a call through a pointer.
        CALL DWORD PTR [GetLastError]

        // If symbols are loaded, the Disassembly window will show
        // CALL DWORD PTR [__imp__GetLastError@0 (00402000)].

        // If symbols are not loaded, the Disassembly window will show
        // CALL DWORD PTR [00402000].

        ////////////////////////////////////////////////////////////////
        // Call a function inside this file.
        CALL NOPFuncOne

        // If symbols are loaded, the Disassembly window will show
        // CALL NOPFuncOne (00401000).

        // If symbols are not loaded, the Disassembly window will show
        // CALL 00401000.
    }
}
```

The RET instruction returns to the caller by using the address that's at the top of the stack, with no checking whatsoever when the instruction is executed. Buffer overrun security exploitations attempt to replace the return address so that you'll return to code that implements the virus. As you can imagine, a corrupt stack can cause you to return anywhere in your application. The RET instruction is sometimes followed by a fixed number. This number specifies how many bytes to pop off the stack to account for parameters pushed on the stack and passed to the function.

Calling Conventions

In the discussion of CALL and RET, I briefly touched on parameters. In order to understand parameters, it's vital you understand calling conventions. The few instructions presented in the preceding section will help you do some excellent debugging. However, I need to tie procedure calling and calling conventions together so that I can start showing you how to decipher the Disassembly window.

A calling convention specifies how parameters are passed to a function and how stack cleanup occurs when the function returns. The programmer who codes a function dictates the calling convention that everyone must follow when calling that function. The CPU doesn't dictate any specific calling conventions. If you understand the calling conventions, you'll find it much easier to look up parameters in the Memory window and to determine the flow of the assembly language in the Disassembly window.

There are five calling conventions in all, but only three are common: the standard call (`__stdcall`), the C declaration (`__cdecl`), and the `this` call. Although you can specify the standard call and the C declaration yourself, the `this` call is automatically applied when you're using C++ code and dictates how the `this` pointer is passed. The other two calling conventions are the fast call (`__fastcall`) and the provocatively named `naked` calling convention. By default, Win32 operating systems don't use the fast-call calling convention in user-mode code because it isn't portable to other CPUs. The naked calling convention is used when you want to control the prolog and epilog generation yourself, as you'll see in Chapter 15.

Table 7-8 lists all the calling conventions. Recall from earlier in this chapter the description of the name decoration scheme for setting breakpoints on system functions. In Table 7-8, you'll see that the calling convention dictates the name decoration scheme.

Changing the calling convention is done as part of the function declaration and definition. For example, the following shows where to place the calling convention. There are also compilation switches to CL.EXE that you can specify to change the default calling conventions for the compile, but I would recommend against using those switches and explicitly specify the calling convention on each function so there is no possible confusion for maintenance programmers.

```
// Declaring a __stdcall function:
void __stdcall ImAStandardCallFunction ( void ) ;
```

If you've never been exposed to the different calling conventions, you might wonder why the different types exist. The differences between the C declaration and the standard call are subtle. In a standard call function, the callee cleans up the stack, so it has to know exactly how many parameters to expect. Therefore, a standard call function can't be a variable argument function such as `printf`. Because C declaration functions have the caller cleaning up the stack, variable argument functions are just fine. Additionally, standard call functions produce smaller code than C declaration functions. With C declaration, each time you make a call to a function, the compiler has to generate the code to clean up the stack. Since you can call that C declaration function from many places in your program, you'll have that stack cleanup after each call, thus bloating your program. Standard call functions, on the other hand, take care of their own cleanup inside the function itself, so the compiler doesn't have to generate any code after the call. Standard call is the default for Win32 system functions for precisely this reason. However, a great quiz question for someone who says they really know Win32 development is this: "What are the only two functions in Win32 that are not standard calls, and what calling convention do they use?" Although I'm tempted to not supply the answer and make you look it up, I'm also feeling benevolent: `wsprintfA` and `wsprintfW`.

Table 7-8 Calling Conventions

Calling Convention	Argument Passing	Stack Maintenance	Name Decoration	Notes
`__cdecl`	Right to left.	Caller removes arguments from the stack. This calling convention is the only one that allows variable argument lists.	Underscore prefixed to function names, as in `_Foo`.	The default for C and C++ functions.
`__stdcall`	Right to left.	Callee removes its own arguments from the stack.	Underscore prefixed to function name, and `@` appended followed by the number of decimal bytes in the argument list, as in `_Foo@12`.	Used by almost all system functions; the default for Visual Basic internal functions.
`__fastcall`	First two `DWORD` parameters are passed in `ECX` and `EDX`; the rest are passed right to left.	Callee removes its own arguments from the stack.	An `@` is prefixed to the name, and `@` is appended followed by the number of decimal bytes in the argument list, as in `@Foo@12`.	Applies only to Intel CPUs. This calling convention is the default for Borland Delphi compilers.

Table 7-8 Calling Conventions *(continued)*

Calling Convention	Argument Passing	Stack Maintenance	Name Decoration	Notes
`this`	Right to left. The `this` parameter is passed in the ECX register.	Caller removes arguments from the stack.	None.	Used automatically by C++ class methods unless you specify standard call. COM methods are declared as standard call.
`naked`	Right to left.	Caller removes arguments from the stack.	None.	Used when you need custom prolog and epilog.

Calling Conventions Example

To tie together the instructions I've shown so far and the calling conventions, Listing 7-3 shows an example of all the calling conventions from the Visual Studio .NET debugger's Disassembly window. The sample source code, CALLING.CPP, is included with this book's sample code if you want to take a look at it.

The code in Listing 7-3 is a debug build with all extra switches such as `/RTCs` and `/GS` removed to make the code easier to follow; also, the code doesn't actually do anything. I call each calling convention function in turn. Pay special attention to how the parameters are pushed to each function and to how the stack is cleaned up. I inserted `NOP` instructions between each of the functions to make the listing easier to read.

```
/*----------------------------------------------------------------------
"Debugging Applications in Microsoft .NET and Microsoft Windows"
Copyright (c) 1997-2003 John Robbins -- All rights reserved.
----------------------------------------------------------------------*/
#include "stdafx.h"

// The strings passed to each function.
static char * g_szStdCall   = "__stdcall"   ;
static char * g_szCdeclCall = "__cdecl"     ;
static char * g_szFastCall  = "__fastcall"  ;
static char * g_szNakedCall = "__naked"     ;

// The extern "C" turns off all C++ name decoration.
extern "C"
{

// The __cdecl function.
void CDeclFunction ( char *        szString ,
```

Listing 7-3 Calling conventions example *(continued)*

```
19:                         unsigned long ulLong    ,
20:                         char          chChar    ) ;
21:
22: // The __stdcall function.
23: void __stdcall StdCallFunction ( char *        szString ,
24:                                  unsigned long ulLong   ,
25:                                  char          chChar   ) ;
26: // The __fastcall function.
27: void __fastcall FastCallFunction ( char *        szString ,
28:                                    unsigned long ulLong   ,
29:                                    char          chChar   ) ;
30:
31: // The naked function. The declspec goes on the definition, not the
32: // declaration.
33: int NakedCallFunction ( char *        szString  ,
34:                         unsigned long ulLong    ,
35:                         char          chChar    ) ;
36: }
37:
38: void main ( void )
39: {
00401000  push        ebp
00401001  mov         ebp,esp
40:     // Call each function to generate the code. I separate each of them
41:     // with a couple of NOP bytes to make it easier to read the
42:     // disassembly.
43:     __asm NOP __asm NOP
00401003  nop
00401004  nop
44:     CDeclFunction ( g_szCdeclCall , 1 , 'a' ) ;
00401005  push        61h
00401007  push        1
00401009  mov         eax,dword ptr [g_szCdeclCall (403028h)]
0040100E  push        eax
0040100F  call        CDeclFunction (401056h)
00401014  add         esp,0Ch
45:     __asm NOP __asm NOP
00401017  nop
00401018  nop
46:     StdCallFunction ( g_szStdCall , 2 , 'b' ) ;
00401019  push        62h
0040101B  push        2
0040101D  mov         ecx,dword ptr [g_szStdCall (40301Ch)]
00401023  push        ecx
00401024  call        StdCallFunction (40105Dh)
47:     __asm NOP __asm NOP
00401029  nop
0040102A  nop
48:     FastCallFunction ( g_szFastCall , 3 , 'c' ) ;
0040102B  push        63h
0040102D  mov         edx,3
00401032  mov         ecx,dword ptr [g_szFastCall (403038h)]
```

```
00401038  call        FastCallFunction (401066h)
49:     __asm NOP __asm NOP
0040103D  nop
0040103E  nop
50:     NakedCallFunction ( g_szNakedCall , 4 , 'd' ) ;
0040103F  push        64h
00401041  push        4
00401043  mov         edx,dword ptr [g_szNakedCall (403044h)]
00401049  push        edx
0040104A  call        NakedCallFunction (40107Ah)
0040104F  add         esp,0Ch
51:     __asm NOP __asm NOP
00401052  nop
00401053  nop
52:
53: }
00401054  pop         ebp
00401055  ret
54:
55: void CDeclFunction ( char *        szString ,
56:                      unsigned long ulLong   ,
57:                      char          chChar    )
58: {
00401056  push        ebp
00401057  mov         ebp,esp
59:     __asm NOP __asm NOP
00401059  nop
0040105A  nop
60: }
0040105B  pop         ebp
0040105C  ret
61:
62: void __stdcall StdCallFunction ( char *        szString ,
63:                                  unsigned long ulLong   ,
64:                                  char          chChar    )
65: {
0040105D  push        ebp
0040105E  mov         ebp,esp
66:     __asm NOP __asm NOP
00401060  nop
00401061  nop
67: }
00401062  pop         ebp
00401063  ret         0Ch
68:
69: void __fastcall FastCallFunction ( char *        szString ,
70:                                    unsigned long ulLong   ,
71:                                    char          chChar    )
72: {
00401066  push        ebp
00401067  mov         ebp,esp
00401069  sub         esp,8
0040106C  mov         dword ptr [ebp-8],edx
```

(continued)

```
0040106F  mov         dword ptr [ebp-4],ecx
73:       __asm NOP __asm NOP
00401072  nop
00401073  nop
74: }
00401074  mov         esp,ebp
00401076  pop         ebp
00401077  ret         4
75:
76: __declspec(naked) int NakedCallFunction ( char *         szString  ,
77:                                           unsigned long ulLong    ,
78:                                           char          chChar     )
79: {
80:       __asm NOP __asm NOP
0040107A  nop
0040107B  nop
81:     // Naked functions must EXPLICITLY do a return.
82:       __asm RET
0040107C  ret
```

Variable Access: Global Variables, Parameters, and Local Variables

Now let's turn to accessing variables. Global variables are the easiest to access because they're just a memory reference with a fixed address. If you have symbols for the particular module at the address, you might get to see the name of the global variable. The following example shows how to access a global variable through the inline assembler. With the inline assembler, you can use your variables as either the source or the destination, depending on the instruction, just as you would in straight C programming.

```
int g_iVal = 0 ;

void AccessGlobalMemory ( void )
{
    __asm
    {
        // Set the global variable to 48,059.
        MOV g_iVal , 0BBBBh

        // If symbols are loaded, the Disassembly window will show
        // MOV DWORD PTR [g_iVal (4030B4)],0BBBBh.

        // If symbols are not loaded, the Disassembly window will show
        // MOV DWORD PTR [4030B4],0BBBBh.
    }
}
```

If a function has standard stack frames, parameters are positive offsets from the EBP register. If you don't change EBP for the life of the function, parameters appear at the same positive offsets because you push the parameters on the stack before you call the procedure. The following code shows parameter access:

```
void AccessParameter ( int iParam )
{
    __asm
    {
        // Move the iParam value into EAX.
        MOV EAX , iParam

        // If symbols are loaded, the Disassembly window will show
        // MOV EAX,DWORD PTR [iParam].

        // If symbols are not loaded, the Disassembly window will show
        // MOV EAX,DWORD PTR [EBP+8].
    }
}
```

The second key phrase to remember after "source to destination" when moving your index finger from the second to the first operand while looking at assembly language is "Parameters are positive!" The fact that standard stack frames give you consistent offsets from `EBP` make it easy to figure out which parameter you're accessing in an instruction, because the first parameter will always be at `[EBP+8]`, the second at `[EBP+0Ch]`, the third at `[EBP+10h]`, and so on. If you're into algebra formulas, the *n*th parameter can be calculated using the formula [`EBP` + (4 + (*n*×4))]. A little later in this chapter, after I discuss local variables, I'll show you an example using standard stack frames and describe exactly why these values are hard coded.

If you're debugging through optimized code and you see references that are positive offsets from the `ESP` stack register, you're looking at a function that has FPO data. Because `ESP` can change throughout the life of the function, you have to work a little harder to keep the parameters straight. When dealing with optimized code, you'll need to keep track of the items pushed onto the stack because a reference to `[ESP+20h]` can be the same reference as `[ESP+8h]` earlier in the function. In the process of debugging optimized code, I always take notes about where parameters are located when I'm single-stepping through the assembly language.

If the standard frames are used, local variables are negative offsets from EBP. The SUB instruction reserves the space, as shown in a preceding section "Common Sequence: Function Entry and Exit." The following code shows how to set a local variable to a new value:

```
void AccessLocalVariable ( void )
{
    int iLocal ;
```

(continued)

```
    __asm
    {
        // Set the local variable to 23.
        MOV iLocal , 017h

        // If symbols are loaded, the Disassembly window will show
        // MOV DWORD PTR [iLocal],017h.

        // If symbols are not loaded, the Disassembly window will show
        // MOV [EBP-4],017h.
    }
}
```

If standard frames aren't used, finding local variables can be difficult—if you can find them at all. The problem is that local variables appear as positive offsets from ESP, just as parameters do. The trick in that case is to try to find the SUB instruction so that you can see how many bytes are devoted to local variables. If the ESP offset is larger than the number of bytes set aside for local variables, that offset reference is probably a parameter.

Stack frames are a bit confusing the first time you encounter them, so I think a final example and a couple of illustrations might help clarify the subject. The following code, a very simple C function, will show you why parameters are at positive offsets from EBP and why local variables are at negative offsets with standard stack frames. After the C function, AccessLocalsAndParamsExample, is the code to make the actual call and parameter setup. The last piece is the disassembly for the function as it was compiled in the ASMer sample program.

```
// The C function itself.
void AccessLocalsAndParamsExample ( int * pParam1 , int * pParam2 )
{
    int iLocal1 = 3 ;
    int iLocal2 = 0x42 ;

    iLocal1 = *pParam1 ;
    iLocal2 = *pParam2 ;
}

// The code that calls AccessLocalsAndParamsExample
void DoTheCall ( void )
{
    int iVal1 = 0xDEADBEEF ;
    int iVal2 = 0xBADDF00D ;
    __asm
    {
        LEA  EAX , DWORD PTR [iVal2]
        PUSH EAX
        LEA  EAX , DWORD PTR [iVal1]
        PUSH EAX
        CALL AccessLocalsAndParamsExample
```

```
        ADD  ESP , 8
    }
}
// The disassembly of AccessLocalsAndParamsExample
void AccessLocalsAndParamsExample ( int * pParam1 , int * pParam2 )
{
0040107A  push        ebp
0040107B  mov         ebp,esp
0040107D  sub         esp,8
    int iLocal1 = 3 ;
00401080  mov         dword ptr [iLocal1],3
    int iLocal2 = 0x42 ;
00401087  mov         dword ptr [iLocal2],42h

    iLocal1 = *pParam1 ;
0040108E  mov         eax,dword ptr [pParam1]
00401091  mov         ecx,dword ptr [eax]
00401093  mov         dword ptr [iLocal1],ecx
    iLocal2 = *pParam2 ;
00401096  mov         edx,dword ptr [pParam2]
00401099  mov         eax,dword ptr [edx]
0040109B  mov         dword ptr [iLocal2],eax
}
0040109E  mov         esp,ebp
004010A0  pop         ebp
004010A1  ret
```

If you set a breakpoint at the start of the `AccessLocalsAndParamsExample` function, address 0x0040107A, you'll see the stack and register values depicted in Figure 7-11.

Figure 7-11 Stack before the `AccessLocalsAndParamsExample` function prolog

The first three assembly-language instructions in `AccessLocalsAndParams-Example` constitute the function prolog. The result of prolog execution is that the stack and the base pointer have been set up, the parameters are accessible through positive offsets from `EBP`, and the local variables are accessible through negative offsets from `EBP`. Figure 7-12 shows the stack and the base pointer values after each of the prolog instructions executes. I'd encourage you to walk through this example in both the text and in the ASMER.CPP program included with this book's sample code.

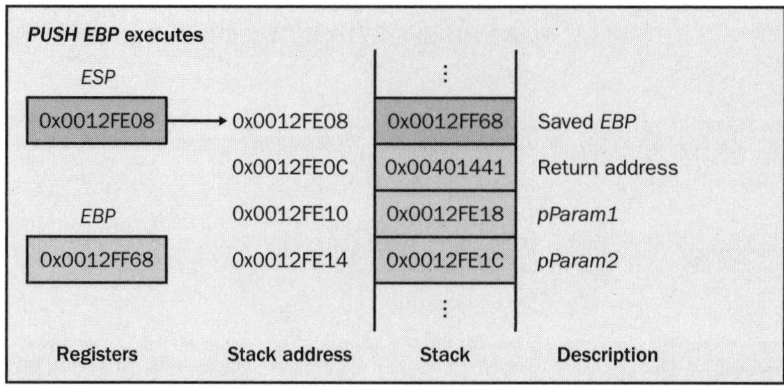

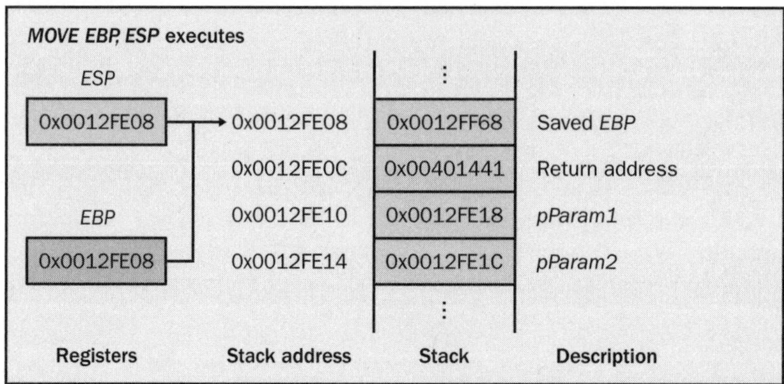

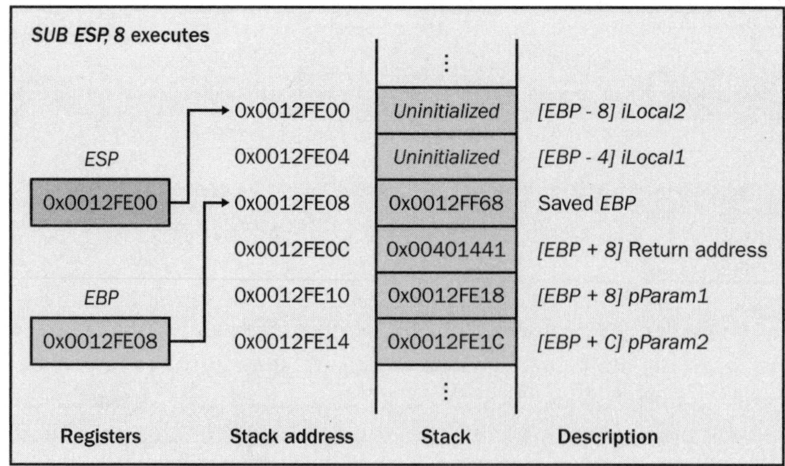

Figure 7-12 Stack during and after execution of the `AccessLocals-AndParamsExample` function prolog

More Instructions You Need to Know

The instructions covered in this section apply to data and pointer manipulation, comparing and testing, jumping and branching, looping, and string manipulation.

Data Manipulation

AND Logical-AND
OR Logical-OR (inclusive)

The AND and OR instructions perform the logical bitwise operations that should be familiar to everyone because they are the basis of bit manipulation.

NOT One's complement negation
NEG Two's complement negation

The NOT and NEG instructions sometimes cause some confusion because although they look similar, they certainly don't indicate the same operation. The NOT instruction is a bitwise operation that turns each binary 1 into a 0 and each 0 into a 1. The NEG instruction is the equivalent of subtracting the operand from 0. The following code snippet shows the differences between these two instructions:

```
void NOTExample ( void )
{
    __asm
    {
        MOV EAX , 0FFh
        MOV EBX , 1
        NOT EAX     // EAX now holds 0FFFFFF00h.
        NOT EBX     // EBX now holds 0FFFFFFFEh.
    }
}

void NEGExample ( void )
{
    __asm
    {
        MOV EAX , 0FFh
        MOV EBX , 1
        NEG EAX     // EAX now holds 0FFFFFF01h ( 0 - 0FFh ).
        NEG EBX     // EBX now holds 0FFFFFFFFh ( 0 - 1 ).
    }
}
```

XOR Logical-OR (exclusive)

You'll see the XOR instruction used quite a bit, not because people are keenly interested in exclusive OR operations but because it's the fastest way to zero out a value. Using XOR on two operands will set each bit to 1 if the same bit in each operand is different. If each bit is the same, the result is 0. Because `XOR EAX, EAX` is faster than `MOV EAX, 0` (because the former takes fewer clock cycles), the Microsoft compilers use it to zero out registers.

INC Increment by 1

DEC Decrement by 1

These instructions are straightforward, and you can figure out what they do just from their names. The compiler often uses these instructions when optimizing certain code sequences because each of them executes in a single clock cycle. Additionally, these instructions map directly to the C integer ++ and the -- arithmetic operators.

SHL Shift left, multiply by 2

SHR Shift right, divide by 2

Binary manipulation bit shifts are faster than the corresponding multiplication and division instructions in x86 CPUs. These instructions are akin to the C `<<` and `>>` bitwise operators, respectively.

DIV Unsigned division

MUL Unsigned multiplication

These seemingly straightforward instructions are in fact a little odd. Both instructions perform their unsigned operations on the `EAX` register. But the output implicitly uses the `EDX` register. The high bytes of double-word and higher size multiplications are placed in the `EDX` register. The `DIV` instruction stores the remainder in `EDX` and the quotient in `EAX`. Both instructions operate on the value in `EAX` only with register or memory values.

IDIV Signed division

IMUL Signed multiplication

These instructions are similar to the `DIV` and `MUL` instructions except that they treat operands as signed values. The same result gyrations happen with the `IDIV` and `IMUL` instructions as with the `DIV` and `MUL` instructions. An `IMUL` instruction sometimes has three operands. The first operand is the destination, and the last two are source operands. `IMUL` is the only three-operand instruction in the x86 instruction set.

LOCK Assert LOCK# signal prefix

`LOCK` isn't an actual instruction but rather a prefix to other instructions. The `LOCK` prefix tells the CPU that the memory accessed by the following instruction needs to be an atomic operation, so the CPU executing the instruction locks the memory bus and prevents any other CPUs on the system from accessing that memory. If you'd like to see the LOCK prefix in action, disassemble `InterlockedIncrement` in Windows XP or a later operating system version.

MOVSX Move with sign-extend
MOVZX Move with zero-extend
These two instructions copy smaller size values to larger size values and dictate how the larger values fill the upper bits. `MOVSX` indicates that the sign value on the source operand will extend through the upper bits of the destination register. `MOVZX` fills the upper bits of the destination register with 0. These are two instructions to watch for when you're tracking down sign errors.

Comparing and Testing

CMP Compare two operands
The `CMP` instruction compares the first and second operands by subtracting the second operand from the first operand, discarding the results, and setting the appropriate flags in the EFLAGS register. You can think of the `CMP` instruction as the conditional part of the C `if` statement. Table 7-9 shows the different flags and the values they correspond to when the `CMP` instruction executes.

Table 7-9 Result Values and Their Flag Settings

Result (First Operand Compared to Second Operand)	Register Window Flag Settings	Intel Manual Flag Settings
Equal	ZR = 1	ZF = 1
Less than	PL != OV	SF != OF
Greater than	ZR = 0 and PL = OV	ZF = 0 and SF = OF
Not equal	ZR = 0	ZF = 0
Greater than or equal	PL = OV	SF = OF
Less than or equal	ZR = 1 or PL != OV	ZF = 1 or SF != OF

TEST Logical compare
The `TEST` instruction does a bitwise logical AND of the operands and sets the `PL`, `ZR`, and `PE` (`SF`, `ZF`, and `PF` for the Intel manuals) flags accordingly. The `TEST` instruction checks whether a bit value was set.

Jump and Branch Instructions

JMP Absolute jump
Just as the name implies, the `JMP` moves execution to the absolute address.

JE Jump if equal
JL Jump if less than
JG Jump if greater than
JNE Jump if not equal
JGE Jump if greater than or equal
JLE Jump if less than or equal

The CMP and TEST instructions aren't much good if you don't have a way to act on their results. The conditional jumps allow you to branch accordingly. These instructions are the most common ones you'll see in the Disassembly window, though there are 62 different conditional jumps in the Pentium Xeon II manual, many of which perform the same action except that the mnemonic is expressed with "not." For example, JLE (jump if less than or equal) has the same opcode as JNG (jump if not greater than). If you're using a disassembler other than the Visual Studio .NET debugger, you might see some of the other instructions. You should get the Intel manuals and look up the "Jcc" codes so that you can decode all the jump instructions.

I listed the conditional jump instructions in the same order they're shown in Table 7-9 so that you can match them up. One of the conditional jumps closely follows any CMP or TEST instructions. Optimized code might have a few instructions interspersed between the check and the jump, but those instructions are guaranteed not to change the flags.

When you're looking at a disassembly, you'll notice that the conditional check is generally the opposite of what you typed in. The first section in the following code shows an example.

```
void JumpExamples ( int i )
{
    // Here is the C code statement. Notice the conditional is "i > 0".
    // The compiler generates the opposite. The assembler that I show
    // is very similar to what the compiler generates. Different
    // optimization methods generate different code.
    // if ( i > 0 )
    // {
    //     printf ( "%i > 0\n" ) ;
    // }
    char szGreaterThan[] = "%i > 0\n" ;
    __asm
    {
        CMP  i , 0           // Compare i to zero by subtracting (i - 0).
        JLE  JE_LessThanOne // If i is less than zero jump around to
                             // the label.
        PUSH i               // Push the parameter on the stack.
        LEA  EAX , szGreaterThan // Push the format string.
        PUSH EAX
```

```
        CALL DWORD PTR [printf]  // Call printf. Notice that you can
                                 // tell printf probably comes from a DLL
                                 // because I am calling through a pointer.
        ADD  ESP , 8             // printf is __cdedcl so I need to clean up
                                 // the stack in the caller.

JE_LessThanOne:                  // With the inline assembler, you can jump
                                 // to any C label.
    }

    ///////////////////////////////////////////////////////////////////

    // Take the absolute value of the parameter and check again.
    // The C code:
    // int y = abs ( i ) ;
    // if ( y >=5 )
    // {
    //      printf ( "abs(i) >= 5\n" ) ;
    // }
    // else
    // {
    //     printf ( "abs(i) < 5\n" ) ;
    // }

    char szAbsGTEFive[] = "abs(i) >= 5\n" ;
    char szAbsLTFive[] = "abs(i) < 5\n" ;
    __asm
    {
        MOV  EBX , i              // Move i's value into EBX.
        CMP  EBX , 0              // Compare EBX to zero (EBX - 0).
        JG  JE_PosNum             // If result is greater than zero, EBX
                                  // is negative.
        NEG  EBX                  // Turn negative into positive.

JE_PosNum:

        CMP  EBX , 5              // Compare EBX to 5.
        JL   JE_LessThan5         // Jump if less than five.
        LEA  EAX , szAbsGTEFive // Get the pointer to the correct string
                                  // into EAX.
        JMP  JE_DoPrintf          // Go to the printf call.

JE_LessThan5:

        LEA  EAX , szAbsLTFive  // Get the correct pointer into EAX.

JE_DoPrintf:

        PUSH EAX                  // Push the string.
        CALL DWORD PTR [printf] // Print it.
        ADD  ESP , 4              // Restore the stack.
    }
}
```

Looping

LOOP Loop according to ECX counter

You might not run into too many LOOP instructions because the Microsoft compilers don't generate them that much. In some parts of the operating system core, however (parts that look as if Microsoft wrote them in assembly language), you'll occasionally see them. Using the LOOP instruction is easy. Set ECX equal to the number of times to loop, and then execute a block of code. Immediately following the code is the LOOP instruction, which decrements ECX and then jumps to the top of the block if ECX isn't equal to 0. When ECX reaches 0, the LOOP instruction falls through.

Most of the loops you'll see are a combination of conditional jumps and absolute jumps. In many ways, these loops look like the if statement code presented a moment ago except that the bottom of the if block is a JMP instruction back to the top. The following example is representative of your average code-generation loop.

```
void LoopingExample ( int q )
{
    // Here's the C code:
    // for ( ; q < 10 ; q++ )
    // {
    //     printf ( "q = %d\n" , q ) ;
    // }

    char szFmt[] = "q = %d\n" ;
    __asm
    {
        JMP  LE_CompareStep      // First time through, check against
                                 // 10 immediately.

LE_IncrementStep:
        INC  q                   // Increment q.

 LE_CompareStep:
        CMP  q , 0Ah             // Compare q to 10.
        JGE   LE_End             // If q is >= 10, this function is done.

        MOV  ECX , DWORD PTR [q] // Get the value of q into ECX.
        PUSH ECX                  // Get the value onto the stack.
        LEA  ECX , szFmt          // Get the format string.
        PUSH ECX                  // Push the format string onto the stack.
        CALL DWORD PTR [printf]   // Print the current iteration.
        ADD  ESP , 8              // Clean up the stack.

        JMP  LE_IncrementStep    // Increment q, and start again.

LE_End:                          // The loop is done.

    }
}
```

String Manipulation

The Intel CPUs are adept at manipulating strings. In the vernacular of CPUs, being good at string manipulation means that the CPU can manipulate large chunks of memory in a single instruction. All the string instructions I'll show you have several mnemonics, which you'll see if you look them up in the Intel reference manuals, but the Visual Studio .NET Disassembly window always disassembles string instructions into the forms I show. All these instructions can work on byte, word, and double-word size memory.

`MOVS` Move data from string to string

The `MOVS` instruction moves the memory address at `ESI` to the memory address at `EDI`. The `MOVS` instruction operates only on values that `ESI` and `EDI` point to. You can think of the `MOVS` instruction as the implementation of the C `memcpy` function. The Visual Studio .NET Disassembly window always shows the size of the operation with the size specifier, so you can tell at a glance how much memory is being moved. After the move is completed, the `ESI` and `EDI` registers are incremented or decremented depending on the Direction Flag in the `EFLAGS` register (shown as the `UP` field in the Visual Studio .NET Registers window). If the `UP` field is 0, the registers are incremented. If the `UP` field is 1, the registers are decremented. In all Microsoft compiler-generated code, the `UP` flag is always set to 1. The increment and decrement amounts depend on the size of the operation: 1 for bytes, 2 for words, and 4 for double words.

`SCAS` Scan string

The `SCAS` instruction compares the value at the memory address specified by the `EDI` register with the value in `AL`, `AX`, or `EAX`, depending on the requested size. The various flag values in `EFLAGS` are set to indicate the comparison values. The flag settings are the same as those shown in Table 7-9 on page 329. If you scan the string for a `NULL` terminator, the `SCAS` instruction can be used to duplicate the functionality of the C `strlen` function. Like the `MOVS` instruction, the `SCAS` instruction auto-increments or auto-decrements the `EDI` register.

`STOS` Store string

The `STOS` instruction stores the value in `AL`, `AX`, or `EAX`, depending on the requested size, into the address specified by the `EDI` register. The `STOS` instruction is similar to the C `memset` function. Like both the `MOVS` and `SCAS` instructions, the `STOS` instruction auto-increments or auto-decrements the `EDI` register.

`CMPS` Compare strings

The `CMPS` instruction compares two string values and sets the flags in `EFLAGS` accordingly. Whereas the `SCAS` instruction compares a string with a single value, the `CMPS` instruction walks the characters in two strings. The `CMPS` instruction is similar to the C `memcmp` function. Like the rest of the string manipulators, the CMPS instruction compares different size values and auto-increments and auto-decrements the pointers to both strings.

REP Repeat for ECX count

REPE Repeat while equal or ECX count isn't 0

REPNE Repeat while not equal or ECX count isn't 0

The string instructions, though convenient, aren't worth a great deal if they can manipulate only a single unit at a time. The repeat prefixes allow the string instructions to iterate for a set number of times (in ECX) or until the specified condition is met. If you use the Step Into key when a repeat instruction is executing in the Disassembly window, you'll stay on the same line because you're executing the same instruction. If you use the Step Over key, you'll step over the entire iteration. If you're looking for a problem, you might want to use the Step Into key to check the strings in ESI or EDI as appropriate. Another trick when looking at a crash in a repeat prefixed string instruction is to look at the ECX register to see which iteration crashed.

In talking about the string instructions, I mentioned which C run-time library function each was similar to. The following code shows, without obvious error checking, what the assembly-language equivalents could look like:

```
void MemCPY ( char * szSrc , char * szDest , int iLen )
{
    __asm
    {

        MOV ESI , szSrc           // Set the source string.
        MOV EDI , szDest          // Set the destination string.

        MOV ECX , iLen            // Set the length to copy.

                                  // Copy away!
        REP MOVS BYTE PTR [EDI] , BYTE PTR [ESI]
    }
}

int StrLEN ( char * szSrc )
{
    int iReturn ;
    __asm
    {
        XOR EAX , EAX             // Zero out EAX.
        MOV EDI , szSrc           // Move the string to check into EDI.
        MOV ECX , 0FFFFFFFFh      // The maximum number of characters to
                                  // check.

        REPNE SCAS BYTE PTR [EDI] // Compare until ECX=0 or found.
```

```
        CMP ECX , 0                 // If ECX is 0, a
        JE  StrLEN_NoNull           // NULL wasn't found in the string.

        NOT ECX                     // ECX was counted down, so convert it
                                    // to a positive number.
        DEC ECX                     // Account for hitting the NULL.
        MOV EAX , ECX               // Return the count.
        JMP StrLen_Done             // Return.

StrLEN_NoNull:
        MOV EAX , 0FFFFFFFFh        // Because NULL wasn't found, return -1.

StrLEN_Done:

    }
    __asm MOV iReturn , EAX ;
    return ( iReturn ) ;
}

void MemSET ( char * szDest , int iVal , int iLen )
{
    __asm
    {
        MOV EAX , iVal              // EAX holds the fill value.
        MOV EDI , szDest            // Move the string into EDI.
        MOV ECX , iLen              // Move the count into ECX.

        REP STOS BYTE PTR [EDI]     // Fill the memory.
    }
}

int MemCMP ( char * szMem1 ,  char * szMem2 , int iLen )
{
    int iReturn ;
    __asm
    {
        MOV ESI , szMem1            // ESI holds the first memory block.
        MOV EDI , szMem2            // EDI holds the second memory block.
        MOV ECX , iLen              // The maximum bytes to compare

                                    // Compare the memory blocks.
        REPE CMPS BYTE PTR [ESI], BYTE PTR [EDI]

        JL  MemCMP_LessThan         // If szSrc < szDest
        JG  MemCMP_GreaterThan      // If szSrc > szDest

                                    // The memory blocks are equal.
        XOR EAX , EAX               // Return 0.
        JMP MemCMP_Done

MemCMP_LessThan:
        MOV EAX , 0FFFFFFFFh        // Return -1.
        JMP MemCMP_Done
```

(continued)

```
MemCMP_GreaterThan:
        MOV EAX , 1                 // Return 1.
        JMP MemCMP_Done

MemCMP_Done:
    }
    __asm MOV iReturn , EAX
    return ( iReturn ) ;
}
```

Common Assembly-Language Constructs

Up to this point, I've just been covering basic assembly-language instructions. Now I want to start looking at various assembly-language constructs that you'll encounter and explain how you identify them and translate them into higher-level operations.

FS Register Access

In Win32 operating systems, the FS register is special because the pointer to the thread information block (TIB) is stored in it. The TIB is also called the thread environment block (TEB). The TIB holds all the thread-specific data so that the operating system can keep your thread access straight. This thread-specific data includes all the structured exception handling (SEH) chains, thread local storage, the thread stack, and other information needed internally. For more information about SEH, see Chapter 13. For an example of thread local storage, see the MemStress discussion in Chapter 17.

The TIB is stored in a special memory segment, and when the operating system needs to access the TIB, it converts the FS register plus an offset into a normal linear address. When you see an instruction accessing the FS register, one of the following operations is underway: an SEH frame is being created or destroyed, the TIB is being accessed, or thread local storage is being accessed.

Creating or Destroying an SEH Frame The first instructions after setting up the stack frame are often something like the following code, which is standard code to start a `__try` block. The first node in the chain of SEH handlers is at offset 0 in the TIB. In the following disassembly, the compiler is pushing a data value and a pointer to a function on the stack. That function is `__except_handler3` in Windows 2000 code. In Windows XP operating system code, the special function is `_SEH_prolog`. The first `MOV` instruction is accessing the TIB; the offset of 0 indicates that a node is being added to the top of the exception chain. The last two instructions indicate where the code moves the actual node to the chain.

```
PUSH 004060d0
PUSH 004014a0
MOV  EAX , FS:[00000000]
```

```
PUSH EAX
MOV  DWORD PTR FS:[0] , ESP
```

Although this example is nice and clean, the compiler doesn't always produce such tidy code. Sometimes it spreads the SEH frame creation throughout the code. Depending on the code generation and optimization flags, the compiler moves instructions around to take better advantage of the CPU's pipelining. The following disassembly example, in which KERNEL32.DLL symbols are loaded, shows the start of the Microsoft Windows 2000 `IsBadReadPtr` function:

```
PUSH EBP
MOV  EBP , ESP
PUSH 0FFFFFFFFh
PUSH 77E86F40h
PUSH OFFSET __except_handler3
MOV  EAX , DWORD PTR FS:[00000000h]
PUSH EAX
MOV  DWORD PTR FS:[0] , ESP
```

What's interesting about Windows XP is that the operating system code seems to have custom exception handling that generates a call to `_SEH_prolog`, where most of the preceding code executes. That leads to much smaller code, and based on looking at the assembly language, it looks as if Windows XP functions that use SEH are using custom prolog and epilog to do their magic.

Destroying an SEH frame is much more mundane than creating one, as the following code shows. The key item to remember is that any access of `FS:[0]` means SEH.

```
MOV ECX , DWORD PTR [EBP-10h]
MOV DWORD PTR FS:[0] , ECX
```

Accessing the TIB The value at `FS:[18]` is the linear address of the TIB structure. In the following code, the Windows XP implementation of `GetCurrentThreadId` gets the linear address of the TIB, and at offset 0x24, it gets the actual thread ID.

```
GetCurrentThreadId:
MOV EAX , FS:[00000018h]
MOV EAX , DWORD PTR [EAX+024h]
RET
```

Accessing Thread Local Storage Thread local storage is a Win32 mechanism that allows you to have variables that are global, but each thread has its own instance of the global variables. Offset 0x2C in the TIB structure is the pointer to the thread local storage array. The following disassembly shows how to access the thread local storage pointer.

```
MOV ECX , DWORD PTR FS:[2Ch]
MOV EDX , DWORD PTR [ECX+EAX*4]
```

Structure and Class References

Because so much of Windows development is structures and classes, I want to spend some time going over how you access that memory. Although structures and classes are convenient to deal with in high-level languages, at the assembly-language level they really don't exist. In high-level languages, a structure and a class are just shorthand ways to specify offsets into a blob of memory.

For the most part, the compilers lay out memory for your structures and classes just as you specify. Occasionally, the compiler will pad fields to keep them on natural memory boundaries, which for x86 CPUs is 4 or 8 bytes.

Structure and class references are denoted by a register and a memory offset. In the following `MyStruct` structure, the comments to the right of each member show the offset from the beginning of the structure for each member. After the `MyStruct` definition, I show various ways of accessing the structure fields.

```
typedef struct tag_MyStruct
{
    DWORD dwFirst ;                 // 0-byte offset
    char  szBuff[ 256 ] ;           // 4-byte offset
    int   iVal ;                    // 260-byte offset
} MyStruct , * PMyStruct ;

void FillStruct ( PMyStruct pSt )
{
    char szName[] = "Pam\n" ;

    __asm
    {
        MOV  EAX , pSt  // Place pSt into EAX. Below, I'm using the
                        // direct offsets in the assembly language to show
                        // what they look like in a disassembly. The
                        // inline assembler allows you to use the normal
                        // <struct>.<field> references.

        // C code : pSt->dwFirst = 23 ;
        MOV  DWORD PTR [EAX] , 17h

        // C code: pSt->iVal = 0x33 ;
        MOV  DWORD PTR [EAX + 0104h] , 0x33

        // C code: strcpy ( pSt->szBuff , szName ) ;
        LEA  ECX , szName       // Push szName on the stack.
        PUSH ECX

        LEA  ECX , [EAX + 4]    // Get to the szBuff field.
        PUSH ECX

        CALL strcpy
        ADD  ESP , 8            // strcpy is a __cdecl function.
```

```
        // C code: pSt->szBuff[ 1 ] = 'A' ;
        MOV  BYTE PTR [EAX + 5] , 41h

        // C code: printf ( pSt->szBuff ) ;
        MOV  EAX , pSt          // Get pSt back. EAX was destroyed
                                // on the call to strcpy.
        LEA  ECX , [EAX + 4]
        PUSH ECX
        CALL DWORD PTR [printf]
        ADD ESP , 4             // printf is a __cdecl function.
    }
}
```

A Complete Example

Now that I've covered all the important parts of Intel assembly language, I want to show a complete example of a Win32 API function before turning to the Disassembly window. Listing 7-4 shows the completely commented disassembly of the `lstrcpyA` function from the Windows 2000 Service Pack 2 KERNEL32.DLL. The `lstrcpyA` function copies one string into another string. I chose this function because it shows a little bit of everything that I've discussed so far in this chapter and because the purpose of the function is easily understood. I made the comments, delineated by semicolons, as detailed as possible.

```
; Function prototype:
; LPTSTR __stdcall lstrcpy ( LPTSTR lpString1 , LPCTSTR lpString2 )

_lstrcpyA@8:

; Set up the standard stack frame prolog.
PUSH        EBP
MOV         EBP , ESP

; Take care of setting up the SEH __try block. The address 0x77E88000
; points to -1. This is the default setup to indicate an __except block
; with EXCEPTION_EXECUTE_HANDLER.
PUSH        0FFFFFFFFh
PUSH        77E88000h
PUSH        OFFSET __except_handler3 (77E8615Bh)
MOV         EAX , DWORD PTR FS:[00000000h]
PUSH        EAX
MOV         DWORD PTR FS:[0] , ESP

; Instead of doing a "SUB ESP , 8" to reserve space for some more items
; on the stack related to SEH, the code generator chose to simply do
; two PUSH instructions. "PUSH ECX" is a single opcode (0x51) so this
; is the fastest way to go.
```

Listing 7-4 `lstrcpyA`, a complete assembly language example *(continued)*

```
PUSH      ECX
PUSH      ECX

; Save off registers that may be stepped on by the function. EBX is not
; used. However, it might be pushed for pipelining purposes.
PUSH      EBX
PUSH      ESI
PUSH      EDI

; The last little bit of SEH setup to record where the try block starts
; on the stack and the code is entering the try block.
MOV       DWORD PTR [EBP-18h] , ESP
AND       DWORD PTR [EBP-4] , 0

; The first step after setting up is to get the length of the string to
; copy. The string to copy is the second parameter.

; Move the second parameter, the string to be copied, into EDI.
MOV       EDI , DWORD PTR [EBP+0Ch]

; lstrcpy will look through 4,294,967,295 bytes for the NULL terminator.
; Remember that ECX is what REPNE SCAS uses to count the loop.
OR        ECX , 0FFFFFFFFH

; Zero out EAX to indicate what value to look for when scanning.
XOR       EAX , EAX

; Use the SCAS string instruction to rip through the string for NULL.
REPNE SCAS  BYTE PTR [EDI]

; Because ECX is counted down, switch all the bits so that the length of
; the string is in ECX. The length here includes the NULL character.
NOT       ECX

; Because the REPNE SCAS also incremented EDI, subtract the length of the
; string from EDI so that EDI points back to the start of the string.
SUB       EDI , ECX

; Hold the length of the string in EDX. EDX is not saved in this
; function as it is not required to be saved across C/C++ function
; calls.
MOV       EDX , ECX

; Move the second parameter into ESI since ESI is the source operand for
; the string instructions.
MOV       ESI , EDI

; Move the first parameter, the destination string, into EDI.
MOV       EDI , DWORD PTR [EBP+8]

; Save the second parameter into EAX. Again, EAX does not have to be
; saved across function calls.
MOV       EAX , EDI
```

```
; The string length was counted in bytes. Divide the string length by
; 4 to get the number of DWORDs. If the number of characters is odd,
; the REPE MOVS won't copy them all. Any remaining bytes are copied
; right after the REPE MOVS.
SHR         ECX , 2

; Copy the second parameter string into the first parameter string.
REP MOVS    DWORD PTR [EDI] , DWORD PTR [ESI]

; Move the saved string length into ECX.
MOV         ECX , EDX

; AND the count with 3 to get the remaining bytes to copy.
AND         ECX , 3

; Copy the remaining bytes from string to string.
REP MOVS    BYTE PTR [EDI] , BYTE PTR [ESI]

; Set the local variable to -1, which indicates that the function is
; leaving this try/except block.
OR          DWORD PTR [EBP-4] , 0FFFFFFFFh

; Get the previous SEH frame.
MOV         ECX , DWORD PTR [EBP-10h]

; Undo the SEH frame.
MOV         DWORD PTR FS:[0] , ECX

; Restore the registers saved earlier on the stack.
POP         EDI
POP         ESI
POP         EBX

; LEAVE does the same as the following instructions:
; MOV ESP , EBP
; POP EBP
LEAVE

; Remove 8 bytes from the stack (the parameters) and return to the
; caller.
; lstrcpy is a __sdtcall function.
RET         8
```

The Disassembly Window

Now that you've learned some assembly language, the Visual Studio .NET debugger Disassembly window shouldn't be so daunting. The Disassembly window offers many features that will help you with your debugging work. In this section, I'll talk about some of those features and how to minimize the time you spend in the Disassembly window.

Navigating

If you've ever worked with a debugger that didn't have navigation features that let you steer a course through disassembled code, you know that the lack of good navigation tools can lead to a very frustrating debugging experience. Fortunately, the Disassembly window offers several efficient ways to get where you need to go in the debuggee.

The first avenue for getting to a specific location in the debuggee is via the Address combo box at the top left corner of the Disassembly window. If you know the address you want to go to, simply type it in and jump right to it. The Address combo box can also interpret symbols and context information, so you can jump to areas even if you don't know the exact address.

The only small problem is that you're stuck with the symbol formatting issues I brought up in the "Advanced Breakpoint Syntax" section earlier in the chapter. You'll have to do the same translations to account for name decoration that you have to do when setting a breakpoint on a system or an exported function. For example, if you have symbols loaded for KERNEL32.DLL and you want to jump to `LoadLibrary` in the Disassembly window, you'll need to enter `{,,kernel32}_LoadLibraryA@4` in the Address combo box to jump to the correct place.

One cool capability that the Disassembly window supports is drag and drop. If you're working through a section of assembly language and you need to quickly check where in memory an operation is going, you can select the address and drag it to the Address combo box. When you release the mouse button, the Disassembly window automatically jumps to that address.

As you're frolicking around the Disassembly window with abandon, don't be surprised if you realize that you've forgotten where you started—it's easy to get lost in the Disassembly window. To get back to where the instruction pointer is sitting, just right-click in the Disassembly window and select Show Next Statement. The Show Next Statement command is also available in source code windows. A great improvement over previous versions of Visual Studio is that the combo box will also keep track of all the places you've jumped to so that you can work your way back through a heavy round of jumping.

Viewing Parameters on the Stack

In the "Advanced Breakpoint Syntax" section earlier in this chapter, you saw how to set breakpoints on system and exported functions. One of the main reasons for setting breakpoints on these functions is so that you can view the parameters that go into a given function. To demonstrate how to look up items on the stack, I want to use a real-world example instead of a contrived, simple example.

When you download a program from the Internet, you want to make sure it's not starting up other programs behind the scenes. To double-check what it might be spawning off, you need to watch any calls to `CreateProcess`. I'll be using CMD.EXE for this example. Substitute the name of the program you want to monitor.

First, I used the DUMPBIN.EXE program that comes with Visual Studio .NET with the `/IMPORTS` command line option to determine what exactly CMD.EXE is calling. The output shows each DLL implicitly imported and what functions are called. Looking at the imported functions, you'll see that CMD.EXE imports `CreateProcessW` from KERNEL32.DLL. Then, from the Visual Studio .NET environment, I opened CMD.EXE as a new solution by selecting Open Solution from the File menu. (CMD.EXE is located in the %SYSTEMROOT%\System32 directory). Because I have symbols loaded, just as you will after reading this book, I needed to set a breakpoint on `{,,kernel32}_CreateProcessW@40`. After starting CMD.EXE, I typed in `SOL.EXE` on the command line and pressed Enter.

On Windows 2000 Service Pack 2, the breakpoint on `_CreateProcessW@40` stops at 0x77E96F60 when the instruction about to be executed is PUSH EBP to set up the standard stack frame. Because the breakpoint is on the first instruction of `CreateProcess`, the top of the stack contains the parameters and the return address. I opened one of the Memory windows by selecting the Debug menu\Windows popup\Memory popup and then selecting one of the four Memory windows. After opening the Memory window, I right-clicked and selected 4-byte Integer from the context menu, and resized the window so that I had a vertical line of stack addresses and a single value next to each. Finally, I entered ESP, which is the stack pointer register, in the Address field to see what was on the stack.

Figure 7-13 shows the stack in the debugger Memory window at the start of the `CreateProcess` breakpoint. The first value displayed, 0x 4AD0728C, is the return address for the instruction; the next 10 are the parameters to `CreateProcess`. (See Table 7-10.) `CreateProcess` has 40 bytes of parameters; each parameter is 4 bytes long. The stack grows from high memory to low memory, and the parameters are pushed in right-to-left order, so the parameters appear in the Memory window in the same order as in the function definition.

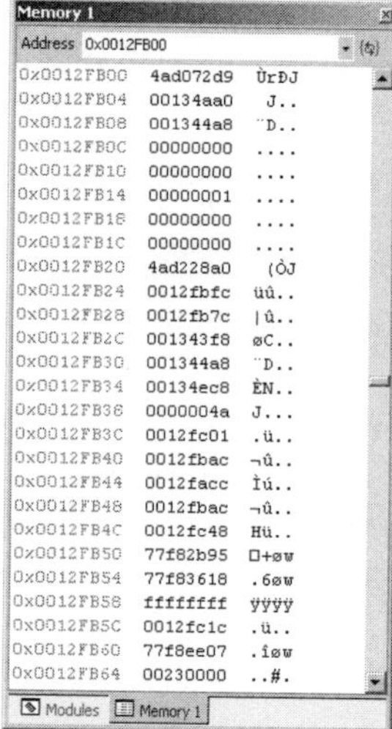

Figure 7-13 The stack displayed in the Visual Studio .NET debugger Memory window

Table 7-10 Parameters That CMD.EXE Passes to `CreateProcessW`

Value	Type	Parameter
0x00134AA0	`LPCWSTR`	`lpApplicationName`
0x001344A8	`LPWSTR`	`lpCommandLine`
0x00000000	`LPSECURITY_ATTRIBUTES`	`lpProcessAttributes`
0x00000000	`LPSECURITY_ATTRIBUTES`	`lpThreadAttributes`
0x00000001	`BOOL`	`bInheritHandles`
0x00000000	`DWORD`	`dwCreationFlags`
0x00000000	`LPVOID`	`lpEnvironment`
0x 4AD228A0	`LPCWSTR`	`lpCurrentDirectory`
0x0012FBFC	`LPSTARTUPINFO`	`lpStartupInfo`
0x0012FB7C	`LPPROCESS_INFORMATION`	`lpProcessInformation`

You can view the individual parameter values for the first two parameters in two ways. The first way is to open a second Memory window and put the address of the parameter into the Address field. Right-click in the window to select any data format you want from the upper portion of context menu. The more important options are toward the bottom of the context menu, where you can select to display the values at the memory address as ANSI or Unicode text.

The second and easier way is to drag the address you want to view to the Watch window. In the Watch window, use a cast operator to view the address. For example, to view the `lpApplicationName` parameter in the example, you'd put `(wchar_t*)0x00134aa0` in the Watch window.

It was easy to get the function parameters in the previous example because I stopped the function on the first instruction before the function had a chance to push additional items. If you need to check the parameters when you're in the middle of a function, you have to do a little more work. Finding the positive offsets from `EBP` helps. Sometimes the best technique is just to open the Memory window and start looking.

The Set Next Statement Command

Like source windows, the Disassembly window has a Set Next Statement command available from the right-click menu, so you can change EIP to another location to execute. You can get away with being a little sloppy when using the Set Next Statement line in a source view while debugging a Debug build, but you must be very careful with the Set Next Statement command in the Disassembly window.

The key to getting EIP set right—so that you don't crash—is to pay attention to the stack. Stack pops should balance out stack pushes; if they don't, you'll eventually crash your program. I don't mean to scare you off from changing execution on the fly; in fact, I encourage you to experiment with it. Changing execution with Set Next Statement is a powerful technique and can greatly speed up your debugging. If you take care of the stack, the stack will take care of you.

For example, if you want to reexecute a function without crashing immediately, make sure to change the execution so that the stack stays balanced. In this example, I want to execute the call to the function at 0x00401005 twice:

```
00401032 PUSH EBP
00401033 MOV  EBP , ESP
00401035 PUSH 404410h
0040103A CALL 00401005h
0040103F ADD  ESP , 4
00401042 POP  EBP
00401043 RET
```

As I step through the disassembly twice, I need to make sure that I let the `ADD` instruction at address 0x0040103F execute to keep the stack balanced. As the discussion of the different calling conventions earlier in the chapter indicated, the assembly-language snippet shows a call to a `__cdecl` function because of the `ADD` instruction right after the call. To reexecute the function, I'd set the instruction pointer to 0x00401035 to ensure that the `PUSH` occurs properly.

Walking the Stack Manually

The Memory windows and the Disassembly window have a symbiotic relationship. As you're trying to determine what a sequence of assembly-language operations is doing in the Disassembly window, you need to have a Memory window open so that you can look at the addresses and values being manipulated. Assembly-language instructions work on memory, and memory affects the execution of assembly language; the Disassembly window and the Memory window together allow you to observe the dynamics of this relationship.

On its own, the Memory window is just a sea of numbers, especially when you crash. By combining the two windows, however, you can start figuring out some nasty crash problems. Using these windows together is especially important when you're trying to debug optimized code and the debugger can't walk the stack as easily. To solve the problem creating the crash, you have to walk the stack manually.

The first step in figuring out how to walk the stack is to know where your binaries are loaded into memory. The new Modules window makes finding out which modules are loaded where in your address space a complete piece of cake because it shows you the module name, the path to the module, the load order, and most important, the address range in which the module was loaded. By comparing items on the stack with the list of address ranges, you can get an idea of which items are addresses in your modules.

After you look at the load address ranges, you need to open both the Memory and Disassembly windows. In the Memory window, enter `ESP`, the stack register, into the Address field and show the values in double-word format by right-clicking within the window and selecting 4-byte Integer. Additionally, it works best if you pull the Memory window out of the docked position in the IDE and shrink it down so that you see only the stack addresses and a single row of 32-bit values. This view shows the stack analogous to how you think of the stack. When you see a number that looks as if it belongs to one of your loaded modules, select the entire number and drag it to the Address combo box in the Disassembly window. The Disassembly window will show the assembly language at that address, and if you built your application with full debugging information, you should be able to see what the caller function was.

If the ESP register dump doesn't show anything that looks like a module address, you can also dump the EBP register in the Memory window and do the same sorts of lookups. As you get more comfortable with assembly language, you'll start looking at the disassembly around the address that crashed. Studying the crash crime scene should give you some hints about where the return address might be located, either in ESP or in EBP.

The downside to looking up items on the stack manually is that you might have to hunt a considerable way down the stack before you start finding addresses that make sense. If you have an idea of where the modules loaded, however, you should be able to pick out the appropriate addresses quickly.

Debugging War Story

What can go wrong in `GlobalUnlock`? It's just a pointer dereference.

The Battle

A team called me in to help them debug an extremely nasty crash—one severe enough to prevent them from releasing the product. The team had spent nearly a month trying to duplicate the crash and still had no idea what was causing it. The only clue they had was that the crash happened only after they brought up the Print dialog box and changed some settings. After they closed the Print dialog box, the crash occurred a little later in a third-party control. The crash call stack indicated that the crash happened in the middle of `GlobalUnlock`.

The Outcome

At first I wasn't sure that anyone was still using the handle-based memory functions (`GlobalAlloc`, `GlobalLock`, `GlobalFree`, and `GlobalUnlock`) in Win32 programming. After looking at a disassembly of the third-party control, however, I saw that the control writer obviously ported the control from a 16-bit code base. My first hypothesis was that the control wasn't properly dealing with the handle-based memory API functions.

To test my hypothesis, I set some breakpoints on `GlobalAlloc`, `GlobalLock`, and `GlobalUnlock` so that I could find the places in the third-party control where memory was being allocated or manipulated. Once I got the breakpoints set in the third-party control, I started watching how the control used the handle-based memory. Everything seemed normal until I started working through the steps to duplicate the crash.

At some point after closing the Print dialog box, I noticed that `GlobalAlloc` was starting to return handle values that ended in odd values, such as 5. Because the handle-based memory in Win32 just needs a pointer dereference to turn the handle into a memory value, I immediately saw that I was on to a critical problem. Every memory allocation in Win32 must end in 0, 4, 8, or a C hex digit, because all pointers must be double-word

(continued)

Debugging War Story *(continued)*

aligned. The handle values coming out of GlobalAlloc were evidence that something serious was corrupted.

Armed with this information, the product manager was ready to jump on the phone and demand the source code for the third-party control because he was sure that the control was causing the crash and holding up his release. After calming him down, I told him that what we had found didn't prove anything and that I needed to be absolutely sure the control was the culprit before we made life miserable for the vendor. I continued to look at the control's memory usage and spent the next several hours chasing down all the handle-based memory manipulations in the control. The control was properly using the handle-based memory, and my new hypothesis became that the team's application contained the real problem. The crash in the third-party control was just a coincidence.

After looking through the team's code, I was more confused than ever because the application was a complete Win32 application and did nothing with handle-based memory. I then turned to their printing code and started looking at it. The code looked fine.

I went back and started to narrow down the cases that would duplicate the crash. After a few runs, I found that all I needed to do to crash was to bring up the Print dialog box and change the paper orientation. After closing the Print dialog box, I just needed to reopen it, and the crash would happen shortly after I closed it the second time. I was happy to get the problem duplicated to this minute level because the page orientation was probably just changing a byte somewhere in memory and causing the problem.

Although the code looked fine on the initial read, I went back through each line and double-checked it against the MSDN documentation. After 10 minutes, I found the bug. The team was saving the PRINTDLG data structure used to initialize the Print dialog box with the PrintDlg API function. The third field in the PRINTDLG structure, hDevMode, is a handle-based memory value that the Print dialog box allocates for you. The bug was that the team was using that memory value as a regular pointer and not properly dereferencing the handle or calling GlobalLock on the handle. When they changed values in the DEVMODE structure, they were actually writing to the global handle table for the process. The global handle table is a chunk of memory in which all handle-based heap allocations are stored. By having the wild writes to the global handle table, a call to GlobalAlloc would use invalid offsets and values calculated from the global handle table so that GlobalAlloc was returning pointers that were incorrect.

The Lesson

The first lesson is to read the documentation carefully. If the documentation says that the data structure is a "movable global memory object," the memory is handle-based memory and you need to dereference that memory handle properly or use `GlobalLock` on it. Even though 16-bit Microsoft Windows 3.1 seems like ancient history, some 16-bit-isms are still in the Win32 API, and you must pay attention to them.

Another lesson I learned was that the global handle table is stored in writable memory. I would have thought that such an important operating system structure would have been in read-only memory. After pondering the reasons Microsoft wouldn't protect that memory, I can only hazard a guess about why they didn't choose to make the global handle table read-only. Technically, the handle-based memory is just for backward compatibility, and Win32 applications should be using the Win32-specific memory types. Protecting the global handle table would require two context switches, from user mode to kernel mode, on each handle-based memory function call. Because those context switches are very expensive in processing time, I can see why Microsoft didn't protect the global handle table.

The final lesson I learned was that I spent too much time concentrating on the third-party control. In all, it took me around seven hours to find the bug. However, the fact that the bug could be duplicated only by bringing up the Print dialog box, which went through the team's code, should have tipped me off that the problem was closer to home.

Tips and Tricks

Earlier in the chapter, I presented some tips and tricks that can make your native debugging life easier. I want to finish up with a few tips that will help you when debugging assembly language.

Endians

The *endianness* of a CPU refers to which end of a byte is stored first. Intel CPUs are *Little Endian*, which means that the little end of a multibyte value is stored first. For example, the value 0x1234 is stored in memory as 0x34 0x12. It's important that you keep the Little Endian storage in mind when you're looking at memory in the debugger. You'll need to convert it in your head so that you're interpreting the correct values. If you use the Memory window to look at one of your link list nodes and the next pointer value is 0x12345678, the value will be displayed in byte format as 0x78 0x56 0x34 0x12.

If you're curious, the term *Endian* comes from Jonathan Swift's *Gulliver's Travels*, and the computer meaning came from a 1980 Request for Comments (RFC) concerning byte ordering by Danny Cohen. Danny's paper is at *http://www.rdrop.com/~cary/html/endian_faq.html#danny_cohen* for those who want to know the entire story.

Garbage Code

As a crash dumps you into the Disassembly window, you have to determine whether or not you're looking at real code, which is sometimes a difficult task. Here are some tips that will help you figure out whether you're looking at something other than executable code.

- I've found that turning on Code Bytes from the Disassembly window's right-click menu to see the opcodes for the instructions is useful. As you'll see in the following tips, knowing what opcode patterns to look for can help you decide whether you're looking at legitimate code.
- If you're looking at a series of identical ADD BYTE PTR [EAX], AL instructions, you're not looking at valid assembly-language code. You're looking at a series of zeros.
- If you see symbols but the offsets added to the symbols are very large numbers, generally over 0x1000, you're probably outside a code section. However, very large numbers can also mean that you're debugging a module that doesn't have private symbols available.
- If you're looking at a bunch of instructions that I didn't cover in this chapter, you're probably looking at data.
- If the Visual Studio .NET disassembler can't disassemble an instruction, it displays "???" as the opcode.
- If the instruction isn't valid, the disassembler will display "db" followed by a number. The "db" stands for data byte and isn't a valid instruction. It means the opcode(s) at that location don't match a valid instruction according to the Intel opcode maps.

Registers and the Watch Window

The Visual Studio .NET debugger Watch window knows how to decode all the registers to values. Therefore, you can put a register in the Watch window and cast it to the type you want to observe. For example, if you're looking at a string manipulation instruction, you can enter `(char*)@EDI` or `(wchar_t*)@EDI` in the Watch window to view the data in a format that's easier to read.

Learn from ASM Files

If you'd like to see more mixed assembly-language and source code, you can have Visual Studio .NET generate the assembly listings for your source files. In the project Property Pages dialog box\C/C++ folder\Output Files property page\Assembler Output field, select Assembly With Source Code (/FAs) to make the compiler generate an ASM file for each of your source code files. You might not want to generate the ASM files for every build, but they can be instructive, letting you see what the compiler is generating. The ASM files don't require you to fire up your application every time you're curious about assembly language.

The files generated are nearly ready to compile with the Microsoft Macro Assembler (MASM), so they can be a challenge to read. Much of the files consist of MASM directives, but the main parts of the files show your C code with the assembly-language code below each construct. After reading this chapter, you shouldn't have any trouble following the flow of ASM files.

Summary

The Visual Studio .NET debugger has many powerful features for debugging, and this chapter introduced you to a set of features for native debugging. The most important conclusion you should have drawn from this chapter is that the debugger can do a considerable amount of work for you if you know how to utilize it effectively. You should strive to make the most of the Visual Studio .NET native debugger so that you can minimize the time you spend in it.

The native enhancements to advanced breakpoints help you avoid the tedium often associated with native debugging by allowing you to specify exactly the place and conditions under which a breakpoint triggers. The context part of the advanced breakpoint syntax is what you use to tell the debugger the scope and exact position of the breakpoints. The pseudoregisters, especially $TIB and $ERR, allow you extra power for your conditional expressions. The global data breakpoints let you set a hardware-assisted breakpoint memory location; then when that data location is written to and changed, the breakpoint fires. Additionally, the hardware breakpoint class provided by Mike Morearty allows true read and write breakpoints in your code.

The Watch window, with its wonderful flexibility, is where you can do amazing things to speed up your debugging. In addition to letting you change your variable values, the Watch window offers all sorts of formatting options so that you can view your data precisely the way you want to. The Watch window also lets you call functions in your program from the debugger. This feature allows you to create and use special debugging functions to automate your most tedious debugging tasks. Additionally, the ability to easily add your own type expansion and HRESULT values will save you many hours of debugging. Finally, the new EEAddIn model, where you can add your own custom display by having your DLLs called by the Watch window, opens up a whole new world of data display.

Although native debugging can take advantage of the excellent DCOM remote debugging, the Pipes solution unique to native debugging has some excellent features. Remote Pipes debugging now allows you to start processes under the debugger on remote machines, which will come in extremely handy for those developers working on large client applications. Additionally, with Pipes debugging, you can attach and debug multiple processes on the remote machine.

The second half of this chapter presented the Intel CPU assembly language that you need to know to survive in the Disassembly window. It started by covering the basics of Intel CPUs, such as setting registers and interpreting status flags, and then moved on to the instructions required to manipulate stacks, data, pointers, and strings; compare and test operands; and jump, branch, and loop, among other actions. After the assembly-language code were tips and tricks that will help you get the most out of debugging at the assembly-language level.

Being able to read assembly language makes all the difference in the world when you're in the debugger trying to figure out why your program crashed. Despite the fact that some people try to avoid it like the plague, assembly language isn't that hard, and there's certainly nothing mysterious about it. The information in this chapter will give you the power to solve many nasty bugs that once stumped you.

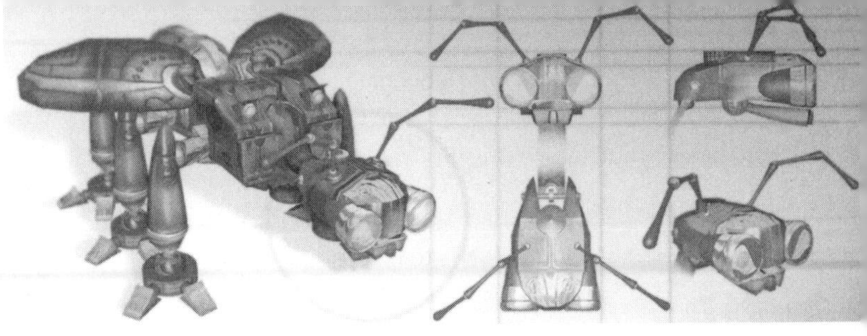

8

Advanced Native Code Techniques with WinDBG

Even though I just spent what seemed like a million pages on the Microsoft Visual Studio .NET debugger, there's still another debugger from Microsoft to talk about—Microsoft WinDBG. I've often wondered why Microsoft has two separate teams working on debuggers, but I'm glad they've gone to the effort, because WinDBG has some extremely powerful features for smacking your bugs into submission. When I've asked folks at Microsoft why there are two debuggers, their answer does make sense. Visual Studio .NET is perfect for application development, but folks working on the operating system need something more extensible so that they can automate the heavy bug-finding tasks necessary to track down problems that occur in 40+ million lines of code.

WinDBG all boils down to raw, unadulterated power. Whereas Visual Studio .NET offers some fine extensibility to control the environment (as you'll see in the next chapter), WinDBG is all about the muscle necessary to poke and prod at the debuggee. Of course, with all this power you'll see some trade-offs, which I'll discuss in a moment.

Many of you are thinking that WinDBG is only for device driver developers, but its power extends to your user-mode native applications. WinDBG can show you more information about your processes than Visual Studio .NET could dream of showing. To entice you to consider WinDBG, I'll mention that WinDBG gives you real memory breakpoints and vastly improved binary handling for minidumps and allows you to see the complete operating system heaps and all handle information in your process.

My goal for this chapter is to help you get past some of the obstacles you'll encounter when starting out using WinDBG. Additionally, I want to show some of the power commands and how you use them. I'll also help you work past some of the strange problems, bugs, and other oddities you'll encounter with WinDBG so that you can be more productive with the tool. Finally, as I promised back in Chapter 6, I'll cover the Son of Strike (SOS) debugger extension for dealing with managed applications and dump files.

Debugging Tools for Windows, the package that contains WinDBG, is available with this book's sample files. The sample files contain the latest version of the tool at the time of this book's printing. You'll also want to check *http://www.microsoft.com/ddk/debugging*, which is where Microsoft posts the latest and greatest information about Debugging Tools for Windows. The development team regularly updates WinDBG to support more debugging features as well as to keep it current with the latest operating system versions. For this chapter, I used the latest version of WinDBG available at the time I wrote it, version 6.1.0017.0.

Before You Begin

Prior to jumping into WinDBG with both feet, I want to go over a few key items to help you get the most out of it. The first is that if you ever have an inkling that you might want to consider writing a WinDBG extension, you'll need to ensure you install the SDK included with the Debugging Tools for Windows. The SDK has the necessary header files as well as some examples to show you the ideas behind extensions. When installing, make sure to select Custom installation from the appropriate setup screen. The custom install screen, shown in Figure 8-1, by default has only one item marked as not installed—the SDK itself. Click on the SDK node and select Entire Feature Will Be Installed On Local Hard Drive. The SDK install directory is, appropriately, named SDK and is directly under the main Debugging Tools for Windows directory.

What makes WinDBG a little weird is that what you and I consider the debugger user interface (UI) isn't where the work takes place at all. The UI is simply a veneer over a debugging engine named DBGENG.DLL. Many people on the operating system teams at Microsoft are used to a debugger named NTSD (Microsoft NT Symbolic Debugger). NTSD is a console application that in the current versions of Debugging Tools for Windows is the console layer over the debugging engine and is part of the Debugging Tools for Windows installation. That means that if you learn to use WinDBG, you can easily use NTSD. Although I prefer the ease of a graphical user interface (GUI), you might want to consider using NTSD because it will scare any roaming managers from sitting in your office and watching over your shoulder as you program. Table 8-1 lists some of the more interesting programs for user-mode developers that are installed as part of Debugging Tools for Windows.

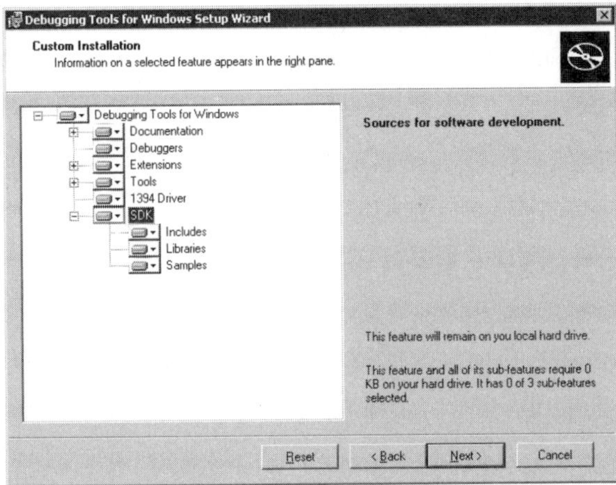

Figure 8-1 SDK installation selected during the Debugging Tools for Windows installation

Table 8-1 Additional Tools Installed with Debugging Tools for Windows

Programs	Description
CDB.EXE	The same debugger as NTSD except it will use the existing command shell when started instead of creating a new one.
LOGGER.EXE, LOG-VIEWER.EXE	A logging system to log all your API calls, record parameters, and return values so that you can track down operating system interaction issues.
LIST.EXE	A console-based text file listing utility.
UMDH.EXE	The user-mode heap dumping utility.
TLIST.EXE	Lists the currently running processes to a console window. (Make sure you pass the `-?` option to see the other interesting command-line options for TLIST.EXE.)
KILL.EXE	An absolute process killer that will remove any user-mode process from memory.
BREAKIN.EXE	Forces a `DebugBreak` call in the process specified on the command line.

The biggest improvement to WinDBG, which is a complete rewrite of previous incantations, is not that it does even more to automatically track down recalcitrant bugs, but that the documentation is actually very good. Before you ever start WinDBG, you need to open DEBUGGER.CHM and read it. You have to read several sections in particular because they are excellent discussions of how to solve problems with WinDBG. As you run through the documentation, keep in mind that much of WinDBG's forte is kernel mode debugging, so you can safely skip those sections unless you're going to be doing device driver development. After perusing "Installation and Setup" as well as the user mode portions under "Debugger Operation," as I mentioned in Chapter 2, you need to read the "Symbols" section completely. Under the "Debugging Techniques" section, make sure to read "Elementary Debugging Techniques," "Stack Traces," and "Processor Architecture." As the Command window is everything in WinDBG, spend a good bit of time reading over the "Reference" section, specifically "Debugger Commands" and "Debugger Extension Commands."

You're probably wondering why, if the WinDBG documentation is so good, I even need to write this chapter. The weakness of the documentation is that it assumes you have either a coworker sitting there showing you how to utilize WinDBG or a phone you can pick up to call one of the developers. I don't think that's an intentional slight, but given that Microsoft developed WinDBG with the operating system developers primarily in mind, it's understandable. In this chapter, my goal is to get you up to speed because WinDBG is quite a bit daunting if you've never used it. Additionally, I'll show you some of the tricks WinDBG can do to make debugging much easier.

The Basics

The biggest problem people face when dealing with WinDBG is getting it set up and wading through a ton of spewed output. I want to turn to a few issues that will help you get past some of those hurdles so that you don't have to bear the scars of learning them. Finally, I'll cover some of the odd quirks of WinDBG so that they won't surprise you and leave you scratching you head wondering what went wrong.

The big thing to remember about WinDBG is that it's kind of a retro debugger. (Heck, the console-based NTSD.EXE should bring tears to some old-timer's eyes!) To that end, it doesn't help you much. Whereas Visual Studio .NET will assist you when it comes to finding symbols and source code, you have to tell WinDBG exactly where to look to find things. If you're debugging a program built on the same machine you're debugging on, the Microsoft Visual C++ .NET compiler and linker embed the complete path to symbols and, inside the PDB, the path to any source files so that you won't have any problems. However, getting the symbols and source lined up if you didn't build the binaries on your debugging machine takes a little doing.

Back in Chapter 2, I introduced the symbol server technology, and without a doubt, it's one of the most important advances in Windows debugging in years. You should have your own symbol server set up by now and be using the `_NT_SYMBOL_PATH` environment variable so that Visual Studio .NET will use the symbol server. WinDBG will automatically pick the `_NT_SYMBOL_PATH` environment variable as the base symbol path to use. WinDBG uses workspaces to store specific information about each process you debug, such as breakpoints, window layout, and symbol paths. Just starting WinDBG before opening a process allows you to change the settings of the base workspace from which all others will inherit their settings. You'll know you're in the base workspace because no MDI child windows are open in the WinDBG frame. By getting the base workspace set with the common values you need across all processes, you'll save yourself a tremendous amount of hassle.

After setting the `_NT_SYMBOL_PATH` environment variable, you'll need to tell WinDBG where to find common source files. Although you can set the source file paths through an environment variable, `_NT_SOURCE_PATH` (see the DEBUGGER.CHM file for all the details), there's an easier way. With the base workspace open in WinDBG, click on the File, Source File Path menu to open the Source Search Path dialog box in which you can enter the paths to common source file locations. At a minimum, you'll always want your default location to look for the C run time and MFC/ATL source code, so you should enter something like the following paths. Note that I separated all the individual paths so that you could see them more easily, but you should enter the values on one line.

```
<Visual Studio .NET Installation Dir>\vc7\crt\src;
<Visual Studio .NET Installation Dir>\vc7\crt\src\intel;
<Visual Studio .NET Installation Dir>\vc7\atlmfc\include;
<Visual Studio .NET Installation Dir>\vc7\atlmfc\src\mfc;
<Visual Studio .NET Installation Dir>\vc7\atlmfc\src\atl;
<Visual Studio .NET Installation Dir>\vc7\atlmfc\src\atl\atls;
<Visual Studio .NET Installation Dir>\vc7\atlmfc\src\atl\atlmincrt;
```

You can separate multiple directories with semicolons just as you can with normal paths. If you really have a burning desire to use NTSD, set the environment variable `_NT_SOURCE_PATH` to the same value.

The final path you'll want to set is the executable image path, which is what WinDBG uses to find binary files. If you're doing live debugging, WinDBG will automatically find the files and load them. However, if you're going to be debugging minidumps, which WinDBG excels at, you'll need to tell WinDBG where it's supposed to look for the binaries. If you followed my recommendations in Chapter 2 when setting up your symbol engine, you put both the operating system and your product symbols and binaries into your symbol server. You can set the executable path for the base workspace by selecting File, Image File Path and entering the same string that you're using for your symbol path or the _NT_SYMBOL_PATH environment variable. WinDBG is smart enough to properly handle getting the binaries on your minidumps directly from your symbol server.

The fact that WinDBG can handle minidumps no matter whether they come from a customer or your manager's machine makes is a key reason you need to spend time with WinDBG. Even if you set the environment variable _NT_EXECUTABLE_IMAGE_PATH to tell Visual Studio .NET where it can find the executables, Visual Studio .NET doesn't load them. Since minidumps are so important for finding problems in production environments, WinDBG is vital to your bug squashing.

After you start opening processes to debug live or minidumps to view, you can update each of those workspaces with symbol, source, and binary paths unique to each project. Every time you change anything on a workspace, which includes set breakpoints; symbol, source, and binary paths; and window layout, WinDBG prompts you to save the workspace whenever the workspace is about to close. It's probably in your best interest to always save the workspace. You can delete unused workspaces or clear specific items saved with a workspace by selecting any of the workspace management items from the File menu.

Finally, you'll want to set in the default workspace some of the color options so that you can see important information in the Command window. If you've never run WinDBG before, you'll notice that WinDBG is verbose to the extreme. Everything goes to the Command window, and you can easily lose track of anything important. Simply loading a large process can result in over 100 lines of spew! Fortunately, WinDBG now allows you to color various reasons for the spew so that you can separate the wheat from the chaff. The color selections appear at the bottom of the Options dialog box, which you can access by selecting Options from the View menu.

The bad news is that the meaning of all the various color items is not quite documented. Some of the items you can color, such as Enabled Breakpoint Background, are self-explanatory, but others, such as Error Level Command

Window Text, only *appear* to be self-explanatory—I never have seen my chosen color. In reality, the most important highlighting you'll want is on any `TRACE` or `OutputDebugString` calls that your programs make. You can get these important values displayed in a different color by setting Debuggee Level Command Window Text to a different color. I personally always choose green as that indicates goodness.

To save your blood pressure, I want to mention a few weird behaviors WinDBG exhibits and how you can work around them. The first piece of very weird behavior concerns what happens when your process ends. In Visual Studio .NET, when your process ends, pressing F5 will restart debugging. With WinDBG, one of two things happens. If you open the process by selecting Open Executable from the File menu, pressing F5 will probably prompt you to save the workspace. After you click a button in the prompt message box, the workspace magically closes, and you're looking at WinDBG with no workspace open. If you happen to start WinDBG with the program to debug on the command line, pressing F5 after the process ends again prompts you to save the workspace. This time, after the prompt goes away, so does WinDBG! Yes, it's completely counterintuitive, but that's how WinDBG works. If you want to restart debugging, select Restart from the Debug menu or press Ctrl+Shift+F5.

Finally, WinDBG is extremely anal-retentive about window placement. It wants to put the child window where it thinks best whether you like it or not! If you're tired of seeing the message box each time you attempt to move a child window, uncheck the Auto-Arrange item on the Window menu. Even though WinDBG is a little rough around the edges, I forgive it because of the power it brings to debugging.

Before I jump into the Command window, I strongly suggest you use WinDBG as a normal GUI debugger for a day or so. It allows normal source-level debugging, so you can open a source file, put the cursor on a line, and press F9 to set a breakpoint. As WinDBG does not load symbol files until needed, you'll probably see a message box prompting you about loading symbols. Always click Yes and you should be fine. I'll talk more about symbol loading issues later in this chapter. In addition to Source windows, the View menu lists all the different types of windows available. WinDBG has the full complement of debugger windows such as Registers, Memory, and Locals. Interestingly, WinDBG also has a Scratch Pad window if you're too lazy to press Alt+Tab to access Notepad to paste debugging information or take notes. As you'll see when you start using WinDBG, the tool certainly doesn't have the UI polish of Visual Studio .NET, but it's certainly serviceable.

Common Debugging Question

How can I change the command-line argument to my process when it's opened in WinDBG?

Unfortunately, you can't. After you have opened a process, the only way to run the debuggee again with different command-line arguments is to close the workspace and either reopen the process with a new arguments in the Open Executable dialog box or restart WinDBG with new arguments.

You can set the command-line arguments to your process in one of two ways. The first is in the Open Executable dialog box when you choose to open an executable from the File menu. Figure 8-2 shows the Open Executable dialog box; the highlighted area shows the spot where you type the command-line arguments to the debuggee.

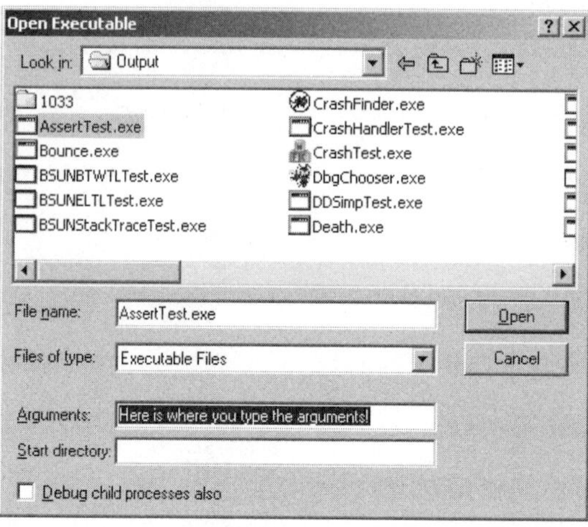

Figure 8-2 The WinDBG Open Executable dialog box

The other option for setting the command-line arguments is to type in the debuggee arguments following the debuggee name on the WinDBG command line.

Debugging Situations

Now that you have an idea of what WinDBG can do and how to avoid some of the issues it presents, I want to turn to various debugging situations you'll encounter and explain how to tackle them using the Command window. The Command window is the root of everything in WinDBG, and although it's harder to learn than using a UI, you can debug much faster once you get familiar with the commands. It all comes down to how much effort you want to put in.

Before we jump into the various commands, I need to mention a couple of issues related to commands. The first is just to remind you that pressing Alt+1 will bring the Command window front and center when debugging. The second is the syntax to calculate addresses because so many commands rely on them. The primary way to specify a particular address based on a symbol is to use the *module*!*symbol* format, in which the module and symbol comparison is case-insensitive. For example, to get the address of `LoadLibraryW`, the syntax is `kernel32!LoadLibraryW`. To specify an address based on a source and line, the syntax is `` `[[module!]filename][:linenumber]` ``. Pay careful attention to the delimiters; they are grave accents (`). The module and filename are optional. If you omit the module (`` `foo.cpp:23` ``), WinDBG will look through the symbols for all loaded modules. Omitting the filename (`` `:23` ``) will assume the filename based on the current executing instruction.

WinDBG has three types of commands: regular commands, meta commands (also called dot commands), and extension commands. These commands are generally described in the following ways. *Regular commands* control the debuggee. For example, tracing, stepping, and viewing memory are regular commands. *Meta commands* mostly control the debugger and the act of debugging. For example, creating log files, attaching to processes, and writing dump files are meta commands. *Extension commands* are where the action is, as they are commands that dig into the debuggee and perform analysis on situations or states. Examples of extension commands include handle dumping, critical section analysis, and crash analysis.

Getting Help

When you're staring at the blinking cursor in the bottom of the Command window wondering what command you'll need, you need to turn to the help. If you just need a tip on what a regular command name is or what its syntax is, the `?` (Command Help) command will bring up a couple of pages of listings so that you can see information about the various regular commands. Some of the regular commands do support passing `-?` as a parameter, so you can get quick help on their parameters. You'll have to use trial and error to find out which ones support `-?`. For meta commands, use `.help` (Meta-command Help) to see the quick listing. Because help for the extension commands is on a case-by-case basis and the syntax is a little different, I'll describe help for those in the "Magical Extensions" section later in this chapter. Also, for regular and meta commands, the commands are case-insensitive, but for extension commands, the commands are all lowercase.

Probably the most important command is the `.hh` (Open HTML Help File) meta command. Passing any command type as a parameter to `.hh` will open the DEBUGGER.CHM help file to the Index tab with the specified command highlighted. Simply press Enter to see the help information for that command. I hope that in a future version of WinDBG, the development team will fix the `.hh` command so that it opens to the help topic of the specified command automatically.

When looking at the command help in DEBUGGER.CHM, pay careful attention to the Environment section that appears with each command. The table in that section tells you the situations in which WinDBG can run the command. Obviously, for user-mode debugging, the Modes field will need to identify user mode. Nearly all the user-mode commands work during live debugging as well as while looking at minidumps.

One thing that's not very clear in the help for any of the commands is why there is a complete lack of consistency when it comes to parameters you can pass to commands. Some commands take parameters that must be delimited by a dash, some take parameters that must be delimited by a slash, and others take parameters that have no delimiters at all. Pay close attention to the documentation for how to specify parameters for any given command.

Ensuring Correct Symbols Are Loaded

WinDBG excels at symbol handling. Whereas Visual Studio .NET gives you no chance to see exactly what's loaded, WinDBG shows you everything. When I'm doing native debugging, I use WinDBG to ensure I have all my symbols aligned before moving over to the ease of Visual Studio .NET. That way I know exactly where I stand and don't have the surprise of stepping through comments or having an operating system symbol point into never-never land.

The most important feature of WinDBG's symbol handling is that you can force all symbols to reload at any time. At the bottom of the Symbol Search Path dialog box is the Reload check box. After you change the symbol path, checking Reload and clicking the OK button will make WinDBG unload any loaded symbols and reload them based on the new symbol path. This is an incredibly powerful feature to allow you to get the best symbols possible. There are also commands to reload symbols, but first I need to show how you can determine what symbols you have loaded.

Whenever the Command window is active, the `LM` (List Loaded Modules) command will display the list of modules and their corresponding symbol files. As an example, I loaded the ASSERTTEST.EXE program (available with this book's sample files), the program to help test SUPERASSERT, into WinDBG.

With WinDBG stopped at the loader breakpoint, issuing the LM command shows the following output:

```
0:000> lm
start    end        module name
00400000 0040a000   AssertTest (deferred)
10200000 10287000   MSVCR71D   (deferred)
10480000 1053c000   MSVCP71D   (deferred)
60000000 6004a000   BugslayerUtil  (deferred)
6d510000 6d58d000   dbghelp    (deferred)
70a70000 70ad4000   SHLWAPI    (deferred)
71950000 71a34000   COMCTL32   (deferred)
77c00000 77c07000   VERSION    (deferred)
77c10000 77c63000   msvcrt     (deferred)
77c70000 77cb0000   GDI32      (deferred)
77d40000 77dc6000   USER32     (deferred)
77dd0000 77e5d000   ADVAPI32   (deferred)
77e60000 77f46000   kernel32   (deferred)
77f50000 77ff7000   ntdll      (pdb symbols)
                    \\zeno\WebSymbols\ntdll.pdb\3D6DE29B2\ntdll.pdb
78000000 78086000   RPCRT4       (deferred)
```

Since loading symbols takes up huge amounts of memory, WinDBG uses lazy symbol loading so that it loads the symbols only when needed. Since WinDBG's original mission is to debug the entire operating system (OS), loading all the OS symbols when it first attaches through kernel debugging would make WinDBG unusable. Thus, the output just shown reveals that the only symbols I have loaded are those for NTDLL.DLL. The rest are marked as "(deferred)" because WinDBG didn't have a reason to access them. If I pulled up a source file in ASSERTTEST.EXE and pressed F9 to set a breakpoint on the line, WinDBG would start loading these symbols until it found one that contained the source file. That's the reason for the message box that prompts you to load symbols. However, at the command-line level, you have finer grained control for choosing which symbols to load.

To force a symbol load, the LD (Load Symbols) command does the trick. LD takes only a module name on the command line, so to force the loading of symbols for ASSERTTEST.EXE, I'd issue `ld asserttest` and get the following output:

```
0:000> ld asserttest
*** WARNING: Unable to verify checksum for AssertTest.exe
Symbols loaded for AssertTest
```

WinDBG is very particular about symbols and tells you about anything that could potentially be wrong with the symbols. Since I'm using a debug build of ASSERTTEST.EXE, I didn't have the /RELEASE switch turned on when I linked the program because it turns off incremental linking. As I mentioned in Chapter 2, the /RELEASE switch is misnamed, and it really should be /CHECKSUM because all it does is add the checksum to the binary and the PDB file.

To force all symbol loading, specify the wildcard character as this LD parameter: `ld *`. As you poke through the WinDBG documentation, you'll see another command, .RELOAD (Reload Module), which essentially does the same thing as LD. To load all symbols with .RELOAD, use the /f parameter: .RELOAD /f. If you're debugging on a large program, the .RELOAD command might be a little better to use because it will report only those modules that have symbol problems, whereas LD will show the result of every module load. Either way, you'll know immediately which symbols aren't correct.

You can also verify proper symbol loading through the LM command. After forcing all symbols to load, the output of the LM command shows the following. (I folded the last item on each line to fit the width of the page.)

```
 0:000> lm
start    end          module name
00400000 0040a000    AssertTest   C (pdb symbols)
                     D:\Dev\BookTwo\Disk\Output\AssertTest.pdb
10200000 10287000    MSVCR71D     (pdb symbols)
                     e:\winnt\system32\msvcr71d.pdb
10480000 1053c000    MSVCP71D     (pdb symbols)
                     e:\winnt\system32\msvcp71d.pdb
60000000 6004a000    BugslayerUtil  C (pdb symbols)
                     D:\Dev\BookTwo\Disk\Output\BugslayerUtil.pdb
6d510000 6d58d000    dbghelp      (pdb symbols)
                     \\zeno\WebSymbols\dbghelp.pdb\
                     819C4FBAB64844F3B86D0AEEDDCE632A1\dbghelp.pdb
70a70000 70ad4000    SHLWAPI      (pdb symbols)
                     \\zeno\WebSymbols\shlwapi.pdb\3D6DE26F2\shlwapi.pdb
71950000 71a34000    COMCTL32     (pdb symbols)
                     \\zeno\WebSymbols\MicrosoftWindowsCommon-Controls-
                     60100-comctl32.pdb\3D6DD9A81\
                     MicrosoftWindowsCommon-Controls-
                     60100-comctl32.pdb
77c00000 77c07000    VERSION      (pdb symbols)
                     e:\winnt\symbols\dll\version.pdb
77c10000 77c63000    msvcrt       (pdb symbols)
                     \\zeno\WebSymbols\msvcrt.pdb\3D6DD5921\msvcrt.pdb
77c70000 77cb0000    GDI32        (pdb symbols)
                     \\zeno\WebSymbols\gdi32.pdb\3D6DE59F2\gdi32.pdb
77d40000 77dc6000    USER32       (pdb symbols)
                     \\zeno\WebSymbols\user32.pdb\3DB6D4ED1\user32.pdb
77dd0000 77e5d000    ADVAPI32     (pdb symbols)
                     \\zeno\WebSymbols\advapi32.pdb\3D6DE4CE2\advapi32.pdb
77e60000 77f46000    kernel32     (pdb symbols)
                     \\zeno\WebSymbols\kernel32.pdb\3D6DE6162\kernel32.pdb
77f50000 77ff7000    ntdll        (pdb symbols)
                     \\zeno\WebSymbols\ntdll.pdb\3D6DE29B2\ntdll.pdb
78000000 78086000    RPCRT4       (pdb symbols)
                     \\zeno\WebSymbols\rpcrt4.pdb\3D6DE2F92\rpcrt4.pdb
```

Those module names followed by a "C" indicate symbols that don't have the checksums set in the module or in the symbol file. An octothorpe "#" following a module indicates symbols that don't match between the symbol file and the executable. (Yes, WinDBG will load the closest symbols, even if they're not correct.) In the preceding example, life is good and all the symbols match. However, you'll normally see the octothorpe next to COMCTL32.DLL. Because it seemingly changes with every single Microsoft Internet Explorer security patch, the odds of getting correct symbols with COMCTL32.DLL are almost nonexistent. To get more detailed information about which modules and corresponding symbol files are loaded, pass the `v` option to `LM`. To show a single module in the next example, I used the `m` option to match a specific module.

```
0:000> lm v m gdi32
start    end        module name
77c70000 77cb0000   GDI32         (pdb symbols)
                                  \\zeno\WebSymbols\
                                  gdi32.pdb\3D6DE59F2\gdi32.pdb
    Loaded symbol image file: E:\WINNT\system32\GDI32.dll
    Image path: E:\WINNT\system32\GDI32.dll
    Timestamp: Thu Aug 29 06:40:39 2002 (3D6DFA27)  Checksum: 0004285C
    File version:     5.1.2600.1106
    Product version:  5.1.2600.1106
    File flags:       0 (Mask 3F)
    File OS:          40004 NT Win32
    File type:        2.0 Dll
    File date:        00000000.00000000
    CompanyName:      Microsoft Corporation
    ProductName:      Microsoft® Windows® Operating System
    InternalName:     gdi32
    OriginalFilename: gdi32
    ProductVersion:   5.1.2600.1106
    FileVersion:      5.1.2600.1106 (xpsp1.020828-1920)
    FileDescription:  GDI Client DLL
    LegalCopyright:   © Microsoft Corporation. All rights reserved.
```

To see exactly where WinDBG is loading symbols and why, the extension command `!sym` from DBGHELP.DLL offers the `noisy` option. The output in the Command windows shows you exactly what process the WinDBG symbol engine goes through to find and load the symbols. Armed with the output, you should be able to solve any possible symbol-loading problem you'll encounter. To turn off the noisy output, issue the `!sym quiet` command.

The final point I want to make about symbols is that WinDBG has built-in symbol browsing. The `X` (Examine Symbols) command allows you to look at symbols globally, specific to a module, or in the local context. Using the `module!symbol` format, you should have no trouble tracking down where a symbol is stored. Additionally, the `X` command is case-insensitive to make life even easier. To see the address where LoadLibraryW is in memory, the command and output is the following:

```
0:000> x kernel32!LoadLibraryw
77e8a379  KERNEL32!LoadLibraryW
```

The module!symbol format supports wildcards, so, for example, if you want to see anything in KERNEL32.DLL with "lib" in the symbol name, x kernel32!*Lib* works great and is also case-insensitive. To see all the symbols in a module, use a single wildcard in place of the symbol name. Using only a wildcard as the parameter will show the local variables in the current scope, which is identical to the DV (Display Variables) command I'll discuss later in the chapter in the section "Looking at and Evaluating Variables."

Processes and Threads

With the symbol story behind us, I can now turn to the various means of getting processes running under WinDBG. Like Visual Studio .NET, WinDBG can debug any number of disparate processes at a time. What makes WinDBG a little more interesting is that you have better control over debugging processes spawned from a process being debugged.

Debugging Child Processes

If you look back at the Open Executable dialog box in Figure 8-2, you'll notice that the very bottom of the dialog box has a check box titled Debug Child Processes Also. By checking it, you're telling WinDBG that you also want to debug any processes started by debuggees. When running Microsoft Windows XP or Microsoft Windows Server 2003, if you forget to check that box when opening a process you can use the .CHILDDBG (Debug Child Processes) command to change the option on the fly. By itself, .CHILDDBG will tell you the current state. Issuing a .CHILDDBG 1 command will turn on debugging child processes. Issue .CHILDDBG 0 to turn it off.

To show you some of the multiple process and thread options, in the next section I'll provide some of the output resulting from debugging the command prompt, CMD.EXE, and choosing to debug child processes as well. After I get CMD.EXE loaded up and executing, I'll start NOTEPAD.EXE. If you follow the same steps and have child debugging enabled, as soon as you start NOTEPAD.EXE, WinDBG will stop at the loader breakpoint for NOTEPAD.EXE. It makes sense that WinDBG stopped NOTEPAD.EXE, but that also stops CMD.EXE because both processes are now sharing the debugger loop.

To see in the UI the processes that are currently running, choose Processes And Threads from the View menu. You'll see a layout similar to that in Figure 8-3. In the Processes And Threads window, the processes are all the root nodes, with each processes' threads as their children. The numbers next to

CMD.EXE, 000:9AC, are the WinDBG process number followed by the Win32 process ID. In CMD.EXE, the thread 000:9B0 indicates the WinDBG thread ID and the Win32 thread ID. The WinDBG process and thread numbers are unique the entire time WinDBG is running. That means there can never be another process number 1 until I restart WinDBG. The WinDBG process and thread numbers are important because they are used to set per-process and per-thread breakpoints and can be used as modifiers to various commands.

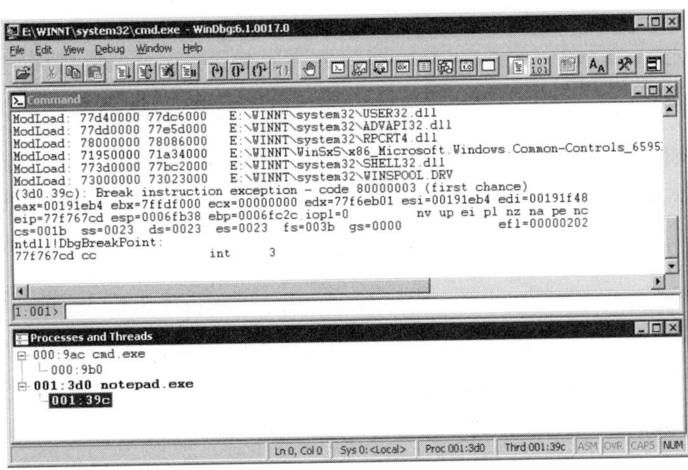

Figure 8-3 The Processes And Threads window

Viewing Processes and Threads in the Command Window

As with anything in WinDBG, if WinDBG displays it in a window, there's a Command window command to get at the same information. To view the processes being debugged, the | (Process Status) command does the trick. The output for the two processes shown in Figure 8-3 is as follows:

```
1:001> |
   0     id: 9ac     create    name: cmd.exe
.  1     id: 3d0     child     name: notepad.exe
```

The dot in the far left column indicates the active process, meaning that any commands you execute will be working on that process. The other interesting field is the one that tells how the process came to run under the debugger. "Create" means WinDBG created the process, and "child" indicates a process that was spawned by a parent process.

The overloaded `S` command—`|S` for Set Current Process and `~S` for Set Current Thread—does the work to change which process is active. You can also use the Processes And Threads window and double-click on the process you'd like to make active. The bold font indicates the active process. When using the `S` command, you need to specify the process as a prefix to the command. For example, to switch from the second process to the first, you'd issue `|0s`. To quickly see which process is active, look at the numbers to the left of the Command window input line. As you swap between the processes, you'll see the numbers update. When I switched to the first process using the CMD.EXE and NOTEPAD.EXE examples and issued the | command again, the output looked a little different:

```
0:000> |
.  0      id: 9ac     create     name: cmd.exe
#  1      id: 3d0     child      name: notepad.exe
```

The difference is the octothorpe in front of the NOTEPAD.EXE process. The octothorpe indicates the process that caused the exception to stop in WinDBG. Since NOTEPAD.EXE is sitting at its loader breakpoint, the exception was a breakpoint.

Viewing threads is almost identical to viewing processes. I'm going to let NOTEPAD.EXE start, so I'll press F5 in WinDBG. When NOTEPAD.EXE appears, I'll open the File Open dialog box because it creates a bunch of threads, and in WinDBG I'll press Ctrl+Break to break into the debugger. If you do the same and have the Processes And Threads window open, you should see that NOTEPAD.EXE has four threads in it and CMD.EXE has two threads.

The ~ (Thread Status) command shows the active threads in the current process. Switching to the NOTEPAD.EXE process and issuing the ~ command creates the following output on Windows XP (SP1):

```
1:001> ~
.  1  Id: 3d0.39c Suspend: 1 Teb: 7ffde000 Unfrozen
   2  Id: 3d0.1a4 Suspend: 1 Teb: 7ffdd000 Unfrozen
   3  Id: 3d0.8f0 Suspend: 1 Teb: 7ffdc000 Unfrozen
   4  Id: 3d0.950 Suspend: 1 Teb: 7ffdb000 Unfrozen
```

As with the | command, the ~ command uses a dot to indicate the current thread and an octothorpe to signify the thread that either caused the exception or was active when the debugger attached. The WinDBG thread number is the next displayed item. As with process numbers, there will only ever be one thread number 2 for the life of the WinDBG instance. Next come the ID values, which are the Win32 process ID followed by the thread ID. The suspend count is a little confusing. A suspend count of 1 indicates the thread is NOT suspended. The help on ~ shows a suspend count of 0, which I've never seen in the output. After the suspend count is the linear address of the Thread Environment Block (TEB) for the thread. The TEB is the same thing as the Thread Information Block (TIB) I discussed in Chapter 7 and is the address of the per-thread data block that contains the thread instance information such as the stack and COM initialization. Finally, Unfrozen indicates whether you've used the ~F (Freeze Thread) command to freeze a thread. (Freezing a thread from the debugger is akin to calling `SuspendThread` on that thread from your program. You'll stop that thread from executing until it is unfrozen.)

A command will work on the current thread by default, but sometimes you'll want to see information about a different thread. For example, to see the registers of a different thread, you use the thread modifier in front of the `R` (Registers) command: `~2r`. If you have multiple processes open, you can also apply the process modifier to the commands. The command `|0~0r` shows the registers for the first process and first thread no matter which process and thread are active.

Creating Processes from the Command Window

Now that you're armed with the ability to view processes and threads, I can move into some of the more advanced tricks you can perform to get processes started under WinDBG. The `.CREATE` (Create Process) command lets you start up any arbitrary processes on the machine. This is extremely helpful when you need to debug multiple sides of a COM+ or other cross-process application. The main parameters to `.CREATE` are the complete path to the process to start and any command-line parameters to that process. As when you start any processes, it's best to put the path and process name in quotation marks to avoid issues with spaces. The following shows using the `.CREATE` command to start Solitaire on one of my development machines:

```
.create "e:\winnt\system32\sol.exe"
```

After pressing Enter, WinDBG indicates that the process will be created on the next execution. What that means is that WinDBG must allow the debugger loop to spin over in order to handle the process creation notification. WinDBG has already made the `CreateProcess` call, but the debugger hasn't seen it yet. By pressing F5, you will release the debug loop. The create process notification comes through and WinDBG will stop on the loader breakpoint. If you use the `|` command to view the processes, WinDBG shows any processes started with `.CREATE` marked as "create," as if you started the session with that process.

Attaching to and Detaching from Processes

If a process is already running on the machine and you want to debug it, the `.ATTACH` (Attach to Process) command does the trick. In this section I'll discuss the full debugging attach. In the next section, I'll discuss the noninvasive attach in which the process does not run under a debugger loop.

The `.ATTACH` command requires the process ID in order to perform the attach. If you have physical access to the machine the process is running on, you can look up the process ID with Task Manager, but for remote debugging, that's a little hard to do. Fortunately, the WinDBG developers thought of everything and added the `.TLIST` (List Process IDs) command to list the running processes on the machine. If you're debugging Win32 services, use the –v parameter to .TLIST to see which services are running in which processes. The output of the .TLIST command looks like the following:

```
0n1544 e:\winnt\system32\sol.exe
0n1436 E:\Program Files\Windows NT\Pinball\pinball.exe
0n2120 E:\WINNT\system32\winmine.exe
```

When I first saw the output, I thought there was a bug in the command and somebody accidentally typed "0n" instead of "0x." However, I've since learned that 0n as a prefix is the ANSI standard for decimal in the same way 0x is for hexadecimal.

Once you have the decimal process ID for the process, you'll pass it as the parameter to .ATTACH (ensuring you use the 0n prefix or it won't work). Like when creating processes, WinDBG will say something about the attach occurring on the next execution, so you'll need to press F5 to let the debugger loop spin. From that point on, you're debugging the process you attached to. The only difference is that the | command will report the process as "attach" in its output.

If you're debugging on Windows XP or Windows Server 2003, you have the .DETACH (Detach from Process) command available to allow debuggees the ability to run free once again. As it only works on the current process, you'll need to switch to the process you want to detach from before you execute the .DETACH command. At any point, you can re-attach to the process to do full debugging.

If you simply want to attach to a process right after starting WinDBG, when it does not have a Command window open, either press F6 or select Attach To A Process from the File menu. In the subsequent Attach To Process dialog box, you can expand the nodes in the tree to view the command lines for the processes. If the process happens to contain Win32 services, you'll see those as well. After selecting the process, click OK and you're debugging away.

Noninvasive Attaching

The full attach I just described is great because you have full access to all the debugging options such as breakpoints. However, on Microsoft Windows 2000, once the process is running under the debugger, it's running under it for life. That's not always the best option when you're attempting to debug production servers, because you must always leave someone with full administrator rights logged on to that server so that WinDBG can run—not to mention that running under a debugger slows down the process. Fortunately, Microsoft finally added in Windows XP and Windows Server 2003 the ability to detach from debugging processes (something I know I asked for back in the Microsoft Windows 3.1 days!).

To make Windows 2000 production debugging a little bit easier, WinDBG offers the noninvasive attach. WinDBG suspends the process so that you can examine it with many commands, but you can't do normal debugging tasks such as set breakpoints. This is a decent trade-off in that you can see a lot of useful information like handle states while still allowing the process to run at full speed later.

Probably the best way to do noninvasive debugging is from a dedicated instance of WinDBG. As you'll see in a moment, to continue the process, which resumes all the threads, you need to close the workspace. If you're already debugging processes, WinDBG will have to immediately shut down those processes. In the bottom of the Attach To Process dialog box, shown in Figure 8-4, make sure the first thing you do is check the Noninvasive check box before you select the process to debug. That way you won't accidentally fall into full debugging.

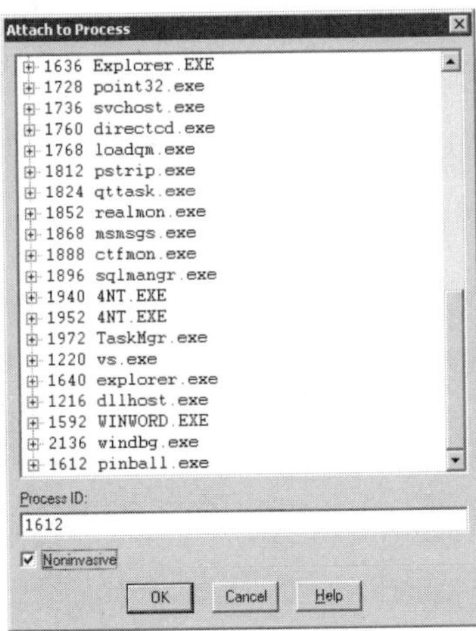

Figure 8-4 Getting ready to do noninvasive debugging

After you click OK, WinDBG will look like it's cranking up to do regular debugging. However, the warning near the top of the Command window, shown here, will help you remember what you're doing:

```
WARNING: Process 1612 is not attached as a debuggee
         The process can be examined but debug events will not be received
```

Once attached, you can examine the process all you want. When finished examining, you'll need to release the processes so that it can continue running. The best way to release the debuggee is by issuing the `Q` (Quit) command. This will close the workspace and leave WinDBG running so that you can attach again. If you use the `.DETACH` command, which does work, you have to shut down WinDBG because there's no way to reattach with that instance.

General Debugging with the Command Window

In this section I want to help you get started debugging with WinDBG by covering some of the key commands you'll have to become familiar with to effectively debug with the Command window. My focus will be on how you can use these commands better and tricks for helping you solve debugging challenges; I won't rehash the existing documentation. I strongly suggest that you also read the documentation on these commands.

Looking at and Evaluating Variables

Peeking at the local variables is the domain of the `DV` (Display Local Variables) command. One thing that's a little confusing about using WinDBG is seeing local variables up the stack. It actually takes a couple of commands to do what clicking in the Call Stack window does automatically.

The first step is to use the `K` (Display Stack Backtrace) command with the `N` modifier to see the call stack with the frame numbers in the far left column of each stack entry. (By the way, my favorite stack display command is `KP`, which shows the stack and, for each entry, the values of parameters to the function.) The frame numbers are regular in that the top of the stack is always 0, the next item is 1, the next value down is 2, and so on. Those frame numbers are important because you need them to specify to the `.FRAME` (Set Local Context) command to move down the stack. Therefore, to view the local variables in the function that called the current function, you use the following command sequence. To move the context back to the top of the stack, simply issue a `.frame 0` command.

```
.frame 1
dv
```

The `DV` command returns enough information to give you the basic gist of what's happening in the local variables. The following output is the result of the `DV` command when debugging the PDB2MAP.EXE program from Chapter 12.

```
    cFuncFMT = CResString
         cIM = CImageHlp_Module
  szBaseName = Array [260]
       pMark = cccccccc
      dwBase = 0x400000
   bEnumRet = 0xcccccccc
        argc = 2
        argv = 00344e18
```

```
   fileOutput = 00000000
 szOutputName = Array [260]
    iRetValue = 0
         bRet = 1
        hFile = 000007c8
          cRS = CResString
```

To see more, you need to use the DT (Display Type) command. The DT command is quite amazing in that it can do some very advanced tricks such as walking linked lists and grinding through arrays. Fortunately, you can pass a -? parameter to the DT command to quickly get some help while you're in the middle of the debugging wars.

One additional trick I'll mention about the DT command is that it can also search for symbol types. Instead of passing the name or address of a variable, you pass a parameter in the format *module*!*type*, where type either is a full type name or contains a wildcard to search for subexpressions. For example, to see any types that start with "IMAGE" in PDB2MAP, the command is this: dt pdb2map!IMAGE*. If you pass the full type, you'll see all the fields that make up the type if it's a class or structure, or the underlying base type if it's a typedef.

The last of the evaluation commands is ?? (Evaluate C++ Expression), which you'll use to check pointer arithmetic and to handle other C++ evaluation needs. Make sure you read the documentation about working with expressions because the process isn't as straightforward as you would expect. Now that you can view and evaluate all your variables, it's time to turn to executing, stepping, and stopping your program.

Executing, Stepping, and Tracing

As you've probably figured out by now, pressing F5 continues execution when you're stopped in WinDBG. You might not have noticed it, but pressing F5 simply causes a G (Go) command. What's neat about the G command is that you can also specify an address as the parameter. WinDBG uses that address as a one-time breakpoint, so you'll run to that location. Have you ever noticed that pressing Shift+F11, the Step Out command, executes the G command followed by an address (sometimes in the form of an expression)? That address is the return address at the top of the stack. You can do the same thing in the Command window, but instead of having to calculate the return address manually, you can use the $ra pseudoregister as the parameter to have WinDBG do the grunt work of finding the return address. There are other pseudoregisters, but you can't use them all in user mode. Search for "Pseudo-Register Syntax" in WinDBG help to find the rest of the pseudoregisters. To clarify, I want to mention that these WinDBG pseudoregisters are unique to WinDBG and aren't usable in Visual Studio .NET.

To handle tracing and stepping, use the `T` (Trace) and `P` (Step) commands, respectively. Just to remind you, tracing will step into any function calls encountered, whereas stepping will step over those function calls. One aspect that makes WinDBG different from Visual Studio .NET is that WinDBG doesn't automatically switch between stepping source code lines and assembly instructions just because you happen to have the focus at a Source and Disassembly window. By default, WinDBG steps source lines when lines are loaded for the current executing location. If you want to step by assembly instructions, either uncheck Source Mode on the Debug menu or use the `.LINES` (Toggle Source Line Support) command with the `–d` parameter.

As with the `G` command, `T` and `P` are what the F11 (also F8) and F10 keystrokes jam into the Command window. Also, you can pass either an address to step/trace to or, interestingly, the number of steps/traces to make. This comes in very handy because it's sometimes easier than setting a breakpoint. In essence, it's a manual "run-to-cursor" type command.

Two relatively new commands for stepping and tracing are the `TC` (Trace to Next Call) and `PC` (Step to Next Call) commands. The difference with these commands is that they step/trace up until the next `CALL` instruction. The only difference between `TC` and `PC` is that with the `PC` command, if the instruction pointer is sitting on a `CALL` instruction, the `CALL` will execute until it returns. A `TC` command will step into the `CALL` and stop on the next `CALL`. I find `TC` and `PC` useful when I want to move past any work the function does but not leave the function.

Trace and Watch Data

One of the biggest problems with tracking down performance issues is that some code is nearly impossible to read and see exactly what it does. For example, Standard Template Library (STL) code creates one of the largest performance problems we see when debugging other programmers' applications. Release builds jam in so many inline functions, and general STL code is nearly impossible to read, so analysis by reading isn't feasible. But because STL allocates so much memory behind the scenes and acquires various synchronization locks left and right, it's vital to have some way to see what a function that uses STL is really doing. Fortunately, WinDBG has an answer to this conundrum and it's one of the key differences between WinDBG and Visual Studio .NET: the `WT`

(Trace and Watch Data) command. This command is so powerful that it's a key reason you need to take the time to learn WinDBG.

What the `WT` command does is show you in a hierarchical display every function a single function calls! At the end of the tracing, the `WT` command displays exactly which functions were called along with how many times each was called. Additionally—and this is extremely important for performance—the `WT` command shows you how many kernel mode transitions your code made. The key to great performance is to avoid kernel mode transitions if you can, so the fact that the `WT` command is one of the few ways you can see this information makes it doubly valuable.

As you can imagine, all of this tracing can generate tons of stuff in the Command window, which you probably want to save to a file. Fortunately, the WinDBG developers met the need for saving this information with a complete logging system. Opening a log file is as simple as passing the name of the log file you want as a parameter to the `.LOGOPEN` (Open Log File) command. Alternatively, you can append to an existing log file with `.LOGAPPEND` (Append Log File). When finished logging, call `.LOGCLOSE` (Close Log File).

Using `WT` effectively so that you get meaningful output without getting more than you can wade through takes a little bit of planning. `WT` traces until it hits the current return address. This means you must carefully position the instruction pointer on one of two places before you call `WT`. The first place is directly on the call instruction of the function you want to execute. You have to do this at the assembly-language level, so you'll need to either set a breakpoint on the call instruction directly or set the stepping to assembly mode and step to the call instruction. The second place is on the first instruction for the function. You can either step to the `PUSH EBP` or set a breakpoint on the open curly brace for the function in a Source window.

Before I jump into the parameter options for `WT`, I want to discuss the output. To keep things simple, I created a small program that has just a few functions that call themselves. It is WTExample included with this book's sample files. I set a breakpoint at the first instruction in `wmain` and issued a `WT` command to get the output on Windows XP SP1, as shown in Listing 8-1. (Note that I trimmed some spaces and wrapped some lines to get the listing to fit within the page width.)

```
0:000> wt
Tracing WTExample!wmain to return address 0040139c
 3     0 [ 0] WTExample!wmain
 3     0 [ 1]   WTExample!Foo
 3     0 [ 2]     WTExample!Bar
 3     0 [ 3]       WTExample!Baz
 3     0 [ 4]         WTExample!Do
 3     0 [ 5]           WTExample!Re
 3     0 [ 6]             WTExample!Mi
 3     0 [ 7]               WTExample!Fa
 3     0 [ 8]                 WTExample!So
 3     0 [ 9]                   WTExample!La
 3     0 [10]                     WTExample!Ti
 6     0 [11]                       WTExample!Do2
 3     0 [12]                         kernel32!Sleep
 3     0 [13]                           kernel32!SleepEx
18     0 [14]                             kernel32!_SEH_prolog
15    18 [13]                           kernel32!SleepEx
16     0 [14]                             ntdll!
                 RtlActivateActivationContextUnsafeFast
20    34 [13]                           kernel32!SleepEx
15     0 [14]                             kernel32!BaseFormatTimeOut
26    49 [13]                           kernel32!SleepEx
 3     0 [14]                             ntdll!ZwDelayExecution
 2     0 [15]                               SharedUserData!
                                                      SystemCallStub
 1     0 [14]                             ntdll!ZwDelayExecution
31    55 [13]                           kernel32!SleepEx
 3     0 [14]                             kernel32!SleepEx
14     0 [15]                               ntdll!
               RtlDeactivateActivationContextUnsafeFast
 4    14 [14]                             kernel32!SleepEx
36    73 [13]                           kernel32!SleepEx
 9     0 [14]                             kernel32!_SEH_epilog
37    82 [13]                           kernel32!SleepEx
 4   119 [12]                         kernel32!Sleep
 8   123 [11]                       WTExample!Do2
 2     0 [12]                         WTExample!_RTC_CheckEsp
11   125 [11]                       WTExample!Do2
 2     0 [12]                         WTExample!_RTC_CheckEsp
13   127 [11]                       WTExample!Do2
 5   140 [10]                     WTExample!Ti
 2     0 [11]                       WTExample!_RTC_CheckEsp
 7   142 [10]                     WTExample!Ti
 5   149 [ 9]                   WTExample!La
 2     0 [10]                     WTExample!_RTC_CheckEsp
 7   151 [ 9]                   WTExample!La
 5   158 [ 8]                 WTExample!So
```

Listing 8-1 WinDBG `wt` output

```
2      0 [ 9]                  WTExample!_RTC_CheckEsp
7    160 [ 8]                 WTExample!So
5    167 [ 7]                WTExample!Fa
2      0 [ 8]                 WTExample!_RTC_CheckEsp
7    169 [ 7]                WTExample!Fa
5    176 [ 6]               WTExample!Mi
2      0 [ 7]                WTExample!_RTC_CheckEsp
7    178 [ 6]               WTExample!Mi
5    185 [ 5]              WTExample!Re
2      0 [ 6]               WTExample!_RTC_CheckEsp
7    187 [ 5]              WTExample!Re
5    194 [ 4]             WTExample!Do
2      0 [ 5]              WTExample!_RTC_CheckEsp
7    196 [ 4]             WTExample!Do
5    203 [ 3]            WTExample!Baz
2      0 [ 4]             WTExample!_RTC_CheckEsp
7    205 [ 3]            WTExample!Baz
5    212 [ 2]           WTExample!Bar
2      0 [ 3]            WTExample!_RTC_CheckEsp
7    214 [ 2]           WTExample!Bar
5    221 [ 1]          WTExample!Foo
2      0 [ 2]           WTExample!_RTC_CheckEsp
7    223 [ 1]          WTExample!Foo
6    230 [ 0] WTExample!wmain
2      0 [ 1]          WTExample!_RTC_CheckEsp
8    232 [ 0] WTExample!wmain

240 instructions were executed in 239 events (0 from other threads)

Function Name                           Invocations MinInst MaxInst AvgInst
SharedUserData!SystemCallStub                     1       2       2       2
WTExample!Bar                                     1       7       7       7
WTExample!Baz                                     1       7       7       7
WTExample!Do                                      1       7       7       7
WTExample!Do2                                     1      13      13      13
WTExample!Fa                                      1       7       7       7
WTExample!Foo                                     1       7       7       7
WTExample!La                                      1       7       7       7
WTExample!Mi                                      1       7       7       7
WTExample!Re                                      1       7       7       7
WTExample!So                                      1       7       7       7
WTExample!Ti                                      1       7       7       7
WTExample!_RTC_CheckEsp                          13       2       2       2
WTExample!wmain                                   1       8       8       8
kernel32!BaseFormatTimeOut                        1      15      15      15
kernel32!Sleep                                    1       4       4       4
kernel32!SleepEx                                  2       4      37      20
kernel32!_SEH_epilog                              1       9       9       9
kernel32!_SEH_prolog                              1      18      18      18
ntdll!
  RtlActivateActivationContextUnsafeFast          1      16      16      16
ntdll!
```

(continued)

```
  RtlDeactivateActivationContextUnsafeFast 1        14        14        14
ntdll!ZwDelayExecution                     2         1         3         2

1 system call was executed

Calls  System Call
    1  ntdll!ZwDelayExecution
```

The beginning part of the output (displaying the hierarchical tree) is the call information. In front of each call, WinDBG displays three numbers. The first number is the assembly instruction count that the function executed before calling the next function. The second number is undocumented, but looks to be a running total of assembly-language instructions executed in the tracing on returns. The final number in brackets is the current nesting level for the hierarchical tree.

The second portion of the output is a summary display, which is a little more understandable. In addition to providing a summary of each function called, it shows the function call count as well as the minimum number of assembly-language instructions called in an invocation, the maximum number of assembly-language instructions called in an invocation, and the average number of instructions called. The final lines of the summary display show how many system calls occurred. You can see that WTExample eventually calls `Sleep` to force a transition to kernel mode. The fact that you can get the number of kernel-mode transitions is extremely cool.

As you can imagine, using the `WT` command can produce a huge amount of output and can really slow down your application since each line of output requires a couple of cross process transitions between the debugger and debuggee to get the information. If you want to see the all-important summary information, passing `–nc` as a parameter to `WT` will suppress the hierarchy. Of course, if you're interested in just the hierarchy, pass `–ns` as the parameter. To see the return value register (`EAX` in x86 assembly language), use the `–or` parameter; and to see the address, source, and line information (if available) for each call, use the `–oa` parameter. The final parameter is `–l`, which allows you to set the maximum depth of calls to display. Using `–l` can be helpful when you want to see the high points of what's executed or keep the display to just the functions in your program.

I strongly encourage you to look at key loops and operations in your own programs with the `WT` command so that you can truly see what's happening under the covers. I don't know how many performance problems and language and technology misuse problems I've been able to track down by being able to see what's actually executing. The `WT` command is one of the best tools in my debugging toolbox.

Common Debugging Question

Some of my C++ names are gigantic. Is there any way I can get WinDBG to help so that I don't get carpal tunnel syndrome from typing them each time?

Fortunately, WinDBG now supports text aliasing. Use the `AS` (Set Alias) command to define a user named alias and an expansion equivalent. For example, you can use `as LL kernel32!LoadLibraryW` to set the string "LL" to expand to `kernel32!LoadLibraryW` whenever you enter it on the command line. You can see any aliases you have defined with `AL` (List Aliases) as well as delete existing aliases with `AD` (Delete Alias).

Another place you can define what the documentation refers to as fixed-name aliases is, strangely enough, the `R` (Registers) command. The fixed-name aliases are `$u0, $u1, …, $u9`. Although user-named aliases are a little easier to remember, fixed-name aliases expand even when no white space is around the name. To define a fixed-name alias, you must put a period in front of the `u`: `r $.u0=kernel32!LoadLibraryA`. The only way to see what a fixed-name alias is defined as is to use the `.ECHO` (Echo Comment) command: `.echo $u0`.

Breakpoints

WinDBG offers all the same breakpoints as Visual Studio .NET plus some that are unique to WinDBG. What's important is that WinDBG offers much more power and complete fine-tuning of exactly when the breakpoints trigger and what occurs after a breakpoint triggers. Older versions of WinDBG had a very nice dialog box that made setting advanced breakpoints very easy. Unfortunately, that dialog box is not in the rewritten version of WinDBG we have now, so we must do all the breakpoint setting manually.

General Breakpoints

The first breakpoint concept I want to address concerns the two commands that you use to set breakpoints: `BP` and `BU`. Both commands take identical parameters and modifiers. You can think of the `BP` version as a hard breakpoint that WinDBG always associates with an address. If the module containing that breakpoint is unloaded, WinDBG removes the `BP` breakpoint from the list of breakpoints. `BU` breakpoints, on the other hand, are associated with a symbol, so WinDBG tracks on the symbol instead of an address. If the symbol moves, the BU breakpoint moves. That means a BU breakpoint will remain active but disabled when the module unloads from the process, but will immediately reactivate when the module comes back into the process, even if the operating system has to relocate the module. A big difference between BP breakpoints and BU breakpoints is that WinDBG saves BU breakpoints in WinDBG workspaces, but BP breakpoints aren't saved there. Finally, when setting breakpoints in the Source code window using F9, WinDBG sets BP breakpoints. My recommendation is to use BU breakpoints instead of BP breakpoints.

There is a limited Breakpoints dialog box (click the Edit menu and then Breakpoints), but I prefer to manipulate breakpoints from the Command window because I find it easier. The BL (Breakpoint List) command allows you to see all the breakpoints that are currently active. You can read the documentation on the output of BL, but I want to point out that the first field is the WinDBG breakpoint number and the second field is a letter that indicates the breakpoint status: d (disabled), e (enabled), and u (unresolved). You can enable and disable breakpoints with the BE (Breakpoint Enable) and BD (Breakpoint Disable) commands, respectively. Passing an asterisk (*) to each of these commands will apply the enable or disable to all breakpoints. Finally, you can enable and disable specific breakpoints by number using the BE and BD commands.

The syntax for setting an x86 user-mode breakpoint is this:

```
[~Thread] bu[ID] [Address [Passes]] ["CommandString"]
```

If you type BU by itself, WinDBG sets a breakpoint on the current instruction pointer. The *thread* modifier is simply the WinDBG thread number, which makes setting per-thread breakpoints trivial. If you'd like to set the WinDBG breakpoint ID, follow BU by the number of the breakpoint. If a breakpoint with that number exists, WinDBG will replace the existing breakpoint with the new one you're setting. The *address* field is any valid WinDBG address expressed in the address syntax I described at the beginning of the "Debugging Situations" section. In the *passes* field, you indicate how many times you'd like this breakpoint skipped before stopping. The *passes* field is a greater than or equal comparison, and the maximum value is 4,294,967,295. As with Visual Studio .NET native debugging, passes are decremented only if running full speed past the breakpoint, not stepping or tracing.

The final field you can set with breakpoints is the amazing, magical command string. That's right, you can associate commands with a breakpoint! This opens up a world of excellent bugslaying techniques that you can add to your arsenal. Probably the best way to demonstrate this awesome power is with a story about how I used this technique to solve an almost impossible bug. I had a situation in which the bug manifested itself only after a long series of data cases went through a specific section of code. As usual, it took quite a while for the right conditions to hit, so there was no way I could simply spend a day or week looking at the variable states each time I hit the breakpoint. (Unfortunately, I wasn't paid by the hour for this job!) I needed a way to log all the variable values so that I could inspect the data flow through the system. Since you can concatenate multiple commands with a semicolon, I built up a huge command that logged out all the variables using `DT` and `??`. I also sprinkled in a few `.ECHO` commands so that I could see where I was and have a common string that I could look for each time the breakpoint triggered. I finished off the command string with a `";G"`, so the breakpoint continued executing after dumping the variable values. Of course, I turned on logging and just let the process run until it crashed. After looking over the log, I immediately saw the pattern and quickly fixed the bug. If it weren't for WinDBG's excellent breakpoint extensibility, I would have never found this bug!

One command in particular, `J` (Execute If – Else), is particularly well suited for use in a breakpoint command string. This command gives you the ability to conditionally execute commands based on a particular condition. In other words, `J` gives you a conditional breakpoint capability in WinDBG. The format of the `J` command is this:

```
j expression 'if true command' ; 'if false command'
```

The *expression* is any expression that the WinDBG expression evaluators can handle. The values in single quotation marks indicate the command strings for true or false evaluation. Make sure you always use the single quotation marks around the command strings because you can embed semicolons to do big operations on values. It's also perfectly valid to include sub `J` commands inside the true and false command strings. One thing that isn't clear in the documentation is what to do when you want to leave one of the true or false conditions empty (i.e., you don't want to execute any commands for that condition): you simply enter two single quotation marks side by side for the omitted condition.

Memory Access Breakpoints

In conjunction with the excellent execution breakpoints, WinDBG also has the phenomenal `BA` (Break On Access) command, which allows you to stop when any piece of memory is read or written in your process. Visual Studio .NET offers only memory change breakpoints, and you have to use Mike Morearty's hardware breakpoint class to have access to all the power supplied by the Intel x86 hardware breakpoints. However, WinDBG has all the power built right in!

The format for Intel x86 user-mode memory breakpoints is as follows:

```
[~Thread] ba[ID] Access Size [Address [Passes]] ["CommandString"]
```

As you can see from the format, the `BA` command offers quite a bit more power than simply stopping on a memory access. As you can with the `BP` and `BU` commands, you can specify to stop only when specific threads are doing the touching, set a pass count, and associate that wonderful command string with any accesses. The *access* field is a single character field that indicates whether you want to stop on read/write (`r`), write (`w`), or execute (`e`). Since the x86 CPU family doesn't have an option to set memory as execute only, specifying execute will simply set a `BP` style breakpoint. The *size* field indicates how many bytes you want to watch. Since the `BA` command uses the Intel Debug Registers to do their magic, you're limited to watching 1, 2, or 4 bytes at a time, and you're limited to four `BA` breakpoints. Like when setting Data breakpoints in Visual Studio .NET, you need to keep in mind the memory alignment issues, so if you want to watch 4 bytes, the memory address must end in 0, 4, 8, or C. The *address* field is the address on which you want to break on access. While WinDBG is a little more forgiving about using variables, I still much prefer to use the actual hexadecimal addresses to ensure the breakpoint is set on the exact place I want it.

If you'd like to see the `BA` command in action, you can use the MemTouch program included with this book's sample files for experimenting. The program simply allocates a local piece of memory, `szMem`, which it passes to one function that touches the memory and another function that reads the memory. You'll have to set the `BA` breakpoint on the address of `szMem` in order to locate the break. To get the address of a local variable, use the `DV` command. Once you've got the address, you can use that value with the `BA` command. To learn what you can do with commands, you might want to use the command string `"kp;g"` so that you can see the stack at the time of the access and then continue execution.

Exceptions and Events

WinDBG's breakpoints offer a tremendous amount of power, and the ability to finely control the debuggee doesn't stop there. WinDBG offers advanced handling of exceptions and events as well. The exceptions are all the hard exceptions like access violations that cause your programs to crash. The events are for the standard events passed to debuggers by the Microsoft Win32 Debugging API. This means that, for example, you can have WinDBG break whenever a module is loaded so that you can gain control before the entry point for that module executes.

There are commands for manipulating the exceptions and events from the Command window, `SX`, `SXD`, `SXE`, `SXI`, `SXN` (Set Exceptions), but they are quite confusing. Fortunately, WinDBG offers a nice dialog box to make manipulating them easier. The Event Filters dialog box is accessible from the Debug, Event Filters menu and is shown in Figure 8-5.

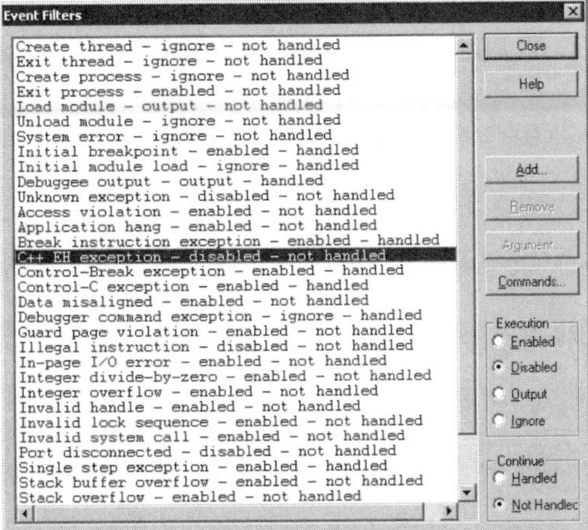

Figure 8-5 The Event Filters dialog box

However, even with a dialog box to help you, it's still a little confusing to figure out what happens with an exception because WinDBG uses some odd terminology in the `SX*` commands and the Event Filters dialog box. The Execution group box in the lower right-hand corner of the dialog box indicates how you want WinDBG to handle the exception. Table 8-2 explains the meanings of the values in the Exception group box. When reading over the table or looking at the defaults in the Event Filter dialog box, keep in mind the discussion of the `ContinueDebugEvent` API back in Chapter 4, because the Exceptions group is indicating what you want WinDBG to pass to that API.

Table 8-2 Exception Break Status

Status	Description
Enabled	When the exception occurs, execution occurs and the target will break into the debugger.
Disabled	The first time the exception occurs, the debugger will ignore it. The second time it occurs, execution will halt and the target will break into the debugger.
Output	When the exception occurs, it won't break into the debugger. However, a message informing the user of this exception will be displayed.
Ignore	When the exception occurs, the debugger will ignore it. No message will be displayed.

You can ignore the Continue group in the lower right-hand corner. It's only important when you want different handling on breakpoint, single step, and invalid handle exceptions. If you add your own structured exception handling (SEH) errors to the list, leave the Continue option at the default, Not Handled. That way any time the exception comes through WinDBG, WinDBG will properly pass the exception directly back to the debuggee. You don't want the debugger eating exceptions other than those it caused, such as a breakpoint or a single step.

After selecting a particular exception, the most important button on the dialog box is the Commands button. The name alone should give you a hint about what it does. Clicking on the Commands button brings up the Filter Command dialog box shown in Figure 8-6. The first edit control is misnamed and should be labeled First-Chance Exception.

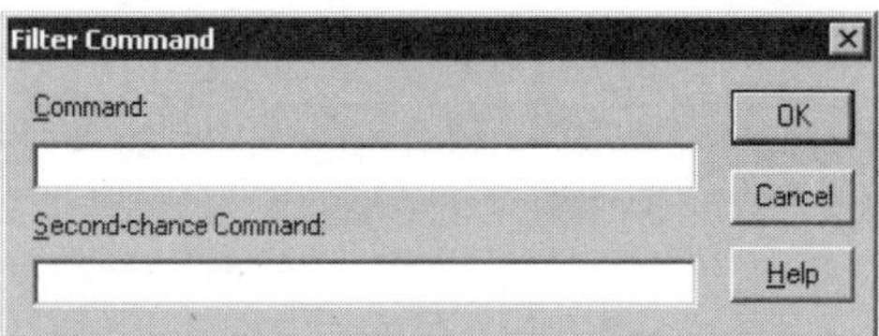

Figure 8-6 Filter Command dialog box

In the Filter Command dialog box, you can enter WinDBG commands to execute when the debuggee generates a particular exception. When I discussed using the Visual Studio .NET Exception dialog box in the "Exception Monitoring" section of Chapter 7, I showed how you should set C++ exceptions to stop on the first chance exception so that you could monitor where your programs did the `throw`s, and after pressing F10, the `catch`. The problem is that Visual Studio .NET stops each time a C++ exception occurs, so you have to sit there pressing F5 over and over when your application has numerous C++ `throw`s.

What's great about WinDBG and the ability to associate commands with the exceptions is that you can use a command to log out all the important information and, most usefully, continue execution so that you don't have to monitor the run. To set up C++ exception handling, select C++ EH Exception from the list of exceptions in the Event Filter dialog box and click the Commands button. In the Filter Command dialog box, enter `kp;g` in the Command edit box to have WinDBG log a stack walk and continue execution. Now you'll have a call stack each time a `throw` occurs, and WinDBG will keep right on executing. By the way, to see the last event or exception that occurred in a process, use the `.LASTEVENT` (Display Last Event) command.

Controlling WinDBG

Now that you've seen the important commands for debugging, I want to turn to a few meta commands that I haven't already covered. You can use these to control or make better use of WinDBG while debugging. Those I discuss are by no means a complete list of all the commands but rather a list of cool meta commands I use on a daily basis when debugging with WinDBG.

The simplest but extremely useful command is `.CLS` (Clear Screen). This allows you to clear the Command window so that you can start fresh. Since WinDBG can spew a tremendous amount of information, which takes memory to store, it's good to clean the slate occasionally.

If you're dealing with Unicode strings in your application, you'll want to set the display to show `USHORT` pointers as Unicode strings. The `.ENABLE_UNICODE` (Enable Unicode Display) command issued with a parameter of 1 will set everything up so that the `DT` command displays your strings correctly. If you'd like to set the locale so that Unicode strings display correctly, the `.LOCALE` (Set Locale) command takes the locale as a parameter. If you're dealing with bit manipulation and want to see the bit values, the `.FORMATS` (Show Number Formats) command will display the value passed as a parameter in all number formats, including binary.

Another extremely useful command is `.SHELL` (Command Shell), which allows you to start up an MS-DOS window from the debugger and redirect output to the Command window. Debugging on the same machine the debuggee is running on and pressing Alt+Tab might be an easier approach, but the beauty of `.SHELL` is that when doing remote debugging, the MS-DOS window runs on the remote machine. You can also use the `.SHELL` command to run a single external program, redirecting output, and return to the Command window. After issuing a `.SHELL` command, the Command window input line says `INPUT>`, indicating that the MS-DOS window is waiting for input. To end the MS-DOS window and return to the Command window, use either the MS-DOS `exit` command or, more preferably, the `.SHELL_QUIT` (Quit Command Prompt) command because it will terminate the MS-DOS window even when the window is frozen.

The final meta command I'll mention is one I've wanted in a debugger for years but has only now shown up. When writing error handling, you usually know that by the time you're executing the error handling, your process is in serious trouble. You also know 9 times out of 10 that if you hit a particular piece of error handling, you're probably going to look at specific variable values or the call stack, or will want to record specific information. What I've always wanted was a way to code the commands I would normally execute directly into my error handling. By doing that, the commands would execute, enabling the maintenance programmers and me to debug a problem faster. My idea was that since `OutputDebugString` calls go through the debugger, you could embed the commands into an `OutputDebugString`. You'd tell the debugger what to look for at the front of the `OutputDebugString` text, and anything after it would be the commands to execute.

What I've just described is exactly how WinDBG's `.OCOMMAND` (Expect Commands from Target) command works. You call `.OCOMMAND`, identifying the string prefix to look for, at the front of any `OutputDebugString` calls. If the command is present, WinDBG will execute the rest of the text as a command string. Obviously, you'll want to be careful with the string you use or WinDBG could go nuts trying to execute `OutputDebugString` calls all through your programs. I like to use `WINDBGCMD:` as my string. I love this command and sprinkle WinDBG command strings all over my programs!

When using `.OCOMMAND`, you need to follow the command string with a `";g"` or WinDBG stops when the command ends. In the following function, I ensure that the commands all end with `";g"` so that execution continues. To get the commands to execute, I issue a `.ocommand WINDBGCMD:` as the program starts.

```
void Baz ( int )
{
    // To see the following convert into WinDBG commands, issue the
    // command ".ocommand WINDBGCMD:" inside WinDBG
    OutputDebugString ( _T ( "WINDBGCMD: .echo \"Hello from WinDBG\";g" ));
    OutputDebugString ( _T ( "WINDBGCMD: kp;g" ) ) ;
    OutputDebugString ( _T ("WINDBGCMD: .echo \"Stack walk is done\";g")) ;
}
```

The Magical Extensions

At this point, you've seen enough commands (representing only a fraction of the commands available) to make your head spin, and you're probably wondering why I'm spending this much time discussing WinDBG. WinDBG is harder to use than Visual Studio .NET and the learning curve isn't just steep—it's nearly vertical! You've seen that WinDBG offers some very cool breakpoint possibilities, but at this point, you're still probably wondering why the hassle is worth it.

WinDBG is worth the investment because of the extension commands. These are commands that extend the debugger and allow you to see things you can't see any other way. Microsoft has supplied a bunch of great extensions that will quickly make you a WinDBG convert. These extensions are what the ninja master debuggers are using to solve the nastiest problems in the business.

I'm going to concentrate on a few of the most important extension commands. I highly recommend that you take the time to read the documentation about all the rest of the extensions. Under the Reference\Debugger Extension Commands node in the WinDBG documentation are the two key sections, General Extensions and User-Mode Extensions.

Physically, the extensions are dynamic-link library (DLL) files that export specific function names to do the work. Under the Debugging Tools For Windows directory are several directories such as W2KFRE (Windows 2000 Free Build) and WINXP. Those directories contain the various operating-system versions of the extension commands. You can read about how to write your own extension in the README.TXT file that accompanies the EXTS sample in the <Debugging Tools for Windows Dir>\SDK\SAMPLES\EXTS directory.

Loading and Controlling Extensions

Before we start looking at individual extension commands, I need to talk about how you can see which extensions you've loaded, how to load your own, and how to get help from an extension. To see what extensions you have loaded, use the `.CHAIN` (List Debugger Extensions) command. This command also shows you the search order for commands from the top of the display down to the bottom as well as the path that WinDBG searches for the extension DLLs. Under Windows 2000, the display looks like the following (depending on the path to your Debugging Tools for Windows directory) for the four default user-mode extensions DLLs (DBGHELP.DLL, EXT.DLL, UEXT.DLL, and NTSDEXTS.DLL):

```
0:000> .chain
Extension DLL search Path:
    G:\windbg\winext;G:\windbg\pri;G:\windbg\WINXP;G:\windbg;
Extension DLL chain:
    dbghelp: image 6.1.0017.1, API 5.2.6, built Sat Dec 14 15:32:30 2002
        [path: G:\windbg\dbghelp.dll]
    ext: image 6.1.0017.0, API 1.0.0, built Fri Dec 13 01:46:07 2002
        [path: G:\windbg\winext\ext.dll]
    exts: image 6.1.0017.0, API 1.0.0, built Fri Dec 13 01:46:07 2002
        [path: G:\windbg\WINXP\exts.dll]
    uext: image 6.1.0017.0, API 1.0.0, built Fri Dec 13 01:46:08 2002
        [path: G:\windbg\winext\uext.dll]
    ntsdexts: image 5.2.3692.0, API 1.0.0, built Tue Nov 12 14:16:20 2002
        [path: G:\windbg\WINXP\ntsdexts.dll]
```

Loading an extension is as simple as passing the name of the extension DLL as the parameter, without the .DLL extension, to the `.LOAD` (Load Extension DLL) command. Of course, to unload an extension DLL, pass the name of the extension to the `.UNLOAD` (Unload Extension DLL) command.

By convention, extension commands are all lowercase, and unlike regular and meta commands, are case sensitive. Also by convention, any extension DLL is supposed to provide a command named, appropriately, `help` to give you a quick clue as to what's in the extension DLL. With the default extensions loaded, issuing the `!help` command doesn't show all the help available. To call an extension command out of a specific extension DLL, you append the DLL name and a period to the extension command: `!dllname.command`. Therefore, to see the help out of NTSDEXTS.DLL, the command is `!ntsdexts.help`.

The Important Extension Commands

Now that you're armed with a little background on how to deal with extensions, I want to turn to the important extension commands that will make your life easier. All these extensions are part of the default extension set which is always loaded, so unless you specifically unload any of the default extensions, these commands will always be available.

The first important command is the `!analyze -v` command, which allows you to get a quick analysis about the current exception. I specifically showed this command with the `-v` parameter because without it, you don't see much information. The `!analyze` command won't automatically solve all your bugs, but the idea is that it will give you all the information you'd normally want to see at the time of the crash, such as the exception record and the call stack.

Because critical sections are lightweight synchronization objects, many developers are using them. WinDBG offers two extension commands for getting a peek inside the critical section to see the objects' lock state and which thread owns them. If you have the address of the critical section, you can view the extension by passing the address as a parameter to the `!critsec` command. If you want to see all locked critical sections, the `!locks` command allows you to do just that. If you want to see all critical sections in a process, pass the `-v` parameter to `!locks`. On Windows XP and Windows Server 2003, the additional `-o` parameter will show you orphaned critical sections.

If you're doing Win32 security programming, it's rather difficult figuring out what the current security information applied to the current thread is. The `!token` (Windows XP/Windows Server 2003) `!threadtoken` (Windows 2000) command will show the impersonation state of the current thread as well as all sorts of other security information such as the user's identity and any groups, plus a textual display of all privileges associated with the thread.

One extension command that has saved me countless hours debugging is the `!handle` command. As you can tell by the name, the command has something to do with the handles in a process. Just typing `!handle` by itself will show you the handle values, what type of object that handle contains, and a summary section listing how many of each type of object is in the process. Some of the types displayed might not make sense if you haven't done device drivers or read David Solomon and Mark Russinovich's *Inside Microsoft Windows 2000*. Table 8-3 provides a translation from the `!handle` command into user-mode terminology for some of the types you'll see.

Table 8-3 Handle Type Translations

`!handle` Term	User-Mode Term
Desktop	Win32 desktop
Directory	Win32 object manager namespace directory
Event	Win32 event synchronization object
File	Disk file, communication endpoint, or device driver interface
IoCompletionPort	Win32 IO completion port
Job	Win32 job object
Key	Registry key
KeyedEvent	Non-user-creatable events used to avoid critical section out of memory conditions
Mutant	Win32 mutex synchronization object
Port	Interprocess communication endpoint
Process	Win32 process
Thread	Win32 thread
Token	Win32 security context
Section	Memory-mapped file or page-file backed memory region
Semaphore	Win32 semaphore synchronization object
SymbolicLink	NTFS symbolic link
Timer	Win32 timer object
WaitablePort	Interprocess communication endpoint
WindowStation	Top level of window security object

Just showing you the handle values is great, but if you pass the `-?` parameter to `!handle`, you'll see that the command can do a whole lot more. If you want to see more information about a handle, you can pass that handle value as the first parameter and, in the second parameter, a bit field that specifies what you want to see from that handle. In the second parameter, you should always pass `F` because that will show you everything. As an example, I'm debugging the WDBG program from Chapter 4, and the handle 0x1CC is an Event. The following shows how to retrieve the detailed information about that handle:

```
0:006> !handle 1cc f
Handle 1cc
  Type         Event
  Attributes   0
  GrantedAccess0x1f0003:
         Delete,ReadControl,WriteDac,WriteOwner,Synch
         QueryState,ModifyState
  HandleCount  3
  PointerCount 6
  Name         \BaseNamedObjects\WDBG_Happy_Synch_Event_614
  Object Specific Information
    Event Type Manual Reset
    Event is Waiting
```

Not only do you see the granted access information, but you see the name and, more important, that the event is waiting (meaning it's not signaled). Since the `!handle` command will show this information for all types, you now have the ability to easily look for deadlocks because you can check the states of all events, semaphores, and mutexes to see who's blocked and who's not.

You can look at all the detailed handle information for every handle in a process by passing `0` and `F` as the two parameters. If you're working on a large process, it might take a while to grind through all the details. To see just the details for a particular class of handles, pass `0` and `F` as the first two parameters, and for the third parameter, pass the handle class value. For example, to see all the events, the command is `!handle 0 f Event`.

In the preceding discussion I mentioned using `!handle` to view event states so that you can deduce why your application is deadlocking. Another wonderful use of `!handle` is to keep an eye on a potential resource leak. Since `!handle` shows you the complete count of all current handles in your process, you can easily compare before and after `!handle` snapshots. If you see the total handle counts change, you'll be able to tell exactly which type of handle was leaked. Because much of the detailed handle information is displayed, such as registry keys and the name of the handle, you can easily see exactly which handle you're leaking.

I've tracked down countless resource leaks and deadlocks with the `!handle` command and I strongly encourage you to spend some time familiarizing yourself with it and the data it shows. The `!handle` command is the only way you'll get handle information while debugging, so it's extremely valuable in your bag of tricks.

Common Debugging Question

The Win32 API functions that create handles, like `CreateEvent`, have an optional name parameter. Should I be assigning a name to my handles?

Absolutely, positively, YES! As I pointed out in the discussion of the WinDBG `!handle` command, the command can show you the states of each of your handles. However, that's only a small part of what you need to find problems. If the handles aren't named, it's very hard to match up handle values with debugging challenges such as deadlocks. By not naming your handles, you're making your life much more difficult than it needs to be.

However, you can't just go off and start slapping names in the optional parameter field. When you create an event, for example, the name you give that event, such as "`MyFooEventName`," is global to all processes on the machine. Although you might think that the second process, which calls `CreateEvent`, is getting a unique event internally, in reality, `CreateEvent` calls `OpenEvent` and returns to you the globally named event handle. Now suppose you have two of your processes running and they each have a thread waiting on the `MyFooEventName` event. When one of the processes signals the event, *both* processes will see the signal and start running. Obviously, if you intended to signal only one process, you just created an extremely difficult bug to track down.

To properly name handles, you'll have to ensure you generate unique names for those handles that you want available only in a single process. Look at what I did in WDBG in Chapter 4. I appended the process ID or the thread ID to the name to ensure uniqueness.

Other Interesting Extension Commands

Before I move on to dump file handling, I want to mention several extension commands that you'll find useful in critical situations, like when you need to solve that one really challenging bug. These are the kind of commands that when you need them, you *really* need them. The first interesting one was `!imgreloc`. It simply runs through all loaded modules and tells whether all modules are loaded at your preferred address. Now you have no excuse for not checking. The output looks like the following. The operating system had to relocate the second module, TP4UIRES.

```
0:003> !imgreloc
00400000 tp4serv - at preferred address
00c50000 tp4uires - RELOCATED from 00400000
5ad70000 uxtheme - at preferred address
6b800000 S3appdll - at preferred address
76360000 WINSTA - at preferred address
76f50000 wtsapi32 - at preferred address
77c00000 VERSION - at preferred address
77c10000 msvcrt - at preferred address
77c70000 GDI32 - at preferred address
77cc0000 RPCRT4 - at preferred address
77d40000 USER32 - at preferred address
77dd0000 ADVAPI32 - at preferred address
77e60000 kernel32 - at preferred address
77f50000 ntdll - at preferred address
```

If you're too lazy to run an MS-DOS box in order to run `NET SEND` so that you can send messages to other users, you can simply enter `!net_send`. Actually, this comes in handy when you need to get someone's attention when doing remote debugging. Entering `!net_send` by itself will show you the parameters necessary to send the message.

Whereas you have `!dreg` to display registry information, you have the `!evlog` to display the event log. If you enter both of these commands on the command line by themselves, you'll get help on how to use them. Both are wonderful for helping you see what you're about to read from the registry or event log. If you use them, especially when remote debugging, you won't have any surprises.

If you're having issues with exception handling, you can use the `!exchain` command to walk the current thread's exception handling chain so that you can see exactly which functions have registered exception handlers. The following shows the output when debugging the ASSERTTEST.EXE.

```
0012ffb0: AssertTest!except_handler3+0 (004027a0)
  CRT scope  0, filter: AssertTest!wWinMainCRTStartup+22c (00401e1c)
                func:   AssertTest!wWinMainCRTStartup+24d (00401e3d)
0012ffe0: KERNEL32!_except_handler3+0 (77ed136c)
  CRT scope  0, filter: KERNEL32!BaseProcessStart+40 (77ea847f)
                func:   KERNEL32!BaseProcessStart+51 (77ea8490)
```

For dealing with operating system heaps (those heaps created with the `CreateHeap` API), you have the `!heap` command at your disposal. You might not think you're using any operating system heaps, but the operating-system code running inside your process is making considerable use of them. If you corrupt memory from one of those heaps, which you'll learn more about in Chapter 17, you can use the `!heap` command to figure out which heap was corrupted and where it was corrupted.

Finally, I want to mention a very interesting and useful undocumented command, `!for_each_frame`, from the EXT.DLL extension. As you can tell from the name, this instruction will execute a command string passed as a parameter for each frame up the stack. The perfect use of this command is `!for_each_frame dv`, which will show each frame's local variables up the stack.

Dealing with Dump Files

With an understanding of the types of commands WinDBG can execute, you can turn to the final set of commands: dump file commands. As I mentioned in "The Basics" section at the beginning of this chapter, WinDBG's forte is handling dump files. In this section, I'll discuss all the gyrations necessary to create and use dump files in WinDBG. The beauty of WinDBG and dump files is that nearly all the informational commands work on the dump files, so it's almost like you're right there at the time the problem occurred.

Creating Dump Files

At any point when you're doing live debugging, you can call the `.DUMP` (Create Dump File) command to create a dump file. Before mentioning anything about what can be in a dump file, I need to point out that it's up to you to specify the extension for any dump file you create. The `.DUMP` command will happily write the file exactly as you specify the complete name and path, without adding any missing file extension. The extension you should always use is .DMP.

With the extension issue out of the way, I want to discuss some of the general options the `.DUMP` command offers before jumping into the types of dump files. The first is the `/u` option, which will append the date, time, and PID to the filename so that you can get unique dump names without having to struggle with naming them. Since dump files are such great tools for taking snapshots of a debugging session so that you can analyze behaviors later, the `/u` option makes your life much easier. To provide a better idea of what was happening at a particular time, another option, `/c`, allows you to specify a comment that will be displayed as you load the dump file. Finally, if you're debugging multiple processes as at a time, the `/a` option will write out dump files for all loaded processes. Make sure you use the `/u` switch with `/a` to ensure every process gets a unique name.

WinDBG produces two types of dump files, full and mini. A full dump file includes everything about the process, from the current thread stacks to all memory data to even the actual binaries loaded in the process. A full dump is specified with the `/f` option. Although having the full dump file is convenient because there are fewer things you need to match up when loading it, you'll chew up a tremendous amount of disk space creating it.

On the minidump side, you can specify numerous options. To create a general minidump file, you just need to use the `/m` option, which happens to be the default if you don't specify any options to the `.DUMP` command. The produced minidump will be the same as the default minidump that Visual Studio .NET creates, and it will contain the loaded modules' versions and enough of the stack information to produce call stacks for all active threads.

You can also tell WinDBG to add more information to the minidumps by specifying various flags as part of the `/m` option. The most useful minidump option is `h` (`/mh`), which, in addition to the default minidump information, also writes the active handle information to the minidump. That means you'll be able to use the `!handle` command to view all handle states at the time the dump was created. If you think you'll be analyzing pointer problems in the dump file, you might also want to specify the `i` option (`/mi`) to have WinDBG include secondary memory. This option looks at pointers on the stack or backing store and records memory referenced by them as well as a small bit of memory around those locations. That way you can follow pointers to see what they contain. There are numerous other minidump options you can specify to record additional pieces of information, but the `h` and `i` options are the ones I always use.

One final option that can save you a ton of disk space is `/b`, which will compress the dump file into a .CAB file. This is a great option, but in the same way that a missing extension is problematic with the general `.DUMP` command, a missing extension is compounded when using the `/b` switch. Since `.DUMP` doesn't append an extension, your first instinct is to add .CAB to get the extension onto the file. However, by specifying the .CAB extension, WinDBG creates the temporary .DMP file with a name of <name>.CAB.DMP inside the actual .CAB file. Fortunately, WinDBG will read the oddly named .DMP file from the .CAB file just fine.

Even given these tiny problems with the .CAB writing option, I still like to use it. In addition to storing only the .DMP file in the .CAB, you can specify the `/ba` option when you'd like to also store the *currently loaded* symbols into the .CAB! If you want to ensure you get all the symbols for the process, make sure to execute a `ld *` (load all symbols) command before creating the dump file. This way you can be assured that you'll have the correct symbols when you take the .CAB to a machine that might not have access to your symbol store. Another thing to keep in mind with the `/b` option is that WinDBG writes the dump file and builds the corresponding .CAB file in the `%TEMP%` directory on the machine. As you can imagine, if you have a large process, use `/f` to create a full dump, and use `/ba` to create a .CAB with symbols, you'll need gobs of disk space free in the `%TEMP%` directory.

Opening Dump Files

Dump files aren't much good if you can't open them. The easiest way to open a dump file is from a new instance of WinDBG. On the File menu, select Open Crash Dump or press Ctrl+D to bring up the Open Crash Dump dialog box, and browse to the directory in which the dump file is located to open it. Interestingly, although it's not documented, WinDBG will open .CAB files that contain .DMP files directly as well. After opening the dump file, WinDBG automatically gets everything loaded so that you can start looking at the dump.

If you created the dump on the machine where you built the process, your life is very easy, as WinDBG will do a good job of getting the symbols and source information lined up. However, most of us will be analyzing dump files created on other machines and other operating system versions. After opening the dump file comes the work of getting the symbol, source, and binary paths set up.

Your first step is to determine which modules have symbol information missing by doing an `LM` command with the `v` option. If any modules report "no symbols loaded," you'll need to get the symbol path adjusted to find the symbols. Look at the version information associated with those modules and update the Symbol File Path (from the File, Symbol File Path menu) appropriately.

The second step is to get the image paths set. As I mentioned in the discussion of symbol servers in Chapter 2, WinDBG needs access to the binaries before it can load the symbols for minidumps. If you followed my recommendation and put your programs and the various operating system binaries and symbols into your symbol server, getting the binaries lined up is trivial. In the Executable Image Search Path dialog box, which is accessible by choosing Image File Path from the File menu, you can simply paste the same string you set for your symbol path. WinDBG will automatically search your symbol server for the matching binaries.

If you don't have the binaries in a symbol store, you're going to have to set the image path manually and hope you point to the correct versions to get them loaded. This is especially difficult with operating system binaries because a hot fix can change any number of binaries. In fact, every time you apply any hot fix or service pack, you should reload your symbol store by running my OSSYMS.JS file discussed in Chapter 2.

The final path you'll need to set up is the source path, which is accessible from the File menu, Source File Path option. After setting all three paths, you should force a symbol reload with the `.RELOAD /f` command followed by an `LM` command to see which symbols are still mismatched. If the minidump came from a customer site, you might not be able to get all the binaries and symbols loaded because that site might have different hot-fix levels or third-party products that jam DLLs into other processes. However, your goal is to get all your product's symbols loaded and as much of the operating system's symbols as possible. After all, having all the symbols loaded makes debugging easy!

Debugging the Dump

Once you've got the symbols and binaries properly loaded, debugging the dump file is almost identical to live debugging. Obviously, some commands such as `BU` won't work on dump files, but most will, especially the extension commands. If you're having trouble with a command, make sure to look at the environment table in the documentation for the command and verify that you can use it with dump files.

If you have a situation in which you created multiple dump files at the same time, you can also debug them side by side with the `.OPENDUMP` (Open Dump File) command. Once you open a dump file this way, you'll need to issue a `G` (Go) command so that WinDBG can get everything started.

Finally, one command that's only available when debugging dump files is the `.DUMPCAB` (Create Dump File CAB) command. This will create a .CAB file from the current dump file. If you add the `–a` parameter, all symbols will be written to the file.

Son of Strike (SOS)

There's great support for debugging dumps for native applications but not for managed applications, and although managed applications are a lot less error prone, they are much harder to debug. For example, consider those many projects that already have a considerable investment in COM+ or other native technologies. You might and want to create new .NET front-ends or components that leverage your existing COM components using COM interop. When those applications crash or hang, you're instantly in a lot of pain because it's almost impossible to hack through the assembly language and walk call stacks or even find the source and line for those .NET portions of the application.

To help you see the .NET portions of a dump or live application, some very smart people at Microsoft came up with a debugger extension called SOS, or Son of Strike. The basic documentation for SOS is in the SOS.HTM file in the <Visual Studio .NET Installation Dir>\SDK\v1.1\Tool Developers Guide\Samples\SOS directory. If you open the documentation, you'll definitely see that "basic" is the operable term here. In essence, it's the list of commands in the SOS.DLL extension and a brief bit about their usage.

If you're dealing with larger .NET systems, especially heavy ASP.NET transactions, you'll also want to download the 170-page PDF file "Production Debugging for .NET Framework Applications," from *http://msdn.microsoft.com/library/default.asp?url=/library/en-us/dnbda/html/DBGrm.asp*. If you want to know how to handle hung ASNET_WP.EXE processes, deal with potential .NET memory management issues, and take charge of other extreme-edge problems, this is an excellent document. The folks writing the document have definitely done their debugging of numerous live production systems and their knowledge can save you quite a bit of hassle.

With these two documentation sources, you'll get a quick discussion of the SOS commands and an extreme hardcore tricks document, but there's still something missing: just how do you get started with SOS inside WinDBG? In this section, I want to help you get a leg up on starting. My hope is that you'll get enough information out of this section to understand what's going on in the "Production Debugging for .NET Framework Applications" document. I won't be covering everything, like all the garbage collector commands, because those are covered in detail in "Production Debugging for .NET Framework Applications."

Before I start, I want to show you the easy way to get SOS.DLL loaded into WinDBG. SOS.DLL is part of the .NET Framework itself, so the trick involves getting the appropriate directories in your path so that WinDBG can easily load SOS.DLL. You need to open a MS-DOS command window and execute VSVARS32.BAT, which is located in <Visual Studio .NET Installation Dir>\Common7\Tools directory. VSVARS32.BAT gets your environment set up so that all the .NET appropriate directories are in your path.

Once you've executed VSVARS.BAT, starting WinDBG from that MS-DOS command window allows you to load SOS.DLL simply by executing `.load sos` from the WinDBG Command window. WinDBG always puts the last loaded extension DLL onto the top of the chain, so executing `!help` shows you a quick listing of all the SOS.DLL commands.

Using SOS

Probably the best way to show SOS usage is with a live example. The ExceptApp program included with this book's sample files will show you how to get started with important commands. To keep things at a manageable level, I wrote this code to simply call a few methods with local variables and finally throw an exception. I'll walk through an example of debugging EXCEPTAPP.EXE with SOS so that you can learn about the important commands for finding where you are when an application using managed code crashes or hangs. With that information, you'll be in a position to more easily apply SOS to the problems you'll encounter and understand "Production Debugging for .NET Framework Applications."

After you've compiled EXCEPTAPP.EXE and set up a MS-DOS command prompt as I described earlier, open up EXCEPTAPP.EXE in WinDBG and stop at the loader breakpoint. To make WinDBG stop when a .NET application throws an exception, you have to tell WinDBG about the exception number that .NET throws. The easiest way to do this is to go into the Event Filters dialog box, click the Add button, and in the Exception Filter dialog box, enter 0xE0434F4D. Select Enabled in the Execution group box, and select Not Handled in the Continue group box. Once you click OK, you've successfully set WinDBG to stop whenever any EXCEPTAPP.EXE throws a .NET exception. If the value 0xE0434F4D looks somewhat familiar, you can always see what it stands for by using the `.formats` command.

After you have the exception set, run EXCEPTAPP.EXE until it stops on the .NET exception. WinDBG will report it as a first chance exception and stop the application on the actual Win32 API `RaiseException` call. After getting SOS loaded with a `.load sos` command, execute `!threads` (first command you'll always want to execute in SOS) so that you can see which threads in the application or dump have .NET code in them. With EXCEPTAPP.EXE, the WinDBG thread command ~ indicates that three commands are running in the application. However, the all-important `!threads` command lists that only threads 0 and 2 have any .NET code in them, as shown in the following output. (To get everything to fit in on the page, I show the individual thread information in a table. In WinDBG, you see it as a long horizontal display.)

```
0:000> !threads
PDB symbol for mscorwks.dll not loaded
 succeeded
Loaded Son of Strike data table version 5 from "e:\WINNT\Microsoft.NET\Frame-
work\v1.1.4322\mscorwks.dll"
ThreadCount: 2
UnstartedThread: 0
BackgroundThread: 1
PendingThread: 0
DeadThread: 0


Row Heading
WinDBG Thread ID       0                            2
Win32 Thread ID        884                          9dc
ThreadObj              00147c60                     001631c8
State                  20                           1220
PreEmptive GC          Enabled                      Enabled
GC Alloc Context       04a45f24:04a45ff4            00000000:00000000
Domain                 00158300                     00158300
Lock Count             0                            0
APT                    Ukn                          Ukn
Exception              System.ArgumentException     (Finalizer)
```

The important information in the `!threads` display consists of the Domain field, because that tells you whether multiple AppDomains are running in this process; and the Exceptions field, which happens to be overloaded. In the EXCEPTAPP.EXE example, the first thread has thrown the `System.ArgumentException`, so you can see the current exception for any thread. The third thread in EXCEPTAPP.EXE shows the special value `(Finalizer)`, which indicates the thread is, as you can guess, the finalizer thread for the process. You'll also see `(Theadpool Worker)`, `(Threadpool Completion Port)`, or `(GC)` in the Exception field. When you see one of those special values, you'll know they represent runtime threads, not your threads.

Since we've determined that the WinDBG thread 0 contains the EXCEPTAPP.EXE exception, you'll want to take a look at the call stack with `!clrstack -all` to see all the details about the stack, including parameters and locals. Although `!clrstack` has switches to see the locals (`-l`) and parameters (`-p`), if you specify them together, they seem to cancel each other out and you see neither. If you'd like to walk all thread call stacks at once, you can use the command `~*e !clrstack`.

```
** Note, I excised the registers from this display **
0:000> !clrstack -all
Thread 0
ESP       EIP
0012f5e0  77e73887 [FRAME: HelperMethodFrame]
0012f60c  06d3025f [DEFAULT] [hasThis] Void ExceptApp.DoSomething.Doh
                                          (String,ValueClass ExceptApp.Days)
   at [+0x67] [+0x16] c:\junk\cruft\exceptapp\class1.cs:14
    PARAM: this: 0x04a41b5c (ExceptApp.DoSomething)
    PARAM: value class ExceptApp.Days StrParam
    PARAM: unsigned int8 ValueParam: 0x07
0012f630  06d301e2 [DEFAULT] [hasThis] Void ExceptApp.DoSomething.Reh
                                                        (I4,String)
  at [+0x6a] [+0x2b] c:\junk\cruft\exceptapp\class1.cs:23
    PARAM: this: 0x04a41b5c (ExceptApp.DoSomething)
    PARAM: class System.String i: 0x00000042
    PARAM: int8 StrParam: 77863812
    LOCAL: class System.String s: 0x04a45670 (System.String)
    LOCAL: value class ExceptApp.Days e: 0x003e5278 0x0012f63c
 :
```

In the parameter display, there seems to be a bug because `!clrstack` doesn't always display the parameter types correctly. In the `DoSomething.Doh` method, you can see it takes a `String` (`StrParam`) and a `Days` (`ValueParam`) value enumeration in the prototype. However, the `PARAM:` information shows the `StrParam` parameter as `value class ExceptApp.Days` and `ValueParam` as `unsigned int8`. Fortunately for value parameters, even when the type is wrong, the correct value displays next to the parameter name. In the `ValueParam` example, the value passed in is 7, which corresponds to the enumeration `Fri`.

Before I jump into figuring out the values of the value classes and objects, I want to mention one other stack walking command you might find useful. If you're dealing with heavy cross–.NET and native calls and you'd like to see a call stack that includes everything, the `!dumpstack` command is your friend. Overall, it does a good job, but it looks like having full PDB symbols for the .NET Framework would make it better. Occasionally, the `!dumpstack` command reports "Use alternate method which may not work", which seems to indicate that it's attempting to walk the stack when it's missing certain symbol information.

In the `LOCAL:` display under the call to `DoSomething.Reh` are two local variables: `s`, a `String` object; and `e`, a `Days` value class. After each comes the hexadecimal address describing the type. For the `Days` value, there are two numbers, 0x003E5278 and 0x0012F63C. The first number is the method table and the second is the location in memory for the value. Seeing the value in memory is simple using one of WinDBG's memory dumping commands such as `dd 0x0012F63C`.

Seeing the method table that describes the method data, the module information, and the interface map, among other things, is done through SOS's `!dumpmt` command. Executing `!dumpmt 0x003E5278` with the EXCEPTAPP.EXE example shows the following:

```
0:000> !dumpmt 0x003e5278
EEClass : 06c03b1c
Module : 001521a0
Name: ExceptApp.Days
mdToken: 02000002  (D:\Dev\ExceptApp\bin\Debug\ExceptApp.exe)
MethodTable Flags : 80000
Number of IFaces in IFaceMap : 3
Interface Map : 003e5380
Slots in VTable : 55
```

With the method table, in the first two numbers displayed, you can see which module a method comes from as well as its execution engine class. For interfaces, the SOS documentation has an excellent example of how to walk the interface maps, and I would encourage you to look it over. If you have a burning desire to see all the methods in the v-table for a particular class or object along with their method descriptors, you can specify the `–md` option in front of the method table value. In the case of EXCEPTAPP.EXE's value class `ExceptApp.Days`, you'll see all 55 methods listed. As the SOS documentation mentions in the "How Do I… ?" section, getting the method descriptors is important to setting breakpoints on specific methods.

Since we're looking at the class and module information for the `ExceptApp.Days` method table, I want to take a little detour. Once you have an execution engine class address, the `!dumpclass` command will show you everything you ever wanted to see about a class, with the important information being all the data fields in the class. To see the information about a module, use the `!dumpmodule` command. The `!dumpmodule` output documentation has examples of how to walk through memory and find classes and method tables for a module.

Now that we've ground through the value class, let's take a look at making sense out of the `String` local variable `s`, in `DoSomething.Reh`, which was displayed as follows:

```
LOCAL: class System.String s: 0x04a45670 (System.String)
```

As `s` is an object, only one hexadecimal value is displayed after the variable name—the location of that object in memory. Using the `!dumpobj` command, you'll see all the information about that object.

```
0:000> !dumpobj 0x04a45670
Name: System.String
MethodTable 0x79b7daf0
EEClass 0x79b7de3c
Size 92(0x5c) bytes
mdToken: 0200000f  (e:\winnt\microsoft.net\framework\v1.1.4322\mscorlib.dll)
String: Tommy can you see me? Can you see me?
FieldDesc*: 79b7dea0
      MT    Field   Offset          Type       Attr    Value Name
79b7daf0  4000013        4  System.Int32   instance       38 _arrayLength
79b7daf0  4000014        8  System.Int32   instance       37 m_stringLength
79b7daf0  4000015        c   System.Char   instance       54 m_firstChar
79b7daf0  4000016        0         CLASS     shared   static Empty
    >> Domain:Value 00158298:04a412f8 <<
79b7daf0  4000017        4         CLASS     shared   static WhitespaceChars
    >> Domain:Value 00158298:04a4130c <<
```

As you can see from the output, some of the fields, MethodTable, EEClass, and MT (aka Method Table), can be used with commands I've previously discussed. For the field members, the `!dumpobj` command will show the values directly in the table for simple value types. In the `String` display in the preceding output, the `m_stringLength` value is the 37 characters currently in the string. As you'll see in a moment, for object field members, the `Value` field will contain the object instance, and you can use the `!dumpobj` command on to see the value.

The entries delineated by >> and << are showing you the domain instance and location in that domain for the static field prior to the >>. If I had multiple AppDomains in EXCEPTAPP.EXE, you'd see two domains and value information output for the static `WhitespaceChars` field.

Now that I've covered some of the basic commands, I want to tie them together and show how you'll look up useful data with them. With EXCEPTAPP.EXE stopped in WinDBG because of an exception, it would be nice to see what the exception is and what some of the fields are so we can see why EXCEPTAPP.EXE stopped in the middle of execution.

We know from executing the `!threads` command that the first thread is currently processing an exception, `System.ArgumentException`. If you look carefully at the output for `!clrstack` or `!dumpstack`, you'll notice that no locals or parameters that show any type of `System.ArgumentException` are displayed. The good news is that an excellent command, `!dumpstackobjects`, shows all objects currently on the stack of the current thread:

```
0:000> !dumpstackobjects
ESP/REG  Object   Name
ebx      04a45670 System.String    Tommy can you see me? Can you see me?
0012f50c 04a45f64 System.ArgumentException
0012f524 04a45f64 System.ArgumentException
0012f538 04a45f64 System.ArgumentException
0012f558 04a44bc4 System.String    Reh =
0012f55c 04a45f64 System.ArgumentException
0012f560 04a45670 System.String    Tommy can you see me? Can you see me?
0012f564 04a4431c System.Byte[]
0012f568 04a43a58 System.IO.__ConsoleStream
0012f5a0 04a45f64 System.ArgumentException
⋮
```

Since the `!dumpstackobjects` command is wandering up the stack, you'll see some items multiple times as they are passed a parameter to multiple functions. In the preceding output, you can see multiple `System.ArgumentException` objects, but if you look at the object value next to each object, you'll notice they are all referring to the same object instance, 0x04A45F64.

To look at the `System.ArgumentException` object, I'll use the `!dumpobj` command. I had to wrap the Name column to get everything to fit on the page.

```
0:000> !dumpobj 04a45f64
Name: System.ArgumentException
MethodTable 0x79b87b84
EEClass 0x79b87c0c
Size 68(0x44) bytes
mdToken: 02000038  (e:\winnt\microsoft.net\framework\v1.1.4322\mscorlib.dll)
FieldDesc*: 79b87c70
      MT    Field   Offset          Type       Attr    Value Name
79b7fcd4  400001d        4         CLASS   instance 00000000 _className
79b7fcd4  400001e        8         CLASS   instance 00000000
                                                       _exceptionMethod
79b7fcd4  400001f        c         CLASS   instance 00000000
```

```
                                                    _exceptionMethodString
79b7fcd4  4000020       10         CLASS   instance 04a456cc _message
79b7fcd4  4000021       14         CLASS   instance 00000000
                                                       _innerException
79b7fcd4  4000022       18         CLASS   instance 00000000 _helpURL
79b7fcd4  4000023       1c         CLASS   instance 00000000 _stackTrace
79b7fcd4  4000024       20         CLASS   instance 00000000
                                                      _stackTraceString
79b7fcd4  4000025       24         CLASS   instance 00000000
                                                _remoteStackTraceString
79b7fcd4  4000026       2c  System.Int32   instance        0
                                                      _remoteStackIndex
79b7fcd4  4000027       30  System.Int32   instance -2147024809 _HResult
79b7fcd4  4000028       28         CLASS   instance 00000000 _source
79b7fcd4  4000029       34  System.Int32   instance        0 _xptrs
79b7fcd4  400002a       38  System.Int32   instance -532459699 _xcode
79b87b84  40000d7       3c         CLASS   instance 04a45708 m_paramName
```

Inside an exception, the `Message` property is the important property. Because I can't call a method directly from WinDBG to see its value, I'll have to look at the `_message` field because that's where the `Message` property stores the actual string. Since the `_message` field is marked with `CLASS`, the hexadecimal number in the Value column is the object instance. To look at the object, I'll do another `!dumpobj` command to view it. As we've seen, the `String` object will have a special field in it, so we can see its actual value, which turns out to be the innocuous "Thowing an exception."

```
0:000> !dumpobj 04a456cc
Name: System.String
MethodTable 0x79b7daf0
EEClass 0x79b7de3c
Size 60(0x3c) bytes
mdToken: 0200000f  (e:\winnt\microsoft.net\framework\v1.1.4322\mscorlib.dll)
String: Thowing an exception
FieldDesc*: 79b7dea0
      MT     Field  Offset          Type       Attr     Value Name
79b7daf0  4000013        4  System.Int32   instance        21 m_arrayLength
79b7daf0  4000014        8  System.Int32   instance        20 m_stringLength
79b7daf0  4000015        c   System.Char   instance        54 m_firstChar
79b7daf0  4000016        0         CLASS     shared    static Empty
    >> Domain:Value 00158298:04a412f8 <<
79b7daf0  4000017        4         CLASS     shared    static WhitespaceChars
    >> Domain:Value 00158298:04a4130c <<
```

Summary

Although you might think I've covered everything about WinDBG, I really covered only about half of the power of WinDBG. My goal was to show you the power of the debugger and help get you past the hurdles you'll encounter along the way. In case I haven't stressed it enough, let me say again that you really do need to read the WinDBG documentation.

The biggest trick with WinDBG is getting the symbols and source set up, and for dump file debugging, getting the image path set. WinDBG offers tremendous flexibility for controlling exactly where symbols are found and loaded. This helps tremendously in ensuring that you have the right symbols.

In addition to the ability to debug multiple processes at once, WinDBG offers outstanding breakpoint control, so you can stop exactly when and where you want. With the ability to execute commands on both breakpoints and exceptions, you now have extra super powers to track down extremely difficult bugs. With the extension commands, you can see things inside your process that you've never been able to see before.

One of the most important reasons for using WinDBG is its dump file handling. Visual Studio .NET, although finally allowing you to read dump files, is only suitable for dump files created on development machines. WinDBG, on the other hand, is the tool you'll be using to read real dump files from customer sites. That alone makes expending the effort to learn WinDBG well worth it.

Finally, I hope I was able to give you a starting point for using the interesting SOS extension DLL that supports .NET debugging. Although it's definitely hard-core for most developers, it's the only way to debug those combined managed and native applications that many developers are doing. As you can tell, you'll need to spend some time with SOS to take full advantage of it. Additionally, reading "Production Debugging for .NET Framework Applications" is crucial to understanding those tough conditions you might encounter with the largest heavy-duty applications.

Part III

Power Tools and Techniques for .NET

9

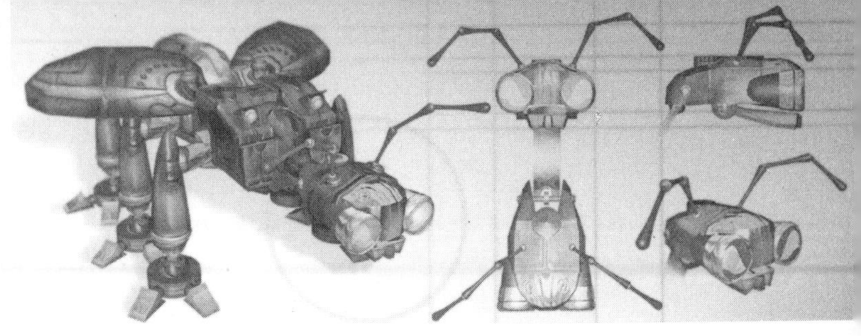

Extending the Visual Studio .NET IDE

The sign of an effective development tool is that it offers sufficient flexibility so that it works for you instead of forcing you to change your lifestyle to accommodate it. Until Microsoft Visual Studio .NET appeared, previous versions, in my opinion, were only good enough for debugging, not for editing and general use. I'm pleased to say that Visual Studio .NET, although still having some quirks, is what I'm using for my editing and development needs. The main reason is that compared to previous versions of Visual Studio, Visual Studio .NET is a paragon of extensibility. If you don't think something behaves correctly or you think a feature is missing, you'll find that Visual Studio .NET finally contains the capabilities to actually correct and fix the shortcoming.

Even better is that today I have an answer to one of the most common questions I used to get when I worked at NuMega: How did you guys get a window inside Visual Studio? Well, my answer doesn't matter anymore because anyone can do it. Nearly every developer has an idea for a tool or a view that belongs inside the IDE but until now has had no way of getting that tool or view in there. With the new Visual Studio .NET extensibility model, anyone can now put his or her own windows inside the IDE. The means of doing this is also documented and supported much better than the special Package Partner Program you had to go through in previous versions of Visual Studio to hook into the IDE.

There are three elements to the extensibility functionality: macros, add-ins, and wizards. Visual Studio .NET allows you to create macros with the built-in Visual Studio Macros IDE editor. This editor looks and behaves just like the

Visual Studio .NET environment, so your investment in learning about that environment pays off when writing macros. The one limitation is that you can write macros only in Microsoft Visual Basic .NET. Since .NET is supposed to be language-agnostic, I can't see why Microsoft limited the environment by not supporting C#. Basically, this limitation means that it doesn't matter that you had decided to stick to C#—maybe because you have a thing for semicolons—you'll still need to learn Visual Basic .NET to write macros.

The second option is through add-ins. Whereas macros are nice for small, non-UI-related tasks, add-ins are COM components that allow you to write true extensions to the IDE. For example, you can create tool windows (your own windows), add property pages to the Options dialog box, and respond to menu commands from add-ins. Anyone you give a macro to can see your macro source code, but add-ins are distributed in binary form, and you can use any language that supports COM to write them.

The final extensibility option is the wizard. Wizards are most useful for tasks that require you to lead the user through the steps necessary for accomplishing a task. A perfect example is the Smart Device Application Wizard that walks you through creating a smart device application. Of the three extensibility options, wizards are the least used.

My goal for this chapter is to give you an idea of what macros and add-ins can do by presenting three real-world tools that I can't live without. By seeing what these tools do, you'll get a good overview of the trials and tribulations you'll run into when writing your particular Tool That No One Can Live Without. Given the fact that very few developers do wizards, I won't discuss those. When it comes to macros and add-ins, I won't be taking you through the usual "click this Wizard button to make an add-in pop out" steps that other books will. I'm assuming that you've read the Visual Studio .NET documentation, so I'll spend my time pointing out the holes and problems I ran into in order to save you all the time I wasted getting things to work.

The first tool I'll show you is CommenTater, a cool macro that ensures your C# documentation comments are included and up to date. The first add-in, SuperSaver, fixes a problem with the way Visual Studio .NET saves files, adds background saving, and lets you add property pages to the Options dialog box. It's an excellent example of a complete add-in but is small enough to wrap your mind around. The final add-in is SettingsMaster, which allows you to batch set or custom set build options so that with no work whatsoever you can use, for all types of projects, the build settings I recommended back in Chapter 2. Armed with SettingsMaster, keeping your team projects properly coordinated should be trivial. You won't have to manually change settings in a bunch of projects ever again! All these tools are available with this book's sample files.

Extending with Macros

Before I discuss the CommenTater macro, I want to spend a little bit of time discussing a few key things about macros and some of the issues you'll encounter. The biggest point I want to make is that even if you think you have the coolest add-in idea in the world and can't wait to get started, you need to spend a lot of time writing macros before you jump into building add-ins. Since macros access all the same objects and properties as add-ins, they provide the best opportunity to learn about the ins and outs of the Visual Studio .NET object model. As you'll see later in the chapter, the object model has lots of quirks, and getting add-ins working is sometimes problematic. Macros are much easier to write and debug, so you'll want to use them first to prototype.

Before finding the Macro option on the Tools menu, you should spend some time reading the documentation about macros and the object model. Macros themselves are discussed in the Visual Studio .NET documentation under Visual Studio .NET\Developing With Visual Studio .NET\Manipulating The Development Environment\Automating Repetitive Actions By Using Macros. The all-important object model is discussed in Visual Studio .NET\Developing With Visual Studio .NET\Reference\Automation And Extensibility Reference.

After perusing the documentation for a while to see what the various objects are, start recording macros so that you can see some of the objects in action. Keep in mind that recording works primarily on the code editors (including the Find/Replace dialog boxes), Solution Explorer, and window activation. You won't be able to record things like building up a Web form or Windows form with controls. Also make sure to take a look at the macro samples provided by Microsoft, which are automatically loaded into the Macro Explorer as part of the Samples macro project. The Macro Explorer is shown in Figure 9-1. The macro samples are good examples of how to use the object model to solve problems. The MakeAddinFromMacroProj macro (in the MakeAddin macro project) is my personal favorite because it takes a macro and converts it to an add-in. It shows the power we now have at our fingertips with Visual Studio .NET.

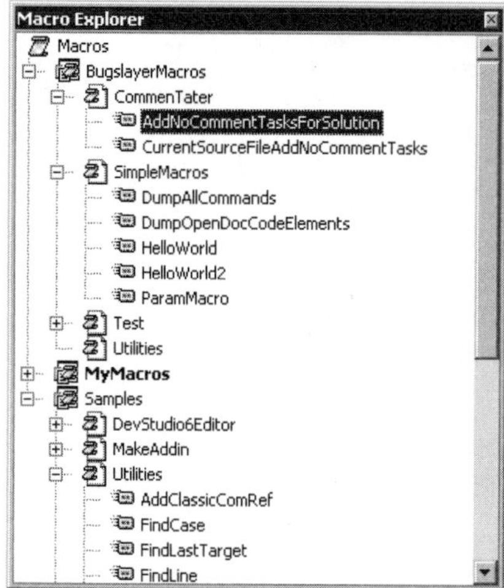

Figure 9-1 Macro Explorer window

There are two ways to execute macros: by double-clicking the macro function name in the Macro Explorer and by using the Command window. If you start typing "macro," the Command window's IntelliSense popup, shown in Figure 9-2, will allow you to choose the macro to run.

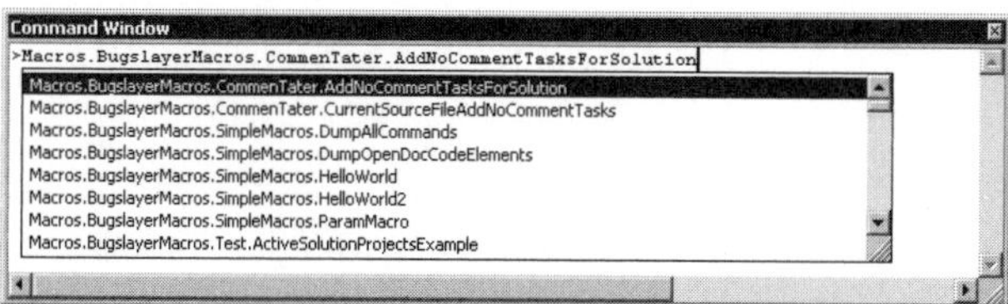

Figure 9-2 Command window's IntelliSense popup executing a macro

If you're really into using the Command window to run macros or any of the other built-in commands, the built-in `alias` command allows you to redefine shorter text commands so that you don't have to type something like this every time you want to run a macro:

```
Macros.BugslayerMacros.CommenTater.AddNoCommentTasksForSolution
```

You also can remove aliases by passing a `/d` in front of the defined alias.

Macro Parameters

One fact that's not very clear from the Macro Explorer window and the Command window's IntelliSense popup is that the only macros shown in both windows are macros that don't take any parameters. That makes sense in Macro

Explorer because it would be pretty difficult to pass parameters when you're double-clicking on an item. However, if you're using the Command window, you probably do want to pass some form of parameter. The trick is to declare the macro subroutine as taking a single optional string parameter, as in the following:

```
Sub ParamMacro(Optional ByVal Param As String = "")
```

Handling multiple parameters is almost as easy; you add an additional optional string parameter for each subsequent one, as in the following code, which shows a macro that takes three parameters:

```
Sub ParamMacroWithThree(Optional ByVal Param1 As String = "", _
                        Optional ByVal Param2 As String = "", _
                        Optional ByVal Param3 As String = "")
```

Although using multiple optional strings for parameters works great for Visual Studio .NET 2003, if you want your macros to be backward compatible with Visual Studio .NET 2002, you're out of luck: you'll find that your macro won't work even from the Command window. You can have only a single optional string parameter for Visual Studio .NET 2002. However, if you want to pass multiple parameters in the Command window, the situation gets a little strange. If you have any spaces whatsoever other than the one separating the macro name from the parameters, your macro won't be called. This means that when you want to pass three parameters, you pass them as a single string but with the parameters separated by commas. If you have a string parameter that has spaces, you have to pass the individual string surrounded by quotes. What's odd is that the quotes won't be in the actual string your macro processes. Interestingly, there's no way to pass a quote-delimited string with a comma in it. The following are examples of proper string passing and how the strings would appear when you go to process the parameter in the macro:

```
Command window call     : MyMacro x,y,z
Macro parameter string  : x,y,z

Command window call     : MyMacro x,"a string",y
Macro parameter string  : x,a string,y
```

To make macro life a little easier in writing macros that work in both versions, this book's sample files includes a utility macro module (Utilities.VB, contained in the Macros directory) with a function named `SplitParams` that takes care of splitting up the parameters into a string array for you. I also provided some convenient wrappers around the Command window and Output window objects in the same utility module. We'll use these objects when we work with the SimpleMacros macro discussed in the section "Code Elements."

Problems with Projects

One key point I need to make that's not completely clear when you start reading the documentation is that the different languages have different project object models. In the common environment object model discussion, the `Project` object lists all sorts of cool methods for manipulating and saving projects. I wasted a huge amount of time because I had the mistaken impression that the common project was the root of all language and technologies projects. In fact, nothing is further from the truth. There are only two properly documented project types, `VSProject` for C# and Visual Basic .NET projects, and `VCProject` for C++ projects. Other types of projects, such as CAB and Setup, aren't documented and will sling exceptions all over the place if you access them using a generic `Project` object. This is especially annoying since methods that you'd expect to work, such as `Save`, throw Not Implemented exceptions. Make sure you're using lots of exception handling when dealing with projects!

When enumerating a solution's projects, you're given the generic `Project` object. Your best route is to use the `Kind` property to retrieve the GUID that will help you determine the type of the project. Table 9-1 lists the project kind GUID strings. If you're working on a C++ project, immediately use the `Object` property to convert the `Project` into a `VCProject`, and then branch off to deal with that `VCProject` because few of the `Project` methods will work. `VSProject` objects are a little more forgiving about being accessed through the generic `Project` object.

Table 9-1 Documented Project GUID Strings

Project Language	GUID
C#	{FAE04EC0-301F-11D3-BF4B-00C04F79EFBC}
Visual Basic .NET	{F184B08F-C81C-45F6-A57F-5ABD9991F28F}
C++	{8BC9CEB8-8B4A-11D0-8D11-00A0C91BC942}
J#	{E6FDF86B-F3D1-11D4-8576-0002A516ECE8}

An alternative method of determining the project type is to use the `Project.CodeModel` property, which describes the code elements present in the project files. I'll be discussing the code elements more in a moment. The `CodeModel` object contains a `Language` property that returns a GUID string identifying the language. This is the technique I used to determine the project type in the SettingsMaster add-in because I needed to work with all language types.

Note that the documentation is wrong in saying the language strings returned by the `Language` property are `vsCMLanguage` constants—that constant doesn't exist. The real constant is `CodeModelLanguageConstants`.

Code Elements

One of the most amazing aspects of Visual Studio .NET is that all the programming constructs for source files can be accessed easily through the object model. The fact we can now simply add, change, or remove items such as methods in all languages supported by Visual Studio .NET without having to do the parsing ourselves opens up huge opportunities for all sorts of unique tools that might never have been created because parsing is so hard. Every time I use the code elements to manipulate the code in a file, I'm amazed at how cool this capability really is.

To show you how easy it is to access and utilize the code elements, I created a macro, shown in Listing 9-1, that dumps the code elements out of the active document. What's not obvious is that the code works for any language. The output reports the name of the code element along with its code element type. You can find this macro with this book's sample code in Macros\SimpleMacros.VB along with its supporting file, Utilities.VB. The following output shows a partial listing of the results returned from calling this macro on the SETTINGSMASTER.VB file from the SettingsMaster project:

```
SettingsMaster.SettingsMaster(vsCMElementClass)
  SettingsMaster.SettingsMaster.RegSettings(vsCMElementVariable)
  SettingsMaster.SettingsMaster.m_ApplicationObject(vsCMElementVariable)
  SettingsMaster.SettingsMaster.New(vsCMElementFunction)
    ApplicationObject(vsCMElementParameter)
    AddInInstance(vsCMElementParameter)
```

One issue that's a little problematic when you're dealing with the code elements is consistency in how child items for an element are retrieved. For example, a `CodeClass` object uses the `Members` property to retrieve the subelements for the class when the class is a Visual Basic .NET or C# class. However, when the class is a C++ class described by the `CodeClass` object, the `Children` property retrieves the subelements. Toward the end of the `DumpElements` function, I use some nested `Try…Catch` blocks to find the appropriate child elements. As you can see, `CodeFunction` objects use yet another property, `Parameters`, to get child objects. What's important is that you know there are possibly more ways than one to get child elements.

```
' Dumps all the code elements for the open document of a project.
Public Sub DumpActiveDocCodeElements()
    ' Where the output goes. Note that the OutputPane class comes
    ' from the Utilities macro project.
    Dim ow As OutputPane = New OutputPane("Open Doc Code Elements")
    ' Clear the output pane.
    ow.Clear()

    ' See if there's a document open.
    Dim Doc As Document = DTE.ActiveDocument
    If (Doc Is Nothing) Then
        ow.WriteLine("No open document")
        Exit Sub
    End If

    ' Get the code model for the doc. You have to get the project
    ' item to diddle down to the code elements
    Dim FileMod As FileCodeModel = Doc.ProjectItem.FileCodeModel

    If (Not (FileMod Is Nothing)) Then
        DumpElements(ow, FileMod.CodeElements, 0)
    Else
        ow.WriteLine("Unable to get the FileCodeModel!")
    End If
End Sub

Private Sub DumpElements(ByVal ow As OutputPane, _
                         ByVal Elems As CodeElements, _
                         ByVal Level As Integer)

    Dim Elem As CodeElement
    For Each Elem In Elems

        Dim i As Integer = 0

        While (i < Level)
            ow.OutPane.OutputString("  ")
            i = i + 1
        End While

        ' If there's an exception accessing the FullName property,
        ' it's probably an unnamed parameter.
        Dim sName As String
        Try
            sName = Elem.FullName
        Catch e As System.Exception
            sName = "'Empty Name'"
        End Try
        ow.WriteLine(sName + "(" + Elem.Kind.ToString() + ")")
```

Listing 9-1 DumpActiveDocCodeElements

```
        ' This is kinda weird. Some CodeElements use a Children property
        ' to get sub elements while others use Members. Then again,
        ' functions use the Parameters property.
        Dim SubCodeElems As CodeElements = Nothing

        Try
            SubCodeElems = Elem.Children
        Catch
            Try
                SubCodeElems = Elem.Members
            Catch
                If (TypeOf Elem Is CodeFunction) Then
                    SubCodeElems = Elem.Parameters
                Else
                    SubCodeElems = Nothing
                End If
            End Try
        End Try

        If (Not (SubCodeElems Is Nothing)) Then
            If (SubCodeElems.Count > 0) Then
                DumpElements(ow, SubCodeElems, Level + 1)
            End If
        End If
    Next
End Sub
```

CommenTater: The Cure for the Common Potato?

One absolutely cool part of C# is the XML documentation comments. They are XML tags that appear in comments describing properties or methods in a file. In fact, the IDE helps you out by automatically inserting the appropriate documentation comments for a program construct when you type in `///` above that construct. There are three very important reasons you should always fill out C# documentation comments. The first is that doing so enforces a consistent commenting standard across teams and, well, the C# programming universe. The second is that the IDE IntelliSense automatically picks up any specified `<summary>` and `<param>` tags, which is a great help to others using your code because it gives them much more valuable information about the item. If the code is in the project, you don't have to do anything to get the benefits of using documentation comments. If you're providing a binary-only solution, the documentation comments can be gathered into an XML file at compile time, so you can still provide the cool summary tips to users. All you need to do is have the resultant XML file in the same directory as the binary, and Visual Studio .NET automatically picks up the comments to show in the IntelliSense tips.

The last reason you should fill out the documentation comments is that the resulting XML file can simply have a good dose of XSLT applied to it to build a complete documentation system for your product. Please note that I'm not talking about the Build Comment Web Pages option on the Tools menu. There is plenty of important information not picked up by that command, such as `<exceptions>`, so it's not that useful. Far better tools can generate the documentation, as I'll discuss in a moment.

I encourage you to read about all the XML documentation comment tags in the Visual Studio .NET documentation so that you can do the best job possible documenting your code. To create the XML document file, fill out the XML Documentation File field on the project Property Pages dialog box, Configuration Properties folder, Build page, as shown in Figure 9-3. Make sure you fill out the field individually for all configurations so that the document file is built every time.

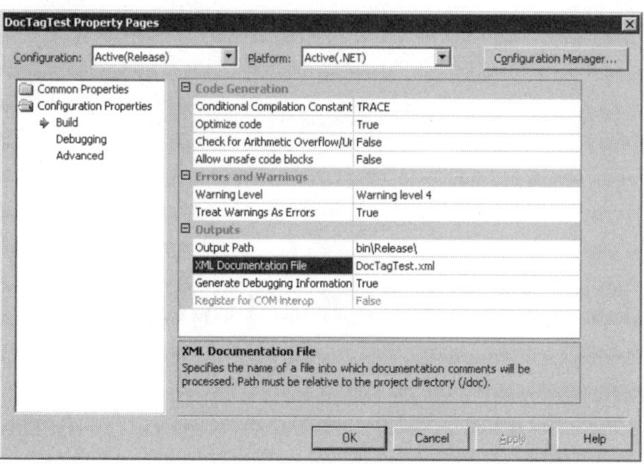

Figure 9-3 Setting the `/doc` command-line option to produce an XML documentation comment file

To produce full output from the XML documentation comment files, I included an XSL transform file and cascading style sheet in the DocCommentsXSL directory available with this book's sample files. However, a far better tool to use is the NDoc tool available from *http://ndoc.sourceforge.net*. NDoc sucks up the XML documentation comments and creates an HTML Help file that looks just like the MSDN .NET Framework class library documentation. NDoc even provides links to general methods such as `GetHashCode`, so you can jump right into the MSDN documentation! NDoc is an excellent way to document your team's code, and I highly recommend its use. In fact, with Visual Studio

.NET 2003's new ability to do post build processing, you can easily make NDoc part of your build.

Since documentation comments are so important, I wanted some way of automatically adding them to my C# code. About the same time I was thinking about this, I found that the Task List window automatically shows any comments in your code that start with key phrases such as "TODO" when you right-click in the Task List window and select either All or Comment from the Show Tasks option on the shortcut menu. My idea was to have either a macro or an add-in that would add any missing documentation comments and use "TODO" in the comments so that I could easily go through and ensure all the documentation comments were properly filled out. The result was CommenTater. The following shows a method that's been processed by CommenTater.

```
/// <summary>
/// TODO - Add Test function summary comment
/// </summary>
/// <remarks>
/// TODO - Add Test function remarks comment
/// </remarks>
/// <param name="x">
/// TODO - Add x parameter comment
/// </param>
/// <param name="y">
/// TODO - Add y parameter comment
/// </param>
/// <returns>
/// TODO - Add return comment
/// </returns>
public static int Test ( Int32 x , Int32 y )
{
return ( x ) ;
}
```

Visual Studio .NET makes iterating the code elements in a source file trivial, so I was pretty excited because I thought that all I'd have to do was wind through the code elements, grab any lines above the method or property, and if the documentation comment wasn't present, poke in the documentation comment for that method or property. That's when I discovered that the code elements all come with a property named `DocComment` that returns the actual documentation comment for the item. I immediately tipped my hat to the developers for thinking ahead and really making the code elements useful. Now all I needed to do was set the `DocComment` property to the value I wanted, and life was good.

At this point, you might want to open up the CommenTater.VB file in the CommenTater directory. The source code for the macro is too large to include in the book pages, but consider looking at the file as I discuss the ideas behind its implementation. My main idea was to create two functions, `AddNoCommentTasksForSolution` and `CurrentSourceFileAddNoCommentTasks`. You can tell from the names what level the functions were to work on. For the most part, the basic algorithm looks relatively similar to the examples in Listing 9-1 in that I just recurse through all the code elements and manipulate the `DocComment` property for each code element type.

The first issue I ran into was what I considered a small weakness in the code element object model. The `DocComment` property is not a common property on the `CodeElement` class, which can be substituted as a base for any general code element. So I had to jump through the hoops necessary to convert the generic `CodeElement` object into the actual type based on the `Kind` property. That's why the `RecurseCodeElements` function has the big `Select…Case` statement in it.

The second problem I ran into was completely self-inflicted. For some reason, it never dawned on me that the `DocComment` property for a code construct needed to be treated as a fully formed XML fragment. I'd build up the documentation comment string I wanted, and when I'd try to assign it to the `DocComment` property, an `ArgumentException` would be thrown. I was quite confused because it looked like the `DocComment` property was both readable and writable, but it was acting like it was only readable. For some bizarre reason, I had a brain cramp and didn't realize that the reason for the exception was that I wasn't properly bracketing my documentation comment XML with the necessary `<doc></doc>` element. Instead I figured I was running into a bug and therefore looked for alternative means for getting the documentation comment text in.

Since the individual code elements included a `StartPoint` property, I just needed to create the appropriate `EditPoint` and start jamming in the text. A little experimentation quickly proved that worked just fine, so I implemented a set of routines to squirt in the necessary text. Since there are plenty of times when manually inserting the text is required, I left the routines in the bottom of the CommenTater.VB file so that you can see the work necessary to add text and keep it aligned, but I commented them out.

For the first version of the macro, I was pretty happy with the way everything worked and used CommenTater quite a bit in my own development. I thought I might have to port CommenTater over to a full add-in because a macro might be too slow, but the macro was always plenty fast for me. The first version of CommenTater added only missing documentation comments. That was fine, but I quickly realized that I really wanted CommenTater to get some smarts and compare existing function comments with what was currently in the code. Many times I had changed a function prototype by adding or removing parameters but didn't remember to update the documentation comment to reflect the change. By adding this comparison functionality, CommenTater would be even more useful.

When I first started looking at what it was going to take to update existing comments, I was a little disheartened. Since at this point I thought the DocComment property was read-only, I realized I was going to have to do quite a bit of text manipulation to properly update comments—and that wasn't looking appealing. However, as I looked at CommenTater in the macro debugger, the big, fat, juicy clue slapped me hard in the forehead, and it dawned on me that I simply needed to put in the <doc></doc> elements around any documentation comments to write to the DocComment property. Once I got over my own stupidity, writing the ProcessFunctionComment function was much easier. It's shown in Listing 9-2.

The beauty of the Microsoft .NET Framework class library certainly came into play. I could use the excellent XmlDocument class to do all the heavy lifting necessary to get the information out of the existing documentation comment string, allowing me to build up a new version. The ProcessFunctionComment function might reorder your documentation comments; I had to pick an order for putting the individual nodes in the file. Additionally, I format the comments as I like to see them, so CommenTater might change your careful formatting of your documentation comments, but it won't lose any information.

```
' Does all the work to take an existing function comment and ensure
' that everything in it is kosher. This might reorder your
' comments, so you might want to change it.
Private Sub ProcessFunctionComment(ByVal Func As CodeFunction)

    Debug.Assert("" <> Func.DocComment, """""" <> Func.DocComment")

    ' Holds the original doc comment.
    Dim XmlDocOrig As New XmlDocument()
    ' I LOVE THIS!  By setting PreserveWhitespace to true, the
    ' XmlDocument class will keep most of the formatting...
    XmlDocOrig.PreserveWhitespace = True
    XmlDocOrig.LoadXml(Func.DocComment)

    Dim RawXML As New StringBuilder()

    ' Get the summary node.
    Dim Node As XmlNode
    Dim Nodes As XmlNodeList = XmlDocOrig.GetElementsByTagName("summary")
```

Listing 9-2 ProcessFunctionComment from CommenTater.VB *(continued)*

```
    If (0 = Nodes.Count) Then
        RawXML.Append(SimpleSummaryComment(Func.Name, "function"))
    Else
        RawXML.AppendFormat("<summary>{0}", vbCrLf)
        For Each Node In Nodes
            RawXML.AppendFormat("{0}{1}", Node.InnerXml, vbCrLf)
        Next
        RawXML.AppendFormat("</summary>{0}", vbCrLf)
    End If

    ' Get the remarks node.
    Nodes = XmlDocOrig.GetElementsByTagName("remarks")
    If (Nodes.Count > 0) Then
        RawXML.AppendFormat("<remarks>{0}", vbCrLf)
        For Each Node In Nodes
            RawXML.AppendFormat("{0}{1}", Node.InnerXml, vbCrLf)
        Next
        RawXML.AppendFormat("</remarks>{0}", vbCrLf)
    ElseIf (True = m_FuncShowsRemarks) Then
        RawXML.AppendFormat("<remarks>{0}TODO - Add {1} function " + _
                                    "remarks comment{0}</remarks>", _
                               vbCrLf, Func.Name)
    End If

    ' Get any parameters described in the doc comments.
    Nodes = XmlDocOrig.GetElementsByTagName("param")

    ' Does the function have parameters?
    If (0 <> Func.Parameters.Count) Then

        ' Slap any existing doc comment params into a hash table with
        ' the parameter name as the key.
        Dim ExistHash As New Hashtable()
        For Each Node In Nodes
            Dim ParamName As String
            Dim ParamText As String
            ParamName = Node.Attributes("name").InnerXml
            ParamText = Node.InnerText
            ExistHash.Add(ParamName, ParamText)
        Next

        ' Loop through the parameters.
        Dim Elem As CodeElement
        For Each Elem In Func.Parameters
            ' Is this one in the hash of previous filled in params?
            If (True = ExistHash.ContainsKey(Elem.Name)) Then
                RawXML.AppendFormat("<param name=""{0}"">{1}{2}{1}" + _
                                            "</param>{1}", _
                                  Elem.Name, _
                                  vbCrLf, _
                                  ExistHash(Elem.Name))
                ' Get rid of this key.
```

```
                ExistHash.Remove(Elem.Name)
            Else
                ' A new parameter was added.
                RawXML.AppendFormat("<param name=""{0}"">{1}TODO - Add " + _
                                    "{0} parameter comment{1}</param>{1}", _
                                    Elem.Name, vbCrLf)
            End If
        Next

        ' If there is anything left in the hash table, a param
        ' was either removed or renamed. I'll add the remaining
        ' with TODOs so the user can do the manual deletion.
        If (ExistHash.Count > 0) Then
            Dim KeyStr As String
            For Each KeyStr In ExistHash.Keys
                Dim Desc = ExistHash(KeyStr)
                RawXML.AppendFormat("<param name=""{0}"">{1}{2}{1}{3}" + _
                                            "{1}</param>{1}", _
                                    KeyStr, _
                                    vbCrLf, _
                                    Desc, _
                                    "TODO - Remove param tag")
            Next
        End If
    End If

    ' Take care of returns if necessary.
    If ("" <> Func.Type.AsFullName) Then
        Nodes = XmlDocOrig.GetElementsByTagName("returns")
        ' Do any returns nodes.
        If (0 = Nodes.Count) Then
            RawXML.AppendFormat("<returns>{0}TODO - Add return comment" + _
                                                    "{0}</returns>{0}", _
                                vbCrLf)
        Else
            RawXML.AppendFormat("<returns>{0}", vbCrLf)

            For Each Node In Nodes
                RawXML.AppendFormat("{0}{1}", Node.InnerXml, vbCrLf)
            Next

            RawXML.AppendFormat("</returns>{0}", vbCrLf)
        End If
    End If

    ' Do any example nodes.
    Nodes = XmlDocOrig.GetElementsByTagName("example")
    If (Nodes.Count > 0) Then
        RawXML.AppendFormat("<example>{0}", vbCrLf)
        For Each Node In Nodes
            RawXML.AppendFormat("{0}{1}", Node.InnerXml, vbCrLf)
        Next
        RawXML.AppendFormat("</example>{0}", vbCrLf)
```

(continued)

```
        End If

        ' Do any permission nodes.
        Nodes = XmlDocOrig.GetElementsByTagName("permission")
        If (Nodes.Count > 0) Then
            For Each Node In Nodes
                RawXML.AppendFormat("<permission cref=""{0}"">{1}", _
                                    Node.Attributes("cref").InnerText, _
                                    vbCrLf)
                RawXML.AppendFormat("{0}{1}", Node.InnerXml, vbCrLf)
                RawXML.AppendFormat("</permission>{0}", vbCrLf)
            Next
        End If

        ' Finally exceptions.
        Nodes = XmlDocOrig.GetElementsByTagName("exception")

        If (Nodes.Count > 0) Then
            For Each Node In Nodes
                RawXML.AppendFormat("<exception cref=""{0}"">{1}", _
                                    Node.Attributes("cref").InnerText, _
                                    vbCrLf)
                RawXML.AppendFormat("{0}{1}", Node.InnerXml, vbCrLf)
                RawXML.AppendFormat("</exception>{0}", vbCrLf)
            Next
        End If
        Func.DocComment = FinishOffDocComment(RawXML.ToString())
    End Sub
```

Once I had everything working with documentation comment updating, I thought it'd be a good idea to go ahead and implement the code necessary to handle an undo context. That way you could do a single Ctrl+Z and restore all changes to CommenTater in case of a bug. Unfortunately, the undo context causes a real problem. When I don't have an undo context open, all the changes I make to documentation comments works just fine. However, when an undo context is open before doing all changes, everything is completely messed up—it looks like the undo context interferes with the code elements. When CommenTater writes to a `DocComment` property, the code element start points are no longer updated, so the updates occur in the old positions, not the updated positions, thus corrupting the file. I found that if, instead of using the undo context to globally account for all changes, I used it each time I updated a method or property's documentation comment, it worked. Although not as good as a global undo of all changes, at least it's some form of undo. I hope Microsoft fixes the undo context problem so that you can use the undo context globally for large-scale changes.

One interesting problem I ran into when developing CommenTater was related to reserved characters in XML that were perfectly fine as function names. Although you can have an `operator &` function, the second you attempt to use `&` in an XML documentation comment, you get an exception indicating an invalid character. Of course, the same functionality applies to `>` and `<`, so all the following operators will cause problems: `operator <`, `operator >`, `operator <<`, and `operator >>`. To keep the XML parser happy, the `BuildFunctionComment` function in CommenTater ensures the appropriate symbols are substituted (such as `&` for `&`).

CommenTater is a very useful macro, but one big enhancement would be an excellent addition and teach you a tremendous amount about the IDE object model. The `<exception>` documentation comment tag is there so that you can document which exceptions a function throws. What I'd like to see is an enhancement that searches the function for any `throw` statements and automatically adds a new entry for that particular exception type. Of course, you should also do the proper thing and mark any existing `<exception>` documentation comment tags as needing to be removed when the method no longer throws the exception.

Common Debugging Question

Are there any tricks to debugging macros and add-ins that are written in managed code?

One of the first things you'll notice about both macro and add-in development is that the Visual Studio .NET IDE eats exceptions like crazy. Although it makes sense for the IDE not to allow any exceptions to percolate up and crash the IDE, the IDE chomps so hard on any unhandled exceptions, you might not even realize you're causing exceptions. When I developed my first macros, I sat for 20 minutes wondering why I could never seem to hit a breakpoint I set.

What I end up doing to ensure there are no surprises is to open the Exceptions dialog box, select the Common Language Runtime Exceptions node in the Exceptions tree control, and in the When The Exception Is Thrown group box, ensure Break Into The Debugger is selected. Figure 9-4 shows the proper settings. Probably this will cause you to stop in the debugger a lot more, but at least you won't have any surprises when it comes to your code.

In Figure 9-4, I didn't set JScript Exception, which is generated by JScript .NET, to stop in the debugger because I don't use it for my add-in development. If you're brave enough to whip up an add-in in JScript .NET, make sure to set the JScript Execution node to stop on all exceptions.

(continued)

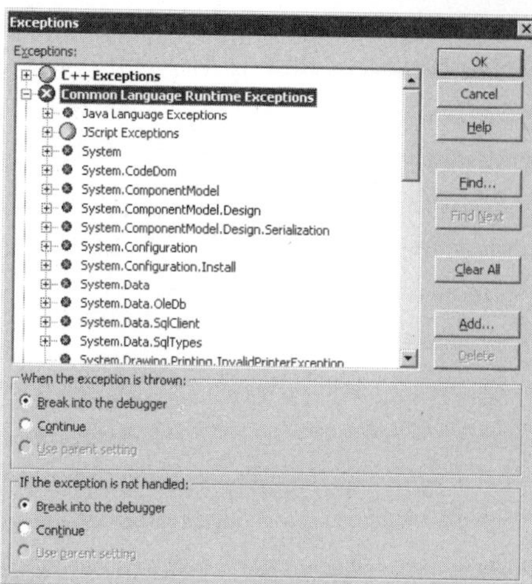

Figure 9-4 Setting the Exceptions dialog box to stop on all exceptions

One thing I've also noticed about debugging macros is that even when you set the Exceptions dialog box to stop on all exceptions, it might not. The trick to getting the macro debugger to start working correctly is to set a breakpoint somewhere in your code after you've set the Exceptions dialog box settings.

Introduction to Add-Ins

Macros are excellent for those smaller isolated tasks, but if you have more advanced UI or input needs or you want to protect your source code, you're going to have to turn to writing add-ins. Although writing a macro is much easier, add-ins allow you to handle the following tasks, which you can't handle in macros:

- Add your own tool windows and dialog boxes to the IDE.
- Add your own command bars (that is, menus and toolbars) to the IDE.
- Add custom property pages to the Options dialog box.

As you'll see in a moment, developing and debugging is much more difficult with add-ins than it is with macros, so I'd highly recommend trying to do all you can in macros instead of going through the hassle of add-ins.

Basically, add-ins are COM objects that plug into the IDE. If you were worried about losing all that COM knowledge you've learned over the last few years, don't be—you'll still need some of it in the add-in world. What's interesting is that since managed languages support COM, you can write your add-ins using Visual Basic .NET or C#. Although I like C++ as much as the next developer, I like the productivity enhancement of .NET even more, so in this chapter I'll concentrate on those issues related to writing add-ins in managed languages.

As usual, you should start your add-in journey by reading the documentation. Second, you need to visit *http://msdn.microsoft.com/vstudio/downloads/samples/automation.asp*, which is the page that contains all the add-in and wizard samples Microsoft has released. You'll definitely want to spend a good deal of time reading the code for those samples as that's the best way to learn.

Many of the add-ins are written in multiple languages, so you shouldn't have any trouble with them. Some of the more advanced samples, such as RegExplore, are available only in C++. I have to point out that the C++ code in Microsoft's samples is a perfect example of poor coding. Much of the code is rife with magic macros that do error handling through gotos and that rely on assumed names. Sadly, the same bad code is generated from the Add-In wizard. If you do choose to use C++ for writing add-ins, please don't follow Microsoft's example!

One item you'll want to make sure to check out is Unsupported Tools. You can either download it or find the current version in the UnsupportedAddInTools directory in this book's sample code. The tools contain a program named Generate ICO Data for Extensibility (GenerateIcoData.exe) that's necessary to get the hex stream for an icon so that you can put a custom icon in the About box. I'll show you how to do this in the next section. An additional tool contained in Unsupported Tools is a nice add-in named the Extensibility Browser (ExtBrws.dll), which will show you all the late-bound properties for the `DTE` (Development Tools Environment) object, which is the root of everything in the Visual Studio .NET extensibility model. Since some of these properties are not very well documented, having ExtBrws.dll to show them to you is helpful. If you're a COM programmer from way back, you can also use OLE/COM Object Viewer to browse these properties as well.

Fixing the Add-In Wizard–Generated Code

When you first create a C# or Visual Basic .NET add-in using the Visual Studio .NET Add-In Wizard, which you can find in the Other Projects\Extensibility Projects directory of the New Project dialog box, the code can stand some fixing up. In this section, I want to discuss what you want to do immediately after generating a skeleton add-in so that you can streamline your development and not drive yourself crazy with problems from the stock code. Along the way, I'll point out some key facts about how add-ins work so that you'll have an idea about why I make certain suggestions.

The very first task you need to do after clicking the Finish button in the Add-In wizard is open the Registry Editor. The Add-In wizard creates some registry entries you need to export to a .REG file. The registry key starts at either `HKEY_LOCAL_MACHINE` or `HKEY_CURRENT_USER` depending on whether you wanted the add-in available to all users. The rest of the key is the same: `\Software\Microsoft\VisualStudio\7.1\AddIns\`<*Add In Name*>. You'll want to save all the keys and values that are under your add-in name, which for the rest of this discussion I'll call the add-in key.

If you look at the key created by the Add-In wizard, you'll notice that some of the value names make perfect sense, such as `AboutBoxDetails`, `AboutBoxIcon`, `FriendlyName`, and `Description`. A couple of other keys need more explanation because they're extremely important to debugging and developing your add-in. The first is the `CommandPreload` key, which indicates whether the add-in needs to be told to register any commands it might want. Many of the problems I've run into while debugging add-ins are related to the commands not getting registered correctly.

The documentation for the `CommandPreload` key appears to be wrong; it's not a Boolean field. When the `CommandPreload` key is 1, Visual Studio .NET loads the add-in to register its commands. When the `CommandPreload` value is 2, Visual Studio .NET assumes the add-in has already registered its commands. If you're having trouble with your commands executing, forcing `CommandPreload` to 1 and restarting the IDE can ensure you get the command registered.

The `LoadBehavior` value in your add-in key describes how your add-in is loaded. It's a bit field where 0 indicates your add-in is not loaded. A value of 1 indicates your add-in should be loaded when the IDE starts up. A value of 4 indicates your add-in should be loaded when doing command-line builds. In Visual Studio .NET 2002, there were problems because add-ins were always loaded during command-line builds even when you marked your add-in as not used with command-line builds. Fortunately, this bug was fixed for Visual Studio .NET 2003.

Two registry keys that are not in the default Add-In wizard–generated code, but which you'll be adding if you want to have your own command bar bitmaps or other Win32 resources, are `SatelliteDllName` and `SatelliteDll-Path`. Although having your managed bitmaps and resources work in managed add-ins would be quite convenient, Visual Studio .NET speaks only COM, so you'll have to put your resources in Microsoft Win32 resource DLLs. As you can guess from its name, `SatelliteDllName` is only the filename of the DLL. The other value, `SatelliteDllPath`, indicates where the satellite DLL resides. The documentation for `SatelliteDllPath` indicates that the IDE will eventually look for the DLL in the path specified (prior searches will append locale-specific IDs to the directory path specified), but the IDE won't load it from that location, so you won't get any resources. For example, if you enter C:\FOO\ as your `SatelliteDllPath` and you're using American English as your locale, your satellite DLL *must* reside in C:\FOO\1033.

If you do have a satellite DLL specified, you can localize the values you specify in your add-in's registry key. If the string value you specify is an octothorpe (#) followed by a number, the IDE will look that value up in your satellite DLL's string table. Both the SuperSaver and SettingsMaster add-ins from this chapter demonstrate using satellite DLLs.

The odd, and final, registry value is `AboutBoxIcon`. It contains the bytes for the add-in icon you want displayed in the About box. As I mentioned earlier, the GenerateIcoData program that comes with the unsupported add-in tools generates the appropriate hexadecimal bytes necessary to plunk in the `AboutBoxIcon REG_BINARY` field.

If you look at the SuperSaver and SettingsMaster projects included with this book's sample files, you'll see that each has a *<project name>*.ADDIN.REG file that sets all the appropriate settings for each add-in. These REG files allow me to remove and quickly restore the appropriate registry settings without messing with installs. The one drawback is that you'll have to hard code the `SatelliteDllPath` value in it.

After getting the registry values for your add-in straightened out, you need to turn to getting the wizard-generated code corrected. Probably you'll want to first change the `ProgId` attribute associated with the generated `Connect` class. The wizard likes to add a ".Connect" to the add-in name, which is superfluous. Unfortunately, the Add-In wizard hard codes in the command name in numerous places, so if you remove the ".Connect" from the `ProgId` attribute, you'll need to change the name in the following places:

- The add-in registry key
- The command usage in the `QueryStatus` method (in CONNECT.CS/.VB)
- The command usage in the `Exec` method (in CONNECT.CS/.VB)

I'd highly recommend that you put your command names in a constant and reference that constant from any place that needs the names. In my add-ins, I have a file named RESCONSTANTS.CS/.VB that contains all constants associated with any commands. That way I ensure there are no typo problems, and if I want to change the command name, doing so is trivial.

Probably the biggest problem with the wizard-generated code is that it eats exceptions when registering commands and adding items to the toolbars. When I first started with add-ins, I went nuts wondering why some of my commands weren't available. It came down to the fact that the command was not registered because the registration had thrown an exception, which skips the rest of the function. The generated code looks like the following snippet, and that's quite dangerous. You should make it part of your code reviews to ensure that if empty `catch` expressions are used, they are something you truly feel safe allowing.

```
try
{
    Command command = commands.AddNamedCommand (...) ;
    CommandBar commandBar = (CommandBar)commandBars["Tools"] ;
    CommandBarControl commandBarControl =
                          command.AddControl ( commandBar ,
                                               1          ) ;
}
catch(System.Exception /*e*/)
{
}
```

All add-in command and toolbar creation occurs by default in the `OnConnection` method when the connection mode parameter contains `ext_cm_UISetup`. I always move my command and toolbar creation to a separate method outside of my `OnConnection` method. By the way, when you receive `ext_cm_UISetup` as the connection mode, your add-in is unloaded immediately after your `OnConnection` method returns. When the `ext_cm_Startup` or `ext_cm_AfterStartup` connection modes occur, your add-in is reloaded.

Before you register your commands and add any command bars, you'll want to remove any commands and toolbars you might have already added. That way you ensure that any commands you register and command bars you create for your add-in are created fresh. Removing added commands and toolbars will also allow you to safely change options for the commands or command bars and avoid any issues with exceptions that could occur if previous items of the same name exist.

To help with add-in development, I also always create a macro that will remove the commands and any command bars my add-ins create. That way I can also use the macro to get rid of the add-in traces. Before your remove commands macro can run, your add-in must be completely unloaded. That means you must uncheck the add-in from the Add-In Manager dialog box, shut down all running copies of the IDE, and delete the add-in registry key.

The command and toolbar creation methods all throw exceptions when anything is out of whack. You'll definitely want to make sure that you surround life with a `try...catch` block and that you report what failed inside the `catch` so that you'll know what's going on. You can look at both SuperSaver and SettingsMaster for examples of how to remove and install commands and command bars.

Handling Toolbar Button Issues

After getting the Add-In wizard–generated code straightened out, probably the next problem you'll run into is getting custom toolbar bitmaps to show up correctly. It's not that hard; it's just undocumented. It took me a while to get the magic incantations figured out, so hopefully this discussion will save you some time and frustration.

For custom toolbar bit maps to be loaded, they have to be placed in a Win32 satellite DLL; there's no way to use managed embedded bitmaps as toolbar bitmaps. When creating the command with `Commands.AddNamedCommand`, you'll pass `false` to the `MSOButton` parameter and the resource ID for the bitmap in your satellite DLL in the `Bitmap` parameter.

The biggest problem with custom toolbar bitmaps is the bitmaps themselves! The first problem is that only 16-color bitmaps are supported. If you're staring at your bitmap and it appears weird, you've got a high-resolution bitmap. The second problem is getting the mask right.

When I first looked at the sample add-ins custom bitmaps from the RegExplorer sample, green looked like the mask color. Getting the mask right is important as that's what allows the bitmap to look 3-D when the mouse cursor slides over the button. After creating my bitmap buttons, I used green as the mask. When I loaded my add-in, the mask sure didn't work, and all the places I wanted transparent were a bright, ugly green instead. After some poking around, I stumbled on the fact that it wasn't really green I was supposed to use as the mask but the RGB value 0, 254, 0. (Green is RGB 0, 255, 0).

However, even after changing my green in the palette to 0, 254, 0, the mask was still showing up as full green. I happened to be using an older painting program that was being "helpful" and "correcting" my palette to show green as 0, 255, 0 instead of the setting I needed. After I switched to using the Visual Studio .NET bitmap editor and reset one of the palette colors (I always reset the default pink to 0, 254, 0), life was good. Keep in mind that when you reopen the bitmap in the Visual Studio .NET bitmap editor, the editor will shift the green palette entry to 0, 254, 0 because that's the closest color to green. That means you'll need to change another entry to 0, 255, 0 if you want to use green in your bitmap.

After you get the mask color correct, you'll also want to update your code to ensure the toolbars look like the rest of the toolbars on the user's screen. By default, the toolbar buttons you add to a `CommandBar` object show up as buttons with text. To get the buttons to show up as the default buttons only, you'll have to manually loop through the `CommandBarControl` items in the `CommandBar` and set the style to `MsoButtonStyle.msoButtonIcon`. The following snippet from SuperSaver shows what you'll need to do.

```
foreach ( CommandBarControl ctl in
                                SuperSaverCmdBar.Controls )
{
    if ( ctl is CommandBarButton )
    {
        CommandBarButton btn = (CommandBarButton)ctl ;
        btn.Style = MsoButtonStyle.msoButtonIcon ;
    }
}
```

Creating Tool Windows

Whereas nearly every add-in that adds a command will offer a bitmap toolbar, some add-ins will want to move past simple commands and show a user interface in Visual Studio .NET. Bringing up a managed dialog box from an add-in is as simple as doing it from a Windows Forms application. Showing a full window, called a tool window, takes a little more work.

There are two types of windows in the Visual Studio .NET IDE, documents and tool windows. Document windows are where you edit code. Any other window is a tool window. Examples of supplied tool windows are the Task List window, Solution Explorer, and the Toolbox window. Tool windows can be docked in views, or if you right-click in the tool window title bar and deselect the Dockable option, they can appear as full windows in the main editing area.

As all tool windows are COM objects, you can always create them in C++ and live with any pain that entails. Although there's no documentation on creating tool windows in managed code, one of the supplied samples, appropriately called ToolWindow, shows how to properly get everything hooked up.

The basic idea for creating a managed tool window is to have your managed add-in create an ActiveX component that in turn hosts the common language runtime (CLR). Once that's going, you can direct the ActiveX component to load and display the desired user control inside the ActiveX window. This

ActiveX component is sometimes referred to as a *host shim control* because it simply pokes its way into the managed code operation so that you can get everything hooked up.

This host shim sounds like it might be pretty wild to write, but the good news is that Microsoft supplies a host shim control you can use with the ToolWindow sample. The bad news is that this host shim does nearly zero error checking, and, if anything fails, you're left scratching your head and wondering why things didn't work. The best news is that I went through the code and did some better error checking and added assertions so that you'll know what's going on when you use the host shim.

I renamed my host shim to VSNetToolHostShim and included it with a sample project named SimpleToolWindow, which is included with this book's sample files. SimpleToolWindow does nothing more than add a scratch edit window, a la WinDBG's scratch window, to the Visual Studio .NET IDE. Since creation of the host shim control is controlled by your managed add-in, any of your tool window projects can use VSNetToolHostShim directly.

The simplest way to explain how to get everything hooked up is to show you the `OnConnection` handler from SimpleToolWindow. The operation is to create the tool window with the VSNetToolWinShim control, which will return a reference to the VSNetToolHostShim control. Using the returned `VSNetToolHostShim` object, call the `HostUserControl2` method so that your managed control gets loaded and the button for the tool window tab gets created. Listing 9-3 shows everything in action.

```
public void OnConnection ( object             application ,
                           ext_ConnectMode    connectMode ,
                           object             addInInst   ,
                           ref System.Array   custom      )
{
    try
    {
        ApplicationObject = (_DTE)application;
        AddInInstance = (AddIn)addInInst;

        // Your tool window must have a unique GUID.
        String guid = "{E16579A4-5E96-4d84-8905-566988322B37}" ;

        // This'll contain the VSNetToolHostShim on output.
        Object RefObj = null ;

        // Create the main tool window by loading the host shim.
```

Listing 9-3 Using VSNetToolHostShim

```
        TheToolWindow = ApplicationObject.Windows.
            CreateToolWindow ( AddInInstance                        ,
                               "VSNetToolHostShim.VSNetToolWinShim",
                               "Scratch Pad Window"                 ,
                               guid                                 ,
                               ref RefObj                           );

        // Make the window visible. You must do this before calling
        // the HostUserControl method or things won't get hooked
        // up right.
        TheToolWindow.Visible = true ;

        // Get the shim. (This is a class level variable):
        // private VSNetToolHostShimLib.IVSNetToolWinShim ShimObj ;
        ShimObj = (VSNetToolHostShimLib.VSNetToolWinShimClass)
                    RefObj ;

        // Get this assembly so I can pass the location to the shim.
        System.Reflection.Assembly CurrAsm =
               System.Reflection.Assembly.GetExecutingAssembly ( ) ;

        // Get the directory to this Add-In and append the name of
        // the resources DLL to the path so I can load the tab
        // button.
        StringBuilder StrSatDll = new StringBuilder ( ) ;

        String StrTemp = CurrAsm.Location.ToLower ( ) ;
        int iPos = StrTemp.IndexOf ( "simpletoolwindow.dll" ) ;
        StrSatDll.Append ( CurrAsm.Location.Substring ( 0 , iPos ));
        StrSatDll.Append ( "SimpleToolWindowResources.DLL" ) ;

        // Load the managed control into the ActiveX control and
        // have it load the bitmap.
        ShimObj.HostUserControl2 ( TheToolWindow                    ,
                                   CurrAsm.Location                 ,
                            "SimpleToolWindow.ScratchPadControl" ,
                                   StrSatDll.ToString ( )           ,
                                   1                                );
    }
    catch ( System.Exception eEx )
    {
        MessageBox.Show ( eEx.Message + "\r\n" +
                              eEx.StackTrace.ToString ( )  ,
                          "ExceptBion in OnConnection"      ) ;
    }
}
```

Creating Options Property Pages with Managed Code

Creating managed tool windows is relatively easy. Trying to create managed property pages that plug into the Options dialog box is a little weirder. It's important to get your pages into the Options dialog box because that's the common place users will look to modify your add-in settings, and it gives you a polished look. Figure 9-5 shows the SettingsMaster options property page.

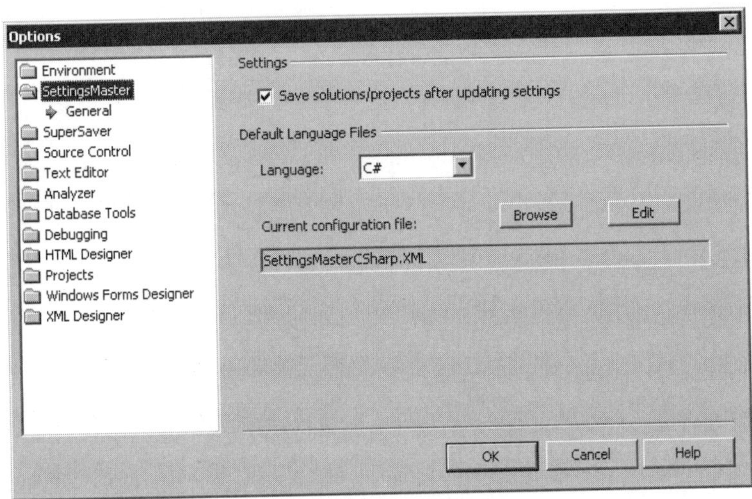

Figure 9-5 SettingsMaster Options property page

As you've probably guessed by now, an options property page is an ActiveX control that implements the `IDTToolsOptionsPage` interface. Visual Studio .NET finds out whether you have an options property page by looking in the add-in registry key. Under the main add-in key, it looks for an `Options` key. Under the `Options` key will be one or more keys that will be added as top-level nodes to the `Options` dialog box tree. By convention, you'll have one key and that's the name of the add-in. Under that key will be another set of keys that will form the subnodes underneath the top tree node. By convention, the first value will be `General`. Inside each final key will be a string value, `Control`, which contains the `ProgID` of the ActiveX control to create in order to show the property page.

It's probably easiest to show a complete key as an example. For the SettingsMaster property page in Figure 9-5, the registry keys are as follows:

```
HKEY_CURRENT_USER\
  Software\
    Microsoft\
      VisualStudio\
```

```
    7.1\
      AddIns\
        SettingsMaster\             <-- Add-In key
          Options\                  <-- Options key
            SettingsMaster\         <-- Root node in Options dialog
              General               <-- Sub node under SettingsMaster

Value item inside the General key
Control REG_SZ SettingsMasterShim.SettingsMasterOption
```

The Options dialog box, not your add-in, controls creation and management of the property pages, which is a small problem when it comes to writing your individual property pages in managed code. The problem is that because the specific control started up is the ActiveX control specified in the `Control` string value. This means the ActiveX control created will have to have a priori knowledge of the managed control you want to show. I was really scratching my head over this one when the February 2002 issue of *MSDN Magazine* landed on my desk and Leo Notenboom had an excellent solution for the problem in an article.

Leo's trick was to write the C++ ActiveX shim control so that it did all the work. Because there's no possible way to write a generic ActiveX control for option property pages, as you can for tool windows, you're going to have to create a new control for each project. Fortunately, all you really need to do is lift Leo's code, change the GUID and name of the control in the control's .RGS files and, in the C++ code, change the GUID of the control to load. You'll want to read Leo's excellent article on add-ins for a complete description of how his code works.

I took Leo's code and added a few assertions and some more error handling to make it easier to find problems. If you borrow either SuperSaverOptionsShim or SettingsMasterShim from this book's sample files, search for the `k_HOSTCLSID` string in the main .CPP files and replace the GUID that is embedded in the string with the GUID of your particular option page. Of course, change the control's name and GUID in the .RGS files.

When I first got my option pages to show up, I thought life was good. When I moved my add-in to my laptop and looked at the option property page, I realized something was wrong because my option property page didn't look anything like the other property pages in the Options dialog box. I'd used a little known trick on my laptop to get dialog boxes and tool windows to show up better (as my laptop has a pretty insane screen resolution): I changed the Dialogs And Tool Windows font in the Environment folder, Fonts And Colors node. Since managed controls default to a fixed Microsoft Sans Serif 8.25-point font instead of asking their host for the correct font, I needed to do the work myself to find the host-specified font.

Look in the SuperSaver project and see the control named OptionPropPageBase.CS. It's a base class that looks up the current dialog box font and size and applies those settings to all the controls on the page. You would think getting the font and size would be a trivial matter, but late-binding properties such as these are mostly undocumented. That's why the unsupported Extensibility Browser I mentioned earlier in the chapter is something very worth using. Once I figured out the magic incantations, I was home free. Listing 9-4 shows the magic in the `OptionPropPageBase.OnAfterCreated` method that gets the appropriate font, creates it, and sets the dialog box and all controls.

```
public virtual void OnAfterCreated ( DTE DTEObject )
{
    // To ensure this option property page looks right, I need to
    // set all the fonts to what the user chose as the Dialog and
    // Tool Windows font. I'll use the late-binding stuff to get
    // the values out of the DTE properties.
    Properties Props = DTEObject.get_Properties ( "FontsAndColors",
                                        "Dialogs and Tool Windows" );

    String FntName = (String)Props.Item ( "FontFamily" ).Value ;

    Object ObjTemp = Props.Item ( "FontSize" ).Value ;
    Int32  FntSize = Convert.ToInt32 ( ObjTemp ) ;

    // Create the font.
    Font DlgFont = new Font ( FntName              ,
                              FntSize              ,
                              GraphicsUnit.Point   ) ;

    // Set the font on the dialog.
    this.Font = DlgFont ;

    // Loop through all the controls on the dialog and set their
    // fonts as well. Some controls will pick the above up, but
    // not all so that's why I need to do this manually.
    foreach ( Control Ctl in this.Controls )
    {
        Ctl.Font = DlgFont ;
    }
}
```

Listing 9-4 Getting and setting the fonts for an option property page

Of course, simply setting the font is only part of the final job. Although the label controls can be set to automatic sizing, most controls can't be, so you'll need to loop through and increase the sizes for any controls that don't automatically resize. You can look at my `SuperSaverOptions.OnAfterCreated` method to see how I handle resizing for a specific dialog box.

You might be wondering why I don't have any code hooked up to change the dialog box fonts on the fly after someone requests they change. The good news is that for dialog box fonts, they can be changed just by restarting the IDE. Interestingly, Visual Studio .NET lets you change all other fonts on the fly, except dialog box fonts.

My cool OptionPropPageBase.CS code will take care of some work for you, but it does expose a bug in Visual Studio .NET that makes the tool very difficult to use. If you derive your option control from `OptionPropPageBase`, the IDE will no longer open your option control in design mode and will simply treat it as a straight text file. What you'll need to do is temporarily set the base class to your option control to `System.Windows.Forms.UserControl` so that Visual Studio .NET can load the control into the design view, allowing you to edit it with the designer. I certainly hope Microsoft gets this fixed in a service pack or a future version.

Common Debugging Question

I have an assembly that's loaded only in my add-in. Do I have to install it in the global assembly cache (GAC)?

The GAC is a special place, and you shouldn't install anything in it unless absolutely necessary. Fortunately, the Visual Studio .NET IDE designers were thinking smart, and under the <VS.NET Installation Dir>\Common7\IDE directory are two directories for add-in or macro-only assemblies: PublicAssemblies and PrivateAssemblies. If you want to allow other add-ins or macros to call code in your assembly, place the assembly in the PublicAssemblies directory. If you want the assembly callable only by your add-in, put it in the PrivateAssemblies directory.

Common Debugging Question

Are there easier ways of debugging add-ins since they can load into the IDE that you're using to debug?

Debugging an add-in can be a huge pain because you have to remove the add-in's registry key, open the add-in project in the target IDE, and restore the add-in keys so that spawned instances of the IDE you want to debug will have everything set up. Though not too onerous a task, you can easily mess these steps up. Additionally, if you need to compile the add-in because you fixed a bug, and the add-in gets loaded by the IDE, your build will never work

Fortunately, there's an undocumented command-line switch, `/rootsuffix`, that comes to the rescue. What `/rootsuffix` does is tell Visual Studio .NET to append a suffix to the normal registry key and load all packages, add-ins, and settings from that registry key instead of from the default. It's almost like having two separate installs of Visual Studio .NET on your machine.

The first thing you need to do is start up REGEDIT.EXE and scoot to the key HKEY_LOCAL_MACHINE\SOFTWARE\Microsoft\VisualStudio\7.1. After selecting the key, select Export from the File menu and save the registry keys to a file. Once you've saved the file, open it in NOTEPAD.EXE and replace all instances of "HKEY_LOCAL_MACHINE\SOFTWARE\Microsoft\VisualStudio\7.1" with "HKEY_LOCAL_MACHINE\SOFTWARE\Microsoft\VisualStudio\7.1NoAddIns." Notice the "NoAddIns" added as the suffix to the registry key. After replacing all the keys, save the file. Back in REGEDIT.EXE, select Import from the File menu, and import the changed file into the registry. If you'd like to move your user settings over to the same export (minus any add-ins, of course!), change and import steps with HKEY_CURRENT_USER\Software\Microsoft\VisualStudio\7.1.

To start Visual Studio .NET and have it use the key with the NoAddIns suffix, simply start Visual Studio.NET in the following way:

```
devenv /rootsuffix NoAddIns
```

This allows you to have a copy of Visual Studio .NET running in which you can play all you want with your add-in code without running into any problems.

The SuperSaver Add-In

Now that you have some idea of the issues associated with add-ins, I thought it best to discuss some real-world add-ins because they offer the best way to learn. The first add-in I created was SuperSaver, which originally appeared in a Bugslayer column I wrote in *MSDN Magazine*. However, the add-in version in this book is completely and radically different from the original and is an excellent example of the trials and tribulations associated with writing add-ins.

SuperSaver's job in life is to solve two problems. The first is to add a background automatic save to the Visual Studio .NET IDE so that you don't lose any changed documents. The second is to trim white space off the ends of lines when saving files. With C++ and C# files, the Visual Studio .NET IDE contradicts the computer gods and leaves the white space on the ends of lines. In order to make everything right with the world, I simply had to fix that.

Solving the background file saving was almost too easy. I set up a background timer, and whenever the timer triggers, I execute the command associated with the File Save All menu option, `File.SaveAll`. The problem was implementing the white space trimming.

As I played around with saving the active item, I noticed that the command that actually executed was `File.SaveSelectedItems`. Interestingly, instead of saving just the current document being edited, that command also saved the project as well as any items that were selected in Solution Explorer. (You can select multiple items with a Ctrl+left mouse click.) Since I wanted my command to be a drop-in replacement for `File.SaveSelectedItems`, I needed to mimic that behavior. My initial design was the following algorithm:

```
get the DTE.SelectedItems collection
foreach item in the selected items
    if it's a document and not saved
        get the text document
        call ReplacePattern on the text document
    end if
    call Save on the item
next
```

An algorithm that seems so simple certainly caused all sorts of problems for me. In all, I ended up writing seven completely unique versions of SuperSaver trying to work around issues. The first problem I ran into was related to the projects themselves. Not all project types support the `Save` method. The setup projects are a good example. This meant there was no guarantee I could save all the projects. I tried to special-case the calls to the `Save` method, but there was no way I could properly handle all the future project types that might not support the save.

The second issue I stumbled into was a bug in the `TextDocument` object. I was calling the `ReplacePattern` method with "[\t]+$" (without the quotes) as the regular expression search pattern and an empty string as the replacement text. Life was good, but that expression also will clear any blank lines that are simply indented white space. So if I saved the active file with the cursor indented 20 characters using tabs or spaces, the save would remove the automatic indenting and I'd end up having to type it all back in. Though I like my tab key as much as the next guy, I thought it would be better to fix SuperSaver to trim the white space only on the lines that actually contained text.

After many hours of messing around with regular expressions, I found the ultimate search expression, "{[^ \t]+}{[\t]#$}", and replacement expression, "\1". Subexpression replacement like this is one of the coolest things about regular expressions. In case you're not a regular expression maven, the search expression says to match any expression in the first group (delineated by the first set of braces) that contains any characters other than a space or a tab. This ensures that the match will occur *only* on lines that have characters in them. The second group (delineated by the second set of braces) says to match one or more space or tab characters at the end of a line. These two groupings will match only when there is white space at the end of the line. The replacement string "\1" tells the regular expression parser to replace the text with that matching the first grouping. In this case, the matching text is the characters at the end of the string *without* any white space. Thus, the white space is removed from the string.

I changed the parameter for `TextDocument.ReplacePattern` to my new search expression and let a save rip. The result was that any lines ending with extra spaces now ended with the ending text plus a "\1" that replaced the extra spaces! This was an interesting result, but the idea of actually corrupting the code probably would not make SuperSaver that useful. Come to find out, `TextDocument.ReplacePattern` has a bug in it that prevents subexpression substitution from working.

If I couldn't get regular expression subexpression substitution to work, SuperSaver wasn't going to be that useful. While playing around with different workaround possibilities, I recorded a find-and-replace macro that used a global `Find` object and worked with subexpression substitution. Although not as clean as the `ReplacePattern` method, it was at least the start of a workaround.

The first thing I realized about using the `Find` object was that because it's a global object, any changes I make to it while doing my regular expression subexpression substitution inside SuperSaver modifies the current values the user leaves in the Find dialog box. I created the `SafeFindObject` to wrap the `Find` object so that I could save and restore all the values, preventing the user from losing any settings.

An additional issue I found when using the global `Find` object was that when a Windows Forms designer was the active document, I could get the

TextDocument object for the document. However, the Find.Execute method, which does the actual search and replace, caused an exception. In SafeFindObject, I decided that the only thing I could do was to eat any exceptions thrown out when calling Find.Execute.

Everything was moving along when I decided I really wanted the auto save to strip trailing white space as well. After all the major work of simply trying to get the active document properly stripped and saved, I thought I was home free. Unfortunately, if I told the global Find object to do its magic on all files and any read-only files were open, things were not so good. Therefore, I simply looped through all open files and, if any of them were marked as read-only, I didn't call my SafeFindObject to do the trim white-space save.

Although I thought I had something going with the auto save, I noticed a problem when I had "virgin files," which are files created with File New but not saved. Calling the Save method on those files brought up the Save File As dialog box. I thought that since the dialog box was up, I'd find a blocking call inside the Save method. However, there wasn't a blocking call, so if I left the IDE running, I'd eventually have a bunch of Save File As dialog boxes up and life would become unhappy in the IDE.

At this point, I became a little obsessed with getting auto file saving to work in a way that would strip the white space off the end of lines. You might want to pull up TrimAndSave.CS and move to the TrimAndSave.SaveAll method to follow along with this discussion. Look for the commented out region marked "Original Attempt." I'll discuss why this code does not work in a moment.

Since I had the Find object working on the current file, I thought I could pop each file that needed saving to the foreground and save it quickly. That seemed reasonable until I ran into a whopper of a problem. If I had a Windows Forms document open in both design view and code view, calling the Active method for the document always activated the design view, even when the code view was the active window for that Windows Forms code. That meant that while I was typing along in the code view for a Windows form, an auto save would kick off, and I'd end up staring at the design view. Amazingly, there's no way to activate a code view from a document in the automation model.

My quest was to find the active document caption, i.e., the active window under the tab strip. Although you can call the DTE.ActiveWindow, doing so returns the window that currently has focus in all the IDE windows, not the window in which you're editing or designing. After a lot of poking, I saw that the Window command bar happens to always have the active document caption in the menu option that starts with "&1" (the ampersand indicates the item in the menu is to be underlined). It's really ugly to poke through a menu to get the actual active document caption, but there was no way to get it in the automation model. Armed with the active document caption string as well as the value returned by `DTE.ActiveWindow`, I could finally consider how to do the saving because I could at least restore the current active document window and the actual focus window.

As I looped through the documents, I needed to do a couple of things before I could save the file. The first was to determine whether the file was a virgin file by looking at the first character in the filename. If the first character was a ~ (tilde), the file was created but never saved. Because I wanted `TrimAndSave.SaveAll` to behave like a real auto save (see SlickEdit's Visual SlickEdit for the perfect auto save), I had the option of telling `TrimAndSave.SaveAll` not to save virgin files or read-only files. Doing that would allow me to avoid being inundated with Save File As dialog boxes each time the auto save was triggered. I could specify in SuperSaver's option dialog box that I wanted to skip virgin files and read-only files. If the file was a virgin file or a read-only file, `TrimAndSave.SaveAll` would skip the current file and loop back for the next one.

After I determined that the document needed saving, it was time to bring the document to the foreground so that the `DTE.Find` object could work on it. Since I needed to ensure that the text editing window of the file got brought to the foreground, I had to look for a window caption that had the same name as the document. If I found that window, I could finally strip the white space from the lines. If I didn't find a text window, I simply moved on to save the file.

If the file is a virgin file, I do my own Save File As dialog box, which is no big deal. If the file already has a name, I can simply call the `Document.Save` method. Interestingly, the `Document.Save` method is a classic example of how *not* to design your exception handling. If the file is read-only, `Document.Save` will pop up the dialog box that asks whether you want to overwrite the read-only file or save the file to a new name. If you click Cancel to skip saving the file, `Document.Save` throws a `COMException` class whose message is "User pressed escape out of save dialog." Because this is a normal user interaction, it should have been reported through a return value.

After winding through all the documents, I could finally turn to restoring the original active document window as well as the active window itself. After restoring the windows, I could turn to saving the projects and the solution.

With a project that needs saving, the first action is to determine whether the project is read-only. There's no property on a `Project` object that will tell you whether a file is read-only. Consequently, I have to get the project's file attributes and check them. If the project is read-only and the user doesn't want to be prompted on auto saves, I won't save that project.

If the project needs to be saved, some more fun begins. As I mentioned back in the "Problems with Projects" section, the project object model in Visual Studio .NET isn't completely thought out or well documented. Because the `Project` object doesn't map well onto a `VCProject` in particular, I attempt to get the `VCProject` out of a project by first checking the project's language. If the project is a C++ project, I call `Project.Object` and cast the return to a `VCProject`. Armed with the `VCProject`, I can call `VCProject.Save` with confidence. If the project isn't a `VCProject`, I attempt first to call `Save`, and if calling `Save` causes an exception, I call `SaveAs`, passing the full project name in each case. Because Microsoft hasn't fully documented the different types of projects, this is the best I can do to get the project saved.

Once the projects are taken care of, I can finally save the solution, if necessary. Like projects and documents, when the solution is read-only and the user doesn't want to be bothered with Save File As dialog boxes, I don't save the solution.

While I thought I had a working implementation, a little bit of testing quickly disabused me of that notion. As I tested the auto save a little bit with the white space strip option turned on, I thought there was too much flashing going on because of all the text windows being brought to the foreground. I remembered reading that the `DTE` object supported a `SuppressUI` property that, if set to `true`, blocked UI display when code was running. Figuring that `SuppressUI` would solve the flashing taskbar issues, I set it to `true` near the beginning of `TrimAndSave.SaveAll`. Alas, that seemed to have no effect whatsoever; the flashing continued unabated.

While I could have lived with the flashing, the other problem with using the `Window.Active` method was that it attempted to bring the whole IDE to the foreground, not just activating a particular document window. Additionally, if the IDE was minimized, `Window.Active` restored the window.

The final problem was that by using the `Find` object in the background save, which occurs on a different thread because of the timer, seems to mess up its state. Calling `SuperSaver.SuperSaverSave`, which I assigned to Ctrl+S worked fine. However, after a background save, whenever I used `SuperSaver.SuperSaverSave`, the Find/Replace message box that pops up after you've used the Find dialog box started appearing. While I loathe requiring you to turn off the Find/Replace message boxes to use SuperSaver, I was willing to consider it. You can turn off the Find/Replace message box by unchecking Show message boxes in the Options dialog box, Environment folder, Documents property page. With the Find/Replace message boxes turned off, I heard the default beep, like you do with the Find dialog box, every time SuperSaver.SuperSaverSave executed.

At this point, I was extremely frustrated, but bound and determined to get something working. Fortunately, my final attempt, while not perfect, got me mostly what I wanted. Since I was stuck using the Find object with the vsFindTarget.vsFindTargetOpenDocuments option, which dictates to search and replace in open documents only, I had to be careful. I could safely strip only white space in the background only if there were no read-only or virgin files in the active documents. While I would have really liked white space stripping on all files when doing a background save, this was the best I could do. To handle the save itself, the only option I had was to call the real File.SaveAll. Because I still wanted the option of not facing Save File As dialogs or overwrite warning message boxes popping up, I will not call File.SaveAll if the user has unchecked Save New And Read-only Files When Auto Saving in the SuperSaver options; there are no read-only files that need saving or virgin files in the active documents.

Of course, even though the above paragraph describes a fairly straight forward algorithm, I would have to run into one more bug. The Document.ReadOnly property, which is supposed to return true if the file is read-only, does not work. I had to manually check the file read-only state with the File.GetAttributes method.

I finally had two commands in my add-in, SuperSaver.SuperSaverSaveAll and SuperSaver.SuperSaverSave, that I thought were working fairly well. I turned my attention to creating a command toolbar for them and ran into the bitmap masking issues that I discussed earlier. After fixing those, I ran into the final problem with SuperSaver.

Since my intention was to write replacement commands for File.SaveSelectedItems and File.SaveAll, I wanted to make sure my toolbar buttons reacted in the same way they do on real toolbars. With lots of experimentation, I noticed that only the File.SaveSelectedItems button greyed out to indicate it was disabled. I tried everything I could think of to get my SuperSaver.SuperSaverSave toolbar button to behave the same way. Since the active state was controlled by what was selected in the current solution and project, I could not find the magic incantation of checks that File.SaveSelectedItems was performing to enable and disable its button.

Just as I was about to give up, it dawned on me that I certainly didn't need to go about it the hard way. All I had to do was retrieve the File.SaveSelectedItems command object and check whether the IsAvailable property was true; if it was, the toolbar button was enabled. Consequently, in my IDTCommandTarget.QueryStatus method, when the File.SaveSelectedItems command is not active, I return vsCommandStatus.vsCommandStatusUnsupported and all is right with my buttons and the world.

SuperSaver was a total pain in the neck to develop, but I'm glad I did it. Not only did it teach me a tremendous amount about the foibles of add-ins and the Visual Studio .NET IDE automation model, but I made the programming gods very happy by killing those spaces at the end of lines. In comments in SuperSaver, I left all the algorithms of what should work so that you can implement the commands again using the fixed versions of the automation problems in future versions of Visual Studio .NET.

The SettingsMaster Add-In

After all the fun I had on SuperSaver, I really wasn't looking forward to the next add-in I had to write for this chapter. In the end, SettingsMaster was not only problem-free but one of the most useful tools I've ever written. I certainly hope you find it useful as well.

As the name implies, SettingsMaster's purpose in life is to get all your settings straight. By settings, I mean all your build settings. Many of the bugs I've worked on over the years have come down to build problems, so I wanted some way, once and for all, to ensure the proper settings were actually in a project. Additionally, Visual Studio .NET is pretty poor when it comes to team development; the only way to set the build settings for multiple projects worked on by multiple developers is manually. This is a huge and very troubling hole in Visual Studio .NET. I wanted to solve these two build settings problems for both .NET and native C++ projects.

SettingsMaster adds two commands to the IDE. The first, SettingsMaster.CorrectCurrentSolution, uses the default configuration file (more on this file later) to automatically apply the settings you want. The second command, SettingsMaster.CustomProjectUpdate, prompts you with the Open File dialog box to select a configuration file for updating the project currently selected in Solution Explorer.

The idea is that you'll put all your common team settings in the common files, and whenever anyone creates a new project, he or she can click the SettingsMaster.CorrectCurrentSolution button and immediately start the project with the correct team settings. The SettingsMaster.CustomProjectUpdate command is for custom updating a project as you're prompted for the input file that contains the changes you want to apply. For example, if you decide to have a new define value in your C# projects, you can easily add that define value to them all.

The SettingsMaster property page in the Options dialog box, shown earlier (in Figure 9-5), allows you to set the default language files for each supported language. The initial version I provide supports C#, Visual Basic .NET, and native C++. It's an excellent exercise for the read to add J# to the mix. You can also choose to have the SettingsMaster commands automatically save the projects it updates after it fixes the build settings.

The configuration files that contain the settings are relatively simple XML files for ease of parsing and to be buzzword-compliant. Because the nature of the project systems for the .NET languages and native C++ is so different, each has different schemas. The basic idea is that the configuration files are language-specific and define the individual settings for each project configuration for that language.

For .NET projects, the basic schema is as follows. Table 9-2 lists the individual fields and what they mean.

```
<Configurations>
    <ProgLanguage></ProgLanguage>
    <Configuration>
        <ConfigName></ConfigName>
        <Properties>
            <Property>
                <PropertyName></PropertyName>
                <PropertyType></PropertyType>
                <PropertyValue></PropertyValue>
            </Property>
        </Properties>
    </Configuration>
</Configurations>
```

Table 9-2 .NET Project Configuration Schema

Node	Description
`<Configurations>`	The main element that contains one or more configurations.

`<ProgLanguage>`	Contains the string that describes the GUID string for the programming language supported by this file.
	
	Example:
	
	`<ProgLanguage>`
	`{B5E9BD34-6D3E-4B5D-925E-8A43B79820B4}`
	`</ProgLanguage>`

`<Configuration>`	The collection of properties for a single build configuration.

(continued)

Table 9-2 .NET Project Configuration Schema *(continued)*

Node	Description
`<ConfigName>`	The name of the configuration. Corresponds to a target configuration in the Visual Studio .NET IDE configuration manager. Example: `<ConfigName>Debug</ConfigName>`
`<Properties>`	The collection of properties for this configuration.
`<Property>`	The description of an individual property.
`<PropertyName>`	The name of a `Project` object property. This property must exist in the specific language's `Project` automation object. Example: `<PropertyName>CheckForOverflowUnderflow</PropertyName>`

`<PropertyType>`	Indicates the type for the property name. This can be only `Boolean`, `String`, or `Enum`. If the type is `String`, you must include an attribute type `OpType`, either `Overwrite` or `Append`, which determines how the string value will be changed. If the type is `Enum`, you must include an attribute type `Name`, which is the name of the enumerated type utilized by the specific `Project` property.
	Example:
	`<PropertyType>Boolean</PropertyType>`
	Example:
	`<PropertyType Name="prjWarningLevel">`
	`Enum</PropertyType>`

`<PropertyValue>`	The value you want the property to have. For `Boolean` types, this is either 1 or 0. For `String` types, it is the string you want either appended or overwritten. For `Enum` types, it is the numeric value of the enumeration. Example: `<PropertyValue>1</PropertyValue>`

Probably the easiest way to illustrate what a .NET configuration looks like is to show two stripped-down examples. Listing 9-5 shows the minimal configuration file necessary to turn on incremental building in a debug build and turn it off for a release build of a Visual Basic .NET project. Listing 9-6 shows how to set the warning level to `prjWarningLevel4` in a C# release build project only.

```
<Configurations>
    <ProgLanguage>{B5E9BD33-6D3E-4B5D-925E-8A43B79820B4}</ProgLanguage>
    <Configuration>
        <ConfigName>Debug</ConfigName>
        <Properties>
            <Property>
                <!--Turn on (/incremental+)-->
                <PropertyName>IncrementalBuild</PropertyName>
                <PropertyType>Boolean</PropertyType>
                <PropertyValue>1</PropertyValue>
            </Property>
        </Properties>
    </Configuration>
    <Configuration>
        <ConfigName>Release</ConfigName>
        <Properties>
            <Property>
                <!--Turn off (/incremental-)-->
                <PropertyName>IncrementalBuild</PropertyName>
                <PropertyType>Boolean</PropertyType>
                <PropertyValue>0</PropertyValue>
            </Property>
        </Properties>
    </Configuration>
</Configurations>
```

Listing 9-5 Visual Basic .NET SettingsMaster project for turning on incremental linking in a debug build and off in a release build

```
<Configurations>
    <ProgLanguage>{B5E9BD34-6D3E-4B5D-925E-8A43B79820B4}</ProgLanguage>
    <Configuration>
        <ConfigName>Release</ConfigName>
            <Properties>
                <Property>
                    <!--Turn on to level 4-->
                    <PropertyName>WarningLevel</PropertyName>
                    <PropertyType Name="prjWarningLevel">Enum</PropertyType>
                    <PropertyValue>4</PropertyValue>
                </Property>
        </Properties>
    </Configuration>
</Configurations>
```

Listing 9-6 C# SettingsMaster project for turning on warning level 4 in a release build

For native C++ applications, the configuration file schema is similar but has to take into account that native applications specify the tool you want to work on. The following code shows the basic schema, and Table 9-3 lists the individual schema fields and what they do.

```
<Configurations>
    <ProgLanguage></ProgLanguage>
    <Configuration>
        <ConfigName></ConfigName>
        <Tools>
            <Tool>
                <ToolName></ToolName>
                <Properties>
                    <Property>
                        <PropertyName></PropertyName>
                        <PropertyType></PropertyType>
                        <PropertyValue></PropertyValue>
                    </Property>
                </Properties>
            </Tool>
        </Tools>
    </Configuration>
</Configurations>
```

Table 9-3 Native C++ Project Configuration Schema

Node	Description
<Configurations>	The main element that contains one or more configurations.

<ProgLanguage>	Contains the string that describes the GUID string for native C++. This will always be the value in the following example.
	Example:
	`<ProgLanguage>`
	`{B5E9BD32-6D3E-4B5D-925E-8A43B79820B4}`
	`</ProgLanguage>`

<Configuration>	The collection of properties for a single build configuration.
<ConfigName>	The name of the configuration. Corresponds to a target configuration in the Visual Studio .NET IDE configuration manager. Example: `<ConfigName>Debug</ConfigName>`
<Tools>	The collection of tools for this configuration.
<Tool>	The properties for an individual tool.
<ToolName>	The name of the particular tool. This can be any of the specified tool objects supported by the VCProject object: VCAlinkTool, VCAuxiliaryManaged-WrapperGeneratorTool, VCCLCompilerTool, VCCustomBuildTool, VCLibrarianTool, VCLinkerTool, VCManagedResourceCompilerTool, VCManagedWrapperGeneratorTool, VCMidlTool, VCNMakeTool, VCPostBuildEventTool, VCPreBuildEventTool, VCPreLinkEventTool, VCPrimaryInteropTool, VCResourceCompilerTool, or VCXMLData-GeneratorTool. You can also specify the special VCProject object VCConfiguration to access the general options for projects. Example: `<ToolName>VCCLCompilerTool</ToolName>`

Table 9-3 Native C++ Project Configuration Schema *(continued)*

Node	Description
`<Properties>`	The collection of properties for this tool configuration.
`<Property>`	The description of an individual property.

`<PropertyName>`	The name of a project property. This property must exist in the `VCProject` automation object. If the property for the tool applies only to a DLL, add a `Type` attribute and set the value to `"DLL"`, and if the property applies only to EXEs, set the value to `"EXE"`. If the property applies to both EXEs and DLLs, do not include the `Type` attribute.
	Example:
	`<PropertyName>BasicRuntimeChecks</PropertyName>`
	Example:
	`<PropertyName Type="EXE">`
	`OptimizeForWindowsApplication</PropertyName>`

`<PropertyType>`	Indicates the type for the property name. This can be only `Boolean`, `String`, or `Enum`. If the type is `String`, you must include an attribute type `OpType`, either `Overwrite` or `Append`, which determines how the string value will be changed. If the type is `Enum`, you must include an attribute type `Name`, which is the name of the enumerated type utilized by the specific `Project` property.
	Example:
	<PropertyType>Boolean</PropertyType>
	Example:
	`<PropertyType Name="basicRuntimeCheckOption">`
	`Enum</PropertyType>`

`<PropertyValue>`	The value you want the property to have. For `Boolean` types, this is either 1 or 0. For `String` types, it is the string you want either appended or overwritten. For `Enum` types, it is the numeric value of the enumeration. Example: `<PropertyValue>4</PropertyValue>`

As with the .NET configuration, I want to show a couple of simple examples of native C++ project configurations. Listing 9-7 shows how to turn on whole program optimization for a release build. Listing 9-8 shows setting the .DEF file for debug and release builds.

```
<Configurations>
    <ProgLanguage>{B5E9BD32-6D3E-4B5D-925E-8A43B79820B4}</ProgLanguage>
    <Configuration>
        <ConfigName>Release</ConfigName>
        <Tools>
            <Tool>
                <ToolName>VCConfiguration</ToolName>
                <Properties>
                    <Property>
                        <!--Turns on /GL and /LTCG.-->
                        <!--(Whole program optimization!)-->
                        <PropertyName>WholeProgramOptimization</PropertyName>
                        <PropertyType>Boolean</PropertyType>
                        <PropertyValue>1</PropertyValue>
                    </Property>
                </Properties>
            </Tool>
        </Tools>
    </Configuration>
</Configurations>
```

Listing 9-7 Native C++ SettingsMaster project for turning on whole program optimizations in release builds

```
<Configurations>
  <ProgLanguage>{B5E9BD32-6D3E-4B5D-925E-8A43B79820B4}</ProgLanguage>
  <Configuration>
    <ConfigName>Debug</ConfigName>
      <Tools>
        <Tool>
          <ToolName>VCLinkerTool</ToolName>
            <Properties>
              <Property>
                <!--Sets the .DEF file for the project.-->
                <PropertyName Type="DLL">ModuleDefinitionFile</PropertyName>
                <PropertyType OpType="Overwrite">String</PropertyType>
                <PropertyValue>.\$(ProjectName).DEF</PropertyValue>
              </Property>
            </Properties>
          </Tool>
      </Tools>
  </Configuration>
  <Configuration>
    <ConfigName>Release</ConfigName>
      <Tools>
        <Tool>
          <ToolName>VCLinkerTool</ToolName>
            <Properties>
              <Property>
```

Listing 9-8 Native C++ SettingsMaster project to set the .DEF file in debug and release builds

```
                <!--Sets the .DEF file for the project.-->
                <PropertyName Type="DLL">ModuleDefinitionFile</PropertyName>
                <PropertyType OpType="Overwrite">String</PropertyType>
                <PropertyValue>.\$(ProjectName).DEF</PropertyValue>
                </Property>
              </Properties>
            </Tool>
        </Tools>
    </Configuration>
</Configurations>
```

If you want to look at complete examples for any language, the common files I've included with the SettingsMaster project set up your projects based on all the recommendations I discussed in Chapter 2. You can use the .NET projects as is, but you might want to change some of the defaults for the native C++ projects. In the C++ projects I turn on Unicode character strings and a few other settings I personally like, but these might cause problems for your projects. I marked each node that you might want to change with comments in the XML files.

SettingsMaster Implementation Highlights

Many of you might be happy just using SettingsMaster, but the implementation is moderately interesting. When I first started thinking about SettingsMaster, I started the work in a macro because it's so much simpler to deal with than a full add-in. I included the original macro with this book's sample files in the SettingsMaster\OriginalMacro directory if you want to look at it. Once I had the macro working, I didn't want to translate all that code into C#, so I went ahead and just implemented the add-in in Visual Basic .NET. Since Visual Basic .NET is simply C# without semicolons, it's trivial to slide between languages.

The hardest part of SettingsMaster was defining the XML schema. Since the files are relatively small, I could use the wonderful `XmlDocument` class to make navigating through the document trivial. If I were to do it all over again, I would look at the XML schema to see whether I could combine everything into one file. When you look at the code, you'll see that I have slightly more duplicated code in processing the two project types than I wanted.

The real magic to SettingsMaster is the wonderful trick of .NET *reflection*. The ability to create a class on the fly and call methods or set and get properties is one of the greatest features of .NET. Since I had the configurations and projects, I used reflection to create the individual tools and properties. I put a ton of comments in the code, so you should have no trouble following how everything works.

The biggest hurdle I faced writing SettingsMaster was creating an enumerated type value. Since .NET is strongly typed, if I couldn't create a specific `Enum` value, it was going to be hard to set the numerous settings both the `Project` and `VCProject` object exposed. After numerous false starts, I finally had to ask for help. Francesco Balena came through and reminded me that the `System.Enum.Parse` method does the job just fine. Once I had that method, everything else was simple grunt work through the XML files.

SettingsMaster Future Enhancements

SettingsMaster is very useful as is, but if you're looking for a project, there are plenty of enhancements you could add to SettingsMaster to make it even better:

- There is no configuration editor for the XML configuration files. Since the property grids are fairly easy to program, you might want to consider writing a configuration file editor so that you don't have to edit the configuration files by hand. This configuration editor should be accessible from the SettingsMaster command bar as well as the Options dialog box property page.
- One feature that would be relatively easy to add would be an event handler that watches when projects load and automatically updates the project settings.
- The `VCPlatform` object is where you can set some of the global options that pertain to native C++ projects. A neat feature to add would be support for this object so that users could set include directories and other properties to help with team development.
- A nice feature would be to add a command to write out the current project settings to a SettingsMaster configuration file so that you could apply those settings to other projects.
- To provide additional user feedback, you could also write out changes made by SettingsMaster to the Output window.

Summary

With the new macro and add-in capabilities present in the Visual Studio .NET IDE, developers now have the ultimate power to make the environment do exactly what they need to do to help solve their problems faster. In this chapter I wanted to show some of the gyrations necessary to build real-world–level macros and add-ins. Although there are still some quirks in the IDE, the overall picture more than makes up for it. I hope the holes I stumbled into and discussed will save you some time in developing your extensions to the Visual Studio .NET IDE.

Developers have been asking for the full power of Visual Studio .NET for a long time. We now have it, and I encourage you to implement the tools you've always dreamed about. The rest of us could use them!

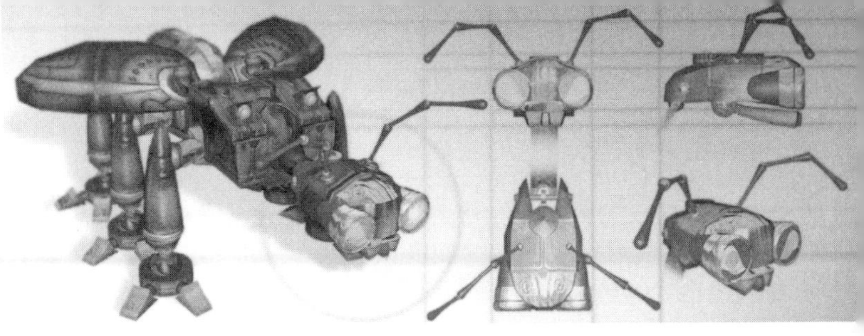

10

Managed Exception Monitoring

You might have guessed by now that Microsoft Visual Studio .NET development involves a lot more exceptions than traditional Microsoft Win32 development. The beauty of .NET is that exception handling was built in right from the beginning. It doesn't reflect the bolted and grafted feel for exceptions we've been wrestling with for the last umpteen years when working with Microsoft Windows applications and C++. Now exceptions are natural and fully supported.

As always, however, exceptions are for exceptional conditions. You don't want to use exceptions in place of constructs, such as `switch` and `case` statements, unless you're really into slow-moving code. In this chapter, I'll present a utility, ExceptionMon, that allows you to easily monitor the exceptions that occur in your application. Although you could always set all common language runtime (CLR) exceptions to stop when thrown in the debugger's exception dialog box, doing so would take forever because you'd have to do a ton of Continue-button pressing. With ExceptionMon, you can monitor the exceptions with almost no hassle.

ExceptionMon uses one of the coolest features of .NET, the Profiling API. I've written profilers and error detection tools without operating system support, and when I saw the .NET Profiling API, I immediately praised the development gods. The Profiling API is incredibly well thought out and works exactly as advertised. Its power allows you to see things that would essentially be impossible to view any other way. Interestingly, the name *Profiling API* is a little misleading because the Profiling API does so much more than allow you to time operations. By the end of the chapter, your head will be spinning with ideas for other advanced tools you can write with the Profiling API. In fact, I'll use the Profiling API in subsequent chapters as the basis for other cool tools.

Our journey to ExceptionMon will start with a discussion of the hows and whys of the Profiling API. After getting that out of the way, I'll explain how to use ExceptionMon and how it's implemented. Finally, I'll discuss exception usage as I see it in the .NET world.

Introduction to the Profiling API

The documentation and examples for the .NET Profiling API are not available from MSDN, but they are on your machine if you've installed Visual Studio .NET. The magic place is <Visual Studio .NET Installation Dir>\SDK\v1.1\Tools Developers Guide. In that directory, you'll find the Docs directory, which contains all the Word documents that describe everything from the Profiling API, to the Debugging API, to the Metadata API, as well as the complete ECMA specifications for the Common Language Infrastructure (CLI). The Samples directory contains examples of .NET compilers, Profile API examples, and an assembly dependency walker. There are many hidden gems among the documents and examples, and if you're at all curious as to how things work in .NET, the Samples directory is an excellent place to start your research. The document that describes the Profiling API is, appropriately enough, Profiling.DOC.

There are two ways to do profiling. The first way is though a process called *sampling*, in which the profiler peeks at the profilee at a specific number of millisecond intervals and checks what's running—hence the name *sampling profiler*. The other method is *nonsampling*, where the profiler monitors every call and returns synchronously so that it can track everything that occurs in the profilee. The .NET Profiling API handles both types of profiling very easily. As I mentioned in the introduction to this chapter, the Profiling API allows you to do much more than simple profiling. Table 10-1 provides the complete list of items you can be notified about when you write a program using the Profiling API. It's relatively trivial to get these notifications, so you'll probably see all sorts of very neat tools in the future.

Table 10-1 Profiling API Support

Item	Notification Types
Run time	Managed execution (all threads) suspended and resumed, individual managed thread suspend and resume
AppDomain	Startup, shutdown
Assembly	Load, unload
Module	Load, unload, attach
Class	Load, unload
Function	JIT Compilation, cache function search, pitched (removed from memory), inlined, unload
Thread	Created, destroyed, assigned to an OS thread
Remoting	Client invocation, client message sending, client receiving reply, server receiving message, invocation, server sending reply
Transitions	Managed to unmanaged, unmanaged to managed, COM VTable creation, COM VTable destruction
Run time suspension	Suspend, suspend aborted, resume, thread suspended, thread resumed
Garbage collection	Object allocated, allocations by class, moved reference, object references, root references
Exception	Thrown, search, filter, catcher entered, catcher found, call OS handler, unwind function, unwind finally, CLR catcher found, CLR catcher executed

The interface you'll implement to write a profiler is `ICorProfilerCallback`. Although writing profilers in managed code would be wonderful, because of the architecture supported by the Profiling API, you can't. Your profiler runs in the address space of the managed application you're profiling. If you could use managed code, you'd end up in all sorts of extremely dangerous situations. For example, if you were notified of a garbage collection operation taking place and you needed to allocate managed memory to store the items being collected, you'd end up triggering recursive garbage collection. Needless to say, Microsoft's architects chose the smarter route, which allows for minimal impact. To support managed profilers, all the notifications would have to occur cross-process, which would really slow down the profilee.

Since profilers are just COM DLLs, anyone who's been doing Windows development since 2000 should be familiar with the concepts. I encapsulated all the drudge work into a library that allows you to concentrate on the important stuff instead of messing around with the COM goo. I'll discuss ProfilerLib more in the next section. One key COM point I do want to make is that your profile

COM code will be called in a completely free-threaded model, so you'll need to do all the work to protect your data structures from multithreaded corruption.

In the ICorProfilerCallback interface, the only two methods that are always required are Initialize and Shutdown. Initialize is the very first method called. You are passed an IUnknown interface, at which point you'll immediately query for the ICorProfilerInfo interface and store the returned interface so that you can request information about the profilee.

Many of the ICorProfilerCallback methods are passed an ID of some kind. You'll use your stored ICorProfilerInfo interface to change the ID into a useful value. For example, the ICorProfilerCallback::ModuleLoadFinished method is passed a ModuleID value, which is the ID of the module just loaded. To determine the module name as well as other useful information such as the load address and the assembly ID, you call the ICorProfilerInfo::GetModuleInfo method. Additional tasks you can perform with the interface methods include getting the metadata interfaces, forcing garbage collection, and starting up in process debugging. I won't discuss everything about the ICorProfilerInfo interface but rather will refer you to the Profiling.DOC file for the whole scoop.

After saving on the ICorProfilerInfo interface in your ICorProfilerCallback::Initialize method, your next step is to tell the CLR which notifications you're interested in seeing. The beauty of the ICorProfilerCallback system is that you'll get notified for only the items you request, so the CLR can minimize resource usage and run the profilee as fast as possible. To indicate which items you'd like notifications on, you'll call the ICorProfilerInfo::SetEventMask method, which takes a bit field indicating the particular items you're interested in.

Table 10-2 lists each bit flag you can set. Most are self-explanatory. Some values—those with a Yes entry in the Immutable column—can be set only during the ICorProfilerCallback::Initialize method call. If a notification bit flag is not immutable, you can toggle the notifications at any time your profiler is running. If you want to see which notification flags are turned on, you can call the ICorProfilerInfo::GetEventMask method. Most flags are self-explanatory, but COR_PRF_ENABLE_OBJECT_ALLOCATED and COR_PRF_MONITOR_OBJECT_ALLOCATED need a little explanation. The former is set in your ICorProfilerCallback::Initialize method to indicate you want the CLR to set up to monitor object allocation. The latter is to toggle the notification on and off.

Table 10-2 `SetMethod` Notification Flags

Flag*	Immutable	Description
`ALL`	Yes	Turn on all notification flags.
`APPDOMAIN_LOADS`	No	Notify on each AppDomain load or unload.
`ASSEMBLY_LOADS`	No	Notify on each assembly load or unload.
`CACHE_SEARCHES`	No	Notify whenever the install-time code finds functions that have been run through Native Image Generator (NGEN).
`CCW`	No	Notify on each COM-callable wrapper.
`CLASS_LOADS`	No	Notify on each class load or unload.
`CLR_EXCEPTIONS`	No	Notify on each internal CLR exception handling.
`CODE_TRANSITIONS`	Yes	Notify on each transition from managed to unmanaged code or the reverse.
`DISABLE_INLINING`	Yes	Turn off method inlining for the entire process. If left enabled (i.e., not set), inlining notifications come through the `ICorProfilerCallback.JITInlining` notification.
`DISABLE_OPTIMIZATIONS`	Yes	Force the JIT compiler to disable optimizations.
`ENABLE_IN_PROC_DEBUGGING`	Yes	Enable in-process debugging to be used with the Profiling API.
`ENABLE_JIT_MAPS`	Yes	Enable JIT-map tracking.
`ENABLE_OBJECT_ALLOCATED`	Yes	Notify on each object allocated from the garbage collected heap.
`ENABLE_REJIT`	Yes	Force rejitting of install-time (NGEN) code generation so that JIT notifications are enabled for those functions.
`ENTERLEAVE`	No	Call function entry and exit hooks.
`EXCEPTIONS`	No	Notify on each non-CLR exception (i.e., all general exceptions).

Table 10-2 SetMethod Notification Flags *(continued)*

Flag*	Immutable	Description
FUNCTION_UNLOADS	No	Notify when functions are being unloaded.
GC	Yes	Notify when a garbage collection is about to occur.
JIT_COMPILATION	No	Notify on each function just before and after it's JIT-compiled.
MODULE_LOADS	No	Notify on each module load and unload.
NONE	No	Send no notifications.
OBJECT_ALLOCATED	No	Notify on each object being allocated on the garbage collected heap.
REMOTING	Yes	Notify on each remoting context crossing.
REMOTING_ASYNC	Yes	Notify on each remoting asynchronous event.
REMOTING_COOKIE	Yes	Generate cookies so that the profiler can pair remoting callbacks.
SUSPENDS	No	Notify when the CLR is suspended.
THREADS	No	Notify on each thread creation and destruction.

* COR_PRF_ or COR_PRF_MONITOR_ have been removed from flag names for clarity.

Once you return S_OK from your ICorProfilerCallback::Initialize method, you'll receive the notifications you requested through the appropriate ICorProfilerCallback method. I'll discuss more about what you'll do with those in a moment because I want to make a point about the only other required method, the ICorProfilerCallback::Shutdown method.

If the process you're profiling starts life as a managed application, your Shutdown method will always be called. However, if your application starts running as a native application that loads the CLR, such as Visual Studio .NET, your Shutdown method will never be called. To fully handle your profiler being stopped, you'll need to process the DLL_PROCESS_DETACH flag in your profiler's DllMain and check whether your Shutdown method has been called. If it hasn't, you'll need to manually clean up, keeping in mind that because the application is ending, you need to be cognizant of what operations you perform. For an example of how to handle this situation, see the ExceptionMon code.

Other than the specific algorithms necessary to implement your particular profile, the bulk of your work will be looking up the values passed to the different `ICorProfilerCallback` notification methods. Many of the notification methods are passed an ID value that you can use to retrieve the particular object information. These IDs, which are unique to the Profiling API, are simply memory addresses to the items. Fortunately, the `ICorProfilerInfo` interface offers methods to help turn these IDs into real values. This generally involves calling the appropriate `ICorProfilerInfo` method, getting the metadata interface directly related to the ID, and using the metadata interface to do the heavy lifting.

Metadata refers to the data that describes each .NET object. Making objects self-describing with metadata is the crux of .NET. When doing managed development, the metadata is accessible through reflection. When doing native development that needs to access metadata, there's a reader interface, `IMetaDataImport`, and a writer interface, `IMetaDataEmit`. Most of the work you'll be doing with your profilers will involve reading data with `IMetaDataImport`. The `IMetaDataEmit` interface is what compilers use to create the metadata in a .NET compiled binary. The metadata interfaces are discussed in detail in the Metadata Unmanaged API.DOC file, so I'll refer you there because much of the metadata manipulation is pure grunt work.

Probably the best way to show you how to deal with the IDs and metadata is to show how to return the class and method name from a function ID. Function ID values are passed to numerous `ICorProfilerCallback` methods such as `ExceptionUnwindFunctionEnter` (to indicate which function is being unwound), `JITCompilationFinished` (to indicate which function was just JIT compiled), and `ManagedToUnmanagedTransition` (to indicate which function is transitioning native code). The code in listing 10-1 shows the `GetClassAndMethodFromFunctionId` method from ProfilerLib, which takes care of getting the class and method name from a function ID. As you can see, it's just a matter of grinding through the metadata interface.

```
BOOL CBaseProfilerCallback ::
            GetClassAndMethodFromFunctionId ( FunctionID uiFunctionId ,
                                              LPWSTR     szClass      ,
                                              UINT       uiClassLen   ,
                                              LPWSTR     szMethod     ,
                                              UINT       uiMethodLen   )
{
```

Listing 10-1 `GetClassAndMethodFromFunctionId`

```
// The magic of metadata is how I'll find this information.

// The return value.
BOOL bRet = FALSE ;

// The token for the function id.
mdToken MethodMetaToken = 0 ;
// The metadata interface.
IMetaDataImport * pIMetaDataImport = NULL ;

// Ask ICorProfilerInfo for the metadata interface for this
// functionID
HRESULT hr = m_pICorProfilerInfo->
            GetTokenAndMetaDataFromFunction ( uiFunctionId        ,
                                              IID_IMetaDataImport ,
                                (IUnknown**) &pIMetaDataImport    ,
                                              &MethodMetaToken     );
ASSERT ( SUCCEEDED ( hr ) ) ;
if ( SUCCEEDED ( hr ) )
{
    // The token for the class.
    mdTypeDef ClassMetaToken ;
    // The total chars copies.
    ULONG ulCopiedChars ;

    // Look up the method information from the metadata.
    hr = pIMetaDataImport->GetMethodProps ( MethodMetaToken ,
                                            &ClassMetaToken ,
                                            szMethod        ,
                                            uiMethodLen     ,
                                            &ulCopiedChars  ,
                                            NULL            ,
                                            NULL            ,
                                            NULL            ,
                                            NULL            ,
                                            NULL             ) ;
    ASSERT ( SUCCEEDED ( hr ) ) ;
    ASSERT ( ulCopiedChars < uiMethodLen ) ;
    if ( ( SUCCEEDED ( hr )                ) &&
         ( ulCopiedChars < uiMethodLen )    )
    {
        // Armed with the class meta data token, I can look up the
        // class.
        hr = pIMetaDataImport->GetTypeDefProps ( ClassMetaToken ,
                                                 szClass        ,
                                                 uiClassLen     ,
                                                 &ulCopiedChars ,
                                                 NULL           ,
                                                 NULL            ) ;
        ASSERT ( SUCCEEDED ( hr ) ) ;
        ASSERT ( ulCopiedChars < uiClassLen ) ;
        if ( ( SUCCEEDED ( hr )             ) &&
```

```
                ( ulCopiedChars < uiClassLen )   )
            {
                bRet = TRUE ;
            }
            else
            {
                bRet = FALSE ;
            }
        }
        else
        {
            bRet = FALSE ;
        }
        pIMetaDataImport->Release ( ) ;
    }
    else
    {
        bRet = FALSE ;
    }

    return ( bRet ) ;
}
```

Getting Your Profiler Started

Up to now I've been discussing how profilers work but still haven't mentioned how you can get them started. Unfortunately, this process is the weakest link of the whole profiling system.

Two environment variables determine which profiler is loaded. The first environment variable you need to set to a nonzero value is `Cor_Enable_Profiling`, which tells the CLR that it's supposed to turn on profiling. The second environment variable is `Cor_Profiler`, which you'll set to either the CLSID or the ProgID of your profiler. The following shows how to set up the ExceptionMon profiler from the command line:

```
set Cor_Enable_Profiling=0x1
set COR_PROFILER={F6F3B5B7-4EEC-48f6-82F3-A9CA97311A1D}
```

Setting environment variables works great for Windows Forms and .NET console applications, but what about profiling Microsoft ASP.NET applications? Ah, there's the big rub. Since we're forced to set environment variables, you'll need to set the two environment variables in the system environment as shown in Figure 10-1 because that's where Microsoft Internet Information Services (IIS) and, in turn, ASPNET_WP.EXE/W3WP.EXE, will read the environment variables.

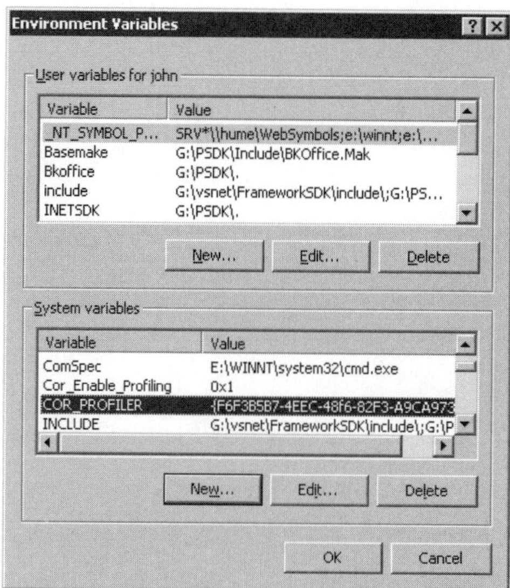

Figure 10-1 Setting the system environment variables

With Visual Studio .NET 2003 and the .NET Framework 1.1, you can restart IIS so that the new instance of ASPNET_WP.EXE picks up the new global environment variables. To restart IIS, bring up the Internet Information Services console, right-click on the machine name, point to All Tasks, and select Restart IIS from the shortcut menu. In the Start/Stop/Reboot dialog box, choose Restart Internet Services On <computer name> from the drop-down list and click OK. ASPNET_WP.EXE/W3WP.EXE won't start until you ask IIS for an ASP.NET application. To ensure your environment variables are set, you can use Process Explorer, which I introduced in Chapter 3: double-click on ASPNET_WP.EXE/W3WP.EXE in the upper window, and in the Properties dialog box, move to the Environment tab.

By setting the system environment variables, you'll run into another issue. Because these are system-wide, any process that loads the CLR is automatically profiled. That might be your intention, but with more and more processes loading the CLR, you can really get into trouble quickly. For example, if you have a bug in your profiler (which I know won't happen, but just humor me), and you go to debug your profiler with Visual Studio .NET, you'll also get your profiler loaded into Visual Studio .NET, which can end up ruining your debugging experience. One option is to use remote debugging, but the option I prefer is to set up another environment variable to indicate which process or processes you want your profiler to run in. That way you can check a specific environment variable at startup and determine whether you're supposed to run in that particular process. If you don't want to run in the process, simply call ICorProfilerInfo::SetEventMask, passing COR_PRF_MONITOR_NONE as the mask in your ICorProfilerCallback::Initialize method.

Since checking to see whether you want your profiler running in a particular process is such a common operation, I implemented the method CBaseProfilerCallback::SupposedToProfileThisProcess in ProfilerLib to do the check for you. Pass the environment variable to check because the parameter and the function will return TRUE in the following conditions:

1. The environment variable is not set, which assumes you want to profile all processes.
2. The value of the environment variable matches the current process drive, path, and name completely.
3. The value of the environment variable matches just the filename of the current process.

At this point, I want to end the basic introduction to the Profiling API. You can do quite a bit more with it, which I didn't cover. However, instead of making your eyes glaze over with detail after detail and leaving you to wonder about how you'd apply the Profiling API, I think the best approach to explaining it is to show you some of the more advanced features as they apply to solving problems. By the end of these two chapters that touch on the Profiling API, you'll have a much more in-depth understanding than you'd have from just the Profiling.DOC.

ProfilerLib

Before we get into the guts of the ExceptionMon profiler, I want to spend a little time talking about ProfilerLib. As you can probably guess from the discussions about the COM Profiling API so far, there's a lot of boilerplate code. Since I'm not really into typing the same thing over and over when I develop software, I quickly realized that I needed a library to do the grunt work, especially given the large number of methods supported by the ICorProfilerCallback interface.

The two sample profilers that come with the Visual Studio .NET also take the tack of reusing all the COM goo code, but the way their code is written is a little ugly in that it mixes all the infrastructure stuff in with some helper data structures. I was working on fixing this when Matt Pietrek's December 2001 "Under the Hood" column came out in *MSDN Magazine*. Matt had taken the profiler sample code and cleaned out some of the messy stuff. I figured that was a good starting point, so I took Matt's code and spiffed it up even more, making the writing of a profiler even simpler.

Setting up to use ProfilerLib is quite easy. The first step is to create a DLL project and set it up to link against ProfilerLib.LIB, and in your project's STDAFX.H, include ProfileLib.H. In one of your CPP files, define the following variables and assign their values to the particular values necessary for your profiler:

```
//The profiler GUID string
wchar_t * G_szProfilerGUID
// The profiler CLSID
GUID G_CLSID_PROFILER
// The profiler ProgID prefix
wchar_t * G_szProgIDPrefix
// The profiler name
wchar_t * G_szProfilerName

// As an example, here's the values specified for ExceptionMon
wchar_t * G_szProfilerGUID =
                            L"{F6F3B5B7-4EEC-48f6-82F3-A9CA97311A1D}" ;

GUID G_CLSID_PROFILER =
    { 0xf6f3b5b7 , 0x4eec , 0x48f6 ,
    { 0x82 , 0xf3 , 0xa9 , 0xca , 0x97 , 0x31 , 0x1a , 0x1d } } ;

wchar_t * G_szProgIDPrefix = L"ExceptionMonProfiler" ;

wchar_t * G_szProfilerName = L"ExceptionMon" ;
```

After declaring the unique COM goo values, add a `DllMain` to your CPP file, like the following:

```
    HINSTANCE G_hInst = NULL ;
    extern "C" BOOL WINAPI DllMain ( HINSTANCE hInstance ,
                                     DWORD     dwReason  ,
                                     LPVOID              )
    {
        switch ( dwReason )
        {
            case DLL_PROCESS_ATTACH:
                DisableThreadLibraryCalls ( hInstance ) ;
                G_hInst = hInstance ;
                break ;
            default :
                break ;
        }
        return( TRUE ) ;
    }
```

ProfilerLib has a base class in it, `CBaseProfilerCallback`, that implements all the methods necessary for the `ICorProfilerCallback` interface. You'll derive your particular profiler callback class from `CBaseProfilerCallback` and override the particular methods you're interested in receiving notifications for. That way you can concentrate on the important parts that you need, not the rest of the methods that will just get in the way.

After you've named your derived class, you'll need to implement a function, `AllocateProfilerCallback`, with the following prototype. In that function, allocate your `CBaseProfilerCallback`-derived class and return it. The rest of the code in ProfilerLib.h will take care of everything else.

```
ICorProfilerCallback * AllocateProfilerCallback ( ) ;
```

Finally, you'll need to take the EXAMPLE.DEF file out of ProfilerLib, copy it to your project, rename it, and replace the `LIBRARY` statement in it to properly do all the exports necessary to make a COM DLL.

In addition to taking care of all the COM goo for you, ProfilerLib also adds additional methods to `CBaseProfilerCallback` that will make your life easier. Some of them I've already mentioned in this chapter, but there are others. Whenever I run across anything that I think I might want to reuse, I add it to ProfilerLib, so make sure you check out the project files to see what other time-saving routines are already written for you.

As you'd expect by now from my code, there's a sample program, DoNothing, in the Tests directory under the ProfilerLib directory. It's the simplest profiler you can make and shows you exactly how to use ProfilerLib. It does process all notifications, but it simply beeps when initializing and unloading. That's my patented "Debug-by-Ear" method of development. Additionally, all the other utilities I wrote that utilize the Profiling API use ProfilerLib as their base classes, so you can see more advanced usage. ProfilerLib has saved me a ton of time, and I hope it will save you a great deal of time as well.

ExceptionMon

Once I had ProfilerLib up and running, I was able to start ExceptionMon. Looking at the `ICorProfilerCallback` interface, you'll see that you have all sorts of amazing callbacks to let you know exactly what processing is happening when an exception occurs. It's almost like someone at Microsoft was reading my mind! At an initial glance, you might think that ExceptionMon was absolutely trivial to implement. As usual, reality was a little bit different.

In my design for ExceptionMon, I wanted to record which exception was thrown, which finally handlers were called, and where the exception was handled. The exception handling notification methods in the `ICorProfilerCallback` interface, listed in the following code, fit the bill exactly. The fact that you also get the function IDs as well as the object ID of the exception thrown and caught is icing on the cake.

```
STDMETHOD ( ExceptionThrown ) ( ObjectID thrownObjectId ) ;
STDMETHOD ( ExceptionUnwindFinallyEnter ) ( FunctionID functionId ) ;
STDMETHOD ( ExceptionCatcherEnter ) ( FunctionID functionId ,
                                      ObjectID   objectId     ) ;
```

I quickly whipped up the initial ExceptionMon using ProfilerLib, writing the output to a logging file in the same directory the process ExceptionMon is loaded into. The first small issue I ran into was how to best debug ExceptionMon. Since the CLR does all the work to bring the specified profiler into the address space, I wanted to ensure I could start debugging right from the beginning. Since you already have to utilize environment variables to get the profiler started, I decided to go ahead and add one, `EXPMONBREAK`, which, if set, would cause ExceptionMon to call `DebugBreak` so that I could get a debugger attached.

Although you can debug the profiler like you would with any native DLL loaded into a process, I prefer the `DebugBreak` call because the profiler will be loaded into Visual Studio .NET since it hosts the CLR. You can always limit the process loading by setting the `EXPMONPROC` environment variable to set just the single process to debug. However, for development and testing purposes, I like to run multiple programs to test. By using the `EXPMONBREAK` scheme, I can get multiple debuggers attached to multiple processes easily.

Because I am mentioning environment variables, I need to talk about two that are primarily for handling ASPNET_WP.EXE/W3WP.EXE exception monitoring. By default, ExceptionMon doesn't flush the output file, so you need to stop ASPNET_WP.EXE/W3WP.EXE to see any reported exceptions. However, if you set the `EXPMONFLUSH` environment variable, all writes are flushed immediately.

The other issue with file writing is that ExceptionMon will put the logging file into the same directory as the process, but that's a problem because the default ASPNET account probably doesn't have permission to create files in %SYSTEMROOT%\Microsoft.NET\Framework\%FRAMEWORKVERSION%, which is where ASPNET_WP.EXE resides. For Windows Server 2003, the account is NETWORK SERVICE and W3WP.EXE resides in %SYSTEMROOT%\System32\inetsrv. The `EXPMONFILENAME` environment variable is where you can specify the complete path and filename for the output file for ExceptionMon. Obviously, you'll have to double-check that the ASPNET user account has create and write permission to the directory.

The initial version of ExceptionMon worked great because you were handed the function ID and object IDs and could simply call the appropriate methods in the `ICorProfilerInfo` interface to acquire the class and function tokens to look up names in the metadata. The code in Listing 10-1, `CBaseProfilerCallback::GetClassAndMethodFromFunctionId`, shows all the work necessary to look up the class and method names from a function ID.

In-Process Debugging and ExceptionMon

Once the basic version was up and running, I thought a useful feature would be to add a stack trace whenever an exception was thrown. That way you could see how you got into the situation in the first place and could take a look at the conditions. Looking at the documentation for the profiling API, I noticed you could pass a bit option to `ICorProfilerInfo::SetEventMask`—`COR_PRF_ENABLE_INPROC_DEBUGGING`—to turn on in-process debugging.

With in-process debugging, the profiling API gives you notifications of events, but you'll need some way of gathering more detailed information that you can get through the `ICorProfilerInfo` interface. Since Microsoft has already developed a fine advanced debugging API that works hand-in-hand with the CLR, the idea was to give us a limited version of the debugging API, which can perform tasks like look up live variable values and walk the stack.

The complete debugging API is discussed in the DebugRef.DOC in the same directory as the profiling API and metadata API documents. As with all documents found in the Tools Developers Guide directory, DebugRef.DOC is long on describing the interface, method, and parameter values, and pretty short on usage. The Samples directory contains a working debugger that's about 98 percent of the real CORDBG source code, but the actual code is sometimes confusing to follow although it will eventually reveal its secrets.

When reading over the debugging API documentation, pay special attention to which methods are callable from in-process debugging. If the method has "Not Implemented In-Process" in green text below its name, you can't use the method. What you'll find is that most of the methods you can't use are related to setting breakpoints and changing values. Since the main reason you'll need the in-process debugging is simply for information gathering, the important parts are fully accessible.

The first step to using in-process debugging with the profiling API is to set the `COR_PRF_ENABLE_INPROC_DEBUGGING` flag when calling `ICorProfilerInfo::SetEventMask`. Interestingly, simply setting that flag causes two side effects. The first is that once you request in-process debugging, the profilee will run slower. That's because the CLR won't use any precompiled code that is compiled with NGEN.EXE, thus forcing that code to be jitted like it normally would. You might not be using NGEN.EXE, but the .NET Framework uses it quite a bit, so that's where you'll take the hit.

If you've run NGEN.EXE, you might have noticed that you have a command-line option named /PROF that adds profiling information to generated code. Although you might think it's worth a shot, the profiling API currently doesn't support it, so you can't use it. I still think the limitations of slower code are worth it because of the benefits.

The second issue you'll run into is undocumented and completely confused me when I first encountered it. The ICorProfilerCallback::ExceptionThrown method is passed an object ID that describes the class being thrown. With my first implementation, which didn't use in-process debugging, I always got an ID I could pass to CBaseProfilerCallback::GetClassAndMethodFromFunctionId. Simply adding the COR_PRF_ENABLE_INPROC_DEBUGGING flag to ICorProfilerInfo::SetEventMask and not even using the actual in-process debugging API changes something internally so that an object ID of 0 is the only thing passed. Even though the in-process debugging API had the necessary methods to find the information, it was quite disconcerting to wonder what had happened to my object ID simply because I tripped a flag!

To use the debugging interfaces, you first have to call the ICorProfilerInfo::BeginInprocDebugging method to start the process of acquiring the appropriate interface. As part of that call, you'll pass a DWORD pointer to a context cookie. You'll need to save that cookie so that you can pass it to the ICorProfilerInfo::EndInProcDebugging method you have to call to indicate you're stopping in-process debugging. The second step is to acquire the appropriate debugging interface. If you're interested only in the current thread, you call the ICorProfilerInfo::GetInprocInspectionIThisThread method to get the IUnknown interface, which you can query for the ICorDebugThread interface. If you want to do process-wide debugging, you call the ICorProfilerInfo::GetInprocInspectionInterface and query the return IUnknown for ICorDebug. Personally, I don't see why the two ICorProfilerInfo methods can't simply return the appropriate interfaces.

Once you have the debugging interface, you're all set to access the debugging API to get the information you need from it. In my case, I wanted to get the last exception on the thread, so all I needed to do was call the ICorDebugThread::GetCurrentException method to get the ICorDebugValue interface, which describes the last exception thrown. The odd thing was that every time I called the ICorDebugThread::GetCurrentException method, it failed, so I was really starting to wonder if I was ever going to get ExceptionMon working!

After a very careful read of the profiling and debugging API documents, I came across a statement saying that in order to have in-process debugging do any stack operations, you need to call ICorDebugThread::EnumerateChains. The debugging API uses the concept of stack chains to string together the managed and native stack traces, which add up to the complete stack trace. I couldn't see that calling ICorDebugThread::GetCurrentException would have anything to do with the stack, but I figured it was worth a try to call ICorDebugThread::EnumerateChains before I did anything else. Though not documented—at least not clearly—I figured out that to do anything with the debugging API, you need to call ICorDebugThread::EnumerateChains first or most methods will fail. Listing 10-2 shows the wrapper method I use inside ExceptionMon to get in-process debugging started.

```
HRESULT CExceptionMon ::
    BeginInprocDebugging ( LPDWORD              pdwProfContext    ,
                           ICorDebugThread **   pICorDebugThread  ,
                           ICorDebugChainEnum ** pICorDebugChainEnum )
{
    // Tell the profiling API I want to get the in-process debugging
    // stuff.
    HRESULT hr = m_pICorProfilerInfo->
                       BeginInprocDebugging ( TRUE           ,
                                              pdwProfContext );

    ASSERT ( SUCCEEDED ( hr ) ) ;
    if ( SUCCEEDED ( hr ) )
    {
        IUnknown * pIUnknown = NULL ;

        // Ask the profiling API for the IUnknown I can get the
        // ICorDebugThread interface from.
        hr = m_pICorProfilerInfo->
                    GetInprocInspectionIThisThread ( &pIUnknown ) ;
        ASSERT ( SUCCEEDED ( hr ) ) ;
        if ( SUCCEEDED ( hr ) )
        {
            hr = pIUnknown->
                     QueryInterface ( __uuidof ( ICorDebugThread ) ,
                                      (void**)pICorDebugThread      ) ;
            ASSERT ( SUCCEEDED ( hr ) ) ;

            // No matter what happens, I don't need the IUnknown any
            // more.
            pIUnknown->Release ( ) ;

            // I'm doing this as part of the normal processing because
            // if you don't call ICorDebugThread::EnumerateChains as
            // the first thing called off ICorDebugThread, many of the
```

Listing 10-2 BeginInprocDebugging

```
            // other methods will fail.
            if ( SUCCEEDED ( hr ) )
            {
                hr = (*pICorDebugThread)->
                            EnumerateChains ( pICorDebugChainEnum ) ;
                ASSERT ( SUCCEEDED ( hr ) ) ;
                if ( FAILED ( hr ) )
                {
                    (*pICorDebugThread)->Release ( ) ;
                }
            }
        }
    }
    return ( hr ) ;
}
```

Once I was able to get `ICorDebugThread::GetCurrentException` to return a proper value, I thought I was home free because all I had to do was get the class name from the `ICorDebugValue`. Alas, looking through all the interfaces related to values—`ICorDebugGenericValue`, `ICorDebugHeapValue`, `ICorDebugObjectValue`, `ICorDebugReferenceValue`, and `ICorDebugValue`—I realized there was obviously a lot more to it because only `ICorDebugObjectValue` had the `GetClass` method necessary to get the class interface that would get the name. That meant I had to do some work to translate the original `ICorDebugValue` from `ICorDebugThread::GetCurrentException` into the `ICorDebugObjectValue`. The easiest thing for me to do is show you the code that does all the work in Listing 10-3. As you can see, it's a matter of dereferencing the object and querying for the `ICorDebugObjectValue` interface.

```
HRESULT CExceptionMon ::
    GetClassNameFromValueInterface ( ICorDebugValue * pICorDebugValue ,
                                     LPTSTR           szBuffer        ,
                                     UINT             uiBuffLen        )
{
    HRESULT hr = S_FALSE ;

    ICorDebugObjectValue * pObjVal = NULL ;

    ICorDebugReferenceValue * pRefVal = NULL ;

    // Get the reference to this value. Exceptions should come in this
    // way. If getting the ICorDebugReferenceValue fails, the type is
    // ICorDebugGenericValue. There's nothing I can do with a
    // ICorDebugGenericValue as I need the class name.
    hr = pICorDebugValue->
```

Listing 10-3 `GetClassNameFromValueInterface`

```
            QueryInterface ( __uuidof ( ICorDebugReferenceValue ),
                             (void**)&pRefVal                    );
    if ( SUCCEEDED ( hr ) )
    {
        // Dereference the value.
        ICorDebugValue * pDeRef ;
        hr = pRefVal->Dereference ( &pDeRef ) ;

        if ( SUCCEEDED ( hr ) )
        {
            // Now that I dereferenced, I can ask for the object value.
            hr = pDeRef->
                    QueryInterface ( __uuidof ( ICorDebugObjectValue ),
                                     (void**)&pObjVal                 );

            // I no longer need the dereference.
            pDeRef->Release ( ) ;
        }
        // I no longer need the reference.
        pRefVal->Release ( ) ;
    }

    ASSERT ( SUCCEEDED ( hr ) ) ;
    if ( SUCCEEDED ( hr ) )
    {
        // Get the class interface for this object.
        ICorDebugClass * pClass ;

        hr = pObjVal->GetClass ( &pClass ) ;

        // I don't need the object reference any more.
        pObjVal->Release ( ) ;

        ASSERT ( SUCCEEDED ( hr ) ) ;
        if ( ( SUCCEEDED ( hr ) ) )
        {
            // Gotta have the class type def token value.
            mdTypeDef ClassDef ;
            hr = pClass->GetToken ( &ClassDef ) ;

            ASSERT ( SUCCEEDED ( hr ) ) ;
            if ( SUCCEEDED ( hr ) )
            {
                // In order to look up the class token, I need the
                // module so I can query for the meta data interface.
                ICorDebugModule * pMod ;
                hr = pClass->GetModule ( &pMod ) ;

                ASSERT ( SUCCEEDED ( hr ) ) ;
                if ( SUCCEEDED ( hr ) )
                {
                    // Get the metadata.
```

(continued)

```
                IMetaDataImport * pIMetaDataImport = NULL ;

                hr = pMod->
                    GetMetaDataInterface ( IID_IMetaDataImport ,
                               (IUnknown**)&pIMetaDataImport    ) ;

                ASSERT ( SUCCEEDED ( hr ) ) ;
                if ( SUCCEEDED ( hr ) )
                {
                    // Finally, get the class name.
                    ULONG ulCopiedChars ;

                    hr = pIMetaDataImport->
                              GetTypeDefProps ( ClassDef          ,
                                                szBuffer          ,
                                                uiBuffLen         ,
                                                &ulCopiedChars    ,
                                                NULL              ,
                                                NULL              ) ;
                    ASSERT ( ulCopiedChars < uiBuffLen ) ;
                    if ( ulCopiedChars == uiBuffLen )
                    {
                        hr = S_FALSE ;
                    }

                    pIMetaDataImport->Release ( ) ;
                }
                pMod->Release ( ) ;
            }
        }
        pClass->Release ( ) ;
    }
}
return ( hr ) ;
}
```

After getting the class name of the exception, I just had to walk the stack. I'd already gotten the `ICorDebugChainEnum` interface, so walking the stack was a simple matter of following the algorithm discussed in the DebugRef.DOC file. The only interesting issue regarding the stack walking is that you can't walk native stacks with the debugging API. To check whether a chain is a native, call `ICorDebugChain::IsManaged`.

I've found ExceptionMon to be invaluable to help me keep an eye on the exceptions my applications are generating. I'm perfectly happy with the text file output, but you might want to consider adding an option to push the output over to a GUI application so that you can see the exceptions in almost real time. Adding that option isn't a huge programming exercise and would be an excellent way to learn about Windows Forms programming!

Exception Usage in .NET

Now that ExceptionMon is keeping an eye on your exceptions, I want to discuss using exceptions in .NET. The fact that .NET has exceptions built right in is certainly a cause for rejoicing. For those of us who came from C++ Win32 land, C++ exceptions were a great idea, but the implementation left a huge amount to be desired. Because .NET has a clean and consistent manner for handling exceptions from the .NET Framework class library (FCL) out, development will get quite a bit easier in .NET-land.

I was all set to write a complete chapter on exception handling, but my coworker Jeffrey Richter already did an outstanding job in his books *Applied Microsoft .NET Framework Programming* (Microsoft Press, 2002) and *Applied Microsoft .NET Framework Programming in Microsoft Visual Basic .NET* (Microsoft Press, 2003). His chapters on exception handling (Chapter 18, in both books) are mandatory reading for anyone doing .NET development. However, I do want to emphasize a few points on using and developing your own exceptions for your products.

The first key point is that *exceptions are for exceptional events.* We've all heard that phrase, but I've found that many developers have trouble actually defining it. My definition is that only when you encounter an error or unexpected condition do you throw the exception. One mistake I've seen developers make is using exceptions instead of a `switch…case` statement. (I really have!) The only time you throw is when something is wrong. Don't return general status codes by using exceptions.

One argument for always using exceptions is that developers never check return values. To me, that's a complete red herring argument, because if developers aren't checking return values, they aren't doing their jobs and should be fired. The reason I'm mentioning this is that I've seen people overusing exceptions when the code would be much cleaner and faster if they would simply return a value. The general rule I apply to my code is that I will always throw exceptions out of public methods and properties on error conditions. That way there's a consistent means of error handling for anyone using my code. Internally to my class, I will use return values instead of throwing on internal helper functions so that I can keep my exception throwing in the main methods. Of course, if one of those internal-only methods encounters a true error condition, I'll do the throw right there. It's all a matter of common sense.

I've mentioned the performance hit because even though exceptions seem to be free in .NET, they are implemented internally with standard structured exception handling (SEH). If you want to verify this, simply debug a .NET application using native mode–only debugging—you'll see all those first-chance exceptions being reported when you cause an exception. That means a happy trip to kernel mode on each exception. The idea, again, is to throw an exception on errors, not as part of normal program flow.

The biggest problem with using exceptions is that it's difficult to know what you should be catching when using the FCL. As Jeffrey points out in his chapter on exceptions (a rule you've probably had beaten into your head), catch only the exceptions germane to the objects you are using. Each method and property in the FCL documentation has a section named Exceptions. I always double-check the help when using each property or method (fortunately the F1 help has gotten smart enough to jump to the correct item) and check any exceptions thrown so that I can ensure I'm catching only what the documentation says is thrown. Keep your exception catching focused so that you don't accidentally chomp those you didn't expect.

Microsoft uses the same documentation comments in C# that you use to generate the MSDN help documentation, and as I pointed out in Chapter 9, you can generate nearly identical documentation with the excellent NDoc tool available from *http://ndoc.sourceforge.net*. To make life easier for anyone using your objects, you have to fill out the `<exception></exception>` tag and indicate any exceptions you throw in your code. It's also an excellent idea to double-check all FCL calls you make and to indicate which exceptions can be thrown from those methods so that you are giving the full report. When I'm doing code reviews, ensuring that exceptions are completely documented is one of my hot buttons and I always look to make sure they are.

Since I'm mentioning code reviews and exceptions, I'll point out three other things I always look for. The first is `finally` blocks in any methods or properties that are opening anything that could be construed as a handle-based resource, which ensures those items get cleaned up. I also look for any `catch (Exception) {…}` or `catch {…}` blocks and ensure they are doing a throw. Finally, I always double-check to make sure that re-throws *never* have a parameter after them like the following:

```
try
{
    // Do some stuff.
}
catch (DivideByZeroException e )
{
    // DON'T DO THIS!!
    throw e ;
}
```

When you re-throw the exception, you lose the information about where the exception originated.

The final issue I want to mention about exceptions concerns the C# `using` statement. The `using` statement expands into the same Intermediate Language code as a `try…finally` block and calls the `Dispose` method on the single object specified inside the `using` statement. It's perfectly reasonable to use the `using` statement, but I prefer not to because what's happening behind the scenes isn't as obvious.

Summary

Exceptions are a radically different concept in .NET that they were in the Win32 world. With ExceptionMon, you now have a way to monitor them, which means you can use them more efficiently. I encourage you to experiment with ExceptionMon—you'll be quite surprised about what goes on in your applications.

The magic of ExceptionMon is the incredible Profiling API. Since the Profiling API allows you to see all sorts of interesting happenings inside the CLR, you have at your fingertips extreme power for writing the kind of tools you've in the past only dreamed about. As you'll see in subsequent chapters, there's much more you can do with the Profiling API.

I hope I gave you some food for thought when it comes to actually using and implementing exceptions inside your own .NET projects. The bible when it comes to learning about exceptions is still the chapters in Jeffrey Richter's books, and I encourage you to read it. The key, though, is to think about and plan your exception usage right from the beginning. We have this wonderful tool at our disposal now, but if we use it improperly, we can really cause development trouble as our product matures.

11

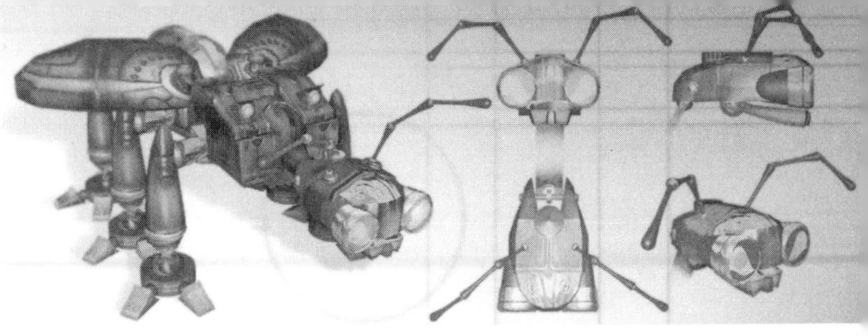

Flow Tracing

In the last chapter, I barely made a dent in the topic of what the Profiling API can do. In this chapter, I want to delve a little bit deeper and build a tool I've always wanted. Back in Chapter 6, I mentioned the amazingly cool `wt` (Watch and Trace) command built into the console-base managed debugger, CORDBG.EXE. With `wt`, you can see the flow of method calls, which means that you can also see the flow of your entire code. The `wt` command offers a fantastic way to learn about bottlenecks—because so many things happen behind the scenes, you can't rely on scrutinizing the code to find them.

Unfortunately, the `wt` command works only in a console application, which is not the most intuitive debugger in the world. Additionally, CORDBG uses the debugging stepping mechanism to do the tracing, so it's slow. I want the tracing output to be fast and easy to use. That's where my favorite utility, FlowTrace, comes into play. It gives you the power of `wt` with none of the bitter aftertaste!

I'll start this chapter with a discussion of how the Profiling API allows you to hook method calls easily and efficiently. After explaining how to use FlowTrace, I'll turn to some of the implementation highlights so that you'll understand how it works. Finally, because FlowTrace is one of those tools that begs to be extended in many different ways, I'll give you some good ideas for taking it to the next level.

Hooking Functions in the Profiling API

One of the most difficult parts of writing a real profiler in Microsoft Win32 was that hooking into the function call stream was nearly impossible without considerable help from the compiler or by changing the binary on disk. Without this capability, you couldn't even come close to getting accurate timings that related to anything in the user's application. Microsoft has built this function-call notification right into the Profiling API—yet another instance where they deserve great credit for doing the heavy lifting. Now tool developers can concentrate on solving hard profiling problems without having to spend six months or more developing just the infrastructure.

Requesting Enter and Leave Notifications

With the Profiling API, you'll get notified whenever a method is called and whenever that method returns. The `/Gh` and `/GH` switches (which enable the `_penter` and `_pexit` hook functions, respectively) in the native C++ compiler follow the same basic strategy as the Profiling API, but the Profiling API makes notifications even easier by also handing you the `FunctionID` of the executing function.

As with any of the other notifications, you first have to tell the run time that you'd like the notifications by ORing in the flag `COR_PRF_MONITOR_ENTERLEAVE` to the `ICorProfilerInfo::SetEventMask` method. I would have bet that once you ask for enter and leave notifications, the notifications would be immutable for the life of the process. However, the smart folks at Microsoft allow you to set and unset the enter and leave notifications as much as you want. Keep that in mind, because you could create some very interesting tools with this capability, for example, one that times only exception processing.

After setting the options, you need to tell the run time which functions you want called, so you'll call `ICorProfilerInfo::SetEnterLeaveFunctionHooks`. The three parameters are pointers to the functions you want called: the entry function, exit function, and tailcall exit function. The first two functions are self-explanatory, but the third is a little weird. In the current version of the common language runtime (CLR), the tailcall exit function is never called. A *tailcall* is when the current method's stack frame is removed before the actual call instruction is executed. In other words, the stack gets cleaned up before the method executes because nothing on the stack is needed. Future versions of the CLR will utilize the tailcall compiler optimization, so you'll need it. Since for most Profile API users, the tailcall exit function performs the same thing as exiting the function, you can simply use your regular exit function if you'd like.

Implementing the Hook Functions

The special part of the function hooking process is defining your actual hook functions. To keep performance as fast as possible, the Profiling API requires that you write the functions using the `naked` calling convention. In essence, your function is inlined right inside the Just In Time (JIT) compiler, so you have to handle the function prolog and epilog needs.

The `typedef` for any of the hook functions is as follows:

```
typedef void FunctionEnter ( FunctionID funcID ) ;
```

However, what's not too clear from the documentation but fortunately is shown in the profiling samples is that the hook functions are like standard calls in that they are responsible for popping the `FunctionID` parameter off the stack. The comments in CorProf.IDL, whose word you should always take over Profiling.DOC, mention that your hook functions are also required to save any registers your code will touch, including any floating-point registers.

Listing 11-1 shows you my enter hook function, so you can see one in action. The hook functions use the naked calling convention, so you're required to write your own prolog and epilog. `CFlowTrace::FuncEnter` is where the real work is being done, so the hook function is really just a wrapper to call it. The prolog (the first three `PUSH` instructions) preserves the registers that are modified by this function. The last four instructions are the epilog, which restores the saved registers and returns. `RET 4` returns and clears the function ID passed to the enter hook function off the stack, saving me a `POP` instruction.

The middle four instructions call `CFlowTrace::FuncEnter`, passing it the class instance and the function ID. The function ID was passed to the enter hook function. It's now 16 (0x10) bytes up the stack, before the three registers we saved and the return address. `PUSH [ESP + 10]` pushes a copy onto the stack to pass to `CFlowTrace::FuncEnter`. Eagle-eyed readers will note that the declaration of `CFlowTrace::FuncEnter` takes only a single parameter. That's because C++ class methods always pass the instance pointer (or `this` pointer) as the first, hidden parameter. I played around with the inline assembly language in the hook functions quite a bit to see whether I could get anything smaller, but what you see in Listing 11-1 is about as small as you can safely go.

```
void __declspec ( naked ) NakedEnter ( FunctionID /*funcID*/ )
{
    __asm
    {
        PUSH EAX                        // Save off whacked registers.
        PUSH ECX
        PUSH EDX

        PUSH [ESP + 10h]                // Push the function ID as the
                                        //  parameter.
        MOV  ECX , g_pFlowTrace         // Push the instance data on the
        PUSH ECX                        //  stack.
```

Listing 11-1 Hook function example *(continued)*

```
        CALL CFlowTrace::FuncEnter      // Call the FuncEnter method.

        POP  EDX                        // Restore saved registers.
        POP  ECX
        POP  EAX

        RET 4                           // Return and clear the function
                                        //  ID off the stack as it was
                                        //  passed to this function.
    }
}
```

Inlining

One very important issue with the hooked function notifications is inlining. The CLR execution engine is highly optimized and will inline code like crazy to eke out a couple of clock cycle savings. This means that although you think you might be seeing everything that's going on in your program, you're seeing only the calls and returns for methods that were not inlined and nothing for the inlined methods.

If you want a complete graph of all calls actually made in a program, you have two options for turning off inlining. However, as you can imagine, disabling inlining can have a dramatic performance hit on the managed code. The easiest way to turn off inlining is to OR in the `COR_PRF_DISABLE_INLINING` flag to `ICorProfilerInfo::SetEventMask` when processing the `ICorProfilerCallback::Initialize` notification. The drawback is that `COR_PRF_DISABLE_INLINING` is an immutable flag, so you've turned it off for the entire life of the process, no matter where your code executes.

A second way, while allowing finer grained control, requires much more work on your part. One of the JIT notifications you get is `JITInlining`, which as you can tell by the name, indicates that a function is being inlined into another function. (You'll have to OR in `COR_PRF_MONITOR_JIT_COMPILATION` in the event mask to get the JIT notifications.) The `JITInlining` parameters, in order, are the caller `FunctionID`, the callee `FunctionID` (the function being inlined), and a pointer to a `BOOL`, which, if set to `FALSE`, will prevent inlining.

You could do some very interesting things with the `JITInlining` notification. For example, you could leave inlining on for the .NET Framework class library (FCL) classes but turn it off when executing non-FCL code. You have to be careful, however, because the CLR will call `JITInlining` billions of times and your code will look up caller and/or callee `FunctionID` values, which could cause a much worse performance hit than simply disabling globally in the process. Although you might think about storing the `FunctionID` values you do look up, keep in mind that the CLR garbage collector can rejiggle those values, so you'll have to handle garbage collection notifications to keep your data tables straight.

The Function ID Mapper

In addition to the very cool hooking functions, I need to tell you about one other special function: `FunctionIDMapper`. The purpose of this function is to allow you to change the value of the `FunctionID` passed to the three separate hook functions. The CLR calls it right before any of the hook functions. You don't have to set the `FunctionIDMapper` function if you don't want to, but doing so can open up some very interesting development possibilities.

Setting the `FunctionIDMapper` is immutable and you should do it in the `ICorProfilerCallback::Initialize` method by passing the function pointer to `ICorProfilerInfo::SetFunctionIDMapper`. One thing that caused me some problems is that the Profiling.DOC discussion of the function prototype is wrong. The `FunctionIDMapper` function returns a `UINT_PTR`, the underlying type for a `FunctionID`, instead of the `void` documented. The correct prototype is this:

```
UINT_PTR __stdcall FunctionIDMapper ( FunctionID functionId ,
                                      BOOL *pbHookFunction ) ;
```

Interestingly, `FunctionIDMapper` is a normal standard call function, not one of the naked functions required by the other hook functions. The `FunctionID` parameter is the function that the CLR is about to call one of the hook functions for. The Boolean pointer parameter allows you to control whether the CLR calls the hook function. If you want to allow the hook call, set `*pbHookFunction` to `TRUE`. If you set it to `FALSE`, the hook function isn't called. If you want to change the value passed as the hook parameter, return that value from your `FunctionIDMapper` function.

I see `FunctionIDMapper` as being quite interesting for larger projects that use the Profiling API. For example, you have to look up the function class and method name on nearly all calls into the hooking functions. You could use the `FunctionIDMapper` function to handle the function lookup instead and pass the values onto the hook function. That way you have a single place in which you're performing the lookups. 

With the option to control whether the hook function is actually called, you have more power at your disposal. For example, when you want to do logging or analysis for only a single thread, you can use `FunctionIDMapper` to determine the thread ID, and if you're not interested in watching the thread, you can skip the hook function. The option to skip the hook function can make the design of your profiler much easier to implement. In fact, I took advantage of it in the FlowTrace program.

Using FlowTrace

Now that you have a basic understanding of what function hooking looks like with the Profiling API, I want to turn to describing how to use FlowTrace. Knowing how to use it will make understanding some of its implementation issues easier. As with anything that uses the Profiling API, you face environment variable city to get your profiler set up and running. Like ExceptionMon from Chapter 10, FlowTrace lets you specify whether you'd like to trigger a `DebugBreak` call on startup (`FLOWTRACEBREAK`) as well as specify exactly which process you want to profile (`FLOWTRACEPROC`). Additionally, to specify where you want the output files written, you can set the `FLOWTRACEFILEDIR` environment variable to point to a specific directory. I'll discuss the FlowTrace .FLS settings file in a moment, but if you specify `FLOWTRACEFILEDIR`, FlowTrace will look for the .FLS file in that directory instead of the directory in which the executable resides.

To keep everything straight for multithreaded applications, FlowTrace's output writes each thread to a different file. The file naming is as follows:

```
<process name>_<Win32 process ID>_<managed thread ID>.FLOW
```

The different parts of the filename should be self-explanatory. The only interesting part is that I used the managed thread ID instead of a Win32 thread ID. As you'll see later in the implementation section, there's no correlation between a managed thread and a Win32 thread.

Your final task before using FlowTrace is setting up the optional settings file. The file is a simple initialization file located in the same directory as the executable or where the `FLOWTRACEFILEDIR` environment variable points, and it is the program name with an .FLS extension. Although I could have used the ultramodern technique of an XML file, I just didn't feel like spending several months writing and testing code that uses MSXML3.DLL from C++ and bloating the FlowTrace working set by tens of megabytes. There is no sense in making things more complicated than they have to be.

The first of the three optional settings supported by FlowTrace is determining whether inlining should be on. By default, inlining is turned on so that the process running under FlowTrace will run faster. The second option is disabling logging of the finalizer thread. All .NET processes have the garbage collector running in a separate thread. I found that the majority of calls made on the finalizer thread were related to cleaning up the CLR-created objects. To keep the output to a minimum, I preferred to record only the real process flow on the other threads because that's more informational in my opinion. Therefore, by default, FlowTrace doesn't record the finalizer thread, but you can easily enable that recording. The third option lets you decide whether to record the startup code for the initial `AppDomain` created on the main thread since the `System.AppDomain.SetupDomain` method creates huge amounts of trace output. By default, I don't record the startup. In Listing 11-2 is a default .FLS file. To enable a particular option, set it to 1; a 0 (zero) disables it.

```
; This is an example .FLS configuration file. Name this file
; the same name as the executable and put it in the same
; directory as the EXE.

; All general options are here. All values shown are the defaults
; if no .FLS file is present for the executable.
[General Options]
; Turns off inlining if set to 1. This will lead to much
; larger trace flows.
TurnOffInlining=0

; Does not process anything in the finalizer thread.
IgnoreFinalizerThread=1

; Skips all AppDomain startup calls on the main thread.
SkipStartupCodeOnMainThread=1
```

Listing 11-2 A Default .FLS File

FlowTrace Implementation Highlights

Now I want to discuss a few of the implementation highlights. The first big issue I ran into was that in the future, managed threads won't have a one-to-one mapping with Win32 threads. The first versions of the Microsoft .NET Framework do have a one-to-one mapping. I first implemented FlowTrace using the reliable standby of thread local storage to ensure each thread had specific data. As I was perusing through Profiling.DOC, I noticed a special thread notification, `ICorProfilerCallback::ThreadAssignedToOSThread`. The description mentions that in the context of a CLR runtime thread, "During its execution lifetime, a given Runtime thread may be switched between different threads, or not—at the whim of both the Runtime and external components running within the process." That sure got my attention, and after checking with Microsoft, I realized the simple thread local storage solution wasn't going to work because FlowTrace would break in the future.

Fortunately, thread creation and destruction notifications in `ICorProfilerCallback` will give you the managed thread ID as a parameter, and you can call `ICorProfilerInfo::GetCurrentThreadID` to learn the thread ID at any time, so you'll have no issues identifying a managed thread. The downside is that I had to create my own "managed thread local storage" in a global Standard Template Library (STL) map class. Of course, to protect against multithreaded corruption, I had to protect it with a critical section. Since many of the Profiling API callback methods in `ICorProfilerCallback` make very explicit warnings against blocking when processing the methods, I was a little concerned. However, after a huge amount of testing, I don't think it has any noticeable effect.

The second big issue I had to deal with was how to support skipping all the startup code calls done by the `System.AppDomain.SetupDomain` method in the main thread. After doing some experimentation on numerous managed applications, I noticed that three threads run the application at startup. The Profiling API documentation mentions that by injecting a profiler into the managed process, a special thread dedicated to just the profiler starts up, but, fortunately, does not execute any managed code. I found that the first thread creation notification was always the main thread in the application, and the second thread notification was always the finalizer thread. Once I discovered how to identify the threads, I could come up with a plan for how to do the skip startup code processing. When skipping startup code, I have to shift to a state in which I don't record any processing on the main thread until after the function leave hook sees the call to `System.AppDomain.ResetBindingRedirects` come through.

I could see which thread was running as the finalizer, but I wanted to add the option to ignore it. My original idea was to set the `FunctionIDMapper` hook so that I could check the managed thread ID. If the managed thread ID was the finalizer thread, I could set the `pbHookFunction` parameter to `FALSE` so that the CLR would not call the hook function. When testing with the simplest IL assembly language program, everything worked great.

However, when I tested FlowTrace with a simple Microsoft Windows Forms application, I got assertions that the managed thread-specific data was `NULL`. Since I was ignoring the finalizer thread, I didn't add that managed thread to the managed map because I wanted to keep the map as small as possible. When I broke in the assertions, I noticed that the enter function hook was called on the finalizer thread. I thought for sure I had screwed up the algorithm, but a very careful inspection didn't explain why I was seeing a call on the finalizer thread.

After recording just those special cases on the finalizer thread and scouring the documentation, I finally figured out what was going on. In Windows Forms applications, you still have some of the oddities of COM, including the annoyance of apartment threading models. What I was seeing were cross-thread marshaled calls from the main thread into the finalizer thread. Interestingly, the CLR never called the `FunctionIDMapper` hook. Therefore, there was no way for me to short-circuit the hook calls. I was hoping I wouldn't have to check for the finalizer thread in the hook functions for performance reasons, but there was nothing I could do. So to avoid logging the finalizer calls, I had to check for the finalizer thread.

That worked like a charm, and if requested, I turned off the finalizer logging. A day or so later after I'd written the code, I realized I needed to utilize the `FunctionIDMapper` only when the user specifically requested I not monitor the finalizer thread. Originally, I was setting it in all cases.

The last item I had to tackle was ensuring that I kept my output straight no matter what. That meant I had to monitor any exceptions that unwound out of functions because I'd never see the leave function hook for them. Handling exception unwinding turned out to be quite simple to accomplish. All I needed to do was keep a running unwind count for the thread when the CLR called `ICorProfilerCallback::ExceptionUnwindFunctionLeave`. Once the exception hit `ICorProfilerCallback::ExceptionCatcherLeave`, I simply subtracted the number of unwound functions from the current indenting level.

What's Next for FlowTrace

I've found the output to FlowTrace to be a great learning tool. As with all utilities, there's still some room for it to grow. If you're looking for an interesting project, here is some cool functionality you could add to FlowTrace:

- Add to the .FLS file a start-and-stop logging feature based on specific classes and methods. This would allow you to control exactly what you wanted to see traced without being overwhelmed by all the other stuff going on. Ideally, you should make this work on a per-thread basis as well as a global thread basis. You'll also get extra credit if you make the class and method matching as regular expressions, which would give you extra power in deciding what you don't want to see.
- It would be nice to start with no logging happening at all and have an external trigger tell FlowTrace to start logging from a specific point. Of course, you should also implement the stop logging as well!
- The infrastructure is already in FlowTrace, so you might want to add function timings to the output.

- Instead of saving the output to a text file, you could record and display the output in a GUI application that was pseudo-real time.
- Finally, the output files for an application can be quite large. What would be nice is an option to filter out common bottom-level calls such as `Object..ctor`.

Summary

Figuring out who calls what in an application can be a difficult task to accomplish from reading the source code. I hope that FlowTrace will make seeing the flow of your managed applications easier so that you can do better debugging and performance tuning. I strongly encourage you to think about what other types of utilities you could develop now that the profiling API makes hooking function entry and exit trivial. Even though there are some gotchas along the way, I'm finding the Profiling API to be one of the most exciting things going in .NET development.

Part IV

Power Tools and Techniques for Native Code

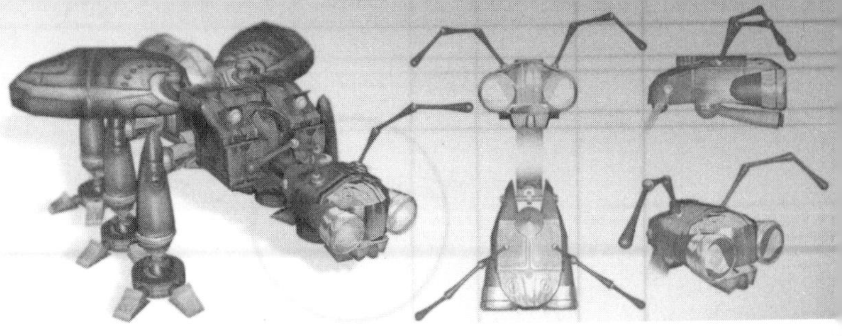

12

Finding Source and Line Information with Just a Crash Address

Your program has crashed. You have the crash address because the operating system is nice enough to give it to you when your application dies. Now what do you do? My friend Chris Sells calls this scenario the "my program went on vacation and all I got was this lousy address" problem. Although having the address is better than nothing, having the source file and the line number of the crash would be much more convenient. I suppose you could always give the source code to your users and have them debug it for you, but I just don't see that happening any time soon.

That crash address is generally all you're going to get if you're very lucky. Microsoft has worked hard to make it easier for their people to track down issues on Microsoft Windows 2000, Windows XP, and Windows Server 2003. Troubleshooting is a little more confusing when your users tell you that your application has had a problem. The default unhandled exception handler displays the fancy new "We are sorry for the inconvenience" dialog box shown in Figure 12-1. The big problem is that the crash dialog box no longer shows you the crash address! This is a classic case of a change that is friendlier for users but worse for us developers.

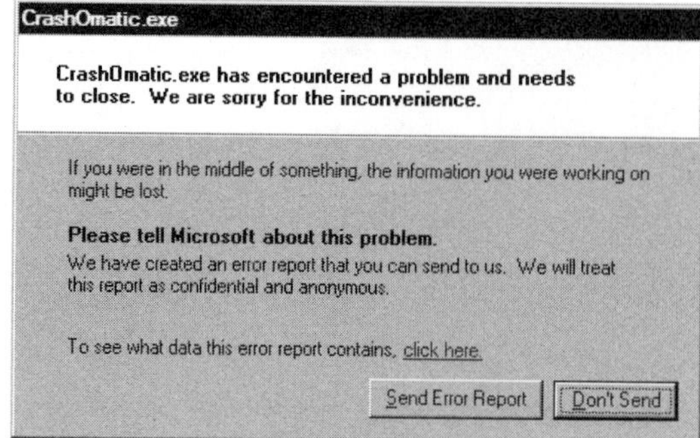

Figure 12-1 Standard Windows XP crash dialog box

To get the crash address, click the To See What Data This Error Report Contains, Click Here link and, in the next dialog box, click the To View Technical Information About The Error Report, Click Here link. In the Error Report Contents dialog box, shown in Figure 12-2, you'll see the crash address and all the loaded modules. Additionally, you'll get a really useful stack dump that's big enough to see almost to the beginning of time for the thread that crashed. Amazingly, someone made a really bad decision and put all that great information in a static control, so you can't copy it. I certainly hope Microsoft will fix this annoying oversight in a future service pack of Windows XP. The good news is that Windows 2000 and Windows Server 2003 always show the crash address in the crash dialog box.

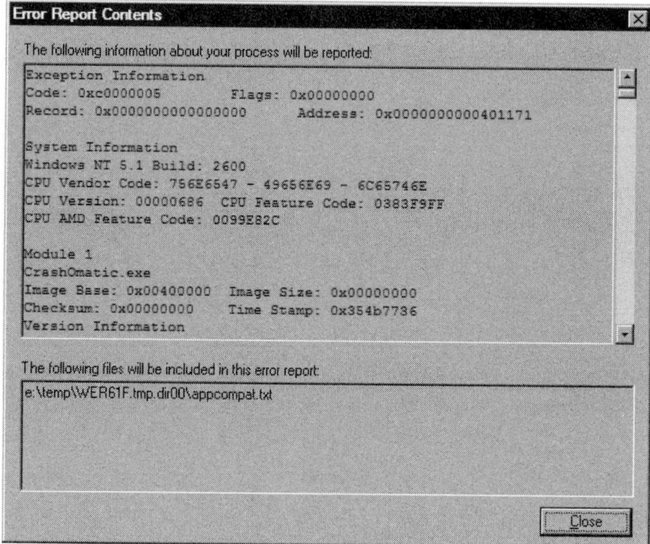

Figure 12-2 Error Report Contents dialog box in Windows XP

The good news is that Dr. Watson will still run no matter what button you click in the crash dialog box provided Dr. Watson is set as the debugger to launch, which it should be for default installations. If it's not, have your users run `DRWTSN32.EXE -i` to set Dr. Watson as the default debugger. To get the information out of Dr. Watson, you'll just need to make sure your users know to start Dr. Watson with the DRWTSN32.EXE command and to copy the crash out of the Dr. Watson user interface (UI). (Refer to Appendix A for detailed information about Dr. Watson logs and how to interpret them.) If you're lucky, your users will be able to send you the minidump files, so make sure they check Create Crash Dump File in the Dr. Watson UI and note where the files are written. Of course, most of us are doing well if we get just a crash address. If you're totally proactive, you'll have your crashing application sending you the minidump automatically, which I'll also discuss in Chapter 13. Obviously, you need a way to convert that crash address to the source file and line number in your application. In this chapter, I'll explain how to accomplish that. I'll concentrate on the two main ways of converting the address: using MAP files and using CrashFinder, a utility included with this book's sample files.

To maximize the techniques in this chapter, you need to have your program compilation set up as I described in Chapter 2. You need to be building your release builds with full debugging symbols and generating MAP files for them. Additionally, you must fix any DLL load address conflicts. If you don't take these steps, the techniques I present in this chapter won't completely work and the only way you'll be able to figure out the source file and line number for a crash address is through pure guessing.

Creating and Reading a MAP File

Many people have asked me why I keep recommending that everyone create MAP files with their release builds. Simply put, MAP files are the only textual representation of your program's global symbols and source file and line number information. Although using CrashFinder is far easier than deciphering a MAP file, your MAP files can be read anywhere and anytime, without requiring a supporting program and without requiring all your program's binaries to get the same information. Trust me, at some point in the future, you're going to need to figure out where a crash happened on an older version of your software, and the only way you'll be able to find the information is with your MAP file.

MAP files are useful only for release builds because when creating a MAP File, the linker has to turn off incremental linking. Setting up to generate MAP files is much easier in Microsoft Visual C++ .NET than in previous versions. In your project Property Pages dialog box, Linker folder, Debugging property page, you just have to set the Generate Map File field, Map Exports, and the Map Lines fields to Yes. Doing so turns on the linker `/MAP`, `/MAPINFO:EXPORTS`, and `/MAPINFO:LINES` options. As you can guess, SettingsMaster from Chapter 9, with the default project files, will add these settings automatically.

If you're working on a real-world project, you probably have your binary files going to their own output directory. By default, the linker writes the MAP file to the same directory as the intermediate files, so you need to specify that the MAP file goes to the binary file output directory. In the Map File Name edit box, you can type `$(OutDir)/$(ProjectName).map`. The `$(OutDir)` is a built-in macro that the build system will substitute with the real output directory, and `$(ProjectName)` substitutes the project name. Figure 12-3 shows the completed MAP file settings for the release build of the MapDLL project, which is included with this book's sample files.

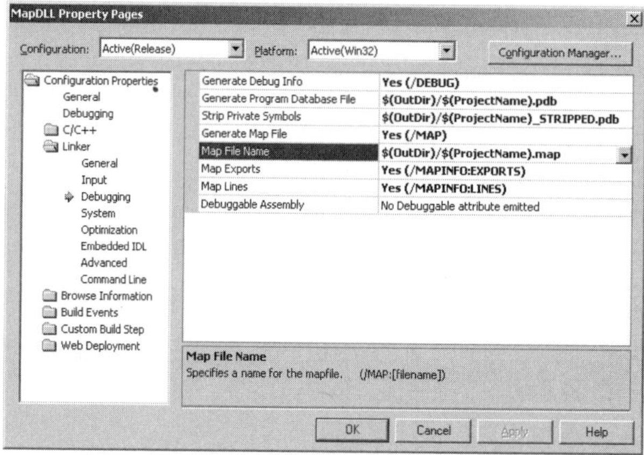

Figure 12-3 The MAP file settings in the project Property Pages dialog box

Although you might not need the MAP files in your day-to-day operation, chances are that you'll need them in the future. CrashFinder and your debugger rely on symbol tables and a symbol engine to read them. If the format of the symbol table changes or if you forget to save the Program Database (PDB) files, you're completely out of luck. Forgetting to save the PDB files is your fault, but you have no control over symbol table formats. They change frequently. For example, many people who upgraded from Microsoft Visual Studio 6 to Microsoft Visual Studio .NET noticed that tools such as CrashFinder quit working with programs compiled with Visual Studio .NET. Microsoft changed the symbol table format and does so on a regular basis. MAP files are your only savior at that time.

Even though you, as a developer, might be up to Window Server 2008 with Visual Studio .NET 2007 Service Pack 6 in five years, I can assure you that you'll still have customers who will be running the software you released back in 2003. When they call you in alarm and give you a crash address, you could spend the next two days trying to find the Visual Studio .NET CDs so that you can read your saved PDB files. Or if you have the MAP files, you can find the problem in five minutes.

MAP File Contents

Listing 12-1 shows an example MAP file. The top part of the MAP file contains the module name, the timestamp indicating when LINK.EXE linked the module, and the preferred load address. After the header comes the section information that shows which sections the linker brought in from the various OBJ and LIB files.

After the section information, you get to the good stuff, the public function information. Notice the "public" part. If you have static-declared functions, they are placed in a similar table after the public functions table. Fortunately, the line numbers are not separated out and appear together.

The important parts of the public function information are the function names and the information in the Rva+Base column, which is the starting address of the function. The `f` after some of the Rva+Base addresses indicates that the address is an actual function and not a global variable or imported address of some kind. The line information follows the public function section. The lines are shown as follows:

```
24 0001:00000006
```

The first number is the line number, and the second is the offset from the beginning of the code section in which this line occurred. Yes, that sounds confusing, but later I'll show you the calculation you need to convert an address into a source file and line number.

If the module contains exported functions, the final section of a MAP file lists the exports. You can get this same information by running `DUMPBIN /EXPORTS` <*modulename*>.

```
 MapDLL

 Timestamp is 3e2b44a3 (Sun Jan 19 19:36:51 2003)

 Preferred load address is 03900000

 Start         Length     Name                   Class
 0001:00000000 00000304H .text                   CODE
 0002:00000000 00000028H .idata$5                DATA
 0002:00000030 000000f8H .rdata                  DATA
 0002:00000128 00000063H .rdata$debug            DATA
 0002:00000190 00000004H .rdata$sxdata           DATA
 0002:00000194 00000004H .rtc$IAA                DATA
 0002:00000198 00000004H .rtc$IZZ                DATA
 0002:0000019c 00000004H .rtc$TAA                DATA
 0002:000001a0 00000004H .rtc$TZZ                DATA
 0002:000001a4 00000014H .idata$2                DATA
 0002:000001b8 00000014H .idata$3                DATA
 0002:000001cc 00000028H .idata$4                DATA
 0002:000001f4 00000082H .idata$6                DATA
 0002:00000280 0000007bH .edata                  DATA
 0003:00000000 00000004H .CRT$XCA                DATA
 0003:00000004 00000004H .CRT$XCZ                DATA
 0003:00000008 00000004H .CRT$XIA                DATA
 0003:0000000c 00000004H .CRT$XIZ                DATA
 0003:00000010 00000004H .data                   DATA
 0003:00000014 00000014H .bss                    DATA

  Address         Publics by Value              Rva+Base       Lib:Object

 0000:00000001       ___safe_se_handler_count      00000001     <absolute>
 0001:00000000       _DllMain@12                   03901000 f   MapDLL.obj
 0001:00000006       ?MapDLLFunction@@YAHXZ        03901006 f   MapDLL.obj
 0001:00000023       ?MapDLLHappyFunc@@YAPADPAD@Z 03901023 f   MapDLL.obj
 0001:0000003c       __CRT_INIT@12                 0390103c f   MSVCRT:crtdll.obj
 0001:000000fa       __DllMainCRTStartup@12        039010fa f   MSVCRT:crtdll.obj
 0001:000001de       __initterm                    039011de f   MSVCRT:MSVCR71.dll
 0001:000001e4       __onexit                      039011e4 f   MSVCRT:atonexit.obj
 0001:0000020a       _atexit                       0390120a f   MSVCRT:atonexit.obj
 0001:0000021c       __RTC_Initialize              0390121c f   MSVCRT:initsect.obj
 0001:00000260       __RTC_Terminate               03901260 f   MSVCRT:initsect.obj
 0001:000002a4       ___CppXcptFilter              039012a4 f   MSVCRT:MSVCR71.dll
 0001:000002ac       __SEH_prolog                  039012ac f   MSVCRT:sehprolg.obj
 0001:000002e7       __SEH_epilog                  039012e7 f   MSVCRT:sehprolg.obj
 0001:000002f8       __except_handler3             039012f8 f   MSVCRT:MSVCR71.dll
 0001:000002fe       ___dllonexit                  039012fe f   MSVCRT:MSVCR71.dll
 0002:00000000       __imp__printf                 03902000     MSVCRT:MSVCR71.dll
 0002:00000004       __imp__free                   03902004     MSVCRT:MSVCR71.dll
 0002:00000008       __imp___initterm              03902008     MSVCRT:MSVCR71.dll
 0002:0000000c       __imp__malloc                 0390200c     MSVCRT:MSVCR71.dll
```

Listing 12-1 Example MAP file

```
0002:00000010   __imp___adjust_fdiv        03902010     MSVCRT:MSVCR71.dll
0002:00000014   __imp____CppXcptFilter     03902014     MSVCRT:MSVCR71.dll
0002:00000018   __imp___except_handler3    03902018     MSVCRT:MSVCR71.dll
0002:0000001c   __imp____dllonexit         0390201c     MSVCRT:MSVCR71.dll
0002:00000020   __imp___onexit             03902020     MSVCRT:MSVCR71.dll
0002:00000024   \177MSVCR71_NULL_THUNK_DATA 03902024     MSVCRT:MSVCR71.dll
0002:0000007c   ??_C@_0CE@EBHAJKCA@Whoops?0?5a?5crash?5is?5about?5to?5occu@
                                           0390207c     MapDLL.obj
0002:000000a0   ??_C@_0CD@OILENIKO@Hello?5from?5InternalStaticFunctio@
                                           039020a0     MapDLL.obj
0002:000000c4   ??_C@_0BM@DFMPKPOD@Hello?5from?5MapDLLFunction?$CB?6?$AA@
                                           039020c4     MapDLL.obj
0002:000000e0   __load_config_used         039020e0     MSVCRT:loadcfg.obj
0002:00000190   ___safe_se_handler_table   03902190     <linker-defined>
0002:00000194   ___rtc_iaa                 03902194     MSVCRT:initsect.obj
0002:00000198   ___rtc_izz                 03902198     MSVCRT:initsect.obj
0002:0000019c   ___rtc_taa                 0390219c     MSVCRT:initsect.obj
0002:000001a0   ___rtc_tzz                 039021a0     MSVCRT:initsect.obj
0002:000001a4   __IMPORT_DESCRIPTOR_MSVCR71 039021a4     MSVCRT:MSVCR71.dll
0002:000001b8   __NULL_IMPORT_DESCRIPTOR   039021b8     MSVCRT:MSVCR71.dll
0003:00000000   ___xc_a                    03903000     MSVCRT:cinitexe.obj
0003:00000004   ___xc_z                    03903004     MSVCRT:cinitexe.obj
0003:00000008   ___xi_a                    03903008     MSVCRT:cinitexe.obj
0003:0000000c   ___xi_z                    0390300c     MSVCRT:cinitexe.obj
0003:00000010   ___security_cookie         03903010     MSVCRT:seccook.obj
0003:00000018   __adjust_fdiv              03903018     <common>
0003:0000001c   ___onexitend               0390301c     <common>
0003:00000020   ___onexitbegin             03903020     <common>
0003:00000024   __pRawDllMain              03903024     <common>

entry point at         0001:000000fa

Static symbols

0001:00000016       ?InternalStaticFunction@@YAXXZ 03901016 f   MapDLL.obj

Line numbers for .\Release\MapDLL.obj(d:\dev\booktwo\disk\chapter examples\ch
apter 12\mapfile\mapdll\mapdll.cpp) segment .text

11 0001:00000000  20 0001:00000000  21 0001:00000003  26 0001:00000006
25 0001:00000006  27 0001:00000012  28 0001:00000015  31 0001:00000016
32 0001:00000016  33 0001:00000022  37 0001:00000023  36 0001:00000023
38 0001:00000028  39 0001:00000033  41 0001:0000003b

Line numbers for R:\VSNET2003\Vc7\lib\MSVCRT.lib(f:\vs70builds\2292\vc\crtbld
\crt\src\atonexit.c) segment .text

81 0001:000001e4  76 0001:000001e4  90 0001:00000209  96 0001:0000020a
95 0001:0000020a  97 0001:0000021b

Line numbers for R:\VSNET2003\Vc7\lib\MSVCRT.lib(f:\vs70builds\2292\vc\crtbld
\crt\src\crtdll.c) segment .text
```

```
134 0001:0000003c  129 0001:0000003c  135 0001:00000044  136 0001:0000004c
158 0001:00000052  163 0001:00000065  168 0001:0000007a  170 0001:0000007e
172 0001:00000081  178 0001:0000008b  179 0001:00000090  184 0001:0000009a
189 0001:000000ab  192 0001:000000b2  219 0001:000000b8  220 0001:000000c1
225 0001:000000c3  226 0001:000000cf  234 0001:000000e5  236 0001:000000ec
234 0001:000000f3  240 0001:000000f4  241 0001:000000f7  249 0001:000000fa
250 0001:00000106  252 0001:0000010c  257 0001:00000111  258 0001:0000011e
260 0001:00000124  262 0001:0000012d  263 0001:00000136  265 0001:00000142
266 0001:0000014b  268 0001:0000015a  269 0001:0000015c  272 0001:0000015e
275 0001:0000016e  283 0001:00000177  286 0001:00000181  288 0001:0000018a
289 0001:00000198  291 0001:0000019b  292 0001:000001a9  298 0001:000001b7
294 0001:000001bc  295 0001:000001d4  299 0001:000001d6

Exports

 ordinal    name

 1      ?MapDLLFunction@@YAHXZ (int __cdecl MapDLLFunction(void))
 2      ?MapDLLHappyFunc@@YAPADPAD@Z (char * __cdecl MapDLLHappyFunc(char *))
```

Finding the Source File, Function Name, and Line Number

The algorithm for extracting the source file, function name, and line number from a MAP file is straightforward, but you need to do a few hexadecimal calculations when using it. As an example, let's say that a crash in MAPDLL.DLL, the module shown in Listing 12-1, occurs at address 0x03901038.

The first step is to look in your project's MAP files for the file that contains the crash address. First look at the preferred load address and the last address in the public function section. If the crash address is between those values, you're looking at the correct MAP file.

To find the function, scan down the Rva+Base column until you find the first function address that's greater than the crash address. The preceding entry in the MAP file is the function that had the crash. For example, in Listing 12-1, the first function address greater than the 0x03901038 crash address is 0x03901023, so the function that crashed is `?MapDLLHappyFunc@@YAPADPAD@Z`. Any function name that starts with a question mark is a C++ decorated name.

You're probably wondering why I didn't mention the C++ name decoration when I talked about the calling convention name decoration in Chapter 6. Although both serve similar purposes, they come from different places. The calling convention name decoration simply tells the code generator how to generate the parameter pushes and stack cleanup, and it comes from the operating system definitions. C++ name decoration comes as a result of the language. Since you can have overloaded methods, the compiler has to have some way to differentiate them. It "decorates" the name with the return type, calling convention, and parameter information. That way it will know exactly what function you meant to call. To translate the name, pass it as a command-line parameter to the program UNDNAME.EXE, which is included with Visual Studio .NET. In the example, `?MapDLLHappyFunc@@YAPADPAD@Z` translates into `char * __cdecl MapDLLHappyFunc(char *)`. You probably could have figured out that `MapDLLHappyFunc` was the function name just by looking at the decorated name. Other C++ decorated names are harder to decipher, especially when overloaded functions are used.

To find the line number, you get to do a little hexadecimal subtraction by using the following formula:

```
(crash address) - (preferred load address) - 0x1000
```

Remember that the addresses are offsets from the beginning of the first code section, so the formula does that conversion. You can probably guess why you subtract the preferred load address, but you earn extra credit if you know why you still have to subtract 0x1000. The crash address is an offset from the beginning of the code section, but the code section isn't the first part of the binary. The first part of the binary is the PE (portable executable) header and associated DOS stub, which is 0x1000 bytes long. Yes, all Win32 binaries still have that MS-DOS heritage in them.

I'm not sure why the linker still generates MAP files that require this odd calculation. The linker team put in the Rva+Base column a while ago, so I don't see why they didn't just fix up the line number at the same time.

Once you've calculated the offset, look through the MAP file line information until you find the closest number that isn't over the calculated value. Keep in mind that during the generation phase the compiler can jiggle the code around so that the source lines aren't in ascending order. With my crash example, I used the following formula:

```
0x03901038 - 0x03900000 - 0x1000 = 0x38
```

If you look through the MAP file in Listing 12-1, you'll see that the closest line that isn't over 0x38 is 39 0001:00000033 (Line 39) in MAPDLL.CPP.

PDB2MAP—Map Files After the Fact

One issue that keeps coming up when I discuss finding crash addresses with other developers is the lament that you've already got code out in the field in which you don't have MAP files. Other eagle eye developers have also pointed out that having perfect MAP files means you have to set the base address of all your DLLs as part of the build. If you're working on an existing project that's about to ship, you might not want to destabilize the build by changing a bunch of settings. Additionally, without SettingsMaster from Chapter 9, Visual Studio doesn't make it convenient to make those global project settings changes. That's a primary reason why people simply default to using REBASE.EXE to take care of setting their DLL's base addresses.

Being one not to let any challenge go unmet, I took a look at the problem. Really all I needed was a way to enumerate functions, source files, and source lines. Given that the DBGHELP.DLL symbol engine already does that, it was a piece of cake to take the next step to generate a MAP file from a PDB file.

The first problem I ran into was that the `SymGetSymNext` and `SymGetSymPrev` functions don't return what you would expect. I thought I could get an address in a source file, call `SymGetSymPrev` until I got to the beginning of the source file, and roll down the end of the source file with `SymGetSymNext`. What I forgot to take into account are small things called inline functions. Those functions and source lines can occur in the middle of a function, so the source line information is really stored in ranges. This meant that I had to come up with a scheme to keep track of all the ranges so that I could condense the source and line information. Once I got over that hurdle, the program was pretty easy to develop.

The only other thing that got me had nothing to do with symbol engines—it was the Standard Template Library (STL). I first started out implementing my data structures in STL and quickly found that even a partial implementation of PDB2MAP.EXE was excruciatingly slow. That was mostly my fault because I was using the vector class in a linear search way that was just plain stupid. After fiddling some more, I realized that STL was always going to be much slower as it was doing quite a bit of memory allocation and copying behind the scenes. After much gnashing of teeth trying to make sense of some of the STL implementation details, I figured out I was making the problem much more complicated than it needed to be. I ended up manually coding a simple multiple array system that was blindingly fast and super simple to understand. It also had the added benefit of being much more maintainable than anything I could have created in STL.

The files produced by PDB2MAP are close to actual MAP files. Since the DBGHELP.DLL symbol engine doesn't return static functions, there's no way for me to output that information. As you look at a .P2M file, you'll see that you should have no trouble reading it. I considered using the crazy MAP file line number system for old-times' sake, but instead used PDB2MAP, which I brought into the modern age. My line information is generated using real addresses that appear in memory.

One other interesting tidbit of data that you might be interested in is output in your .P2M file. As I mentioned back in Chapter 2, small code is good code. However, other than looking at the total size of the binary, there's no way to see how different compiler switches will affect the size of individual functions. Additionally, there's no way to see what effect inline functions have on a particular function. Since I was doing PDB2MAP, I figured I might as well report symbol sizes because DBGHELP.DLL's symbol engine can report the individual sizes. After the header information in your .P2M file, the function information shows the size of each function between the function address and name, as shown in Listing 12-2, which is an abbreviated .P2M file. Although nearly all functions will have their sizes, DBGHELP.DLL doesn't guarantee that sizes will be returned, so you might see sizes of 0.

```
PDB2MAP Generated Map File

Image: AssertTest

Timestamp is 3E0E7E2A -> Sat Dec 28 23:46:34 2002

Preferred load address is 00400000

Address       Size  Function
0x00401050      36  ??2@YAPAXI@Z
0x00401080     260  ?MyThread@@YGKPAX@Z
0x00401190      38  ?SleepThread@@YGKPAX@Z
0x004011C0     535  ?TestThree@@YAXPAD@Z
0x004013E0     258  ?TestTwo@@YAXXZ
0x004014F0     421  ?TestOne@@YAXPAG@Z
0x004016A0     453  _wWinMain@16
0x00401A5E       6  _InitCommonControls@0
0x00401A64       6  _SuperAssertionW
. . .
Line numbers for d:\dev\booktwo\disk\bugslayerutil\tests\asserttest\assertes
t.cpp

16 : 0x00401080      18 : 0x0040109F      19 : 0x004010CB      20 : 0x004010DE
21 : 0x004010E5      22 : 0x0040113C      23 : 0x0040113E      26 : 0x00401190
27 : 0x00401194      28 : 0x004011A8      29 : 0x004011AA      32 : 0x004011C0
33 : 0x004011D7      39 : 0x004011DE      40 : 0x00401201      41 : 0x00401207
43 : 0x00401223      44 : 0x0040127A      45 : 0x0040129D      46 : 0x004012B2
47 : 0x0040131A      48 : 0x0040131F      49 : 0x00401334      50 : 0x0040139C
53 : 0x004013E0      55 : 0x004013F7      57 : 0x0040140F      59 : 0x00401427
60 : 0x0040143A      61 : 0x0040143C      62 : 0x0040143E      63 : 0x00401498
64 : 0x004014A5      67 : 0x004014F0      68 : 0x00401515      70 : 0x00401527
74 : 0x0040153E      76 : 0x00401548      78 : 0x004015CF      80 : 0x00401632
81 : 0x00401638      82 : 0x0040163D      90 : 0x004016A0      91 : 0x004016C4
92 : 0x0040171B      93 : 0x00401772      94 : 0x004017D2      96 : 0x00401829
97 : 0x00401838      98 : 0x00401845      99 : 0x00401852     100 : 0x00401854

Line numbers for f:\vs70builds\2292\vc\crtbld\crt\src\atonexit.c

76 : 0x00402810      81 : 0x00402814      90 : 0x0040284B      95 : 0x00402850
96 : 0x00402853      97 : 0x00402866
⋮
```

Listing 12-2 An abbreviated .P2M file

Using CrashFinder

As you just saw, reading a MAP or P2M file isn't too terribly difficult. It is rather tedious, however, and certainly not a scalable solution to others on your team, such as quality engineers, technical support staff, and even pointy haired managers. To address the issue of scalability in CrashFinder, I decided to make CrashFinder usable for all members of the development team, from individual developers, through test engineers, and on to the support engineers so that all crash reports include as much information as possible about the crash. If you follow the steps outlined in Chapter 2 for creating the appropriate debug symbols, everyone on your team will be able to use CrashFinder without a problem.

When using CrashFinder in a team setting, you need to be especially vigilant about keeping the binary images and their associated PDB files accessible because CrashFinder doesn't store any information about your application other than the paths to the binary images. CrashFinder stores only the paths to your binary files, so you can use the same CrashFinder project throughout the production cycle. If CrashFinder stored more detailed information about your application, such as symbol tables, you'd probably need to produce a CrashFinder project for each build. If you take this advice and allow easy access to your binaries and PDB files, when your application crashes, all your test or support engineers will have to do is fire up CrashFinder and add a vital piece of information to the bug report. As we all know, the more information an engineer has about the particular problem, the easier correcting the problem will be.

Depending on your application, you might want to have multiple CrashFinder projects for it. For example, you could have one project that points to the daily build location as well as different projects for each milestone release. If you opt to include system DLLs as part of your CrashFinder project, you'll need to create separate CrashFinder projects for each operating system you support. You'll also need to have a CrashFinder project for each version of your application that you send to testers outside your immediate development team, so you'll have to store separate binary images and PDBs for each version you send out.

CrashFinder has been quite a bit of fun to develop. I've been extremely honored by all the people who have told me that they've found it invaluable on their projects and that it's helped them do their jobs better. What's been even cooler is how many smart developers have jumped in with UI and capabilities improvements. The CrashFinder version with this edition had lots of great work added by Scott Bloom, Ching Ming Kwok, Jeff Shanholtz, Rich Peters, Pablo Presedo, Julian Onions, and Ken Gladstone. I want to thank them for the code and for making CrashFinder even better.

Figure 12-4 shows the CrashFinder user interface with one of my personal projects loaded as a project. The top portion of the child window is a tree control that shows the executable and its associated DLLs. The green check marks indicate that the symbols for each of the binary images have been loaded properly. If CrashFinder couldn't load the symbols, a red X would indicate a problem. Additionally, the tree for the problem item would be expanded to show you exactly why CrashFinder could not properly load the binary.

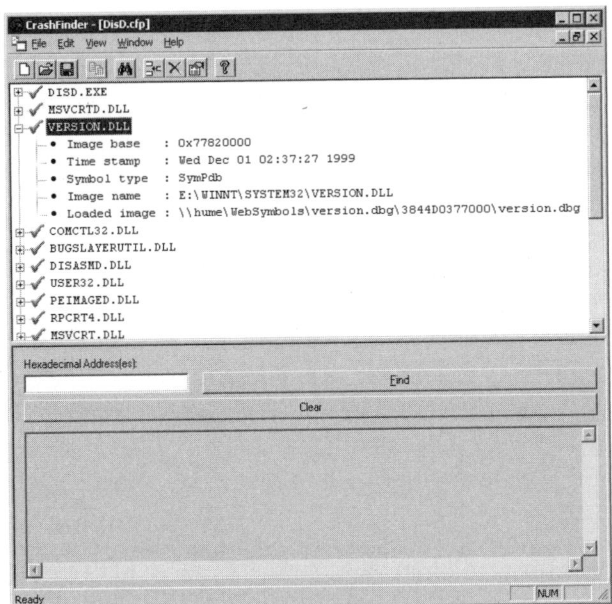

Figure 12-4 The CrashFinder user interface

There are three reasons CrashFinder shows the X. The first is that it can't find the PDB file associated with the binary. Your best bet is to always keep the binary and its PDB file together; if you do, you shouldn't have problems. The second reason is because CrashFinder opens a saved project and can no longer find the binary. The last reason is that CrashFinder sees address load conflicts with any of the DLLs in the project. Since the operating system won't allow you to have any conflicting DLLs, CrashFinder won't either. If you do have a load conflict, you can change the conflicting DLL's address just for the current instance of the CrashFinder project. As I've pointed out several times in this book, having your DLLs rebased is vital to your bug hunting success.

The bottom part of the child window is where the magic of turning a mystical address into a source, function, and line takes place. Before I describe that, I need to tell you how to get your binaries into a CrashFinder project. When you click the New button on the toolbar, you are prompted to add a binary image with a common file dialog box. You should add your EXE first, if you have one. You can select multiple binaries with the Add Binary Image dialog box, so you can add your entire project at once.

After selecting Open, lots of action takes place. One of the great enhancements to the new version of CrashFinder is that it automatically hunts down all implicitly loaded DLLs and adds them to the project. If you have explicitly loaded DLLs such as COM objects, click Add Image on the Edit menu to add each of them. CrashFinder will also bring in any additional implicitly linked modules.

When you're adding binary images, keep in mind that CrashFinder will accept only a single EXE for the project. For your applications comprising multiple EXEs, create a separate CrashFinder project for each EXE. Because CrashFinder is a multiple-document interface (MDI) application, you can easily open all the projects for each of your EXEs to locate the crash location. When you add DLLs, CrashFinder checks that there are no load address conflicts with any other DLLs already in the project. If CrashFinder detects a conflict, it will allow you to change the load address for the conflicting DLL just for the current instance of the CrashFinder project. This option is handy when you have a CrashFinder project for a debug build and you accidentally forget to rebase your DLLs.

As your application changes over time, you can remove binary images by selecting the Remove Image command from the Edit menu. At any time, you can also change a binary image's load address through the Image Properties command on the Edit menu. Since CrashFinder will automatically add the system DLLs used by your binaries, as I mentioned in Chapter 2, your symbol server helps you immensely when debugging. Now you have an even better reason for installing a symbol server—CrashFinder can use them, so you can look up crashes even in system modules. If you look at the information displayed for VERSION.DLL, you'll see it's loading the symbols out of my symbol server.

CrashFinder's raison d'être is to turn a crash address into a source file, function name, and line number. The Hexadecimal Address(es) box in the bottom half of the child window is where you enter the address you want to look up. When you click the Find button, the source file, function name, and line number are displayed in the edit box at the bottom of the window. If you like, you can enter multiple addresses at once, separated by spaces or commas. For example, you can drop in the complete call stack addresses from a Dr. Watson log and find all the sources at once.

By default, CrashFinder doesn't show the function or source displacements. If you would like to see them, you can indicate this in the Options dialog box. The function displacement shows how many code bytes from the start of the function the address is. The source displacement tells you how many code bytes from the start of the closest source line the address is. Remember that many assembly-language instructions can make up a single source line, especially if you use function calls as part of the parameter list. When using CrashFinder, keep in mind that you can't look up an address that isn't a valid instruction address. If you blow out the `this` pointer, you can cause a crash in an address such as 0x00000001. Fortunately, those types of crashes aren't as prevalent as the usual memory access violation crashes, which you can easily find with CrashFinder.

Implementation Highlights

CrashFinder itself is a straightforward Microsoft Foundation Class (MFC) library application, so most of it should be familiar. I want to point out three key areas and explain their implementation highlights so that you can extend CrashFinder more easily with some of the suggestions I offer in the section "What's Next for CrashFinder?" later in the chapter. The first area is the symbol engine, the second is where the work gets done in CrashFinder, and the last is the data architecture.

CrashFinder uses the DBGHELP.DLL symbol engine introduced in Chapter 4. The only detail of interest is that I need to force the symbol engine to load all source file and line number information by passing the `SYMOPT_LOAD_LINES` flag to `SymSetOptions`. The DBGHELP.DLL symbol engine doesn't load source file and line number information by default, so you must explicitly tell the symbol engine to load it.

The second point about CrashFinder's implementation is that all the work is essentially done in the document class, `CCrashFinderDoc`. It holds the `CSymbolEngine` class, does all the symbol lookup, and controls the view. The key function, `CCrashFinderDoc::LoadAndShowImage`, is shown in Listing 12-3. This function is where the binary image is validated and checked against the existing items in the project for load address conflicts, the symbols are loaded, and the image is inserted at the end of the tree. This function is called both when a binary image is added to the project and when the project is opened. By letting `CCrashFinderDoc::LoadAndShowImage` handle all these chores, I ensure that the core logic for CrashFinder is always in one place and that the project needs to store only the binary image names instead of copies of the symbol table.

```
BOOL CCrashFinderDoc :: LoadAndShowImage ( CBinaryImage * pImage      ,
                                           BOOL           bModifiesDoc ,
                                           BOOL           bIgnoreDups  )
{
    // Check the assumptions from outside the function.
    ASSERT ( this ) ;
    ASSERT ( NULL != m_pcTreeControl ) ;

    // A string that can be used for any user messages
    CString   sMsg                      ;
    // The state for the tree graphic
    int       iState = STATE_NOTVALID ;
    // A Boolean return value holder
    BOOL      bRet                      ;

    // Make sure the parameter is good.
    ASSERT ( NULL != pImage ) ;
    if ( NULL == pImage )
    {
        // Nothing much can happen with a bad pointer.
        return ( FALSE ) ;
    }

    // Check to see whether this image is valid. If it is, make sure
    // that it isn't already in the list and that it doesn't have
    // a conflicting load address. If it isn't a valid image, I add
    // it anyway because it isn't good form just to throw out user
    // data. If the image is bad, I just show it with the invalid
    // bitmap and don't load it into the symbol engine.
    if ( TRUE == pImage->IsValidImage ( ) )
    {

        // Here I walk through the items in the data array so that I can
        // look for three problem conditions:
        // 1. The binary image is already in the list. If so, I can
        //    only abort.
        // 2. The binary is going to load at an address that's already
        //    in the list. If that's the case, I'll display the
        //    Properties dialog box for the binary image so that its
        //    load address can be changed before adding it to the list.
        // 3. The project already includes an EXE image, and pImage is
        //     also an executable.

        // I always start out assuming that the data in pImage is valid.
        // Call me an optimist!
        BOOL bValid = TRUE ;
        INT_PTR iCount = m_cDataArray.GetSize ( ) ;
        for ( INT_PTR i = 0 ; i < iCount ; i++ )
```

Listing 12-3 The `CCrashFinderDoc::LoadAndShowImage` function

```
{
    CBinaryImage * pTemp = (CBinaryImage *)m_cDataArray[ i ] ;

    ASSERT ( NULL != pTemp ) ;
    if ( NULL == pTemp )
    {
        // Not much can happen with a bad pointer!
        return ( FALSE ) ;
    }

    // Do these two CString values match?
    if ( pImage->GetFullName ( ) == pTemp->GetFullName ( ) )
    {
        if ( FALSE == bIgnoreDups )
        {
            // Tell the user!!
            sMsg.FormatMessage ( IDS_DUPLICATEFILE      ,
                                 pTemp->GetFullName ( )  ) ;
            AfxMessageBox ( sMsg ) ;
        }
        return ( FALSE ) ;
    }

    // If the current image from the data structure isn't
    // valid, I'm up a creek. Although I can check
    // duplicate names above, it's hard to check load
    // addresses and EXE characteristics. If pTemp isn't valid,
    // I have to skip these checks. Skipping them can lead
    // to problems, but since pTemp is marked in the list as
    // invalid, it's up to the user to reset the properties.
    if ( TRUE == pTemp->IsValidImage ( FALSE ) )
    {

        // Check that I don't add two EXEs to the project.
        if ( 0 == ( IMAGE_FILE_DLL &
                    pTemp->GetCharacteristics ( ) ) )
        {
            if ( 0 == ( IMAGE_FILE_DLL &
                        pImage->GetCharacteristics ( ) ) )

            {
                // Tell the user!!
                sMsg.FormatMessage ( IDS_EXEALREADYINPROJECT ,
                                     pImage->GetFullName ( ) ,
                                     pTemp->GetFullName ( )   ) ;
                AfxMessageBox ( sMsg ) ;
                // Trying to load two images marked as EXEs will
                // automatically have the data thrown out for
                // pImage.
                return ( FALSE ) ;
            }
        }
```

```
            // Check for load address conflicts.
            if ( pImage->GetLoadAddress ( ) ==
                 pTemp->GetLoadAddress( )        )
            {
                sMsg.FormatMessage ( IDS_DUPLICATELOADADDR      ,
                                     pImage->GetFullName ( )    ,
                                     pTemp->GetFullName ( )      ) ;

                if ( IDYES == AfxMessageBox ( sMsg , MB_YESNO ) )
                {
                    // The user wants to change the properties by
                    // hand.
                    pImage->SetProperties ( ) ;

                    // Check that the load address really did
                    // change and that it doesn't now conflict with
                    // another binary.
                    int iIndex ;
                    if ( TRUE ==
                            IsConflictingLoadAddress (
                                       pImage->GetLoadAddress(),
                                       iIndex                   ))
                    {
                        sMsg.FormatMessage
                                  ( IDS_DUPLICATELOADADDRFINAL ,
                                    pImage->GetFullName ( )    ,
              ((CBinaryImage*)m_cDataArray[iIndex])->GetFullName());
                        AfxMessageBox ( sMsg ) ;

                        // The data in pImage isn't valid, so go
                        //  ahead and exit the loop.
                        bValid = FALSE ;
                        break ;
                    }
                }
                else
                {
                    // The data in pImage isn't valid, so go
                    // ahead and exit the loop.
                    bValid = FALSE ;
                    pImage->SetBinaryError ( eAddressConflict ) ;
                    break ;
                }
            }
        }
    }
    if ( TRUE == bValid )
    {
        // This image is good (at least up to the symbol load).
        iState = STATE_VALIDATED ;
    }
```

```
        else
        {
            iState = STATE_NOTVALID ;
        }
    }
    else
    {
        // This image isn't valid.
        iState = STATE_NOTVALID ;
    }

    if ( STATE_VALIDATED == iState )
    {
        bRet = (BOOL)
           m_cSymEng.SymLoadModule64 ( NULL                        ,
                                       (PWSTR)pImage->
                                               GetFullNameString ( ) ,
                                       NULL                        ,
                                       pImage->GetLoadAddress ( )  ,
                                       0                            );
        // Watch out. SymLoadModule returns the load address of the
        // image, not TRUE.
        ASSERT ( FALSE != bRet ) ;
        if ( FALSE == bRet )
        {
            TRACE ( "m_cSymEng.SymLoadModule failed!!\n" ) ;
            iState = STATE_NOTVALID ;
        }
        else
        {
            CImageHlp_Module cModInfo ;
            BOOL bRet =
                  m_cSymEng.SymGetModuleInfo64(pImage->GetLoadAddress(),
                                               &cModInfo             );
            ASSERT ( TRUE == bRet ) ;
            if ( TRUE == bRet )
            {
                // Check if the symbols type is not SymNone.
                if ( SymNone != cModInfo.SymType )
                {
                    iState = STATE_VALIDATED ;
                    // Set the image symbol information.
                    pImage->SetSymbolInformation ( cModInfo ) ;
                }
                else
                {
                    iState = STATE_NOTVALID ;
                    // Unload the module. The symbol engine loads a
                    // module even without symbols so I need to unload
                    // them here. I only want good loads to happen.
                    m_cSymEng.SymUnloadModule64(
                                               pImage->GetLoadAddress());
                    pImage->SetBinaryError ( eNoSymbolsAtAll ) ;
                }
```

```
            }
            else
            {
                iState = STATE_NOTVALID ;
            }
        }
    }

    // Set the extra data value for pImage to the state of the symbol
    // load.
    if ( STATE_VALIDATED == iState )
    {
        pImage->SetExtraData ( TRUE ) ;
    }
    else
    {
        pImage->SetExtraData ( FALSE ) ;
    }

    // Put this item into the array.
    m_cDataArray.Add ( pImage ) ;

    // Does adding the item modify the document?
    if ( TRUE == bModifiesDoc )
    {
        SetModifiedFlag ( ) ;
    }

    // Get the image into the tree.
    bRet = m_cTreeDisplay.InsertImageInTree ( pImage ,
                                              iState   ) ;
    ASSERT ( bRet ) ;

    // All OK, Jumpmaster!!
    return ( bRet ) ;
}
```

The last point I want to mention is about CrashFinder's data architecture. The main data structure is a simple array of `CBinaryImage` classes. The `CBinaryImage` class represents a single binary image added to the project and serves up any core information about a single binary—details such as load address, binary properties, and name. When a binary image is added, the document adds `CBinaryImage` to the main data array and puts the pointer value for it into the tree node's item data slot. When selecting an item in the tree view, the tree view passes the node back to the document so that the document can get `CBinaryImage` and look up its symbol information.

What's Next for CrashFinder?

The first version of CrashFinder got the job done, but it needed some usability help that the fine folks I mentioned earlier and I added, which took care of many issues people had raised. However, tweaks and additions can always make CrashFinder even better and also more powerful. If you want to learn more about binary images, I encourage you to add some of the following features to CrashFinder:

- Set up the different operating system binaries and have CrashFinder automatically switch between the different versions to give you better control over finding crashes originating in operating system code. Right now CrashFinder just looks for the system DLLs you are running on your machine.
- Show more information in the tree control under each binary. The `CBinaryImage` class has the functionality to show more information after the symbol information through the `GetAdditionalInfo` method. You could add the ability to show information from the binary image, such as header information, imported functions, and exported functions.
- Allow pasting in of DLL lists to automatically add them to the project. The debugger Output window lists all the DLLs that an application loads. You could extend CrashFinder to allow the user to paste in the Output window text and have CrashFinder scan through the text looking for DLL names.
- Coordinate CrashFinder with any crash dumps you get from the field. CrashFinder could double-check the crash against the crash dump and see exactly what went wrong.

Summary

This chapter helped demystify the process of what you do to pinpoint the location of a crash when the only information you have is the crash address. The first technique for finding out the source file and line number of a particular crash is to refer to a MAP file. MAP files are the only textual representation of your symbols, and you should create them routinely for every release build of your application. The second technique for converting a crash address to a source file, function name, and line number is to use CrashFinder. The CrashFinder utility takes all the work out of making this conversion and allows others on your team to report as much information as possible when the application crashes on them. Although CrashFinder is easier to use than MAP files, you still need to get into the habit of creating MAP files because symbol file formats change—and when they do, only your MAP files will save your soul when the ghost of applications past comes knocking at your door.

13

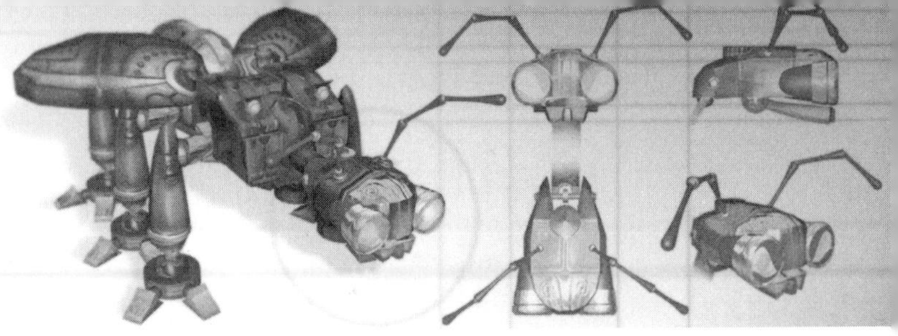

Crash Handlers

This news flash shouldn't come as a shock, but I'm going to let you in on a little secret: your users really hate seeing that Application Error or error report dialog box pop up when your application crashes. The fact that you're reading this book means that you're trying hard to avoid crashes in the first place. As we all know, however, crashes happen even in the best applications, and you need to be prepared for them.

Instead of just letting the Application Error dialog box make an appearance and irritate your users, wouldn't it be nice if a user-friendly dialog box popped up and reported the problem, and asked the users exactly what they were doing at the time of the crash? Wouldn't it be even better if, in addition to recording the usual crash address and call stack that utilities such as Dr. Watson give you, this kinder and gentler dialog box recorded the internal state of your program so that you could get the processing and data states at the time of the crash? And wouldn't it just be icing on the cake if the dialog box automatically e-mailed the crash information to you and logged a bug report directly into your bug tracking system?

Crash handlers can turn such wishful thinking into reality, providing you with all the cool information I fantasized about in the preceding paragraph. *Crash handlers* is the term I've come up with to describe both exception handlers and unhandled exception filters. If you've done any C++ programming, you should be familiar with exception handlers. You might know less about unhandled exception filters, which are interesting routines that allow you to gain control right before that Application Error dialog box that drives your users crazy pops up. Whereas exception handlers are C++ specific, unhandled exception filters work for both C and C++ code.

In this chapter, I'll present code that you can drop into your applications to get crash information such as registers and call stacks. In addition, the code will hide much of the dirty work of gathering this information for you so that you can concentrate on reporting the information that is unique to your application and on presenting a better face to the user. As part of this information gathering, I'll also cover how to get the most out of the excellent `MiniDumpWriteDump` API function so that you can get minidumps any time you need them. Before I can jump into the code, however, I need to spend some time describing the various types of exception handling in Microsoft Win32 systems.

Structured Exception Handling vs. C++ Exception Handling

Getting up to speed on exception handling can be tough partly because C++ can use two main types of exception handling: structured exception handling (SEH), which the operating system provides, and C++ exception handling, which the C++ language provides. Just figuring out which type of exception handling to use when can be a challenge, and it doesn't help that many people talk about both types as if they were interchangeable. I assure you that each type of exception handling has a distinctly different approach. The one common aspect is that exceptions of either type are for exceptional conditions, not for normal processing and logic. I think what confuses some people are the rumors that you can combine both types. In the following sections, I'll touch on the differences and similarities between these two types of exception handling. I'll also discuss how to avoid the biggest bug generator of them all when it comes to exceptions.

Structured Exception Handling

The operating system provides SEH, and it deals directly with crashes such as access violations. SEH is language-independent but is usually implemented in C and C++ programs with the `__try`/`__except` and `__try`/`__finally` keyword pairs. The way you use the `__try`/`__except` pair is to set your code inside a `__try` block and then determine how to handle the exception in the `__except` block (also called an exception handler). In a `__try`/`__finally` pair, the `__finally` block (also called a termination handler) ensures that a section of code will always be executed upon leaving a function, even if the code in the `__try` block terminates prematurely, so you can be guaranteed that resources will be cleaned up.

Listing 13-1 shows a typical function with SEH. The `__except` block looks almost like a function call, but the parentheses specify the value of a special expression called an exception filter. The exception filter value in Listing 13-1 is `EXCEPTION_EXECUTE_HANDLER`, which indicates that the code in the `__except` block must be executed every time any exception occurs inside the `__try` block. The two other possible exception filter values are `EXCEPTION_CONTINUE_EXECUTION`, which allows an exception to be ignored, and `EXCEPTION_CONTINUE_SEARCH`, which passes the exception up the call chain to the next `__except` block. You can make the exception filter expression as simple or as complicated as you like so that you target only those exceptions you're interested in handling.

```
void Foo ( void )
{
    __try
    {
        __try
        {
            // Execute code to accomplish something.
        }
        __except ( EXCEPTION_EXECUTE_HANDLER )
        {
            // This block will be executed if the code in the __try
            // block causes an access violation or some other hard crash.
            // The code in here is also called the exception handler.
        }
    }
    __finally
    {
        // This block will be executed regardless of whether the function
        // causes a crash. Mandatory cleanup code goes here.
    }
}
```

Listing 13-1 Example SEH handler

The process of finding and executing an exception handler is sometimes called *unwinding the exception*. Exception handlers are kept on an internal stack; as the function call chain grows, the exception handler (if one exists) for each new function is pushed onto this internal stack. When an exception occurs, the operating system finds the thread's exception handler stack and starts calling the exception handlers until one exception handler indicates that it will handle the exception. As the exception works its way down the exception handler stack, the operating system cleans up the call stack and executes any termination handlers it finds along the way. If the unwinding continues to the end of the exception handler stack, the Application Error dialog box or the installed JIT debugger pops up.

Your exception handler can determine the exception value by calling the special `GetExceptionCode` function, which can be called only in exception filters. If you were writing a math package, for example, you might have an exception handler that handles divide-by-zero attempts and returns NaN (not a number). The code in Listing 13-2 shows an example of such an exception handler. The exception filter calls GetExceptionCode, and if the exception is divide-by-zero, the exception handler executes. If any other exception occurs, EXCEPTION_CONTINUE_SEARCH tells the operating system to execute the next __except block up the call chain.

```
long IntegerDivide ( long x , long y )
{
    long lRet ;

    __try
    {
        lRet = x / y ;
    }
    __except ( EXCEPTION_INT_DIVIDE_BY_ZERO ==
                GetExceptionCode ( )
                    ? EXCEPTION_EXECUTE_HANDLER
                    : EXCEPTION_CONTINUE_SEARCH
              )
    {
        lRet = NaN ;
    }
    return ( lRet ) ;
}
```

Listing 13-2 Example SEH handler with exception filter processing

If your exception filter requires more complexity, you can even call one of your own functions as the exception filter as long as it specifies how to handle the exception by returning one of the valid exception filter values. In addition to calling the special GetExceptionCode function, you can also call the GetExceptionInformation function in the exception filter expression. GetExceptionInformation returns a pointer to an EXCEPTION_POINTERS structure that completely describes the reason for a crash and the state of the CPU at that time. You might have guessed that the EXCEPTION_POINTERS structure will come in handy later in this chapter.

SEH isn't limited just to handling crashes. You can also create your own exceptions with the RaiseException API function. Most developers don't use RaiseException, but it does offer a way to quickly leave deeply nested conditional statements in code. The RaiseException exit technique is cleaner than using the old setjmp and longjmp run-time functions.

Before you dive in and start using SEH, you need to be aware of two of its limitations. The first is minor: your custom error codes are limited to a single unsigned integer. The second limitation is a little more serious: SEH doesn't mix well with C++ programming because C++ exceptions are implemented internally with SEH and the compiler complains when you try to combine them indiscriminately. The reason for the conflict is that when straight SEH unwinds out of a function, it doesn't call any of the C++ object destructors for objects created on the stack. Because C++ objects can do all sorts of initialization in their constructors, such as allocating memory for internal data structures, skipping the destructors can lead to memory leaks and other problems.

If you'd like to learn more about the basics of SEH, I recommend two references in addition to perusing the Microsoft Developer Network (MSDN). The best overview of SEH is in Jeffrey Richter's *Programming Applications for Microsoft Windows* (Microsoft Press, 1999). If you're curious about the actual SEH implementation, check out Matt Pietrek's article "A Crash Course on the Depths of Win32 Structured Exception Handling" in the January 1997 *Microsoft Systems Journal*.

One advanced feature of SEH I do want to mention, which first appeared with Microsoft Windows XP and Microsoft Windows Server 2003, is vectored exception handling. With regular SEH, there's no way to get globally notified when an exception occurs. Although generally not something you'd like to have as part of your day-to-day development, vectored exception handling allows you to get either the first notification or the last notification of all SEH exceptions occurring in your application. The first time I realized that Microsoft had added vectored exception handling to the operating system, I immediately saw how to write an exception monitor for SEH so that you could keep an eye on what exceptions your application was generating without running your application under a debugger.

To set up receiving vectored exceptions, simply call the `AddVectoredExceptionHandler` function, where the second parameter is a pointer to the function you want called when any first-chance exceptions occur in your application. The first parameter is a Boolean value that indicates whether you want notifications before or after the normal exception chain unwinding. Your callback function will get a pointer to an `EXCEPTION_POINTERS` structure describing the exception. As you can guess, armed with that information, getting the exceptions is a piece of cake.

The XPExceptMon project, which you can find with this book's sample files, shows exactly how to use the vectored exceptions because it writes out each exception your application encounters. All the work for setting up and tearing down the vectored exception hook takes place in the `DllMain` for XPExceptMon.DLL, so utilizing it from your applications is trivial. My interest was showing vectored exceptions, so all XPExceptMon does is report the exception type and the faulting address to a text file. If you're looking for a place to get some practice using the DBGHELP.DLL symbol engine, feel free to add function lookup and stack walking to XPExceptMon.

If you'd like to get exception notifications on earlier Windows versions, you're in luck. Eugene Gershnik wrote an excellent article, "Visual C++ Exception-Handling Instrumentation," in the December 2002 issue of *Windows Developer Magazine*. In addition to showing you how to hook exception handling, Eugene has a great discussion of how exception handling works.

C++ Exception Handling

Because C++ exception handling is part of the C++ language specification, it's probably more familiar to most programmers than SEH. The keywords for C++ exception handling are `try` and `catch`. The `throw` keyword allows you to initiate an exception unwind. Whereas SEH error codes are limited to just a single unsigned integer, a C++ `catch` statement can handle any variable type, including classes. If you derive your error handling classes from a common base class, you can handle just about any error you need to in your code. This class hierarchy approach to error handling is exactly what the Microsoft Foundation Class (MFC) library does with its `CException` base class. Listing 13-3 shows C++ exception handling in action with an MFC `CFile` class read.

```
BOOL ReadFileHeader ( CFile * pFile , LPHEADERINFO pHeader )
{
    ASSERT ( FALSE == IsBadReadPtr ( pFile , sizeof ( CFile * ) ) ) ;
    ASSERT ( FALSE == IsBadReadPtr ( pHeader ,
                                     sizeof ( LPHEADERINFO ) ) ) ;
    if ( ( TRUE == IsBadReadPtr ( pFile , sizeof ( CFile * ) ) ) ||
         ( TRUE == IsBadReadPtr ( pHeader ,
                                  sizeof ( LPHEADERINFO )     ) )    )
    {
        return ( FALSE ) ;
    }

    BOOL bRet ;
    try
    {
        pFile->Read ( pHeader , sizeof ( HEADERINFO ) ) ;
        bRet = TRUE ;
    }
    catch ( CFileException * e )
    {
        // If the header couldn't be read because the file was
        // truncated, handle it; otherwise, continue the unwind.
        if ( CFileException::endOfFile == e->m_cause )
```

Listing 13-3 C++ exception handler example

```
        {
            e->Delete();
            bRet = false;
        }
        else
        {
            // The throw keyword just by itself throws the same exception
            // as passed to this catch block.
            throw ;
        }
    }
    return ( bRet ) ;
}
```

You need to keep in mind the following drawbacks when you're using C++ exception handling. First, it doesn't handle your program crashes automatically. Second, C++ exception processing isn't free. The compiler might do a great deal of work setting up and removing the `try` and `catch` blocks even if you never throw any exceptions, so if you're working on performance-sensitive code you might not be able to afford that much overhead. If you're new to C++ exception handling, MSDN is a great place to start learning about it.

Avoid Using C++ Exception Handling

Probably one of the most consistently confusing issues that comes up for development shops in my company's consulting business is the issue of C++ exception handling. Developers have wasted more effort on C++ exception handling problems than on anything else (except memory corruptions) when it comes to Windows development. Based on all the horrific situations we've resolved, my recommendation is to avoid C++ exception handling because your life will get infinitely simpler and your code will be easier to debug.

The first problem with C++ exception handling is that it isn't a clean feature of the language. In many ways, it looks grafted on and unfinished. The fact that we don't have an ANSI standard class that contains information about an exception means that there's no consistent way of handling generic errors. Some of you might be thinking about the `catch (...)` construct as the standard approved catchall mechanism, but in the next section I'll permanently scare you off from ever using that construct again.

C++ exception handling is also one of those technologies that looks great in theory but breaks down the minute you implement anything more than "Hello World!" Repeatedly I've seen completely insane situations on teams where someone becomes enamored with C++ exceptions and starts implementing tons of them in his code. This forces the rest of the team to deal with C++ exception handling across the application, even though very few developers can deal with the ramifications of designing and using them. What invariably happens is that some code forgets to catch some random unexpected exception, and the application goes down. Additionally, the maintenance nightmare of trying to extend code that mixes return value failures as well as C++ exceptions means that many companies find it better to throw out the code and start again, thus massively increasing their costs.

Many people throw (pun intended!) out the argument that the best reason for using C++ exceptions is that developers never check return values from functions. Not only is this a complete red herring argument, but it's also an excuse for bad programming. If a developer on your team has a consistent problem checking return values, she needs counseling on the correct way to do it. If she still can't check return values, fire her. She is simply not doing her job.

Up to this point, I've been discussing issues with the design and management of C++ exceptions. What many developers fail to consider is that C++ exceptions have quite a bit of overhead associated with them. The code necessary to set up the `try` and `catch` blocks takes a lot of work, adding to your performance woes even if you rarely (if ever) cause an exception.

Another implementation issue is that Microsoft implemented C++ exceptions under the covers with SEH, meaning that every C++ throw is calling `RaiseException`. There's nothing wrong with that, but each throw causes the happy trip to kernel mode. Although the actual transition from user mode to kernel mode is very fast, the work done in kernel mode to manipulate your exception leads to a ton of overhead. Back in Chapter 7's "Tips and Tricks" section, I discussed monitoring C++ exceptions in your applications to help pinpoint this overhead.

Developers sometimes seem oblivious to the cost of C++ exception handling. Working on one company's code performance problem, I couldn't understand why the `_except_handler3` function, which is executed as part of exception processing, was called so many times. As I inspected the code, it dawned on me that a developer on the team was using C++ exception handling in place of the tried-and-true `switch...case` construct. To speed up the application, the company had to redesign large portions of that developer's code simply to return enumerated type values. When I asked the developer why he used C++ exception handling, he told me that he thought a `throw` statement just changed the instruction pointer. Only code for which performance isn't important can use C++ exception handling.

Absolutely, Positively, *NEVER EVER* Use `catch ( ... )`

The `catch (...)`construct has been very good to my bank account because it has caused more bugs in people's code than you can ever imagine. There are two huge problems with `catch (...)`. The first is with its design as specified by the ANSI standard. The ellipsis means that the `catch` block catches any type of throw.

However, since there's no variable in the catch, you have absolutely no way of knowing how you got there and why. The design of catch (...) means you might as well change the instruction pointer to random spots in your code and start executing. With no ability to know what was thrown or how you got there, the only safe and logical action you can take is to terminate the application. Some of you might be thinking that's a drastic step, but there's nothing else you can safely do.

The second problem with catch (...) concerns implementation. What many people don't realize is that in the Windows C run time, catch (...) eats not only C++ exceptions but also SEH exceptions! Not only do you have a situation in which you don't know how you ended up executing inside the catch block, but you also might have ended up in the catch block because of an access violation or another hard error. In addition to being lost, your program is probably completely unstable in the catch block, so you have to terminate the process immediately.

It boggles my mind how many times I've seen developers—and senior developers at that—implement code like the following:

```
BOOL DoSomeWork ( void )
{
    BOOL bRet = TRUE ;
    try
    {
        ...Do a bunch of code...
    }
    catch ( ... )
    {
        // NOTICE THERE'S NO CODE IN HERE!
    }
    return ( bRet ) ;
}
```

What happens in these catch (...) situations is that your code will have some sort of access violation, which gets eaten so you don't even know it happened. After 20 minutes or more, your program crashes and you have no earthly idea why it crashed because the call stack doesn't capture the causal relationship. You're left wondering how the problem occurred. Based on what I've seen while debugging many applications, the number-one cause of unexplained bugs is catch (...). You're far better off letting the application crash, because at least you'll stand a reasonable chance of finding the bug. With catch (...) involved, the odds decrease to less than a 5 percent chance of finding it.

If you can't tell, I'm passionate about ridding your code of catch (...) statements. In fact, I expect you to put this book down, search your source files, and remove any catch (...)'s immediately. If you don't, you'll probably be hiring me soon to help find the bug—and while you're at it, helping me make another car payment.

Debugging War Story

The Case Against `catch (...)`

The Battle

I was sitting in my car driving to the airport to go visit a client. Our office manager called and said that we'd gotten a call for consulting work that sounded not only desperate but also absolutely frantic. As we were in the business of helping frantic people, I called to see what was up. The manager wasn't just frantic—he was apoplectic! He said they had a completely random bug, still unsolved, which was holding up their release. He also said that this was the least of his problems, because if they couldn't fix this bug and ship their product, their company was going out of business. They also had over 10 engineers working on this bug for three weeks straight, with no luck whatsoever. Because I don't get much excitement in my life these days compared with what I experienced in previous jobs, the opportunity to save a company certainly piqued my interest. This person then asked how fast I could make it down to their site. I told him that I was driving to the airport on my way to Seattle for the week and so I couldn't make it down until after that. We'd recently started Wintellect and didn't have anyone else on staff who was free.

At this point, he started speaking much, much louder (OK, screaming), exclaiming that he couldn't wait that long. He asked if my work in Seattle was a 24-hour-a-day job. It wasn't, so he told me I could work on his problem in the evenings. That sounded fine to me, and I told him I'd work on his bug until midnight, at which point he pulled the phone away from his ear and screamed, "He's gonna be in Seattle. Get on a plane now!" He told me that he had two engineers on their way to the airport with all the equipment necessary to debug the problems. When I asked what was going to happen if we didn't get it fixed before I had to leave Seattle, his response was, "We'll be following you to New Hampshire." This bug had already moved into the super-serious category.

The next evening I showed up at the apartment the engineers had rented and was confronted with two people who were so tired they were wobbling on their feet. They'd been working on this bug for nearly three weeks straight without much of a break. After showing me their application, I immediately broke out in a complete and utter flop sweat! They were working on a custom GINA (Graphical Identification and Authentication), the logon screen that used a custom smart card reader to log all across a custom terminal server session! Talk about a nasty application to debug! Since much of the application ran inside LSASS.EXE, you could get debugging started, but if you clicked anywhere outside the debugger, you locked the machine. To make my life even more interesting, the engineers used the Standard Template Library (STL) all over the place, so in addition to a very tough debugging problem, they had unreadable code. As we all should know, STL's main claim to fame isn't reusable data structures but rather job security. Since STL code is unreadable and unmaintainable, your company will be forced to keep paying you because only you can understand the code.

I asked them whether they could show me anything resembling duplicable crashes or data corruption. They had a document listing the 10 or 12 places they had seen crashes. My initial hypothesis was that they had a wild write to uninitialized memory. After spending a few hours figuring out how the system fit together and getting used to debugging their application, I started trying to determine whether we could find those uninitialized pointers. Grinding through the source code, I noticed they had lots of `catch (...)` statements all over the place. At the end of the first evening, I told them they needed to remove all the `catch (...)` statements so that we could see the corruption immediately and try to start narrowing down the problem.

The Outcome

When I went back to the apartment the second day, these engineers were pushed right to the edge of their physical limits. They told me that once they'd commented out the `catch (...)` statements, the application didn't initialize. While the developers took a nap, I started looking through the startup code and quickly found the following:

```
//catch ( ... )
//{
    return ( FALSE ) ;
//}
```

In their sleep-addled state, they'd forgotten to comment out the `return` statement. I commented it out, recompiled, and ran the program. It crashed almost immediately. On the second run, it crashed in the same place, which was the first time they'd seen a consistent crash. The third crash was a charm, and I started inspecting every single thing happening up the stack.

After carefully reading the code, we found the error in only a couple of hours. The documentation called for a buffer that was passed to another function to be 250 characters in size. A developer was passing a

(continued)

Debugging War Story *(continued)*

local variable as the buffer and had typed 25 instead of 250. Once we fixed the typo, we were able to run the application to completion!

The Lesson

The lesson is simple: don't use `catch (...)`! This particular company had already wasted weeks of work (and tons of money) attempting to track down a bug that was completely solvable but not reproducible because `catch (...)` was involved.

Don't Use _set_se_translator

In the first edition of this book, I covered the use of an interesting API named `_set_se_translator`. It has the magical ability to turn your SEH errors into C++ exceptions by calling a translation function that you define, which simply calls `throw` on the type you want to use for the conversion. I might as well confess now that although I was well intentioned, my advice was wrong. When you use `_set_se_translator`, you quickly find out that it doesn't work in release builds.

The first problem with `_set_se_translator` is that it isn't global in scope; it works only on a per-thread basis. That means you probably have to redesign your code to ensure that you call `_set_se_translator` at the beginning of each thread. Unfortunately, doing that isn't always easy. Additionally, if you're writing a component used by other processes you don't control, using `_set_se_translator` can and will completely mess up those processes' exception handling if they are expecting SEH exceptions and getting C++ exceptions instead.

The bigger problem with `_set_se_translator` has to do with the arcane implementation details of C++ exception handling. C++ exception handling can be implemented in two ways: asynchronous and synchronous. In asynchronous mode, the code generator assumes that every instruction can throw an exception. In synchronous mode, exceptions are generated explicitly only by a `throw` statement. The differences between asynchronous and synchronous exception handling don't seem that great, but they certainly are.

The drawback of asynchronous exceptions is that the compiler must generate what's called *object lifetime tracking code* for every function. Since the compiler is assuming that every instruction can throw an exception, every function that puts a C++ class onto the stack has to have code in it to hook up the destructor calls for each object in case an exception is thrown. Since exceptions are supposed to be rare or nearly impossible events, the downside to asynchronous exceptions is that you're paying quite a performance cost for all that object lifetime tracking code you'll never use.

Synchronous exception handling, on the other hand, solves the overhead problem by generating the object lifetime tracking code only when a method in the call tree for that method has an explicit `throw`. In fact, synchronous exception handling is such a good idea that it's the exception type the compiler uses. However, with the compiler assuming that exceptions occur only with an explicit `throw` in the call stack, the translator function does the `throw`, which is outside the normal code flow and is thus asynchronous. Consequently your carefully constructed C++ exception wrapper class never gets handled and your application crashes anyway. If you want to experiment with the differences between asynchronous and synchronous exception handling, add `/EHa` to the compiler command line to turn on asynchronous and remove any `/GX` or `/EHs` switches.

What makes using `_set_se_translator` even worse is that it works correctly in debug builds. Only in release builds will you experience the problems. That's because debug builds use synchronous exception handling instead of the release-build default of asynchronous. Because of the inherent problems with `_set_se_translator`, you'll definitely want to look for it in your code reviews to ensure that no one is using it.

The `SetUnhandledExceptionFilter` API Function

Interestingly, crashes have a habit of never happening where you expect them. Unfortunately, when your users experience crashes in your program, they just see the Application Error dialog box, and then maybe Dr. Watson gives them a little information to send to you to figure out the problem. As I mentioned earlier in this chapter, you can devise your own dialog boxes and handlers to get the information you really need to solve the crash. I've always referred to these exception handlers along with their corresponding exception filters as crash handlers.

In my experience, crash handlers have excellent debugging capabilities. I've worked on numerous projects where we'd gain control right as the application died, gather all the information about the crash (including the state of the user's system) into a file, and if the project was a client application, pop up a dialog box with a technical support number. In some cases, we architected the application so that we could iterate through the program's main objects, enabling us to report down to the class level which objects were active and what they contained. We were logging almost too much information about the program's state. With a crash report, we had a 90 percent chance of duplicating the user's problem. If that isn't proactive debugging, I don't know what is!

You create crash handlers through the magic of the SetUnhandledExceptionFilter API function. Amazingly, this functionality has been in Win32 since Microsoft Windows NT 3.5, but it's almost never mentioned in the documentation. At the time I wrote this chapter, in MSDN Online, this function was mentioned only eight times.

Needless to say, I find SetUnhandledExceptionFilter powerful. Just by looking at the function name—SetUnhandledExceptionFilter—you can probably guess what the function does. SetUnhandledExceptionFilter allows you to specify an unhandled exception filter function that should be called when an unhandled exception occurs in a process. The one parameter to SetUnhandledExceptionFilter is a pointer to an exception filter function that is called in the final __except block for the application. This exception filter returns the same value that any exception filter would return: EXCEPTION_EXECUTE_HANDLER, EXCEPTION_CONTINUE_EXECUTION, or EXCEPTION_CONTINUE_SEARCH. You can do any exception handling you want in the exception filter, but you need to be careful about blown stacks in your exception filter. To be on the safe side, you might want to avoid any C run-time library calls as well as MFC. Although I'm obligated to warn you about these possibilities, I can assure you that the vast majority of your crashes will be access violations—you shouldn't have any problems if you write a complete crash handling system in your exception filter and exception handler, provided you check the exception reason first and avoid function calls when the stack is blown.

Your exception filter also gets a pointer to an EXCEPTION_POINTERS structure. In Listing 13-4, I'll present several routines that translate this structure for you. Because each company has different crash handler needs, I'll let you write your own.

You need to keep in mind a couple of issues when you're using SetUnhandledExceptionFilter. The first is that you can't use standard user-mode debuggers to debug any unhandled exception filter you set. This restriction actually makes sense, because the operating system needs to take over the final exception filter when running under a debugger so that the operating system can properly report the final crash to the debugger. However, it can make debugging your final crash handler a bit of a pain. One workaround you can use to debug your unhandled exception filter is to call it from a regular SEH exception filter. You can find an example of this workaround in the Baz function in BugslayerUtil\Tests\CrashHandler\CrashHandler.CPP, which is part of this book's source code.

Another issue is that the exception filter you specify by calling SetUnhandledExceptionFilter is global to your process. If you build the coolest crash handler in the world for your ActiveX control and the container crashes—even if it's not your fault—your crash handler will be executed. Don't let this possibility keep you from using `SetUnhandledExceptionFilter`, though. I have some code that might help you out.

Common Debugging Question

Is there anything you can do to fix blown stacks from infinite recursion?

Infinite recursion is not, thank goodness, that common, but when it does happen, it's nearly impossible to debug. If you've ever seen an application appear to pause for a second or so and completely disappear without displaying an Application Error dialog box, you're almost certainly looking at infinite recursion. If you can't even get a chance to debug the application, it's very hard to figure out what went wrong with it.

Fortunately, the new `_resetstkoflw` C run-time function attempts to get you some stack space so that you can at least report the error. If you'd like to see how `_resetstkoflw` does its magic, check out its implementation, which is included in RESETSTK.C.

Using the `CrashHandler` API

In the reusable module BUGSLAYERUTIL.DLL, I wrote the CrashHandler API, which you can use to limit your crash handler to a specific module or modules. I limit your crash handler by making all unhandled exceptions pass through an unhandled exception filter that I set. When my unhandled exception filter is called, I check the module that the exception came from. If the exception is from one of the specified modules, I call your crash handler, but if it's from a module outside those that were specified, I call the unhandled exception filter I replaced. Calling the replaced exception filter means that multiple modules can use my CrashHandler API without stepping on one another. If no modules are specified, your crash handler will always be called. You can see all the CrashHandler API functions in Listing 13-4. I strongly encourage you to read the code over because if you understand it, you'll learn quite a bit about exception handling, using the DBGHELP.DLL symbol engine, and how to walk the stack.

```
/*----------------------------------------------------------------------
Debugging Applications for Microsoft .NET and Microsoft Windows
Copyright © 1997-2003 John Robbins -- All rights reserved.
----------------------------------------------------------------------*/

#include "pch.h"
#include "BugslayerUtil.h"
#include "CrashHandler.h"

// The project internal header file
#include "Internal.h"

/*//////////////////////////////////////////////////////////////////////
// File Scope Defines
//////////////////////////////////////////////////////////////////////*/
// The maximum symbol size handled in the module
#define MAX_SYM_SIZE  512
#define BUFF_SIZE 2048
#define SYM_BUFF_SIZE 1024

// String format constants. To avoid doing tons of ANSI to UNICODE
// conversions myself, I rely on wsprintf to do them. In order to make
// this file happy for ANSI compiles, I need keep the %S out of the
// format strings.
#ifdef UNICODE
#define k_NAMEDISPFMT       _T ( " %S()+%04d byte(s)" )
#define k_NAMEFMT           _T ( " %S " )
#define k_FILELINEDISPFMT   _T ( " %S, line %04d+%04d byte(s)" )
#define k_FILELINEFMT       _T ( " %S, line %04d" )
#else
#define k_NAMEDISPFMT       _T ( " %s()+%04d byte(s)" )
#define k_NAMEFMT           _T ( " %s " )
#define k_FILELINEDISPFMT   _T ( " %s, line %04d+%04d byte(s)" )
#define k_FILELINEFMT       _T ( " %s, line %04d" )
#endif

#ifdef _WIN64
#define k_PARAMFMTSTRING   _T ( " (0x%016X 0x%016X 0x%016X 0x%016X)" )
#else
#define k_PARAMFMTSTRING   _T ( " (0x%08X 0x%08X 0x%08X 0x%08X)" )
#endif

// Define the machine type.
#ifdef _X86_
#define CH_MACHINE IMAGE_FILE_MACHINE_I386
#elif _AMD64_
#define CH_MACHINE IMAGE_FILE_MACHINE_AMD64
```

Listing 13-4 CRASHHANDLER.CPP

```
#elif _IA64_
#define CH_MACHINE IMAGE_FILE_MACHINE_IA64
#else
#pragma FORCE COMPILE ABORT!
#endif

/*//////////////////////////////////////////////////////////////////////
// File Scope Global Variables
//////////////////////////////////////////////////////////////////////*/
// The custom unhandled exception filter (crash handler)
static PFNCHFILTFN g_pfnCallBack = NULL ;

// The original unhandled exception filter
static LPTOP_LEVEL_EXCEPTION_FILTER g_pfnOrigFilt = NULL ;

// The array of modules to limit crash handler to
static HMODULE * g_ahMod = NULL ;
// The size, in items, of g_ahMod
static UINT g_uiModCount = 0 ;

// The static buffer returned by various functions. This buffer
// allows data to be transferred without using the stack.
static TCHAR g_szBuff [ BUFF_SIZE ] ;

// The static symbol lookup buffer
static BYTE g_stSymbol [ SYM_BUFF_SIZE ] ;

// The static source file and line number structure
static IMAGEHLP_LINE64 g_stLine ;

// The stack frame used in walking the stack
static STACKFRAME64 g_stFrame ;

// The flag indicating that the symbol engine has been initialized
static BOOL g_bSymEngInit = FALSE ;

// The original version of this code changed the CONTEXT structure when
// passed through the stack walking code. Therefore, if the user
// utilized the containing  EXCEPTION_POINTERS to write a mini dump, the
// dump wasn't correct. I now save off the CONTEXT as a global, much
// like the stack frame.
static CONTEXT g_stContext ;

/*//////////////////////////////////////////////////////////////////////
// File Scope Function Declarations
//////////////////////////////////////////////////////////////////////*/
// The exception handler
LONG __stdcall CrashHandlerExceptionFilter ( EXCEPTION_POINTERS *
                                                  pExPtrs             ) ;

// Converts a simple exception to a string value
LPCTSTR ConvertSimpleException ( DWORD dwExcept ) ;
```

(continued)

```
// The internal function that does all the stack walking
LPCTSTR __stdcall InternalGetStackTraceString ( DWORD dwOpts ) ;

// Initializes the symbol engine if needed
void InitSymEng ( void ) ;

// Cleans up the symbol engine if needed
void CleanupSymEng ( void ) ;

/*//////////////////////////////////////////////////////////////////////
// Destructor Class
//////////////////////////////////////////////////////////////////////*/
// See the note in MEMDUMPERVALIDATOR.CPP about automatic classes.
// Turn off warning : initializers put in library initialization area
#pragma warning (disable : 4073)
#pragma init_seg(lib)
class CleanUpCrashHandler
{
public  :
    CleanUpCrashHandler ( void )
    {
    }
    ~CleanUpCrashHandler ( void )
    {
        // Are there any outstanding memory allocations?
        if ( NULL != g_ahMod )
        {
            VERIFY ( HeapFree ( GetProcessHeap ( ) ,
                                0                  ,
                                g_ahMod             ) ) ;
            g_ahMod = NULL ;
            // FIXED BUG - Thanks to Gennady Mayko.
            g_uiModCount = 0 ;
        }
        if ( NULL != g_pfnOrigFilt )
        {
            // Restore the original unhandled exception filter.
            SetUnhandledExceptionFilter ( g_pfnOrigFilt ) ;
            g_pfnOrigFilt = NULL ;
        }
    }
} ;

// The static class
static CleanUpCrashHandler g_cBeforeAndAfter ;

/*//////////////////////////////////////////////////////////////////////
// Crash Handler Function Implementation
//////////////////////////////////////////////////////////////////////*/

BOOL __stdcall SetCrashHandlerFilter ( PFNCHFILTFN pFn )
{
    // A NULL parameter unhooks the callback.
    if ( NULL == pFn )
```

```
    {
        if ( NULL != g_pfnOrigFilt )
        {
            // Restore the original unhandled exception filter.
            SetUnhandledExceptionFilter ( g_pfnOrigFilt ) ;
            g_pfnOrigFilt = NULL ;
            if ( NULL != g_ahMod )
            {
                // FIXED BUG:
                // Previously, I called "free" instead of "HeapFree."
                VERIFY ( HeapFree ( GetProcessHeap ( ) ,
                                    0                  ,
                                    g_ahMod             ) ) ;
                g_ahMod = NULL ;
                // FIXED BUG - Thanks to Gennady Mayko.
                g_uiModCount = 0 ;
            }
            g_pfnCallBack = NULL ;
        }
    }
    else
    {
        ASSERT ( FALSE == IsBadCodePtr ( (FARPROC)pFn ) ) ;
        if ( TRUE == IsBadCodePtr ( (FARPROC)pFn ) )
        {
            return ( FALSE ) ;
        }
        g_pfnCallBack = pFn ;

        // If a custom crash handler isn't already in use, enable
        // CrashHandlerExceptionFilter and save the original unhandled
        // exception filter.
        if ( NULL == g_pfnOrigFilt )
        {
            g_pfnOrigFilt =
               SetUnhandledExceptionFilter(CrashHandlerExceptionFilter);
        }
    }
    return ( TRUE ) ;
}

BOOL __stdcall AddCrashHandlerLimitModule ( HMODULE hMod )
{
    // Check the obvious cases.
    ASSERT ( NULL != hMod ) ;
    if ( NULL == hMod )
    {
        return ( FALSE ) ;
    }

    // Allocate a temporary array. This array must be allocated from
    // memory that's guaranteed to be around even if the process is
    // toasting. If the process is toasting, the RTL heap probably isn't
    // safe, so I allocate the temporary array from the process heap.
```

(continued)

```
    HMODULE * phTemp = (HMODULE*)
                    HeapAlloc ( GetProcessHeap ( )                    ,
                                HEAP_ZERO_MEMORY |
                                   HEAP_GENERATE_EXCEPTIONS           ,
                                (sizeof(HMODULE)*(g_uiModCount+1))   ) ;
    ASSERT ( NULL != phTemp ) ;
    if ( NULL == phTemp )
    {
        TRACE ( "Serious trouble in the house! - "
                "HeapAlloc failed!!!\n"              );
        return ( FALSE ) ;
    }

    if ( NULL == g_ahMod )
    {
        g_ahMod = phTemp ;
        g_ahMod[ 0 ] = hMod ;
        g_uiModCount++ ;
    }
    else
    {
        // Copy the old values.
        CopyMemory ( phTemp     ,
                     g_ahMod    ,
                     sizeof ( HMODULE ) * g_uiModCount ) ;
        // Free the old memory.
        VERIFY ( HeapFree ( GetProcessHeap ( ) , 0 , g_ahMod ) ) ;
        g_ahMod = phTemp ;
        g_ahMod[ g_uiModCount ] = hMod ;
        g_uiModCount++ ;
    }
    return ( TRUE ) ;
}

UINT __stdcall GetLimitModuleCount ( void )
{
    return ( g_uiModCount ) ;
}

int __stdcall GetLimitModulesArray ( HMODULE * pahMod , UINT uiSize )
{
    int iRet ;

    __try
    {
        ASSERT ( FALSE == IsBadWritePtr ( pahMod ,
                                          uiSize * sizeof ( HMODULE ) ) ) ;
        if ( TRUE == IsBadWritePtr ( pahMod ,
                                     uiSize * sizeof ( HMODULE ) ) )
        {
            iRet = GLMA_BADPARAM ;
            __leave ;
        }
```

```
        if ( uiSize < g_uiModCount )
        {
            iRet = GLMA_BUFFTOOSMALL ;
            __leave ;
        }

        CopyMemory ( pahMod       ,
                     g_ahMod      ,
                     sizeof ( HMODULE ) * g_uiModCount ) ;

        iRet = GLMA_SUCCESS ;
    }
    __except ( EXCEPTION_EXECUTE_HANDLER )
    {
        iRet = GLMA_FAILURE ;
    }
    return ( iRet ) ;
}

LONG __stdcall CrashHandlerExceptionFilter (EXCEPTION_POINTERS* pExPtrs)
{
    LONG lRet = EXCEPTION_CONTINUE_SEARCH ;

    // If the exception is an EXCEPTION_STACK_OVERFLOW, there isn't much
    // you can do because the stack is blown. If you try to do anything,
    // the odds are great that you'll just double-fault and bomb right
    // out of your exception filter. Although I don't recommend doing so,
    // you could play some games with the stack register and
    // manipulate it so that you could regain enough space to run these
    // functions. Of course, if you did change the stack register, you'd
    // have problems walking the stack.
    // I take the safe route and make some calls to OutputDebugString
    // here. I still might double-fault, but because OutputDebugString
    // does very little on the stack (something like 8-16 bytes), it's
    // worth a shot. You can have your users download Mark Russinovich's
    // DebugView (www.sysinternals.com) so they can at least tell you
    // what they see.
    // The only problem is that I can't even be sure there's enough
    // room on the stack to convert the instruction pointer.
    // Fortunately, EXCEPTION_STACK_OVERFLOW doesn't happen very often.
    // You might be wondering why I don't call the new _resetstkoflw
    // function here. This function is only called on fatal exceptions
    // so attempting to reset the stack will not do anything useful as
    // the application is going down. The _resetstkoflw function is
    // only useful if you call it before you get here.
    __try
    {

        // Note that I still call your crash handler. I'm doing the logging
        // work here in case the blown stack kills your crash handler.
        if ( EXCEPTION_STACK_OVERFLOW ==
                               pExPtrs->ExceptionRecord->ExceptionCode )
```

(continued)

```
        {
            OutputDebugString(_T("!!!!!!!!!!!!!!!!!!!!!!!!!!!!!!!!!!!\n"));
            OutputDebugString(_T("EXCEPTION_STACK_OVERFLOW occurred\n"));
            OutputDebugString(_T("!!!!!!!!!!!!!!!!!!!!!!!!!!!!!!!!!!!\n"));
        }

        if ( NULL != g_pfnCallBack )
        {

            // The symbol engine has to be initialized here so that
            // I can look up the base module information for the
            // crash address as well as get the symbol engine
            // ready.
            InitSymEng ( ) ;

            // Check the g_ahMod list.
            BOOL bCallIt = FALSE ;
            if ( 0 == g_uiModCount )
            {
                bCallIt = TRUE ;
            }
            else
            {
                HINSTANCE hBaseAddr = (HINSTANCE)
                    SymGetModuleBase64( GetCurrentProcess ( )       ,
                                        (DWORD64)pExPtrs->
                                             ExceptionRecord->
                                                       ExceptionAddress);
                if ( NULL != hBaseAddr )
                {
                    for ( UINT i = 0 ; i < g_uiModCount ; i ++ )
                    {
                        if ( hBaseAddr == g_ahMod[ i ] )
                        {
                            bCallIt = TRUE ;
                            break ;
                        }
                    }
                }
            }
            if ( TRUE == bCallIt )
            {
                // Check that the crash handler still exists in memory
                // before I call it. The user might have forgotten to
                // unregister, and the crash handler is invalid because
                // it got unloaded. If some other function loaded
                // back into the same address, however, there isn't much
                // I can do.
                ASSERT ( FALSE == IsBadCodePtr((FARPROC)g_pfnCallBack));
                if ( FALSE == IsBadCodePtr ( (FARPROC)g_pfnCallBack ) )
                {
                    lRet = g_pfnCallBack ( pExPtrs ) ;
                }
```

```
            }
            else
            {
                // Call the previous filter but only after it checks
                // out. I'm just being a little paranoid.
                ASSERT ( FALSE == IsBadCodePtr((FARPROC)g_pfnOrigFilt));
                if ( FALSE == IsBadCodePtr ( (FARPROC)g_pfnOrigFilt ) )
                {
                    lRet = g_pfnOrigFilt ( pExPtrs ) ;
                }
            }
            CleanupSymEng ( ) ;
        }
    }
    __except ( EXCEPTION_EXECUTE_HANDLER )
    {
        lRet = EXCEPTION_CONTINUE_SEARCH ;
    }
    return ( lRet ) ;
}

/*//////////////////////////////////////////////////////////////////////
// EXCEPTION_POINTER Translation Functions Implementation
//////////////////////////////////////////////////////////////////////*/

LPCTSTR __stdcall GetFaultReason ( EXCEPTION_POINTERS * pExPtrs )
{
    ASSERT ( FALSE == IsBadReadPtr ( pExPtrs ,
                                     sizeof ( EXCEPTION_POINTERS ) ) ) ;
    if ( TRUE == IsBadReadPtr ( pExPtrs ,
                                sizeof ( EXCEPTION_POINTERS ) ) )
    {
        TRACE0 ( "Bad parameter to GetFaultReason\n" ) ;
        return ( NULL ) ;
    }

    // The variable that holds the return value
    LPCTSTR szRet ;

    __try
    {

        // Initialize the symbol engine in case it isn't initialized.
        InitSymEng ( ) ;

        // The current position in the buffer
        int iCurr = 0 ;
        // A temporary value holder. This holder keeps the stack usage
        // to a minimum.
        DWORD64 dwTemp ;

        iCurr += BSUGetModuleBaseName ( GetCurrentProcess ( ) ,
                                        NULL                  ,
```

(continued)

```
                                        g_szBuff                ,
                                        BUFF_SIZE               ) ;

        iCurr += wsprintf ( g_szBuff + iCurr , _T ( " caused an " ) ) ;

        dwTemp = (DWORD_PTR)
            ConvertSimpleException(pExPtrs->ExceptionRecord->
                                                         ExceptionCode);

        if ( NULL != dwTemp )
        {
            iCurr += wsprintf ( g_szBuff + iCurr ,
                                _T ( "%s" )      ,
                                dwTemp           ) ;
        }
        else
        {
            iCurr += FormatMessage( FORMAT_MESSAGE_IGNORE_INSERTS |
                                         FORMAT_MESSAGE_FROM_HMODULE,
                                    GetModuleHandle (_T("NTDLL.DLL"))  ,
                                    pExPtrs->ExceptionRecord->
                                                      ExceptionCode ,
                                    0                                  ,
                                    g_szBuff + iCurr                   ,
                                    BUFF_SIZE                          ,
                                    0                                  );
    }

        ASSERT ( iCurr < ( BUFF_SIZE - MAX_PATH ) ) ;

        iCurr += wsprintf ( g_szBuff + iCurr , _T ( " in module " ) ) ;

        dwTemp =
            SymGetModuleBase64( GetCurrentProcess ( ) ,
                                (DWORD64)pExPtrs->ExceptionRecord->
                                                ExceptionAddress ) ;
        ASSERT ( NULL != dwTemp ) ;

        if ( NULL == dwTemp )
        {
            iCurr += wsprintf ( g_szBuff + iCurr , _T ( "<UNKNOWN>" ) );
        }
        else
        {
            iCurr += BSUGetModuleBaseName ( GetCurrentProcess ( ) ,
                                            (HINSTANCE)dwTemp     ,
                                            g_szBuff + iCurr      ,
                                            BUFF_SIZE - iCurr     ) ;
        }

#ifdef _WIN64
        iCurr += wsprintf ( g_szBuff + iCurr     ,
                            _T ( " at %016X" )   ,
```

```
                          pExPtrs->ExceptionRecord->ExceptionAddress);
#else
        iCurr += wsprintf ( g_szBuff + iCurr                     ,
                          _T ( " at %04X:%08X" )                 ,
                          pExPtrs->ContextRecord->SegCs          ,
                          pExPtrs->ExceptionRecord->ExceptionAddress);
#endif

        ASSERT ( iCurr < ( BUFF_SIZE - 200 ) ) ;

        // Start looking up the exception address.
        PIMAGEHLP_SYMBOL64 pSym = (PIMAGEHLP_SYMBOL64)&g_stSymbol ;
        ZeroMemory ( pSym , SYM_BUFF_SIZE ) ;
        pSym->SizeOfStruct = sizeof ( IMAGEHLP_SYMBOL64 ) ;
        pSym->MaxNameLength = SYM_BUFF_SIZE -
                                    sizeof ( IMAGEHLP_SYMBOL64 ) ;

        DWORD64 dwDisp ;
        if ( TRUE ==
             SymGetSymFromAddr64 ( GetCurrentProcess ( )              ,
                                   (DWORD64)pExPtrs->ExceptionRecord->
                                                ExceptionAddress ,
                                    &dwDisp                          ,
                                    pSym                             ))
        {
            iCurr += wsprintf ( g_szBuff + iCurr , _T ( "," ) ) ;

            // Copy no more of the symbol information than there's
            // room for. Remember, symbols names are ANSI!
            int iLen = lstrlenA ( pSym->Name ) ;
            // Make sure there's enough room for the longest symbol
            // and the displacement.
            if ( iLen > ( ( BUFF_SIZE - iCurr) -
                          ( MAX_SYM_SIZE + 50 )  ) )
            {
#ifdef UNICODE
                // Get some room on the stack to convert the string.
                TCHAR * pWideName = (TCHAR*)_alloca ( iLen + 1 ) ;

                BSUAnsi2Wide ( pSym->Name , pWideName , iLen + 1 ) ;

                lstrcpyn ( g_szBuff + iCurr      ,
                           pWideName             ,
                           BUFF_SIZE - iCurr - 1  ) ;
#else
                lstrcpyn ( g_szBuff + iCurr      ,
                           pSym->Name            ,
                           BUFF_SIZE - iCurr - 1  ) ;
#endif  // UNICODE
                // Gotta leave now
                szRet = g_szBuff ;
                __leave ;
            }
```

(continued)

```
        else
        {
            if ( dwDisp > 0 )
            {
                iCurr += wsprintf ( g_szBuff + iCurr ,
                                    k_NAMEDISPFMT    ,
                                    pSym->Name       ,
                                    dwDisp           ) ;
            }
            else
            {
                iCurr += wsprintf ( g_szBuff + iCurr ,
                                    k_NAMEFMT        ,
                                    pSym->Name       ) ;
            }
        }
    }
    else
    {
        // If the symbol wasn't found, the source and line won't
        // be found either, so leave now.
        szRet = g_szBuff ;
        __leave ;
    }

    ASSERT ( iCurr < ( BUFF_SIZE - 200 ) ) ;

    // Look up the source file and line number.
    ZeroMemory ( &g_stLine , sizeof ( IMAGEHLP_LINE64 ) ) ;
    g_stLine.SizeOfStruct = sizeof ( IMAGEHLP_LINE64 ) ;

    DWORD dwLineDisp ;
    if ( TRUE ==
          SymGetLineFromAddr64 ( GetCurrentProcess ( )       ,
                                 (DWORD64)pExPtrs->
                                          ExceptionRecord->
                                            ExceptionAddress ,
                                 &dwLineDisp                 ,
                                 &g_stLine                   ) )
    {
        iCurr += wsprintf ( g_szBuff + iCurr , _T ( "," ) ) ;

        // Copy no more of the source file and line number
        // information than there's room for.
        int iLen = lstrlenA ( g_stLine.FileName ) ;
        if ( iLen > ( BUFF_SIZE - iCurr -
                      MAX_PATH - 50       ) )
        {
#ifdef UNICODE
            // Get some room on the stack to convert the string.
            TCHAR * pWideName = (TCHAR*)_alloca ( iLen + 1 ) ;

            BSUAnsi2Wide(g_stLine.FileName , pWideName , iLen + 1);
```

```
                lstrcpyn ( g_szBuff + iCurr       ,
                           pWideName              ,
                           BUFF_SIZE - iCurr - 1  ) ;
#else
                lstrcpyn ( g_szBuff + iCurr       ,
                           g_stLine.FileName      ,
                           BUFF_SIZE - iCurr - 1  ) ;

#endif  // UNICODE
                // Gotta leave now
                szRet = g_szBuff ;
                __leave ;
            }
            else
            {
                if ( dwLineDisp > 0 )
                {
                    iCurr += wsprintf ( g_szBuff + iCurr              ,
                                        k_FILELINEDISPFMT             ,
                                        g_stLine.FileName             ,
                                        g_stLine.LineNumber           ,
                                        dwLineDisp                    );
                }
                else
                {
                    iCurr += wsprintf ( g_szBuff + iCurr     ,
                                        k_FILELINEFMT        ,
                                        g_stLine.FileName    ,
                                        g_stLine.LineNumber   ) ;
                }
            }
        }
        szRet = g_szBuff ;
    }
    __except ( EXCEPTION_EXECUTE_HANDLER )
    {
        ASSERT ( !"Crashed in GetFaultReason" ) ;
        szRet = NULL ;
    }
    return ( szRet ) ;
}

// Helper function to isolate filling out the stack frame, which is CPU
// specific.
void FillInStackFrame ( PCONTEXT pCtx )
{
    // Initialize the STACKFRAME structure.
    ZeroMemory ( &g_stFrame , sizeof ( STACKFRAME64 ) ) ;

#ifdef _X86_
    g_stFrame.AddrPC.Offset       = pCtx->Eip    ;
    g_stFrame.AddrPC.Mode         = AddrModeFlat ;
    g_stFrame.AddrStack.Offset    = pCtx->Esp    ;
```

(continued)

```
    g_stFrame.AddrStack.Mode       = AddrModeFlat ;
    g_stFrame.AddrFrame.Offset     = pCtx->Ebp    ;
    g_stFrame.AddrFrame.Mode       = AddrModeFlat ;
#elif  _AMD64_
    g_stFrame.AddrPC.Offset        = pCtx->Rip    ;
    g_stFrame.AddrPC.Mode          = AddrModeFlat ;
    g_stFrame.AddrStack.Offset     = pCtx->Rsp    ;
    g_stFrame.AddrStack.Mode       = AddrModeFlat ;
    g_stFrame.AddrFrame.Offset     = pCtx->Rbp    ;
    g_stFrame.AddrFrame.Mode       = AddrModeFlat ;
#elif  _IA64_
    #pragma message ( "IA64 NOT DEFINED!!" )
    #pragma FORCE COMPILATION ABORT!
#else
    #pragma message ( "CPU NOT DEFINED!!" )
    #pragma FORCE COMPILATION ABORT!
#endif
}

LPCTSTR BUGSUTIL_DLLINTERFACE __stdcall
            GetFirstStackTraceString ( DWORD                dwOpts  ,
                                       EXCEPTION_POINTERS * pExPtrs  )
{
    ASSERT ( FALSE == IsBadReadPtr ( pExPtrs                      ,
                                     sizeof ( EXCEPTION_POINTERS * ))) ;
    if ( TRUE == IsBadReadPtr ( pExPtrs                       ,
                                sizeof ( EXCEPTION_POINTERS *  ) ) )
    {
        TRACE0 ( "GetFirstStackTraceString - invalid pExPtrs!\n" ) ;
        return ( NULL ) ;
    }

    // Get the stack frame filled in.
    FillInStackFrame ( pExPtrs->ContextRecord ) ;

    // Copy over the exception pointers fields so I don't corrupt the
    // real one.
    g_stContext = *(pExPtrs->ContextRecord) ;

    return ( InternalGetStackTraceString ( dwOpts ) ) ;
}

LPCTSTR BUGSUTIL_DLLINTERFACE __stdcall
            GetNextStackTraceString ( DWORD                dwOpts  ,
                                      EXCEPTION_POINTERS * /*pExPtrs*/)
{
    // All error checking is in InternalGetStackTraceString.
    // Assume that GetFirstStackTraceString has already initialized the
    // stack frame information.
    return ( InternalGetStackTraceString ( dwOpts ) ) ;
}
```

```
BOOL __stdcall CH_ReadProcessMemory ( HANDLE                              ,
                                      DWORD64     qwBaseAddress           ,
                                      PVOID       lpBuffer                ,
                                      DWORD       nSize                   ,
                                      LPDWORD     lpNumberOfBytesRead     )
{
    return ( ReadProcessMemory ( GetCurrentProcess ( )  ,
                                 (LPCVOID)qwBaseAddress ,
                                 lpBuffer               ,
                                 nSize                  ,
                                 lpNumberOfBytesRead     ) ) ;
}

// The internal function that does all the stack walking
LPCTSTR __stdcall InternalGetStackTraceString ( DWORD dwOpts )
{

    // The value that is returned
    LPCTSTR szRet ;
    // The module base address. I look this up right after the stack
    // walk to ensure that the module is valid.
    DWORD64 dwModBase ;

    __try
    {
        // Initialize the symbol engine in case it isn't initialized.
        InitSymEng ( ) ;

        // Note:  If the source file and line number functions are used,
        //        StackWalk can cause an access violation.
        BOOL bSWRet = StackWalk64 ( CH_MACHINE                         ,
                                    GetCurrentProcess ( )              ,
                                    GetCurrentThread ( )               ,
                                    &g_stFrame                         ,
                                    &g_stContext                       ,
                                    CH_ReadProcessMemory               ,
                                    SymFunctionTableAccess64           ,
                                    SymGetModuleBase64                 ,
                                    NULL                               );
        if ( ( FALSE == bSWRet ) || ( 0 == g_stFrame.AddrFrame.Offset ))
        {
            szRet = NULL ;
            __leave ;
        }

        // Before I get too carried away and start calculating
        // everything, I need to double-check that the address returned
        // by StackWalk really exists. I've seen cases in which
        // StackWalk returns TRUE but the address doesn't belong to
        // a module in the process.
        dwModBase = SymGetModuleBase64 ( GetCurrentProcess ( )   ,
                                         g_stFrame.AddrPC.Offset  ) ;
```

(continued)

```
        if ( 0 == dwModBase )
        {
            szRet = NULL ;
            __leave ;
        }

        int iCurr = 0 ;

        // At a minimum, put in the address.
#ifdef _WIN64
        iCurr += wsprintf ( g_szBuff + iCurr         ,
                            _T ( "0x%016X" )          ,
                            g_stFrame.AddrPC.Offset   ) ;
#else
        iCurr += wsprintf ( g_szBuff + iCurr         ,
                            _T ( "%04X:%08X" )        ,
                            g_stContext.SegCs         ,
                            g_stFrame.AddrPC.Offset   ) ;
#endif

        // Output the parameters?
        if ( GSTSO_PARAMS == ( dwOpts & GSTSO_PARAMS ) )
        {
            iCurr += wsprintf ( g_szBuff + iCurr          ,
                                k_PARAMFMTSTRING          ,
                                g_stFrame.Params[ 0 ]     ,
                                g_stFrame.Params[ 1 ]     ,
                                g_stFrame.Params[ 2 ]     ,
                                g_stFrame.Params[ 3 ]      ) ;
        }
        // Output the module name.
        if ( GSTSO_MODULE == ( dwOpts & GSTSO_MODULE ) )
        {
            iCurr += wsprintf ( g_szBuff + iCurr  , _T ( " " ) ) ;

            ASSERT ( iCurr < ( BUFF_SIZE - MAX_PATH ) ) ;
            iCurr += BSUGetModuleBaseName ( GetCurrentProcess ( ) ,
                                            (HINSTANCE)dwModBase  ,
                                            g_szBuff + iCurr      ,
                                            BUFF_SIZE - iCurr      ) ;
        }

        ASSERT ( iCurr < ( BUFF_SIZE - MAX_PATH ) ) ;
        DWORD64 dwDisp ;

        // Output the symbol name?
        if ( GSTSO_SYMBOL == ( dwOpts & GSTSO_SYMBOL ) )
        {

            // Start looking up the exception address.
            PIMAGEHLP_SYMBOL64 pSym = (PIMAGEHLP_SYMBOL64)&g_stSymbol ;
            ZeroMemory ( pSym , SYM_BUFF_SIZE ) ;
            pSym->SizeOfStruct = sizeof ( IMAGEHLP_SYMBOL64 ) ;
```

```
            pSym->MaxNameLength = SYM_BUFF_SIZE -
                                  sizeof ( IMAGEHLP_SYMBOL64 ) ;
            pSym->Address = g_stFrame.AddrPC.Offset ;

            if ( TRUE ==
                  SymGetSymFromAddr64 ( GetCurrentProcess ( )      ,
                                        g_stFrame.AddrPC.Offset    ,
                                        &dwDisp                    ,
                                        pSym                      ) )
            {
                if ( dwOpts & ~GSTSO_SYMBOL )
                {
                    iCurr += wsprintf ( g_szBuff + iCurr , _T ( "," ));
                }

                // Copy no more symbol information than there's room
                // for. Symbols are ANSI
                int iLen = ( lstrlenA ( pSym->Name ) * sizeof ( TCHAR));
                if ( iLen > ( BUFF_SIZE - iCurr -
                            ( MAX_SYM_SIZE + 50 ) ) )
                {
#ifdef UNICODE
                    // Get some room on the stack to convert the string.
                    TCHAR * pWideName = (TCHAR*)_alloca ( iLen + 1 ) ;

                    BSUAnsi2Wide ( pSym->Name , pWideName , iLen + 1 ) ;

                    lstrcpyn ( g_szBuff + iCurr      ,
                               pWideName             ,
                               BUFF_SIZE - iCurr - 1  ) ;
#else
                    lstrcpyn ( g_szBuff + iCurr      ,
                               pSym->Name            ,
                               BUFF_SIZE - iCurr - 1  ) ;

#endif  // UNICODE
                    // Gotta leave now
                    szRet = g_szBuff ;
                    __leave ;
                }
                else
                {
                    if ( dwDisp > 0 )
                    {
                        iCurr += wsprintf ( g_szBuff + iCurr    ,
                                            k_NAMEDISPFMT       ,
                                            pSym->Name          ,
                                            dwDisp             ) ;
                    }
                    else
                    {
                        iCurr += wsprintf ( g_szBuff + iCurr ,
                                            k_NAMEFMT        ,
```

(continued)

```
                                                  pSym->Name        ) ;
                }
            }
        }
        else
        {
            // If the symbol wasn't found, the source file and line
            // number won't be found either, so leave now.
            szRet = g_szBuff ;
            __leave ;
        }

    }

    ASSERT ( iCurr < ( BUFF_SIZE - MAX_PATH ) ) ;

    // Output the source file and line number information?
    if ( GSTSO_SRCLINE == ( dwOpts & GSTSO_SRCLINE ) )
    {
        ZeroMemory ( &g_stLine , sizeof ( IMAGEHLP_LINE64 ) ) ;
        g_stLine.SizeOfStruct = sizeof ( IMAGEHLP_LINE64 ) ;

        DWORD dwLineDisp ;
        if ( TRUE == SymGetLineFromAddr64 ( GetCurrentProcess ( )  ,
                                            g_stFrame.AddrPC.Offset,
                                            &dwLineDisp            ,
                                            &g_stLine             ))
        {
            if ( dwOpts & ~GSTSO_SRCLINE )
            {
                iCurr += wsprintf ( g_szBuff + iCurr , _T ( "," ));
            }

            // Copy no more of the source file and line number
            // information than there's room for.
            int iLen = lstrlenA ( g_stLine.FileName ) ;
            if ( iLen > ( BUFF_SIZE - iCurr -
                         ( MAX_PATH + 50     ) ) )
            {
#ifdef UNICODE
                // Get some room on the stack to convert the string.
                TCHAR * pWideName = (TCHAR*)_alloca ( iLen + 1 ) ;

                BSUAnsi2Wide ( g_stLine.FileName ,
                               pWideName         ,
                               iLen + 1           ) ;

                lstrcpyn ( g_szBuff + iCurr       ,
                           pWideName             ,
                           BUFF_SIZE - iCurr - 1  ) ;
#else
                lstrcpyn ( g_szBuff + iCurr       ,
                             g_stLine.FileName     ,
```

```
                                BUFF_SIZE - iCurr - 1  ) ;
#endif
                    // Gotta leave now
                    szRet = g_szBuff ;
                    __leave ;
                }
                else
                {
                    if ( dwLineDisp > 0 )
                    {
                        iCurr += wsprintf( g_szBuff + iCurr      ,
                                           k_FILELINEDISPFMT     ,
                                           g_stLine.FileName     ,
                                           g_stLine.LineNumber   ,
                                           dwLineDisp            ) ;
                    }
                    else
                    {
                        iCurr += wsprintf ( g_szBuff + iCurr     ,
                                            k_FILELINEFMT        ,
                                            g_stLine.FileName    ,
                                            g_stLine.LineNumber  ) ;
                    }
                }
            }
        }

        szRet = g_szBuff ;
    }
    __except ( EXCEPTION_EXECUTE_HANDLER )
    {
        ASSERT ( !"Crashed in InternalGetStackTraceString" ) ;
        szRet = NULL ;
    }
    return ( szRet ) ;
}

LPCTSTR __stdcall GetRegisterString ( EXCEPTION_POINTERS * pExPtrs )
{
    // Check the parameter.
    ASSERT ( FALSE == IsBadReadPtr ( pExPtrs                      ,
                                     sizeof ( EXCEPTION_POINTERS ) ) ) ;
    if ( TRUE == IsBadReadPtr ( pExPtrs                      ,
                                sizeof ( EXCEPTION_POINTERS ) ) )
    {
        TRACE0 ( "GetRegisterString - invalid pExPtrs!\n" ) ;
        return ( NULL ) ;
    }

#ifdef _X86_
    // This call puts 48 bytes on the stack, which could be a problem if
    // the stack is blown.
```

(continued)

```
    wsprintf(g_szBuff ,
             _T ("EAX=%08X  EBX=%08X  ECX=%08X  EDX=%08X  ESI=%08X\n")\
             _T ("EDI=%08X  EBP=%08X  ESP=%08X  EIP=%08X  FLG=%08X\n")\
             _T ("CS=%04X   DS=%04X  SS=%04X  ES=%04X   ")\
             _T ("FS=%04X  GS=%04X" ) ,
                 pExPtrs->ContextRecord->Eax      ,
                 pExPtrs->ContextRecord->Ebx      ,
                 pExPtrs->ContextRecord->Ecx      ,
                 pExPtrs->ContextRecord->Edx      ,
                 pExPtrs->ContextRecord->Esi      ,
                 pExPtrs->ContextRecord->Edi      ,
                 pExPtrs->ContextRecord->Ebp      ,
                 pExPtrs->ContextRecord->Esp      ,
                 pExPtrs->ContextRecord->Eip      ,
                 pExPtrs->ContextRecord->EFlags   ,
                 pExPtrs->ContextRecord->SegCs    ,
                 pExPtrs->ContextRecord->SegDs    ,
                 pExPtrs->ContextRecord->SegSs    ,
                 pExPtrs->ContextRecord->SegEs    ,
                 pExPtrs->ContextRecord->SegFs    ,
                 pExPtrs->ContextRecord->SegGs      ) ;
#elif _AMD64_
    wsprintf ( g_szBuff ,
        _T ("RAX=%016X  RBX=%016X  RCX=%016X  RDX=%016X  RSI=%016X\n")\
        _T ("RDI=%016X  RBP=%016X  RSP=%016X  RIP=%016X  FLG=%016X\n")\
        _T (" R8=%016X   R9=%016X  R10=%016X  R11=%016X  R12=%016X\n")\
        _T ("R13=%016X  R14=%016X  R15=%016X" ) ,
        pExPtrs->ContextRecord->Rax      ,
        pExPtrs->ContextRecord->Rbx      ,
        pExPtrs->ContextRecord->Rcx      ,
        pExPtrs->ContextRecord->Rdx      ,
        pExPtrs->ContextRecord->Rsi      ,
        pExPtrs->ContextRecord->Rdi      ,
        pExPtrs->ContextRecord->Rbp      ,
        pExPtrs->ContextRecord->Rsp      ,
        pExPtrs->ContextRecord->Rip      ,
        pExPtrs->ContextRecord->EFlags   ,
        pExPtrs->ContextRecord->R8       ,
        pExPtrs->ContextRecord->R9       ,
        pExPtrs->ContextRecord->R10      ,
        pExPtrs->ContextRecord->R11      ,
        pExPtrs->ContextRecord->R12      ,
        pExPtrs->ContextRecord->R13      ,
        pExPtrs->ContextRecord->R14      ,
        pExPtrs->ContextRecord->R15        ) ;
#elif _IA64_
    #pragma message ( "IA64 NOT DEFINED!!" )
    #pragma FORCE COMPILATION ABORT!
#else
    #pragma message ( "CPU NOT DEFINED!!" )
    #pragma FORCE COMPILATION ABORT!
#endif
```

```
    return ( g_szBuff ) ;

}

LPCTSTR ConvertSimpleException ( DWORD dwExcept )
{
    switch ( dwExcept )
    {
        case EXCEPTION_ACCESS_VIOLATION         :
            return ( _T ( "EXCEPTION_ACCESS_VIOLATION" ) ) ;
        break ;

        case EXCEPTION_DATATYPE_MISALIGNMENT    :
            return ( _T ( "EXCEPTION_DATATYPE_MISALIGNMENT" ) ) ;
        break ;

        case EXCEPTION_BREAKPOINT               :
            return ( _T ( "EXCEPTION_BREAKPOINT" ) ) ;
        break ;

        case EXCEPTION_SINGLE_STEP              :
            return ( _T ( "EXCEPTION_SINGLE_STEP" ) ) ;
        break ;

        case EXCEPTION_ARRAY_BOUNDS_EXCEEDED    :
            return ( _T ( "EXCEPTION_ARRAY_BOUNDS_EXCEEDED" ) ) ;
        break ;

        case EXCEPTION_FLT_DENORMAL_OPERAND     :
            return ( _T ( "EXCEPTION_FLT_DENORMAL_OPERAND" ) ) ;
        break ;

        case EXCEPTION_FLT_DIVIDE_BY_ZERO       :
            return ( _T ( "EXCEPTION_FLT_DIVIDE_BY_ZERO" ) ) ;
        break ;

        case EXCEPTION_FLT_INEXACT_RESULT       :
            return ( _T ( "EXCEPTION_FLT_INEXACT_RESULT" ) ) ;
        break ;

        case EXCEPTION_FLT_INVALID_OPERATION    :
            return ( _T ( "EXCEPTION_FLT_INVALID_OPERATION" ) ) ;
        break ;

        case EXCEPTION_FLT_OVERFLOW             :
            return ( _T ( "EXCEPTION_FLT_OVERFLOW" ) ) ;
        break ;

        case EXCEPTION_FLT_STACK_CHECK          :
            return ( _T ( "EXCEPTION_FLT_STACK_CHECK" ) ) ;
        break ;
```

(continued)

```
        case EXCEPTION_FLT_UNDERFLOW          :
            return ( _T ( "EXCEPTION_FLT_UNDERFLOW" ) ) ;
        break ;

        case EXCEPTION_INT_DIVIDE_BY_ZERO     :
            return ( _T ( "EXCEPTION_INT_DIVIDE_BY_ZERO" ) ) ;
        break ;

        case EXCEPTION_INT_OVERFLOW           :
            return ( _T ( "EXCEPTION_INT_OVERFLOW" ) ) ;
        break ;

        case EXCEPTION_PRIV_INSTRUCTION       :
            return ( _T ( "EXCEPTION_PRIV_INSTRUCTION" ) ) ;
        break ;

        case EXCEPTION_IN_PAGE_ERROR          :
            return ( _T ( "EXCEPTION_IN_PAGE_ERROR" ) ) ;
        break ;

        case EXCEPTION_ILLEGAL_INSTRUCTION    :
            return ( _T ( "EXCEPTION_ILLEGAL_INSTRUCTION" ) ) ;
        break ;

        case EXCEPTION_NONCONTINUABLE_EXCEPTION :
            return ( _T ( "EXCEPTION_NONCONTINUABLE_EXCEPTION" ) ) ;
        break ;

        case EXCEPTION_STACK_OVERFLOW         :
            return ( _T ( "EXCEPTION_STACK_OVERFLOW" ) ) ;
        break ;

        case EXCEPTION_INVALID_DISPOSITION    :
            return ( _T ( "EXCEPTION_INVALID_DISPOSITION" ) ) ;
        break ;

        case EXCEPTION_GUARD_PAGE             :
            return ( _T ( "EXCEPTION_GUARD_PAGE" ) ) ;
        break ;

        case EXCEPTION_INVALID_HANDLE         :
            return ( _T ( "EXCEPTION_INVALID_HANDLE" ) ) ;
        break ;

        case 0xE06D7363                       :
            return ( _T ( "Microsoft C++ Exception" ) ) ;
        break ;

        default :
            return ( NULL ) ;
        break ;
    }
}
```

```
// Initializes the symbol engine if needed
void InitSymEng ( void )
{
    if ( FALSE == g_bSymEngInit )
    {
        // Set up the symbol engine.
        DWORD dwOpts = SymGetOptions ( ) ;

        // Turn on line loading.
        SymSetOptions ( dwOpts                |
                        SYMOPT_LOAD_LINES      ) ;

        // Force the invade process flag on.
        BOOL bRet = SymInitialize ( GetCurrentProcess ( ) ,
                                    NULL                  ,
                                    TRUE                   ) ;
        ASSERT ( TRUE == bRet ) ;
        g_bSymEngInit = bRet ;
    }
}

// Cleans up the symbol engine if needed
void CleanupSymEng ( void )
{
    if ( TRUE == g_bSymEngInit )
    {
        VERIFY ( SymCleanup ( GetCurrentProcess ( ) ) ) ;
        g_bSymEngInit = FALSE ;
    }
}
```

To set your exception filter function, simply call `SetCrashHandlerFilter`. Internally, `SetCrashHandlerFilter` saves your exception filter function to a static variable and calls `SetUnhandledExceptionFilter` to set the real exception filter, `CrashHandlerExceptionFilter`. If you don't add any modules that limit the exception filtering, `CrashHandlerExceptionFilter` will always call your exception handler no matter which module had the hard crash. Calling your exception handler when no modules are added was by design so that you'd have to use only one API call to set your final exception handling. It's best if you call `SetCrashHandlerFilter` as soon as you can and make sure that you call it again with `NULL` right before you unload so that you allow my crash handler code to remove your filter function. Figure 13-1 shows a diagram of how a crash handler works.

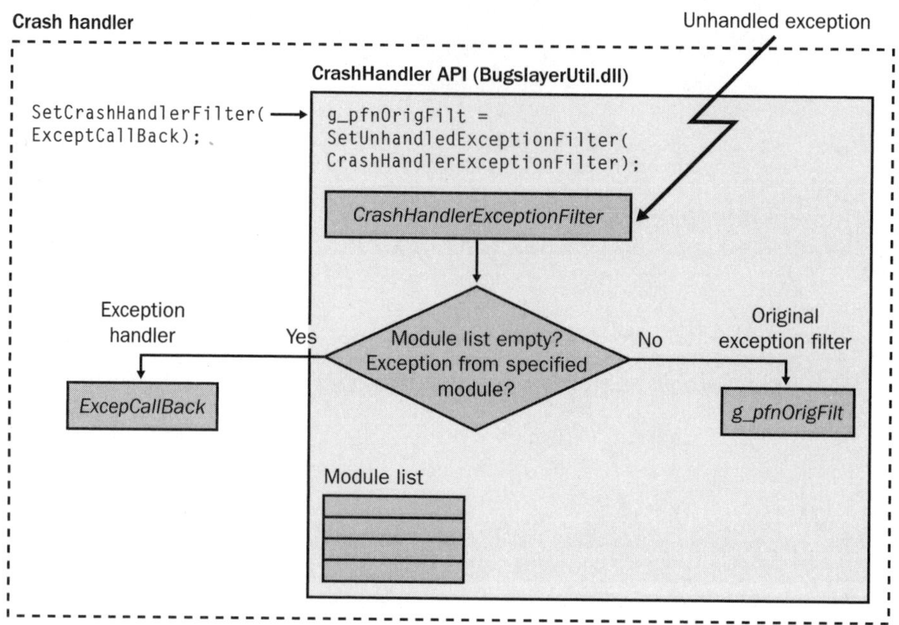

Figure 13-1 Diagram of a crash handler

`AddCrashHandlerLimitModule` is where you add a module to limit the crash handling. All you need to pass to this function is the `HMODULE` for the module in question. If you have multiple modules that you want to limit crash handling to, just call `AddCrashHandlerLimitModule` for each one. The array of module handles is allocated from the main process heap.

As you look at the various functions in Listing 13-4, you'll notice that I don't make any C run-time library calls. Because the crash handler routines are called only in extraordinary situations, I can't rely on the run time being in a stable state. To clean up any memory that I allocated, I use an automatic static class whose destructor is called when BUGSLAYERUTIL.DLL is unloaded. I also provide a couple of functions that allow you to get the size of the limit module array and a copy of the array—`GetLimitModuleCount` and `GetLimitModulesArray`. I'll leave it up to you to write a `RemoveCrashHandlerLimitModule` function.

One interesting aspect of the implementation in CRASHHANDLER.CPP is how I handle initializing the DBGHELP.DLL symbol engine. Because the crash handler code can be called at any time, I needed a way to get all the process's modules loaded at the time of the crash. `SymInitialize` will take care of this automatically for you by setting its third parameter, `fInvadeProcess`, to `TRUE`.

Another interesting aspect to the code is the way I deal with ANSI characters in a Unicode world. Since the CrashHandler code, which I provided in the first edition of this book, has proven extremely popular and countless products are using it, I had to balance the needs of developers who will want to drop the new CRASHHANDLER.CPP into their existing projects. Consequently, I didn't feel comfortable relying on my large symbol engine wrapper SYMBOLENGINE.LIB to handle the character conversions because it would prevent direct upgrades. I finally settled on using `wsprintf` to do many of the translations by specifying `%S` formatting, which indicates an ANSI character string is a parameter when compiling for full Unicode.

For those spots in which I needed to do the conversions myself, I decided to use the `_alloca` function to allocate the memory off the stack instead of using the C run time or operating system heaps because the heaps might be corrupted and be the reason for the crash. If the crash was caused by a stack overflow, because there's so little room on the stack, any code I executed would probably cause a double fault long before the code hit one of the `_alloca` calls.

Translating `EXCEPTION_POINTERS` Structures

Now that you've written your exception handlers and crash handlers, it's time to talk about those `EXCEPTION_POINTERS` structures that each is passed. Because these structures are where all the interesting information about the crash is stored, I wanted to develop a set of functions that you can call to translate the information into human-readable form. With these functions, all you need to concentrate on is the display of information to the user in a manner that's appropriate for your particular application. You can find all these functions in Listing 13-4.

I tried to keep the functions as simple as possible. All you need to do is to pass in the `EXCEPTION_POINTERS` structures. Each function returns a pointer to a global string that holds the text, which allows me to write the code so that it doesn't rely on any heap memory and so that the big buffers it needs are always present. Some of you might look at the code and cringe because it uses global variables and recycles buffers, but it's the safest code I could possibly write.

The `GetRegisterString` function simply returns the formatted register string. The `GetFaultReason` function is a little more interesting in that it returns a complete description of the problem. The returned string shows the process, the reason for the exception, the module that caused the exception, the address of the exception, and—if symbol information is available—the function, source file, and line number where the crash occurred.

```
CrashHandlerTest.exe caused an EXCEPTION_ACCESS_VIOLATION in module
CrashHandlerTest.exe at 001B:004011D1, Baz()+0088 byte(s),
d:\dev\booktwo\disk\bugslayerutil\tests\crashhandler\crashhandler.cpp,
line 0061+0003 byte(s)
```

The most interesting functions are GetFirstStackTraceString and GetNextStackTraceString. As their names indicate, these functions let you walk the stack. As with the FindFirstFile and FindNextFile API functions, you can call GetFirstStackTraceString and then continue to call GetNextStackTraceString until it returns FALSE to walk the entire stack. The second parameter these functions take is the EXCEPTION_POINTERS structure that is passed to your crash handler function. The crash handler code does the right thing and caches the value passed to GetFirstStackTraceString, so the EXCEPTION_POINTERS structure in your crash handler function is kept pristine if you subsequently want to pass it on to the minidump writing functions. Although GetNextStackTraceString doesn't actually use the passed-in EXCEPTION_POINTERS structure, I didn't want to break any code that was already using CRASHHANDLER.CPP.

The first parameter to the GetFirstStackTraceString and GetNextStackTraceString functions is a flag option parameter that lets you control the amount of information that you want to see in the resultant string. The following string shows all the options turned on:

```
001B:004017FD (0x00000001 0x00000000 0x00894D00 0x00000000)
CrashHandlerTest.exe, wmain()+1407 byte(s), d:\dev\booktwo\disk\bugslayerutil\t
ests\crashhandler\crashhandler.cpp,
line 0226+0007 byte(s)
```

The values in parentheses are the first four possible parameters to the function. Table 13-1 lists the options and what each will include in the output string. Some of you might wonder why I didn't include local variables as one of the output options. There were two main reasons. The first is that the main use of my CrashHandler code is intended to be at customer sites. Unless you like giving away your proprietary secrets, you're probably not distributing PDB files with private information to your customers. The second reason is that local variables, especially when you want them expanded, take up quite a bit of memory. I felt I was already pushing the limits with the static buffers I was using and that adding more to cover local variables would be prohibitive.

Table 13-1 GetFirstStackTraceString and GetNextStackTraceString Options

Option	Output
0	Just the stack address
GSTSO_PARAMS	The first four possible parameters
GSTSO_MODULE	The module name
GSTSO_SYMBOL	The symbol name of the stack address
GSTSO_SRCLINE	The source file and line number information of the stack address

To show you the `GetFirstStackTraceString` and `GetNextStackTraceString` functions in action, I included two sample test programs with the sample files for this book. The first, BugslayerUtil\Tests\CrashHandler, exercises the CrashHandler methods. The second program, CrashTest, shows a full dialog box example you could display in the event of an unhandled crash. Between these two programs, you should get a pretty good idea of how to use all the functions I've presented. Figure 13-2 shows CrashTest displaying its crash dialog box.

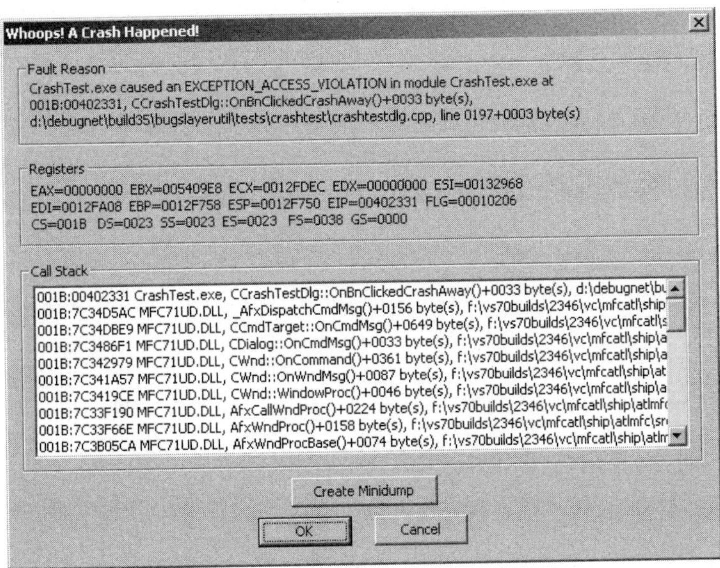

Figure 13-2 CrashTest dialog box

Minidumps

Some of you might be wondering why I went to the trouble to write and continue to support the `EXCEPTION_POINTERS` manipulation code in the CrashHandler library because you've heard about or used a thing called minidumps. The main reason is that there are many companies out there using my code in their applications and I didn't want to break compatibility. However, the minidump capabilities are so amazingly cool, I'm sure that many folks will rip out the existing code inside their crash handlers and simply replace it with a call to the minidump-creation functions as soon as they can.

I've already talked about how to read minidump files with both Microsoft Visual Studio .NET and WinDBG in Chapter 7 and Chapter 8, respectively. What I want to turn to now is how you can create your own minidumps right from your own code. After the symbol server technology and Visual Studio .NET itself, I think that minidumps API is the second greatest thing Microsoft has released for native developers in the last couple of years! However, there are a few quirks with creating your own, so I want to show you how to get the very best minidumps possible so that you can solve your bugs much faster.

The MiniDumpWriteDump API

DBGHELP.DLL contains the `MiniDumpWriteDump` function, which does all the work. DBGHELP.DLL version 5.1 or later contains the function. This means that the versions that come with stock Microsoft Windows 2000 (up through Service Pack 3) are earlier versions and don't export `MiniDumpWriteDump`. Additionally, versions of DBGHELP.DLL earlier than version 6.0 had a bug in `MiniDumpWriteDump` that caused a deadlock when you called it to write a minidump from the current process. Fortunately, those versions were distributed only with Debugging Tools for Windows, so they should not be on users' machines. To ensure life is good for your application, your best bet is to include DBGHELP.DLL 6.1.17.1 or later with your application and install it into your application's directory because it's now fully redistributable. Do not install it into the %SYSTEMROOT%\System32 directory. DBGHELP.DLL is a part of Debugging Tools for Windows (that is, WinDBG), which is included with the sample files for this book. To get the latest version of DBGHELP.DLL, go to *http://www.microsoft.com/ddk/debugging/* and download Debugging Tools for Windows. After you install everything, you can extract DBGHELP.DLL from the Debugging Tools for Windows directory.

The next snippet of code is the prototype for `MiniDumpWriteDump`. The parameters are generally self-explanatory, but I want to discuss a few highlights. The first parameter, the handle to the process, must have read and query rights. Since many of our programs are not running with full Administrator rights, you might need to do the security dance to ensure you have the rights to call `MiniDumpWriteDump` if you're doing impersonation or other cross user/rights programming. However, in all the different types of applications I've used `MiniDumpWriteDump` in, I've never needed to do any security work on the process handle.

```
BOOL MiniDumpWriteDump ( HANDLE                            hProcess       ,
                         DWORD                             ProcessId      ,
                         HANDLE                            hFile          ,
                         MINIDUMP_TYPE                     DumpType       ,
                         PMINIDUMP_EXCEPTION_INFORMATION   ExceptionParam ,
                         PMINIDUMP_USER_STREAM_INFORMATION UserStreamParam,
                         PMINIDUMP_CALLBACK_INFORMATION    CallbackParam );
```

The fourth parameter is the type of dump you want to write. This enumeration seems to be updated with every release of Debugging Tools for

Windows, so make sure you do a custom installation of Debugging Tools for Windows and install the SDK components to get the latest DBGHELP.H header file. What's not clear from the documentation is that you can OR together the various `MINIDUMP_TYPE` enumeration flags to request that additional bits of information be written to the dump. No matter what you do, you'll always want to ensure `MiniDumpWithHandleData` is included so that you can get the handle information.

If you're working with secure applications or have customers that are extremely concerned about protecting data, `MiniDumpWriteDump` can expose information in the dump that you shouldn't see. To protect users, Microsoft introduced two flags with DBGHELP.DLL 6.1.17.1 and later versions: `MiniDumpFilterMemory` and `MiniDumpFilterModulePaths`. The former removes private data unnecessary for stack walking, and the latter filters pathnames for usernames and important directory names. Although useful, `MiniDumpFilterModulePaths` can make finding the modules in a minidump harder.

The final parameter of interest is the fifth, `ExceptionParam`. You'll set this parameter to a pointer to an `EXCEPTION_POINTERS` structure to get the crash information added to the minidump. For the final two parameters, you'll almost always pass `NULL`. However, if you do want to consider writing custom information—the key program state, user preferences, object lists, or anything else your heart desires—you can plop information into the `UserStreamParam` parameter and get it written to the minidump file. It'll be up to you to read the user streams out with `MiniDumpReadDumpStream`, but the good news is that you're limited only to your imagination regarding what you want to have in a minidump.

Pacifying `MiniDumpWriteDump`

When I first looked at `MiniDumpWriteDump`, I immediately realized that I needed a wrapper function around it to accomplish two things: hiding the grunge of `GetProcAddress` because I wanted to ensure my code ran on a stock copy of Windows 2000; and avoiding having to open the file before every call to `MiniDumpWriteDump`. After I'd done the first version of my simple wrapper, I realized I was never going to do more than set the `ExceptionParam` parameter to point to the `EXCEPTION_POINTERS` structure I was processing in a crash. My minidump function for writing dumps in your crash handler function is `CreateCurrentProcessCrashDump`. I also added a function, `IsMiniDumpFunctionAvailable`, that returns `TRUE` when `MiniDumpWriteDump` is available in the address space. You can see both functions in the BugslayerUtil MINIDUMP.CPP file.

Everything was going along well until one day, I decided I wanted a function that would snap out a minidump at any point during program execution, not just when I crashed. I was working on a server application and we wanted to be able to snap out the minidump when a specific event was signaled externally to the application. That way we could look at application states after the fact without attaching a debugger to the machine. Alas, the minidumps created by `MiniDumpWriteDump` weren't always readable.

WinDBG always reported what looked like a bogus call stack in those snapped minidumps. Visual Studio .NET did a better job but sometimes reported weird stack walks even though I had perfect symbols all around. After a little bit of head scratching, it dawned on me what was going on. `MiniDumpWriteDump` was writing the call stack for the thread that was writing the dump, starting deep in the bowels of `MiniDumpWriteDump` itself. Even though I had perfect symbols, walking back into my code was proving very difficult.

Since I was snapping out a dump file and not responding to a crash, I was a little stumped about how to proceed. Any dump files I wrote as part of a crash were perfectly formed and readable by both debuggers. Of course, to get WinDBG to read a true crash dump file, I had to issue the `.ecxr;kp` commands to get the exception record set and to look at the stack. That gave me the idea to set up the `MINIDUMP_EXCEPTION_INFORMATION` structure and fake the same information as a crash so that I could get a minidump file with good call stacks.

The whole key to setting up the `MINIDUMP_EXCEPTION_INFORMATION` structure is getting the `CONTEXT` (register) information correct so that the debuggers think the fake crash looks like a real one. After much trial and error, I came up with the `SnapCurrentProcessMiniDump` function. Now snapping a minidump at any time will always walk the stack. You might want to examine the code in Listing 13-5 because the way it works is a little interesting.

My first challenge was figuring out where I should grab the registers and what value I should use for the exception address. I finally decided that the best thing to do would be to use the exact registers as they came into my `SnapCurrentProcessMiniDump` function because they were the users' registers at the time they called my function. To cleanly get registers coming into a function, I had to get a crack at the registers before the compiler-generated code whacked them, so I used the `naked` calling convention.

What I ended up doing was utilizing a `CONTEXT` structure on the stack and writing the inline assembly language to copy the registers into the appropriate structure fields. I caused the first bug myself because I copied the 16-bit segment registers into their `CONTEXT` member fields and didn't realize that the structure still utilized 32-bit values for those members. Consequently, I left garbage in the upper world. Copying the segment registers in the `EAX` register and using that value to fill the structure worked just fine. The only real work necessary was to get the `EBP` and `ESP` values because I had to use those to build my local variables, but getting them was no big deal. For `ESP` and `EBP`, I copied the values as they were at the time SnapCurrentProcessMiniDump was called. The SNAPPROLOG macro in Listing 13-5 shows the prolog, and SNAPEPILOG handles the epilog code necessary for naked calling convention functions. The one CONTEXT register value not filled out is the EIP register, which takes a little more work.

My initial thought was that the general registers I captured would be enough, but I was unsure whether the debuggers needed other values, such as the floating point values or extended registers, to properly display the user's information. Therefore, I thought it was safe enough to call GetThreadContext on the executing thread to get these other values. Since my code didn't touch any of those registers, I was going to get the actual values at the time of the call. Of course, I made the call with a second CONTEXT structure so that I wouldn't overwrite my carefully saved values. Once I had the registers retrieved by GetThreadContext, I copied the specific values I saved at the beginning of the function over the retrieved values.

At this point I had the register state correct when the call to SnapCurrentProcessMiniDump occurred. My original thought was to put the return address onto the stack as the EIP register as well as the exception address. Accessing the return address is now easy because Microsoft documented the _ReturnAddress intrinsic function. _ReturnAddress will give you the address anywhere in the function. To use _ReturnAddress, you'll need to add the following two lines to your code so that the compiler doesn't complain the function is undefined. I like to put these lines in my precompiled header file so that they are globally accessible.

```
extern "C" void * _ReturnAddress ( void ) ;
#pragma intrinsic ( _ReturnAddress )
```

Because I had the rest of the registers set as they were before the call, very few people would have noticed the difference if I had simply used the return address as the EIP and exception address. Given that I can be quite anal-retentive, I went ahead and looked a few bytes back from the return address for the 0xE8 and 0xFF opcodes, which are the near CALL instruction and the far CALL instruction, respectively. That way the register set is completely aligned and appears at the instance of the call. You can see the work of determining the appropriate CALL type in CalculateBeginningOfCallInstruction.

The rest of the work after getting the register squared away is simply setting up the MINIDUMP_EXCEPTION_INFORMATION structure, opening the file handle, and calling MiniDumpWriteDump. You can see all this in action in the CommonSnapCurrentProcessMiniDump function in Listing 13-5.

Opening up a file created with SnapCurrentProcessMiniDump is just like opening any other minidump. The only difference is that the debugger will report the exception number as zero and show the instruction pointer on the

CALL instruction itself. Now you have no excuse for not snapping minidumps all the time. Set up a background thread that waits on an event, and when that even is signaled from an external program, call SnapCurrentProcessMiniDump in your thread to get perfect dumps all along the execution of your program.

```
// The following are snippets from MINIDUMP.CPP so you can see
// how SnapCurrentProcessMiniDump works.

// The distances (in bytes) from a return address to the call
// instruction for near and far calls. These are used in the
// CalculateBeginningOfCallInstruction function.
#define k_CALLNEARBACK  5
#define k_CALLFARBACK   6

// The common prolog for the naked functions,
// SnapCurrentProcessMiniDumpA and SnapCurrentProcessMiniDumpW.
#define SNAPPROLOG(Cntx)                                               \
__asm PUSH  EBP                    /* Save EBP explictly.           */ \
__asm MOV   EBP , ESP              /* Move the stack.               */ \
__asm SUB   ESP , __LOCAL_SIZE     /* Space for the local variables. */ \
/* Copy over all the easy current registers values. */                  \
__asm MOV   Cntx.Eax , EAX                                              \
__asm MOV   Cntx.Ebx , EBX                                              \
__asm MOV   Cntx.Ecx , ECX                                              \
__asm MOV   Cntx.Edx , EDX                                              \
__asm MOV   Cntx.Edi , EDI                                              \
__asm MOV   Cntx.Esi , ESI                                              \
/* Zero put the whole EAX register and just copy the segments into   */ \
/* the lower word. This avoids leaving the upper word uninitialized */ \
/* as the context segment registers are really 32-bit values.       */ \
__asm XOR   EAX , EAX                                                   \
__asm MOV   AX , GS                                                     \
__asm MOV   Cntx.SegGs , EAX                                            \
__asm MOV   AX , FS                                                     \
__asm MOV   Cntx.SegFs , EAX                                            \
__asm MOV   AX , ES                                                     \
__asm MOV   Cntx.SegEs , EAX                                            \
__asm MOV   AX , DS                                                     \
__asm MOV   Cntx.SegDs , EAX                                            \
__asm MOV   AX , CS                                                     \
__asm MOV   Cntx.SegCs , EAX                                            \
__asm MOV   AX , SS                                                     \
__asm MOV   Cntx.SegSs , EAX                                            \
/* Get the previous EBP value. */                                       \
__asm MOV  EAX , DWORD PTR [EBP]                                        \
__asm MOV  Cntx.Ebp , EAX                                               \
/* Get the previous ESP value. */                                       \
__asm MOV  EAX , EBP                                                    \
/* Two DWORDs up from EBP is the previous stack address. */             \
```

Listing 13-5 SnapCurrentProcessMiniDump and friends from MINIDUMP.CPP

```
__asm ADD  EAX , 8                                                    \
__asm MOV  Cntx.Esp , EAX                                             \
/* Save changed registers. */                                         \
__asm PUSH ESI                                                        \
__asm PUSH EDI                                                        \
__asm PUSH EBX                                                        \
__asm PUSH ECX                                                        \
__asm PUSH EDX

// The common epilog for the naked functions,
// SnapCurrentProcessMiniDumpA and SnapCurrentProcessMiniDumpW.
#define SNAPEPILOG(eRetVal)                                           \
__asm POP     EDX            /* Restore saved registers.  */          \
__asm POP     ECX                                                     \
__asm POP     EBX                                                     \
__asm POP     EDI                                                     \
__asm POP     ESI                                                     \
__asm MOV     EAX , eRetVal  /* Set the return value.     */          \
__asm MOV     ESP , EBP      /* Restore the stack pointer. */         \
__asm POP     EBP            /* Restore the frame pointer. */         \
__asm RET                    /* Return to caller.          */

BSUMDRET CommonSnapCurrentProcessMiniDump ( MINIDUMP_TYPE eType      ,
                                            LPCWSTR       szDumpName ,
                                            PCONTEXT      pCtx       )
{
    // Assume the best.
    BSUMDRET eRet = eDUMP_SUCCEEDED ;

    // Have I even tried to get the exported MiniDumpWriteDump function
    // yet?
    if ( ( NULL == g_pfnMDWD ) && ( eINVALID_ERROR == g_eIMDALastError))
    {
        if ( FALSE == IsMiniDumpFunctionAvailable ( ) )
        {
            eRet = g_eIMDALastError ;
        }
    }
    // If the MiniDumpWriteDump function pointer is NULL, I'm done.
    if ( NULL == g_pfnMDWD )
    {
        eRet = g_eIMDALastError ;
    }

    if ( eDUMP_SUCCEEDED == eRet )
    {
        // Armed with the context at the time of the call to this
        // function, I can now look to actually writing the dump. To
        // make everything work, I need to make it look like an
        // exception happened. Hence, all this work to fill out the
        // MINIDUMP_EXCEPTION_INFORMATION structure.
```

(continued)

```
    EXCEPTION_RECORD stExRec ;
    EXCEPTION_POINTERS stExpPtrs ;
    MINIDUMP_EXCEPTION_INFORMATION stExInfo ;

    // Zero out all the individual values.
    ZeroMemory ( &stExRec , sizeof ( EXCEPTION_RECORD )) ;
    ZeroMemory ( &stExpPtrs , sizeof ( EXCEPTION_POINTERS ) ) ;
    ZeroMemory ( &stExInfo ,sizeof(MINIDUMP_EXCEPTION_INFORMATION));

    // Set the exception address to the start of the CALL
    // instruction. Interestingly, I found I didn't have to set the
    // exception code. When you open up a .DMP file created
    // with this code in VS.NET, you'll see the exception code
    // reported as:
    // 0x00000000: The operation completed successfully.

    // warning C4312: 'type cast' : conversion from 'DWORD'
    // to 'PVOID' of greater size
#pragma warning ( disable : 4312 )
    stExRec.ExceptionAddress = (PVOID)(pCtx->Eip) ;
#pragma warning ( default : 4312 )

    // Set the exception pointers.
    stExpPtrs.ContextRecord = pCtx ;
    stExpPtrs.ExceptionRecord = &stExRec ;

    // Finally, set up the exception info structure.
    stExInfo.ThreadId = GetCurrentThreadId ( ) ;
    stExInfo.ClientPointers = TRUE ;
    stExInfo.ExceptionPointers = &stExpPtrs ;

    // Create the file to write.
    HANDLE hFile = CreateFile ( szDumpName                        ,
                                GENERIC_READ | GENERIC_WRITE ,
                                FILE_SHARE_READ                   ,
                                NULL                              ,
                                CREATE_ALWAYS                     ,
                                FILE_ATTRIBUTE_NORMAL             ,
                                NULL                               ) ;
    ASSERT ( INVALID_HANDLE_VALUE != hFile ) ;
    if ( INVALID_HANDLE_VALUE != hFile )
    {
        // Do the dump file.
        BOOL bRetVal = g_pfnMDWD ( GetCurrentProcess ( )   ,
                                   GetCurrentProcessId ( ) ,
                                   hFile                   ,
                                   eType                   ,
                                   &stExInfo               ,
                                   NULL                    ,
                                   NULL                     ) ;
        ASSERT ( TRUE == bRetVal ) ;
        if ( TRUE == bRetVal )
```

```
            {
                eRet = eDUMP_SUCCEEDED ;
            }
            else
            {
                eRet = eMINIDUMPWRITEDUMP_FAILED ;
            }
            // Close the file.
            VERIFY ( CloseHandle ( hFile ) ) ;
        }
        else
        {
            eRet = eOPEN_DUMP_FAILED ;
        }
    }
    return ( eRet ) ;
}

BSUMDRET __declspec ( naked )
            SnapCurrentProcessMiniDumpW ( MINIDUMP_TYPE eType      ,
                                          LPCWSTR       szDumpName  )

{
    // Where the registers coming into this function are stored.
    CONTEXT stInitialCtx ;
    // Where the final registers are stored.
    CONTEXT stFinalCtx ;
    // The return value.
    BSUMDRET    eRet ;
    // Boolean return value local.
    BOOL        bRetVal ;

    // Do the prolog.
    SNAPPROLOG ( stInitialCtx ) ;

    eRet = eDUMP_SUCCEEDED ;

    // Check the string parameter.
    ASSERT ( FALSE == IsBadStringPtr ( szDumpName , MAX_PATH ) ) ;
    if ( TRUE == IsBadStringPtr ( szDumpName , MAX_PATH ) )
    {
        eRet = eBAD_PARAM ;
    }

    if ( eDUMP_SUCCEEDED == eRet )
    {
        // Zero out the final context structure.
        ZeroMemory ( &stFinalCtx , sizeof ( CONTEXT ) ) ;

        // Indicate I want everything in the context.
        stFinalCtx.ContextFlags = CONTEXT_FULL                  |
                                    CONTEXT_CONTROL             |
                                    CONTEXT_DEBUG_REGISTERS     |
```

(continued)

```
                                             CONTEXT_EXTENDED_REGISTERS |
                                             CONTEXT_FLOATING_POINT      ;

        // Get all the groovy context registers and such for this
        // thread.
        bRetVal = GetThreadContext ( GetCurrentThread ( ) ,&stFinalCtx);
        ASSERT ( TRUE == bRetVal ) ;
        if ( TRUE == bRetVal )
        {
            COPYKEYCONTEXTREGISTERS ( stFinalCtx , stInitialCtx ) ;

            // Get the return address and hunt down the call instruction
            // that got us into this function. All the rest of the
            // registers are set up before the call so I'll ensure the
            // instruction pointer is set that way too.
            UINT_PTR dwRetAddr = (UINT_PTR)_ReturnAddress ( ) ;
            bRetVal = CalculateBeginningOfCallInstruction ( dwRetAddr );
            ASSERT ( TRUE == bRetVal ) ;
            if ( TRUE == bRetVal )
            {
                // Set the instruction pointer to the beginning of the
                // call instruction.
                stFinalCtx.Eip = (DWORD)dwRetAddr ;

                // Call the common function that does the actual write.
                eRet = CommonSnapCurrentProcessMiniDump ( eType      ,
                                                          szDumpName ,
                                                          &stFinalCtx );
            }
            else
            {
                eRet = eGETTHREADCONTEXT_FAILED ;
            }
        }
    }
    // Do the epilog.
    SNAPEPILOG ( eRet ) ;
}

// I had to pull this out of SnapCurrentProcessMiniDumpA/W as it's naked
// so can't use SEH.
BOOL CalculateBeginningOfCallInstruction ( UINT_PTR & dwRetAddr )
{
    BOOL bRet = TRUE ;
    // Protect everything inside exception handling. I need to be extra
    // careful here as I'm reading up the stack and could possibly bump
    // off the top. As I don't want SnapCurrentProcessMiniDump whacking
    // the application when you call it, I've got to eat any possible
    // exception I could run into here.
    __try
    {
        BYTE * pBytes = (BYTE*)dwRetAddr ;
```

```
        if ( 0xE8 == *(pBytes - k_CALLNEARBACK) )
        {
            dwRetAddr -= k_CALLNEARBACK ;
        }
        else if ( 0xFF == *(pBytes - k_CALLFARBACK) )
        {
            dwRetAddr -= k_CALLFARBACK ;
        }
        else
        {
            bRet = FALSE ;
        }
    }
    __except ( EXCEPTION_EXECUTE_HANDLER )
    {
        bRet = FALSE ;
    }
    return ( bRet ) ;
}
```

Summary

This chapter covered crash handlers, which are exception handlers and unhandled exception filters. Crash handlers allow you to get more information about a crash and provide a better face to the user when your application does have problems. The key to debugging faster is also getting the information you need when confronted with a problem, and crash handlers allow you to do that.

C++ exceptions and SEH exceptions are sometimes confused. The C++ language specification provides C++ exceptions, whereas the operating system provides SEH; the two kinds of exception handling are completely different, though intertwined in the dirty implementation details.

I hope I was able to show you the ugly truth about the love affair with C++ exception handling and make you think twice about using it in your application. With the overhead associated with C++ exception handling, you'll take a performance hit. However, the fact that `catch (...)` eats SEH errors with the Microsoft compiler implementation means it's one of the most evil constructs you'll ever see in your code. Additionally, `_set_se_translator` doesn't work as advertised, so you need to avoid it. Even though some C++ and object-oriented purists might find my stance on C++ exception harsh, the only purity that matters in my opinion is shipping high-quality code on time. By avoiding C++ exception handling, you'll achieve the purest code of all.

The magic function that does the work to make crash handlers possible is `SetUnhandledExceptionFilter`, which allows you to set the final SEH exception filter. The final exception filter allows you to gain control right before the Application Error dialog box pops up so that you can record all sorts of great information about why you crashed. The CrashHandler code presented will make it easier to set unhandled exception filters and will do the hard work of translating the crash information for you so that you can concentrate on the display and the unique parts of your application.

Finally, one of the coolest new APIs around is `MiniDumpWriteDump`. It has a few idiosyncrasies, but I was able to take care of them and make your minidump creation and subsequent reading as smooth as possible. Armed with minidumps created exactly when you need them, you should be able to solve any problems encountered by your customers.

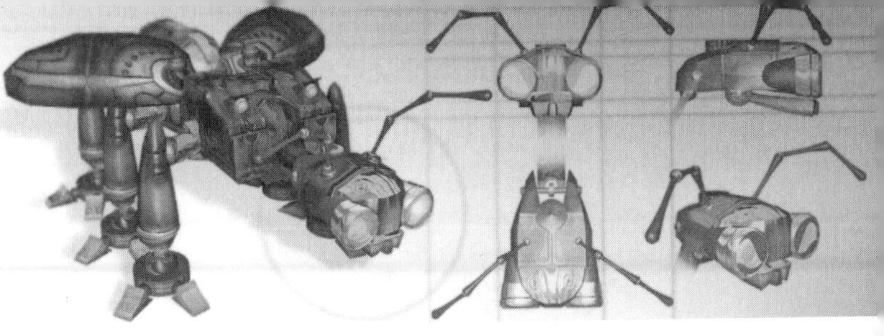

14

Debugging Windows Services and DLLs That Load into Services

Next to device drivers, the hardest code to debug involves Microsoft Windows services and DLLs that load into services. You might think that because services are really just user-mode processes without a user interface, debugging them would be as easy as debugging a console application. Unfortunately, the story isn't that simple. In fact, so many issues come into play with Windows services and with DLLs that load into services, especially issues related to Windows security, that you might find yourself wanting to pull out your hair in frustration trying to work with them. In the early days of Microsoft Windows NT, very few developers wrote services or even knew what they were. However, in today's world of COM+, Microsoft Internet Information Services (IIS), Microsoft Exchange Server extensions, and Windows Clustering, many developers must start dealing with services—and debugging them.

In this chapter, I'll provide an overview of the basic characteristics of services. To understand how to debug services and DLLs that load into services, such as ISAPI filters and extensions, you need to know how services operate. I'll then explain issues directly related to debugging services. As I walk you through the different stages of debugging a service, I'll point out issues that apply to specific Microsoft service technologies.

Service Basics

A service has three basic characteristics:

- A service might run all the time, even when the computer doesn't have anyone logged on or when the computer first starts.
- A service doesn't have a user interface.
- A service can be managed and controlled by both local and remote clients.

When deciding whether you need to write your application as a service or as a normal user-mode application, you need to ask yourself whether the development problem you're trying to solve has these three requirements. If it does, you should consider writing your application as a service. And if you do decide to write a service—and want to be able to debug it—you need to make sure you have a solid understanding of how a service operates. The information I'll present in this section will be just enough to give you an idea of what you're getting yourself into. If you'd like to learn more about services, I suggest you take a look at the excellent book by Jeffrey Richter and Jason Clark, *Programming Server-Side Applications for Microsoft Windows 2000* (Microsoft Press, 2000).

A perfect example of when to write a service is when you're writing an application that needs to monitor an uninterruptible power supply (UPS). All the UPS software needs to do is to monitor when the UPS hardware reports a power failure, and when the power does go out, the UPS software needs to initiate a controlled shutdown. Obviously, if the UPS software isn't running all the time (the first criterion for deciding whether your application should be a service), the shutdown won't happen and the computer will just stop when the UPS hardware runs out of battery power. The UPS software doesn't really need a user interface (the second criterion) because it just needs to run in the background and monitor the UPS hardware. Finally, if you're working on UPS hardware for use in data centers, system administrators will definitely want to check on the health of remote UPS hardware (the third criterion).

Sounds simple enough—so far. Now we'll turn to the way services operate. The first aspect of services I'll cover is the specific API functions that you call to turn a normal user-mode process into a service.

The API Dance

Services have some unique qualities that will require some maneuvering on your part to accommodate. First, the entry point you use in services—`main` or `WinMain`—doesn't matter. Because your service doesn't have any user interface, you can use console or graphical user interface (GUI) entry points interchangeably.

Inside your main or WinMain processing, the first call you have to make is to the StartServiceCtrlDispatcher API function. You pass a SERVICE_TABLE_ENTRY structure to StartServiceCtrlDispatcher in which you indicate your service name and the main entry point of your service. The Service Control Manager (SCM), which starts all services and is what StartServiceCtrlDispatcher eventually talks to in order to set up your service, is an operating system feature that, as its name implies, controls all services. If your service doesn't call StartServiceCtrlDispatcher within 30 seconds of starting, the SCM will terminate your service. As you'll see later in the chapter, this time limit can make debugging startup a little more interesting.

As soon as you call into the SCM, the SCM spawns a thread to call your service's entry point. Your service's entry point has one hard requirement: it must register a handler with RegisterServiceCtrlHandlerEx and call SetServiceStatus within 82 seconds of starting. If your service doesn't make the calls within that time, the SCM thinks your service has failed, though it doesn't terminate the service. If your service eventually does call RegisterServiceCtrlHandlerEx, your service will run normally. Although you'd expect that the SCM would terminate your service if it thought your service had failed, it doesn't. Odd as this behavior is, it does make debugging as your service continues to run much easier.

RegisterServiceCtrlHandlerEx takes yet another pointer to a function, called the handler function. The SCM calls into the handler function to control your service's performance on operations such as stopping, pausing, or continuing.

When your service is transitioning from the states of starting, stopping, and pausing, it communicates with the SCM through the SetServiceStatus API function. Most services just need to call SetServiceStatus and indicate the basic state to which they're changing—there's nothing fancy about this API function.

I've glossed over a few of the details involved with the API functions, but basically the calls to StartServiceCtrlDispatcher, RegisterServiceCtrlHandlerEx, and SetServiceStatus are all that the operating system requires of your service to get it up and running. Notice that I didn't mention anything about requirements concerning communications protocols your service uses to communicate between a controller user interface you write and your service. Fortunately, services have access to all the regular Windows API functions, so you can use memory-mapped files, mail slots, named pipes, and so on. With services, you really have all the same options as you do in normal cross-process communications. The most challenging issue with services, as I pointed out at the beginning of the chapter, is security.

The Security Dance

Unless you specify otherwise, services run in a special account called the System account. Because Windows has user-based security for all objects, the System account is validated for the machine, not for the network as a whole. Consequently, a System account process can't access network resources. For many services, such as the UPS example mentioned earlier in this chapter, the security issues might never arise during development. But if you're trying to share mapped memory from your service to the UI client application, for example, and your security isn't set correctly, you'll run into access-denied errors from your client applications as they attempt to map the shared memory.

Unfortunately, no amount of debugging will solve security problems; you have to make sure that you program both your services and your client applications with the security aligned correctly. Complete Windows security programming is a book unto itself, so be prepared to spend some time planning your security programming from the beginning of development. For a quick introduction to the range of security issues with services, I strongly suggest that you read Frank Kim's article "Why Do Certain Win32 Technologies Misbehave in Windows NT Services?" in the March 1998 *Microsoft Systems Journal*. Other excellent resources are Keith Brown's "Security Briefs" column in *Microsoft Systems Journal* and his book *Programming Windows Security* (Addison-Wesley, 2000). Finally, one of the best books ever written about real-world Windows security is *Writing Secure Code, Second Edition* by Michael Howard and David LeBlanc (Microsoft Press, 2003).

Now that you've had a whirlwind tour of services, let's turn to the real heart of this chapter: how to debug services.

Debugging Services

As you've seen, the unique nature of services alone means that you need to deal with many issues that don't come up when you're programming regular user-mode applications. Keep in mind that the discussion so far has been about the bare minimum functionality necessary for getting a service up and running. I haven't even touched on the fundamental requirement of ensuring that your general algorithms and implementation work for the one-of-a-kind pieces of your service. The easiest and best way to debug services without becoming completely overwhelmed is to approach the debugging in stages.

Two main stages are involved when you're debugging services:

- Debugging the core code
- Debugging the basic service

In the following sections, I'll describe what you need to do in each stage to make sure that you stand the best chance of debugging your service with a minimal amount of hassle.

Debugging the Core Code

Before you even consider running your application as a service, you need to run and test your application as a standard user-mode executable until you've debugged all your core code. Once you've done that, you can start working on the issues specific to services.

When debugging your core code, you should debug everything on the same machine, running under your developer account; that is, your service core code as well as any client code should be on the same machine. With this approach, you won't have to worry about any security or network issues. Once you debug your logic, you can move on to the joy of other problems you'll encounter with services, such as security and service initialization orders.

COM+ Services

If you're building a COM+ service with the Active Template Library (ATL), you don't have to do anything with security. By default, ATL runs as a user-mode executable until you register your application with the `-Service` command-line option.

ISAPI Filters and Extensions

The exported functions you must provide for your filters and extensions are fairly simple, and you can easily write a test harness that acts as a fake IIS system. You can test all your core algorithms in a controlled environment so that you have them completely debugged before you run your service under IIS proper.

Exchange Server

You can build Exchange Server services that run as console applications if you use the helper functions in WINWRAP.LIB. Starting your service with the `notserv` startup parameter will force running as a normal process. The `notserv` parameter must be the first parameter specified.

Debugging the Basic Service

After you test and debug your general logic, you can start debugging your code while running as a service. All your initial debugging should take place on a system on which you can control everything. Ideally, you should have a second machine sitting right next to your main development machine that you can use for your initial debugging. The second machine should have the version and flavor of Windows you're recommending to your customers for the environment your service will run under. Whereas the reason for debugging the core code was to verify your basic logic, the reason for preliminary service debugging is to shake out your basic service-specific code. You need to complete four tasks as part of debugging your first-cut service code:

- Turn on Allow Service To Interact With Desktop.
- Set your service identity.
- Attach to your service.
- Debug your startup code.

As I discuss each task, I'll mention particular issues relevant to the different technologies as appropriate.

Turn On Allow Service To Interact With Desktop

No matter what type of service you're debugging, you'll want to turn on Allow Service To Interact With Desktop on the Log On tab of your service's Properties dialog box. Although you shouldn't have any user interface elements with your service, having assertion notifications that allow you to gain control with the debugger is very helpful. Assertion notifications combined with excellent logging code, such as the code that ATL gives you for writing to the event log, can make it much easier to debug services.

In the initial stages of development, I turn on SUPERASSERT dialog assertions just so that I can quickly gauge the general health of my code. (For more information on SUPERASSERT, see Chapter 3.) As I get more and more of the service running, however, I set the assertion options so that all assertions just go through trace statements.

Until I'm confident of the service code, I generally leave the Allow Service To Interact With Desktop setting checked. One nasty bug that cropped up in a service I once wrote took me a while to track down because I turned off this option and I still had a message box that popped up. Because the operating system security won't allow normal services to show a message box, my service just appeared to hang. Before I do turn off Allow Service To Interact With Desktop,

I double-check that my service—and any DLLs that it uses—don't call message boxes by using DUMPBIN /IMPORTS to verify that neither `MessageBoxA` nor `MessageBoxW` are imported when I don't expect them to be.

If you're using `SUPERASSERT` as your assertion code, you're in luck. Even when you forget to turn off its dialog notifications, `SUPERASSERT` checks to see whether the process is running with a visible desktop before it shows the cool notification dialog box. In fact, this feature is so useful that I encapsulated it in the `BSUIsInteractiveUser` function (BSUFUNCTIONS.CPP) in BugslayerUtil.DLL.

Set Your Service Identity

To avoid security problems when you're trying to get your service running, you can set the identity of your service. By default, all services run under the System account, which is sometimes referred to as the LocalSystem account. However, you can set your service to start under a user account with higher security access, such as someone who is a member of a group with higher rights.

In your service's Properties dialog box, click on the Log On tab. Select the This Account radio button, click the Browse button, and choose the appropriate account from the Select User dialog box. After selecting the user, you'll need to type in and confirm the password for that account. For COM+ executable services, the DCOMCNFG.EXE can also set the logon identity of your service if you're more comfortable using it.

Attach to Your Service

Once your service has started, debugging isn't usually that difficult. All you need to do is to attach to your service process from the Microsoft Visual Studio .NET debugger. Depending on your service and the complexity of your code, attaching to the service with a debugger might be all you need to do to debug. Follow these simple steps to attach to an active process from the Visual Studio .NET debugger:

1. Start DEVENV.EXE.
2. From the Tools menu, select Debug Processes to bring up the Processes dialog box.
3. Check the Show System Processes check box, and click the Refresh button so that you can see all the service processes. Select the process you want to debug from the list, and click the Attach button. If you hold down either Ctrl key while clicking the Attach button, you'll automatically start Native debugging, bypassing the Attach To Process dialog.

4. If the Attach To Process dialog box does appear, ensure that Native is checked and click OK.

One very nice new feature of the Visual Studio .NET debugger is that you can now avoid going through the preceding steps every time you want attach to your service because you can create a project that will attach to the service as you start debugging. Set up your special attach projects with the following steps. Please note that these steps assume you're running the debugger under an account that has full administrator privileges and is in the Debugger Users group for the machine.

1. Build your application. When the build finishes, close the existing solution.
2. From the File menu, select Open Solution.
3. In the Open Solution dialog box, change the Files Of Type drop-down list to Executable Files and navigate to where the built service EXE resides. Select the EXE as the solution and click the Open button.
4. Save the solution by selecting Save All from the File menu and give the solution a name such as <*project*>_Attach.SLN in the Save File As dialog box.
5. Right-click on the .EXE node in the Solution Explorer window, and select Properties from the shortcut menu.
6. In the Debugging page of the project Property Pages dialog box, set the Attach field to Yes, as shown in Figure 14-1.

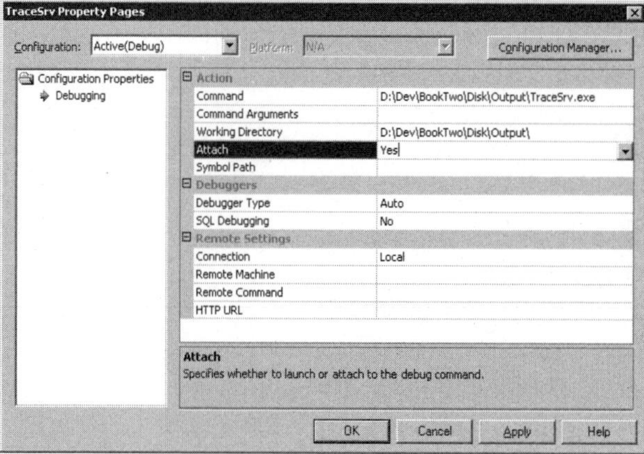

Figure 14-1 The Attach Debugging property page

7. Click OK in the project Property Pages dialog box.
8. Install and start your service in the usual manner.
9. When you're ready to debug the service, simply press F5 in Visual Studio .NET with your attach project loaded and you'll be all set.

An alternative method of attaching the debugger is just to call the `DebugBreak` API function. When the Application Error dialog box pops up, simply click the Cancel (Windows 2000) or Debug (Microsoft Windows XP and Windows Server 2003) button and debug as you normally would. Keep in mind that if you're building a COM+ service, you should make the `DebugBreak` call outside any COM method or property invocations. If you don't, COM will eat the breakpoint exception generated by `DebugBreak` and you'll never get a debugger attached. In addition, you shouldn't call `DebugBreak` as part of your service's initial startup code; see the section "Debug Your Startup Code" later in this chapter for reasons why.

Yet another means to attach the debugger to your service—if you're logged in with Administrator rights—is to use Task Manager. Bring up Task Manager, select the Processes tab, right-click on the process you want to debug, and select Debug from the shortcut menu. The operating system makes it easy to attach your debugger if you know what process you want to debug.

Only users who are authenticated as Administrators on the local machine are allowed to attach a debugger to services. If you're not an Administrator, the Debug option will show you an Unable To Attach Debugger message box when you try to debug a process that's not running under your user account.

IIS ISAPI filters and extensions Prior to IIS 5, all ISAPI filters ran inside INETINFO.EXE, the main IIS service, which meant you simply connected to INETINFO.EXE and debugged the single process. In IIS 5 and later versions, extensions run in DLLHOST.EXE because of the new pooled out-of-process model. ISAPI filters still run inside the IIS process, INETINFO.EXE. The new model makes IIS much more stable, and according to Microsoft, much more scalable. The only problem for debugging is that you might not know which DLLHOST.EXE process your extension is running under.

The IIS documentation mentions that you should set up your extensions to run inside IIS so that you can debug them. The only problem with changing where your extensions run is that you should deploy your extensions so that you use the pooled out-of-process model. Because I'm a believer in debugging in scenarios like those your users will experience, I want to show you the trick to debugging extensions even when they're running under DLLHOST.EXE, which is how your extensions will run.

Before I talk about using the debugger, though, I need to talk about how to figure out which process is running your filter or extension because multiple instances of DLLHOST.EXE will be running. First, you need to download a fantastic free utility, Process Explorer, from Mark Russinovich and Bruce Cogswell's Web site, *www.sysinternals.com.* I first mentioned Process Explorer in Chapter 2 because it's an excellent tool you can use to determine whether DLLs loading in your address space are being relocated.

Process Explorer will show you the handles that a process has open and, most important, which DLLs are loaded into which processes. To find your DLL using Process Explorer, first press Ctrl+D to indicate you want to view DLLs, then press Ctrl+F, and in the Process Explorer Search dialog box, type the filename of your DLL in the DLL Substring edit control. Click the Search button, and Process Explorer will list the names and process IDs (PIDs) of the processes that have your DLL loaded. After you have the PID, you can attach the Visual Studio .NET debugger to the process using the Debug Process command on the Tools menu. Make sure you read the sidebar about what other tasks Process Explorer can perform because it's one of the best tools you can put on your hard disk.

If you're looking for the command-line equivalent tool to Process Explorer, it's the TLIST.EXE program that comes with the Debugging Tools for Windows (that is, WinDBG). It can show you the MTS packages as well as which processes have which DLLs loaded. Running `TLIST -?` will show you all the command-line options supported by TLIST.EXE. The `–k` command-line switch shows all processes that have MTS packages in them. The `–m` command-line switch shows which processes have a particular DLL loaded in them. The `–m` switch supports regular expression syntax. So, for example, to see all modules that load KERNEL32.DLL, you'd specify `*KERNEL32.DLL` as the pattern.

Because you're looking for a loaded DLL, you obviously have to make sure that it loads before you can debug it. Filters run inside INETINFO.EXE, so you can't attach the debugger before the IIS service starts. Therefore, you're out of luck if you want to debug the initialization. If you're debugging extensions, you can debug your initialization if you're ingenious. The idea is to create a dummy extension that you force IIS to load by connecting to your Web site with Microsoft Internet Explorer, which will make IIS start the DLLHOST.EXE pooled out-of-process executable. After you hunt down the PID for the new DLLHOST.EXE, you can attach the debugger. You can then set a breakpoint on `LdrpRunInitializeRoutines` so that you can step directly into your extension's DllMain. Matt Pietrek clarifies exactly what you need to do to set the LdrpRunInitializeRoutines breakpoint in his "Under the Hood" column from the September 1999 *Microsoft Systems Journal*. After you've set the breakpoint, you can load your real extension with Internet Explorer and debug your initialization.

Debug Your Startup Code

The hardest part of debugging services is debugging the startup code. The SCM will wait only 30 seconds for a service to get started and call StartServiceCtrlDispatcher to indicate that the service is running fine. Although this time is almost a lifetime on the CPU, you can easily spend that amount of time single-stepping through your code looking at variables.

The only clean way to debug your service startup code is to use trace statements if all you have is the Visual Studio .NET debugger. Using Mark Russinovich's DebugView, which I refer to in Chapter 3, you can see the statements as your service rolls along. Fortunately, your service startup code is generally more lightweight than the main service code, so debugging with trace statements isn't too painful.

The SCM timeout limit can cause problems for services that can't start quickly. A slow piece of hardware or the nature of your service can sometimes dictate a long startup time. The SERVICE_STATUS structure you pass to SetServiceStatus has two fields, dwCheckPoint and dwWaitHint, which might help you if your service is likely to time out on startup.

When your service does start, you can tell the SCM that you're entering the SERVICE_START_PENDING state, place a large hint in the dwWaitHint field (the time is in milliseconds), and set the dwCheckPoint field to 0 so that the SCM won't use the default times. If you need more time in your service startup, you can repeat the call to SetServiceStatus as many times as necessary as long as you increment the dwCheckPoint field before each successive call.

The final point I want to address about debugging startup code is that the SCM will add entries to the event log explaining why it can't start a particular service. In the Event Viewer, look in the Source column for "Service Control Manager." If you also use the event log for your lightweight tracing, between the SCM entries and your tracing, you should be able to solve many of your startup problems. If you use the event log, make sure your service dependencies are set so that your service will be started after the event log service.

Common Debugging Question

Why does every developer need Process Explorer?

I've already mentioned that Mark Russinovich's wonderful Process Explorer program makes it trivial to find which instance of DLLHOST.EXE has a particular DLL loaded and to determine whether you have relocated DLLs in a process. However, there's so much more to Process Explorer—such as being an outstanding debugging tool—and I want to take a moment to discuss some of its excellent features.

By default, Process Explorer updates periodically, just like Task Manager. Although this updating is great for general monitoring, it can make you miss some details when debugging. It's best to set Process Explorer to manual updating by selecting the View menu, and then setting Update Speed to Paused.

Probably the best way to show you the power of Process Explorer is to run through a little demonstration. You might want to follow along so that you can see the tool in action. The first step is to start Process Explorer followed by NOTEPAD.EXE because I'll use it for the demonstration. Set Process Explorer to manual updating by selecting the View menu, and then setting Update Speed to Paused.

The first trick you can perform with Process Explorer is determining which DLLs are coming into your address space because of a particular operation. In Process Explorer, press F5 to refresh the display, select the instance of NOTEPAD.EXE you started up a moment ago, and then press Ctrl+D to change the view to show the DLLs for Notepad. Activate Notepad and select Open from Notepad's File menu. Leave the Open dialog box open in Notepad and switch back to Process Explorer. Press F5 to refresh Process Explorer's display and you'll see a bunch of lines appear in green in NOTEPAD.EXE's DLL view, as shown in Figure 14-2. The green indicates which DLLs came into the address space since the last refresh. Of course, you can also see which DLLs leave the address space by switching back to Notepad and closing the Open dialog box, returning to Process Explorer, and refreshing the display with F5. All DLLs that have left the address space are shown in red. This ability to quickly see what's coming into and out of your processes is very helpful in determining what's causing module loads and unloads. An added benefit is that the color highlighting showing what's been loaded and unloaded also applies to the EXE listing in the upper half of the Process Explorer display.

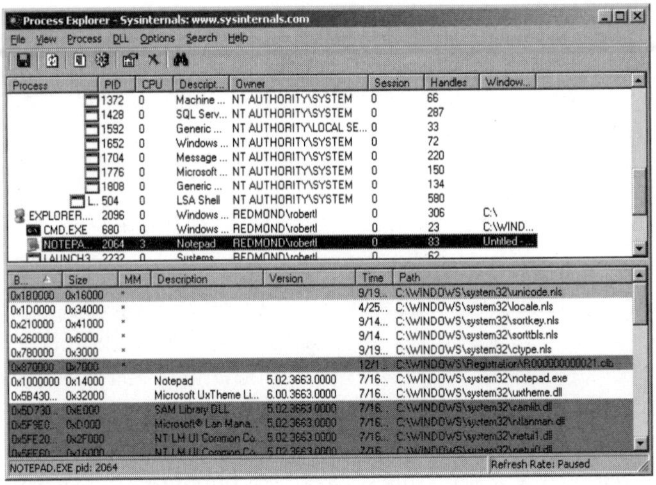

Figure 14-2 DLL view for Process Explorer showing new DLLs added to the Notepad process

Process Explorer's second trick lets you peek at all sorts of excellent information about a process simply by double-clicking it. The dialog box that pops up shows you four or five tabs depending on the process. The first tab, Image, shows you information such as the path and current directory for the process, as well as offers a button to let you kill the process. The second tab, Performance, shows you the important performance data information related to the CPU, memory, I/O, and GDI handles. The third tab, Security, shows you the security information such as groups for the process and granted access. If the process is a Microsoft Win32 service or host, the Services tab shows you the name of the particular services running in that process. The final tab, Environment, lists the environment variables active for that process. In using the Security and Environment tabs, I've tracked down some very interesting problems related to security programming because Process Explorer is about the only tool that makes this information easy to see.

The final trick with Process Explorer lets you see which handles are currently open for any process! I've utilized this feature to track down many different handle problems in the past. In Process Explorer, press Ctrl+H to change the bottom half of the display to handle viewing. The first column displayed is the handle value, and the second column is the type of handle (see the explanation in Chapter 8 in the discussion of `!handle`). The third column contains the access bits for that handle, and

(continued)

Common Debugging Question *(continued)*

the fourth column is the name of the object. As I mentioned back in Chapter 8, naming your handles is crucial to tracking down problems. If you want more details about a particular handle, double-click it to see the handle properties and more than you ever wanted to know about that handle's particular permission values.

As with DLL view, you can see handles being created and closed inside your process. Select the instance of NOTEPAD.EXE you started earlier. Press Ctrl+H to get the handle view, and refresh the display by pressing F5. Switch back to Notepad, and reopen the Open dialog box. Once the dialog box is open, switch back to Process Explorer and refresh the display again. All new handles in the Notepad process show up with green highlighting. If you close Notepad's Open dialog box and refresh Process Explorer once more, all the closed handles will show up with red highlighting.

I've used the handle view in Process Explorer to help track down handle leaks more times than I can count. By default, Process Explorer will show you only those handles that have names. You can also view all unnamed handles by pressing Ctrl+U. If you're tracking down handle issues, you'll probably want to view all the handles so that you can see all types that might be leaking.

One pretty interesting feature in handle view gives you the option to forcibly close a particular handle by right-clicking on it and selecting Close Handle. When I asked Mark why he put that feature in, he said, "Because I could." When I laughed and said that it was pretty dangerous, he said it was my job to come up with a reason for having it. The key reason for randomly closing handles in Process Explorer is so that you can sneak into your manager's office and close half the handles in Outlook to keep him from sending you annoying e-mail. I figure that's a plenty good enough reason!

Summary

This chapter covered some of the trials and tribulations that are a part of debugging Windows services and DLLs that load into services. Services have a special status in the operating system, and because of the security issues involved, you need to have an excellent understanding of what services are and how they behave. Service debugging takes more planning up front than most debugging.

The first step in debugging services and any DLLs that load into services is to debug as much of the core code as possible while running as a normal application. The second step is to ensure that you take advantage of the environment for services, such as by turning on interaction with the desktop and by using tools such as Process Explorer to find the information you need to debug faster.

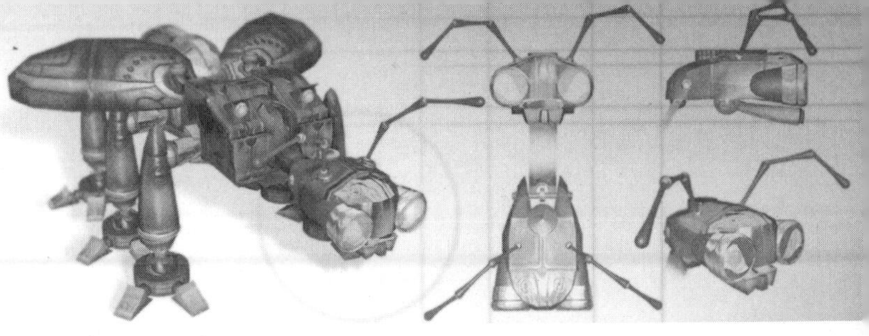

15

Multithreaded Deadlocks

Without a doubt, the hardest problems to solve in modern software development are multithreaded deadlocks. Even if you think you planned for every situation, your multithreaded application can stop dead when you least expect it. The biggest obstacle to debugging multithreaded deadlocks is that by the time your application is deadlocked, it's almost too late to start debugging.

In this chapter, I'll go over some tricks and techniques that have worked for me when I've done multithreaded programming. I'll also present a utility I wrote, DeadlockDetection, that lets you see the flow of events that led up to your deadlock, which is about the only evidence you'll have to help you track down what went wrong and figure out how to avoid the same deadlock in the future. The information in this chapter and the DeadlockDetection utility will help you avoid the minefield of multithreaded deadlocks.

Multithreading Tips and Tricks

As I've been emphasizing throughout this book, one of the keys to debugging is up-front planning. With multithreaded programming, up-front planning is the only way you can avoid the dreaded deadlocks. I break down the necessary planning for multithreaded applications into the following categories:

- Don't do it.
- Don't overdo it.
- Multithread only small, discrete pieces.
- Synchronize at the lowest level.
- Spin your critical sections.

- Don't use `CreateThread`.
- The default memory manager might kill you.
- Get the dump in the field.
- Review the code—and review the code again.
- Test on multiprocessor machines.

Don't Do It

This first tip might seem a little facetious, but I'm absolutely serious. Make sure there's no other way you can structure your program before you decide to incorporate multithreading into your application. When you include multithreading in your application, you're easily adding a minimum of an extra month of development and testing to your schedule.

If you're coding thick client applications and you need your program to do some lightweight background processing, check to see whether the work can be handled either through the Microsoft Foundation Class (MFC) library `OnIdle` processing or through a background periodic timer event. With a little creative thinking, you can probably find a way to avoid multithreading and the headaches that go with it.

Don't Overdo It

When it comes to server-based applications, you also have to be extremely careful not to create too many threads. One common mistake we've all seen is that some developers end up with a server application in which each connection runs on its own thread. The average development team is doing well to get 10 concurrent connections during their heaviest testing, and it looks like their code works fine. The code might work fine when first deployed, but as soon as business picks up, the server starts bogging down because it's not scalable.

When working on server applications, you'll definitely want to take advantage of the excellent support Microsoft Windows 2000, Windows XP, and Windows Server 2003 has for thread pooling with the `QueueUserWorkItem` family of functions. That way you can fine-tune the tradeoff between the number of threads and the amount of work you want to get done. Developers are used to things like Microsoft Internet Information Services (IIS) and COM+ handling thread pooling, but developing your own thread pooling system is not something most developers have much experience at, so make sure you spend extra time prototyping your particular situation. For instance, it's much easier to deadlock with misused thread pools than you can ever imagine.

Multithread Only Small, Discrete Pieces

If you must multithread, try to keep it to small, discrete pieces. With thick client applications, you should stick to small pieces of work that are generally devoid of any user interface (UI) elements. For example, printing in the background is a smart use of multithreading because your application's UI will be able to accept input while data is printing.

In server applications, it's slightly different in that you need to judge whether the overhead of thread creation and work will actually speed up your application. Although threads are much more lightweight than processes, they still take quite a bit of overhead. Consequently, you'll want to make sure that the benefit of cranking up that thread will be worth the effort. For example, many server applications have to transfer data back and forth between some type of database. The cost of waiting for the write to that database can potentially be high. If you have a situation in which you don't need to do transactional recording, you can plop parts of the database write into a thread pool object and let it complete on its own time, and thus continue your processing. That way you'll be more responsive to the calling process and get more work done.

Synchronize at the Lowest Level

Since writing the first edition of this book, I have seen that this particular multithread rule is broken more than any other. You have to keep your synchronization methods at the lowest level possible in your code. This might sound like common sense, but the mistake I see made over and over is that developers are using fancy C++ wrapper classes that grab the synchronization object in the constructor and release it in the destructor. The following code shows an example class you'll find in CRITICALSECTION.H in this book's source code:

```
class CUseCriticalSection;

class CCriticalSection
{
public      :

    CCriticalSection ( DWORD dwSpinCount = 4000 )
    {
        InitializeCriticalSectionAndSpinCount ( &m_CritSec   ,
                                                dwSpinCount  ) ;
    }
    ~CCriticalSection ( )
    {
        DeleteCriticalSection ( &m_CritSec ) ;
    }
```

```
    friend CUseCriticalSection ;
public     :
    CRITICAL_SECTION m_CritSec ;
} ;

class CUseCriticalSection
{
public      :
    CUseCriticalSection ( const CCriticalSection & cs )
    {
        m_cs = &cs ;
        EnterCriticalSection ( ( LPCRITICAL_SECTION)&(m_cs->m_CritSec));
    }

    ~CUseCriticalSection ( )
    {
        LeaveCriticalSection ( (LPCRITICAL_SECTION)&(m_cs->m_CritSec) );
        m_cs = NULL ;
    }

private     :
    CUseCriticalSection ( void )
    {
        m_cs = NULL ;
    }
    const CCriticalSection * m_cs ;
} ;
```

These classes look great from an object-oriented standpoint, but the implementation issues absolutely kill your performance. The constructor for a wrapper class such as `CUseCriticalSection` is called at the top of the scope, where it's declared and destroyed when that scope ends. Nearly everyone uses the synchronization class as it is shown in the following code:

```
void DoSomethingMultithreaded ( )
{
    CUseCriticalSection ( g_lpCS ) ;

    for ( . . . )
    {
        CallSomeOtherFunction ( . . . ) ;
    }

    // Here's the only piece of data really needing protection.
    m_xFoo = z ;

    YetAnotherCallHere ( . . . ) ;
}
```

The constructor grabs the critical section at the top curly brace, that is, right after the prolog, yet the destructor is not called until the bottom curly brace, right before the epilog. That means you hold onto the critical section for the life of the function, even though DoSomethingMultithreaded is probably calling functions that don't need to be holding onto the critical section. All you are succeeding in doing is killing performance.

As you look at DoSomethingMultithreaded, you're probably thinking, "How expensive can acquiring a synchronization object really be?" If there's no contention for the synchronization object, the cost is very small. However, with multiple threads, the instant a thread can't acquire a synchronization object, you begin a potentially astronomical cost!

Let's start by taking a look at what happens when you call WaitForSingleObject to acquire a synchronization object. Since you are an assembly language demigod from reading Chapter 7, you might want to follow along in the Disassembly window as it will show you exactly what I'm about to discuss. Note that I'm doing the work on Windows XP; the Windows 2000 version of WaitForSingleObject might be slightly different. WaitForSingleObject itself is simply a wrapper around WaitForSingleObjectEx, which does about 40 lines or so of assembly language and calls two functions to set up some data. Down toward the bottom of WaitForSingleObjectEx is a call to NtWaitForSingleObject from NTDLL.DLL. So the WaitForSingleObject function is a call to a wrapper of a wrapper. If you disassemble the address where NtWaitForSingleObject is in memory (use {,,ntdll}_NtWaitForSingleObject@12 in the Address field of the Disassembly window), you'll see that it's really a call to some weird function, ZwWaitForSingleObject, which is also out of NTDLL.DLL. (On Windows 2000, you'll stop at NtWaitForSingleObject.) As you look at the disassembly for ZwWaitForSingleObject, you'll see that it looks something like the following:

```
_ZwWaitForSingleObject@12:
77F7F4A3  mov         eax,10Fh
77F7F4A8  mov         edx,7FFE0300h
77F7F4AD  call        edx
77F7F4AF  ret         0Ch
77F7F4B2  nop
```

The real action is at that address, 0x7FFE0300. If you dump what's at that address, you'll see the following:

```
7FFE0300  mov         edx,esp
7FFE0302  sysenter
7FFE0304  ret
```

The middle line in the preceding code, showing the SYSENTER, is the magical assembly language instruction. It's one that you'll see only in this context and you won't ever see generated in your code, so I didn't cover it in Chapter 7. Just from the name you can probably guess what it does: it's the instruction that transitions you from user mode to kernel mode. On Windows 2000, the `INT 2E` call does the same thing as the `SYSENTER` instruction. Why did I go through this long drawn-out discussion to show you that `WaitForSingleObject` eventually calls `SYSENTER` and transitions to kernel mode? I did it simply because that call to `SYSENTER` sends your thread on a journey into kernel mode, and I wanted to show all the overhead associated with moving your thread out of the thread queue and figuring out what you're waiting on, as well as all the rest of the necessary work for thread coordination. Of course, when you get up to kernel mode, if you actually have to wait on that kernel object you passed to `WaitForSingleObject`, you'll have thousands of instructions doing the work to pull your thread out of the active thread queue and to place it in the waiting thread queue.

Some eagle-eyed readers are thinking that if you call `WaitForSingleObject` when waiting on a kernel handle, you're going to hit that cost no matter what. That's true because kernel handles used for cross-process synchronization give you no choice. However, for that reason, most people doing internal synchronization that don't require the cross-process synchronization use the trusty standby of a critical section, as I showed earlier in the `CUseCriticalSection` class. As most of us have read at one time or another, critical sections are great because you can acquire them without going to kernel mode. That's exactly correct, but most people forget one crucial detail. What happens if you can't acquire that critical section? There obviously has to be some sort of synchronization going on if you can't acquire that critical section. There is—and it's a Microsoft Win32 semaphore handle.

I went through this long discussion because I wanted to fully explain the problem of holding onto those synchronization objects too long. I've seen applications where we've been able to track down the critical contention issues and remove the wrapping classes and gain a significant performance boost. I've found it's much better to explicitly call the synchronization acquire and release functions only around the actual data accesses—even when you might be doing those calls two, three, or more times per function. With critical-section synchronization in particular, the increase in speed is considerable. The other benefit of keeping the synchronization around the actual data accesses is also one of your best defenses against inadvertent deadlocks.

I just want to reiterate that the wrapper classes like `CUseCriticalSection` are not evil in themselves, it's just the improper use that's the issue. What I've seen done that's perfectly acceptable is code like the following:

```
void DoSomeGoodMultithreaded ( )
{

    for ( . . . )
    {
```

```
        CallSomeOtherFunction ( . . . ) ;
    }

    // Protect this data access but not hold onto the lock too long.
    {
        CUseCriticalSection ( g_lpCS ) ;
        m_xFoo = z ;
    }

    YetAnotherCallHere ( . . . ) ;
}
```

The `CUseCriticalSection` helper class is still present, but by introducing it inside the separate standalone curly braces, it's given a scope so that it's acquired and released just around the one necessary spot, and it isn't held too long.

Spin Your Critical Sections

As I mentioned in the previous section, critical sections are the preferred method of synchronization when you are only synchronizing inside a process. However, you can get a considerable performance boost using critical sections if you remember to spin!

Years ago, some folks at Microsoft were wondering about multithreaded application performance, so they came up with several testing scenarios to find out more. After lots of study, they found something quite counterintuitive, though not unheard of in computer science. They found that in certain cases it was much faster to poll than to actually perform an operation. We've all been told since we were wee programmers never to poll, but in the case of critical sections, that's exactly what you want to do.

The vast majority of critical-section protection was for small data protection cases. As I described in the last section, a critical section is protected by a semaphore, and making the call into kernel mode to acquire that critical section is extremely expensive. The original implementation of `EnterCriticalSection` simply looked to see whether the critical section could be acquired. If it couldn't, `EnterCriticalSection` went right into kernel mode. In most cases, by the time the thread got into kernel mode and back down, the other thread had released the critical section a million years ago in computer time. The counterintuitive idea the Microsoft researchers came up with on multiple CPU systems was to check whether the critical section was available and, if it wasn't, spin the CPU, then check again. On single CPU systems, the spin count, obviously, is ignored. If after the second check the critical section wasn't available, finally transition to kernel mode. The idea was that keeping the thread in user mode, even though it was spinning on nothing, was tremendously faster than transitioning to kernel mode.

Two functions allow you to set the critical-section spin count. The first is `InitializeCriticalSectionAndSpinCount`, which you should use in place of `InitializeCriticalSection`. For the second function, `SetCriticalSectionSpinCount`, you want to change the value you originally started with, or you need to change the value for library code that uses only `InitializeCriticalSection`. Of course, I am assuming that you can access the critical-section pointer in your derived code.

Determining your spin count can be problematic. If you work in an environment in which you have the two to three weeks to run through all the scenarios, grab all those interns sitting around and have fun. However, most of us aren't that lucky. I always use the value 4,000 for my spin count. That's what Microsoft uses for the operating system heaps, and I always figured that my code was probably less intensive than those. Using that number also would be big enough should I keep my code in user mode almost all the time.

Don't Use `CreateThread/ExitThread`

One of the more insidious mistakes that people make in multithreaded development is using `CreateThread`. Of course, that begs this question: if you can't use `CreateThread` to start a thread, how can you get any threads cranked up? Instead of `CreateThread`, you should always use `_beginthreadex`, the C run-time function to start your threads. As you'd expect, since `ExitThread` is paired with `CreateThread` to end a thread, `_beginthreadex` has its own matching exit function, `_exitthreadex`, that you'll need to use instead as well.

You might be using `CreateThread` in your application right now and not be experiencing any problems whatsoever. Unfortunately, some very subtle bugs can occur because the C run time is not initialized when you use `CreateThread`. The C run time relies on some per-thread data, so certain standard C run-time functions designed before high speed multithreaded applications were the norm. For example, the function `strtok` holds the string to parse in per-thread storage. Using `_beginthreadex` ensures that the per-thread data is there along with other things the C run time needs. To ensure proper thread cleanup, use `_exitthreadex`, which will ensure the C run time resources are cleaned up when you need to exit the thread prematurely.

The `_beginthreadex` function works the same way and takes the same type of parameters as `CreateThread`. To end your thread, simply return from the thread function or call `_endthreadex`. However, if you want to leave early, use the `_endthreadex` C run time function to end your threads. As with the `CreateThread` API function, `_beginthreadex` returns the thread handle, which you must pass to `CloseHandle` to avoid a handle leak.

If you look up _beginthreadex, you'll also see a C run time function named _beginthread. You'll want to avoid using that function like the plague because its default behavior is a bug, in my opinion. The handle returned by _beginthread is cached, so if the thread ends quickly, another spawned thread could overwrite that location. In fact, the documentation on _beginthread indicates that it's safer to use _beginthreadex. When reviewing your code, make sure to note calls to _beginthread and _endthread so that you can change them to _beginthreadex and _endthreadex, respectively.

The Default Memory Manager Might Kill You

A client of ours wanted to make the fastest possible server application. When they brought us in to tune the application, they found that adding threads to the application, which according to their design should have scaled the processing power, was having no affect. One of the first things I did when their server application was warmed up and cooking along was to stop it in the debugger and, from the Threads window, look at where each thread was sitting.

This application made use of quite a bit of the Standard Template Library (STL), which as I pointed when discussing WinDBG in the "Trace and Watch Data" section of Chapter 8, can be a performance killer all its own because it allocates tons of memory behind your back. By stopping the server application, I was looking to see which threads were in the C run time memory management system. We all have the memory management code (you install the C run time source code every time you install Microsoft Visual Studio, right?), and I'd seen that a single critical section protects the whole memory management system. That was always scary to me because I thought it could lead to performance issues. When I looked at our client's application, I was horrified to see that 38 out of 50 threads were blocked on the C run-time memory management critical section! More than half of their application was waiting and doing nothing! Needless to say, they were not very thrilled to find this out.

For most applications, the Microsoft supplied C run time is perfectly fine and will not cause you memory problems. However, in the larger, high-volume server applications, that single critical section can eat you up. My first recommendation is to always think long and hard about using STL, and if you insist on using STL, take a look at the STLPort version I discussed back in Chapter 2. I've already discussed numerous issues with STL earlier in this book. In the context of high-volume, multithreaded applications, the Microsoft-supplied STL can lead to bottlenecks.

The bigger problem is what to do about the C run-time single critical section problem. What we really need is each thread with its own heap instead of a single global heap for all threads. That way each thread would never make that kernel mode transition to allocate or deallocate memory. Of course, you can probably see that the solution is not as simple as making a single heap per thread, because you have the problem of handling the case in which memory is allocated in one thread and deallocated in another. Fortunately, there are three solutions to the conundrum.

The first solution is the commercial memory management systems on the market, which handle the per-thread heap code for you. Unfortunately, the pricing models for those products are borderline extortion and your manager will never buy anything that expensive. The second solution, one of the big performance boosts with Windows 2000, is the major improvements Microsoft made to how the operating system heaps work (those heaps created with `HeapCreate` and accessed with `HeapAlloc` and `HeapFree`). To take advantage of the operating system heap, you can easily replace your `malloc`/`free` allocations with the appropriate `Heap*` functions. For the C++ `new` and `delete` functions, you'll need to provide replacement global functions. The third and last solution, if you'll be running on multiprocessor machines, is to use Emery Berger's excellent Hoard multiprocessor memory management code (*http://www.hoard.org*). It's a drop-in replacement for the C and C++ memory routines and is very fast on multiprocessor machines. If you have trouble getting it to link in because of duplicate symbols, you'll have to use the `/FORCE:MULTIPLE` command line option to LINK.EXE. Keep in mind that Hoard is for multiprocessor machines and can actually run slower than the default allocators on single processor systems.

Get the Dump in the Field

One of the most frustrating experiences is when your program appears to be deadlocking in the field and no matter how hard you try, you can't duplicate the deadlock. However, with the latest improvements in DBGHELP.DLL, you should never want in that situation ever again. The new minidump functions will allow you to take a snapshot of the deadlock so that you can debug it at your leisure. In Chapter 13, I discussed the particulars of the minidump function and my improved wrapper around it, `SnapCurrentProcessMiniDump`, in BUGSLAYERUTIL.DLL.

To get the dump in the field, you'll want to create a background thread that simply creates and waits on an event. When that event is signaled, it will call `SnapCurrentProcessMiniDump`, and snap the dump to disk. The following pseudo code snippet shows the function. To tickle the event, have a separate executable that the user will execute to set the event.

```
DWORD WINAPI DumperThread ( LPVOID )
{
    HANDLE hEvents[2] ;
```

```
    hEvents[0] = CreateEvent ( NULL                    ,
                               TRUE                    ,
                               FALSE                   ,
                               _T ( "DumperThread" )  ) ;
    hEvents[1] = CreateEvent ( NULL                    ,
                               TRUE                    ,
                               FALSE                   ,
                               _T ( "KillDumperThread" ) ) ;

    int iRet = WaitForMultipleObjects ( 2 , hEvents , FALSE , INFINITE);
    while ( iRet != 1 )
    {
        // You might want to create a unique filename each time.
        SnapCurrentProcessMiniDump ( MiniDumpWithFullMemory ,
                                     _T ( "Program.DMP" )  ) ;
        iRet = WaitForMultipleObjects ( 2 , hEvents , FALSE , INFINITE);
    }
    VERIFY ( CloseHandle ( hEvents[ 0 ] ) ) ;
    VERIFY ( CloseHandle ( hEvents[ 1 ] ) ) ;
    return ( TRUE ) ;
}
```

Review the Code—And Review the Code Again

If you really do need to multithread your application, you must allow plenty of time to walk through your multithreaded code in full code reviews. The trick is to assign one person to each thread in your code and one person to each synchronization object. In many ways, the code review in multithreaded programming is really a "multithreaded" review.

When you review the code, pretend that each thread is running at real-time priority on its own dedicated CPU and that the thread is never interrupted. Each "thread person" walks through the code, paying attention only to the particular code that his thread is supposed to be executing. When the "thread person" is ready to acquire a synchronization object, the "object person" literally moves behind the "thread person." When the "thread person" releases a synchronization object, the "object person" goes to a neutral corner of the room. In addition to the thread and object representatives, you should have some developers who are monitoring the overall thread activity so that they can assess the program's flow and help determine the points at which different threads deadlock.

As you're working through the code review, keep in mind that the operating system has its own synchronization objects that it applies to your process and that those objects can cause deadlocks as well. The process critical section, explained in the next section's Debugging War Story "The Deadlock Makes No Sense," and the infamous Microsoft Windows 9x/Me Win16 mutex are both synchronization objects that the operating system uses in your process. Be sure to pay attention to anything that could possibly cause any sort of contention in your application.

Test on Multiprocessor Machines

As I mentioned, a multithreaded application requires a much higher level of testing than a single-threaded one. The most important tip I have for testing your multithreaded application is to test it thoroughly on multiprocessor machines. And I don't mean simply running your application through a few paces; I mean continually testing your program in all possible scenarios. Even if your application runs perfectly on single-processor machines, a multiprocessor machine will turn up deadlocks you never thought possible.

The best approach to this kind of testing is to have the team's developers running the application on multiprocessor machines every day. If you're a manager and you don't have any multiprocessor machines in your shop, stop reading right now and immediately equip half your developers and QA testers with multiprocessor machines! If you're a developer without a multiprocessor machine, show this chapter to your manager and demand the proper equipment to do your job! Several people have written me and mentioned that showing this chapter really did help them get a multiprocessor machine, so don't hesitate to tell your manager that John Robbins said the company owed you one.

Debugging War Story

Saving Some Jobs

The Battle

When a vice president of development called and said he wanted me to work on his team's deadlock *now*, I knew this job was going to be tough. The guy was abrupt and not too happy that he had to bring a consultant in to help his team. He called his two key developers together and the four of us got into a conference call. The VP was ranting and raving that the developers had slipped too long because of this deadlock bug, and he was not happy. I could just imagine the two engineers cringing as their dirty laundry got aired to some guy on the phone they didn't know. They were porting the application from, in the VP's words, "a real operating system" (UNIX) to "this (censored) toy operating system called Windows," and that just "ruined his year." Of course, when I asked him why, he did have to admit that "it was to stay in business." I had to smile on my end of the phone quite a bit about that!

The engineers mailed me the code and we started going through it with the VP stalking around the conference room. As I got my bearings in the code and got toward the area where the deadlock was, I immediately broke out in a huge flop sweat and felt my heart pounding. I knew that if

I'd said that all they had to do was backspace over a D, an N, an E, and an S, and type a P, an O, an S, and a T, the VP was going to blow a fuse and probably fire those two engineers.

The Outcome

I didn't say anything for quite a bit until I collected my thoughts. After a long exhale and saying "Whew, this looks really, really tough," I told the development manager that it was going to take a few hours to sort this out. It was best if the engineers and I worked on it alone because I'm sure he had much more important things to do than to listen to three engineers read hexadecimal numbers to each other over the phone. Fortunately, he bought it and I told the engineers I would call them back in their computer lab.

When I called the engineers I told them they had made a very common mistake that a lot of UNIX developers make: calling a function to send a message from one thread to another in some versions of UNIX immediately returns. However, in Windows, `SendMessage` doesn't return until the message is processed. I saw in the code the place where the thread they were sending to was already blocked on the synchronization object, and that `SendMessage` was the reason for the deadlock. They felt a little bad when I told them that to fix their problem they just needed to change `SendMessage` to `PostMessage`. I told them it was perfectly understandable they misunderstood what was going on. We spent the rest of the day going over other things they were running into such as DLL relocations and building their applications with full debug symbols. When we got back on the phone with the VP, I just told him it was one of the toughest bugs I'd worked on, but his engineers really went the extra mile to help make it right. In the end, everyone was happy. The VP got his bug fixed, the engineers learned a bunch of hints to help them develop better, and I didn't get anyone fired!

The Lesson

If you've got multiple threads and you want to use message communications between threads, think long and hard about how those synchronization objects and messages will interact. If you're in that situation, try always to use `PostMessage`. Of course, if you're using the messages to pass more than 32-bit data values across, `PostMessage` calls won't work because the parameters you pass can be corrupted by the time the other thread processes the message. In that case, use `SendMessageTimeOut` so that you'll at least return at some point and then can look to see whether the other thread is deadlocked or could not process the message.

Debugging War Story

The Deadlock Makes No Sense

The Battle

A team was developing an application and ran into a nasty deadlock that made no sense. After struggling with the deadlock for a couple of days—an ordeal that brought development to a standstill—the team asked me to come help them figure out the bug.

The product they were working on had an interesting architecture and was heavily multithreaded. The deadlock they were running into occurred only at a certain time, and it always happened in the middle of a series of DLL loads. The program deadlocked when `WaitForSingleObject` was called to check whether a thread was able to create some shared objects.

The team was good and had already double-checked and triple-checked their code for potential deadlocks—but they remained completely stumped. I asked if they had walked through the code to check for deadlocks, and they assured me that they had.

The Outcome

I remember this situation fondly because it was one of the few times I got to look like a hero within 5 minutes of starting the debugger. Once the team duplicated the deadlock, I took a quick look at the Call Stack window and noticed that the program was waiting on a thread handle inside `DllMain`. As part of their architecture, when a certain DLL loads, that DLL's `DllMain` starts another thread. It then immediately calls `WaitForSingleObject` on an acknowledge event object to ensure that the spawned thread was able to properly initialize some important shared objects before continuing with the rest of the `DllMain` processing.

What the team didn't know is that each process has something named a *process critical section* that the operating system uses to synchronize various actions happening behind the scenes in a process. One situation in which the process critical section is used is to serialize the execution of `DllMain` for the four cases in which `DllMain` is called: `DLL_PROCESS_ATTACH`, `DLL_THREAD_ATTACH`, `DLL_THREAD_DETACH`, and `DLL_PROCESS_DETACH`. The second parameter to `DllMain` indicates the reason the call to `DllMain` occurred.

In the team's application, the call to LoadLibrary caused the operating system to grab the process critical section so that the operating system could call the DLL's DllMain for the DLL_PROCESS_ATTACH case. The DLL's DllMain function then spawned a second thread. Whenever a process spawns a new thread, the operating system grabs the process critical section so that it can call the DllMain function of each loaded DLL for the DLL_THREAD_ATTACH case. In this particular program, the second thread blocked because the first thread was holding the process critical section. Unfortunately, the first thread then called WaitForSingleObject to ensure that the second thread was able to properly initialize some shared objects. Because the second thread was blocked on the process critical section, held by the first thread, and the first thread blocked while waiting on the second thread, the result was the usual deadlock.

The Lesson

The obvious lesson is to avoid doing any Wait* or EnterCriticalSection calls inside DllMain so that you avoid those kernel object blocks because the process critical section blocks any other thread. As you can see, even experienced developers can get bitten by multithreaded bugs—and as I mentioned earlier, this kind of bug is often in the place you least expect it.

DeadlockDetection Requirements

As you might have noticed in the preceding tips and tricks section, I didn't provide very many suggestions about what to do when an unexpected deadlock paralyzes your code. Most of the recommendations there were more preventive measures you can take to try to avoid deadlocks in the first place rather than prescriptions for fixing them when they do occur. As you know, solving deadlocks with just the debugger isn't easy. In this section, you'll get the additional help you need, in the DeadlockDetection utility.

Here's the list of basic requirements I worked with when I developed DeadlockDetection:

1. Show exactly where the deadlock happens in the user's code. A tool that tells only that EnterCriticalSection is blocked doesn't help

much. To be really effective, the tool needs to let you get back to the address, and consequently the source file and line number, where the deadlock occurred so that you can fix it quickly.

2. Show which synchronization object caused the deadlock.
3. Show which Windows function is blocked and the parameters passed to the function. It helps to see timeout values and the values passed to the function.
4. Determine which thread caused the deadlock.
5. The utility must be lightweight so that it interferes with the user's program as little as possible.
6. The information output processing must be extensible. The information collected in a deadlock detection system can be processed in many ways, and the utility needs to allow others, not just you, to extend the information as they see fit.
7. The tool must integrate easily with the user's programs.

One of the key points to keep in mind with a utility such as DeadlockDetection is that it definitely affects the behavior of the application it's observing. Once again, it's the Heisenberg uncertainty principle in action. DeadlockDetection can produce deadlocks in your programs you might not otherwise see because the work it does to gather information slows down your threads. I almost defined this behavior as a feature because any time you can cause a deadlock in your code, you've identified a bug, which is the first step toward correcting it—and as always, it's better for you to find the bugs than for your customers to find them.

High-Level Design Issues with DeadlockDetection

I had to figure out how to implement DeadlockDetection given the preceding requirements. I first needed to determine which functions I needed to monitor so that I could report the complete deadlock trace. Table 15-1 lists all the functions, grouped by type, that I decided I needed to monitor to implement DeadlockDetection.

Table 15-1 Functions That DeadlockDetection Monitors

Type	Function
Thread-related functions	CreateThread, ExitThread, SuspendThread, ResumeThread, TerminateThread, _beginthreadex, _beginthread, _exitthreadex, _exitthread, FreeLibraryAndExitThread
Critical-section functions	InitializeCriticalSection, InitializeCriticalSectionAndSpinCount, DeleteCriticalSection, EnterCriticalSection, LeaveCriticalSection, SetCriticalSectionSpinCount, TryEnterCriticalSection
Mutex functions	CreateMutexA, CreateMutexW, OpenMutexA, OpenMutexW, ReleaseMutex
Semaphore functions	CreateSemaphoreA, CreateSemaphoreW, OpenSemaphoreA, OpenSemaphoreW, ReleaseSemaphore
Event functions	CreateEventA, CreateEventW, OpenEventA, OpenEventW, PulseEvent, ResetEvent, SetEvent
Blocking functions	WaitForSingleObject, WaitForSingleObjectEx, WaitForMultipleObjects, WaitForMultipleObjectsEx, MsgWaitForMultipleObjects, MsgWaitForMultipleObjectsEx, SignalObjectAndWait
Special functions	CloseHandle, ExitProcess, GetProcAddress, LoadLibraryA, LoadLibraryW, LoadLibraryExA, LoadLibraryExW, FreeLibrary

After pondering the problem of how to collect the information I needed to satisfy the first four requirements, I realized that I was going to have to intercept (or hook) the functions in Table 15-1 to record the acquisition and release of synchronization objects. Hooking functions isn't a trivial task, and I'll explain how I implemented the code in the section "Hooking Imported Functions" later in this chapter. The one constraint that hooking imported functions imposed on DeadlockDetection is that the code for DeadlockDetection must reside in a DLL because the hooks apply only to the address space in which they're created. This constraint means that the user must load the DeadlockDetection DLL into her address space, a requirement that isn't too harsh given the benefits. As a DLL, the utility would integrate easily with a user program, requirement 7 specified in the list in the preceding section.

As you're looking over Table 15-1, you might have noticed that I didn't include certain potentially blocking message functions such as `SendMessage`, `PostMessage`, and `WaitMessage`. Originally, I'd intended to include these functions, but when I ran Charles Petzold's canonical "Hello World!" GUI program under DeadlockDetection, DeadlockDetection reported so many calls that the program essentially fell over. In the effort of keeping DeadlockDetection as lightweight as possible, I had to forego them.

Gathering the information to satisfy requirements 1 through 4 follows as a direct consequence of choosing the in-process function hooking approach. This approach means that each of the multithreading and synchronization functions will be calling directly into the DeadlockDetection code with all the information I need.

Making DeadlockDetection as lightweight as possible (requirement 5) was a tough condition to satisfy. I tried to code efficiently, but efficient code went only so far toward fulfilling the goal I set out to achieve. Figuring that you know best what types of synchronization objects you're using in your program, I grouped the object types so that you can specify just those functions you want to hook. For example, if you're concerned only about deadlock problems on mutexes, you can process only mutex functions.

To make DeadlockDetection even more useful, you can specify, on the fly, which sets of synchronization object functions you want to watch. You can also turn DeadlockDetection on and off as many times as needed. You might even want to give your application an accelerator key or a special menu option that toggles the entire DeadlockDetection system. Allowing this narrow scope meets requirement 5 and helps with requirement 7.

The only requirement left is number 6: making the output processing as extensible as possible. I wanted to give you the ability to slice and dice the output, rather than force you to make do with some arbitrary, hard-coded format. By keeping the main hooking and processing separate from the output code, I can achieve greater code reuse because the only part being changed, the output side, is much easier to develop than the core side. I named the output portions DeadlockDetection extensions, or DeadDetExt for short. A DeadDetExt is simply a DLL that has several exported functions that DeadlockDetection looks for and calls when appropriate.

Now it's time to explain how to use DeadlockDetection. If you understand the requirements I set out and understand how to use this utility, you'll find it easier to see how I implemented it.

Using DeadlockDetection

The first step in using DeadlockDetection is to put DEADLOCKDETECTION.DLL, its initialization file, and the appropriate DeadDetExt DLL in the same place. The initialization file is a simple INI file that, at a minimum, must specify the name of the DeadDetExt file to load. The following sample is a DEADLOCKDETECTION.INI file that loads the supplied TEXTFILEDDEXT.DLL:

```
[Initialization]
; The only mandatory value, the name of the DeadDetExt file that will
; handle the output.
ExtDll = "TextFileDDExt.dll"

; If this option is 1, DeadlockDetection will initialize in it's DllMain
; so that logging can start at the earliest possible time.
StartInDllMain = 0

; If StartInDllMain is 1, this key specifies the initial options for
; DeadlockDetection. This is the VALUE of the DDOPT_* flags.
; InitialOpts = 0

; The list of modules to ignore when hooking synchronization functions.
; IMM32.DLL is the Input Method Editor DLL that Windows XP puts in all
; processes.
; Keep the list in consecutive number order starting at 1.
[IgnoreModules]
Ignore1=IMM32.DLL
```

As you can see from some of the INI settings, DeadlockDetection can initialize just by having `LoadLibrary` called on it. A good proactive debugging idea would be to create a backdoor in your application initialization that calls `LoadLibrary` on the specified DLL name if your application sees a special registry key or an environment variable. This alternate approach to initializing your application would mean that you wouldn't need conditional compilation and you'd have a means of getting DLLs into your address space cleanly. Of course, all this assumes that the DLLs you're loading in this way are smart enough to initialize themselves completely in their `DllMains` and don't require you to call any other exported functions in the DLL.

Having your code set the DeadlockDetection initialization options, rather than using an INI file, means that you'll need to include DEADLOCKDETECTION.H in your application and have your application link against DEADLOCKDETECTION.LIB. If you want to initialize DeadlockDetection yourself, all you need to do is call `OpenDeadlockDetection` when appropriate. `OpenDeadlockDetection` takes a single parameter, the initial reporting options. Table 15-2 lists all the `DDOPT_*` flags. You'll want to call `OpenDeadlockDetection` before your application starts creating threads so that you can record all the key information about your synchronization objects.

At any point, you can change the reporting options by calling `SetDeadlockDetectionOptions`. This function takes the same OR'd set of flags as the `OpenDeadlockDetection` function. To see what the current options are, call `GetDeadlockDetectionOptions`. You can change the current options as many times as you like during your program's execution. If you want to suspend and resume logging, call the `SuspendDeadlockDetection` and `ResumeDeadlockDetection` functions.

Table 15-2 DeadlockDetection Reporting Options

Flag	Limits Logging to
DDOPT_WAIT	Wait-related functions
DDOPT_THREADS	Thread-related functions
DDOPT_CRITSEC	Critical-section functions
DDOPT_MUTEX	Mutex functions
DDOPT_SEMAPHORE	Semaphore functions
DDOPT_EVENT	Event functions
DDOPT_ALL	All hooked functions

Along with the DeadlockDetection source code that comes with this book's sample files, I've included a DeadDetExt DLL that I wrote, TEXTFILEDDEXT.DLL. This relatively simple extension writes all the information to a text file. When you run DeadlockDetection with TEXTFILEDDEXT.DLL, the extension creates a text file in the same directory as the executable program. The text file will use the name of the executable with a .DD extension. For example, if you run DDSIMPTEST.EXE, the resulting file will be DDSIMPTEST.DD. Listing 15-1 shows some sample output from TEXTFILEDDEXT.DLL.

```
TID        Ret Addr     C/R Ret Value  Function & Params
0x00000DF8 [0x004011B2] (R) 0x00000000 InitializeCriticalSection 0x00404150
0x00000DF8 [0x004011CC] (R) 0x000007C0 CreateEventA 0x00000000, 1, 0,
                                               0x004040F0 [The Event Name]
0x00000DF8 [0x004011EF] (R) 0x000007BC CreateThread 0x00000000, 0x00000000,
                                                    0x00401000, 0x00000000,
                                                    0x00000000, 0x0012FF5C
0x00000DF8 [0x00401212] (R) 0x000007B8 CreateThread 0x00000000, 0x00000000,
                                                    0x004010BC, 0x00000000,
                                                    0x00000000, 0x0012FF5C
0x00000DF8 [0x00401229] (C)            EnterCriticalSection 0x00404150
0x000000A8 [0x00401030] (C)            EnterCriticalSection 0x00404150
0x00000F04 [0x004010F3] (R) 0x000007B0 OpenEventA 0x001F0003, 0, 0x004040BC
                                                  [The Event Name]
0x00000DF8 [0x00401229] (R) 0x00000000 EnterCriticalSection 0x00404150
0x00000DF8 [0x0040123E] (C)            WaitForSingleObject 0x000007C0,
                                                           INFINITE
0x00000F04 [0x00401121] (C)            EnterCriticalSection 0x00404150
```

Listing 15-1 DeadlockDetection output using TESTFILEDDEXT.DLL

Notice that the function and parameter information is wrapped in Listing 15-1 so that it displays on the page. The output shows the information in the following order:

1. The ID of the executing thread.
2. The return address to indicate which of your functions called the synchronization function. Using the CrashFinder utility from Chapter 12, you can look up the return addresses and discover how you got into the deadlock situations.
3. The call or return indicator to help identify actions that occur before and after specific functions.
4. The return value of the function if your program is reporting function returns.
5. The synchronization function name.
6. The parameter list for the synchronization function. Items in brackets are the human-readable data. I concentrated on showing string values, but it would be trivial to add more data, such as individual flags.

When you run your application and it deadlocks, kill the process and view the output file to see the last synchronization item called. TEXTFILEDDEXT.DLL keeps the file up to date by flushing the file buffers each time you call a `WaitFor*` function, `EnterCriticalSection`, or `TryEnterCriticalSection`.

A word of caution: if you turn on full logging of all functions, you can generate some extremely large files in no time. Using the MTGDI Visual C++ sample application, I generated an 11-MB text file in a minute or two by creating a couple of threads.

Implementing DeadlockDetection

As you can see, using DeadlockDetection is fairly simple. Beneath the simplicity of use, however, is a fairly sophisticated implementation. The first part of DeadlockDetection's implementation I'll go over is how to hook functions.

Hooking Imported Functions

There are many ways to hook the function calls a program makes. The hard way is to hunt down all the `CALL` instructions and replace the address with one of your own. This approach is difficult and extremely error prone. Fortunately, with DeadlockDetection, the functions I need to hook are imported functions and are much easier to handle than `CALL` instructions.

An imported function is a function that comes out of a DLL. For example, when your program calls `OutputDebugString`, it's calling a function that resides in KERNEL32.DLL. When I first started doing Win32-based programming, I thought that calling an imported function would be just like calling any other function—a `CALL` or branch instruction would jump to an address and start executing the imported function. The only difference might be that with an imported function, the operating system program loader would have to run through the executable and fix up the addresses to reflect where the DLL being called would be loaded into memory. When I looked at how a call to an imported function really is implemented, I was amazed at the simplicity and beauty of the design.

The problem with the way I was thinking becomes apparent when you consider how many API functions there are and that you can easily call the same ones many times throughout your program. If the loader had to find and replace each occurrence of a call to `OutputDebugString`, for example, loading a program could take forever. Even if the linker generated a complete table that specified where each call to `OutputDebugString` took place in the code, the huge amount of looping and memory writing would make load times excruciatingly slow.

So how does the loader tell your application where to find an imported function? The solution is fiendishly clever. If you think about where the calls to `OutputDebugString` go, you'll soon realize that each call must go to the same address: the address where `OutputDebugString` is loaded into memory. Of course, your application can't know this address ahead of time, so instead, all your `OutputDebugString` calls get routed through a single, indirect address. When the program loader loads your executable and its dependent DLLs, the loader fixes up this one indirect address so that it corresponds to the final load address of `OutputDebugString`. The compiler makes this indirect addressing work by generating a jump to the indirect address any time your code calls the imported function. This indirect address is stored in the `.idata` (or `import`) section of the executable. If you import through `__declspec(dllimport)`, instead of being an indirect jump, the code is an indirect call, thus saving a couple of instructions per function call.

Hooking an imported function is a matter of finding the imports section of the executable, looking for the address of the particular function you want to hook, and then writing the hook function address in its place. Although hunting down and replacing function addresses might sound like a lot of work, it's not that bad because the Win32 Portable Executable (PE) file format is so nicely organized.

In Chapter 10 of his excellent book *Windows 95 System Programming Secrets* (IDG Books, 1995), Matt Pietrek describes a method for hooking imported functions. Matt's code simply finds a module's imports section and, using the value returned from a call to `GetProcAddress`, loops through the imported functions. When Matt's code finds the function it's looking for, it overwrites the original imported function address with the hook function.

Not surprisingly, given that 1995 is a past lifetime in software development circles, two small issues have changed since Matt's book came out. The first is that when Matt wrote his book, most developers didn't merge their imports section with other PE sections. Therefore, if the imports section is in read-only memory, you cause an access violation by writing the hook address. I fixed the read-only memory issue by setting the virtual memory protection to read-write before the hook function address is written to memory. The second issue, which is a little tougher to work around, is that under certain conditions you can't hook imported functions under Microsoft Windows Me. Since so many people ask me about how to hook functions, I decided to keep the Microsoft Windows Me support for hooking code, so it's relevant for me to discuss what happens under Windows Me.

When you use DeadlockDetection, you want to be able to have the threading functions redirected any time you run your application, even when the application is running under the debugger. Although you wouldn't think that hooking functions while running under a debugger would be a problem, it is. In Windows XP, or when running a program in Windows Me outside a debugger, when you call `GetProcAddress` to find a function and then look through the imports section for that address, you'll always find it. But under Windows Me, calling `GetProcAddress` in your program while it's running under a debugger returns a different address than when it runs outside a debugger. What `GetProcAddress` actually returns when running under the debugger is a *debug thunk*—a special wrapper around the real call.

The reason for the debug thunk is that Windows Me doesn't implement copy-on-write in the operating system for addresses above 2 GB. Copy-on-write means that when a page of shared memory is written to, the operating system makes a copy of that page and gives it to the process where the write is taking place. For the most part, Windows Me and Windows XP follow the same rules and everything is fine. However, for shared memory above 2 GB, where all the operating system DLLs load on Windows Me, Windows Me doesn't do the copy-on-write for those addresses. That means that when you change the memory inside an operating system DLL to set a breakpoint or to patch a function, it's patched for all processes in the system and will cause a complete system crash if another process executes at that changed location. Therefore, Windows Me goes to quite a bit of trouble to keep you from accidentally messing up that memory.

The debug thunk returned by `GetProcAddress` when running under a debugger is a means by which Windows Me keeps debuggers from attempting to step into system functions above the 2-GB line. Overall, the lack of copy-on-write isn't much of an issue for most developers—only those who write debuggers or who want to hook functions correctly whether or not they're running under a debugger.

Fortunately, getting the real address for an imported function isn't too difficult—it just takes a little more work, and you have to avoid `GetProcAddress`. The PE file `IMAGE_IMPORT_DESCRIPTOR` structure, which holds all the information about functions imported from a specific DLL, has pointers to two arrays in the executable. These arrays are called import address tables (IATs), or sometimes thunk data arrays. The first pointer references the real IAT, which the program loader fixes up when the executable is loaded. The second pointer references the original IAT, which is untouched by the loader and lists the imported functions. To find the real imported function address, simply work your way through the original IAT until you find the named function that you want to hook, and then write the hook address in the corresponding entry in the real IAT, which the program is using. By taking this extra step, the hooking code will always work no matter where it's called.

`HookImportedFunctionsByName` is the function I wrote to take care of your hooking needs. Table 15-3 shows the parameters to `HookImportedFunctionsByName` and describes each one. Because I wanted to make the hooking as generic as possible, I went to the trouble of allowing you to hook multiple functions imported from the same DLL at the same time. As its name implies, the `HookImportedFunctionsByName` function will hook only those functions imported by name. Though I won't be discussing it in this book, I did include another function, `HookOrdinalExport`, that allows you to hook functions exported by ordinal.

Table 15-3 `HookImportedFunctionsByName` Parameter Descriptions

Parameter	Description
`hModule`	The module in which the imports will be hooked.
`szImportMod`	The name of the module whose functions are imported.
`UiCount`	The number of functions to hook. This parameter is the size of the `paHookArray` and `paOrigFuncs` arrays.

Table 15-3 HookImportedFunctionsByName Parameter Descriptions *(continued)*

Parameter	Description
paHookArray	The array of function descriptor structures that indicates which functions to hook. The array doesn't have to be in szFunc name order (though it's wise to keep the array sorted in function name order, because I might implement better searching in the future). Also, if a particular pProc is NULL, HookImportedFunctionsByName skips that item. The structure for each element in paHookArray is simply the name of the function to hook and a pointer to the new hook procedure. Because you might want to hook or unhook functions at will, HookImportedFunctionsByName returns all the original imported function addresses.
paOrigFuncs	The array of original addresses hooked by HookImportedFunctionsByName. If a function wasn't hooked, that item index will be NULL.
pdwHooked	Returns the number of functions hooked out of paHookArray.

Listing 15-2 shows the HookImportedFunctionsByNameA function. In your code, you'll call HookImportedFunctionsByName because that macro maps between ANSI and Unicode. However, since the names in the IAT section are all stored as ANSI, the implementation for HookImportedFunctionsByNameW simply converts the appropriate parameters to ANSI and calls HookImportedFunctionsByNameA.

```
BOOL BUGSUTIL_DLLINTERFACE __stdcall
        HookImportedFunctionsByNameA ( HMODULE         hModule      ,
                                       LPCSTR          szImportMod  ,
                                       UINT            uiCount      ,
                                       LPHOOKFUNCDESC  paHookArray  ,
                                       PROC *          paOrigFuncs  ,
                                       LPDWORD         pdwHooked     )
{
    // Assert the parameters.
    ASSERT ( FALSE == IsBadReadPtr ( hModule                         ,
                                     sizeof ( IMAGE_DOS_HEADER )  ) ) ;
    ASSERT ( FALSE == IsBadStringPtrA ( szImportMod , MAX_PATH ) ) ;
    ASSERT ( 0 != uiCount ) ;
    ASSERT ( NULL != paHookArray ) ;
    ASSERT ( FALSE == IsBadReadPtr ( paHookArray ,
                                     sizeof (HOOKFUNCDESC) * uiCount ));

    // In debug builds, perform deep validation of paHookArray.
#ifdef _DEBUG
```

Listing 15-2 HookImportedFunctionsByNameA from HOOKIMPORTEDFUNCTIONBYNAME.CPP

```
    if ( NULL != paOrigFuncs )
    {
        ASSERT ( FALSE == IsBadWritePtr ( paOrigFuncs ,
                                           sizeof ( PROC ) * uiCount ) );

    }
    if ( NULL != pdwHooked )
    {
        ASSERT ( FALSE == IsBadWritePtr ( pdwHooked , sizeof ( UINT )));
    }

    // Check each item in the hook array.
    {
        for ( UINT i = 0 ; i < uiCount ; i++ )
        {
            ASSERT ( NULL != paHookArray[ i ].szFunc  ) ;
            ASSERT ( '\0' != *paHookArray[ i ].szFunc ) ;
            // If the function address isn't NULL, it is validated.
            if ( NULL != paHookArray[ i ].pProc )
            {
                ASSERT ( FALSE == IsBadCodePtr ( paHookArray[i].pProc));
            }
        }
    }
#endif

    // Perform the error checking for the parameters.
    if ( ( 0    == uiCount      )                                   ||
         ( NULL == szImportMod  )                                   ||
         ( TRUE == IsBadReadPtr ( paHookArray ,
                                  sizeof ( HOOKFUNCDESC ) * uiCount ) ))
    {
        SetLastErrorEx ( ERROR_INVALID_PARAMETER , SLE_ERROR ) ;
        return ( FALSE ) ;
    }
    if ( ( NULL != paOrigFuncs )                                  &&
         ( TRUE == IsBadWritePtr ( paOrigFuncs ,
                                   sizeof ( PROC ) * uiCount ) )  )
    {
        SetLastErrorEx ( ERROR_INVALID_PARAMETER , SLE_ERROR ) ;
        return ( FALSE ) ;
    }
    if ( ( NULL != pdwHooked )                                      &&
         ( TRUE == IsBadWritePtr ( pdwHooked , sizeof ( UINT ) ) )  )
    {
        SetLastErrorEx ( ERROR_INVALID_PARAMETER , SLE_ERROR ) ;
        return ( FALSE ) ;
    }

    // Is this a system DLL above the 2-GB line, which Windows 98 won't
    // let you patch?
    if ( ( FALSE == IsNT ( ) ) && ( (DWORD_PTR)hModule >= 0x80000000 ) )
```

```
    {
        SetLastErrorEx ( ERROR_INVALID_HANDLE , SLE_ERROR ) ;
        return ( FALSE ) ;
    }

    // TODO TODO
    // Should each item in the hook array be checked in release builds?

    if ( NULL != paOrigFuncs )
    {
        // Set all the values in paOrigFuncs to NULL.
        memset ( paOrigFuncs , NULL , sizeof ( PROC ) * uiCount ) ;
    }
    if ( NULL != pdwHooked )
    {
        // Set the number of functions hooked to 0.
        *pdwHooked = 0 ;
    }

    // Get the specific import descriptor.
    PIMAGE_IMPORT_DESCRIPTOR pImportDesc =
                     GetNamedImportDescriptor ( hModule , szImportMod );
    if ( NULL == pImportDesc )
    {
        // The requested module wasn't imported. Don't return an error.
        return ( TRUE ) ;
    }

    // BUG FIX (thanks to Attila Szepesváry!)
    // Make sure the original first thunk and first thunk are not
    // NULL. The original first thunk can be a null import
    // descriptor and cause this routine to crash.
    if ( ( NULL == pImportDesc->OriginalFirstThunk ) ||
         ( NULL == pImportDesc->FirstThunk         )     )
    {
        // I return TRUE here because it's analogous to the case in
        // which the requested module wasn't imported.
        // All OK, JumpMaster!
        SetLastError ( ERROR_SUCCESS ) ;
        return ( TRUE ) ;
    }

    // Get the original thunk information for this DLL. I can't use
    // the thunk information stored in pImportDesc->FirstThunk
    // because the loader has already changed that array to fix up
    // all the imports. The original thunk gives me access to the
    // function names.
    PIMAGE_THUNK_DATA pOrigThunk =
                        MakePtr ( PIMAGE_THUNK_DATA        ,
                                  hModule                  ,
                                  pImportDesc->OriginalFirstThunk  ) ;
    // Get the array the pImportDesc->FirstThunk points to because
    // I'll do the actual bashing and hooking there.
```

```
PIMAGE_THUNK_DATA pRealThunk = MakePtr ( PIMAGE_THUNK_DATA       ,
                                         hModule                 ,
                                         pImportDesc->FirstThunk  );


// Loop through and find the functions to hook.
while ( NULL != pOrigThunk->u1.Function )
{
    // Look only at functions that are imported by name, not those
    // that are imported by ordinal value.
    if (  IMAGE_ORDINAL_FLAG !=
                    ( pOrigThunk->u1.Ordinal & IMAGE_ORDINAL_FLAG ))
    {
        // Look at the name of this imported function.
        PIMAGE_IMPORT_BY_NAME pByName ;

        pByName = MakePtr ( PIMAGE_IMPORT_BY_NAME    ,
                            hModule                  ,
                            pOrigThunk->u1.AddressOfData  ) ;

        // If the name starts with NULL, skip it.
        if ( '\0' == pByName->Name[ 0 ] )
        {
            // BUG FIX (thanks to Attila Szepesváry!)
            // I forgot to increment the thunk pointers!
            pOrigThunk++ ;
            pRealThunk++ ;
            continue ;
        }

        // Determines whether I hook the function
        BOOL bDoHook = FALSE ;

        // TODO TODO
        // Might want to consider bsearch here.

        // See whether the imported function name is in the hook
        // array. Consider requiring paHookArray to be sorted by
        // function name so that bsearch can be used, which
        // will make the lookup faster. However, the size of
        // uiCount coming into this function should be rather
        // small, so it's OK to search the entire paHookArray for
        // each function imported by szImportMod.
        for ( UINT i = 0 ; i < uiCount ; i++ )
        {
            if ( ( paHookArray[i].szFunc[0] ==
                                        pByName->Name[0] ) &&
                 ( 0 == strcmpi ( paHookArray[i].szFunc ,
                                  (char*)pByName->Name   )   )    )
            {
                // If the function address is NULL, exit now;
                // otherwise, go ahead and hook the function.
                if ( NULL != paHookArray[ i ].pProc )
```

```
            {
                bDoHook = TRUE ;
            }
            break ;
        }
    }

    if ( TRUE == bDoHook )
    {
        // I found a function to hook. Now I need to change
        // the memory protection to writable before I overwrite
        // the function pointer. Note that I'm now writing into
        // the real thunk area!

        MEMORY_BASIC_INFORMATION mbi_thunk ;

        VirtualQuery ( pRealThunk                              ,
                       &mbi_thunk                              ,
                       sizeof ( MEMORY_BASIC_INFORMATION ) ) ;

        if ( FALSE == VirtualProtect ( mbi_thunk.BaseAddress ,
                                       mbi_thunk.RegionSize  ,
                                       PAGE_READWRITE        ,
                                       &mbi_thunk.Protect     ))
        {
            ASSERT ( !"VirtualProtect failed!" ) ;
            SetLastErrorEx ( ERROR_INVALID_HANDLE , SLE_ERROR );
            return ( FALSE ) ;
        }

        // Save the original address if requested.
        if ( NULL != paOrigFuncs )
        {
            paOrigFuncs[i] =
                (PROC)((INT_PTR)pRealThunk->u1.Function) ;
        }

        // Hook the function.
        DWORD_PTR * pTemp = (DWORD_PTR*)&pRealThunk->u1.Function ;
        *pTemp = (DWORD_PTR)(paHookArray[i].pProc);

        DWORD dwOldProtect ;

        // Change the protection back to what it was before I
        // overwrote the function pointer.
        VERIFY ( VirtualProtect ( mbi_thunk.BaseAddress ,
                                  mbi_thunk.RegionSize  ,
                                  mbi_thunk.Protect     ,
                                  &dwOldProtect           ) ) ;

        if ( NULL != pdwHooked )
        {
            // Increment the total number of functions hooked.
```

```
                    *pdwHooked += 1 ;
                }
            }
        }
        // Increment both tables.
        pOrigThunk++ ;
        pRealThunk++ ;
    }

    // All OK, JumpMaster!
    SetLastError ( ERROR_SUCCESS ) ;
    return ( TRUE ) ;
}
```

HookImportedFunctionsByName shouldn't be difficult for you to follow. After doing the proactive debugging practice of validating every parameter thoroughly, I call the helper function GetNamedImportDescriptor to find the IMAGE_IMPORT_DESCRIPTOR for the requested module. After getting the pointers to the original and real IATs, I loop through the original IAT, looking at each function imported by name to see whether it's in the paHookArray list. If the function is in the hook list, I simply set the real IAT's memory to PAGE_READWRITE so that the hooked address can be written safely, write the hook into the entry for the real function, and reset the memory protection to its original setting. The unit test function for HookImportedFunctionsByName is included with the BUGSLAYERUTIL.DLL source code, so feel free to use it to step through the code if you don't quite follow what's going on.

Now that you have an idea of how to hook the imported functions, let's move on to implementing the rest of DeadlockDetection.

Implementation Highlights

One of my primary goals in implementing DeadlockDetection was to make the utility as data-driven and table-driven as possible. When you step back and look at what the DLL does in its hook processing, you'll see that the processing is almost identical for each function in Table 15-1. The hooked function gets called, determines whether its class of functions is being monitored, calls the real function, and (if logging is on for that class) logs the information and returns. I had to write a bunch of similar hook functions, and I wanted to make them as simple as possible. Complicated hook functions are a perfect breeding ground for bugs, and even when you try to make things simple, bugs can creep in. In a moment, I'll point out where I had a nasty bug in the DeadlockDetection code for the first edition of this book.

The best way to show this simplicity is to talk about writing a DeadDetExt DLL. A DeadDetExt DLL must have three exported functions. The first two,

DeadDetExtOpen and DeadDetExtClose, are self-explanatory. The interesting function is DeadDetProcessEvent, which each hook function calls when there is information to write. DeadDetProcessEvent takes a single parameter, a pointer to a DDEVENTINFO structure:

```
typedef struct tagDDEVENTINFO
{
    // The identifier that specifies what is contained in the rest of
    // this structure.
    eFuncEnum    eFunc          ;
    // The pre-call or post-call indicator.
    ePrePostEnum ePrePost       ;
    // The return address. This is so the calling function can be
    // found.
    DWORD        dwAddr         ;
    // The thread ID of the calling thread.
    DWORD        dwThreadId     ;
    // The return value for post calls
    DWORD        dwRetValue     ;
    // The parameter information. Cast this to the appropriate
    // structure as, described below, for the function. When accessing
    // the parameters, treat them as read-only.
    DWORD        dwParams       ;
} DDEVENTINFO , * LPDDEVENTINFO ;
```

The entire output for a single function that appears in Listing 15-1 comes from the information in the DDEVENTINFO structure. Although most of the fields in DDEVENTINFO are self-explanatory, the dwParams field needs special mention. The dwParams field is really a pointer to the parameters as they appear in memory.

In Chapter 7, I discussed how parameters are passed on the stack. Just to jog your memory, parameters for __stdcall and __cdecl functions are passed right to left and the stack grows from high memory to low memory. The dwParams field in the DDEVENTINFO structure points to the last parameter on the stack, so the structure lists the parameters in left-to-right order. I applied a little creative casting to make it easy to convert dwParams.

In DEADLOCKDETECTION.H, I provide typedefs that describe each intercepted function's parameter lists. For example, if eFunc were eWaitForSingleObjectEx, you would cast dwParams to LPWAITFORSINGLEOBJECTEX_PARAMS to get the parameters. To see all this creative casting in action, check out the TEXTFILEDDEXT.DLL code included with the sample files.

Although output processing is relatively easy, gathering the information can be difficult. I wanted DeadlockDetection to hook the synchronization functions in Table 15-1, but I didn't want the hook functions to change the behavior of the real functions. I also wanted to get the parameters and the return value and to write the hook functions in C/C++ easily. I spent quite a while with the debugger and the disassembler before I got it right.

Initially, I wrote all the hook functions so that they were just pass-through functions and called the real functions directly. This approach worked great. Then I put the parameters and the return value for the functions into local variables. Getting the value returned from the real function was simple, but because I started implementation of DeadlockDetection with Visual C++ 6, I didn't have a clean way to get the return address in my C/C++ hook function. Visual C++ .NET now offers the `_ReturnAddress` intrinsic, but that was not available in Visual C++ 6. I needed the `DWORD` right before the current stack pointer. Unfortunately, in straight C/C++, the function prolog would've already done its magic by the time I could get control, so the stack pointer would've already moved away from where it needed to be.

You might think that the stack pointer is just offset by the number of local variables, but that isn't always the case. The Visual C++ compiler does an excellent job of optimizing so that the stack pointer isn't in the same place with different optimization flags set. Although you might declare a variable as a local variable, the compiler can optimize the variable by storing it in a register so that it doesn't even appear on the stack.

I needed a guaranteed way to get the stack pointer no matter what optimizations were set. At this point, I started thinking naked (no, not me without clothes): why not declare the hook functions as `__declspec(naked)` and create my own prolog and epilog code? With this approach, I'd have complete control over `ESP` no matter what optimization settings were used. Additionally, getting the return address and parameters would be a snap because they are at `ESP+04h` and `ESP+08h`, respectively. Keep in mind that I'm not doing anything out of the ordinary with the prolog and epilog code, so I still perform the usual `PUSH EBP` and `MOV EBP, ESP` for the prolog and `MOV ESP, EBP` and `POP EBP` for the epilog.

Because each hook function was going to be declared as `__declspec(naked)`, I wrote a couple of macros to handle the prolog and epilog: `HOOKFN_PROLOG` and `HOOKFN_EPILOG`. I also went ahead and declared some common local variables that all hook functions would need in `HOOKFN_PROLOG`. These variables included the last error value, `dwLastError`, and the event information structure to pass to the DeadDetExt DLL, `stEvtInfo`. The `dwLastError` is yet another bit of state that I needed to preserve when intercepting functions.

The Windows API can return a special error code through `SetLastError` to provide more information if a function fails. This error code can be a real boon because it tells you why an API function failed. For example, if `GetLastError` returns 122, you know that the buffer parameter was too small. WINERROR.H contains all the error codes the operating system returns. The problem with hook functions is that they can reset the last error as part of their processing. This behavior can wreak havoc if your application relies on the last error.

If you call CreateEvent and want to see whether the returned handle was created or just opened, CreateEvent sets the last error to ERROR_ALREADY_EXISTS if it just opened the handle. Because the cardinal rule of intercepting functions is that you can't change the expected behavior of the function, I needed to call GetLastError immediately after the real function call so that my hook function could properly set the last error code that the real function returned. The general rule for a hook function is that you need to call GetLastError right after you call the real function and then call SetLastError as the last action before leaving the hook function.

Common Debugging Question

If ReturnAddress is now available, why didn't you use it instead of going to all this trouble?

When it came time to update DeadlockDetection for the second edition of this book, I thought I might want to go through and update the HOOKFN_PROLOG macro to use the new _ReturnAddress intrinsic to make my life a little easier. That would mean I could get rid of the naked declarations and make the functions more normal, and not rely on the special prolog and epilog. However, the one great advantage I get with the existing macros is that I can treat the parameters as a blob in memory and pass them directly to the output function. If I were to use standard functions, I'd have to require some sort of weird address of casting to achieve the same thing. I also had the most powerful argument of all: the code was working quite well and I wasn't going to buy sufficient advantage to consider rewriting the code. Consequently, I left the naked functions as they were.

At this point, I thought I was done except for testing. Unfortunately, my first test uncovered a bug: I wasn't preserving ESI and EDI across the hook call because the documentation on using the inline assembler explicitly stated that you didn't have to save them. After I fixed the ESI/EDI register problem, DeadlockDetection seemed to work fine. When I started doing register comparisons on before, during, and after cases, however, I noticed that I wasn't returning the values the real functions left in EBX, ECX, and EDX, and worse yet, in the flags' registers. Although I didn't see any problems and the documentation said that those registers didn't need to be preserved, I still was concerned that my hook functions were changing the application state. I declared the REGSTATE structure to hold the register values after the real function call so that I could restore the values when my hook function returned. To save and restore the registers, I created two additional macros, REAL_FUNC_PRE_CALL and REAL_FUNC_POST_CALL, which I placed around the real call the hook function makes.

After a little more testing, I found another problem: in release builds with full optimizations, I crashed inexplicably every so often. I finally tracked down those crashes and was able to attribute them to the effect of the optimizer on some of my hook functions. The optimizer was trying to be helpful but ended up doing more harm than good. I was very careful about the register usage in my hook functions and used only EAX or stack memory directly. Even though I was taking every precaution to preserve the registers, I found that the debug build code sequence

```
MOV DWORD PTR [EBP-018h] , 00000002h
MOV DWORD PTR [EBP-014h] , 00000002h
```

was being transformed by the optimizer into

```
PUSH    002h
POP     EBX
MOV     DWORD PTR [EBP-01Ch] , EBX
MOV     DWORD PTR [EBP-018h] , EBX
```

It's easy to see in the second snippet that the POP into EBX was trashing the register. To prevent the optimizer from stealing registers behind my back, I turned optimizations off for all hook function files by placing

```
#pragma optimize("", off )
```

at the top of each file. Turning optimizations off also made debugging easier because the unoptimized code the compiler generates is very similar for both release and debug builds.

Listing 15-3 shows the final version of DD_FUNCS.H, which is the internal header file in which all the special hook function macros are declared. The comment at the top of the file has two sample hook functions that explain how I used each of the special macros. I strongly encourage you to step through the DDSimpTest example that's part of the source code. Make sure that you watch an entire function call at the assembly-language level because that's the only way you'll see all the processing that takes place.

```
/*----------------------------------------------------------------------
Debugging Applications for Microsoft .NET and Microsoft Windows
Copyright © 1997-2003 John Robbins -- All rights reserved.
----------------------------------------------------------------------
The prototypes for all the hook functions and the prolog/epilog code
----------------------------------------------------------------------*/

#ifndef _DD_FUNCS_H
#define _DD_FUNCS_H
```

Listing 15-3 DD_FUNCS.H

```
/*//////////////////////////////////////////////////////////////////////
    All the hook functions are __declspec(naked) functions, so I must
provide the prolog and epilog. I need to provide a custom prolog and
epilog for several reasons:
1. Functions written in C have no control over which registers are used
   or when the compiler saves the original registers. Not having control
   over the registers means that getting the return address is nearly
   impossible. For the DeadlockDetection project, the return address is
   critical.
2. I also wanted to hand the parameters to the extension DLL processing
   function without having to copy massive amounts of data on
   each function call.
3. Because almost all the hook functions behave the same way, I set up
   the common variables needed in all functions.
4. Hook functions can't change any of the return values, including
   the value from GetLastError. By doing my own prolog and epilog, I
   can make it much easier to return the correct value. Also,
   I need to restore the register values to the state they were in
   following the real function call.

A basic hook function only requires two macros, HOOKFN_STARTUP and
HOOKFN_SHUTDOWN.

As you can see, doing a regular function is quite easy!

BOOL NAKEDDEF DD_InitializeCriticalSectionAndSpinCount (
                                LPCRITICAL_SECTION lpCriticalSection,
                                DWORD              dwSpinCount       )
{
    HOOKFN_STARTUP ( eInitializeCriticalSectionAndSpinCount ,
                     DDOPT_CRITSEC                          ,
                     0                                       ) ;

    InitializeCriticalSectionAndSpinCount ( lpCriticalSection ,
                                            dwSpinCount        ) ;

    HOOKFN_SHUTDOWN ( 2 , DDOPT_CRITSEC ) ;
}

If you have to do special processing and don't want to do something the
normal macros don't do, you can use the following macros to do the
necessary behind-the-scenes work:

HOOKFN_PROLOG
REAL_FUNC_PRE_CALL
REAL_FUNC_POST_CALL
HOOKFN_EPILOG

Here's an example of a function using the macros:
HMODULE NAKEDDEF DD_LoadLibraryA ( LPCSTR lpLibFileName )
{
    // Any local variables must be declared before the HOOKFN_PROLOG
    // macro. This sets up the actual function prolog and automatically
```

```
    // defines some key variables such as stEvtInfo (DDEVENTINFO).
    HOOKFN_PROLOG ( ) ;

    // Before doing the call to the real function, you need to specify
    // the REAL_FUNC_PRE_CALL macro to ensure the registers get set
    // up to reflect what they were when the function was called.
    REAL_FUNC_PRE_CALL ( ) ;
    // Make the real function call.
    LoadLibraryA ( lpLibFileName ) ;
    // The macro to save off the registers after the real call. This
    // way I can change the registers before I leave so that it appears
    // this function wasn't even there.
    REAL_FUNC_POST_CALL ( ) ;

    // The work specific to the LoadLibraryA hook.
    if ( NULL != stEvtInfo.dwRetValue )
    {
        HookAllLoadedModules ( ) ;
    }

    // Takes care of the function epilog, restoring the registers as
    // well as the stack. The number passed to the macro is the
    // number of parameters passed to the function. Be very careful
    // and make sure you don't get "editor inheritance" errors when you
    // cut and paste this macro into other functions!
    HOOKFN_EPILOG ( 1 ) ;
}
//////////////////////////////////////////////////////////////////////*/

/*//////////////////////////////////////////////////////////////////////
// The register state structure. I use this structure to ensure that
// ALL registers are returned exactly as they came from the real
// function. Notice that EBP and ESP are handled as part of the
// prolog.
//////////////////////////////////////////////////////////////////////*/
typedef struct tag_REGSTATE
{
    DWORD   dwEAX ;
    DWORD   dwEBX ;
    DWORD   dwECX ;
    DWORD   dwEDX ;
    DWORD   dwEDI ;
    DWORD   dwESI ;
    DWORD   dwEFL ;
} REGSTATE , * PREGSTATE ;

/*//////////////////////////////////////////////////////////////////////
// The macros to save and restore ESI across function calls in debug
// builds.
//////////////////////////////////////////////////////////////////////*/
#ifdef _DEBUG
#define SAVE_ESI()        __asm PUSH ESI
#define RESTORE_ESI()     __asm POP  ESI
```

```
#else
#define SAVE_ESI()
#define RESTORE_ESI()
#endif

/*//////////////////////////////////////////////////////////////////////
// The common prolog code for all DD_* functions
//////////////////////////////////////////////////////////////////////*/
#define HOOKFN_PROLOG()                                                 \
/* All hook functions automatically get the same three local          */\
/* variables.                                                          */\
DDEVENTINFO stEvtInfo   ;   /* The event information for the function*/\
DWORD       dwLastError ;   /* The last error value                  */\
REGSTATE    stRegState  ;   /* The register state to ensure that I   */\
                            /* restore the registers correctly       */\
{                                                                       \
__asm PUSH  EBP             /* Always save EBP explicitly.           */\
__asm MOV   EBP , ESP       /* Move the stack.                       */\
__asm MOV   EAX , ESP       /* Get the stack pointer to calculate the*/\
                            /* return address and the parameters.    */\
SAVE_ESI ( )                /* Save ESI in debug builds.             */\
__asm SUB   ESP , __LOCAL_SIZE /* Save space for the local variables.*/\
__asm ADD   EAX , 04h + 04h /* Account for PUSH EBP and the          */\
                            /* return address.                       */\
                            /* Save start of parameters on the stack.*/\
__asm MOV   [stEvtInfo.dwParams] , EAX                                  \
__asm SUB   EAX , 04h       /* Get back to the return address.       */\
__asm MOV   EAX , [EAX]     /* EAX now holds the return address.     */\
                            /* Save the return address.              */\
__asm MOV   [stEvtInfo.dwAddr] , EAX                                    \
__asm MOV   dwLastError , 0 /* Initialize dwLastError.               */\
                            /* Initialize the event information.     */\
__asm MOV   [stEvtInfo.eFunc] , eUNINITIALIZEDFE                        \
__asm MOV   [stRegState.dwEDI] , EDI /* Save the two registers that  */\
__asm MOV   [stRegState.dwESI] , ESI /* need to be saved across      */\
                                     /* function calls.              */\
}

/*//////////////////////////////////////////////////////////////////////
// The common epilog code for all DD_* functions. iNumParams is the
// number of parameters to the function that is used to restore the
// stack to the proper place after the hook call.
//////////////////////////////////////////////////////////////////////*/
#define HOOKFN_EPILOG(iNumParams)                                       \
{                                                                       \
SetLastError ( dwLastError ) ;      /* Set the real function's last  */\
                                    /* error value.                  */\
__asm ADD   ESP , __LOCAL_SIZE      /* Add back the local variables. */\
__asm MOV   EBX , [stRegState.dwEBX]/* Restore all the registers so  */\
__asm MOV   ECX , [stRegState.dwECX]/* that this call looks          */\
__asm MOV   EDX , [stRegState.dwEDX]/* identical to the intercepted  */\
__asm MOV   EDI , [stRegState.dwEDI]/* function.                     */\
__asm MOV   ESI , [stRegState.dwESI]                                    \
```

```
__asm MOV   EAX , [stRegState.dwEFL]                                    \
__asm SAHF                                                              \
__asm MOV   EAX , [stRegState.dwEAX]                                    \
RESTORE_ESI ( )                     /* Restore ESI in debug builds.  */\
__asm MOV   ESP , EBP               /* Put back ESP.                 */\
__asm POP   EBP                     /* Restore the saved EBP.        */\
__asm RET   iNumParams * 4          /* stdcall restore of the stack  */\
}

/*//////////////////////////////////////////////////////////////////////
// The REAL_FUNC_PRE_CALL macro needs to be placed IMMEDIATELY *BEFORE*
// ANY call to the real function the hook function is handling. The
// macro ensures that EDI and ESI are returned in the same condition
// they were in when passed to the hook function.
//////////////////////////////////////////////////////////////////////*/
#define REAL_FUNC_PRE_CALL()                                            \
{                                                                       \
__asm MOV   EDI , [stRegState.dwEDI]    /* Restore the real EDI.     */\
__asm MOV   ESI , [stRegState.dwESI]    /* Restore the real ESI.     */\
}

/*//////////////////////////////////////////////////////////////////////
// The REAL_FUNC_POST_CALL macro needs to be placed IMMEDIATELY *AFTER*
// ANY call to the real function the hook function is handling. All the
// register values after the real call are saved so that the hook
// function epilog can return the same register values as the real
// function call.
//////////////////////////////////////////////////////////////////////*/
#define REAL_FUNC_POST_CALL()                                           \
{                                                                       \
__asm MOV   [stRegState.dwEAX] , EAX  /* Save the EAX value.         */\
__asm MOV   [stRegState.dwEBX] , EBX  /* Save the EBX value.         */\
__asm MOV   [stRegState.dwECX] , ECX  /* Save the ECX value.         */\
__asm MOV   [stRegState.dwEDX] , EDX  /* Save the EDX value.         */\
__asm MOV   [stRegState.dwEDI] , EDI  /* Save the EDI value.         */\
__asm MOV   [stRegState.dwESI] , ESI  /* Save the ESI value.         */\
__asm XOR   EAX , EAX                 /* Zero out EAX.               */\
__asm LAHF                            /* Load the flag values into AH*/\
__asm MOV   [stRegState.dwEFL] , EAX  /* Save the flag values.       */\
}                                                                       \
dwLastError = GetLastError ( ) ;      /* Save the last error value.  */\
{                                                                       \
__asm MOV   EAX , [stRegState.dwEAX]  /* Restore EAX to its original */\
                                      /* value.                      */\
                                      /* Set the return value for    */\
                                      /* the information.            */\
__asm MOV   [stEvtInfo.dwRetValue] , EAX                                \
}

/*//////////////////////////////////////////////////////////////////////
// A convenient macro to fill out the event information structure
//////////////////////////////////////////////////////////////////////*/
#define FILL_EVENTINFO(eFn)                             \
```

```
    stEvtInfo.eFunc      = eFn        ;                \
    stEvtInfo.ePrePost   = ePostCall ;                 \
    stEvtInfo.dwThreadId = GetCurrentThreadId ( )

/*//////////////////////////////////////////////////////////////////////
// The version 2 macros to make life MUCH, MUCH simpler to define
// hook functions
//////////////////////////////////////////////////////////////////////*/
// Declare this at the beginning of any hook function.
// eFunc          - The function enumeration value.
// SynchClassType - The DDOPT_* flag value for the function class you
//                  are processing.
// bRecordPreCall - Record the entry into this function.
#define HOOKFN_STARTUP(eFunc,SynchClassType,bRecordPreCall)             \
    HOOKFN_PROLOG ( ) ;                                                 \
    if ( TRUE == DoLogging ( SynchClassType ) )                         \
    {                                                                   \
        FILL_EVENTINFO ( eFunc ) ;                                      \
        if ( TRUE == (int)bRecordPreCall )                              \
        {                                                               \
            stEvtInfo.ePrePost = ePreCall ;                             \
            ProcessEvent ( &stEvtInfo ) ;                               \
        }                                                               \
    }                                                                   \
    REAL_FUNC_PRE_CALL ( ) ;

/*//////////////////////////////////////////////////////////////////////
// The ending macro for a hook function.
// iNuMParams     - The number of parameters passed to the function.
// SynchClassType - The synchronization class for the function.
//////////////////////////////////////////////////////////////////////*/
#define HOOKFN_SHUTDOWN(iNumParams,SynchClass)                          \
    REAL_FUNC_POST_CALL ( ) ;                                           \
    if ( TRUE == DoLogging ( SynchClass ) )                             \
    {                                                                   \
        stEvtInfo.ePrePost = ePostCall ;                                \
        ProcessEvent ( &stEvtInfo ) ;                                   \
    }                                                                   \
    HOOKFN_EPILOG ( iNumParams ) ;

/*//////////////////////////////////////////////////////////////////////
// The calling convention declaration for all DD_* definitions.
//////////////////////////////////////////////////////////////////////*/
#define NAKEDDEF __declspec(naked)

/*//////////////////////////////////////////////////////////////////////
// BIG NOTE BIG NOTE BIG NOTE BIG NOTE
// The following prototypes look like cdecl functions. They are
// not--they are all stdcall! The custom prolog and epilog ensure that
// the correct calling convention is used!
//////////////////////////////////////////////////////////////////////*/

////////////////////////////////////////////////////////////////////////
```

```
// The mandatory functions that have to be intercepted to make the
// system work
BOOL DD_FreeLibrary ( HMODULE hModule ) ;
VOID DD_FreeLibraryAndExitThread ( HMODULE hModule    ,
                                   DWORD   dwExitCode  ) ;
HMODULE DD_LoadLibraryA ( LPCSTR lpLibFileName ) ;
HMODULE DD_LoadLibraryW ( LPCWSTR lpLibFileName ) ;
HMODULE DD_LoadLibraryExA ( LPCSTR lpLibFileName ,
                            HANDLE hFile         ,
                            DWORD  dwFlags        ) ;
HMODULE DD_LoadLibraryExW ( LPCWSTR lpLibFileName ,
                            HANDLE  hFile         ,
                            DWORD   dwFlags        ) ;

VOID DD_ExitProcess ( UINT uExitCode ) ;

FARPROC DD_GetProcAddress ( HMODULE hModule , LPCSTR lpProcName ) ;

/////////////////////////////////////////////////////////////////////////
// The thread-specific functions
HANDLE DD_CreateThread (LPSECURITY_ATTRIBUTES  lpThreadAttributes   ,
                        DWORD                  dwStackSize          ,
                        LPTHREAD_START_ROUTINE lpStartAddress       ,
                        LPVOID                 lpParameter          ,
                        DWORD                  dwCreationFlags      ,
                        LPDWORD                lpThreadId            ) ;
VOID DD_ExitThread ( DWORD dwExitCode ) ;
DWORD DD_SuspendThread ( HANDLE hThread ) ;
DWORD DD_ResumeThread ( HANDLE hThread ) ;
BOOL DD_TerminateThread ( HANDLE hThread , DWORD dwExitCode ) ;

// The following are the CRT thread function and are handled properly as
// they are __cdecl.
uintptr_t
    DD_beginthreadex ( void *           security       ,
                       unsigned         stack_size     ,
                       unsigned ( __stdcall *start_address )( void * ) ,
                       void *           arglist        ,
                       unsigned         initflag       ,
                       unsigned *       thrdaddr        ) ;
uintptr_t
    DD_beginthread ( void( __cdecl *start_address )( void * ) ,
                     unsigned   stack_size                   ,
                     void *     arglist                       ) ;
VOID DD_endthreadex ( unsigned retval ) ;
VOID DD_endthread ( void ) ;

/////////////////////////////////////////////////////////////////////////
// Waiting and special functions
DWORD DD_WaitForSingleObject ( HANDLE hHandle        ,
                               DWORD  dwMilliseconds  ) ;
DWORD DD_WaitForSingleObjectEx ( HANDLE hHandle        ,
                                 DWORD  dwMilliseconds ,
                                 BOOL   bAlertable      ) ;
```

```
DWORD DD_WaitForMultipleObjects( DWORD          nCount       ,
                                 CONST HANDLE * lpHandles    ,
                                 BOOL           bWaitAll     ,
                                 DWORD          dwMilliseconds  ) ;
DWORD DD_WaitForMultipleObjectsEx( DWORD          nCount         ,
                                   CONST HANDLE * lpHandles      ,
                                   BOOL           bWaitAll       ,
                                   DWORD          dwMilliseconds ,
                                   BOOL           bAlertable      ) ;
DWORD DD_MsgWaitForMultipleObjects ( DWORD    nCount        ,
                                     LPHANDLE pHandles      ,
                                     BOOL     fWaitAll      ,
                                     DWORD    dwMilliseconds,
                                     DWORD    dwWakeMask     ) ;
DWORD DD_MsgWaitForMultipleObjectsEx ( DWORD    nCount          ,
                                       LPHANDLE pHandles        ,
                                       DWORD    dwMilliseconds  ,
                                       DWORD    dwWakeMask      ,
                                       DWORD    dwFlags          ) ;
DWORD DD_SignalObjectAndWait ( HANDLE hObjectToSignal ,
                               HANDLE hObjectToWaitOn ,
                               DWORD  dwMilliseconds  ,
                               BOOL   bAlertable       ) ;
BOOL DD_CloseHandle ( HANDLE hObject ) ;

////////////////////////////////////////////////////////////////////////////
// Critical-section functions
VOID DD_InitializeCriticalSection(LPCRITICAL_SECTION lpCriticalSection);
BOOL DD_InitializeCriticalSectionAndSpinCount (
                                  LPCRITICAL_SECTION lpCriticalSection,
                                  DWORD              dwSpinCount     );
VOID DD_DeleteCriticalSection(LPCRITICAL_SECTION lpCriticalSection ) ;
VOID DD_EnterCriticalSection ( LPCRITICAL_SECTION lpCriticalSection ) ;
VOID DD_LeaveCriticalSection ( LPCRITICAL_SECTION lpCriticalSection ) ;
DWORD DD_SetCriticalSectionSpinCount (
                                  LPCRITICAL_SECTION lpCriticalSection,
                                  DWORD              dwSpinCount     );
BOOL DD_TryEnterCriticalSection ( LPCRITICAL_SECTION lpCriticalSection);

////////////////////////////////////////////////////////////////////////////
// Mutex functions
HANDLE DD_CreateMutexA ( LPSECURITY_ATTRIBUTES lpMutexAttributes ,
                         BOOL                  bInitialOwner     ,
                         LPCSTR                lpName             ) ;
HANDLE DD_CreateMutexW ( LPSECURITY_ATTRIBUTES lpMutexAttributes ,
                         BOOL                  bInitialOwner     ,
                         LPCWSTR               lpName             ) ;
HANDLE DD_OpenMutexA ( DWORD  dwDesiredAccess ,
                       BOOL   bInheritHandle  ,
                       LPCSTR lpName           ) ;
HANDLE DD_OpenMutexW ( DWORD   dwDesiredAccess ,
                       BOOL    bInheritHandle  ,
                       LPCWSTR lpName           ) ;
BOOL DD_ReleaseMutex ( HANDLE hMutex ) ;
```

```
////////////////////////////////////////////////////////////////////////
// Semaphore functions
HANDLE
    DD_CreateSemaphoreA ( LPSECURITY_ATTRIBUTES lpSemaphoreAttributes ,
                          LONG                  lInitialCount          ,
                          LONG                  lMaximumCount          ,
                          LPCSTR                lpName                 );
HANDLE
    DD_CreateSemaphoreW ( LPSECURITY_ATTRIBUTES lpSemaphoreAttributes ,
                          LONG                  lInitialCount          ,
                          LONG                  lMaximumCount          ,
                          LPCWSTR               lpName                 );
HANDLE DD_OpenSemaphoreA ( DWORD  dwDesiredAccess ,
                           BOOL   bInheritHandle  ,
                           LPCSTR lpName           ) ;
HANDLE DD_OpenSemaphoreW ( DWORD   dwDesiredAccess ,
                           BOOL    bInheritHandle  ,
                           LPCWSTR lpName           ) ;
BOOL DD_ReleaseSemaphore ( HANDLE hSemaphore       ,
                           LONG   lReleaseCount    ,
                           LPLONG lpPreviousCount  ) ;

////////////////////////////////////////////////////////////////////////
// Event functions
HANDLE DD_CreateEventA ( LPSECURITY_ATTRIBUTES lpEventAttributes ,
                         BOOL                  bManualReset      ,
                         BOOL                  bInitialState     ,
                         LPCSTR                lpName             ) ;
HANDLE DD_CreateEventW ( LPSECURITY_ATTRIBUTES lpEventAttributes ,
                         BOOL                  bManualReset      ,
                         BOOL                  bInitialState     ,
                         LPCWSTR               lpName             ) ;
HANDLE DD_OpenEventA ( DWORD  dwDesiredAccess ,
                       BOOL   bInheritHandle  ,
                       LPCSTR lpName           ) ;
HANDLE DD_OpenEventW ( DWORD   dwDesiredAccess ,
                       BOOL    bInheritHandle  ,
                       LPCWSTR lpName           ) ;
BOOL DD_PulseEvent ( HANDLE hEvent ) ;
BOOL DD_ResetEvent ( HANDLE hEvent ) ;
BOOL DD_SetEvent ( HANDLE hEvent ) ;

#endif  // _DD_FUNCS_H
```

One of the dumbest bugs I had in the first edition of DeadlockDetection was of the old "editor inheritance" variety. I created the hook functions for `LoadLibraryA` and `LoadLibraryW` and realized I also needed hook functions for `LoadLibraryExA` and `LoadLibraryExW`. Being the typical engineer, I cut and pasted the `LoadLibraryA/W` hook functions and edited them for the `LoadLibraryExA/W` functions. If you look at the `HOOKFN_EPILOG` macro, you'll see that it takes a parameter that is the number of function parameters. You can probably guess what happened—I forgot to change the value from 1 to 3, so calls to `LoadLibraryExA/W` were removing two extra items from the stack and crashing your programs!

As I looked at the code that I put in the hook functions, I realized it was basically the same thing over and over. To encapsulate the common parts, I came up with the `HOOKFN_STARTUP` and `HOOKFN_SHUTDOWN` macros. As the name implies, `HOOKFN_STARTUP` goes at the start of the hook function and takes care of the prolog as well any necessary pre-call logging. The parameters, in order, are the function enumeration, the `DDOPT_*` flag to indicate which group this function belongs to, and a Boolean flag, which if `TRUE`, will do pre-logging for the function. The pre-logging is for those functions such as `WaitForSingle-Object` that would cause the potential deadlock. The `HOOKFN_SHUTDOWN` macro takes the number of parameters for the function and the same `DDOPT_*` flag passed to `HOOKFN_STARTUP`. Of course, to ensure I didn't make the same mistake I did with the `LoadLibraryExA/W` hooks, I went through and verified that the number of parameters specified in `HOOKFN_SHUTDOWN` was accurate.

I want to mention several other minor points about DeadlockDetection. The first is that DeadlockDetection is always active in your application, even if you suspend DeadlockDetection logging. Instead of hooking and unhooking dynamically, I leave the functions hooked and look at some internal flags to determine how the hook should behave. Keeping all functions hooked makes it easier to toggle different function logging at run time, but it adds some overhead to your application. I felt that allowing hooking and unhooking on the fly would have led to more errors in the DeadlockDetection code.

Second, DeadlockDetection hooks the functions out of a DLL when brought into your program through `LoadLibrary`. However, it can gain control only after that DLL's `DllMain` has executed, so if any synchronization objects are created or used during `DllMain`, DeadlockDetection can miss them.

Third, DeadlockDetection also hooks `GetProcAddress` and `ExitProcess`. The `GetProcAddress` hooking is there in case your program, or a third-party control you might be deadlocking against, calls `GetProcAddress` to find a synchronization method at run time.

I hook `ExitProcess` because when the application is ending, I need to unhook and shut down DeadlockDetection so that it doesn't crash or hang your program. Because there's no way to control the unload order of DLLs during program termination, you can easily get into situations in which a DLL that DeadlockDetection relies on, such as DeadDetExt, has been unloaded before DeadlockDetection itself. Fortunately, very few developers are doing major multithreaded control after the application calls `ExitProcess`.

For `ExitProcess` hooking, you'll see some special processing in DEADLOCKDETECTION.CPP. Because it's so vital to ensure that DeadlockDetection gets shut down, I forcibly hook any calls to `ExitProcess`, even in ignored modules. That way you don't get a surprise crash in which synchronization functions are still hooked after DeadlockDetection has already shut down.

Finally, several test programs are included with DeadlockDetection, which comes with this book's sample files. All of them are included in the main DeadlockDetectionTests solution, and all link against DEADLOCKDETECTION.DLL, so you can use them to see how DeadlockDetection operates.

What's Next for DeadlockDetection?

DeadlockDetection is a fairly complete utility, and I've used it successfully to track down quite a few multithreaded deadlocks. As always, however, I encourage you to look for ways that you can extend DeadlockDetection to make it more useful. Here are some of my ideas for enhancements to DeadlockDetection:

- Create a stand-alone application to manipulate the DEADLOCKDETECTION.INI file. Your program could be even nicer if it allowed you to set the DeadDetExt DLL and validated that the selected DeadDetExt DLL exported the correct functions.
- You could optimize the hook functions better if they weren't doing any logging. In that case, not all the register values need to be copied.
- Right now, DeadlockDetection just skips hooking a couple of DLLs that it knows about. A mechanism for specifying on a program-by-program basis which DLLs to skip would be nifty.

Debugging War Story

Uncommitted Transactions with Pooled COM Objects

The Battle

My good friend Peter Ierardi told me about an interesting multithreading bug he encountered. He was working on a large DCOM project that used a multithreaded DCOM service to coordinate database transactions. The DCOM service managed the transactions by creating a pool of database-centric in-process COM objects, which were used to write data into and read data from his relational database management system (RDBMS). The component-to-component communication took place through Microsoft Message Queue Server (MSMQ). Even though there were explicit, transactional commits, the data didn't seem to be written to the database. The

DCOM service would retry three to five times, and the data would finally appear, as if by magic. Obviously, the excessive retries were taking a toll on the application's performance, and the fact that the data wasn't being written to the database was cause for alarm.

The Outcome

After some heavy debugging sessions, Peter found that the DCOM service was performing the reads and writes on separate, nonsynchronized threads. The read occurred before a separate instance of the database COM object had written the data. This behavior wasn't evident during debugging sessions because the debugger was forcing the proper timing and synchronization. He eventually uncovered the problem through appropriate labeling of object instances in the event log.

The Lesson

The big lesson Peter said he learned from this bug was that in a large-scale distributed application such as the one he was working on, you can't assume that the debug environment will accurately represent the release environment. He solved the problem by adding appropriate synchronization code and wrapping the component-to-component communications, which originally went through MSMQ individually, into the same transaction along with the database writes such that the messages would be sent only upon transactional commits.

What was happening in Peter's bug was that the MSMQ reads/writes, not surprisingly, were cycling much faster than the database reads/writes. Even though Peter and his team had walked through and planned all the multithreading carefully, they were still bitten by some initial misunderstanding about how much faster certain operations outside their project would take in the real world.

Summary

Multithreaded programming is difficult and the area in which you'll encounter some of the hardest bugs you'll ever have to solve. This chapter presented tips, techniques, and key points that should help you avoid deadlocks from the beginning of your project. As I stressed early in the chapter, in multithreaded programming, up-front planning is vital, and you must make sure to allot your team enough time and resources to plan multithreaded applications carefully and correctly. Once you're faced with the inevitable multithreaded deadlocks, however, there's no need to panic: this chapter also covered DeadlockDetection, a utility that will allow you to figure out which threads deadlocked on which synchronization object.

Finally—and I can't stress this point enough—if you're doing multithreaded programming, you must be developing, running, and testing your projects on multiprocessor computers. If you're not, you probably shouldn't be doing multithreaded programming because you're leaving yourself open to some extremely serious bugs.

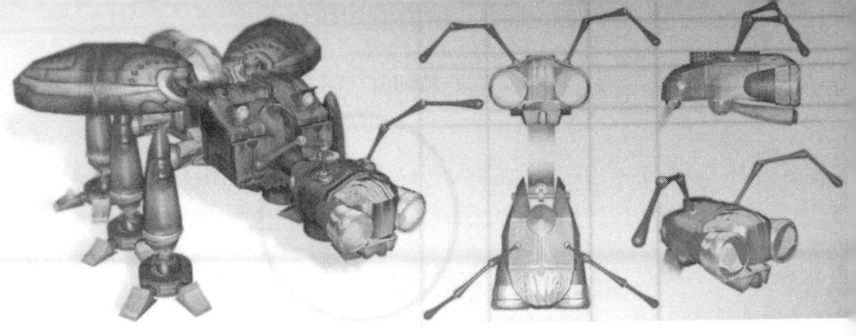

16

Automated Testing

In Chapter 3, I talked about unit tests and explained why unit testing is such a vital part of producing high-quality code. For those of us who work mostly on an application's internal logic, unit tests can be fairly simple. Look at this book's sample files in BugslayerUtil\Tests, and you'll see all the unit tests I used to develop BUGSLAYERUTIL.DLL. Almost all those tests are console applications that do their jobs admirably.

Unfortunately, testing user interface (UI) code is more difficult, no matter whether the application is a Microsoft .NET fat client or is browser based. In this chapter, I'll present a utility I wrote, Tester, that will help you automate your UI testing. Compared with the version of Tester included in the first edition of this book, the new Tester tool now borders on the capabilities of a full-blown commercial regression-testing tool. In fact, I've been extremely pleased to see how many development shops are using Tester. Not only is it easier to deal with than many commercial systems, it's quite a bit less expensive, too.

The Bane of Unit Testing: User Interfaces

I'm firmly convinced that Microsoft Windows developers get their carpal tunnel syndrome not from typing their source code but from hitting the same keystroke combinations over and over to test their applications. After the 5,000th time you type *Alt+F, O,* your wrists are locked tighter than rebar in concrete. Without a tool to automate the tasks involved in accessing the different features of your applications, you generally have to follow some sort of script to ensure that you're doing sufficient unit testing. Testing with manual input scripts is totally boring—and the boredom that results leaves plenty of room for human error.

Automating your unit tests will mean that you don't have to type so much and that you can quickly verify the state of your code. Unfortunately, the Recorder application that used to ship with Microsoft Windows 3.0 and 3.1 doesn't come with any of the 32-bit operating systems. For those of you new to Windows, Recorder wrote your mouse and keyboard interactions to a file so that you could play them back as if they were physical mouse and keyboard events. Although several third-party products are available that will automate your application and a whole lot more (such as completely validate every pixel in a screen comparison and maintain databases of which tests ran when), I wanted something that was lightweight and geared toward development engineers. Thus, the idea for my Tester application was born.

When I started thinking about creating an automation utility, I spent some time considering exactly what I'd expect from such a tool. At first, I thought about developing a utility akin to the old Recorder application. Way back in the days of Windows 3.0, I had a complete set of REC files to drive my tests. However, the big problem with Recorder was that it didn't provide a way to do conditional tests. If my application signaled an error during the test, Recorder just went along its merry way, playing back the recorded keystrokes and mouse clicks, completely oblivious to my application's distress. One time I wiped out half my operating system with Recorder because I was testing a WINFILE.EXE extension, and when my extension had a problem, Recorder played the delete files sequence all over the System directory. My new automation tool definitely had to have an `if...then...else` construct.

To incorporate conditional constructs into my tests, I obviously needed to use some sort of language. Developing my own testing language would've been an intriguing intellectual exercise, but I soon concluded that I was more interested in writing a useful debugging tool than in designing a language and dealing with YACC and FLEX. It took all of two seconds to realize that I should write Tester as a COM object—that way, developers could use my utility and still write tests in their language of choice, and I could concentrate on programming the utility's regression-testing features instead of designing a new language. My personal testing languages of choice are scripting languages, such as Microsoft Visual Basic Scripting Edition (VBScript) and Microsoft JScript, because the testing scripts don't require compiling. The different Microsoft Windows Scripting Host (WSH) scripting engine implementations have a few limitations, however, which I'll point out later in the chapter. For now, let's talk about the requirements that guided my creation of Tester.

Tester Requirements

I wanted to keep Tester focused on doing two things very well: recording your keystrokes and mouse usage, and playing those inputs back to your application so that you can unit test faster. If you've ever explored commercial regression-testing tools, you've undoubtedly seen what a wild ride they can involve, from simply controlling a window on the screen to validating all sorts of complicated and weird data of the most obscure window properties possible. I wanted to concentrate on the developer's needs during unit testing and keep Tester simple to use. Here are the main requirements for Tester:

1. Tester can be controlled through any language that supports COM.
2. Given an input string of keystrokes, in the same format used by the `System.Windows.Forms.SendKeys` class, Tester can play the keystrokes to the active window.
3. Tester can find any top-level or child window by its caption or class.
4. Given any arbitrary `HWND`, Tester can get all the window's properties.
5. Tester must notify the user's script of specific window creation or destruction so that the script can handle potential error conditions or do advanced window handling. Tester doesn't limit developers from extending the code in any direction they need for their shops' requirements.
6. Tester must be able to record keystrokes and place them into a string that is compatible with the Tester playback code.
7. When generating a Tester script, the script is self-contained so that the saved script is ready to run.
8. The user can edit the automatically generated script before saving it.
9. Tester can properly set focus to a specific window, including any child control, to ensure that playback goes to the correct window.

While quite complete, Tester probably isn't a general solution for your 20-person QA department. My intention was to build a tool that you and I, as development engineers, could use to automate our unit testing. To that end, I think Tester fits the bill. I used Tester quite a bit to help develop WDBG, the graphical user interface (GUI) debugger I developed as part of Chapter 4. The best part of using Tester with WDBG was that I saved myself thousands of keystrokes—this far into the book, I can still move my wrists!

Using Tester

Using Tester is relatively simple. I'll start out by discussing the actual Tester object and its use in scripts before I move on to discussing how to use the TESTREC.EXE program to record scripts. By understanding the object Tester presents for your scripts, you'll be able to record them more effectively.

Tester Scripts

In your scripts, the basic idea is to just create a couple of Tester objects, either start or find your application's main window, play some keystrokes to your application, check the results, and end. Listing 16-1 shows a sample VBScript test that starts NOTEPAD.EXE, enters a few lines of text, and closes Notepad. (All the example scripts shown in this chapter are included with the sample files for this book.)

```
' A minimal VBScript Tester example. It just starts Notepad, enters a
' few lines of text, and closes Notepad.

' Get the system and input objects.
Dim tSystem
Dim tInput
Dim tWin
Set tSystem = WScript.CreateObject ( "Tester.TSystem" )
Set tInput = WScript.CreateObject ( "Tester.TInput" )

' Start Notepad.
tSystem.Execute "NOTEPAD.EXE"

' Wait a few seconds.
tSystem.Sleep 3.0

' Try to find Notepad's main window.
Set tWin = tSystem.FindTopTWindowByTitle ( "Untitled - Notepad" )
If ( tWin Is Nothing ) Then
    MsgBox "Unable to find Notepad!"
    WScript.Quit
End If

' Ensure that Notepad is in the foreground.
tWin.SetForegroundTWindow

' Type something.
tInput.PlayInput "Be all you can be!~~~"
' Play it again, Sam.
tInput.PlayInput "Put on your boots and parachutes....~~~"
' Third time's the charm.
tInput.PlayInput "Silver wings upon their chests.....~~~"
```

Listing 16-1 MINIMAL.VBS showing how to use common Tester objects

```
' Wait 3 seconds.
tSystem.Sleep 3.0

' End Notepad.
tInput.PlayInput "%FX"
tSystem.Sleep 2.0
tInput.PlayInput "{TAB}~"

' Script is done!
```

Listing 16-1 shows the three objects Tester uses most often. The `TSystem` object allows you to find top-level windows, start applications, and pause the testing. The `TWindow` object, which is returned by `FindTopTWindowByTitle` in Listing 16-1, is the main workhorse. It is a wrapper around an `HWND` and has all sorts of properties that tell you everything about the window. Additionally, `TWindow` allows you to enumerate all the child windows that belong to a particular parent. The last object in Listing 16-1 is the `TInput` object, which supports the single method `PlayInput` to funnel keystrokes to the window that has the focus.

Listing 16-2 shows the `TNotify` object used in a VBScript test. When developing automation scripts, one of the most difficult cases you'll need to handle is when an unexpected window, such as an `ASSERT` message box, pops up. The `TNotify` object makes it a snap to provide an emergency handler for such events. The simple script in Listing 16-2 just watches for any windows with "Notepad" in their captions. Although you might not use the `TNotify` class much, when you do need it, you really need it.

```
' A VBScript test to show the window notification handlers

' Constants for the TNotify.AddNotification routine.
Const antDestroyWindow    = 1
Const antCreateWindow     = 2
Const antCreateAndDestroy = 3

Const ansExactMatch       = 0
Const ansBeginMatch       = 1
Const ansAnyLocMatch      = 2

' Get the system and input objects.

Dim tSystem
Dim tInput
Set tSystem = WScript.CreateObject ( "Tester.TSystem" )
Set tInput = WScript.CreateObject ( "Tester.TInput" )
```

Listing 16-2 HANDLERS.VBS showing how to use the `TNotify` object

```
' The TNotify object variable
Dim Notifier

' Create the TNotify object.
Set Notifier = _
        WScript.CreateObject ( "Tester.TNotify"         , _
                               "NotepadNotification"     )

' Add the notifications that I want. For this demonstration, I want both
' window destroy and window create notifications. See the TNotify source
' code for all the possible notification combinations.
Notifier.AddNotification  antCreateAndDestroy , _
                          ansAnyLocMatch      , _
                          "Notepad"

' Start Notepad.
tSystem.Execute "NOTEPAD.EXE"

' Pause for one seconds.
tSystem.Sleep 1.0

' Because the apartment model isn't thread-safe, I set up the
' notification scheme to use a timer. However, the message can get
' blocked because all the processing is forced to a single thread. This
' function lets you manually check the window create and window destroy
' conditions.
Notifier.CheckNotification

' The message box in the NotepadNotification_CreateWindow event
' procedure blocks, so the code to end Notepad won't execute until the
' message box is cleared.
tInput.PlayInput "%FX"
tSystem.Sleep 1.0

' Again, check notifications.
Notifier.CheckNotification

' Give TNotify a chance to intercept the window destroy message.
tSystem.Sleep 1.0

' Disconnect the notifications. If you don't do this in WSH, the class
' terminate never gets called so the notification is still active in the
' notification table.
WScript.DisconnectObject Notifier

Set Notifier = Nothing

WScript.Quit


Sub NotepadNotificationCreateWindow ( tWin )
    MsgBox ( "Notepad was created!!" )
```

```
End Sub

Sub NotepadNotificationDestroyWindow ( )
    MsgBox ( "Notepad has gone away...." )
End Sub
```

You need to call the TNotify CheckNotification method every once in a while. (I'll explain the reasons you need to call this method in the section "Implementing Tester" later in the chapter.) Periodically calling the CheckNotification method ensures that the notification messages can get through even though you might not have a message loop in your language of choice. The code in Listing 16-2 shows how to use a message box in the notification event procedures, though you probably don't want to use message boxes in your real scripts because they can cause problems by unexpectedly changing the window with the focus.

Also keep in mind that I allow you to set only a limited number of notifications—five—so you shouldn't use TNotify for general scripting tasks such as waiting for the File Save dialog box to appear. TNotify should be used only for unexpected windows. Depending on how you set up your notification handlers and how they search for the specified text in the window caption, you can easily receive notifications for windows that you might not be interested in. You're most likely to receive unwanted notifications when you use a generic string such as "Notepad" and you specify that the string can appear anywhere in the window caption. To avoid notifications you don't want, you should be as specific as possible with your notifications when calling the TNotify AddNotification method. Your CreateWindow event procedures should also look at the TWindow passed in so that you can verify that it's the window you're interested in. For DestroyWindow event procedures that handle generic notifications, you should search the open windows to ensure that the window you're interested in no longer exists.

Included with the source code that accompanies this book are other samples that you might want to look at to see how you can use Tester. NPAD_TEST.VBS is a more complete VBScript test and has some reusable routines. PAINTBRUSH.JS shows using the mouse playback capabilities in a resolution-independent manner. It takes a bit to run, but the outcome is worth it. TesterTester is the main unit test for the Tester COM object. TesterTester a C# application in the Tester\Tester\Tests\TesterTester directory, should give you an idea of how to use Tester with .NET. Additionally, the sample TesterTester shows the TWindows object, which is a collection that contains TWindow objects.

Although I'm partial to using JScript and VBScript for my unit tests, I realize that getting them to work correctly can be a challenge. Scripting variables are untyped and there's no magic IntelliSense editor, such as the C# editor in

Visual Studio .NET, so you're back to the old run-and-crash style of debugging. The main reason I like using scripting languages is that I don't need to rely on compiling my tests. If you have a flexible build environment—one in which you can easily build other binaries in addition to your main application—you might want to consider using .NET so that you can build your tests as you build your application. Of course, Tester doesn't limit you to the easiest-to-use testing languages. If you're more comfortable using C or the Microsoft Macro Assembler (MASM), you're welcome to use those languages instead.

Although using the objects in Tester is fairly simple, the real work is planning your tests. You should keep your tests as focused and simple as possible. When I first started automating my unit tests in my early development days, I tried to force my tests to do too much. Now I write each script to test just a single operation. A good example of a single-operation test is to limit the script just to sending the keystrokes to open a file. You can chain the scripts together in various ways to maximize script reuse. Once you have the script to open a file, you can use it in three different tests: a test to see whether you can open a valid file, a test to open an invalid file, and a test to open a corrupt file. As in normal development, you should avoid any hard-coded strings if possible. Not only will this make internationalizing your script a piece of cake, but it will also help when you change your menu system and accelerators for the hundredth time.

Another detail to consider when you're designing your Tester scripts is how to verify that the script actually worked. If you're bored and have the time, I guess you could just sit there and watch the scripts run to see whether you get the same results on each run. Probably a better idea is to log states and key points in your script so that you can compare the output to previous runs automatically. If you use the CSCRIPT.EXE WSH executable, you can use `WScript.Echo` and redirect the output to a file. After the script finishes, you can run a difference utility (such as WinDiff) on the output; if the utility turns up any differences, you can check to see that the script executed correctly. Keep in mind that you'll want to normalize the information you log and keep the information free of run-specific details. For example, if you're writing an application that downloads stock quotes, you won't want to include the last price-update time in the logging output.

What about debugging your Tester scripts? Tester doesn't have its own integrated debugger, so you'll need to use whatever debugging tools are available for the language that the Tester script is written in. If you're using a debugger, you need to be careful that you don't stop on a `TInput PlayInput` method call. If the debugger does stop there, the keystrokes will obviously go to the wrong window. To work around this potential problem, I generally force the window to which I'm sending keystrokes to the top of the z-order by calling the `TWindow SetForegroundTWindow` method before each `PlayInput` call. This way, I can break on the `SetForegroundTWindow` call, check the state of the application, and still get the keystrokes to the correct window.

Recording Scripts

Now that you're armed with an understanding of the Tester objects and how to call them from your own scripts, I can turn to the TESTREC.EXE program that you'll use to record the interaction with your applications. When you first fire up TESTREC.EXE, you'll notice that it's a text editor that has a little bit of code already written for you. By default, the language is JScript, but I'll show you how to change the default to VBScript in a moment. Starting the recording is as simple as pressing the Record button on the toolbar or pressing Ctrl+R.

When recording, TESTREC.EXE automatically minimizes itself and changes its caption to "RECORDING!," so you'll know what it's doing. You can stop recording in several different ways. The easiest is to set focus to TESTREC.EXE by either pressing Alt+Tab or clicking on the application. Recording will also stop if you press Ctrl+Break or Ctrl+Alt+Delete; the former is suggested in the hook documentation, and the latter is appropriate when you want the system to forcibly cancel any active journaling hooks (which is how TESTREC.EXE does its magic).

Before you go off and start recording a million scripts, you'll need to do a little planning to take complete advantage of Tester. Although Tester handles mouse recording and playback, your scripts will be much more robust if you can do as much work as possible with keystrokes. One nice feature is that when recording, Tester works hard to keep track of the window with the focus. By default, for single mouse clicks and double-clicks, Tester will generate code to set the focus to the top-level window before processing the click or clicks. In addition, when recoding with keystrokes, Tester monitors Alt+Tab combinations to set the focus when you finish shifting focus.

Since mouse recording can generate a million statements in a script, TESTREC.EXE, by default, records only single mouse clicks, double-clicks, and drag actions every 50 pixels. Of course, I did the right thing and allowed you to specify exactly how you want your scripts recorded. Figure 16-1 shows TESTREC.EXE's Script Recording Options dialog box, which is accessible by pressing Ctrl+T or selecting Script Options from the Scripts menu. All items shown are the default values.

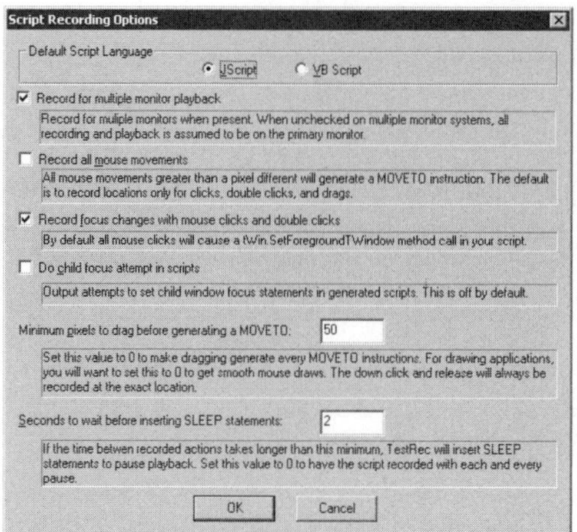

Figure 16-1 Script recording options for Tester

The first thing you'll notice at the top of the Script Recording Options dialog box is the option to choose JScript or VBScript for new scripts. The Record For Multiple Monitor Playback check box, which is checked by default, will insert calls to `TSystem.CheckVirtualResolution` to ensure the screen size for the rest of the recording. If you uncheck this option, any point that falls outside the primary monitor for mouse clicks or windows locations will abort recording. You might want to turn off multiple monitor recording if you plan to use recorded scripts on different machines. However, if you're recording scripts that only you will be running, leave the multiple monitor recording turned on so that you can take advantage of multiple monitors.

For scripts in which you will be doing a lot of click-and-drags and you want to record all the mouse movements between the mouse down and release actions, set the Minimum Pixels To Drag Before Generating A MOVETO value to 0. If your recording will be doing a lot of clicks in the application without shifting focus to other applications, you'll want to uncheck Record Focus Changes With Mouse Clicks And Double Clicks. That will keep TESTREC.EXE from generating the code to force the focus each time the mouse is clicked and will make your script much smaller.

The Do Child Focus Attempt In Scripts option will add code that attempts to set the focus to a specific control or child window you click on. I left this option off by default because I was already generating the statements to set the focus to the top-level window. Although applications like Notepad have only a single child window, other applications have deeply nested window hierarchies, and it can be difficult to track down child windows when all the parents don't have titles and unique classes. For an example, use Spy++ to look at the

Visual Studio .NET editor window hierarchy. I found that setting the top window–level focus before generating the click code usually worked perfectly fine.

Finally, the Seconds To Wait Before Inserting SLEEP Statements option automatically inserts pauses in the script longer than a specific value in seconds. Most of the time, you'll want to let your scripts run as quickly as possible, but to help keep scripts coordinated, the extra pause time can help.

The recording and playback for Tester support the same format as the .NET `System.Windows.Forms.SendKeys` class, except for the repeating keys option. To handle the mouse, I extended the format to allow for it as well as the format modifiers necessary to allow Ctrl, Alt, and Shift key utilization in conjunction with it. Table 16-1 shows the format of the mouse commands to `TInput.PlayInput`.

Table 16-1 The Mouse Commands to `TInput.PlayInput`

Command	Usage
`MOVETO`	{MOVETO *x* , *y*}
`BTNDOWN`	{BTNDOWN *btn* , *x* , *y*}
`BTNUP`	{BTNUP *btn* , *x* , *y*}
`CLICK`	{CLICK *btn* , *x* , *y*}
`DBLCLICK`	{DBLCLICK *btn* , *x* , *y*}
`SHIFT DOWN`	{SHIFT DOWN}
`SHIFT UP`	{SHIFT UP}
`CTRL DOWN`	{CTRL DOWN}
`CTRL UP`	{CTRL UP}
`ALT DOWN`	{ALT DOWN}
`ALT UP`	{ALT UP}
	btn: LEFT, RIGHT, MIDDLE
	x: X screen coordinate value
	y: Y screen coordinate value

There were a few items I wasn't able to add to the mouse recording. The first was mouse wheel processing. I used a journal hook to capture keystrokes and mouse operations, and the mouse wheel message came through. Unfortunately, a bug in the journal hook reporting doesn't pass the mouse wheel direction, so there's no way to know whether you're scrolling up or down. The second item I couldn't process was the new X1 and X2 buttons found on the newer Microsoft Explorer mouse. These `WM_XBUTTON*` messages pass which button was pressed in the high order word of the `wParam`. Since the `WM_MOUSEWHEEL` message does the same thing with the direction, but the journal record hook doesn't receive it, I doubt the X button would come through either.

Implementing Tester

Now that you have an idea of how to use both sides of Tester to record and play back your automation scripts, I want to go over some of the high points of the implementation. If you add up the source and build sizes of the Tester source code and binaries, which include both TESTER.DLL and TESTREC.EXE, you'll see that Tester is the biggest utility in this book. Not only is it the biggest, but it's easily the most complicated because of COM, parsing recursion, and background timers.

The TESTER.DLL Notification and Playback Implementation

In the first version of this book, I implemented TESTER.DLL in Visual Basic 6, because that was the hot COM programming language and environment *de jour*. However, requiring you to keep Visual Basic 6 installed just to compile a single COM DLL didn't seem like a great idea. My first inclination was to move the TESTER.DLL code over to .NET. Since some of the core code, specifically the portion that played back keystrokes, was in C++, I thought it'd be easier to re-implement the Visual Basic 6 portion of Tester in C++ and take advantage of the new attributed COM programming.

In all, attributed COM is quite nice, but it did take me a while to find the `idl_quote` attribute to get my forward interface declarations to work. One very pleasant surprise with the attributed COM was how clean everything felt when combining the IDL/ODL and the C++ code. Additionally, the hugely improved wizards made it a snap to add interfaces and methods and properties to those interfaces. I certainly remember my fair share of times when the wizards broke in prior releases of Visual Studio.

Back when I first started thinking about doing an automated playback utility, I thought I could use the original `SendKeys` statement from Visual Basic 6. After a bit of testing, I found that that implementation didn't suffice, because it did not correctly send keystrokes to programs such as Microsoft Outlook. That meant I needed to implement my own version that would properly send the keystrokes and allow mouse input in the future. Fortunately, I ran across the `SendInput` function, which is part of Microsoft Active Accessibility (MSAA) and replaces all the previous low-level event functions, such as `keybd_event`. It also places all the input information in the keyboard or mouse input stream as a contiguous unit, ensuring that your input isn't interspersed with any extraneous user input. This functionality was especially attractive for Tester.

Once I knew how to send the keystrokes properly, I needed to develop the keystroke input format. Because the Visual Basic 6 `SendKeys` statement or .NET `System.Windows.Forms.SendKeys` class already provides a nice input format, I thought I'd duplicate it for my `PlayInput` function. I used everything but the repeat key code, though as I mentioned earlier, I extended the format to support mouse playback as well. There's nothing too thrilling about the parsing code—if you want to see it, look in the Tester\Tester\ParsePlayInputString.CPP file that accompanies the sample files for this book. Additionally, if you want to see the code in action, you might want to debug through the ParsePlayKeysTest program in the Tester\Tester\Tests\ParsePlayKeysTest directory. As you can tell by the name, this program is one of the unit tests for the Tester DLL.

The `TWindow`, `TWindows`, and `TSystem` objects are straightforward, and you should be able to understand them just by reading their source code. These three classes are essentially wrappers around the appropriate Windows API functions. The only slightly interesting portion of the implementation was writing the code to ensure the `TWindow.SetFocusTWindow` and `TSystem.SetSpecificFocus` methods could bring a window to the foreground. Those functions entailed attaching to the input thread by using the `AttachThreadInput` API before being able to set the focus.

I ran into some interesting obstacles in the `TNotify` class. When I first started thinking about what it would take to determine whether a window with a specific caption was created or destroyed, I didn't expect that creating such a class would be too hard. I discovered that not only was the job moderately difficult, but the window creation notifications can't be made foolproof without heroic effort.

My first idea was to implement a systemwide computer-based training (CBT) hook. The SDK documentation seemed to say that a CBT hook was the best method for determining when windows are created and destroyed. I whipped up a quick sample but soon hit a snag. When my hook got the `HCBT_CREATEWND` notification, I couldn't retrieve the window caption consistently. After I thought about the problem a bit, it started to make sense; the CBT hook is probably called as part of the `WM_CREATE` processing, and very few windows have set their captions at that point. The only windows I could get reliably with the `HCBT_CREATEWND` notification were dialog boxes. The window destruction surveillance always worked with the CBT hook.

After looking through all the other types of hooks, I extended my quick sample to try them all. As I suspected, just watching `WM_CREATE` wasn't going to tell me the caption reliably. A friend suggested that I watch only the

WM_SETTEXT messages. Eventually, to set the caption in a title bar, almost every window will use a WM_SETTEXT message. Of course, if you're doing your own non-client painting and bit blitting, you won't use the WM_SETTEXT message. One interesting behavior I did notice was that some programs, Microsoft Internet Explorer in particular, post WM_SETTEXT messages with the same text many times consecutively.

Having figured out that I needed to watch WM_SETTEXT messages, I took a harder look at the different hooks I could use. In the end, the call window procedure hook (WH_CALLWNDPROCRET) was the best choice. It allows me to watch WM_CREATE and WM_SETTEXT messages easily. I can also watch WM_DESTROY messages. At first, I expected to have some trouble with WM_DESTROY because I thought that the window caption might have been deallocated by the time this message showed up. Fortunately, the window caption is valid until the WM_NCDESTROY message is received.

After considering the pros and cons of handling WM_SETTEXT messages only for windows that didn't yet have a caption, I decided to just go ahead and process all WM_SETTEXT messages. The alternative would've involved writing a state machine to keep track of created windows and the times they get their captions set, and this solution sounded error prone and difficult to implement. The drawback to handling all WM_SETTEXT messages is that you can receive multiple creation notifications for the same window. For example, if you set a TNotify handler for windows that contained "Notepad" anywhere in their captions, you'd get a notification when NOTEPAD.EXE launched, but you'd also get a notification every time NOTEPAD.EXE opened a new file. In the end, I felt it was better to accept a less-than-optimal implementation rather than spend days and days debugging the "correct" solution. Also, writing the hook was only about a quarter of the implementation of the final TNotify class; the other three-quarters addressed the problem of how to let the user know that the window was created or destroyed.

Earlier, I mentioned that using the TNotify object isn't completely hands-off and that you have to call the CheckNotification method every once in a while. The reason you have to call CheckNotification periodically is that Tester supports only the apartment threading model that can't be multithreaded, and I needed a way to check whether a window was created or destroyed and still use the same thread in which the rest of Tester was running.

After sketching out some ideas about the notification mechanisms, I narrowed down the implementation needs to the following basic requirements:

- The `WH_CALLWNDPROCRET` hook has to be systemwide, so it must be implemented in its own DLL.
- The Tester DLL obviously can't be that DLL because I don't want to drag the entire Tester DLL and, in turn, all the COM code into each address space on the user's computer. This condition means that the hook DLL probably has to set a flag or something that the Tester DLL can read to know that a condition is met.
- Tester can't be multithreaded, so I need to do all the processing in the same thread.

The first ramification of the basic requirements is that the hook function had to be written in C. Because the hook function is loaded into all address spaces, the hook DLL couldn't call any functions in the TESTER.DLL that were written in apartment-threaded COM. Consequently, my code would need to check the results of the hook-generated data periodically.

If you've ever developed 16-bit Windows applications, you know that getting some background processing done in a single-threaded, non-preemptive environment seems like the perfect job for the `SetTimer` API function. With `SetTimer`, you can get the background-processing capabilities yet still keep your application single-threaded. Consequently, I set up a timer notification as part of the `TNotify` object to determine when the windows I needed to monitor were created or destroyed.

What made the `TNotify` background processing interesting was that the timer procedure solution seemed like the answer, but in reality, it usually works only in the `TNotify` case. Depending on the length of the script and on whether your language of choice implements a message loop, the `WM_TIMER` message might not get through, so you'll need to call the `CheckNotification` method, which checks the hook data as well.

All these implementation details might seem confusing, but you'll be surprised at how little code it really takes to implement Tester. Listing 16-3 shows the hook function code from TNOTIFYHLP.CPP. On the Tester side, TNOTIFY.CPP is the module in which the timer procedure resides along with the COM code necessary for the object. The `TNotify` class has a couple of C++ methods that the `TNotify` object can access to get the events fired and to determine what types of notifications the user wants. The interesting part of the hook code is the globally shared data segment, `.HOOKDATA`, which holds the array of notification data. When looking at the code, keep in mind that the notification data is global but all the rest of the data is on a per-process basis.

```
/*----------------------------------------------------------------------
Debugging Applications for Microsoft .NET and Microsoft Windows
Copyright © 1997-2003 John Robbins -- All rights reserved.
----------------------------------------------------------------------*/
#include "stdafx.h"

/*//////////////////////////////////////////////////////////////////////
                     File Scope Defines and Constants
//////////////////////////////////////////////////////////////////////*/
// The maximum number of notification slots
static const int TOTAL_NOTIFY_SLOTS = 5 ;
// The mutex name
static const LPCTSTR k_MUTEX_NAME  = _T ( "TNotifyHlp_Mutex" ) ;
// The longest amount of time I'll wait on the mutex
static const int k_WAITLIMIT = 5000 ;

// I have my own trace here because I don't want to drag
// BugslayerUtil.DLL into each address space.
#ifdef _DEBUG
#define TRACE   ::OutputDebugString
#else
#define TRACE   __noop
#endif

/*//////////////////////////////////////////////////////////////////////
// File Scope Typedefs
//////////////////////////////////////////////////////////////////////*/
// The structure for an individual window to look for
typedef struct tag_TNOTIFYITEM
{
    // The PID for the process that created this item
    DWORD   dwOwnerPID  ;
    // The notification type
    int     iNotifyType ;
    // The search parameter
    int     iSearchType ;
    // The handle to the HWND being created
    HWND    hWndCreate  ;
    // The destroy Boolean
    BOOL    bDestroy    ;
    // The title string
    TCHAR   szTitle [ MAX_PATH ] ;
} TNOTIFYITEM , * PTNOTIFYITEM ;

/*//////////////////////////////////////////////////////////////////////
// File Scope Global Variables
//////////////////////////////////////////////////////////////////////*/
// This data is **NOT** shared across processes, so each process gets
// its own copy.
```
Listing 16-3 TNOTIFYHLP.CPP

```
// The HINSTANCE for this module. Setting global system hooks requires
// a DLL.
static HINSTANCE g_hInst = NULL ;

// The mutex that protects the g_NotifyData table
static HANDLE g_hMutex = NULL ;

// The hook handle. I don't keep this handle in the shared section because
// multiple instances could set the hook when running multiple scripts.
static HHOOK g_hHook = NULL ;

// The number of items added by this process. This number lets me know
// how to handle the hook.
static int  g_iThisProcessItems = 0 ;

/*//////////////////////////////////////////////////////////////////////
// File Scope Function Prototypes
//////////////////////////////////////////////////////////////////////*/
// Our happy hook
LRESULT CALLBACK CallWndRetProcHook ( int    nCode  ,
                                      WPARAM wParam ,
                                      LPARAM lParam  ) ;

// The internal check function
static LONG_PTR __stdcall CheckNotifyItem ( HANDLE hItem , BOOL bCreate ) ;

/*//////////////////////////////////////////////////////////////////////
// Funky Shared Data Across All Hook Instances
//////////////////////////////////////////////////////////////////////*/
#pragma data_seg ( ".HOOKDATA" )
// The notification items table
static TNOTIFYITEM g_shared_NotifyData [ TOTAL_NOTIFY_SLOTS ] =
    {
        { 0 , 0 , 0 , NULL , 0 , '\0' } ,
        { 0 , 0 , 0 , NULL , 0 , '\0' } ,
        { 0 , 0 , 0 , NULL , 0 , '\0' } ,
        { 0 , 0 , 0 , NULL , 0 , '\0' } ,
        { 0 , 0 , 0 , NULL , 0 , '\0' }
    } ;
// The master count
static int g_shared_iUsedSlots = 0 ;
#pragma data_seg ( )

/*//////////////////////////////////////////////////////////////////////
// EXTERNAL IMPLEMENTATION STARTS HERE
//////////////////////////////////////////////////////////////////////*/

extern "C" BOOL WINAPI DllMain ( HINSTANCE hInst       ,
                                 DWORD     dwReason    ,
                                 LPVOID    /*lpReserved*/ )
{
#ifdef _DEBUG
```

```
    BOOL bCHRet ;
#endif

    BOOL bRet = TRUE ;
    switch ( dwReason )
    {
        case DLL_PROCESS_ATTACH :
            // Set the global module instance.
            g_hInst = hInst ;
            // I don't need the thread notifications.
            DisableThreadLibraryCalls ( g_hInst ) ;
            // Create the mutex for this process. The mutex is created
            // here but isn't owned yet.
            g_hMutex = CreateMutex ( NULL , FALSE , k_MUTEX_NAME ) ;
            if ( NULL == g_hMutex )
            {
                TRACE ( _T ( "Unable to create the mutex!\n" ) ) ;
                // If I can't create the mutex, I can't continue, so
                // fail the DLL load.
                bRet = FALSE ;
            }
            break ;
        case DLL_PROCESS_DETACH :

            // Check to see whether this process has any items in the
            // notification array. If it does, remove them to avoid
            // leaving orphaned items.
            if ( 0 != g_iThisProcessItems )
            {
                DWORD dwProcID = GetCurrentProcessId ( ) ;
                // I don't need to grab the mutex here because only a
                // single thread will ever call with the
                // DLL_PROCESS_DETACH reason.

                // Loop through and take a gander.
                for ( INT_PTR i = 0 ; i < TOTAL_NOTIFY_SLOTS ; i++ )
                {
                    if ( g_shared_NotifyData[i].dwOwnerPID == dwProcID )
                    {
#ifdef _DEBUG
                        TCHAR szBuff[ 50 ] ;
                        wsprintf ( szBuff ,
                              _T("DLL_PROCESS_DETACH removing : #%d\n"),
                                   i ) ;
                        TRACE ( szBuff ) ;
#endif
                        // Get rid of it.
                        RemoveNotifyTitle ( (HANDLE)i ) ;
                    }
                }
            }
```

```
            // Close the mutex handle.
#ifdef _DEBUG
            bCHRet =
#endif
            CloseHandle ( g_hMutex ) ;
#ifdef _DEBUG
            if ( FALSE == bCHRet )
            {
                TRACE ( _T ( "!!!!!!!!!!!!!!!!!!!!!!!!\n" ) ) ;
                TRACE ( _T ( "CloseHandle(g_hMutex) " ) \
                        _T ( "failed!!!!!!!!!!!!!!!!!!\n" ) ) ;
                TRACE ( _T ( "!!!!!!!!!!!!!!!!!!!!!!!!\n" ) ) ;
            }
#endif
            break ;
        default                     :
            break ;
    }
    return ( bRet ) ;
}


HANDLE TNOTIFYHLP_DLLINTERFACE __stdcall
    AddNotifyTitle ( int     iNotifyType ,
                     int     iSearchType ,
                     LPCTSTR szString     )
{
    // Ensure that the notify type range is correct.
    if ( ( iNotifyType < ANTN_DESTROYWINDOW     ) ||
         ( iNotifyType > ANTN_CREATEANDDESTROY  )    )
    {
        TRACE (
            _T( "AddNotify Title : iNotifyType is out of range!\n" ) ) ;
        return ( INVALID_HANDLE_VALUE ) ;
    }
    // Ensure that the search type range is correct.
    if ( ( iSearchType < ANTS_EXACTMATCH  ) ||
         ( iSearchType > ANTS_ANYLOCMATCH )    )
    {
        TRACE (
            _T( "AddNotify Title : iSearchType is out of range!\n" ) ) ;
        return ( INVALID_HANDLE_VALUE ) ;
    }
    // Ensure that the string is valid.
    if ( TRUE == IsBadStringPtr ( szString , MAX_PATH ) )
    {
        TRACE ( _T( "AddNotify Title : szString is invalid!\n" ) ) ;
        return ( INVALID_HANDLE_VALUE ) ;
    }

    // Wait to acquire the mutex.
    DWORD dwRet = WaitForSingleObject ( g_hMutex , k_WAITLIMIT ) ;
    if ( WAIT_TIMEOUT == dwRet )
```

```
    {
        TRACE (_T( "AddNotifyTitle : Wait on mutex timed out!!\n"));
        return ( INVALID_HANDLE_VALUE ) ;
    }

    // If the slots are used up, abort now.
    if ( TOTAL_NOTIFY_SLOTS == g_shared_iUsedSlots )
    {
        ReleaseMutex ( g_hMutex ) ;
        return ( INVALID_HANDLE_VALUE ) ;
    }

    // Find the first free slot.
    for ( INT_PTR i = 0 ; i < TOTAL_NOTIFY_SLOTS ; i++ )
    {
        if ( _T ( '\0' ) == g_shared_NotifyData[ i ].szTitle[ 0 ] )
        {
            break ;
        }
    }

    // Add this data.
    g_shared_NotifyData[ i ].dwOwnerPID  = GetCurrentProcessId ( ) ;
    g_shared_NotifyData[ i ].iNotifyType = iNotifyType ;
    g_shared_NotifyData[ i ].iSearchType = iSearchType ;
    lstrcpy ( g_shared_NotifyData[ i ].szTitle , szString ) ;

    // Bump up the master count.
    g_shared_iUsedSlots++ ;

    // Bump up the count for this process.
    g_iThisProcessItems++ ;

    TRACE ( _T( "AddNotifyTitle - Added a new item!\n" ) ) ;

    ReleaseMutex ( g_hMutex ) ;

    // If this is the first notification request, enable the hook.
    if ( NULL == g_hHook )
    {
        g_hHook = SetWindowsHookEx ( WH_CALLWNDPROCRET  ,
                                     CallWndRetProcHook ,
                                     g_hInst            ,
                                     0                  ) ;
#ifdef _DEBUG
        if ( NULL == g_hHook )
        {
            TCHAR szBuff[ 50 ] ;
            wsprintf ( szBuff ,
                       _T ( "SetWindowsHookEx failed!!!! (0x%08X)\n" ),
                       GetLastError ( ) ) ;
            TRACE ( szBuff ) ;
        }
```

```
#endif
    }

    return ( (HANDLE)i ) ;

}

void TNOTIFYHLP_DLLINTERFACE __stdcall
    RemoveNotifyTitle ( HANDLE hItem )
{
    // Check the value.
    INT_PTR i = (INT_PTR)hItem ;
    if ( ( i < 0 ) || ( i > TOTAL_NOTIFY_SLOTS ) )
    {
        TRACE ( _T ( "RemoveNotifyTitle : Invalid handle!\n" ) ) ;
        return ;
    }

    // Get the mutex.
    DWORD dwRet = WaitForSingleObject ( g_hMutex , k_WAITLIMIT ) ;
    if ( WAIT_TIMEOUT == dwRet )
    {
        TRACE ( _T ( "RemoveNotifyTitle : Wait on mutex timed out!\n"));
        return ;
    }

    if ( 0 == g_shared_iUsedSlots )
    {
        TRACE ( _T ( "RemoveNotifyTitle : Attempting to remove when " )\
                _T ( "no notification handles are set!\n" ) ) ;
        ReleaseMutex ( g_hMutex ) ;
        return ;
    }

    // Before removing anything, make sure this index points to a
    // NotifyData entry that contains a valid value. If I
    // didn't check, you could call this function with the same value
    // over and over, which would mess up the used-slots counts.
    if ( 0 == g_shared_NotifyData[ i ].dwOwnerPID )
    {
        TRACE ( _T ( "RemoveNotifyTitle : ") \
                _T ( "Attempting to double remove!\n" ) ) ;
        ReleaseMutex ( g_hMutex ) ;
        return ;
    }

    // Remove this item from the array.
    g_shared_NotifyData[ i ].dwOwnerPID   = 0 ;
    g_shared_NotifyData[ i ].iNotifyType  = 0 ;
    g_shared_NotifyData[ i ].hWndCreate   = NULL ;
    g_shared_NotifyData[ i ].bDestroy     = FALSE ;
    g_shared_NotifyData[ i ].iSearchType  = 0 ;
    g_shared_NotifyData[ i ].szTitle[ 0 ] = _T ( '\0' ) ;
```

```
    // Bump down the master item count.
    g_shared_iUsedSlots-- ;

    // Bump down this process's item count.
    g_iThisProcessItems-- ;

    TRACE ( _T ( "RemoveNotifyTitle - Removed an item!\n" ) ) ;

    ReleaseMutex ( g_hMutex ) ;

    // If this is the last item for this process, unhook this process's
    // hook.
    if ( ( 0 == g_iThisProcessItems ) && ( NULL != g_hHook ) )
    {
        if ( FALSE == UnhookWindowsHookEx ( g_hHook ) )
        {
            TRACE ( _T ( "UnhookWindowsHookEx failed!\n" ) ) ;
        }
        g_hHook = NULL ;
    }

}

HWND TNOTIFYHLP_DLLINTERFACE __stdcall
    CheckNotifyCreateTitle ( HANDLE hItem )
{
    return ( (HWND)CheckNotifyItem ( hItem , TRUE ) ) ;
}

BOOL TNOTIFYHLP_DLLINTERFACE __stdcall
    CheckNotifyDestroyTitle ( HANDLE hItem )
{
    return ( (BOOL)CheckNotifyItem ( hItem , FALSE ) ) ;
}

/*//////////////////////////////////////////////////////////////////////
// INTERNAL IMPLEMENTATION STARTS HERE
//////////////////////////////////////////////////////////////////////*/

static LONG_PTR __stdcall CheckNotifyItem ( HANDLE hItem , BOOL bCreate )
{
    // Check the value.
    INT_PTR i = (INT_PTR)hItem ;
    if ( ( i < 0 ) || ( i > TOTAL_NOTIFY_SLOTS ) )
    {
        TRACE ( _T ( "CheckNotifyItem : Invalid handle!\n" ) ) ;
        return ( NULL ) ;
    }

    LONG_PTR lRet = 0 ;

    // Get the mutex.
    DWORD dwRet = WaitForSingleObject ( g_hMutex , k_WAITLIMIT ) ;
```

```
    if ( WAIT_TIMEOUT == dwRet )
    {
        TRACE ( _T ( "CheckNotifyItem : Wait on mutex timed out!\n" ) );
        return ( NULL ) ;
    }

    // If all slots are empty, there's nothing to do.
    if ( 0 == g_shared_iUsedSlots )
    {
        ReleaseMutex ( g_hMutex ) ;
        return ( NULL ) ;
    }

    // Check the item requested.
    if ( TRUE == bCreate )
    {
        // If the HWND value isn't NULL, return that value and NULL it
        // out in the table.
        if ( NULL != g_shared_NotifyData[ i ].hWndCreate )
        {
            lRet = (LONG_PTR)g_shared_NotifyData[ i ].hWndCreate ;
            g_shared_NotifyData[ i ].hWndCreate = NULL ;
        }
    }
    else
    {
        if ( FALSE != g_shared_NotifyData[ i ].bDestroy )
        {
            lRet = TRUE ;
            g_shared_NotifyData[ i ].bDestroy = FALSE ;
        }
    }

    ReleaseMutex ( g_hMutex ) ;

    return ( lRet ) ;
}

static void __stdcall CheckTableMatch ( int     iNotifyType ,
                                        HWND    hWnd        ,
                                        LPCTSTR szTitle      )
{
    // Grab the mutex.
    DWORD dwRet = WaitForSingleObject ( g_hMutex , k_WAITLIMIT ) ;
    if ( WAIT_TIMEOUT == dwRet )
    {
        TRACE ( _T ( "CheckTableMatch : Wait on mutex timed out!\n" ) );
        return ;
    }

    // The table shouldn't be empty, but never assume anything.
    if ( 0 == g_shared_iUsedSlots )
```

```
{
    ReleaseMutex ( g_hMutex ) ;
    TRACE ( _T ( "CheckTableMatch called on an empty table!\n" ) ) ;
    return ;
}


// Search through the table.
for ( int i = 0 ; i < TOTAL_NOTIFY_SLOTS ; i++ )
{
    // Does this entry have something in it, and does the type of
    // notification match?
    if ( ( _T ( '\0' ) != g_shared_NotifyData[ i ].szTitle[ 0 ] ) &&
         ( g_shared_NotifyData[ i ].iNotifyType & iNotifyType   )  )
    {
        BOOL bMatch = FALSE ;
        // Perform the match.
        switch ( g_shared_NotifyData[ i ].iSearchType )
        {
            case ANTS_EXACTMATCH    :
                // This is simple.
                if ( 0 == lstrcmp ( g_shared_NotifyData[i].szTitle ,
                                    szTitle                       ) )
                {
                    bMatch = TRUE ;
                }
                break ;
            case ANTS_BEGINMATCH    :
                if ( 0 ==
                        _tcsnccmp ( g_shared_NotifyData[i].szTitle ,
                                    szTitle                        ,
                           _tcslen(g_shared_NotifyData[i].szTitle)))
                {
                    bMatch = TRUE ;
                }
                break ;
            case ANTS_ANYLOCMATCH   :
                if ( NULL != _tcsstr ( szTitle                     ,
                                   g_shared_NotifyData[i].szTitle ))
                {
                    bMatch = TRUE ;
                }
                break ;
            default                 :
                TRACE ( _T ( "CheckTableMatch invalid " ) \
                        _T ( "search type!!!\n" ) ) ;
                ReleaseMutex ( g_hMutex ) ;
                return ;
                break ;
        }
        // Tell them, Johnny. Do we have a match?
        if ( TRUE == bMatch )
        {
```

```
                // If this is a destroy notification, stick "1" in the
                // table.
                if ( ANTN_DESTROYWINDOW == iNotifyType )
                {
                    g_shared_NotifyData[ i ].bDestroy = TRUE ;
                }
                else
                {
                    // Otherwise, stick the HWND in the table.
                    g_shared_NotifyData[ i ].hWndCreate = hWnd ;
                }
            }
        }
    }
    ReleaseMutex ( g_hMutex ) ;
}

LRESULT CALLBACK CallWndRetProcHook ( int    nCode  ,
                                      WPARAM wParam ,
                                      LPARAM lParam  )
{
    // Buffer for storing the window title
    TCHAR szBuff[ MAX_PATH ] ;

    // Always pass the message to the next hook before I do any
    // processing. This way I don't forget and I can do my processing
    // in peace.
    LRESULT lRet = CallNextHookEx ( g_hHook , nCode , wParam , lParam );

    // The docs say never to mess around with a negative code, so I
    // don't.
    if ( nCode < 0 )
    {
        return ( lRet ) ;
    }

    // Get the message structure. Why are there three (or more)
    // different message structures?  What's wrong with consistently
    // using the stock ol' MSG for all message/proc hooks?
    PCWPRETSTRUCT pMsg = (PCWPRETSTRUCT)lParam ;

    // No caption, no work to do
    LONG lStyle = GetWindowLong ( pMsg->hwnd , GWL_STYLE ) ;
    if ( WS_CAPTION != ( lStyle & WS_CAPTION ) )
    {
        return ( lRet ) ;
    }

    // The WM_DESTROY messages are copacetic for both dialog boxes and
    // normal windows. Just get the caption and check for a match.
    if ( WM_DESTROY == pMsg->message )
    {
        if ( 0 != GetWindowText ( pMsg->hwnd , szBuff , MAX_PATH ) )
```

```
        {
            CheckTableMatch ( ANTN_DESTROYWINDOW , pMsg->hwnd , szBuff ) ;
        }
        return ( lRet ) ;
    }

    // Window creation isn't as clean as window destruction.

    // Get the window class. If it is a true dialog box, the
    // WM_INITDIALOG is all I need.
    if ( 0 == GetClassName ( pMsg->hwnd , szBuff , MAX_PATH ) )
    {
#ifdef _DEBUG
        TCHAR szBuff[ 50 ] ;
        wsprintf ( szBuff                                        ,
                   _T ( "GetClassName failed for HWND : 0x%08X\n" ) ,
                   pMsg->hwnd                                    ) ;
        TRACE ( szBuff ) ;
#endif
        // There's not much point in going on.
        return ( lRet ) ;
    }
    if ( 0 == lstrcmpi ( szBuff , _T ( "#32770" ) ) )
    {
        // The only message I need to check is WM_INITDIALOG.
        if ( WM_INITDIALOG == pMsg->message )
        {
            // Get the caption of the dialog box.
            if ( 0 != GetWindowText ( pMsg->hwnd , szBuff , MAX_PATH ) )
            {
                CheckTableMatch ( ANTN_CREATEWINDOW ,
                                  pMsg->hwnd        ,
                                  szBuff            ) ;
            }
        }
        return ( lRet ) ;
    }
    // That took care of true dialog boxes. Start figuring out what to do
    // for actual windows.

    if ( WM_CREATE == pMsg->message )
    {
        // Very few windows set the title in WM_CREATE.
        // However, a few do and they don't use WM_SETTEXT, so I have
        // to check.
        if ( 0 != GetWindowText ( pMsg->hwnd , szBuff , MAX_PATH ) )
        {
            CheckTableMatch ( ANTN_CREATEWINDOW ,
                              pMsg->hwnd        ,
                              szBuff            ) ;
        }
    }
    else if ( WM_SETTEXT == pMsg->message )
```

```
    {
        // I always default to WM_SETTEXT because that's how captions
        // get set. Unfortunately, some applications, such as Internet
        // Explorer, seem to call WM_SETTEXT a bunch of times with the
        // same title. To keep this hook simple, I just report
        // the WM_SETTEXT instead of maintaining all sorts of weird,
        // hard-to-debug data structures that keep track of the windows
        // that called WM_SETTEXT previously.
        if ( NULL != pMsg->lParam )
        {
            CheckTableMatch ( ANTN_CREATEWINDOW     ,
                              pMsg->hwnd            ,
                              (LPCTSTR)pMsg->lParam   ) ;
        }
    }

    return ( lRet ) ;
}
```

Although the `TNotify` implementation was a brainteaser in some ways, I was pleased at how few troubles I experienced implementing it. If you do want to extend the hook code, be aware that debugging systemwide hooks isn't a simple endeavor. Your best bet is to use remote debugging as I described in Chapter 5. The other way you can debug systemwide hooks is to resort to `printf`-style debugging. Using DebugView from *www.sysinternals.com*, you can watch all the `OutputDebugString` calls to see the state of your hook.

Implementing TESTREC.EXE

With the Tester DLL out of the way, it was time to provide the keystroke and mouse recording capabilities in TESTREC.EXE. When it comes to recording input, there's only one clean way to do it on Windows operating systems: use a journal record hook. There's nothing very exciting about journal hooks except handling the `WM_CANCELJOURNAL` message properly. When the user presses Ctrl+Alt+Delete, the operating system terminates any active journal record hooks. This makes sense because it would be a pretty serious security breach to allow an application to record the keystrokes that make up the user's password. To handle `WM_CANCELJOURNAL` in a manner that keeps the implementation details hidden, I used a message filter to monitor for it coming through. You can see all the hook details in HOOKCODE.CPP in the Tester\TestRec directory.

Processing Keystrokes

The keystroke recording code mainly involves keeping straight what's going on with the Shift, Ctrl, and Alt keys. Before I discuss some of the particulars of wrestling with the individual keystrokes, you'll probably want to look at Figures

16-2 through 16-4, which is a simplified graph of all the keystroke states that the recording code handles.

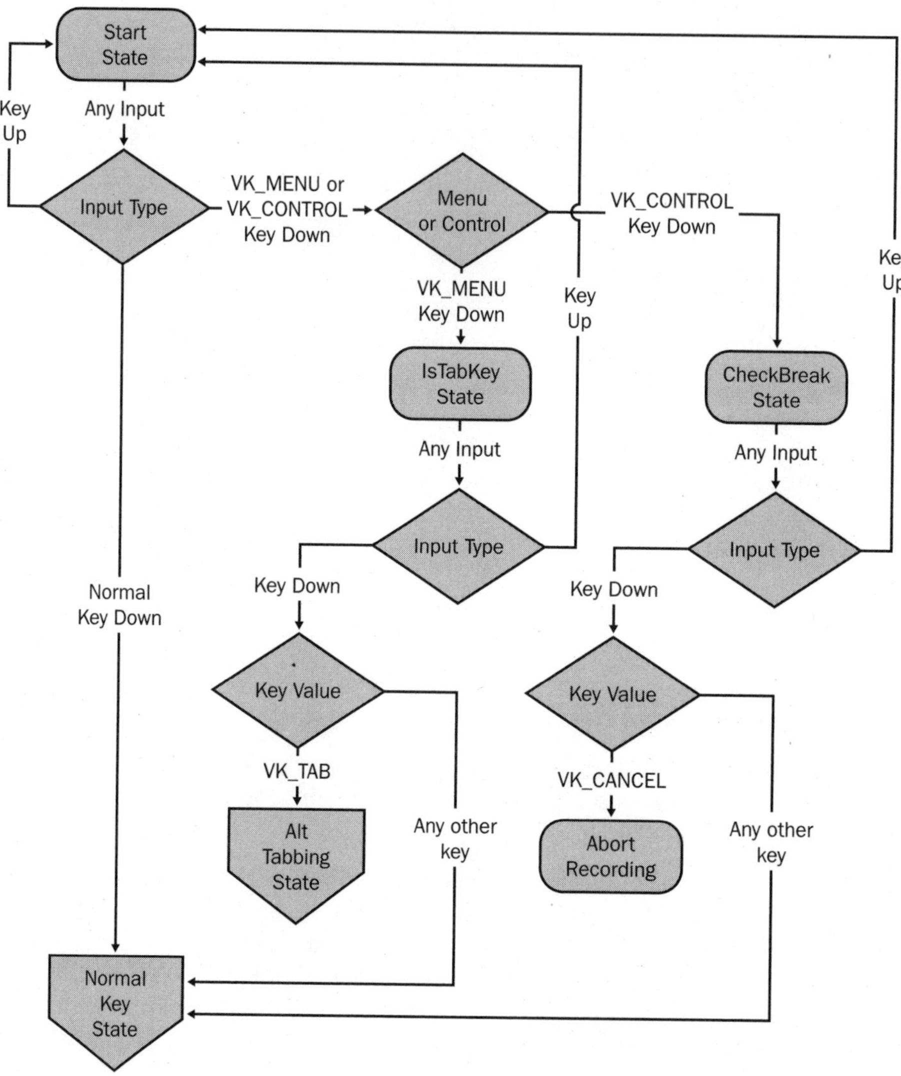

Figure 16-2 Keystroke recording start, tab key, and check break state machines

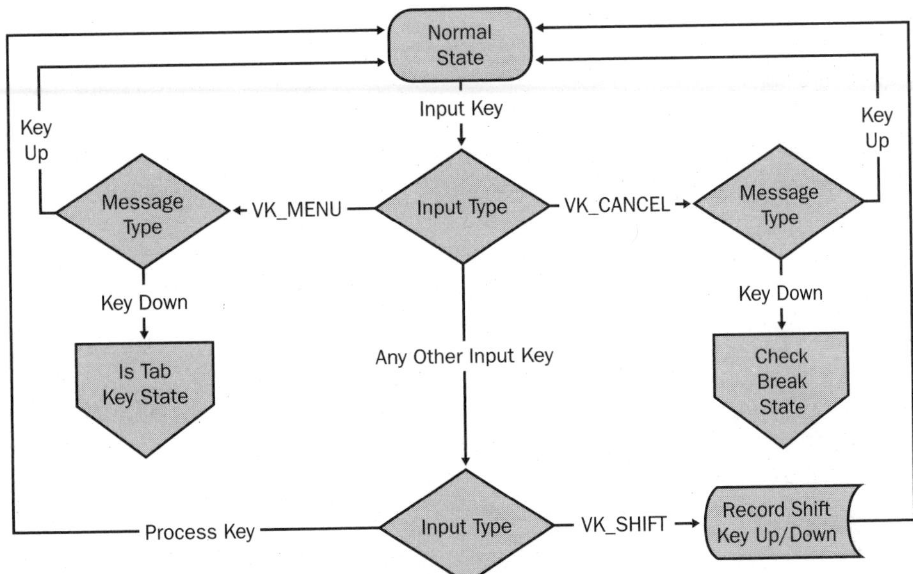

Figure 16-3 Keystroke recording normal key state machine

The first challenge to keystroke recording is getting the keystrokes in a human-readable form from the journal hook. If you've never had the joy of messing with virtual codes and scan codes, you don't know what you're in for! Additionally, I found that the keys for some characters received by the journal record hook were quite a bit different from what I expected.

The last time I messed around with keyboard processing at this level was way back in the old MS-DOS days. (I think my age is showing!) Consequently, I brought some misconceptions to the problem. For example, the first time I typed an exclamation point, I expected to see that exact character come through the journal record hook. What I got instead was a Shift character followed by a 1. That's exactly what the keystroke sequence is on the U.S. English keyboard. The problem is that I wanted any key sequences that I output to be mostly understandable. The `SendKeys` sequence "+1" is technically correct, but you have to go through some mental gymnastics to realize that you're really looking at the "!" character.

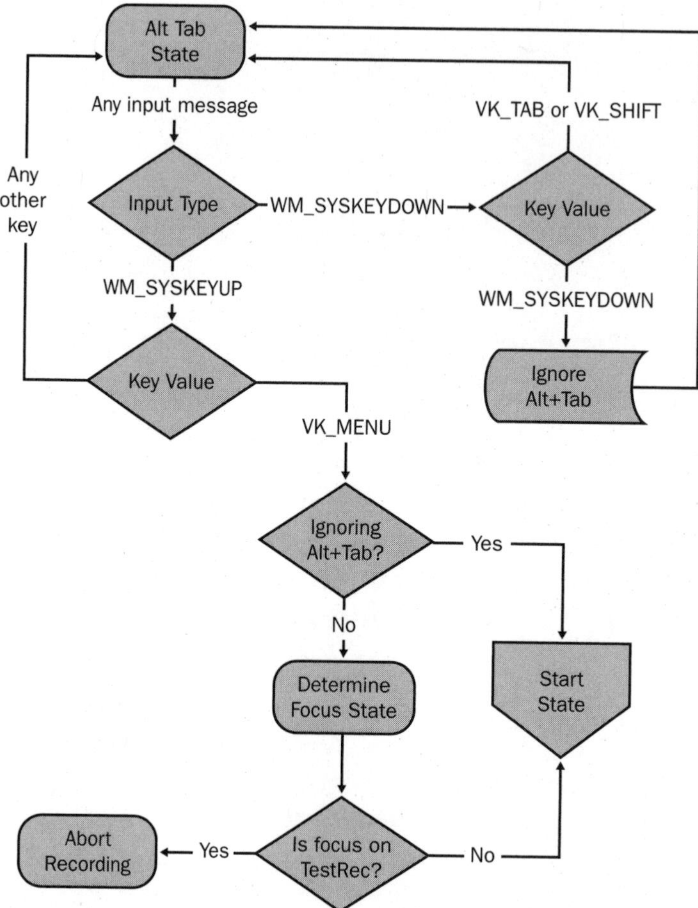

Figure 16-4 Keystroke recording Alt+Tab state machine

To make TESTREC.EXE as useful as possible, I needed to do some special processing to make the output strings readable. Basically, you check the keyboard state to see whether the shift key is down, and if it is, convert the key to its readable form. Fortunately, the `GetKeyboardState` and `ToUnicode` API functions take care of the problem of getting the real key. The best way for you to get the gist of this keystroke processing is to look at `CRecordingEngine::NormalKeyState` in Listing 16-4.

```
void CRecordingEngine :: NormalKeyState ( PEVENTMSG pMsg )
{
    // The state to shift to after processing the key passed in.
    eKeyStates eShiftToState = eNormalKey ;

    UINT vkCode = LOBYTE ( pMsg->paramL ) ;

#ifdef _DEBUG
    {
        STATETRACE (_T("RECSTATE: Normal : ")) ;
        if ( ( WM_KEYDOWN == pMsg->message    ) ||
             ( WM_SYSKEYDOWN == pMsg->message )    )
        {
            STATETRACE ( _T( "KEYDOWN " ) ) ;
        }
        else
        {
            STATETRACE ( _T ( "KEYUP " ) ) ;
        }
        TCHAR szName [ 100 ] ;
        GetKeyNameText ( pMsg->paramH << 16 , szName , 100 ) ;
        CharUpper ( szName ) ;
        STATETRACE ( _T ( "%c %d %04X (%s)\n" ) ,
                      vkCode                ,
                      vkCode                ,
                      vkCode                ,
                      szName                 ) ;

    }
#endif

    // Check that this is not key that will cause a transition out.
    switch ( vkCode )
    {
        case VK_CONTROL :
            // An CTRL down can come through after a ALT key is already
            // down.
            if ( ( WM_KEYDOWN    == pMsg->message ) ||
                 ( WM_SYSKEYDOWN == pMsg->message )    )
            {
                eShiftToState = eCheckBreak ;
                STATETRACE ( _T ( "RECSTATE: Looking for BREAK key\n"));
            }
            else
            {
                m_cKeyBuff += _T( "{CTRL UP}" ) ;
```

Listing 16-4 `CRecordingEngine::NormalKeyState`

```
            m_iKeyBuffKeys++ ;
        }
        m_iKeyBuffKeys++ ;
        break ;
    case VK_MENU    :
        if ( ( WM_KEYDOWN    == pMsg->message ) ||
             ( WM_SYSKEYDOWN == pMsg->message )   )
        {
            eShiftToState = eIsTabKey ;
            STATETRACE (_T("RECSTATE: Looking for TAB key\n")) ;
        }
        else
        {
            m_cKeyBuff += _T( "{ALT UP}" ) ;
            m_iKeyBuffKeys++ ;
        }
        m_iKeyBuffKeys++ ;
        break ;

    case VK_SHIFT   :
        if ( ( WM_KEYDOWN    == pMsg->message ) ||
             ( WM_SYSKEYDOWN == pMsg->message )   )
        {
            // Make sure I only do this once!
            if ( FALSE == m_bShiftDown )
            {
                // The shift key is down so set my flags.
                m_bShiftDown = TRUE ;
                m_bShiftDownInString = FALSE ;
            }
        }
        else
        {
            // If I put a {SHIFT DOWN} earlier, I need to match up
            // with a {SHIFT UP}
            if ( TRUE == m_bShiftDownInString )
            {
                m_cKeyBuff += _T ( "{SHIFT UP}" ) ;
                m_iKeyBuffKeys++ ;

                m_bShiftDownInString = FALSE ;
            }
            // The shift key has popped up.
            m_bShiftDown = FALSE ;
        }
        break ;
    default :
        // It's a normal key.

        // If it's not a key down, I don't care.
        if ( ( WM_KEYDOWN    == pMsg->message ) ||
             ( WM_SYSKEYDOWN == pMsg->message )   )
```

```
        {
            //TRACE ( "vkCode = %04X\n" , vkCode ) ;

            // Is there a key string for the virtual code?
            if ( NULL != g_KeyStrings[ vkCode ].szString  )
            {
                // Is the shift key down?  If so, I need to ensure
                // that I add the {SHIFT DOWN} before adding this
                // key.
                if ( ( TRUE  == m_bShiftDown          ) &&
                     ( FALSE == m_bShiftDownInString )    )
                {
                    m_cKeyBuff += _T ( "{SHIFT DOWN}" ) ;
                    m_iKeyBuffKeys++ ;
                    m_bShiftDownInString = TRUE ;
                }
                // Add the key to the key list.
                m_cKeyBuff += g_KeyStrings[ vkCode ].szString ;
            }
            else
            {
                // I need to translate the key into it's character
                // equivalent. Getting the keyboard state and using
                // ToAscii will properly convert things like
                // "{SHIFT DOWN}1{SHIFT UP}" into "!"

                // First step is to get the current keyboard state.
                BYTE byState [ 256 ] ;

                GetKeyboardState ( byState ) ;

                // Now do the conversion
                TCHAR cConv[3] = { _T ( '\0' ) } ;
                TCHAR cChar ;
#ifdef _UNICODE
                int iRet = ToUnicode ( vkCode                ,
                                       pMsg->paramH          ,
                                       byState               ,
                                       (LPWORD)&cConv        ,
                                       sizeof ( cConv ) /
                                        sizeof ( TCHAR )     ,
                                       0                     ) ;

#else
                int iRet = ToAscii ( vkCode        ,
                                     pMsg->paramH  ,
                                     byState       ,
                                     (LPWORD)&cConv ,
                                     0             ) ;
#endif
                if ( 2 == iRet )
                {
                    // This is an international keystroke.
                    ASSERT ( !"I gotta handle this!" ) ;
```

```
                    }

                    // If it didn't convert, don't use cChar!
                    if ( 0 == iRet )
                    {
                        cChar = (TCHAR)vkCode ;
                    }
                    else
                    {
                        // Before I can use the character, I need to
                        // check if the CTRL key is down. If so,
                        // ToAscii/ToUnicode return the ASCII control
                        // code value. Since I want the key, I'll need
                        // to do some work to get it.
                        SHORT sCtrlDown =
                                   GetAsyncKeyState ( VK_CONTROL ) ;
                        if ( 0xFFFF8000 == ( 0xFFFF8000 & sCtrlDown ))
                        {
                            // Control is down so I need to look if
                            // the CAPSLOCK and SHIFT keys are down.
                            BOOL bCapsLock =
                                ( 0xFFFF8000 == ( 0xFFFF8000 &
                                    GetAsyncKeyState ( VK_CAPITAL)));
                            if ( TRUE == bCapsLock )
                            {
                                // CAPSLOCK is down so if SHIFT is down,
                                // use the lowercase version of the key.
                                if ( TRUE == m_bShiftDown )
                                {
// 'variable' : conversion from 'type' to 'type' of greater size
#pragma warning ( disable : 4312 )
                                    cChar = (TCHAR)
                                        CharLower ( (LPTSTR)vkCode );
#pragma warning ( default : 4312 )
                                }
                                else
                                {
                                    // Us the upper case version.
                                    cChar = (TCHAR)vkCode ;
                                }
                            }
                            else
                            {
                                // CAPSLOCK is not down so just check
                                // the shift state.
                                if ( TRUE == m_bShiftDown )
                                {
                                    cChar = (TCHAR)vkCode ;
                                }
                                else
                                {
// 'variable' : conversion from 'type' to 'type' of greater size
#pragma warning ( disable : 4312 )
```

```
                                    cChar = (TCHAR)
                                        CharLower ( (LPTSTR)vkCode );
#pragma warning ( default : 4312 )
                                }
                            }
                        }
                        else
                        {
                            // The CTRL key is not down so I can use the
                            // converted key directly.
                            cChar = cConv[ 0 ] ;
                        }
                    }

                    switch ( cChar )
                    {
                        // Brackets, braces, and tildes have to be
                        // specially handled. All other keys are
                        // just slapped on the output list.
                        case _T ( '[' ) :
                            m_cKeyBuff += _T ( "{[}" ) ;
                            break ;
                        case _T ( ']' ) :
                            m_cKeyBuff += _T ( "{]}" ) ;
                            break ;
                        case _T ( '~' ) :
                            m_cKeyBuff += _T ( "{~}" ) ;
                            break ;
                        case _T ( '{' ) :
                            m_cKeyBuff += _T ( "{{}" ) ;
                            break ;
                        case _T ( '}' ) :
                            m_cKeyBuff += _T ( "{}}" ) ;
                            break ;
                        default :
                            m_cKeyBuff += cChar ;
                    }
                }
                // Bump up the number of keys processed.
                m_iKeyBuffKeys++ ;

                if ( ( m_iKeyBuffKeys > 20          ) ||
                     (  m_cKeyBuff.Length ( ) > 50 )    )
                {
                    DoKeyStrokes ( TRUE ) ;
                }
            }

            break ;
    }

    // Set the state to move to after this key is processed.
    eCurrKeyState = eShiftToState ;
}
```

The only special processing I do when recording keystrokes is handle Alt+Tab operations. Although I could've recorded the actual Alt and Tab keys, doing that might have prevented the script from running the next time because I'd have to keep the application in the exact same location in the top window z-order with the same number of applications running. Consequently, instead of recording the keystrokes, I shift to a state in which I wait for you to release the Alt key and, on the next journal input of any kind, I determine which application has the focus and generate the appropriate code for the script.

Processing Mouse Input

When I first started looking at adding the mouse support, my first big surprise was realizing that the keystroke recording I had originally implemented wasn't going to handle adding the mouse input to it. My original keystroke recording code had gone to quite a bit of trouble to generate sequences that optimized the Ctrl, Shift, and Alt processing to ensure a single algorithm generated a complete statement for `PlayInput` that put the Ctrl, Shift, or Alt key down and popped it up and the end of a single statement. When I got to thinking about adding the mouse input, I realized that keeping that option might generate a `PlayInput` statement of tens of thousands of characters! To even begin handling the mouse input, I had to change the keystroke recording code to generate special codes such as `{ALT DOWN}` and `{ALT UP}` so that the generated statements would be chewable by whatever scripting language you used.

After taking care of the Ctrl, Alt, and Shift processing, I next had to figure out how I was going to handle single mouse clicks, double-clicks, and drags. What makes the processing fun is that the journal hook I'm using to record keys and mouse moves reports only `WM_xBUTTONDOWN` and `WM_xBUTTONUP` messages. I would've much preferred to get `WM_xBUTTONDBLCLK` messages to make my life easier. This processing was screaming to be a state machine like the one I developed for the keystroke recording. Figures 16-5 and 16-6 show the mouse state machine that I implemented in RECORDINGENGINE.H/.CPP. Keep in mind that I also had to do this state tracking for each button on the system. The mentions of Slot 0 and Slot 1 were to keep track of the previous event for comparison purposes.

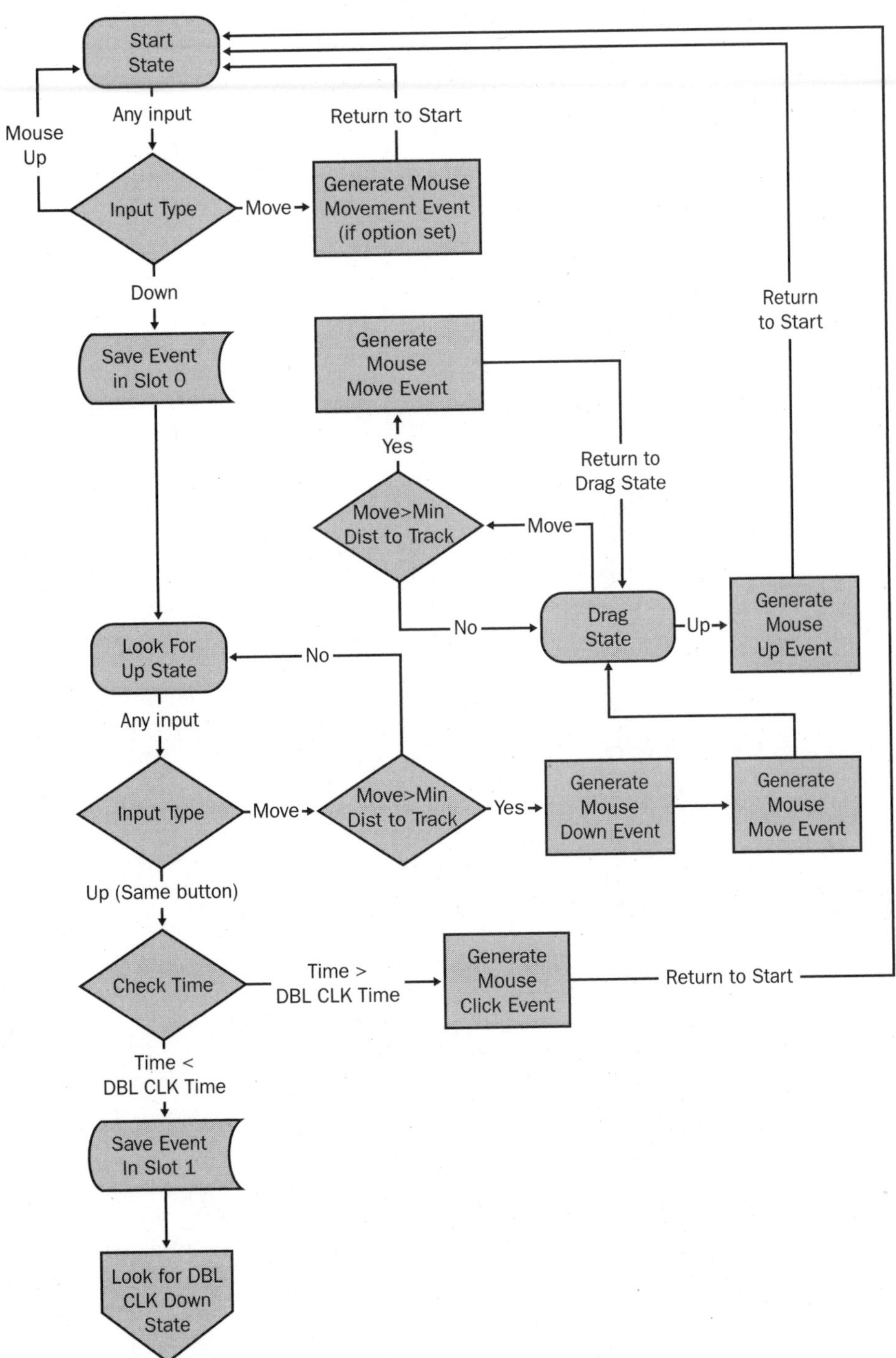

Figure 16-5 Mouse recording normal state machine

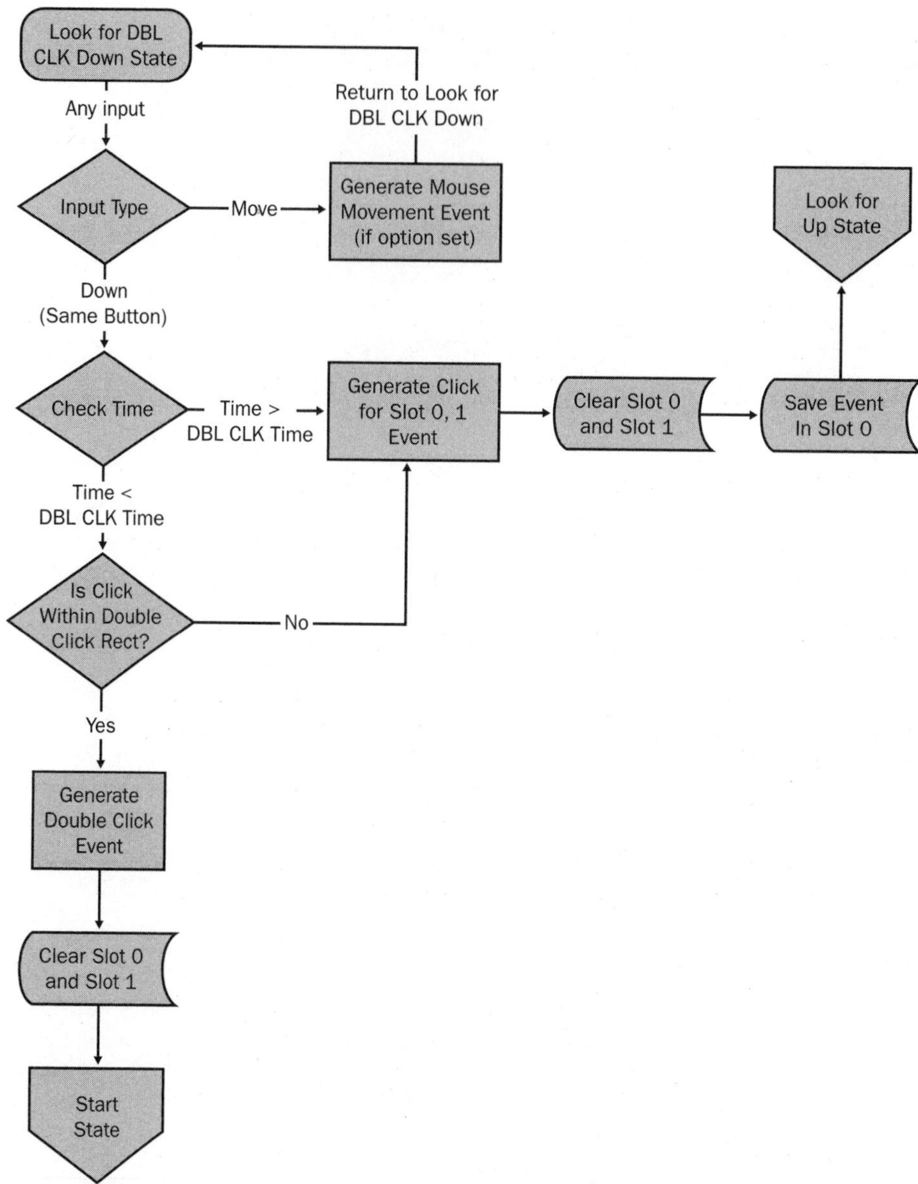

Figure 16-6 Mouse recording double click state machine

After grinding through the code to implement the recording, everything looked good until I started hard testing. Immediately, I saw problems. Recording scripts as I was drawing items in Microsoft Paint worked just fine. Playing them back was a problem. For example, I'd draw a circle freehand but the playback would look like a straight line through the origin of the circle, then the rest of the circle would be drawn. I went back and thoroughly examined my recording and playback code, but found nothing wrong. As it turns out, the script was pumping a bunch of `MOVETO` instructions very quickly, and the Windows operating system input queue dumps extra input when it's getting full. What I needed to do was slow down the mouse message processing so that all the mouse events would have enough time to execute. I was using the `SendInput` function to do the actual playback, so my first idea was to set the time on each event in the `INPUT` structure to allow extra time for the mouse events. That didn't work, and I found that setting the timing long enough would cause the computer to kick into power-save mode, which certainly freaked me out the first time it happened.

I looked at another approach. I thought that since my code parses the input commands into an array of `INPUT` structures to pass to `SendInput`, I might be able to spin through the array one at a time and do extra pauses on the mouse events. The question of how long to wait became an experiment. After playing around, I found it best to sleep for 25 milliseconds before and after each mouse event. This means that recorded scripts will play back much slower with mouse input than when you recorded them.

What's Next for Tester?

As I mentioned earlier, Tester does two things well: recording scripts and playing keystrokes. As with all the utilities in this book, you're welcome to find ways to improve Tester if you're so inclined. Here are some possible enhancements you might pursue:

- Add wrapper classes such as `TListBox`, `TTreeControl`, and `TRadioButton` so that you can check various states and verify that control items contain the proper data. With these classes, you can start validating controls and writing more complicated scripts. You might want to look at the MSAA interfaces to make this work easier.
- Add support during recording for on-the-fly entering of validation and verification code and other necessary code.
- Update the TestRec application to be a little friendlier and offer more help while developing scripts. For example, you could add knowledge of the supported Tester objects to help other developers write their own scripts.

- Add language output options so that you can utilize compiled languages such as C# and Visual Basic .NET (or Microsoft Visual Object Assembler, if Microsoft ever releases it).
- Right now TestRec and Tester support only the US English keyboard. You might want to add true international support to both applications.

Summary

Performing UI unit tests can be a challenge. This chapter introduced a solid utility, Tester, that will automate your testing by recording keystroke and mouse input and playing them back to your application. Although it falls short of being as complete as a commercial regression-testing tool, Tester will certainly save wear and tear on your wrists.

I hope that Tester shows you how valuable tools that automate your application can be. If your application is complex enough, I'd recommend investing in a commercial regression-testing tool so that you can speed up your unit testing. If you spend a little time planning how you're going to use the regression-testing tool, you can grow a system in which your developers are contributing regression scripts that the QA department can then roll into the master QA automated testing scripts. If you play your cards right, your main QA suites will almost appear to write themselves.

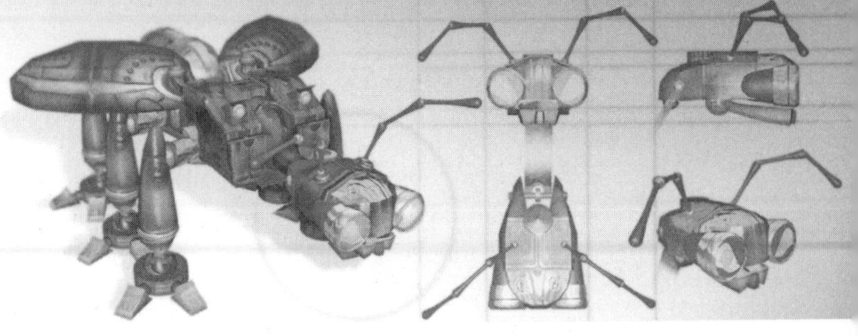

17

The Debug C Run-Time Library and Memory Management

Even after I wrote the first edition of this book, I got many, many questions about memory corruption and memory leaks, and I still do. If developers would just stop using memory in their programs, they wouldn't have so many problems. Right. And if we'd all stop breathing, we'd never have any trouble with our lungs. Memory is the elixir of life for your C and C++ programs, and if you want to do more about memory corruption and memory leaks than just wish they would go away, you need to be proactive about handling them. The first step you need to take is to learn how to use the Microsoft debug C run-time library.

The complexities of memory debugging are legendary and one of the prime motivators for Microsoft to develop the .NET concept. With memory taken care of for you because of the common language runtime (CLR) garbage collector, .NET eliminates probably 50 percent of the bugs you'd normally deal with in the Microsoft Win32 and Microsoft Win64 world. Of course, if raw speed is vital to your application, you'll be dealing with C++ and potential memory woes for a long time to come.

Developers working in C and C++ get to have all the fun of wrangling memory. C and C++ offer all sorts of programming freedom, but they also provide the opportunity to do much more than just shoot yourself in the foot; you can blow off your whole leg when you make even a small mistake. Fortunately, the C run-time (CRT) library developers heard our cries of anguish and, starting a million Internet years ago with Microsoft Visual C++ 4, have built in a wonderful feature: the debug CRT (DCRT) library.

Oddly enough, many C and C++ developers don't seem to realize that the DCRT library exists. The reason the library is something of a mystery is that by default much of it is turned off. Once you get the proper flags switched on, however, you'll find out what you've been missing. In this chapter, I'll start by introducing the DCRT library and build two extensions, MemDumperValidator and MemStress, that will provide you with even more functionality while you're using the library. After introducing the DCRT, I'll discuss the various issues related to memory debugging such as the operating system heaps, how to track down wild writes, and how to use these free and amazing tools from Microsoft that help you with memory issues: the PageHeap and the Application Verifier. Finally, as I promised in Chapter 2, I'll cover the amazing run-time check (`/RTCx`) and security (`/GS`) switches now offered by Visual C++ to make your memory debugging and security better than ever.

Features of the Debug C Run-Time Library

The main claim to fame for the DCRT library is its wonderful heap memory tracking support. All the memory allocated through standard C/C++ memory allocation functions, such as `new`, `malloc`, and `calloc`, can be tracked in debug builds. The tracking checks for memory underwrites, in which your program writes past the beginning of a block of memory, and memory overwrites, in which your program writes past the end of a block of memory. All those errors are reported through an assertion from the DCRT itself. The tracking also monitors and reports memory leaks in your application when the application ends because of calls to `OutputDebugString`, whose output appears in the Output window of the debugger. If you've been writing Microsoft Foundation Class (MFC) library programs, you've probably noticed the memory leak reports when your application ends; those leak reports come from the DCRT library. MFC partially turns on the DCRT library for you automatically.

Another neat feature of the DCRT library is the reporting subsystem, which you and I would call trace, through its `_RPTn` and `RPTFn` macros and assertion support. I introduced the DCRT library assertion support in Chapter 3 and explained some of the issues associated with using it. As I mentioned, the DCRT library assertions are good, but they destroy the last error value and therefore could cause debug and release builds to behave differently. For your assertions, I strongly recommend that you use the `SUPERASSERT` assertion code that's part of BUGSLAYERUTIL.DLL.

Another nice feature of the DCRT library is that its source code is included with the compiler. Table 17-1 lists all the files that make up the DCRT library. If you elected to install the CRT library source code when you installed Microsoft

Visual Studio .NET, which I highly recommend doing, you can find all the CRT and DCRT library source code in the <Visual Studio .NET Installation Directory>\VC7\CRT\SRC directory.

Table 17-1 Debug C Run-Time Library Source Files

Source File	Description
DBGDEL.CPP	The debug global `delete` operator.
DBGHEAP.C	All the debug heap-handling functions.
DBGHOOK.C	The stub memory allocation hook function.
DBGINT.H	The internal debug headers and functions.
DBGNEW.CPP	The debug global `new` operator.
DBGRPT.C	The debug reporting functions.
CRTDBG.H	The header file you include. This file is in the standard include directory.

Common Debugging Question

Why do I need the debug C run-time library if I'm using an error detection tool like BoundsChecker?

Error detection tools such as Compuware's BoundsChecker and Rational Software's Purify automatically handle memory underwrites, memory overwrites, and memory leaks. If you use one of these tools, you might think that using the DCRT library isn't worth your time and effort. Technically, that's true, but to ensure that you find all your memory problems, you need to run your application under your error detection tool every time anyone on the team runs a debug build of the application. "Anyone" includes you, your fellow developers, and if you followed my advice from Chapter 2, even your quality engineers. I just don't see everyone being that vigilant.

Using the DCRT library is like having good fire or theft insurance. You hope you'll never need to use the insurance, but if you do, it can be a lifesaver. Any time you can validate data in your application, you should. The DCRT library doesn't impose a drastic performance hit, and it can unearth some outstanding bugs. You should always use it—even if you have all the tools in the world.

Using the Debug C Run-Time Library

The first step in using the .DCRT library is to include it and turn it on so that you can start benefiting from the memory tracking as early in your project as possible. In your main precompiled header file (or whatever header file all the source files in your project will include), add the following line before any `#include` directive in your precompiled header file:

```
#define _CRTDBG_MAP_ALLOC
```

After the rest of your header files, include CRTDBG.H. Defining `_CRTDBG_MAP_ALLOC` will redirect normal calls to memory allocation and deallocation functions to special versions that record the source file and line number for each allocation or deallocation.

The second step you need to take is to turn on the DCRT library heap code. As I mentioned at the beginning of this chapter, by default, most of the features of the DCRT library are turned off. The documentation states that most of the features are turned off to keep the code small and to increase execution speed. Although size and speed are important for a release build, the whole point of a debug build is to find bugs! The increased size and reduced speed of debug builds is inconsequential. So don't hesitate to turn on all the features you think will help you. The `_CrtSetDbgFlag` function takes a set of flags, shown in Table 17-2, that can be OR'd together to turn on various options in the DCRT library.

Table 17-2 Debug C Run-Time Library Flags

Flag	Description
`_CRTDBG_ALLOC_MEM_DF`	Turn on the debug heap allocations, and use the memory block identifiers. This is the only flag that's on by default.
`_CRTDBG_CHECK_ALWAYS_DF`	Check and validate all memory on each allocation and deallocation request. Turning on this flag catches any underwrites and overwrites as close to when they happen as possible.
`_CRTDBG_CHECK_CRT_DF`	Include `_CRT_BLOCK` memory allocations in all leak detection and state differences. In general, unless you're having a problem with the CRT library functions, you shouldn't turn on this flag. If you do, you'll get CRT library memory allocation reports. Because the CRT library must keep some memory allocated until the true end of the program, which is after the leaked memory reporting, you'll see a large number of false positive leak reports on that memory.

Table 17-2 Debug C Run-Time Library Flags *(continued)*

Flag	Description
_CRTDBG_DELAY_FREE_MEM_DF	Instead of truly freeing memory, keep the block allocated and in the internal heap list. The blocks are filled with the value 0xDD, so you know the memory is freed when you're looking at it in the debugger. By not freeing the memory, this flag allows you to test your program under memory stress conditions. Additionally, the DCRT library will check that you don't access the deallocated block again by ensuring that all values in the block remain 0xDD. You should always turn on this flag, but keep in mind that your program's memory requirements can easily double because the deallocated memory isn't reclaimed by the heap.
_CRTDBG_LEAK_CHECK_DF	Check for memory leaks at the end of the program. Turning on this extremely useful flag is mandatory.

After building your application with the appropriate #includes and #defines, and calling _CrtSetDbgFlag, you now have the DCRT library, with its slew of functions that help you control and report on memory usage, fully available. You can call these functions at any time. Many of them lend themselves to being used in assertions, so you can sprinkle them around freely and catch your memory problems close to the source.

The Bug in the DCRT

If you follow the instructions I just gave you in the previous section, your source code will look something like that shown in Listing 17-1. At the top of the listing, after the rest of the headers, you see the _CRTDBG_MAP_ALLOC define and the include file for CRTDBG.H. The first call inside main is to _CrtSetDbgFlag to set up the DCRT. At the bottom, I've done three allocations, a malloc and two new, and all three pieces of memory are leaked.

```
// This define must occur before any headers are included.
#define _CRTDBG_MAP_ALLOC
#include <stdio.h>
#include <stdlib.h>
#include <string.h>
#include <tchar.h>

// Include CRTDBG.H after all other headers
#include <crtdbg.h>
```

Listing 17-1 Setting up the DCRT and leaking memory

```
void main ( void )
{
    // Turn on the full heap checking
    _CrtSetDbgFlag ( _CRTDBG_ALLOC_MEM_DF       |
                     _CRTDBG_CHECK_ALWAYS_DF    |
                     _CRTDBG_DELAY_FREE_MEM_DF  |
                     _CRTDBG_LEAK_CHECK_DF       ) ;

    // Allocate some more memory.
    TCHAR * pNew = new TCHAR[ 200 ] ;
    TCHAR * pNew2 = new TCHAR[ 200 ] ;
    TCHAR * pMemLeak = (TCHAR*)malloc ( 100 ) ;

    _tcscpy ( pNew , _T ( "New'd memory..." ) ) ;
    _tcscpy ( pNew2 , _T ( "More new'd memory..." ) ) ;
    _tcscpy ( pMemLeak , _T ( "Malloc'd memory..." ) ) ;
}
```

Since I've turned on leak checking in the code for Listing 17-1, you'll see detected memory leak output like the following in the Output window when the program executes:

```
Detected memory leaks!
Dumping objects ->
NewProblem.cpp(22) : {62} normal block at 0x002F2E58, 100 bytes long.
 Data: <M a l l o c ' d > 4D 00 61 00 6C 00 6C 00 6F 00 63 00 27 00 64 00
 G:\vsnet\Vc7\include\crtdbg.h(692) :
 {61} normal block at 0x002F2C88, 400 bytes long.
 Data: <M o r e   n e w > 4D 00 6F 00 72 00 65 00 20 00 6E 00 65 00 77 00
 G:\vsnet\Vc7\include\crtdbg.h(692) :
 {60} normal block at 0x002F4DC0, 400 bytes long.
 Data: <N e w ' d   m e > 4E 00 65 00 77 00 27 00 64 00 20 00 6D 00 65 00
Object dump complete.
```

What's very nice is that the leak output format is such that double-clicking on the source line displayed will automatically jump to that line in the source file. The first leak is on line 22 of NEWPROBLEM.CPP (shown in Listing 17-1), and double-clicking jumps you to the line that did the `malloc`. If you double-click on the second source line listed, you jump to CRTDBG.H (line 692). While you're staring at a `new` call, it's certainly not the `new` in your source code. Since I had multiple calls to `new` in the program, you can see that logically all calls to `new` are going to show up as coming from CRTDBG.H. As you can imagine, this doesn't help much when you're looking for leaks in a huge program!

The problem lies in the declaration of `new` in CRTDBG.H, as shown here:

```
inline void* __cdecl operator new[](size_t s)
        { return ::operator new[](s, _NORMAL_BLOCK, __FILE__, __LINE__); }
```

If you've never experienced the joy of the placement syntax `new`, the preceding code could appear a little strange at first. The `new` operator is a very special construct in C++ in that it can take all sorts of different parameters. The call to

::operator new in the code shows that it's passing three additional parameters to new. This version of new is defined as part of CRTDBG.H. At first glance, the problem with the code isn't obvious. The __FILE__ and __LINE__ macros expand to the source name and line when compiled. However, as you've seen, they don't expand into *your* source and lines. The problem is with the first word in the code: inline. In release builds, inline indicates to the compiler that it's supposed to take the code inside the function and plop it directly into where it is being used instead of making a function call. However, in a debug build, inline-specified functions, as everyone should realize, don't get expanded and are treated as real functions. Hence, the __FILE__ and __LINE__ macros expand into CRTDBG.H and 692.

Since this puts a severe damper on using the DCRT, I certainly had to figure out a way to get any detected memory leaks to point to the allocation location in your source code. My original thought was to change CRTDBG.H, but because it's a system header, that didn't seem like such a great idea. After a lot of pondering, I finally came up with the following macro to be placed immediately after including CRTDBG.H in your precompiled header file. This simply turns any use of new into the placement syntax version of new, which takes the extra parameters.

```
#ifdef _DEBUG
#ifndef NEW_INLINE_WORKAROUND
#define NEW_INLINE_WORKAROUND new ( _NORMAL_BLOCK ,\
                                    __FILE__ , __LINE__ )
#define new NEW_INLINE_WORKAROUND
#endif
#endif  // _DEBUG
```

Sharp-eyed readers might immediately think there's a problem with my NEW_INLINE_WORKAROUND trick. The one big problem with my approach is that if you have a class that defines the new operator, my macro will cause problems because your declarations will be all messed up. Although you might not define new operators for your classes, libraries such as MFC and STL certainly do. The whole trick is to define this only inside your precompiled header file and to include only libraries like MFC and STL inside your precompiled header as well as taking advantage of the improved #pragma push_macro/#pragma pop_macro directives. To see exactly what to do, read the Common Debugging Question appearing later in this section, titled "What are the rules for properly precompiling headers?"

If you do have your own classes or use classes that define the new operator, you can still use the NEW_INLINE_WORKAROUND macro if you're willing to add some code and a few directives to your class. The following code shows a stripped-down class with the necessary parts in it to make NEW_INLINE_WORKAROUND work like a champ.

```
// Save off the definition of new on the macro stack.
#pragma push_macro ( "new" )
// Undefine new so I don't blow the class declaration.
#ifdef new
#undef new
#endif

class TestClass
{
public :

// The placement syntax version of new with the proper prototype needed
// to ensure the source and line information is recorded for the
// allocation.
#ifdef _DEBUG
    // iSize        - The size of the allocation.
    // iBlockType   - The DCRT block type.
    // lpszFileName - The source file name.
    // nLine        - The source line.
    static void * operator new ( size_t nSize        ,
                                 int    iBlockType   ,
                                 char * lpszFileName ,
                                 int    nLine         )
    {
        // Put any special code in here you need.

        // Allocate the actual memory with _malloc_dbg and pass in all
        // the parameters to record the allocation location.
        return ( _malloc_dbg ( nSize        ,
                               iBlockType   ,
                               lpszFileName ,
                               nLine         ) ) ;
    }
#endif  // _DEBUG
} ;

// Restore the new macro to the saved value (i.e., the
// NEW_INLINE_WORKAROUND).
#pragma pop_macro ( "new" )
```

The big trick that allows this to work is the new `#pragma push_macro` and `#pragma pop_macro` directives. These save off an existing macro definition to an internal compiler stack and restore the previous value, respectively. You'll have to include the pragma directives around each class that has the `new` operator overloaded since pragmas cannot be *macroized*. The extra `new` operator you'll have to include is the one that the `NEW_INLINE_WORKAROUND` macros call to affect the actual allocation. Even though the extra `new` operator is a little inconvenient, at least you're going to get all your leaks completely reported. If you want to see how everything works, check out the FixedNewProblem project included with this book's sample files.

Common Debugging Question

What are the rules for properly precompiling headers?

As I mentioned when discussing how to work around the bug in the DCRT so that you can properly get leaks from memory allocated with the `new` operator and display the correct source line, getting your precompiled headers straight is critical. Not only will this make your memory debugging easier, it will speed up your compiles greatly. The precompiled header file is basically the parse tree for those files specified in the .H file (traditionally named STDAFX.H), written to disk. Hence, you're compiling it only once instead of each time you build a .C/.CPP file.

Here are the rules for what to put in your precompiled header file:

1. All CRT/compiler supplied library included headers.
2. If you're using brackets around the name in the include statement, the header files you develop should be in quotes.
3. Any third-party library header files, such as BUGSLAYERUTIL.DLLs.
4. Any headers from your project that haven't changed in more than a month or two.

Useful DCRT Functions

One of the most useful DCRT library functions is `_CrtCheckMemory`. This function walks through all the memory you've allocated and checks to see whether you have any underwrites or overwrites and whether you've used any previously freed blocks. This one function alone makes the entire DCRT library worth using. A great technique for tracking down memory problems is to scatter `ASSERT ( _CrtCheckMemory ( ) ) ;` calls throughout your code. That way you'll catch those underwrites and overwrites as close to where they occur as possible.

Another set of functions allows you to easily check the validity of any piece of memory. The `_CrtIsValidHeapPointer`, `_CrtIsMemoryBlock`, and `_CrtIsValidPointer` functions are perfect for use as debugging parameter validation functions. These functions, combined with `_CrtCheckMemory`, offer excellent memory checking features.

Another neat feature of the DCRT library is the memory state functions: `_CrtMemCheckpoint`, `_CrtMemDifference`, and `_CrtMemDumpStatistics`. These functions make it easy to do before-and-after comparisons of the heap to see whether anything is amiss. For example, if you're using a common library in a team environment, you can take before-and-after snapshots of the heap when you call the library to see whether there are any leaks or to see how much memory the operation uses.

The icing on the memory-checking cake is that the DCRT library allows you to hook into the memory allocation code stream so that you can see each allocation and deallocation function call. If the allocation hook returns `TRUE`, the allocation is allowed to continue. If the allocation hook returns `FALSE`, the allocation fails. When I first discovered this functionality, my immediate thought was that, with a small amount of work, I could have a means to test code in some really nasty boundary conditions that would otherwise be very difficult to duplicate. You can see the result of this brainstorm in MemStress, a feature of BUGSLAYERUTIL.DLL that allows you to force allocation failures in your programs, which I'll present later in the chapter.

The cherry on top of the icing on the memory-checking cake is that the DCRT library also allows you to hook the memory dump functions and to enumerate client blocks (your allocated memory). You can replace the default memory dump functions with custom dump functions that know all about your data. Now, instead of seeing the cryptic dumped memory you get as the default (which besides being hard to decipher isn't that helpful), you can see exactly what the memory block contains and format it exactly as you want. MFC has the `Dump` function for this purpose, but it works only with `CObject`-derived classes. If you're like me, you don't spend your entire coding life in MFC and you need dumping functions that are more generic to accommodate different types of code.

The client block enumeration feature, as the name implies, allows you to enumerate the memory blocks you've allocated. This excellent feature gives you the power to create some interesting utilities. For example, in the MemDumperValidator functions in BUGSLAYERUTIL.DLL, I call the dumping hooks from the client block enumerator so that the enumeration can dump and validate many types of allocated memory in one operation. This extensible validation is critical in that it allows you to do deep validations instead of the surface checks of underwrites and overwrites. By deep validation, I mean an algorithm that knows the data formats in the memory block and walks those formats making sure that each data element is correct.

Choosing the Right C Run-Time Library for Your Application

Some of the confusion surrounding the use of the CRT libraries in Microsoft Windows development revolves around figuring out which library to use. There are six versions of the library, and they fall into two main categories: debug (DCRT) and release (CRT). In each category is a single-threaded static library, a multithreaded static library, and a multithreaded DLL.

The static versions of the CRT libraries link the library functions directly into your application and are the default versions used for non-MFC-wizard-generated applications. The advantage of using the static versions is that you won't have to ship a CRT library DLL with your product. The disadvantage is that the size of your binary files grows tremendously and your application's working set is much larger. The two static CRT library variants, single-threaded and multithreaded, are self-explanatory. If you're building a DLL and want to use a static CRT library, you should link only with a multithreaded version—if you don't, multithreaded applications can't use your DLL because the single-threaded static CRT libraries aren't thread-safe.

The DLL versions of the CRT libraries, named MSVCRT(D).DLL, allow you to import the CRT libraries' functions. The upside of using these DLLs is that your binary's size is drastically smaller, thus reducing your application's working set. Because other applications are loading the same CRT library DLLs, the operating system can share the page tables for the DLLs' code sections across processes and the entire system will run faster. The downside to using the DLL versions is that you might need to distribute another DLL with your application.

For your applications, it's extremely important that you choose one version of the CRT library to use across all binaries that load into your main program's address space. If you have some DLLs using the static CRT library and others using the DLL CRT library, not only are you making your address space larger with duplicated code, but you're also running the risk of introducing one of the most insidious memory bugs there is—a bug that could take months to track down. If you allocate heap memory out of one DLL and attempt to deallocate that heap memory in another DLL that uses a different version of the CRT library, you can easily crash because the deallocating DLL doesn't know where the allocated memory came from. Don't assume that heap memory is heap memory—having different versions of the CRT library running at the same time means that you have multiple versions of heap memory tracking code.

I always use the DLL versions of the CRT libraries, and I suggest that you do the same. The benefit of shrinking the working set and having smaller main binaries overrides any other considerations. In only a few instances—for example, when I'm developing games, where I'm guaranteed never to need multithreading and where performance is supercritical—do I even consider using the single-threaded static versions to avoid the overhead of the multi-threaded locking mechanisms.

I've set up BUGSLAYERUTIL.DLL to use the DLL versions of the CRT libraries. The two extensions I demonstrate in this chapter, MemDumperValidator and MemStress, are also in BUGSLAYERUTIL.DLL. These extensions expect you to be using the DLL versions. If you want to use the extensions in your application but not the DLL versions, however, it's trivial to pull out the source files, MEMDUMPERVALIDATOR.CPP, MEMDUMPERVALIDATOR.H, MEMSTRESS.CPP, MEMSTRESSCONSTANTS.H, and MEMSTRESS.H; change the function linkage specified; and drop them into your application.

I want to mention one additional detail about using BUGSLAYERUTIL.DLL in your projects. You might experience a slowdown in your application depending on how you allocate memory. As part of the MemDumperValidator extension, I turn on all the appropriate flags, including `_CRTDBG_CHECK_ALWAYS_DF`, in the DCRT library to allow full memory tracking and validation. The `_CRTDBG_CHECK_ALWAYS_DF` flag tells the DCRT library to walk through and validate each piece of heap memory each time you allocate or deallocate heap memory. If you're doing thousands of small allocations in your application, you'll see the slowdown. This is a perfect indication that you probably need to look at your data algorithms. Doing lots of small allocations is a huge performance problem, so you'll need to fix it. If you can't change the code, you can turn off the flag by calling `_CrtSetDbgFlag`.

Using MemDumperValidator

The MemDumperValidator extension makes memory debugging much easier. By default, the DCRT library reports memory leaks and validates that memory blocks haven't experienced overwrite or underwrite corruption. Both those reports can be very useful, but when the memory leak report looks something like the following, it can get difficult to figure out exactly which type of memory leaked:

```
Detected memory leaks
Dumping objects ->
TestProc.cpp(104) : {596} normal block at 0x008CD5B0,
    24 bytes long.
 Data: < k         w k  > 90 6B 8C 00 B0 DD 8C 00 00 00 80 77 90 6B 8C 00
Object dump complete.
```

As I mentioned earlier, having more than just the default memory validation helps—having deep memory validation can help you catch some wild writes that you might not otherwise catch. The extra information in MemDumperValidator's leak report and the additional validations the extension supplies provide you with more information when you're debugging. And the more information you have when you debug, the faster you can debug.

The MemDumperValidator extension takes advantage of the DCRT library block identifier capabilities so that it can associate a block type with a set of functions that know something about what the block contains. Each block allocated through the DCRT library is assigned an identifier. The different identifiers are listed in Table 17-3. The block types are a parameter to DCRT library functions that allocate memory: `_nh_malloc_dbg` (`new`), `_malloc_dbg` (`malloc`), `_calloc_dbg` (`calloc`), and `_realloc_dbg` (`realloc`).

Table 17-3 Memory Block Identifiers

Block Identifier	Description
`_NORMAL_BLOCK`	A normal call to `new`, `malloc`, or `calloc` creates a Normal block. Defining `_CRTDBG_MAP_ALLOC` causes all heap allocation to default to Normal blocks and associates the source file and line number that allocated the block with the memory block.
`_CRT_BLOCK`	The memory blocks allocated internally by many run-time library functions are marked as CRT blocks so that they can be handled separately. As a result, you're able to exclude them from leak detection and other memory validation operations. Your application must never allocate, reallocate, or free any block of type CRT.

`_CLIENT_BLOCK`	If you want your application to do special tracking on a type of memory, you can call the debug allocation functions and pass a special Client value as a parameter. You can track subtypes of Client blocks by putting a 16-bit value into the upper 16 bits of the Client block value, as shown here:
	`#define CLIENT_BLOCK_VALUE(x) \`
	`      (_CLIENT_BLOCK|(x<<16))`
	
	`_heap_alloc_dbg ( 10         ,`
	`     CLIENT_BLOCK_VALUE(0xA),`
	`                  __FILE__  ,`
	`                  __LINE__    ) ;`
	
	The application can supply a hook function, through `_CrtSetDumpClient`, for dumping memory registered as Client blocks. The hook will be called whenever a DCRT library function needs to dump a Client block. The `_CrtDoForAllClientObjects` function also allows you to enumerate the Client blocks currently allocated.
	
	MFC uses a Client block identifier for all `CObject`-derived classes. MemDumperValidator also uses the Client hook.

(continued)

Table 17-3 Memory Block Identifiers *(continued)*

Block Identifier	Description
_FREE_BLOCK	Calling a memory deallocation routine normally removes the memory from the debug heap lists. If you set the _CRTDBG_DELAY_FREE_MEM_DF flag with _CrtSetDbgFlag, however, the memory isn't freed but left allocated and filled with 0xDD.
_IGNORE_BLOCK	If you temporarily toggle off DCRT library tracking, any allocations made after the tracking is turned off will be marked as Ignore blocks.

After you set up a class or a C data type to use the MemDumperValidator extension, the DCRT library will call MemDumperValidator when it wants to dump a block. The extension will look at the block value, and if it sees a matching dumping function, it will call the function to dump the memory. The validation portion goes through the same process when called by the DCRT library except that it calls the matching validation function on the memory block.

Describing MemDumperValidator is the easy part—getting it to work is a little more difficult. Listing 17-2 shows MEMDUMPERVALIDATOR.H, which takes care of much of the initialization for you. By including BUGSLAYERUTIL.H in your program, you'll automatically include MEMDUMPERVALIDATOR.H.

```
/*----------------------------------------------------------------------
Debugging Applications for Microsoft .NET and Microsoft Windows
Copyright © 1997-2003 John Robbins -- All rights reserved.
----------------------------------------------------------------------*/

#ifndef _MEMDUMPERVALIDATOR_H
#define _MEMDUMPERVALIDATOR_H

// Don't include this file directly; include BUGSLAYER.H
// instead.
#ifndef _BUGSLAYERUTIL_H
#error "Include BUGSLAYERUTIL.H instead of this file directly!"
#endif  // _BUGSLAYERUTIL_H

#ifdef __cplusplus
extern "C" {
#endif      // __cplusplus

// This library can be used only in _debug builds.
#ifdef _DEBUG

////////////////////////////////////////////////////////////////////////
// The typedefs for the dumper and validator functions
////////////////////////////////////////////////////////////////////////
```

Listing 17-2 MEMDUMPERVALIDATOR.H

```
// The memory dumper function. This function's only parameter is a
// pointer to the block of memory. This function can output the memory
// data for the block in any way it chooses, but to be consistent, it
// should use the same reporting mechanism the rest of the DCRT
// library uses.
typedef void (*PFNMEMDUMPER)(const void *) ;
// The validator function. This function's first parameter is the memory
// block to validate, and the second parameter is the context
// information passed to the ValidateAllBlocks function.
typedef void (*PFNMEMVALIDATOR)(const void * , const void *) ;

///////////////////////////////////////////////////////////////////////
// Useful macros
///////////////////////////////////////////////////////////////////////
// The macro used to set a Client block subtype value. Using this macro
// is the only approved means of setting the value of the dwValue field
// in the BSMDVINFO structure below.
#define CLIENT_BLOCK_VALUE(x) (_CLIENT_BLOCK|(x<<16))
// A macro to pick out the subtype
#define CLIENT_BLOCK_SUBTYPE(x) ((x >> 16) & 0xFFFF)

///////////////////////////////////////////////////////////////////////
// The header used to initialize the dumper and validator for a specific
// Client block subtype
///////////////////////////////////////////////////////////////////////
typedef struct tag_BSMDVINFO
{
    // The subtype value for the Client blocks. This value must be set
    // with the CLIENT_BLOCK_VALUE macro above. See the AddClientDV
    // function to find out how to have the extension assign this
    // number.
    unsigned long   dwValue      ;
    // The pointer to the dumper function
    PFNMEMDUMPER    pfnDump      ;
    // The pointer to the dumper function
    PFNMEMVALIDATOR pfnValidate ;
} BSMDVINFO , * LPBSMDVINFO ;

/*----------------------------------------------------------------------
FUNCTION        :   AddClientDV
DISCUSSION      :
    Adds a Client block dumper and validator to the list. If the
dwValue field in the BSMDVINFO structure is 0, the next value in
the list is assigned. The value returned must always be passed to
 _malloc_dbg as the subtype value of the Client block.
    If the subtype value is set with CLIENT_BLOCK_VALUE, a macro can be
used for the value passed to _malloc_dbg.
    Notice that there's no corresponding remove function. Why run the
risk of introducing bugs in debugging code?  Performance is a nonissue
when it comes to finding errors.
PARAMETERS      :
    lpBSMDVINFO - The pointer to the BSMDVINFO structure
RETURNS         :
```

(continued)

```
    1 - The client block dumper and validator were properly added.
    0 - The client block dumper and validator couldn't be added.
----------------------------------------------------------------------*/
    BUGSUTIL_DLLINTERFACE int __stdcall
            AddClientDV (LPBSMDVINFO lpBSMDVInfo);

/*----------------------------------------------------------------------
FUNCTION        :   ValidateAllBlocks
DISCUSSION      :
    Checks all the memory allocated out of the local heap. Also goes
through all Client blocks and calls the special validator function for
the different subtypes.
    It's probably best to call this function with the VALIDATEALLBLOCKS
macro below.
PARAMETERS      :
    pContext - The context information that will be passed to each
               validator function
RETURNS         :
    None
----------------------------------------------------------------------*/
    BUGSUTIL_DLLINTERFACE void __stdcall
                                ValidateAllBlocks ( void * pContext ) ;

#ifdef __cplusplus
////////////////////////////////////////////////////////////////////////
// Helper C++ class macros
////////////////////////////////////////////////////////////////////////
// Declare this macro in your class just as you would an MFC macro.
#define DECLARE_MEMDEBUG(classname)                                     \
public   :                                                              \
    static BSMDVINFO  m_stBSMDVINFO ;                                   \
    static void ClassDumper ( const void * pData ) ;                    \
    static void ClassValidator ( const void * pData ,                   \
                                 const void * pContext )               ;\
    static void * operator new ( size_t nSize )                         \
    {                                                                   \
        if ( 0 == m_stBSMDVINFO.dwValue )                               \
        {                                                               \
            m_stBSMDVINFO.pfnDump     = classname::ClassDumper ;        \
            m_stBSMDVINFO.pfnValidate = classname::ClassValidator ;     \
            AddClientDV ( &m_stBSMDVINFO ) ;                            \
        }                                                               \
        return ( _malloc_dbg ( nSize                        ,           \
                               (int)m_stBSMDVINFO.dwValue ,             \
                               __FILE__                     ,           \
                               __LINE__                     ) ) ;       \
    }                                                                   \
    static void * operator new ( size_t nSize         ,                 \
                                 char * lpszFileName ,                  \
                                 int    nLine         )                 \
    {                                                                   \
        if ( 0 == m_stBSMDVINFO.dwValue )                               \
        {                                                               \
            m_stBSMDVINFO.pfnDump     = classname::ClassDumper ;        \
```

```
        m_stBSMDVINFO.pfnValidate = classname::ClassValidator ; \
        AddClientDV ( &m_stBSMDVINFO ) ;                       \
    }                                                          \
    return ( _malloc_dbg ( nSize                   ,           \
                           (int)m_stBSMDVINFO.dwValue ,        \
                           lpszFileName            ,           \
                           nLine                   ) ) ;       \
}                                                              \
static void * operator new ( size_t nSize          ,           \
                             int    /*iBlockType*/ ,           \
                             char * lpszFileName   ,           \
                             int    nLine          )           \
{                                                              \
    if ( 0 == m_stBSMDVINFO.dwValue )                          \
    {                                                          \
        m_stBSMDVINFO.pfnDump     = classname::ClassDumper ;   \
        m_stBSMDVINFO.pfnValidate = classname::ClassValidator ; \
        AddClientDV ( &m_stBSMDVINFO ) ;                       \
    }                                                          \
    return ( _malloc_dbg ( nSize                   ,           \
                           (int)m_stBSMDVINFO.dwValue ,        \
                           lpszFileName            ,           \
                           nLine                   ) ) ;       \
}                                                              \
static void operator delete ( void * pData )                   \
{                                                              \
    _free_dbg ( pData , (int)m_stBSMDVINFO.dwValue ) ;         \
}                                                              \
static void __cdecl operator delete ( void * _P ,              \
                                      int       ,              \
                                      char *    ,              \
                                      int       )              \
{                                                              \
    ::operator delete ( _P ) ;                                 \
}                                                              \
static void __cdecl operator delete[] ( void * _P ,            \
                                        int       ,            \
                                        char *    ,            \
                                        int       )            \
{                                                              \
    ::operator delete[]( _P ) ;                                \
}

// Declare this macro at the top of your CPP file.
#define IMPLEMENT_MEMDEBUG(classname)                          \
    BSMDVINFO  classname::m_stBSMDVINFO = { 0 , 0 , 0 }

// The macro for memory debugging allocations. If DEBUG_NEW is defined,
// it can be used.
#ifdef DEBUG_NEW
#define MEMDEBUG_NEW DEBUG_NEW
#else
#define MEMDEBUG_NEW new ( __FILE__ , __LINE__ )
#endif
```

(continued)

```
#endif      // __cplusplus defined

////////////////////////////////////////////////////////////////////////
// Helper C macros
////////////////////////////////////////////////////////////////////////

// Use this macro for C-style allocations. The only problem
// with C is that you need to drag around a BSMDVINFO structure.
#define INITIALIZE_MEMDEBUG(lpBSMDVINFO , pfnD , pfnV )               \
    {                                                                  \
        ASSERT ( FALSE == IsBadWritePtr ( lpBSMDVINFO ,                \
                                 sizeof ( BSMDVINFO ) ) ) ;           \
        ((LPBSMDVINFO)lpBSMDVINFO)->dwValue = 0 ;                      \
        ((LPBSMDVINFO)lpBSMDVINFO)->pfnDump = pfnD ;                   \
        ((LPBSMDVINFO)lpBSMDVINFO)->pfnValidate = pfnV ;               \
        AddClientDV ( lpBSMDVINFO ) ;                                  \
    }

// The macros that map the C-style allocations. It might be easier if
// you use macros to wrap these so that you don't have to remember which
// BSMDVINFO block value to drag around with each memory usage function.
#define MEMDEBUG_MALLOC(lpBSMDVINFO , nSize)                      \
            _malloc_dbg ( nSize                ,                  \
                        ((LPBSMDVINFO)lpBSMDVINFO)->dwValue ,     \
                        __FILE__               ,                  \
                        __LINE__               )
#define MEMDEBUG_REALLOC(lpBSMDVINFO , pBlock , nSize)            \
            _realloc_dbg( pBlock                 ,                \
                        nSize                    ,                \
                        ((LPBSMDVINFO)lpBSMDVINFO)->dwValue   ,   \
                        __FILE__                 ,                \
                        __LINE__                 )
#define MEMDEBUG_EXPAND(lpBSMDVINFO , pBlock , nSize )            \
            _expand_dbg( pBlock                  ,                \
                        nSize                    ,                \
                        ((LPBSMDVINFO)lpBSMDVINFO)->dwValue   ,   \
                        __FILE__                 ,                \
                        __LINE__                 )
#define MEMDEBUG_FREE(lpBSMDVINFO , pBlock)                       \
            _free_dbg ( pBlock                 ,                  \
                        ((LPBSMDVINFO)lpBSMDVINFO)->dwValue )
#define MEMDEBUG_MSIZE(lpBSMDVINFO , pBlock)  \
            _msize_dbg ( pBlock , ((LPBSMDVINFO)lpBSMDVINFO)->dwValue )

// Macro to call ValidateAllBlocks
#define VALIDATEALLBLOCKS(x)   ValidateAllBlocks ( x )

#else       // _DEBUG is not defined.

#ifdef __cplusplus
#define DECLARE_MEMDEBUG(classname)
#define IMPLEMENT_MEMDEBUG(classname)
#define MEMDEBUG_NEW new
#endif      // __cplusplus
```

```
#define INITIALIZE_MEMDEBUG(lpBSMDVINFO , pfnD , pfnV )

#define MEMDEBUG_MALLOC(lpBSMDVINFO , nSize) \
                malloc ( nSize )
#define MEMDEBUG_REALLOC(lpBSMDVINFO , pBlock , nSize) \
                realloc ( pBlock , nSize )
#define MEMDEBUG_EXPAND(lpBSMDVINFO , pBlock , nSize)  \
                _expand ( pBlock , nSize )
#define MEMDEBUG_FREE(lpBSMDVINFO , pBlock) \
                free ( pBlock )
#define MEMDEBUG_MSIZE(lpBSMDVINFO , pBlock) \
                _msize ( pBlock )

#define VALIDATEALLBLOCKS(x)

#endif      // _DEBUG

#ifdef __cplusplus
}
#endif      // __cplusplus

#endif      // _MEMDUMPERVALIDATOR_H
```

Using MemDumperValidator with C++

Fortunately, setting up a C++ class so that MemDumperValidator can handle it is a relatively simple operation. Before your class you want to use with MemDumperValidator, add a `#pragma push_macro ("new")` and undefined `new`. After the class, restore any new macros with a `#pragma pop_macro ("new")`. In the declaration of the C++ class, just specify the `DECLARE_MEMDEBUG` macro with the class name as the parameter. This macro is a little like some of the "magic" MFC macros in that it expands into a couple of data and method declarations. If you're following along in Listing 17-2, you'll notice six inline functions for `new` and `delete` that handle any type of placement syntax calls to those operators. If any of these operators are defined in your class, you'll need to extract the code from the extension operators and place it in your class's operators.

In the implementation file for your C++ class, you need to use the `IMPLEMENT_MEMDEBUG` macro, again with your class name as the parameter. This macro sets up a static variable for your class. The `DECLARE_MEMDEBUG` and `IMPLEMENT_MEMDEBUG` macros expand only in debug builds, so they don't need to have conditional compilation used around them.

After you've specified both macros in the correct place, you'll need to implement the two methods that will do the actual dumping and validating for your class. The prototypes for those methods follow. Obviously, you'll want to use conditional compilation around them so that they aren't compiled into release builds.

```
static void ClassDumper ( const void * pData ) ;
static void ClassValidator ( const void * pData,
                             const void * pContext  ) ;
```

For both methods, the pData parameter is the memory block that points to an instance of the class. All you need to do to get to a usable pointer is to cast the value in pData to the class type. Whatever you do when you're dumping or validating, treat the value in pData as super read-only or you could easily introduce as many bugs into your code as you meant to eliminate. For the ClassValidator method, the second parameter, pContext, is the context parameter you passed to the original call to the ValidateAllBlocks function. I'll talk more about the ValidateAllBlocks function in the "Deep Validations" section later in this chapter.

I have only two recommendations for implementing the ClassDumper method. First, stick to the _RPTn and _RPTFn macros from the DCRT library so that your formatted output will be dumped in the same place as the rest of the DCRT library output. Second, end your output with a carriage return/line feed combination because the DCRT library macros don't do any formatting for you.

Setting up a dumper and a validator for a C++ class seems almost trivial. But what about those C data structures that you'd like to dump cleanly at long last? Unfortunately, handling them takes a little more work.

Using MemDumperValidator with C

You might be wondering why I even bothered to support C. The answer is simple: there's still quite a bit of C code out there in many products you and I are using. And believe it or not, some of these applications and modules use memory too.

The first step you need to take to use MemDumperValidator in a C application is to declare a BSMDVINFO structure for each different type of memory you want to dump and validate. The C++ macros automatically declare dumper and validator methods for you, but in C, you have to do some work. Keep in mind that all the macros I talk about here require a pointer to the specific BSMDVINFO structures.

The prototypes for the C dumper and validator functions are the same as the C++ methods except that the static keyword isn't used. As with declaring the unique memory block BSMDVINFO structures, for convenience, you might want to consider placing all the C memory dumping and validation function implementations in a combined file.

Before you can start allocating, dumping, or validating memory in a C application, you must tell the MemDumperValidator extension about the Client block subtype and the dumper and validator functions for it. You pass all this information to the MemDumperValidator extension by using the INITIALIZE_MEMDEBUG macro, which takes the assigned BSMDVINFO structure, the dump function, and the validation function as parameters. You'll need to execute the macro before you allocate any memory blocks of this type.

Finally—and this is the area in which C++ memory handling is far better than C memory handling—to allocate, free, reallocate, expand, or get the size of a block, you must use an entire set of macros that pass the block value through to the underlying memory function. For example, if your `BSMDVINFO` structure is `stdvBlockInfo`, you need to allocate your C blocks with the following code:

```
MEMDEBUG_MALLOC ( &stdvBlockInfo , sizeof ( x ) ) ;
```

At the bottom of Listing 17-2, you'll see all the different macros for the C memory functions. Remembering the `BSMDVINFO` structure for every type of allocation isn't impossible but it isn't practical either, so you might want to set up wrapper macros to handle the different `BSMDVINFO` structures for you; all you'll need to pass to your wrapper macros are the normal parameters to the memory functions.

Deep Validations

Although the dumping portion of the MemDumperValidator extension is unquestionably useful, you might be wondering why you need the validation method, even if it does allow you to do deep validation of the memory block. In many cases, the validation function might even be an empty function if all the class holds is a couple string variables. Even so, the validation function can be invaluable because it gives you some excellent debugging capabilities. One of the reasons I started using deep validation was to provide a second level of data validation on a set of base classes that I had developed. Although a validation function shouldn't replace good old-fashioned parameter and input checking, it can give you another layer of assurance that your data is correct. Deep validations can also be a second line of defense against wild writes.

The neatest use of the validation function is for double-checking complex data structures after operations have been performed on them. For example, one time I had a relatively complex situation in which two separate self-referential data structures both used the same allocated objects because of space considerations. After filling in the data structures with a large set of data, I used the validation function to look at the individual blocks from the heap and check that they were referentially correct. I could've written a bunch of code to walk each data structure, but I knew that any code I wrote would be an open target for bugs. By using the validation function, I could bounce through the allocated blocks using code that I'd already tested, and I could check the data structures from different positions because the memory was in the order of allocation, not in sorted order.

Although setting up allocations is more difficult in C than in C++, using the memory validation function is the same in both languages. All you need to do is call the `VALIDATEALLBLOCKS` macro. This macro expands in debug builds to a call to the `ValidateAllBlocks` routine. The parameter required is any value that you want to pass on through to the validation functions that you registered with the library. I've used this parameter in the past to determine the depth of the validation that the function will perform. Keep in mind that `ValidateAllBlocks` passes this value to every registered validation routine, so you might need to coordinate the values across your team.

To see the MemDumperValidator functions in action, check out the Dump program shown in Listing 17-3, which is in the BUGSLAYERUTIL\TESTS\DUMP directory in this book's sample files. Dump is a stripped-down program that shows what you need in order to use the extension. Although I didn't provide a code example, the MemDumperValidator extension works well with MFC because MFC will call any previously registered client dump hook functions. With MemDumperValidator, you get the best of both worlds!

```
/*----------------------------------------------------------------------
Debugging Applications for Microsoft .NET and Microsoft Windows
Copyright © 1997-2003 John Robbins -- All rights reserved.
----------------------------------------------------------------------*/
#include <stdio.h>
#include <stdlib.h>
#include <memory.h>
#include <string.h>
#include <tchar.h>
#include "BugslayerUtil.h"

#pragma push_macro ( "new" )
#ifdef new
#undef new
#endif

class TestClass
{
public:
    TestClass ( void )
    {
        _tcscpy ( m_szData , _T ( "TestClass constructor data!" ) ) ;
    }
    ~TestClass ( void )
    {
        m_szData[ 0 ] = _T ( '\0' ) ;
    }

    // The declaration of the memory debugging stuff for C++ classes
    DECLARE_MEMDEBUG ( TestClass ) ;
private     :
    TCHAR m_szData[ 100 ] ;

} ;
```

Listing 17-3 DUMP.CPP

```
#pragma pop_macro ( "new" )

// This macro sets up the static BSMDVINFO structure.
IMPLEMENT_MEMDEBUG ( TestClass ) ;

// The methods you must implement to dump and
// validate
#ifdef _DEBUG
void TestClass::ClassDumper ( const void * pData )
{
    TestClass * pClass = (TestClass*)pData ;
    _RPT1 ( _CRT_WARN                           ,
            " TestClass::ClassDumper : %S\n"    ,
            pClass->m_szData                    ) ;
}
void TestClass::ClassValidator ( const void * pData    ,
                                 const void *          )
{
    // Validate the data here.
    TestClass * pClass = (TestClass*)pData ;
    _RPT1 ( _CRT_WARN                            ,
            " TestClass::ClassValidator : %S\n" ,
            pClass->m_szData                     ) ;
}
#endif

typedef struct tag_SimpleStruct
{
    TCHAR szName[ 256 ] ;
    TCHAR szRank[ 256 ] ;
} SimpleStruct ;

// The dumper and validator for simple string data memory
void DumperOne ( const void * pData )
{
    _RPT1 ( _CRT_WARN , " Data is : %S\n" , pData ) ;
}

void ValidatorOne ( const void * pData , const void * pContext )
{
    // Validate the string data here.
    _RPT2 ( _CRT_WARN                                 ,
            " Validator called with : %s : 0x%08X\n" ,
            pData                                     ,
            pContext                                  ) ;
}

// The dumper and validator for the structure allocations
void DumperTwo ( const void * pData )
{
    _RPT2 ( _CRT_WARN                         ,
            " Data is Name : %S\n"
            "         Rank : %S\n"            ,
```

(continued)

```
             ((SimpleStruct*)pData)->szName  ,
             ((SimpleStruct*)pData)->szRank    ) ;
}

void ValidatorTwo ( const void * pData , const void * /*pContext*/ )
{
    // Validate any structures here.
    _RPT2 ( _CRT_WARN                                   ,
            "  Validator called with :\n"
            "    Data is Name : %s\n"
            "            Rank : %s\n"                   ,
            ((SimpleStruct*)pData)->szName  ,
            ((SimpleStruct*)pData)->szRank    ) ;
}

// Unfortunately, the C functions need to drag around their own
// BSMDVINFO structures. In the real world, you'd define these structures
// as extern references and wrap the MEMDEBUG macros with your own
// macros.
static BSMDVINFO g_dvOne ;
static BSMDVINFO g_dvTwo ;

void main ( void )
{
    _tprintf ( _T ( "At start of main\n" ) ) ;

    // The memory debugging initialization for type one.
    INITIALIZE_MEMDEBUG ( &g_dvOne , DumperOne , ValidatorOne )  ;
    // The memory debugging initialization for type two.
    INITIALIZE_MEMDEBUG ( &g_dvTwo , DumperTwo , ValidatorTwo )  ;

    // Allocate the class with the MEMDEBUG new.
    TestClass * pstClass ;
    pstClass = new TestClass ( ) ;

    // Allocate the two C types.
    TCHAR * p = (TCHAR*)MEMDEBUG_MALLOC ( &g_dvOne , 20 ) ;
    _tcscpy ( p , _T ( "VC VC" ) ) ;

    SimpleStruct * pSt =
            (SimpleStruct*)MEMDEBUG_MALLOC ( &g_dvTwo ,
                                             sizeof ( SimpleStruct ) ) ;

    _tcscpy ( pSt->szName , _T ( "Pam" ) ) ;
    _tcscpy ( pSt->szRank , _T ( "CINC" ) ) ;

    // Validate all the blocks in the list.
    VALIDATEALLBLOCKS ( NULL ) ;

    _tprintf ( _T ( "At end of main\n" ) ) ;

    // Every block will get dumped as part of the memory leak checking.

}
```

Implementing MemDumperValidator

Implementing the MemDumperValidator functions was generally straightforward. The first unexpected problem I had to deal with was that the DCRT library doesn't document a way for the hook functions to get the memory block value. The hook functions are passed only a pointer to the user data, not the whole memory block the DCRT library allocates. Fortunately, with the DCRT library source code, I was able to see exactly how the library allocates memory blocks. Memory blocks are all allocated as a `_CrtMemBlockHeader` structure defined in the DBGINT.H file.

Also in the DBGINT.H file are macros to get at the `_CrtMemBlockHeader` from a user data pointer and to get at the user data from a `_CrtMemBlockHeader` pointer. I copied the `_CrtMemBlockHeader` structure and access macros into a header file, CRTDBG_INTERNALS.H (shown in Listing 17-4), so that I could get at the header information. Although relying on a copy of a structure definition when the definition might change isn't a good practice, it works in this case because the DCRT library `_CrtMemBlockHeader` structure hasn't changed since Visual C++ 4. That doesn't mean that this structure won't change in a future version of Visual C++. If you're using the MemDumperValidator extension, you need to quickly check each service pack and major release of the compiler to see whether the internal structures have changed.

```
/*----------------------------------------------------------------------
Debugging Applications for Microsoft .NET and Microsoft Windows
Copyright (c) 1997-2003 John Robbins -- All rights reserved.
----------------------------------------------------------------------*/

#ifndef _CRTDBG_INTERNALS_H
#define _CRTDBG_INTERNALS_H
#define nNoMansLandSize 4

typedef struct _CrtMemBlockHeader
{
    struct _CrtMemBlockHeader * pBlockHeaderNext        ;
    struct _CrtMemBlockHeader * pBlockHeaderPrev        ;
    char *                      szFileName              ;
    int                         nLine                   ;
    size_t                      nDataSize               ;
    int                         nBlockUse               ;
    long                        lRequest                ;
    unsigned char               gap[nNoMansLandSize]    ;
    /* followed by:
     *  unsigned char           data[nDataSize];
     *  unsigned char           anotherGap[nNoMansLandSize];
     */
```

Listing 17-4 CRTDBG_INTERNALS.H

(continued)

```
} _CrtMemBlockHeader;

#define pbData(pblock) ((unsigned char *) \
                                   ((_CrtMemBlockHeader *)pblock + 1))
#define pHdr(pbData) (((_CrtMemBlockHeader *)pbData)-1)

#endif      // _CRTDBG_INTERNALS_H
```

If you'd feel more comfortable with using DBGINT.H directly, you can replace the structure definition in CRTDBG_INTERNALS.H with `#include DBGINT.H`. You'll also need to add "$(VCInstallDir)VC7\CRT\SRC" to both your master INCLUDE environment variable and the Include files directories in the Options dialog box, Projects folder, VC++ Directories property page. Because not everyone installs the CRT library source code, though they should, I decided it would be easier if I just included the structure definition directly.

You can also use the `_CrtMemBlockHeader` structure definition to get more information from the `_CrtMemState` structures returned by `_CrtMemCheckpoint` because the first item in the structure is a pointer to a `_CrtMemBlockHeader`. I hope a future version of the DCRT library gives us real access functions to get the memory block information.

As you look through the source code in MEMDUMPERVALIDATOR.CPP, part of the BUGSLAYERUTIL.DLL project included with this book's sample files, you might notice that I use straight Windows application programming interface (API) heap functions from the `HeapCreate` family for internal memory management. The reason I use these API functions is that the dump and hook functions you use with the DCRT library will cause reentrancy if you use routines from the standard library. Keep in mind that I'm not talking about multithreaded reentrancy. If my hook code allocates memory with a call to `malloc`, my hook would be reentered because the hooks are called on every memory allocation.

Initialization and Termination in C++

After I finished implementing MemDumperValidator and started to test it, I was pleased that the extension worked as planned. However, as I was pondering all the ways that a program can allocate heap memory, I started to break out in a cold sweat. Were static constructors that possibly allocate memory going to give me any problems? As I looked at my initial code for MemDumperValidator, I discovered a glaring hole in my logic.

Although most developers don't do it much, in some cases, memory is allocated before an application's entry point. The problem with my approach in MemDumperValidator was that I needed to ensure that the appropriate flags to `_CrtSetDbgFlag` are set before any allocations take place.

The last thing I wanted to do with MemDumperValidator was force you to remember to call some goofy initialization function before you could use the library. It's bad enough that you have to drag around your BSMDVINFO structures for C programming. I wanted to make MemDumperValidator as automatic as possible so that more developers would use it—without any hassle.

Fortunately, my cold sweat didn't last too long because I remembered the #pragma init_seg directive, which can be used to control the initialization and destruction order of statically declared values. You can pass one of several options to the #pragma init_seg directive: compiler, lib, user, section name, and funcname. The first three are the important ones.

The compiler option is reserved for the Microsoft compiler, and any objects specified for this group are constructed first and destructed last. Those marked as lib are constructed next and destructed before the compiler-marked group, and those marked user are constructed last and terminated first.

Because the code in MemDumperValidator needs to be initialized before your code, I could just specify lib as the directive to #pragma init_seg and be done with it. However, if you're creating libraries and marking them as lib segments (as you should) and want to use my code, you still need to initialize my code before your code. To handle this contingency, I set the #pragma init_seg directive as compiler. Although you should always follow the rules when it comes to proper segment initializations, using the compiler option with debug code is safe enough.

Because the initialization idea works only with C++ code, MemDumperValidator uses a special static class, named AutoMatic, that simply calls the _CrtSetDbgFlag function. I need to go to all this trouble because it's the only way to set the DCRT flags before any other library's initialization. Additionally, as you'll see in a moment, to get around some limitations in the DCRT library memory leak checking, I need to do some special processing on the class destruction. Even though the MemDumperValidator has only a C interface, I can take advantage of C++ to get the extension up and running so that it's ready when you call it.

Where Have All the Leak Reports Gone?

I survived my bout of anxiety over initialization issues and finally got the MemDumperValidator extension running. I was happy with how it all worked—except that when the program terminated I never saw the nicely formatted output from my dumping functions if I had memory leaks. The memory dumps were just the old standard DCRT library dumps. I tracked down the "missing" leak reports and was surprised to see that the DCRT library termination functions call _CrtSetDumpClient with a parameter of NULL, thus clearing out my dump hook before calling _CrtDumpMemoryLeaks. I was distressed by this behavior until it dawned on me that I just had to do the final memory leak checking myself. Fortunately, I had the perfect place to do it.

Because I was already using the `#pragma init_seg(compiler)` directive to get the `AutoMatic` class initialized before your code and to call the destructor after your code, I just needed to do the leak checking there and then turn off the `_CRTDBG_LEAK_CHECK_DF` flag so that the DCRT library didn't do its own reporting. The only caveat with using this approach is that you need to make sure that the CRT library of your choice comes before BUGSLAYERUTIL.LIB if you link with the `/NODEFAULTLIB` switch. When you link against BUGSLAYERUTIL.LIB, the CRT libraries can't depend on their `#pragma init_seg(compiler)` directive to ensure that their data gets initialized first and destroyed last, so you need to enforce the correct ordering yourself.

If you think about it, having the DCRT library clear out any dump hooks installed makes sense. If your dump hook were using any CRT library functions, such as `printf`, it could crash the termination of your program because the library is in the middle of shutting down when `_CrtDumpMemoryLeaks` is called. If you follow the rules and always link with the DCRT library before any other libraries, you'll be fine because the MemDumperValidator functions are shut down before the DCRT library shuts down. To avoid problems, use the `_RPTn` and `_RPTFn` macros only in your dumper functions anyway, because `_CrtDumpMemoryLeaks` uses only these macros.

Using MemStress

Now it's time to add a little stress to your life. Believe it or not, stress can be a good thing. Unfortunately, stressing Win32 applications is much harder these days than it used to be. In the days of 16-bit Windows systems, we could run our programs through their paces with STRESS.EXE, a neat program that comes with the SDK. STRESS.EXE allowed you to torment your application in all sorts of nasty ways, such as eating up disk space, gobbling up the graphics device interface (GDI) heap, and using up file handles. It even had a cool icon: an elephant walking a tightrope.

To stress your Win32 applications, you can hook into the DCRT library's allocation system and control whether allocations succeed or fail. The MemStress extension gives you a means to stress your C and C++ memory allocation. (I'll leave it up to you to write the disk-eating code.) To make MemStress easy to use, I wrote a Windows Forms front end that lets you specify under exactly what conditions you'd like your allocation to fail.

The MemStress extension lets you force allocation failures based on various criteria: all allocations, on every *n* allocation, after *x* bytes are allocated, on requests over *y* bytes, on all allocations out of a source file, and on a specific line in a source file. In addition, you can have the MemStress extension prompt you with a message box on each allocation asking whether you want this particular allocation to fail, and you can also set the DCRT library flags you'd like in effect for your program. The MemStressDemo program is a sample MFC program (that comes with this book's sample files) that allows you to experiment with setting different options from the MemStress user interface (UI) and see the results. It also serves as the unit test for MemStress itself.

Using the MemStress extension is relatively simple. In your code, include BUGSLAYERUTIL.H and call the `MEMSTRESSINIT` macro with the name of your program. To stop the memory allocation hooking, use the `MEMSTRESSTERMINATE` macro. You can start and stop the hook as many times as you want when running your program.

After you've compiled your program, start the MemStress UI, click the Add Program button, and type the same name that you specified in the `MEMSTRESSINIT` macro. After you've selected the failure options you want, click the Save Program Settings button to save the settings into MEMSTRESS.INI. Now you can run your program and see how it behaves when it fails memory allocations.

You'll probably want to be very selective about using the MemStress extension. For example, if you specify that you want all allocations over 100 bytes to fail and you have the `MEMSTRESSINIT` macro in your MFC application's `InitInstance` function, you'll likely take down MFC because it will be unable to initialize. You'll have the best results with the MemStress extension if you limit its use to key areas in your code so that you can test them in isolation.

Most of the implementation of MemStress is in the reading and processing of the MEMSTRESS.INI file, in which all the settings for individual programs are stored. From the DCRT library perspective, the important function is the call to `_CrtSetAllocHook` during the MemStress initialization because this call sets the hook function, `AllocationHook`, as the allocation hook. If the allocation hook function returns `TRUE`, the allocation request is allowed to continue. By returning `FALSE`, the allocation hook can have the DCRT library fail the allocation request. The allocation hook has only one hard requirement from the DCRT library: if the type of block, as specified by the `nBlockUse` parameter, is marked as a `_CRT_BLOCK`, the hook function must return `TRUE` to allow the allocation to take place.

The allocation hook gets called on every type of allocation function. The different types, as specified in the first parameter to the hook, are `_HOOK_ALLOC`, `_HOOK_REALLOC`, and `_HOOK_FREE`. In my `AllocationHook` function, if the type is `_HOOK_FREE`, I skip all the code that determines whether the memory request should pass or fail. For `_HOOK_ALLOC` and `_HOOK_REALLOC` types, my `AllocationHook` function performs a series of `if` statements to determine whether any of the failure conditions are met. If a failure condition is met, I return `FALSE`.

Interesting Stress Problems

Everything worked great in MemStress on my initial console sample program, and I was feeling fine. As I finished off the MFC-based MemStressDemo program, I noticed a compelling problem. If I elected to have MemStress ask me with a message box whether I wanted allocations to fail, I would hear a series of beeps and MemStressDemo would stop working. I was able to duplicate the problem every time—and to duplicate the serious stress the problem was causing me because I didn't see what the issue could be.

After a few runs, I finally got a message box to show up. Instead of being in the center of the screen, the message box was down in the lower right-hand corner. When message boxes start moving off the lower right-hand corner of the screen, you can be pretty sure that you're stuck in a situation in which calling the `MessageBox` API function somehow became reentrant. I suspected that my allocation hook was getting called in the middle of my call to `MessageBox`. I confirmed my hypothesis by setting a breakpoint on the first instruction of `AllocationHook` just before I stepped over the `MessageBox` call. Sure enough, the debugger stopped on the breakpoint.

I looked up the stack and saw that a direct call to the `MessageBox` API function was somehow going through MFC code. As I poked through the code looking at what was happening, I saw that I was in the `_AfxActivationWndProc` function on a line that was calling `CWnd::FromHandle`, which causes memory allocations so that MFC can create a `CObject`. I was a little stumped about how I got in there, but a comment in the code indicated that `_AfxActivationWndProc` is used to handle activation and make gray dialog boxes. MFC uses a computer-based training (CBT) hook to catch window creations in the process space. When a new window is created—in my case, a simple message box—MFC subclasses the window with its own window procedure.

When I understood all the issues, my personal stress level really shot up because I wasn't sure how to handle the situation. Because the reentrancy was on the same thread, I couldn't use a synchronization object such as a semaphore because that would have deadlocked the thread. After contemplating the problem a bit, I concluded that what I needed was a recursion flag that told me when `AllocationHook` was being reentered—but it had to be on a per-thread basis. I already had a critical section protecting against multiple-thread reentrancy in `AllocationHook`.

When I stated the problem this way, I realized that all I needed was a variable in thread local storage that I would access at the beginning of `AllocationHook`. If the value was greater than 0, `AllocationHook` was being reentered as part of the `MessageBox` processing and I just needed to bail out of the function. I implemented a quick dynamic thread local storage solution and my anxiety dropped considerably because everything started working as planned.

I thought I had everything rolling at this point, but I noticed my second stress problem. When testing the code to fail on a specific source and line, the source filename was coming in as `NULL` and the source line was 0. Because I was using MFC for the MemStressDemo program, I thought it would have done the right thing and properly used the CRTDBG.H versions of the allocation functions to pass in the source and line. Alas, that wasn't the case.

I figured that all I needed to do was to drop in a define of `_CRTDBG_MAP_ALLOC` at the top of STDAFX.H and include CRTDBG.H as the end of the file. Of course, as soon as I compiled, the spew of redefine and unexpected constant errors overwhelmed me. No matter what I tried, I could not make an MFC application compile and use the proper version of the allocation functions. After a while I found that the only thing I could reasonably do was extract the defines from CRTDBG.H and include them manually in STDAFX.H. You can look at the MemStressDemo's STDAFX.H to see exactly what you need to do.

Operating System Heaps

Although you thought I might be done with the heap system after so many pages, there's another set of heaps you'll definitely want to know about—the operating system heaps. As an application starts under a debugger, Windows turns on the operating system heap checking. This heap isn't the C run-time library debug heap; it's the Windows heap code for those heaps created with the `HeapCreate` API function. The C run-time library heap is a separate entity. Because processes use the operating system heaps extensively, for example, to do ANSI to Unicode string conversion when using ANSI functions, you might see information related to operating system heaps in your normal operation, which is why it's important to cover them here. If you attach a debugger to your application rather than start your application under the debugger, you won't activate the operating system heap checking. One of the most common questions I get is: "My application runs fine outside the debugger, but when it runs under the debugger, it has a User breakpoint exception. Why won't my application run?" The answer is the operating system heap checking.

With the operating system heap checking turned on, your application will run slightly slower because the operating system heap checking will validate the heap when your application calls a heap function. This book's code samples include a program named Heaper that corrupts the heap. When you run Heaper under a debugger, you'll see that it calls `DebugBreak` twice on the first

HeapFree. Additionally, you'll see output such as the following that shows what was wrong. Yes, the output stops at "of a" and doesn't show the size of the block, which would be quite useful. If you run the program outside the debugger, it runs to completion without reporting any problems.

```
HEAP[Heaper.exe]: Heap block at 00311E98 modified at 00311EAA past
    requested size of a
```

HEAPER.CPP is shown in Listing 17-5.

```
void main(void)
{
    // Create an operating system heap.
    HANDLE hHeap = HeapCreate ( 0 , 128 , 0 ) ;

    // Allocate a 10-byte block.
    LPVOID pMem = HeapAlloc ( hHeap , 0 , 10 ) ;

    // Write 12 bytes to a 10-byte block (an overwrite).
    memset ( pMem , 0xAC , 12 ) ;

    // Allocate a new 20-byte block.
    LPVOID pMem2 = HeapAlloc ( hHeap , 0 , 20 ) ;

    // Underwrite 1 byte on the second block.
    char * pUnder = (char *)( (DWORD_PTR)pMem2 - 1 );
    *pUnder = 'P' ;

    // Free the first block. This call to HeapFree will trigger a
    // breakpoint from the operating system debug heap code.
    HeapFree ( hHeap , 0 , pMem ) ;

    // Free the second block. Notice that this call won't report
    // a problem.
    HeapFree ( hHeap , 0 , pMem2 ) ;

    // Free a bogus block. Notice that this call won't report a problem.
    HeapFree ( hHeap , 0 , (LPVOID)0x1 ) ;

    HeapDestroy ( hHeap ) ;

}
```

Listing 17-5 HEAPER.CPP, a Windows heap corruption example

If you're using your own operating system heaps, or you'd like to have the application turn on operating system heap checking outside the debugger, you can turn on some additional flags to receive more diagnostic output. The Debugging Tools for Windows package includes a small utility named GFLAGS.EXE. With it, you can set some of the global flags that Windows checks when it first starts an application. Figure 17-1 shows GFLAGS.EXE set up for HEAPER.EXE, which is the program in Listing 17-5. Many of the System Registry and Kernel Mode options are global, so you need to be extremely careful if you set them because they can have a major impact on system performance or can make your machine unbootable. Setting Image File Options, as shown in Figure 17-1, is much safer because the settings are limited to just that one executable. Keep in mind that although GFLAGS.EXE is useful, you can also use the Application Verifier tool to check for heap corruptions, which I'll discuss later in the chapter.

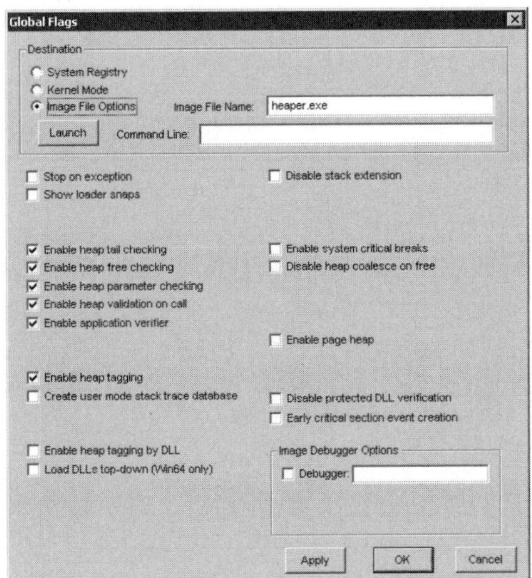

Figure 17-1 GFLAGS.EXE with settings for HEAPER.EXE

Because I'm on the subject of GFLAGS.EXE, I want to take a moment to point out one very useful option, Show Loader Snaps. If you check that box and run your application, you'll see where Windows is loading the DLLs and how it's going about fixing up the imports, called *snapping*, for your application. If you need to see exactly what the Windows loader is doing when it loads your application (in case you have a problem), you'll find it helpful to turn on this option. For more information on loader snaps, see Matt Pietrek's "Under the Hood" column in the September 1999 *Microsoft Systems Journal*.

Tricks for Hunting Down Memory Problems

With a good understanding of the debugging memory systems available to you, I can now turn to tricks and techniques for finding those memory problems that occur only in production systems and don't easily show up in the debugger.

Finding Uninitialized Memory Writes

Nothing is worse than a crash that occurs out of nowhere and that doesn't seem to match up with any known code path. If you're experiencing these symptoms, you're probably looking at an uninitialized write, which is also known as a *wild write*. The cause is a pointer variable that hasn't been initialized and happens to be pointing to valid memory. You'll mostly see this with stack-based pointers, in other words, local variables. Since the stack is being changed all the time as your program is executing, there's no telling what that uninitialized pointer is pointing to, which is why it can appear to be random.

When my company is brought in to help track down one of these insidious problems, we invariably find a team that's at wits' end. When we first meet with the team, someone will tell us that the team has literally tried every possible trick to find the problem. Since they've already done "everything," they're desperate to see what magic we'll do to solve the problem. My response is that we'll have to use the patented and trademarked Magic Ninja Uninitialized Memory Debugging Technique (MNUMDT). Everyone's sitting on the edge of his or her seat waiting for the trick—especially when I mention that the MNUMDT works only if I have the two least experienced developers on the team work with me to find the bug.

By this point the two junior developers are champing at the bit to get going and show the rest of the team they can seriously carry their weight. I have the two come around and stand by me as I spell out the MNUMDT:

- The two developers and I are each going to take one third of the code.
- Each of us is going to read each line of code looking for any pointer declarations.
- When we find a pointer declaration, we're going to initialize that pointer to `NULL` if the pointer isn't initialized in the declaration.
- For each non-class memory allocation we find, we're going to add a call to `memset` or `ZeroMemory` after that call to zero out the memory.
- When we find a deallocation, we'll initialize the pointer value back to zero after the deallocation.
- When we encounter a `memset`, or string copy operation, we're going to verify that each operation properly calculates the memory block size.
- Each class member variable is initialized in the constructor(s).

When I get through the MNUMDT list, the two developers are ready to run out of the room, but because I have them stand next to me, I can grab them and prevent it. If you're thinking that this sounds like a lot of grunt work and a brute force approach, you're exactly right—that's what it is.

Having looked for thousands of uninitialized memory bugs now, I've found that no amount of fancy debugging will get you close. All you'll end up doing is wasting a ton of time. It's much more efficient to go through and follow the steps I just outlined before starting the debugging. The odds are extremely high that one of those pointers we initialize will be the one with the problem. Now, instead of corrupting memory and continuing to run, the application will crash immediately because it's trying to write to `NULL`.

Some of you might think this won't work, but I can give you hundreds of instances where teams have spent weeks looking for the problem and didn't get anywhere. However, when we were brought in, we were able to find the problem in a day or two. Sometimes developers try to outsmart themselves because they don't want to think about brute force. However, brute force is an excellent technique in this case. If you're wondering why I ask for the two junior developers on the team, I've found that they don't make as many assumptions as senior developers and with the eyes of the whole team on them, they are superconscientious about the work they do grinding through the code.

Finding Memory Overruns

Between the DCRT and tools like Compuware's BoundsChecker, you should have scrubbed out all the memory overruns in your application as part of your testing. Sadly, not everyone is testing to the level that readers of this book are, and you'll have to find those pesky overruns in those developers' code. Additionally, some of the memory overruns occur only under the most stressful production situations. To make matters worse, when a release build application overruns memory, there's no slop space on the end of the memory block, so the overrun can subtly corrupt data that you might not notice for weeks, until the server application crashes.

One of the weaknesses of the DCRT overrun checking is that the overrun is reported only after the fact when a memory operation triggers the run through to check for them. It would be better to find a way to immediately stop the instant a program bashed memory just outside its allotted space. Inside Microsoft, they needed a testing tool that would do just that and a few years ago released a tool called PageHeap.

PageHeap is actually baked into the operating system and uses a unique trick to catch those overruns instantaneously. When you allocate 16 bytes, PageHeap actually allocates 8 KB! It allocates a 4 KB page, the smallest block of memory that can have access rights applied to it. PageHeap marks that allocated page with read and write access. PageHeap allocates the very next page in memory directly behind the read/write page and marks that page as no access. PageHeap does some pointer arithmetic and hands your program an address that is 16 bytes off the end of the first page. Thus, when you write into the seventeenth byte off that address, you'll write into the page marked as no access so you immediately access violate. Figure 17-2 shows the layout of a PageHeap allocation so that you can visualize what's happening.

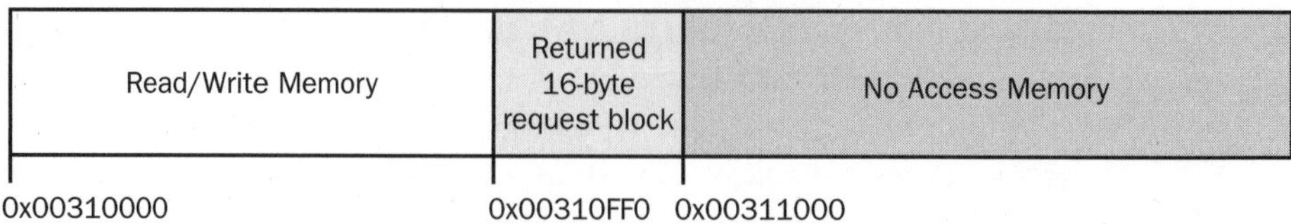

Figure 17-2 PageHeap allocation

As you can imagine, PageHeap uses a ton more memory than normal. However, the cost is dirt cheap if it helps you find the memory overrun. If you've got a large application, slap as much memory as possible into the test machine so that your application will turn over. Go ahead and steal some out of your manager's machine because he or she won't miss it.

One key item I do need to mention about PageHeap is that all pointers returned to you have to be on a 16-byte boundary. That means if you allocate 10 bytes, you'll have to overrun by 7 bytes in order to hit the no access page. The good news is that normally when people overrun a block, it's not just by a byte or two but by a whole gob of them, so PageHeap should still catch them. This also means that PageHeap is worth your while only if you're running a release build of your application. With the debug build padding the memory allocation for its own overrun and underrun bytes, you'll never see the PageHeap overrun crash.

Application Compatibility Toolkit

Although I could walk you through a huge discussion of turning on PageHeap with the weird command-line tool built into GFLAGS, there's a much better way to do it. The Application Compatibility Toolkit (ACT) not only brings PageHeap functionality right into Visual Studio .NET but offers some excellent bug detection tools you should definitely know about. Much of ACT is geared toward helping IT administrators get applications running on Microsoft Windows XP and Windows Server 2003, but the Application Verifier (AppVerifier) portion of ACT is where the developer action is.

ACT is offered with this book's sample files, or you can download the latest version from *http://www.microsoft.com/windowsxp/appexperience/default.asp*. The documentation says that ACT 2.6, the version available to me as I write this book, indicates that AppVerifier runs on Microsoft Windows 2000 SP3 and later, but I've had luck only on Windows XP and Windows Server 2003. On Windows 2000, I've never gotten the AppVerifier to work properly. Additionally, some of the tests and errors the documentation says should work don't seem to produce any output. For the rest of this discussion, I'll assume you are using Windows XP or Windows Server 2003 when running AppVerifier and are running under an account with Administrator privileges (as required for AppVerifier).

AppVerifier has been designed as a standalone executable (APPVERIF.EXE) and as an add-in (VSAPPVERIF.DLL). The AppVerifier add-in included with ACT version 2.6 is integrated into the Debug toolbar of Visual Studio .NET 2002. However, that integration is not migrated over to Visual Studio .NET 2003. Fortunately, because of all the experience I got with add-ins back in Chapter 9, I was able to figure out how to get the AppVerifier add-in working. If you're using a later version of the AppVerifier add-in, it will probably integrate directly into Visual Studio .NET 2003, so you can skip the following steps to make it work.

After you've installed ACT, open a command prompt and navigate to the <ACT installation directory>\Applications directory. You'll need to register the AppVerifier add-in DLL with `REGSVR32 VSAPPVERIF.DLL` so that the COM components are in the registry. The next step is to tell Visual Studio .NET 2003 about the add-in. In the AppVerifierAddIn directory with this book's sample files is a .REG file named AppVerifierAddInReg.reg.REG. You can either double-click the .REG file from Windows Explorer or execute it with `REGEDIT AppVerifierAddInReg.REG`.

In case you're wondering whether bringing an add-in written for a previous version of Visual Studio .NET over to a newer version can be a problem, let me tell you that it can be. If the add-in happens to be written using .NET, pulling in a previous edition of the CLR could cause problems. However, in the case of the AppVerifier add-in, it's written only in C++, so it's safe. I could tell this because I was running REGASM on VSAPPVERIF.DLL, and REGASM reported that the add-in wasn't a .NET assembly. Of course, I still went through and tested all the options in VSAPPVERIF.DLL to ensure everything was safe. If you happen to run Visual Studio .NET with the AppVerifier add-in under an account where you don't have Administrator privileges, you'll get an odd error message box. The title of the box is "Installer Error" and the text is "Error: insufficient permissions to run this program. Administrator access needed."

Once you install ACT or register the AppVerifier add-in manually, you might miss the new buttons added to the Debug toolbar of Visual Studio .NET. This new Debug toolbar is shown in Figure 17-3. You'll need to make the Debug toolbar visible when you aren't debugging because you can set AppVerifier add-in options only before you start debugging. One of the key tenets of the AppVerifier add-in is that it will cause `DebugBreak` calls left and right when you encounter a problem, so you're always going to be running under a debugger. By having it built into Visual Studio .NET, you can avoid the pain of Windows NT Symbolic Debugger (NTSD) or WinDBG.

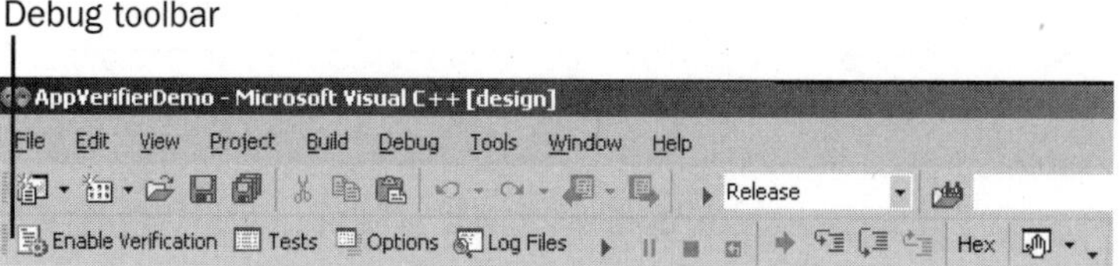

Figure 17-3 Visual Studio .NET Debug toolbar after properly configuring the AppVerifier add-in

The first thing you'll need to do with the AppVerifier add-in is turn on an option that isn't documented but will provide better memory error detection. After loading a project in Visual Studio .NET, on the Debug toolbar, click the new Options button, and in the Options dialog box, check the Use Full Page Heap option as shown in Figure 17-4. This option is not available in the standalone APPVERIF.EXE program, and more checking is always better. Figure 17-4 also shows that I haven't checked Break In The Debugger After Each Logged Event. If this checkbox is checked, you'll be stopping every 15 nanoseconds as the AppVerifier add-in reports something.

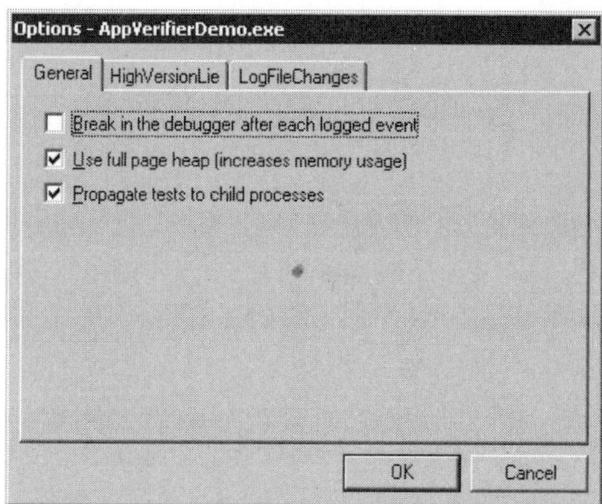

Figure 17-4 The AppVerifier add-in Options dialog box inside Visual Studio .NET

Clicking the Tests button on the Debug toolbar brings up the AppVerifier Test Settings dialog box in which you can specify which tests to run. The tests are all described in Table 17-4. Additionally, I turn on all the tests shown in Figure 17-5. The items set in the AppVerifier Test Settings dialog box are on a per-process basis, so you'll need to set them for each application you want to run under the AppVerifier add-in.

Table 17-4 The AppVerifier Add-in Test Descriptions

Test	Description
Detect heap corruptions	This test performs regular checks of the heap and adds guard pages at the end of each allocation to catch possible heap overruns.
Check lock usage	This test looks for common errors associated with critical sections.
Detect invalid handle usage	With ACT 2.6, this test checks only whether handles are `NULL/INVALID_HANDLE_VALUE` or a TLS parameter is bad.
Check for adequate stack	This test checks for adequate stack in Win32 services. You probably won't use this test.
Log start and stop	This option simply enters log information when the application starts or stops. This helps to make the logs easier to read when reviewing test data.
Checks system path usage	This test monitors the application's attempts to obtain file path information to see if the program uses hard-coded paths, or a non-standard method of gathering the information.
Checks version handling	In the past, many applications have been written to run on a single version of Windows. This test will return a very high version number when the application attempts to determine which version of Windows it's running in.
Checks registry usage	This test monitors the application's use of the system registry for any inappropriate or dangerous calls. Any problems detected will be logged. This test helps to ensure future compatibility for applications because it checks for the usage of specific registry keys that might be dropped or changed in future versions of the Windows operating system.
Logs changes to Windows File Protection files	This test logs changes to Windows File Protection files.
Logs DirectX file checks	This test logs any attempts that an application makes to perform a version check on DirectX libraries.
Logs registry changes	This test logs to an XML file all changes that an application makes to the registry.
Logs file system changes	This test logs to an XML file all changes that an application makes to the file system. You'll receive a warning if the application attempts to write files to the %windir% or Program Files folders.

(continued)

Table 17-4 The AppVerifier Add-in Test Descriptions *(continued)*

Test	Description
Logs calls made to obsolete APIs	This test logs calls made to APIs that have been marked as obsolete in the Microsoft Platform SDK. When using this test, only look for log entries with your binaries in the log. The operating system itself makes quite a few obsolete calls.
Logs installations of kernel-mode drivers	This test logs any attempt made by an application to install a kernel-mode driver.
Logs potential security issues	This test detects and logs potential security issues when using NULL DACL security descriptors and process creation API calls.
RPC Checks	This test checks for incorrect RPC usage. This test applies only to Windows Server 2003. You'll probably never need to turn this test on.

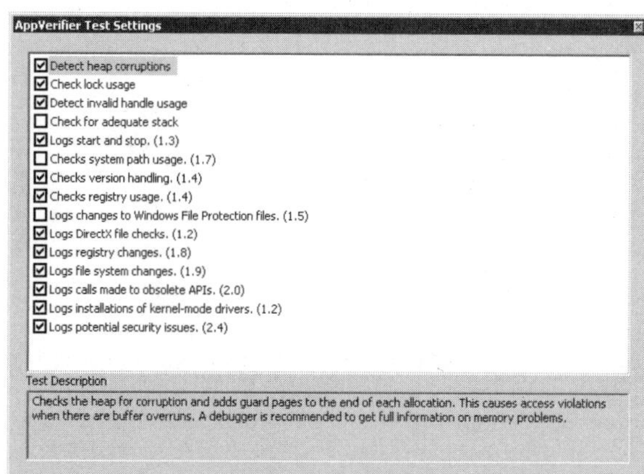

Figure 17-5 AppVerifier Test Settings dialog box

Turning on the AppVerifier add-in for your application is as simple as clicking the Enable Verification button. As you'll notice, you'll need to define your tests and options before you click Enable Verification because the Tests and Options buttons are disabled after clicking it. ACT does come with a demo program, but what it does isn't clear and it doesn't come with source code, so I wrote a quick demo program, AppVerifierDemo, that you can use to see many of the errors that the AppVerifier add-in catches. Simply open the AppVerifier-Demo project (which is included with this book's sample files) to see the errors in action. Some of the buttons don't cause errors—for example, the double critical section initialization. ACT 2.6 documented the error but doesn't actually generate it. The important section to play with is the PageHeap Errors section so that you can see how excellent PageHeap is at detecting those tough overruns and other nasty memory errors.

After you've executed your application a time or two, you can look at the logs of the runs and the output saved by the AppVerifier add-in. Although most of the errors the AppVerifier add-in detects result in an immediate access violation, some, such as obsolete function calls, appear only in the log, which you can access by clicking the Log Files button on the Debug toolbar. When looking at the logs, make sure to set the view option to Show All so that you'll see everything.

Killer Switches

As I mentioned in Chapter 2, there are some new compiler switches in Microsoft Visual C++ .NET that you should always have turned on. In this section, I'll introduce the `/RTCx` and `/GS` switches and explain why they're so important.

The Run-Time Check Switches

If the only feature added to the Visual C++ .NET compiler were the `/RTCx` (Run-Time Error Checks) switches, I would still tell everyone that it's a mandatory upgrade. As the name implies, the four RTC switches watch your code, and when you have certain errors at run time, the debugger pops up and tells you about them. Figure 17-6 shows an error in which some code overwrote past the end of a local variable. As you can see in the message box, the particular local that was blown is shown as well. The part you can't see is that this message box pops up at the end of the function where the error occurred, so it's trivial to find and fix the problem! The RTC switches, by the way, are allowed only in debug builds.

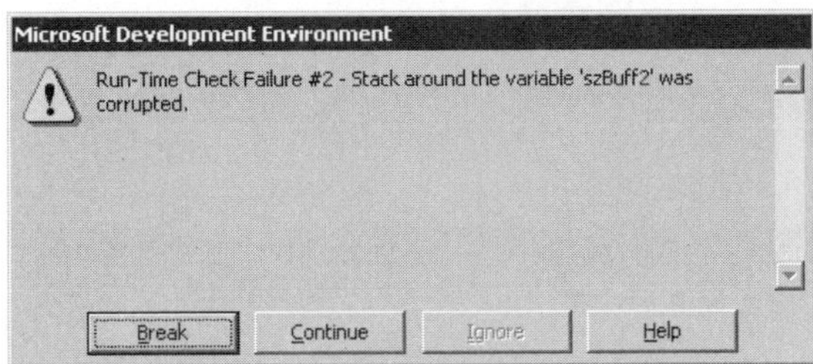

Figure 17-6 The `/RTCs` error report

The first switch, `/RTCs`, whose error report is shown in Figure 17-6, does all sorts of run-time stack checking. It starts by initializing all local variables to nonzero values. This helps you find those pesky release build problems that don't show up in debug builds—specifically the case in which you have an uninitialized pointer variable on the stack. All local variables are filled with 0xCC, the `INT 3` (breakpoint) opcode.

The second helpful stack-checking feature is that `/RTCs` does stack pointer verification around every function call you make to combat against calling convention mismatches. For example, if you declare a function as `__cdecl`, but it's exported as `__stdcall`, the stack will be corrupted upon returning from the `__stdcall` function. If you've been paying attention to compiler switches over the years, you might have guessed that the first two stack-checking options for `/RTCs` do the same thing as the `/GZ` switch in Microsoft Visual C++ 6.

Fortunately for us, Microsoft extended the `/RTCs` switch to also do overrun and underrun checking of all multibyte local variables such as arrays. It does this by adding four bytes to the front and end of those arrays and checking them at the end of the function to ensure those extra bytes are still set to 0xCC. The local checking works with all multibyte locals except those that require the compiler to add padding bytes. In almost all cases, padding is added only when you use the `__declspec(align)` directive, the `/Zp` structure member alignment switch, or the `#pragma pack(n)` directive.

The second switch, `/RTCu`, checks your variable usage and will pop the warning if you use any without initializing them first. If you've been a loyal Bugslayer over the years, you might be wondering why this switch is important. Since all loyal readers (like you) are already compiling their code with warning level 4 (`/W4`) and treating all warnings as errors (`/WX`), you know that compiler warnings C4700 and C4701 will always tell you at compile time where you are definitely using and where you might be using variables without initialization, respectively. With the `/RTCu` switch, those who aren't will still be told they have bugs in their code. What's interesting about the `/RTCu` switch is the code to check for uninitialized variables is inserted if the compiler detects a C4700 or C4701 condition. The third switch, `/RTC1`, is just shorthand for combining `/RTCu` and `/RTCs`.

The final switch, `/RTCc`, checks for data truncation assignments—for example, if you try to assign 0x101 to a `char` variable. Like the `/RTCu`, if you're compiling with `/W4` and `/WX`, data truncation will produce a C4244 error at compilation time. If you get an `/RTCc` error, you have to either mask off the bits you need or cast to the appropriate value. The project Property Pages dialog box, shown in Figure 17-7, allows you to only set `/RTCu`, `/RTCs`, or `/RTC1` in the Basic Runtime Checks option. In order to turn on `/RTCc`, you'll need to select the Smaller Type Check option above the Basic Runtime Checks option, as shown in Figure 17-7.

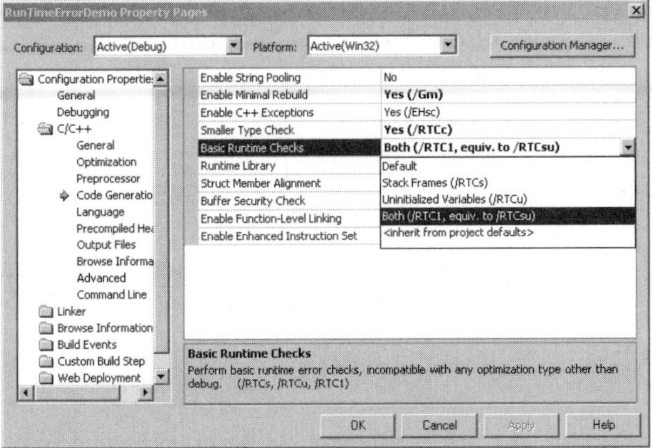

Figure 17-7 Setting the /RTCx switches

At first, I couldn't see why the /RTCc switch was not turned on by the /RTC1. A little thinking showed that /RTCc can show errors on legal C code such as the following:

```
char LoByte(int a)
{
    return ((char)a) ;
}
```

If /RTCc were included in /RTC1, people might think that all the Run-Time Error Checks switches are reporting false positives. However, I vote for always turning on /RTCc because I want to know about any potential problems whenever I run my code.

With the switch descriptions out of the way, I want to turn to the notification you get when you do have an error. When running your programs outside the debugger, the run-time checking code uses the standard C run-time assertion message box. For those of you writing services or code that can't have a user interface, you'll need to redirect the message box using the _CrtSetReportMode function with the _CRT_ASSERT report type parameter. You might think there would be a single, standard way for the /RTCx switches to notify the user, but that's not the case. When running under the debugger, there's a completely different way to do the notifications.

If you happen to look at the Exceptions dialog box in the Visual Studio .NET IDE, you might notice several new classes of exceptions added. The interesting new exception class is Native Run-Time Checks. As you look at it in the Exceptions dialog box, you'll recognize the four different exceptions as matching up with the /RTCx switches. That's your hint that when your program encounters a run-time check while running under the debugger, your program will throw a special exception so that the debugger can handle it.

Controlling Run-Time Check Output

While the default method of output will suffice for many situations, you might want to handle the error output yourself. Listing 17-6 shows a sample custom error handler. The parameter list for run-time check error handlers is a little different in that it takes variable parameters. Evidently, Microsoft is planning to add quite a few different run-time error checks in the future to account for this flexibility. Since your custom handler gets the same parameters as the default version, you can show the errors with variable information and everything else. As you can see from Listing 17-6, it's up to you how you choose to inform the user. The code from Listing 17-6 is with this book's sample files in the RTCHandling sample, so you can play with the error handling all you want.

```
/*//////////////////////////////////////////////////////////////////////
FUNCTION        :   HandleRTCFailure
DESCRIPTION     :
    The Run Time Checking (RTC) handler function when NOT running
under the debugger. When running under a debugger, this function
is ignored. Consequently, you can't debug this puppy at all!
PARAMETERS      :
    iError    - The type of error as reported through _RTC_SetErrorType.
                Note that I don't use this parameter.
    szFile    - The source filename where the error occurred.
    iLine     - The line where the error occurred.
    szModule  - The module where the error occurred.
    szFormat  - The printf-style format string for the variable
                parameters.
                Note that I don't use this parameter except to get the
                values out of the variables parameters.
    ...      - The "variable" length parameter list. There are only
                two values passed here. The first is the RTC Error
                number.
                     1 = /RTCc
                     2 = /RTCs
                     3 = /RTCu
                 The second is the string that appears when the debugger
                 shows the message. This is only important for /RTCs and
                 /RTCu as those show the variable where the problem
                 happened.
RETURN VALUES   :
    TRUE  - Cause a _DebugBreak to be called after this function
            returns.
    FALSE - Continue execution.
//////////////////////////////////////////////////////////////////////*/
// Turn off run time checks for this function so I don't go recursive
// on myself.
#pragma runtime_checks("", off)

// The critical section to protect against reentrancy in the
```

Listing 17-6 /RTCx custom error reporting

```
// HandleRTCFailure function.
CRITICAL_SECTION g_csRTCLock ;

int HandleRTCFailure ( int          /*iError*/    ,
                       const char * szFile        ,
                       int          iLine         ,
                       const char * szModule      ,
                       const char * szFormat      ,
                       ...                        )
{
    // Just say no to reentrant code!
    EnterCriticalSection ( &g_csRTCLock ) ;

    // Get the two variable length parameters. I guess they plan on
    // adding a ton of these RTC checks in the future.
    va_list vl ;

    va_start ( vl , szFormat ) ;

    // The first one is the number of the error that occured.
    _RTC_ErrorNumber RTCErrNum = va_arg ( vl , _RTC_ErrorNumber ) ;

    // The second is the additional description of the error.
    char * szErrorVariableDesc = va_arg ( vl , char * ) ;

    va_end ( vl ) ;

    TCHAR szBuff [ 512 ] ;

    // Get the error description text based off the error number.
    const char *szErr = _RTC_GetErrDesc ( RTCErrNum ) ;

    // Make sure szFile and szModule have something in them.
    if ( NULL == szFile )
    {
        szFile = "Unknown File" ;
    }
    if ( NULL == szModule )
    {
        szModule = "Unknown Module" ;
    }

    // If it's any error other than /RTCc, I can show some cool info
    // that includes the variable in question!
    if ( 1 != RTCErrNum )
    {
        _stprintf ( szBuff                                            ,
                    _T ( "%S\n%S\nLine #%d\nFile:%S\nModule:%S" ) ,
                    szErr                                             ,
                    szErrorVariableDesc                               ,
                    iLine                                             ,
                    szFile                                            ,
                    szModule                                            ) ;
    }
```

(continued)

```
    else
    {
        // Build the string.
        _stprintf ( szBuff                                          ,
                    _T ( "%S\nLine #%d\nFile:%S\nModule:%S" ) ,
                    szErr                                           ,
                    iLine                                           ,
                    szFile                                          ,
                    szModule                                        ) ;
    }

    int iRes = TRUE ;
    if ( IDYES == MessageBox ( GetForegroundWindow ( )           ,
                               szBuff                            ,
                               _T ( "Run Time Check Failure" )   ,
                               MB_YESNO | MB_ICONQUESTION        ) )
    {
        // Returning 1 means DebugBreak will happen when this
        // function returns.
        iRes = 1 ;
    }
    else
    {
        iRes = 0 ;
    }

    // Pop out of the lock.
    LeaveCriticalSection ( &g_csRTCLock ) ;

    return ( iRes ) ;
}
#pragma runtime_checks("", restore)
```

Setting your custom error handler function is trivial; just pass it as the parameter to `_RTC_SetErrorFunc`. There are a few other functions to assist you when handling run-time check errors. The first, `_RTC_GetErrDesc`, retrieves the description string for a particular error. `_RTC_NumErrors` returns the total number of errors supported by the current version of the compiler and run time. One function, which I find a little dangerous, is `_RTC_SetErrorType`. You can use this function to turn off error handling for any or all of the specific run-time checks.

Since the run-time checks rely on the C run time, if your program doesn't use the C run time, you might think you would completely lose the benefits of the RTC switches. If you are wondering why you would ever have a program without the C run time, think about ATL and building with `_ATL_MIN_CRT`. Without the C run time, you need to call `_RTC_Initialize` if you've used `__MSVC_RUNTIME_CHECKS`. You must also provide a function named `_CRT_RTC_INIT`, which returns your custom error handler.

When I first started playing with a custom output handler, I immediately ran into a small problem. I couldn't debug my handler! If you think about it, you can see why it happens. As I've already discussed, the run-time checking code can determine whether you are running under a debugger and display the output either in the debugger or through the normal C run-time assertion dialog box. When you're running under a debugger, the run-time checking code sees that it's under a debugger and just generates the special exception code to talk to the debugger, completely bypassing your custom output handler.

Common Debugging Question

How can I make sure I don't screw up my string processing?

Probably the most common security error as well as an inflection point for bugs is related to handling good old null terminated strings. The problem lies in the original definition of the C run time string handling functions: there's no way to indicate how long a string buffer is. For example, `strcpy` takes an input buffer and an output buffer and blindly copies the date from the input buffer into the output buffer—no matter that the output buffer might be only half the size. Not only is that a memory overrun but one of the key security holes that virus writers take advantage of to overwrite the return value on the stack in order to get code executing.

You could code review yourself to death looking for these errors, but you'll still miss them. Fortunately, some very bright people at Microsoft realized it was time to make a change. A new library, STRSAFE, rides to the rescue to save your string processing from yourself. STRSAFE is part of the July 2002 Platform SDK and is included with Visual Studio .NET 2003.

The whole idea is to include STRSAFE.H in your precompiled header so that you'll have access to a whole slew of functions that take output buffer lengths and ensure those functions don't copy any more than the specified number of characters. When you first compile after including STRSAFE.H, you'll find that all the error-prone string functions are now deprecated and your builds will stop until you fix them.

Unfortunately, STRSAFE came out after I had written nearly all the code for this book. As you'll find with your projects, retrofitting STRSAFE on your code is much like taking the ride to convert ANSI code to Unicode. It takes quite a bit of time, but it's worth it. If the code is not fully converted by the time the book ships, I'll have it moved over soon and posted on Wintellect's Web site.

The Buffer Security Check Switch

The run-time checks are very cool, but another switch that you should always turn on is /GS, the Buffer Security Check switch. Unlike the /RTCx switches, /GS should be turned on for both debug and release builds. The purpose of /GS is to monitor the return address for a function to see whether it's overwritten, which is a common technique used by viruses and Trojan horse programs to take over your application. /GS works by reserving space on the stack before the return address. At the function entry, the function prolog fills in that spot with a security cookie XOR'd with the return address. That security cookie is computed as part of the module load so it's unique to each module. When the function exits, a special function, _security_check_cookie, checks to see whether the value stored at the special spot is the same as it was when entering the function. If the values are different, the code pops up a message box and terminates the program. If you want to see the security code in action, read the source files SECCINIT.C, SECCOOK.C, and SECFAIL.C in the C run-time source code.

As if the security-checking capability of the /GS switch weren't enough, the switch is also a wonderful debugging aid. Even though the /RTCx switches will track numerous errors, a random write to the return address will still sneak through. With the /GS, you get that checking in your debug builds as well. Of course, the Redmondtonians were thinking of us when they wrote the /GS switch, so you can replace the default message box function with your own handler by calling _set_security_error_handler. If you do whack the stack, your handler should call ExitProcess after logging the error.

Summary

The debug C run-time library has many wonderful features—provided you turn them on in your application. Because using memory is a fact of life in our C and C++ programs, we need all the help we can get solving the problems we invariably have with memory. This chapter covered the high points of the DCRT library and presented two utilities I wrote, MemDumperValidator and MemStress, that will help you get more information about the memory your application uses and allow you to better test your application under stressful conditions.

The extensibility of the DCRT library is pretty amazing. If you've been in this business for more than a year or two, you've probably written something like it in the past. I hope I was able to give you some sense of the power of the DCRT library. I encourage you to devise other utilities and helper code that will ease your memory debugging chores.

I also discussed the techniques and tools necessary to handle the nastiest of memory problems in production applications: uninitialized writes and memory overruns. Although the brute force approach might not seem elegant for solving those uninitialized writes, it's the only technique that actually gives you a chance. When it comes to memory overruns, the PageHeap tool accessible from AppVerifier, part of the Application Compatibility Toolkit, makes tracking them down easier. Although AppVerifier has some lumps, I'm sure Microsoft will continue to improve it in the future. Finally, the new Run-Time Error Checks and Buffer Security Check compiler switches are some of the most important advances we've had in compiler tools to help eradicate errors.

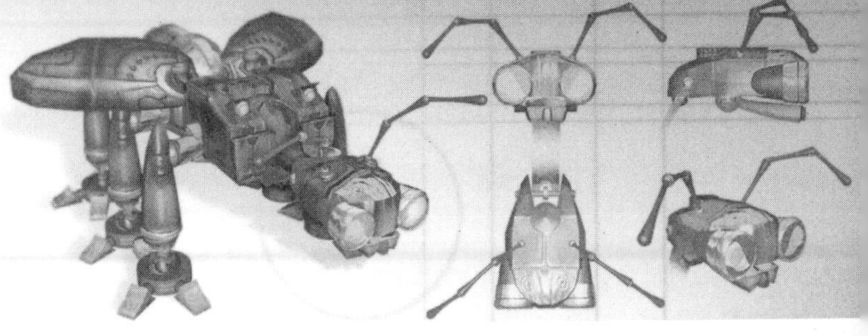

18

FastTrace: A High-Performance Tracing Tool for Server Applications

As we all know, server-based applications put a priority on speed. Every operation you undertake has to be carefully considered, because the longer something takes, the less scalability you'll get out of the application. Many of us are working on applications that have to handle thousands—or even millions—of individual requests, and any extraneous work your application has to manage can have huge consequences. What makes a server application even more "fun" is that it's highly multithreaded, so sometimes it's not even obvious where an application is killing performance.

It's tough enough to write server applications, but it's doubly hard to debug them. You can observe client applications with your own eyeballs to see some bugs, especially performance bottlenecks. However, with server applications, you're left groping at a blob of code that is running in the dark recesses of memory and that you can see only tangentially in response times and by poking at it with tools like debuggers and PerfMon, which show you only snippets of the overall health of the application. To make matters even worse, none of the nontrivial bugs you'll encounter will ever show up in the nice controlled environment of your QA systems; they show up only in the jungles of production.

To debug these server applications, everyone resorts to the old standby of tracing. This is the only way you'll be able to see the big picture, especially on live production systems. I've worked on applications that have some of the most incredible tracing systems you could ever imagine. A lot of thought was put into them so that the developers could truly see what was happening in production, giving them a good chance of finding and solving bugs.

Unfortunately, the balance between "debugability" and performance is extremely delicate when it comes to server applications. In fact, several times in our consulting business, we've been called in to work on performance problems and have run into the situation where the tracing system used by the team *is* the performance problem. What makes these scenarios even more interesting is that in the cases in which the tracing system was the bottleneck, the teams didn't even realize it.

Since I've had numerous opportunities to wrestle with poorly performing tracing systems, I wanted to solve the problem once and for all. For this chapter, I wrote a tool, FastTrace, which should allow you to have as much tracing as you'd like without killing your performance. Before I discuss using FastTrace and its implementation, I want to explain why most of the tracing techniques that people use are such a problem.

The Fundamental Problem and Its Solution

The biggest problem with server applications is that we poor humans find it hard to truly visualize multiple things going on at the same time. Our brains organize linearly. To make our server debugging easier, we subconsciously gravitate toward ensuring that our tracing output is in linear time. However, with multiple processors being the norm on most servers these days and with many applications running with 20 or more threads, many of those linear universes are happening at the same time. In our effort to create order out of this seeming chaos, our tracing resorts to a single file responsible for reporting the whole application's tracing.

When you have a single file containing the tracing and a multithreaded application, you're looking at the situation described in Figure 18-1. The bottleneck comes from trying to make tracing calls from every thread linear. As I mentioned in Chapter 15, your whole job when it comes to multithreaded programming is to keep your threads as busy as possible and waiting as little as possible.

Obviously, taking the processing time necessary to keep things linear out of the normal execution is absolutely critical to having the fastest tracing in the West. If each thread did its own tracing, the situation would be perfect. Well, that's exactly what FastTrace does: it gives each thread its own tracing output file so that none of the threads are waiting or blocking. After the trace output for multiple threads has been saved to log files, you can merge these log files so that you can see the tracing as it exactly occurred. In the section titled "Fast-

Trace Implementation" later in this chapter, you'll see that FastTrace is quite straightforward to implement.

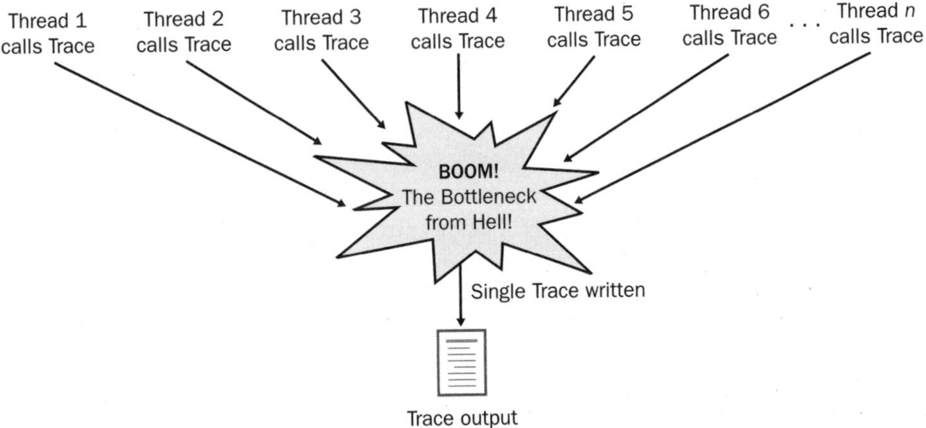

Figure 18-1 The common server tracing system

Using FastTrace

With FastTrace hiding the implementation details, all you need to do is link against FASTTRACE.DLL and start making calls to one of its exports, appropriately named `FastTrace`, whose prototype is shown here:

```
FASTTRACE_DLLINTERFACE void FastTrace ( LPCTSTR szFmt       ,
                                        ...                 ) ;
```

All tracing output you'll generate will go to files in the same directory as the executable process. Each file will have the following format:

```
<EXE Name>_<Process ID>_<Thread ID>.FTL
```

When you open an individual file, you'll notice it's a binary file. Each FastTrace output string is stored with a sequence number so that when merging the files together, the appropriate order can be maintained. Additionally, each output string can have an optional timestamp.

To keep FastTrace simple and fast, I chose to limit the length of a string to 80 characters. If you're running a debug build, you'll get a `SUPERASSERT` assertion to help you cull out longer strings. If you want longer strings, you can simply redefine `MAX_FASTTRACE_LEN` in FastTrace.H and rebuild the FastTrace solution.

The function `SetFastTraceOptions` allows you to set the three options for FastTrace by passing the `FASTTRACEOPTIONS` structure as a parameter. The first option lets you turn on write through writing. You might want to turn this on if you're chasing down a crash and want to ensure you get all traces immediately flushed as soon as they are written. This obviously slows down performance, so you should turn on this option only if needed. The second option allows you to turn on time stamping for each trace. Timestamps are off by default to squeak out a little more performance. You can turn timing on and off at will. The final option that you can specify is the debugging output function, which is prototyped to match `OutputDebugString`. By default, FastTrace doesn't call `OutputDebugString`, as I explained in Chapter 4; it causes an exception and will slow down your application. However, you'll probably want to see those exceptions in debug builds, so the option is there.

Two final functions will help you take control of your tracing. The first is `FlushFastTraceFiles`, which, as the name implies, will flush all the FastTrace buffers to disk. You might want to consider setting up a background thread that monitors when the server application isn't busy and periodically flushes the tracing. That way, you can ensure you get your traces into the file in case you crash.

The other function is `SnapFastTraceFiles`. Server applications don't have a definitive ending point, so you need a way to ensure you can look at your traces at any time. The `SnapFastTraceFiles` function closes any open trace files and renames them to indicate that you have snapped out the files. The naming scheme is as follows:

```
SNAP_<Snap Number>_<EXE Name>_<Process ID>_<Thread ID>.FTL
```

The snap number is a decimal number that is unique per process, so you can see the chain of snaps you have taken. After closing and renaming all active trace files, `SnapFastTraceFiles` reopens tracing files for each thread so that you won't miss a thing. As with `FlushFastTraceFiles`, you'll want a way to trigger your calls to `SnapFastTraceFiles` so that you can generate them when you need them. Also keep in mind that both `SnapFastTraceFiles` and `FlushFastTraceFiles` have to acquire a critical section to protect internal data structures, so it will block any trace calls during that time.

Merging Trace Logs

As I mentioned, the log files are in binary format, so use the FastTraceLog.EXE program to look at individual logs or combine logs to see the linear flow. Dumping a log to the screen is as simple as passing `–d` *<Individual log file>* on the FastTraceLog.EXE command line. The output will show the sequence number and if time stamping was turn on, the date/time followed by the individual trace string done at that time.

Merging, or combining, the log files is only a little more difficult. The command line passed to FastTraceLog.EXE is `–c` *<Optional SNAP and number>_<EXE Name>_<Process ID>*. For example, when you run the test program FTSimpTest.EXE, you'll see that it produces some of these trace file names:

```
FTSimpTest_2720_0400.FTL
FTSimpTest_2720_1644.FTL
FTSimpTest_2720_2332.FTL
FTSimpTest_2720_2368.FTL
FTSimpTest_2720_2424.FTL
FTSimpTest_2720_2560.FTL
FTSimpTest_2720_2584.FTL
FTSimpTest_2720_2640.FTL
FTSimpTest_2720_2688.FTL
```

The command to combine these individual thread logs is as follows:

```
FastTraceLog.exe -c FTSimpTest_2720
```

The merged trace file is written to a text file—in the preceding case, it's FTSimpTest_2720.TXT. The output in the text file looks very similar to the dump, and you can see that time stamping was on and turned off before the last line.

```
[0x0B3C 57 1/1/2003 17:52:47:205]
Hello from CThread -> 3!
[0x0B50 58 1/1/2003 17:52:47:205]
Hello from CThread -> 3!
[0x0B50 59 1/1/2003 17:52:47:486]
Hello from CThread -> 4!
[0x0B20 60 1/1/2003 17:52:47:486]
Hello from CThread -> 4!
[0x0B20 61 1/1/2003 17:52:47:767]
Hello from CThread -> 5!
[0x0830 62]
THIS SHOULD BE THE LAST LINE!
```

The values in brackets represent the particular thread that generated the message, the sequence number, and the optional date/time stamp of the message, and on the line below the bracketed values is the trace message. I'm proud to point out that the date/time stamp is internationalized, so the date will appear as you expect it for your local!

FastTrace Implementation

As you can see, FastTrace is quite simple to use, and as you'll learn in this section, its implementation is nearly that simple as well. The main magic behind FastTrace is per-thread storage. Each thread has its own copy of the file-writing class, so it writes only to a single file. Much of the core implementation is straightforward. All the source code is in the FastTrace project, which accompanies this book's sample files.

I had to make only two interesting decisions while implementing FastTrace. The first thought I had when designing the tool was to store the individual thread trace logs as text files. That way the files were easily readable right off the bat. Of course, when I thought about the work that I was going to cause by merging them, I figured there had to be another way. Consequently, I chose to store each entry with a binary timestamp along with the particular trace string. I originally considered allowing variable length strings in that file format, but I didn't want to slow down the tracing by needing to count the characters in each string on each trace statement. Additionally, variable length strings would have made the reading that much more difficult.

The second issue I needed some time to think about was which time format to store the timestamps in. I don't know if you've ever looked at the Time help for the operating system, but there seems to be a plethora of different formats. After playing around a little bit, I chose to use the `FILETIME` format because it's only 8 bytes, whereas the `SYSTEMTIME` format is 16 bytes. I also looked at the processing involved and determined the fastest way to get the time was to call only `GetSystemTimeAsFileTime` instead of other time functions.

Summary

The difficulties you face in debugging server applications—finding those production-only bugs—means that trace statements are one of the most important tools you can have. However, with the tension between tracing and performance, you need to have something as fast as possible. In this chapter, I provided a tracing mechanism that should work quite well with even the most intense server application imaginable.

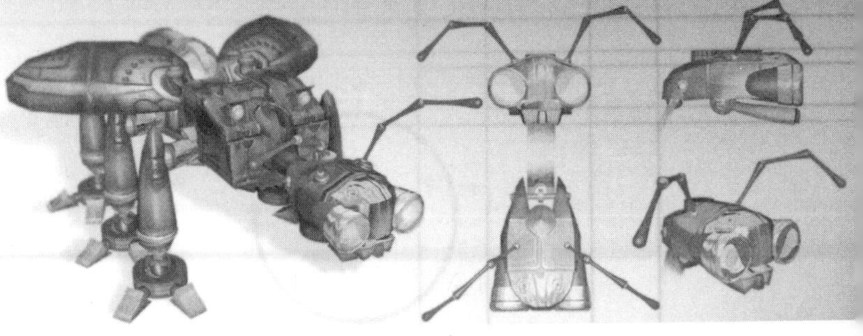

19

Smoothing the Working Set

As the Godzilla movie of a few years ago said, and according to a lot of the spam in your inbox, "size does matter." All developers salivate over bigger and faster machines, but what we really need to be worried about is the size of our binaries. The old adage "small code is good code" still applies in today's world of 512-MB developer machines and 2-GB servers. Just because you have what looks like infinite memory doesn't mean that you have to use it all!

After you've taken care of the obvious performance issues in your code, such as mistakenly calculating pi to a billion digits inside some loop, it's time to ensure that your application's working set is as small as possible. The working set is the amount of memory dedicated to the currently running parts of the program. The smaller you can make the working set, the faster your computer will run because you'll avoid page faults. A page fault occurs when parts of your application are either not in cache memory (soft page faults) or not in memory at all and have to be brought in from the hard disk (hard page faults). As a wise man once told me, "A page fault can ruin your day!"

When you're looking at the Mem Usage column in the Processes tab of Task Manager, you're looking at the current working set of your application. Many other diagnostic and informational tools such as PerfMon also show you the working set. After you've ensured your algorithms are memory frugal, you need to consider the amount of memory taken up by the code itself. I'll start this chapter by discussing the ramifications of page faults when it comes to execution and why these page faults hurt you. As you'd expect, I'll also present a tool, Smooth Working Set (SWS), which will make tuning your working set nearly a snap.

Working Set Tuning

What you might intuitively realize but don't consider the ramifications of is that when you compile and link your binaries, the linker simply orders the functions starting with the first OBJ file first, the second OBJ second, and so on. In other words, the functions are placed in order of link, not in order of execution. However, the problem is that this process doesn't take into account the locality of the most commonly called functions.

Figure 19-1 shows a stylized example of what happens. In this example, the operating system supports only six fixed-length functions per memory page and can hold only four pages in memory at a time. Additionally, the 10 functions being called are the most commonly called functions in the program.

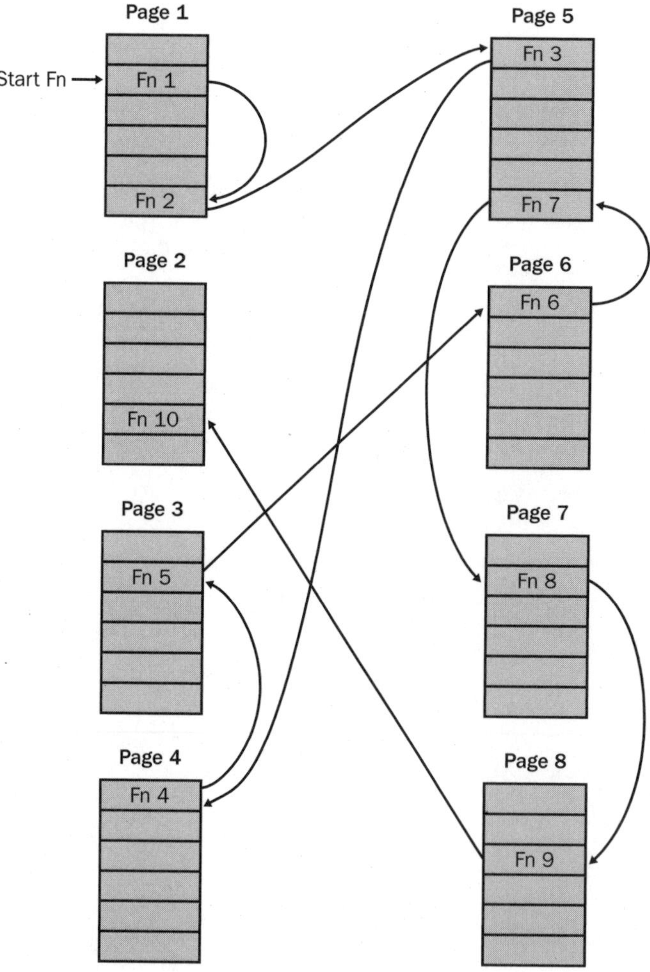

Figure 19-1 Model nonoptimized system

When the operating system loads the program in Figure 19-1, it naturally loads the first four pages of the binary in memory. The first function executes and calls function 2, which happens to reside in the same page. However, function 2 calls function 3, which resides in page 5. Since page 5 isn't in memory, a page fault occurs. Now the operating system has to throw out one of the loaded pages. Since page 4 hasn't been touched, the operating system throws it out and in its place puts page 5. Now it can execute function 3. Unfortunately, function 3 calls function 4, which happens to reside in page 4, which was just swapped out, so our second page fault occurs. The operating system will have to swap out page 3, as it's the least recently used, so it can bring page 4 back into memory to execute function 4. As you can see, another page fault will happen because function 4 calls function 5, which was just swapped out. Feel free to continue to walk through all the calls, but as you can see, there's lots of work going on in those page faults.

The key issue to remember here is that page faults take huge amounts of time to process. The program shown in Figure 19-1 is spending a lot of time in the operating system code instead of executing. If we could specify the function order regarding how the linker puts the code in the pages, we could avoid much of the overhead necessary to process all those page faults.

Figure 19-2 shows the same program after all the most commonly called functions have been packed together and moved to the front of the binary. The program as a whole takes the same amount of memory, the four page limit, but because the most commonly called functions are now packed together, they don't cause any page faults while calling each other, and the application runs faster.

The process of finding the most commonly called functions so that you can reorder them is called *working set tuning* and is a two-stage process. The first stage is to determine which functions are called the most, and the second stage is to tell the linker how to order the functions so that everything is packed together.

The work involved in counting the function executions is all hidden by SWS, and I'll discuss how you do it in the next section, "Using SWS." Telling the linker what order to put the functions in is fairly trivial. You do this through the `/ORDER` command-line option to LINK.EXE. The parameter to the `/ORDER` option is simply a text file, called the order file, which lists each function on a single line in the order in which you want them to appear. Interestingly, each of the functions listed in the order file must be in its full-name decorated glory. Essentially, the idea behind SWS is to produce the order file for your application.

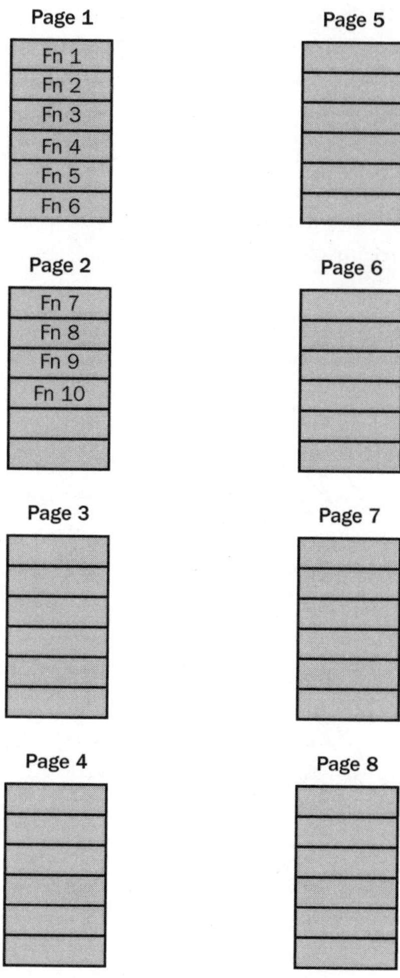

Figure 19-2 Model optimized system

Those of you who are old Microsoft Windows salts like me might have the initials WST floating around in the back of your head right now. WST stands for Working Set Tuner. It was a tool that Microsoft used to distribute with the Platform SDK to do, well, working set tuning. However, you might also remember three distinct facts about WST: the first is that it was extremely difficult to use, the second is that it was broken quite a bit, and the third is that it's no longer on the Platform SDK. SWS is a much easier-to-use replacement for WST.

For more background on working set tuning and an excellent primer on Windows performance, I strongly suggest you see whether you can find Volume 4 of the *Microsoft Windows NT 3.51 Resource Kit*, *Optimizing Windows NT* (Microsoft Press, 1995), which was written by Russ Blake and is an excellent introduction to the topic. Russ was in charge of performance tuning on the Microsoft Windows NT team. The book used to be on MSDN, but alas, it's since disappeared. Russ's team developed WST and in his book, Russ says you should see a 35–50 percent reduction in your working set after using a working set tuning tool. Any time your application can lose that much fat, you should sit up and take notice!

Before I jump into using SWS, I need to pause for a reality check. First, SWS isn't a magic elixir. If you have terrible performance before running SWS, you'll have terrible performance after running SWS. Second, tuning your working set should be the final performance tweak you perform *after* you've perfected your algorithms and taken care of any incidental performance bugs you find. Finally, you should be concerned about running SWS only towards the end of the development cycle. You need the code changes to be on a rapidly decreasing curve to ensure you get the benefits of SWS.

Sometimes you might not need to run SWS. If you have a small application whose total compiled size for all binaries is less than 2 to 3 MB, you might not see any working set reduction at all. The maximum benefit is achieved when you tune the working set on larger applications because the more pages you have, the more room there is for improvement.

Common Debugging Question

Can I check a process for a resource leak on a production server without installing any programs?

Although you can always use PerfMon to perform a quick check, nothing is better than the amazing Task Manager. In the Processes tab, you're allowed to add a column that reports various performance monitor statistics. Since resources are handle-based, you'll need to monitor the handle count for the process. Activate the Processes tab, choose Select Columns from the View menu, and in the Select Columns dialog box, check Handle Count. If you need to watch GDI objects, check GDI Objects as well. Figure 19-3 shows both columns added to Task Manager, sorted by handles.

(continued)

Common Debugging Question *(continued)*

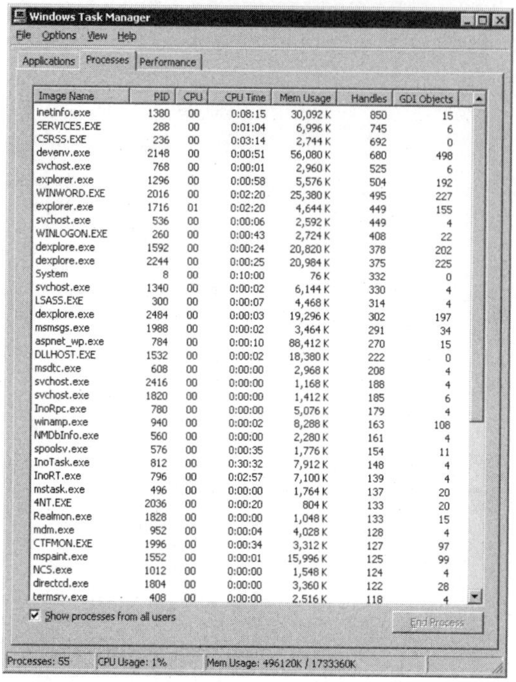

Windows Task Manager

File Options View Help

Applications | Processes | Performance

Image Name	PID	CPU	CPU Time	Mem Usage	Handles	GDI Objects
inetinfo.exe	1380	00	0:08:15	30,092 K	850	15
SERVICES.EXE	288	00	0:01:04	6,996 K	745	6
CSRSS.EXE	236	00	0:03:14	2,744 K	692	0
devenv.exe	2148	00	0:00:51	56,080 K	680	498
svchost.exe	768	00	0:00:01	2,960 K	525	6
explorer.exe	1296	00	0:00:58	5,576 K	504	192
WINWORD.EXE	2016	00	0:02:20	25,380 K	495	227
explorer.exe	1716	01	0:02:20	4,644 K	449	155
svchost.exe	536	00	0:00:06	2,592 K	449	4
WINLOGON.EXE	260	00	0:00:43	2,724 K	408	22
dexplore.exe	1592	00	0:00:24	20,820 K	378	202
dexplore.exe	2244	00	0:00:25	20,984 K	375	225
System	8	00	0:10:00	76 K	332	0
svchost.exe	1340	00	0:00:02	6,144 K	330	4
LSASS.EXE	300	00	0:00:07	4,468 K	314	4
dexplore.exe	2484	00	0:00:03	19,296 K	302	197
msmsgs.exe	1988	00	0:00:02	3,464 K	291	34
aspnet_wp.exe	784	00	0:00:10	88,412 K	270	15
DLLHOST.EXE	1532	00	0:00:02	18,380 K	222	0
msdtc.exe	608	00	0:00:00	2,968 K	208	4
svchost.exe	2416	00	0:00:00	1,168 K	188	4
svchost.exe	1820	00	0:00:00	1,412 K	185	6
InoRpc.exe	780	00	0:00:00	5,076 K	179	4
winamp.exe	940	00	0:00:02	8,288 K	163	108
NMDbInfo.exe	560	00	0:00:00	2,280 K	161	4
spoolsv.exe	576	00	0:00:35	1,776 K	154	11
InoTask.exe	812	00	0:30:32	7,912 K	148	4
InoRT.exe	796	00	0:02:57	7,100 K	139	4
mstask.exe	496	00	0:00:00	1,764 K	137	20
4NT.EXE	2036	00	0:00:20	804 K	133	20
Realmon.exe	1828	00	0:00:00	1,048 K	133	15
mdm.exe	952	00	0:00:04	4,028 K	128	4
CTFMON.EXE	1996	00	0:00:34	3,312 K	127	97
mspaint.exe	1552	00	0:00:01	15,996 K	125	99
NCS.exe	1012	00	0:00:00	1,548 K	124	4
directcd.exe	1804	00	0:00:00	3,360 K	122	28
termsrv.exe	408	00	0:00:00	2,516 K	118	4

Show processes from all users

End Process

Processes: 55 | CPU Usage: 1% | Mem Usage: 496120K / 1733360K

Figure 19-3 Task Manager showing handles and GDI objects

By default, Task Manager automatically updates every few seconds, but you'll have to keep an eye on the handle or GDI values to determine whether the value is sliding up. What I like to do is pause the updating by setting the Update Speed menu to Paused on the View menu. This way I can perform an operation, shift back to Task Manager, and press F5 to update the display. Make sure you also watch the Mem Usage column because handle values are backed by memory—if both are sliding up, you're seeing a resource leak in action.

Using SWS

Using SWS is a three-stage process. The first stage involves recompiling your application to get SWS hooked in so that you can collect the function execution data. The second stage involves running the most common user scenarios using the special compiled version of your application. To use SWS correctly, you must spend some time determining exactly what those user scenarios are so that you can duplicate them precisely. Just running your application randomly under SWS won't help reduce your working set much at all. The third stage involves generating the order file for the linker (which is very simple to do), and integrating that order file into your final build.

Setting Up the SWS Compiles

The reason you're required to do a separate recompile to use SWS is that I based SWS on the same concepts the WST program was based on. Although I could've written a hugely complicated and error-prone tool to patch all the functions in your application on the fly, it's so much easier to use the compiler to do the hooking. The `/Gh` switch (Enable `_penter` Hook Function) tells the compiler to insert a call to a function named `_penter` at the beginning of all generated function prologs. SWS provides the `_penter` implementation that you'll link against so that it can do all it's magic.

Getting your application compiled for SWS is generally straightforward; you simply follow these steps:

1. Before you do anything, you should ensure your project's release build settings are exactly what you want because you'll use that configuration to clone your settings. If you've applied the switches to the compiler and linker I recommended in Chapter 2 by using the SettingsMaster add-in from Chapter 9, you'll be all set.

2. Clone the configuration you want to tune. Right-click on the solution in Solution Explorer and select Configuration Manager from the menu to bring up the Configuration Manager dialog box. The new configuration option is hidden in the Active Solution Configuration drop-down list. Figure 19-4 shows accessing the <New...> field. (It took me a while to find it.) In general, you'll want to clone your release builds. In the New Solution Configuration dialog box, make doubly sure you set the Copy Settings From drop-down list because you'll inherit from <Default> and your build settings won't get moved over. When naming the new project, I like to use the build type immediately followed by "-SWS" so that the full name is Release-SWS. Figure 19-5 shows the New Solution Configuration dialog box with these settings. Keep in mind that when creating new solutions, the output and intermediate directories will change.

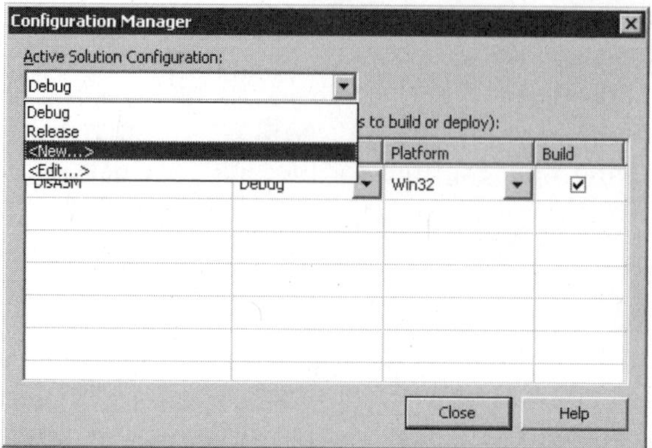

Figure 19-4 Initiating a new configuration from the Configuration Manager dialog box

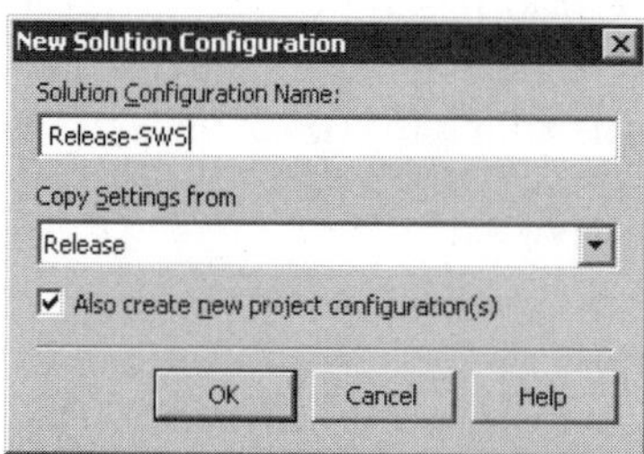

Figure 19-5 Creating a new Release-SWS configuration

3. If you're using SettingsMaster (and you should be), setting the compiler and linker switches is trivial. Click the SettingsMaster Custom Project Update button and, when prompted, choose the Release-SWS.XML file. This will take care of ensuring the minimal settings are all set up. If you want to run SWS on a Debug build, choose the Debug-SWS.XML file. (Both files are in the SettingsMaster\SettingsMaster directory.)

4. If you aren't using SettingsMaster (shame on you!), you'll need to add the following settings to the compiler (CL.EXE) for your Release-SWS project. Please see Chapter 2 for information on how to set these.

   - `/Zi` (Debug Information Format)
   - `/Gy` (Enable Function-Level Linking)
   - `/Gh` (Enable `_penter` Hook Function) There's no standard setting for this switch, so you'll have to select the Command Line node under the C/C++ folder and enter it manually.

The following settings must be added to the linker (LINK.EXE) for your Release-SWS project:

- `/DEBUG` (Generate Debug Info).
- `/OPT:REF` (Optimization, eliminate unreferenced functions).

5. Add SWSDLL.LIB to the dependencies.

For doing a Debug-SWS configuration, you'll just need to add the `/Gh` switch to CL.EXE and the dependency on SWSDLL.LIB.

Running Applications Using SWS

After your application is set up and compiled, you encounter the hardest step in using SWS: running your application. You need to sit down and think long and hard about what the most common usage scenarios are for your application. If you have an existing application, you should probably schedule some customer visits to see which common usage applies to all. If you have a new application, you should sit down with the marketing or customer representative folks to plan the actions. After you've got the scenarios down, you'll need to run your application through each of them on various machines under various loads. You'll probably want to invest in making those scenarios repeatable with an automation tool such as Tester from Chapter 16.

When you first run your application with SWS, you'll notice two new files created in the directory in which each SWS compiled binary resides: <*filename*>.SWS and <*filename*>.1.SWS. The SWS file without the number in it is the base file that contains the addresses and sizes of each function for the module as well as room for the execution counts. This file is copied over to a new file on each live run so that the symbol lookup doesn't have to take place on each run. The files with the number in them indicate a live run and contain execution counts. Each time you run your special compiled binary, a new <*filename*>.#.SWS file is created for each run.

Part of SWS is an executable with the imaginative name SWS.EXE. This is the program that allows you to view individual SWS files, generate new ones, and do the final tuning. If you run SWS.EXE without any parameters or with `-?`, the output is as follows:

```
SWS (Smooth Working Set) 2.0
John Robbins - Debugging Applications for Microsoft .NET and Microsoft Windows

Usage: SWS [-t <module>]|[-d <module>]|[-g <module>]|[-?] [-nologo]
     -t <module> - Tune the module's working set
                   (run from directory with .SWS file)
```

```
-d <module> - Dump the raw data for the module or #.SWS file
-g <module> - Generate the initial SWS file for the module
-?          - Show this help screen
-nologo     - Do not display the program information
```

You can dump out any of the resulting .SWS files so that you can see exactly which functions are being called, which ensures you're executing the functions you think you're executing. The output of a dumped run file (*<filename>*.#.SWS) looks like the following:

```
Link time    : 0x3E13849C
Entry count  : 12
Image base   : 0x00400000
Image size   : 0x00007000
Module name  : SimpleSWSTest.exe

Address     Count     Size  Name
---------- -------- ----- ----
0x00401050        2    22 ?Bar@@YAXXZ
0x00401066        2    22 ?Baz@@YAXXZ
0x0040107C        2    22 ?Bop@@YAXXZ
0x00401092        4    10 ?Foo@@YAXXZ
0x0040109C        1    49 _wmain
0x004010CD        2    10 _YeOlCFunc
0x004011E0        0   422 _wmainCRTStartup
0x00401C50        0    63 __onexit
0x00401C90        0    24 _atexit
0x00401DC0        0    23 __setdefaultprecision
0x00401DE0        0     7 __matherr
0x00401DF0        0     7 __wsetargv
```

While an application is compiled and using the SWS `_penter` function, the initial .SWS file is automatically generated. However, generating the file requires a considerable amount of work with the DBGHELP.DLL symbol engine, so you can save some startup time by pre-generating the module .SWS files with the `-g` option to SWS.EXE.

Producing and Using the Order File

After you've completed all the runs, it's time to tune your application and generate the order file you'll pass to the linker. SWS.EXE provides the front end to the tuning with the `-t` command-line option followed by just the module name of the binary to tune. Tuning produces the actual order file with a .PRF extension, mainly because that's what the old Working Set Tuner tool produced. If you'd like to see the work going on when generating the order file, that is, how it's packing and building the order, pass -v on the SWS command line. An example of the verbose output is fairly easy to understand:

```
Verbose output turned on
Action -> Tuning for : SimpleSWSTest
Initializing the symbol engine.
Loading the symbols
Processing : SimpleSWSTest.1.SWS
Processing : SimpleSWSTest.2.SWS
Processing : SimpleSWSTest.3.SWS
Processing : SimpleSWSTest.4.SWS
Processing : SimpleSWSTest.5.SWS
Order file output: SimpleSWSTest.PRF
Page Remaining (4086) (0010) : (   20) ?Foo@@YAXXZ
Page Remaining (4064) (0022) : (   10) ?Bop@@YAXXZ
Page Remaining (4042) (0022) : (   10) ?Baz@@YAXXZ
Page Remaining (4032) (0010) : (   10) _Ye01CFunc
Page Remaining (4010) (0022) : (   10) ?Bar@@YAXXZ
Page Remaining (3961) (0049) : (    5) _wmain
```

The numbers after the "Page Remaining" text are the page size remaining, the size of the function, and the number of executions for the particular function.

When building the .PRF file, SWS doesn't just produce a text file listing of those functions in most called order because that doesn't take into account the page size of the operating system. If a function happens to cross a page boundary, two pages will have to be in memory for that one function. SWS ensures that the functions appear on a single page and also tries to ensure that every page is filled as completely as possible. To ensure every page is filled, you might see functions that are rarely called in the resulting order file. By avoiding unnecessary page padding, you'll reduce the amount of RAM your program needs.

After you've produced the order file, you just need to specify it to the linker /ORDER switch so that the file is used. You should always store the order file in the same directory as the project file and sources. Here's one confusing issue to note about the /ORDER option: the filename must be preceded by the @ character. If you're not using SettingsMaster, you can specify the order file for the binary in the project Property Pages dialog box, Linker folder, Optimization node, Function Order field for your release build, as shown in Figure 19-6. When using SettingsMaster, simply choose the ReleaseOrderFile.XML file after clicking the SettingsMaster Custom Project Update button.

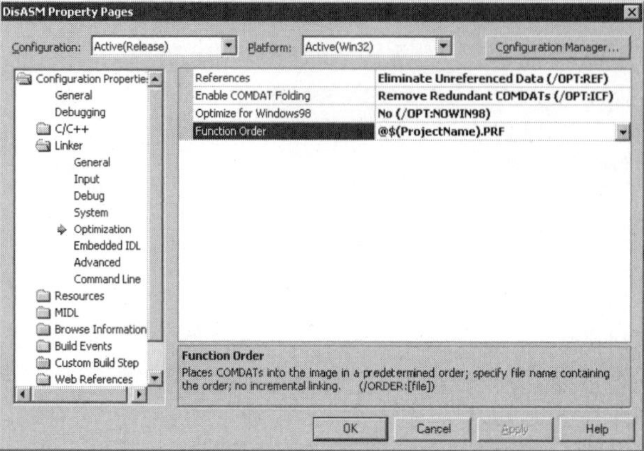

Figure 19-6 Specifying the `/ORDER` file to a release build

Implementing SWS

As happens with many projects, when I first considered implementing SWS, I thought it was going to be a pretty tall task, but as I got into the coding, implementing the tool turned out to be a somewhat simpler operation. My plan was to tackle the `_penter` function, the binary file and symbol enumeration, and the run time and the tuning algorithm, in that order.

The `_penter` Function

I have to admit that before I settled on using the `_penter` function through the `/Gh` compiler switch, I looked at attempting SWS so that it would run on an unmodified binary. While it's certainly doable, it's quite complicated—I'd have to write a debugger to ensure my hooking code was injected before anything else, and I'd have to insert 5-byte jumps over every function I found in the symbol table. Having implemented similar code for commercial products, I knew how much hard work that would be. In the end, I felt it was perfectly acceptable to require a special build, especially when we have tools like SettingsMaster, which make the SWS build trivial to add to your configuration.

With the function-hooking design mercifully out of the way, I started looking at the actions that had to take place each time the `_penter` function was called. Listing 19-1 shows my `_penter` function and its supporting code. As you can see, the code is `naked`, and I generate my own prolog and epilog to handle function setup and teardown. I go `naked` because the `_penter` documentation requires it and it makes getting the return address of the function easier. Fortunately, when the compiler says it will generate _penter before anything else, it means it! The following disassembly shows the effects of the /Gh switch. As you can see, the call to _penter comes even before the PUSH EBP standard function prolog.

```
Bar:
00401050: E8B7000000          call      _penter
00401055: 55                  push      ebp
00401056: 8BEC                mov       ebp,esp
00401058: E8A8FFFFFF          call      ILT+0(?Foo
0040105D: 3BEC                cmp       ebp,esp
0040105F: E8AE000000          call      _chkesp
00401064: 5D                  pop       ebp
00401065: C3                  ret
```

If you daydream a little bit, you can see that the /Gh switch might allow some other interesting utilities. The first one that pops into my mind is a performance tool. Since Microsoft now offers the /GH switch (Enable _pexit Hook Function), using such a tool should be much easier since you'll know when the function ends. I encourage you to do some thinking about the power of _penter and _pexit.

Common Debugging Question

Why do some function calls start with "ILT" in the Disassembly window?

In the discussion of the code generated by the /Gh switch, one of the function calls is CALL ILT+0(?Foo, which has caused confusion for many developers. What you're seeing in action is the magic of incremental linking. ILT stands for Incremental Link Table.

When creating a debug build, the linker wants to link the binary as fast as possible. Consequently, each function is given quite a bit of padding so that if the function changes, the linker only has to overwrite that function in place; it doesn't have to move things around in the binary. By the way, the padding around those functions comprises INT 3 instructions. However, a function can grow larger than the space remaining. In that case, the linker has to move the function in the binary.

If each function that called the now-moved function called the real function address, every time a function moved because of a new link, the linker would have to grind through all the CALL instructions and update each one. To save that processing time, the linker builds the special Incremental Link Table, which it then uses for each call. Instead of updating a

(continued)

Common Debugging Question *(continued)*

bunch of locations when a function changes, the linker now has to update only a single spot in the binary. Listing 19-1 shows an ILT table.

```
@ILT+0(_wmain):
00401005  jmp         wmain (401070h)
@ILT+5(??_GCResString@@UAEPAXI@Z):
0040100A  jmp         CResString::`scalar deleting destructor' (401B40h)
@ILT+10(?ParseCommandLine@@YAHHQAPAGAAUtag_CMDOPTS@@@Z):
0040100F  jmp         ParseCommandLine (401439h)
@ILT+15(?ShowHelp@@YAXXZ):
00401014  jmp         ShowHelp (401644h)
@ILT+20(??1CResString@@UAE@XZ):
00401019  jmp         CResString::~CResString (401A00h)
@ILT+25(?LoadStringW@CResString@@QAEPBGI@Z):
0040101E  jmp         CResString::LoadStringW (401A30h)
@ILT+30(??2@YAPAXI@Z):
00401023  jmp         operator new (401B90h)
@ILT+35(??_GCResString@@UAEPAXI@Z):
00401028  jmp         CResString::`scalar deleting destructor' (401B40h)
@ILT+40(??0CResString@@QAE@PAUHINSTANCE__@@@Z):
0040102D  jmp         CResString::CResString (401990h)
@ILT+45(??BCResString@@QBEPBGXZ):
00401032  jmp         CResString::operator unsigned short const * (401B20h)
```

Therefore, when an instruction is `CALL @ILT+15(?ShowHelp@@YAXXZ)`, the call is the `@ILT+15(?ShowHelp@@YAXXZ)` label, which is a jump to the real instruction.

```
/*----------------------------------------------------------------------
Debugging Applications for Microsoft .NET and Microsoft Windows
Copyright © 1997-2003 John Robbins -- All rights reserved.
----------------------------------------------------------------------*/
/*//////////////////////////////////////////////////////////////////////
                                The Includes
//////////////////////////////////////////////////////////////////////*/
#include "stdafx.h"
#include "SWSDLL.h"
#include "SymbolEngine.h"
#include "VerboseMacros.h"
#include "ModuleItemArray.h"

/*//////////////////////////////////////////////////////////////////////
                        Defines, Constants, & Typedefs
//////////////////////////////////////////////////////////////////////*/
```

Listing 19-1 PENTERHOOK.CPP

```
// The event handle the _penter function checks to see if the processing
// is disabled.
static HANDLE g_hStartStopEvent = NULL ;
// The simple automatic class I used to ensure various things are
// initialized.
class CAutoMatic
{
public  :
    CAutoMatic ( void )
    {
        g_hStartStopEvent = ::CreateEvent ( NULL                 ,
                                            TRUE                 ,
                                            FALSE                ,
                                            SWS_STOPSTART_EVENT   ) ;
        ASSERT ( NULL != g_hStartStopEvent ) ;
    }
    ~CAutoMatic ( void )
    {
        VERIFY ( ::CloseHandle ( g_hStartStopEvent ) ) ;
    }
} ;

/*//////////////////////////////////////////////////////////////////////
                         File Scope Globals
//////////////////////////////////////////////////////////////////////*/
// The automatic class.
static CAutoMatic g_cAuto ;

// The module array.
static CModuleItemArray g_cModArray ;


/*//////////////////////////////////////////////////////////////////////
                        Function Prototypes
//////////////////////////////////////////////////////////////////////*/

/*//////////////////////////////////////////////////////////////////////
//////////////////////////////////////////////////////////////////////*/

extern "C" void SWSDLL_DLLINTERFACE __declspec(naked) _penter ( void )
{
    DWORD_PTR dwCallerFunc ;

    // The function prolog.
    __asm
    {
        PUSH EBP                    // Set up the standard stack frame.
        MOV  EBP , ESP

        PUSH EAX                    // Save off EAX as I need to use it
                                    // before saving all registers.
```

(continued)

```
        MOV  EAX , ESP                // Get the current stack value into
                                      //  EAX.

        SUB  ESP , __LOCAL_SIZE       // Save off the space needed by the
                                      // local variables.

        PUSHAD                        // Save off all general register
                                      // values.

        // Now I can calculate the return address.
        ADD  EAX , 04h + 04h          // Account for the PUSH EBP and the
                                      // PUSH EAX.
        MOV  EAX , [EAX]              // Grab the return address.
        SUB  EAX , 5                  // Take off the 5 byte jump used to
                                      // call _penter to get to the start
                                      // of the function.
        MOV  [dwCallerFunc] , EAX     // Save the caller function.

    }

    // If the start/stop event is signaled, don't do any processing.
    if ( WAIT_TIMEOUT == WaitForSingleObject ( g_hStartStopEvent , 0 ))
    {
        // Do the work.
        g_cModArray.IncrementFunctionEntry ( dwCallerFunc ) ;
    }
    // The function epilog.
    __asm
    {
        POPAD                         // Restore all general purpose
                                      // values.

        ADD ESP , __LOCAL_SIZE        // Remove space needed for locals.

        POP EAX                       // Restore EAX

        MOV ESP , EBP                 // Restore the standard stack frame.
        POP EBP
        RET                           // Return to caller.
    }
}
```

The .SWS File Format and Symbol Enumeration

As you can see from Listing 19-1, the `_penter` function isn't very exciting. Things get more interesting when you start to think about how to organize the address data. Since I need to associate an address with a function name, I use my good friend, the DBGHELP.DLL symbol engine, somewhere in the program. However, looking up symbols in the symbol engine is not the fastest of operations, so I had to find a way to keep the data access small and fast because it will be touched by each function call.

When I thought about it, what I wanted for the data arrangement was just a sorted array of all the function addresses with their associated execution counts. That way, when I had the return address in the `_penter` function, I could just do a quick binary search for the address. This solution seemed relatively straightforward because all I had to do was enumerate the modules' symbols and sort the array of functions. I had all the necessary data to do this.

I thought that SWS, like the WST, should keep each module's execution counts for a run in a separate data file. I favor that approach because if you don't want a particular application run, you can delete it from the overall merged data set. The WST uses the *<module name>.<run number>* naming format, but I wanted SWS to use a *<module name>.<run number>*.SWS scheme so that I could eventually write a graphical program to make combining all the runs easier.

After I decided how I wanted to approach the run-time data processing, I considered how to generate the actual order file. As I already mentioned, I needed to concatenate the individual runs. However, when I thought about producing the actual order file, I realized that I hadn't brought forward all the necessary data. The order file needs the names of the functions as well as their sizes, but all I had planned to store were the function addresses. Although I could have used the symbol engine again when generating the actual order file, the only way to get a symbol's size is to enumerate all the module's symbols. Since I was already handling full symbol enumeration in the initial data generation phases, I thought I should just go ahead and add the function sizes to the file. I didn't need to store the function names because I could always look them up by loading the PDB file for the binary.

If you did find Russ Blake's *Optimizing Windows NT* and you read the chapter "Tuning the Working Set of Your Application," you might wonder why I didn't mention anything about bit sets and time intervals. The Windows NT performance team implemented WST using a scheme in which a bit in a bit set represents each function. Every so many milliseconds, WST writes out the bit set to record which functions executed in that time interval. I've often wondered why they implemented WST that way. At first glance, it seems like you do save some memory with the bit set, but you have to remember that there must be some way of mapping a function address to a bit. I don't think the bit set scheme saves much more memory than my scheme. I believe the Windows NT performance team used the bit set scheme because they were tuning the operating system with WST. In contrast, I'm looking at individual binaries, so it's an issue of scale.

When designing my data structures, I was concerned about one point: I wanted to simply increment a value whenever a function executed. In multithreaded programs, I need to protect that value so that only one thread at a time is manipulating it. My goal was to make the SWS run time as fast as possible, so the best choice was to increment the function count with the `InterlockedIncrement` API function. Since that function uses the hardware locking mechanism (the LOCK prefix on an instruction), I can guarantee data coherency in multithreaded applications. However, in Microsoft Win32, the largest data size that you can pass to `InterlockedIncrement` is a 32-bit value. Therefore, it's possible to wrap after 4,294,967,295 function calls. Four billion is a large number, but some message loops could execute that much if you run your application long enough.

The WST program avoided this problem at run time by recording only when the function executed and then calculating the total executions after the fact, when it's easier to deal with the possible wrapping. When tuning the operating system, the odds are quite good that you could execute some functions more than four billion times. However, with SWS, I'm willing to take the chance during my initial design and perform some testing to determine whether function count wrap is a problem. Function count wrap might be less likely with my design because I left the hooks in so that you can start and stop the data collection at will. Thus, each time you run the application, you can generate data only in the cases in which you need it.

In the extremely rare case in which you do execute a function more than 4 billion times, you have two options. The first is to implement the data counting variable as a 64-bit integer and have a per-module synchronization object to protect all the bits. The other option is drastic in that I will need to implement the SWS run time to work like WST. Of course, the wrapping problem happens only on Win32, so another option would be to implement SWS for Microsoft Win64 only, because there's no way you'll ever hit 18,446,744,073,709,551,615 function executions in your lifetime.

You can see how simple the file format actually is by looking at Listing 19-2. I quickly realized that I needed a common base class to handle all the file manipulation, which is `CSWSFile` defined in SWSFILE.H and SWSFILE.CPP. The class is really nothing more than a wrapper over your normal Win32 file manipulation.

```
/*----------------------------------------------------------------------
Debugging Applications for Microsoft .NET and Microsoft Windows
Copyright © 1997-2003 John Robbins -- All rights reserved.
----------------------------------------------------------------------*/
#ifndef _FILEFORMAT_H
#define _FILEFORMAT_H


/*//////////////////////////////////////////////////////////////////////
                              Defines and Structures
//////////////////////////////////////////////////////////////////////*/
// The SWS file signature (SWS2).
#define SIG_SWSFILE '2SWS'
#define EXT_SWSFILE _T ( ".SWS" )

/*//////////////////////////////////////////////////////////////////////
The SWS file header.
//////////////////////////////////////////////////////////////////////*/
typedef struct tag_SWSFILEHEADER
{
    // The file signature. See the SIG_* defines above.
    DWORD   dwSignature ;
    // The link time for the binary associated with this file.
    DWORD   dwLinkTime ;
    // The load address for the binary.
    DWORD64 dwLoadAddr ;
    // The size of the image.
    DWORD   dwImageSize ;
    // The number of entries in this file.
    DWORD   dwEntryCount ;
    // The flags field.
    DWORD   dwFlags ;
    // The modulename for this file.
    TCHAR   szModuleName[ MAX_PATH ] ;
    DWORD   dwPadding ;
} SWSFILEHEADER , * LPSWSFILEHEADER ;

/*//////////////////////////////////////////////////////////////////////
The entry type for SWS files.
//////////////////////////////////////////////////////////////////////*/
typedef struct tag_SWSENTRY
{
    // The function address.
    DWORD64 dwFnAddr ;
    // The function size.
    DWORD   dwSize ;
    // The execution count.
    DWORD   dwExecCount ;
} SWSENTRY , * LPSWSENTRY ;

#endif  // _FILEFORMAT_H
```

Listing 19-2 FILEFORMAT.H

One key issue I want to point out in the file format is that I store the binary files' load address in the SWS file. Originally I stored only the addresses for the functions, but I remembered the case in which the binary might be relocated in memory. In that situation, the SWSDLL.DLL run time would be called with one address, but I wouldn't have any record of that address in any of the module's loaded SWS files. Even though we should always rebase our DLLs, sometimes we forget, and I wanted to make sure SWS didn't crater when that happened.

One area that did give me a little trouble was generating the symbols for the initial SWS module. Because of the way programs are linked and symbols are generated, many of the symbols reported in a module are not those that have `_penter` calls inserted in them. For example, if you link against the static C run time, your module will have all sorts of C run-time functions added. Since the address lookup would be faster in the SWS run time if there were fewer symbols, I looked at a few ways to minimize the numbers.

Listing 19-3 shows the symbol enumeration callback and how I started limiting the number of symbols. The first step I took was to check whether the symbol had corresponding line information with it. Because I assumed that functions that have `_penter` calls were properly compiled using the steps I specified earlier, I safely got rid of many extraneous symbols. My next step in eliminating symbols was to check whether specific strings are part of the symbols. For example, any symbols that start with `_imp__` are imported functions from other DLLs. There are two other checks that I didn't implement but instead left as exercises for you dear readers. The first is that you should be able to flag symbols from specific files, which SWS should ignore. The main reason for implementing this feature is so that you can add all the C run-time source files to that list. The last symbol elimination trick ensures that the address in question comes only from a code section in the module. You might not need this last check, but it would ensure that only true code symbols are used.

```
/*----------------------------------------------------------------------
FUNCTION        :   SymEnumSyms
DISCUSSION      :
    The symbol enumeration callback. The only thing done here is that
the data is added to the SWS files.
PARAMETERS      :
    szSymbolName    - The symbol name.
    ulSymbolAddress - The symbol address.
    ulSymbolSize    - The size, in bytes, of the symbol.
    pUserContext    - The SWS file.

RETURNS         :
    TRUE  - Everything is cool.
```

Listing 19-3 SWS symbol enumeration

```
    FALSE - There was a problem adding data to the file.
----------------------------------------------------------------------*/
BOOL CALLBACK SymEnumSyms ( PSTR    szSymbolName     ,
                            DWORD64 ulSymbolAddress  ,
                            ULONG   ulSymbolSize     ,
                            PVOID   pUserContext      )
{
    LPENUMSYMCTX pCTX = (LPENUMSYMCTX)pUserContext ;

    CImageHlp_Line cLine ;
    DWORD dwDisp ;
    if ( FALSE == g_cSym.SymGetLineFromAddr ( ulSymbolAddress ,
                                              &dwDisp         ,
                                              &cLine           ) )
    {
        // If no source and line was found for this symbol, ignore
        // it.
        return ( TRUE ) ;
    }

    // Future enhancements to ignoring particular symbols:
    // 1. Add an ignore file list to search here.
    // 2. Check if this address is in the modules code section. This
    // will avoid putting IAT symbols into the output files.

    // Is this symbol in the ignore containing list?
    for ( int i = 0 ; i < IGNORE_CONTAINING_COUNT ; i++ )
    {
        if ( NULL != strstr ( szSymbolName              ,
                              g_szIgnoreContaining[ i ]  ) )
        {
            // Drop out now.
            return ( TRUE ) ;
        }
    }

    if ( NULL != pCTX->pfnVerboseOutput )
    {
#ifdef _WIN64
        pCTX->pfnVerboseOutput(_T("  Adding Symbol : 0x%016I64X %S\n"),
#else
        pCTX->pfnVerboseOutput(_T("  Adding Symbol : 0x%08X %S\n" ) ,
#endif
                               (DWORD_PTR)ulSymbolAddress          ,
                               szSymbolName                         );
    }
    if ( FALSE == pCTX->pSWSFile->AddData ( ulSymbolAddress ,
                                            ulSymbolSize    ,
                                            0                ) )
```

(continued)

```
        {
            ASSERT ( !"Adding to SWS file failed!" ) ;
            return ( FALSE ) ;
        }
        pCTX->iAddedCount++ ;
        return ( TRUE ) ;
}
```

The Run Time and Tuning

One symbol problem I had at run time happened because the symbol engine doesn't return static functions. Being Mr. Contentious, when I didn't find an address that came from a module, I popped up my usual six or seven assertion message boxes. At first I was a little confused that I was seeing the assertions, because one of my test programs didn't have anything declared as static. When I looked at the stack in the debugger, I found I was looking at a symbol named something like $E127. There was a call to `_penter` in the function and everything looked good. It finally dawned on me that I was looking at a compiler-generated function, such as a copy constructor. Although I really would have liked to keep the error checking in the code, I noticed that there were quite a few of those compiler-generated functions in some programs, so all I could do was report the problem with a `TRACE` statement in debug builds.

The last interesting aspect of SWS is the tuning of a module. The code for the `TuneModule` function is large, so Listing 19-4 shows only the algorithm. As you can see, I work to ensure that I pack each code page with as many functions as possible to eliminate padding. The interesting part is where I hunt down the best-fitting function. I decided to try to pack as many functions with execution counts as possible into the pages. If I couldn't find a function with an execution count that fit, I used a function that had no execution counts. My initial algorithm for fitting everything together worked great. However, it started crashing when tuning certain modules.

A little exploration revealed that I was getting into a situation in which I had a page almost filled but also had a function whose size was bigger than the page. That's right—a function size reported by the symbol engine was bigger than a memory page. When I looked more closely, I noticed that those huge functions appeared only when they were the last symbols in the code section. Evidently, the symbol engine treats everything after certain symbols as part of the symbol, so the size is wrong. In the tuning algorithm, you can see that when I get a symbol larger than the page size, the only thing I can do is punt and drop the symbol into the order file. That might not be the best solution, but it's a boundary condition that you shouldn't run into too often.

```
// The TuneModule algorithm.
BOOL TuneModule ( LPCTSTR szModule )
{
    Build the output .SWS filename.

    Copy the base .SWS file to a temporary file

    Open the temporary .SWS file

    for each szModule.#.SWS in the directory
    {
        Verify this #.SWS link time matches the
          temporary .SWS file

        for each address in this #.SWS
        {
            Add this address's execution count to
              the same address in the temporary file
        }
    }

    Get the page size for this computer

    while not done
    {
        Look for the first entry in the temporary
          .SWS file that has an address

        If I looped through each address
        {
            done = TRUE
            break
        }

        If this entry has an execution count of zero
        {
            done = TRUE
            break
        }

        if this entry's size is less than the remaining
          page size
        {
            Output the entry's function name to the PRF
            Zero out the address so I don't use this one
              again
            Subtract this entry size from the remaining
             page remaining size
        }
```

Listing 19-4 The SWS tuning algorithm

```
        else if this entry's size is greater than a
          page size
        {
            Punt and just write out the address to the PRF
              as there's nothing I can do
            Reset the page amount remaining to the page size
        }
        else
        {
            // This entry is too big to fill into the page
            // so find the best fitting function to pack
            // the page.
            for each item in the temporary .SWS file
            {
                if the address is not zero'd out
                {
                    if a best fit has not been found
                    {
                        Set this entry as the best fit overall
                        Set this entry as the best exec count fit
                    }
                    else
                    {
                        if this entry size is > the best fit size
                        {
                            Set this entry as the best fit overall
                        }
                        if this item has an execution count
                        {
                            if this entry size is > the best exec count
                              size
                            {
                                Set this entry as the best exec count fit
                            }
                        }
                    }

                }
            }
            if no best exec count fit was found
            {
                Set the best exec count fit to the best overall fit
            }
            Output the best exec count function name to the PRF
            Reset the page amount remaining to the page size
        }

    }
    Close any temporary files
}
```

What's Next for SWS?

As it stands, SWS is plenty good enough for making your modules svelte. If you're interested in SWS, here are a few cool things you might do in future versions:

- Implement a start and stop program. I have the code hooked up in `_penter` to check whether an event is signaled. You can create a separate program that toggles the event so that you can control SWS's data collection. Just create an event named `SWS_Start_Stop_Event` and set it to when you want to stop data collection.
- Implement the symbol exclusion features I discussed earlier so that you can have the fewest symbols possible in the .SWS files.
- If you're really ambitious, you can write a GUI tool to make viewing data and tuning much easier than it is using a command-line utility.

Summary

The final frontier of performance tuning is ensuring that your binaries are ordered and as packed as possible because there's no excuse for fat code. SWS is the diet your binaries have needed, and it should make reducing your working set relatively painless, especially when matched with the automatic settings control of SettingsMaster.

Part V

Appendixes

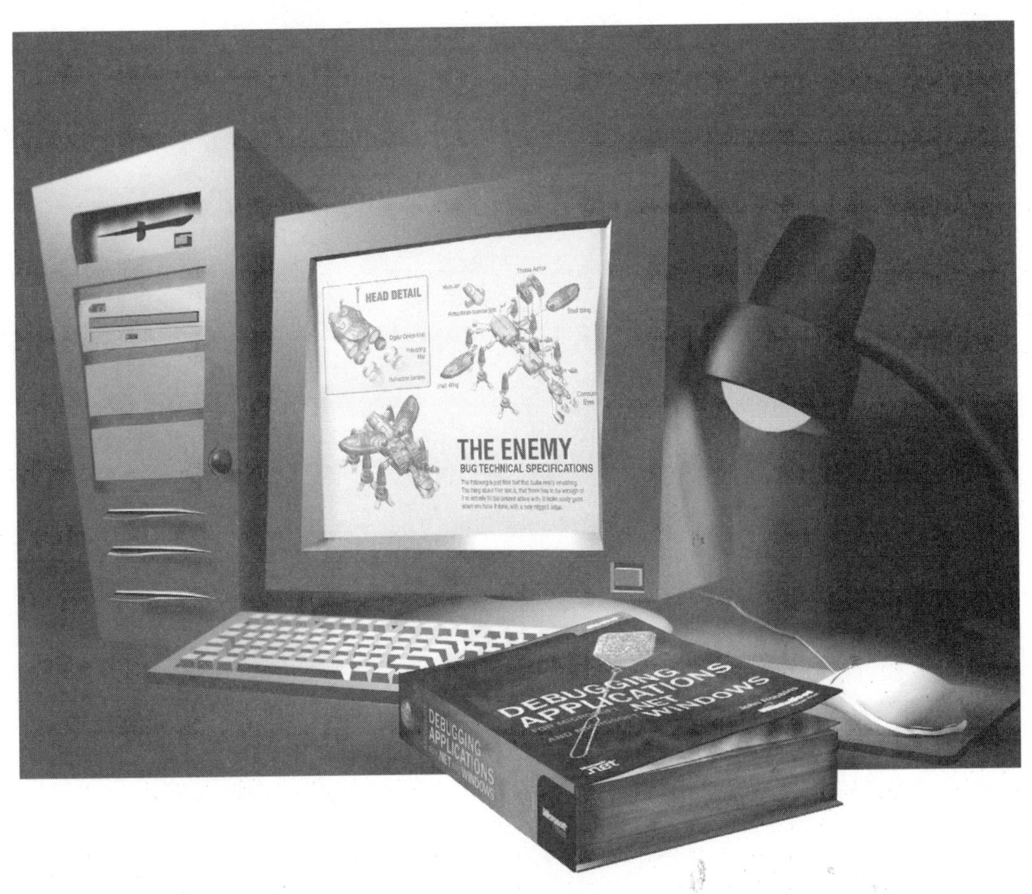

Appendix A

Reading Dr. Watson Logs

I hope that instead of reading Dr. Watson logs, you'll be adding minidump creation to your application, which I described in Chapter 13, to make debugging your crashes extremely simple. However, if you've got an existing application or a customer that won't e-mail you the binary minidump, you've always got Dr. Watson to tell you when and where the problem occurred.

In some ways, Dr. Watson should really be named Dr. Jekyll and Mr. Hyde. In Dr. Jekyll mode, you get the information about a crash on a user's machine and can easily find where the crash occurred and fix it quickly. In Mr. Hyde mode, all you get is another set of numbers that don't tell you anything. In this appendix, I'll explain how to read Dr. Watson logs so that you can see less of Mr. Hyde and more of Dr. Jekyll.

I'll walk you through a complete Dr. Watson log in the following pages, explaining all the pertinent information as we go. (Relevant information in a particular section appears in boldface type.) The crash log in this appendix is for an early version of WDBG.EXE, the debugger I wrote in Chapter 4.

Now that you've read this book, nothing in the Dr. Watson log should come as a big surprise. When it comes to differences between Dr. Watson logs in Microsoft Windows 2000, Windows XP, and Windows Server 2003, there aren't many. However, as you'll see in this appendix, the Windows XP and Windows Server 2003 versions are slightly better.

To get your logs, start Dr. Watson (DRWTSN32.EXE). The Application Errors list box shows recent crashes. If Dr. Watson doesn't list any crashes in the Application Errors list box, Dr. Watson might not be set up as the default debugger. To set up Dr. Watson as the default debugger, run it with the –i switch: `drwtsn32 -i`. To generate a test crash, run CrashTest.EXE from Chapter 13 and click the Crash Away button. Figure A-1 shows the UI for Dr. Watson.

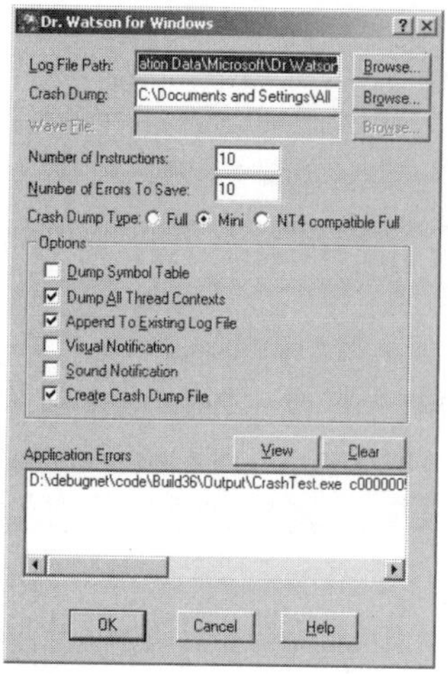

Figure A-1 Dr. Watson UI

In the Application Errors list box, select the crash you're interested in viewing and click the View button. The Log File Viewer dialog box appears as shown in Figure A-2. In Windows 2000, you'll be presented with only the application error numbers and the addresses where you crashed. For Windows XP and Windows Server 2003, you'll see the process name. In the Log File Viewer dialog box, copy the text out of the edit control for the particular crash. If you'd like to get the minidump of the last crash, the Crash Dump edit control in the Dr. Watson window contains the complete path.

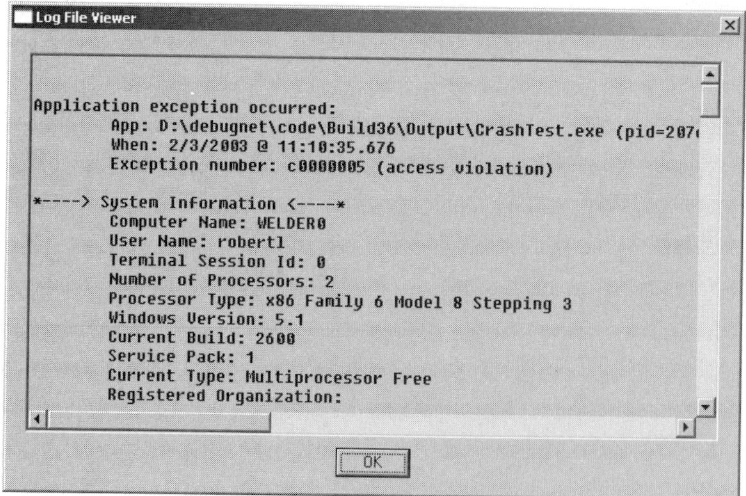

Figure A-2 Dr. Watson Log File View dialog box for Windows XP

Dr. Watson Logs

Here's the first section of a sample Dr. Watson log:

```
Application exception occurred:
        App:  (pid=1796)
        When: 1/2/2003 @ 13:42:56.208
        Exception number: c0000005 (access violation)
```

The header information tells you what caused the crash—in this case, an application exception. The exception numbers for some crashes might not get translated into a human-readable description, such as "access violation" for exception number 0xC0000005. You can see all the possible exception number values by searching for STATUS_ in WINNT.H. The crash values are documented as EXCEPTION_ values returned by the GetExceptionCode function, but the real values are in all the STATUS_ #defines. Once you translate back into the EXCEPTION_ value, you can look up the description for the crash in the GetExceptionCode documentation.

The System Information section should be self-explanatory:

```
*----> System Information <----*
        Computer Name: HUME
        User Name: john
        Number of Processors: 2
        Processor Type: x86 Family 15 Model 0 Stepping 10
        Windows 2000 Version: 5.0
        Current Build: 2195
        Service Pack: 3
        Current Type: Multiprocessor Free
        Registered Organization: Wintellect
        Registered Owner: John Robbins
```

The Task List section looks like this:

```
*----> Task List <----*
   0 Idle.exe
   8 System.exe
 132 smss.exe
 160 csrss.exe
 156 winlogon.exe
 208 services.exe
 220 lsass.exe
 364 svchost.exe
 424 svchost.exe
 472 spoolsv.exe
 504 MWMDMSVC.exe
 528 MWSSW32.exe
 576 regsvc.exe
 592 MSTask.exe
 836 Explorer.exe
```

(continued)

```
904 tp4mon.exe
912 tphkmgr.exe
920 4nt.exe
940 taskmgr.exe
956 tponscr.exe
268 msdev.exe
252 WDBG.exe
828 NOTEPAD.exe
416 drwtsn32.exe
  0 _Total.exe
```

The Task List section shows the processes that were running at the time of the crash. Unfortunately, the list doesn't show the version information, so you'll have to ask the user for the file versions of all the processes in this section. The numbers down the left-hand side are the decimal process IDs (PIDs) at the time of the crash. The numbers are worthless after the fact.

The Module List section contains all the modules loaded into the address space at the time of the crash. The numbers are in the format (load address – maximum address) for each module. This is the first place differences appear between Windows 2000, Windows XP, and Windows Server 2003 Dr. Watson logs. If you're looking at a Windows 2000 log, all you'll see are the address ranges of the modules and nothing else. If you have a Microsoft Visual Studio 6–compiled application and the symbols are accessable, you'll see the name of the loaded symbols next to the address range. Because the DBGHELP.DLL that comes with Windows 2000 knows nothing about Microsoft Visual Studio .NET symbols, you'll never see loaded symbols for binaries compiled with it. Windows 2000 has issues with the modules list, but Dr. Watson on Windows XP and Windows Server 2003 is smart enough to put the names of each DLL next to the address range.

```
Windows 2000 Modules List
(00400000 - 00460000)
(77F80000 - 77FFB000)
(63000000 - 6301B000)
(77E10000 - 77E6F000)
(77E80000 - 77F31000)

Windows XP Modules List
(0000000000400000 - 0000000000460000: d:\Dev\BookTwo\Disk\Output\WDBG.exe
(0000000071c20000 - 0000000071c6e000: E:\WINDOWS\System32\NETAPI32.dll
(0000000075a70000 - 0000000075b15000: E:\WINDOWS\system32\USERENV.dll
(0000000075f40000 - 0000000075f5f000: E:\WINDOWS\system32\appHelp.dll
(00000000763b0000 - 00000000763f5000: E:\WINDOWS\system32\comdlg32.dll
```

On Windows 2000, to figure out what modules were loaded, you have to guess. As I've mentioned several times in this book, it's vital for you to know where your dynamic-link libraries (DLLs) load into the process address space.

You can probably recognize your DLLs just from the load addresses. To find the information for the other DLLs on the user's machine, you could write a small utility that would run through the DLLs on the user's system and report their names, load addresses, and sizes.

The following output is the beginning of the three-part thread state section. (You'll notice that I removed the code bytes from beside the disassembly addresses and wrapped the register display so that it would fit on the page.)

```
*----> State Dump for Thread Id 0xe14 <----*

eax=00000000 ebx=00000000 ecx=011305d8 edx=00000a30 esi=00154b40
edi=0012fae4
eip=00410144 esp=0012faa8 ebp=0012faf0 iopl=0
nv up ei pl nz na pe nc
cs=001b  ss=0023  ds=0023  es=0023  fs=0038  gs=0000 efl=00000202

function: WDBG!CWDBGProjDoc__HandleBreakpoint
        0041012b push    esi
        0041012c push    edi
        0041012d push    ecx
        0041012e lea     edi,[ebp-0x40]
        00410131 mov     ecx,0xd
        00410136 mov     eax,0xcccccccc
        0041013b rep     stosd
        0041013d pop     ecx
        0041013e mov     [ebp-0x10],ecx
        00410141 mov     eax,[ebp+0xc]
FAULT ->00410144 mov     ecx,[eax+0x4]      ds:0023:00000004=????????
        00410147 cmp     dword ptr [ecx],0x80000003
        0041014d jz WDBG!CWDBGProjDoc__HandleBreakpoint+0x90 (004101a0)
        0041014f mov     [ebp-0x14],esp
        00410152 mov     [ebp-0x18],ebp
        00410155 mov     esi,esp
        00410157 push    0x456070
        0041015c push    0x45606c
        00410161 mov     edx,[ebp-0x18]
        00410164 xor     eax,eax
        00410166 push    eax
```

Dr. Watson displays the state information for each thread running in a process at the time it crashed. The thread states contain all the information you need to determine how and why the system crashed.

The register portion shows what all the registers contained at the time of the crash. The important register to look at is EIP, the instruction pointer. The example I show from Windows XP has symbols, so you can see which function this thread was executing when the crash occurred—most Dr. Watson logs won't have symbol information. Of course, it's not a problem if Dr. Watson doesn't give you the function name. Using CrashFinder from Chapter 12, simply load up the CrashFinder project for your application, enter the address into the Hexadecimal Address(es) edit control, and click the Find button.

This thread happened to be the thread that crashed. The only indicator is the FAULT-> pointer in the middle of the disassembly. I've seen a Dr. Watson log or two that didn't display the FAULT-> pointer. If you don't see this pointer in a log, run through each thread state and enter each `EIP` address into CrashFinder to figure out where the thread was sitting at the time of the crash.

The disassembly should look familiar to you if you remember what you read in Chapter 7. The only new elements are the values after the instructions. The Dr. Watson disassembler attempts to look up the effective address of the memory reference for the instruction so that you can see what value the instruction was manipulating. The addresses that start with `ss` indicate that the memory was a stack segment reference; `ds` indicates a data segment reference. On Windows XP and Windows Server 2003, the only effective address display will be next to the line that contains the `EIP` value.

On Windows 2000, the Dr. Watson logs will have an effective address display next to each assembly language line. The only effective address in the disassembly that's guaranteed to be correct is the one at the instruction pointer. The others might be incorrect because the value the instruction refers to could have been changed. For example, let's say that the first instruction disassembled in the thread state had a memory reference at `EBX`. If the crash instruction occurred 10 instructions later, one of the intervening instructions could easily have changed `EBX`. When Dr. Watson on Windows 2000 does its disassembly, however, it uses the value *currently* in `EBX`—that is, the one at the time of the crash—to do the effective address translation. For this reason, the effective address shown in the disassembly could be incorrect. Carefully check whether any instructions could change the register values before you believe what you see in the effective address display.

Using your newfound assembly-language skills, you should be able to figure out that this thread crashed. The big mistake that everyone makes when reading the assembly language listing from Dr. Watson (or the debugger, for that matter) is starting from the top and reading down. The real trick is to start at the location of the crash and read *up* the listing, looking for which instructions set the registers of the crashing instruction.

The preceding thread state crashed at `00410144 MOV ECX, [EAX+0x4]`, where the value in `EAX` was 0. Since any address less than 64 KB on a Microsoft Windows operating system is marked as no access, attempting to read memory from 0x00000004 isn't a good plan. As you read up the assembly language listing, you'll want to look for the instruction that puts a value of 0 into *EAX*. Moving up one instruction, you'll see `MOV EAX, [EBP+0xC]`. Remember that the latter operand, the source, goes into the first operand, the destination. (In other words, remember "source to destination.") That means the value in [EBP+0xC] was copied into EAX. Therefore [EBP+0xC] was 0.

At this point another little trick I taught you in Chapter 7 should be screaming in your head: "parameters are positive"! Parameters are positive offsets from the EBP register with the first one at [EBP+0x8] and each additional parameter above the first by four bytes. Since 0xC is four bytes above 0x8, my hypothesis as to why this function crashed is that the second parameter is NULL. (I hope these last two paragraphs have convinced you how important it is to know enough assembly language to read a Dr. Watson log!)

Here's the second part of the thread state: the Stack Back Trace section. (Notice that I wrapped the function names so that everything would fit on the page. Also, the two underscores (__) in the symbol names is Dr. Watson's way of displaying the scope resolution operator (::).)

```
*----> Stack Back Trace <----*
ChildEBP RetAddr  Args to Child
0012faf0 004100cd 00000a30 00000000 80000003
                           WDBG!CWDBGProjDoc__HandleBreakpoint +0x34
0012fb0c 004075f1 00000a30 0164f8fc 01130b68
                           WDBG!CWDBGProjDoc__HandleExceptionEvent+0x6d
0012fb20 7c3422b2 00000a30 0164f8fc 0000000d
                           WDBG!CDocNotifyWnd__HandleExceptionEvent+0x21
0012fc28 7c341b2e 00000502 00000a30 0164f8fc
                           MFC71UD!CWnd__OnWndMsg+0x752
0012fc48 7c33f2f0 00000502 00000a30 0164f8fc
                           MFC71UD!CWnd__WindowProc+0x2e
0012fcc0 7c33f7ce 01130b68 002502ca 00000502
                           MFC71UD!AfxCallWndProc+0xe0
0012fce0 7c3b072a 002502ca 00000502 00000a30
                           MFC71UD!AfxWndProc+0x9e
0012fd10 77d67ad7 002502ca 00000502 00000a30
                           MFC71UD!AfxWndProcBase+0x4a
0012fd3c 77d6ccd4 7c3b06e0 002502ca 00000502
                           USER32!SetWindowPlacement+0x57
0012fda4 77d445bd 00000000 7c3b06e0 002502ca
                           USER32!DefRawInputProc+0x284
0012fdf8 77d447d4 00593330 00000502 00000a30
                           USER32!TranslateMessageEx+0x78d
0012fe20 77fb4da6 0012fe30 00000018 00593330
                           USER32!DefWindowProcA+0x209
0012fe64 7c34e8e1 00154af8 00000000 00000000
                           ntdll!KiUserCallbackDispatcher+0x13
0012fe90 7c34fb4c 00455e30 0012feb8 7c34f407
                           MFC71UD!AfxInternalPumpMessage+0x21
0012fe9c 7c34f407 00000001 00455e30 00154ac8
                           MFC71UD!CWinThread__PumpMessage+0xc
0012feb8 7c34fe87 00455e30 00434ffa 0040a66b
                           MFC71UD!CWinThread__Run+0x87
```

(continued)

```
0012fecc 7c34865a 1020c034 102682d0 ffffffff
                            MFC71UD!CWinApp__Run+0x57
0012fef0 00430008 00400000 00000000 00020c22
                            MFC71UD!AfxWinMain+0xda
0012ff08 004284b8 00400000 00000000 00020c22
                            WDBG!wWinMain+0x18
0012ffc0 77e814c7 00140000 01f88550 7ffdf000
                            WDBG!wWinMainCRTStartup+0x1f8
0012fff0 00000000 004282c0 00000000 78746341
                            kernel32!GetCurrentDirectoryW+0x44
```

Although my example Windows XP Dr. Watson log has symbols, your user's log probably won't. The RetAddr column lists the return addresses of functions on the call stack. If your user's log doesn't have symbols, all you need to do is load each address in the RetAddr column into CrashFinder to find out the sequence of function calls leading up to the crash.

The Args To Child columns show a function's first three possible parameters on the stack. With highly optimized release builds and no symbols, the values are probably incorrect. However, you can still use them as a starting point for hand-walking your code.

Dr. Watson won't handle symbol values in Windows 2000, so your logs will look something like the following:

```
*----> Stack Back Trace <----*

FramePtr ReturnAd Param#1  Param#2  Param#3  Param#4  Function Name
0012FBA0 004100CD 00000714 00000000 80000003 CCCCCCCC !<nosymbols>
0012FBBC 004075F1 00000714 018EF8FC 016705F8 0012FCD8 !<nosymbols>
0012FBD0 7C3422B2 00000714 018EF8FC 0000000D 016705F8 !<nosymbols>
0012FCD8 7C341B2E 00000502 00000714 018EF8FC 0012FCF4 !Ordinal6841
0012FCF8 7C33F2F0 00000502 00000714 018EF8FC 0013BD01 !Ordinal8666
0012FD70 7C33F7CE 016705F8 00090500 00000502 00000714 !Ordinal1363
0012FD90 7C3B072A 00090500 00000502 00000714 018EF8FC !Ordinal1580
0012FDC0 77E3A244 00090500 00000502 00000714 018EF8FC !Ordinal1581
0012FDE0 77E14730 7C3B06E0 00090500 00000502 00000714
                                             user32!SetWindowPlacement
0012FDFC 77E1558A 00517E40 00000502 00000714 018EF8FC
                                             user32!TranslateMessageEx
0012FE24 77FA02FF 0012FE34 00000018 00517E40 00000502 user32!DefWindowProcA
0012FE64 7C34E8E1 00136BC0 00000000 00000000 00000000
                                             ntdll!KiUserCallbackDispatcher
0012FE90 7C34FB4C 00455E30 0012FEB8 7C34F407 00000001 !Ordinal1462
0012FE9C 7C34F407 00000001 00455E30 00136B90 00000002 !Ordinal7046
0012FEB8 7C34FE87 00455E30 00434FFA 0040A66B 0012FEF0 !Ordinal7554
0012FECC 7C34865A 1020C034 102682D0 FFFFFFFF 0012FEF0 !Ordinal7553
0012FEF0 00430008 00400000 00000000 000209D8 00000005 !Ordinal1578
0012FF08 004284B8 00400000 00000000 000209D8 00000005 !<nosymbols>
0012FFC0 77EA847C 0013BD01 0013BD01 7FFDF000 C0000005 !<nosymbols>
0012FFF0 00000000 004282C0 00000000 000000C8 00000100
                                             kernel32!ProcessIdToSessionId
```

The function names are shown in <*module*>!<*function*> format. Those functions shown as Ordinal# are ordinal exports. If you don't have the source code for the DLL that does the exports by ordinal, you're mostly out of luck. However, because you do have the source code for the Microsoft Foundation Class (MFC) library, you can look up MFC ordinal values. In the WDBG program, I know that MFC71UD.DLL is loaded at 0x7C250000, so I can look up those ordinals because all MFC functions are exported by ordinal value through a linker definition (DEF) file.

The one prerequisite for converting MFC ordinal values to functions is that you must be certain of the version of the MFC DLL on the machine that crashed. On my machine, named \\HUME, I had MFC71UD.DLL from Visual Studio .NET 2003. If you're unsure of the version of MFC on the user's machine, you'll either have to ask for it or beg for it—I'll let you choose the method you're most comfortable with.

Follow these simple steps to turn ordinal values into functions:

1. Open the <Visual Studio .NET installation directory>\VC7\ATLMFC\SRC\MFC\Intel directory.
2. Select the appropriate DEF file for the MFC file you want to look up. For example, MFC71UD.DLL's DEF file is MFC71UD.DEF.
3. Search for the ordinal number. To find Ordinal6841 from the preceding stack, I'd search the MFC71UD.DEF file for 6841. The line with 6841 is "?OnWndMsg@CWnd@@MAEHIIJPAJ@Z @ 6841 NONAME."
4. The name to the left of "@6841 NONAME" is the decorated function name exported at that ordinal value. To undecorate the name, use the UNDNAME.EXE program that comes with the Visual Studio .NET. For 6841, the function is `CWnd::OnWndMsg`.
5. The third part and final part of the thread state is the Raw Stack Dump section:

```
*----> Raw Stack Dump <----*
0012faa8 a8 fc 12 00 40 4b 15 00 - cc cc cc cc cc cc cc cc
                                         ....@K..........
0012fab8 cc cc cc cc cc cc cc cc - cc cc cc cc cc cc cc cc
                                         ................
0012fac8 cc cc cc cc cc cc cc cc - cc cc cc cc cc cc cc cc
                                         ................
0012fad8 cc cc cc cc cc cc cc cc - d8 05 13 01 1c fc 12 00
                                         ................
0012fae8 af 55 43 00 ff ff ff ff - 0c fb 12 00 cd 00 41 00
                                         .UC...........A.
0012faf8 30 0a 00 00 00 00 00 00 - 03 00 00 80 cc cc cc cc
                                         0...............
```

(continued)

```
0012fb08 d8 05 13 01 20 fb 12 00 - f1 75 40 00 30 0a 00 00
                                   .... ....u@.0...
0012fb18 fc f8 64 01 68 0b 13 01 - 28 fc 12 00 b2 22 34 7c
                                   ..d.h...(...."4|
0012fb28 30 0a 00 00 fc f8 64 01 - 0d 00 00 00 68 0b 13 01
                                   0.....d.....h...
0012fb38 00 00 00 00 00 00 00 00 - 00 00 00 00 00 00 00 00
                                   ................
0012fb48 00 00 00 00 00 00 00 00 - 00 00 00 00 00 00 00 00
                                   ................
0012fb58 b2 98 d4 77 85 70 9b c2 - 00 00 00 00 cc a5 30 7c
                                   ...w.p........0|
0012fb68 8c fb 12 00 c7 a7 28 7c - 01 00 00 00 4c f5 25 7c
                                   ......(|....L.%|
0012fb78 5c 01 00 00 03 00 00 00 - 04 00 00 00 e0 f4 25 7c
                                   \.............%|
0012fb88 cc fb 12 00 b4 fb 12 00 - 91 a7 28 7c 4c f2 43 7c
                                   ..........(|L.C|
0012fb98 4c f5 25 7c 5c 01 00 00 - 03 00 00 00 04 00 00 00
                                   L.%|\...........
0012fba8 e0 f4 25 7c cc fb 12 00 - 00 00 00 00 4c fc 12 00
                                   ..%|........L...
0012fbb8 b7 b4 39 7c e8 fb 12 00 - 03 00 00 00 04 00 00 00
                                   ..9|............
0012fbc8 e0 f4 25 7c 68 4f 25 7c - ca 02 25 00 f4 fb 12 00
                                   ..%|hO%|..%.....
0012fbd8 30 0a 00 00 32 b5 39 7c - 00 00 00 00 00 00 00 00
                                   0...2.9|........
```

I rarely look at this information. If I'm really stuck on a crash, however, I might start looking at the information to see whether I can guess at local variable values. The three return addresses I can correlate with the preceding stack walk are shown in boldface.

Appendix B

Resources for .NET and Windows Developers

As I pointed out in Chapter 1, being a good developer is a prerequisite for being a good debugger. The best debuggers also have a solid skill set and, most important, can draw on a broad range of knowledge to help them solve any debugging problem they encounter. Having a solid grasp of the language, the technologies involved, the operating system, and the CPU can make the difference between solving a debugging problem in minutes and spending days in the debugger wondering what's going on.

My motivation for putting together this list of resources is that developers continually ask me what resources I use to learn about Microsoft .NET and Microsoft Windows development. Please keep in mind that the books, tools, and Web sites in this appendix don't constitute an exhaustive list by any means, and you might even disagree with some of my recommendations. All the items I list are suggestions—except for one. The one item you absolutely must have for Windows development is a subscription to the Microsoft Developer Network (MSDN) CDs. If you don't have access to these CDs, there's no way you can do serious, professional Windows development. Microsoft has come out with MSDN Online, but the MSDN CDs are the only place that some information appears. For more information on subscribing to MSDN, see *msdn.microsoft.com/subscriptions*.

Please keep in mind that I've either written some of the tools or worked with some of the authors of the books I recommend. I feel it's only fair to point out the potential conflict of interest.

Books

I've referred to the following books time and time again during my career as a software developer and debugger. I strongly recommend them to you.

Software Development

- *Code Complete* by Steve McConnell (Microsoft Press, 1993)
  This is simply the best book on software construction that I've ever read. Every developer should own a copy and read it cover to cover every year. After reading it annually for nine years, I'm still learning things from this book!
- *Rapid Development* by Steve McConnell (Microsoft Press, 1996)
  This book taught me how to manage teams and schedule projects.
- *Debugging the Development Process* by Steve Maguire (Microsoft Press, 1994)
  This book is a great introduction to the way Microsoft develops software. Obviously, since Microsoft is the most successful software company on the planet, they must be doing something right. You can learn a great deal from this book.
- *Dynamics of Software Development* by Jim McCarthy (Microsoft Press, 1995)
  This book is a very interesting look at software development from the perspective of a manager with a track record for shipping great products. The rules Jim proposes are excellent because they all come from actual experience; he's not just some academic theorizing.
- *Under Pressure and On Time* by Ed Sullivan (Microsoft Press, 2001)
  Ed's the great project manager from whom I stole most of my ideas about how to deliver software. This book discusses real-world project management and how Ed built great teams that delivered great products consistently and always on time. Also, the guy who wrote the forward is probably the sexiest developer working today.
- *The Career Programmer: Guerilla Tactics for an Imperfect World* by Christopher Duncan (APress, 2002)
  All the books on software development address only the manager's perspective. It's about time someone wrote a book for the developers in the trenches! Chris covers tactics and techniques that enable you to concentrate on getting your job done even when your manager might be an idiot.
- *Writing Secure Code, Second Edition,* by Michael Howard and David LeBlanc (Microsoft Press, 2002)
  With security in the forefront of everyone's mind, all developers need to have this book in their collections. Not only does it do a fantastic

job of introducing the issues, it's chock full of real-world recommendations and examples of what you need to do in your software.

- *Don't Make Me Think: A Common Sense Approach to Web Usability* by Steve Krug (New Riders, 2000)
  Everyone is a user interface expert, and this is especially so the higher up the food chain you go in your development shop. This outstanding book discusses real-world Web page design and shows you the techniques necessary to ensure your designs actually work.

- *Philip and Alex's Guide to Web Publishing* by Philip Greenspun (Morgan Kaufmann, 1999)
  If you're designing a Web site, you have to read this book. You might not agree with everything (I sure didn't), but it's one of the most cogent discussions of the issues surrounding how to keep users happy and how to develop Web sites people will come back to. Also, the photographs in the book are excellent. My father, a world class artist, can't seem to figure out why my books don't look so good.

- *High-Performance Client/Server* by Chris Loosley and Frank Douglas (Wiley, 1998)
  This is a great book on designing performance into applications and has an especially excellent discussion of high-speed architectures.

- *Developing International Software, Second Edition* by Dr. International (Microsoft Press, 2003)
  What's the old joke? A person who speaks three languages is trilingual, a person who speaks two is bilingual, and the person who speaks only one is American. Microsoft makes 60 percent of its revenue from outside the United States and you can too if you plan for it. This book shows you how to develop international applications for all of Microsoft's technologies.

Debugging and Testing

- *The Practice of Programming* by Brian W. Kernighan and Rob Pike (Addison-Wesley, 1999)
  This book is a wonderful discussion of developing, debugging, and testing.

- *Writing Solid Code* by Steve Maguire (Microsoft Press, 1993)
  Although it focuses mainly on C programming, this book contains excellent advice on interface definitions and avoiding nasty prob-

lems in the language.

- *Managing the Testing Process* by Rex Black (Microsoft Press, 1999)
To develop better, you need to know how to test better. This excellent book will change the way you develop and the way you interact with your QA teams.
- *How Debuggers Work: Algorithms, Data Structures, and Architecture* by Jonathan B. Rosenberg (John Wiley & Sons, 1996)
This book is an excellent introduction to how debuggers work and to the issues you need to consider when designing a debugger.
- *Debugging Windows Programs: Strategies, Tools, and Techniques for Visual C++ Programmers* by Everett N. McKay and Mike Woodring (Addison Wesley, 2000)
Right after the first edition of the book you're reading now came out, Everett's and Mike's book showed up. It's a fantasic book, and I wish I'd thought of some of the great ideas they put in there, like how to think about debugging.

.NET Technologies

- *Applied Microsoft .NET Framework Programming* by Jeffrey Richter (Microsoft Press, 2002)
- *Applied Microsoft .NET Framework Programming in Microsoft Visual Basic .NET* by Jeffrey Richter and Francesco Balena (Microsoft Press, 2002)
Simply the best introduction to the insides of .NET. This is what all those thousands of "Introduction to .NET" books strive to do but fail miserably at doing.
- *Programming Microsoft .NET* by Jeff Prosise (Microsoft Press, 2002)
This is the perfect book to follow Jeffrey Richter's. Somehow Jeff managed to anticipate every single question I ever had about Microsoft ASP.NET and answer them all in his outstanding book.
- *.NET and COM: The Complete Interoperability Guide* by Adam Nathan (Sams, 2002)
If your .NET application is going to communicate outside the CLR to the big bad world of Windows or COM applications, this book is the bible you need to ensure that communication works.
- *Applied XML Programming for Microsoft .NET* by Dino Esposito (Microsoft Press, 2002)

XML is everywhere today, and Dino's book is an outstanding reference on digesting and emitting XML with Microsoft .NET.

- *.NET Enterprise Design with Visual Basic .NET and SQL Server 2000* by Jimmy Nilsson (Sams, 2002)
  Jimmy's book is one of the few books out there that concentrates on real-world development issues. It's a joy to read and to learn about how to apply many different aspects of real-world tools to solve problems.
- *Performance Testing Microsoft .NET Web Applications* by Microsoft Application Consulting and Engineering (ACE) Team (Microsoft Press, 2003)
  Although .NET takes care of many programming chores for you, you're still responsible for performance. A great introduction to performance testing.
- *Inside Microsoft .NET IL Assembler* by Serge Lidin (Microsoft Press, 2002)
  Although you'll probably never program in IL professionally, it sure is cool to know you can.

C/C++ Language

- *The C Programming Language, Second Edition* by Brian W. Kernighan and Dennis M. Ritchie (Prentice Hall, 1988)
  This book is the definitive guide to C programming and the best-written technical book I've ever read.
- *Learning C++* by Neill Graham (McGraw-Hill, 1991)
  I used this book to learn C++. Unlike other C++ doorstop books, *Learning C++* is short, sweet, and to the point.
- *C++ Programmer's Guide to the Standard Template Library* by Mark Nelson (IDG Books, 1995)
  I have an intense love-hate relationship with the Standard Template Library. Fortunately, Mark's book does a great job of providing samples and explaining the finer points of using this library.

Windows and Windows Technologies

- *Programming Windows, Fifth Edition* by Charles Petzold (Microsoft Press, 1999)
  This one book will teach you everything you need to know about how Windows programs work at the most fundamental level. People could solve many of the problems they ask me about if they only had a better understanding of how message handling, graphics device interface (GDI), and other subjects work at the Microsoft Win32 level.
- *Programming Applications for Microsoft Windows, Fourth Edition* by Jeffrey Richter (Microsoft Press, 1999)
  This book covers all the unique aspects of Win32 development. The chapters on DLLs, threads, synchronization, and structured exception handling are the best descriptions available and all relate directly to debugging your problems more quickly and efficiently.
- *Programming Windows with MFC, Second Edition* by Jeff Prosise (Microsoft Press, 1999)
  This book is the definitive guide to programming with the Microsoft Foundation Class (MFC) library. If you're using MFC, you must have this book.
- *Windows++: Writing Reusable Windows Code in C++* by Paul Dilascia (Addison-Wesley, 1992)
  Unlike other design books, which have only toy examples, this book produces a strong and viable C++ class library for Windows programming. I learn best by example, and this book taught me how to think in terms of objects.
- *Essential COM* by Don Box (Addison-Wesley, 1998)
  In the Disassembly window ("unambiguous mode"), a COM interface is just a pointer to an array of pointers, so COM should be easy to understand. COM is so much more than just a pointer and is so fundamental to programming life, however, that you must understand how it works if you expect to stand a chance of correctly implementing and debugging your code. Don's book will give you a great start along the path of COM enlightenment.
- *Inside Microsoft Windows 2000, Third Edition* by David A. Solomon and Mark E. Russinovich (Microsoft Press, 2000)
  The book is the official "big picture" view of the Microsoft Windows 2000 kernel. Although more directly applicable for device driver writers, this book will help you make sense out of how the different parts of the operating system fit together in Windows 2000.

- *Windows 95 System Programming Secrets* by Matt Pietrek (IDG Books, 1995)
  Matt's book is out of print, but you should really try to find a copy. Debugging anything more than a simple access violation on Microsoft Windows 95 and Microsoft Windows 98 is an exercise in extreme frustration mainly because Windows 95 and Windows 98 are hybrid 16-bit/32-bit operating systems. Much of the information in the book, such as the Portable Executable (PE) file format chapter, applies to Windows 2000 as well.
- *ATL Internals* by Brent Rector and Chris Sells (Addison-Wesley, 1999)
  The Active Template Library (ATL) makes the smallest and fastest COM objects around. To take full advantage of ATL, you have to have this book.
- *Programming Windows Security* by Keith Brown (Addison-Wesley, 2000)
  Simply the best book on Windows security programming.
- *Programming Server-Side Application for Microsoft Windows 2000* by Jeffrey Richter and Jason D. Clark (Microsoft Press, 1999)
  If you're doing native server applications, you have to have this book. The section on scalable I/O is the best ever written.

The Intel CPU and Hardware

- *Structured Computer Organization, Fourth Edition* by Andrew S. Tanenbaum (Prentice-Hall, 1998)
  An excellent introduction to computer architecture, this book is filled with information that I use to debug problems daily. The book has some typos and technical errors, but if you can get past that you'll be glad you read it.
- Intel CPU reference manuals
  Intel makes available, for free, the CPU manuals for their processors. If you're doing serious debugging, these manuals are extremely helpful and informative. You can download the Adobe PDF files from Intel's Literature Center at *developer.intel.com/design/litcentr/index.htm*. Intel also provides the manuals in book form if you prefer having hard copies.
- *The Indispensable PC Hardware Book, Fourth Edition* by Hans-Peter Messmer (Addison-Wesley, 2001)
  This book is the best discussion of PC hardware around. When you need to interact with hardware, this book is an invaluable resource.

Software Tools

- Whole Tomato's Visual Assist (*www.wholetomato.com*)
  This is an excellent add-in to Microsoft Visual Studio .NET that extends the editor and puts in real IntelliSense and other advanced editing tools.
- Source Dynamic's Source Insight (*www.sourceinsight.com*)
  If you need to see how large C++, C#, or Java programs fit together, this is the source browsing tool of choice.
- Compuware DevPartner (*www.compuware.com/products/numega*)
  This is the suite that holds BoundsChecker (error detection), TrueTime (profiler), TrueCoverage (code coverage), CodeReview (static analysis), and Distrbuted Anayzer (cross-machine analysis). These tools all work for .NET as well as native code.
- Bullseye Testing Technology's C-Cover (*www.bullseye.com*)
  This is a fantastic native C++ code coverage tool.
- JPSoft's 4NT (*www.jpsoft.com*)
  This is the ultimate command shell for Windows machines. It's even got a debugger for batch files! On a fresh operating installation, it's the first program I put on the machine.
- Jay Freeman's Anakrino (*www.saurik.com/net/exemplar*)
  This is the easy way to learn about .NET: decompile it!
- Luts Roeder's Reflector (*www.aisto.com/roeder/DotNet*)
  Use this for a better ILDASM.
- WiseOwl's Demeanor for .NET (www.wiseowl.com)
  This is Brent Rector's excellent code obfuscator.
- MindReef's SOAPscope (*www.mindreef.com*)
  If you want to see what's happening with your Web services under the hood, you can't get any better than SOAPscope.
- VMWare (*www.vmware.com*)
  Instead of having 300 machines in your test lab, buy a few big servers and run VMWare. I've seen several organizations save a ton of money by utilizing VMWare to cut down on hardware costs and yet increase their operating system testing coverage considerably.

Web Sites

- MSDN Online (*msdn.microsoft.com*)
  MSDN is the first place to start looking for .NET and Windows information. MSDN Online can be accessed at the address I list as well as through the Microsoft-endorsed magazine *MSDN Magazine*. Keep in mind that MSDN is partly a marketing organization, so sometimes a little hype creeps into various pieces.
- ASP.NET Web (*www.asp.net*)
  This Web site is the official home of the ASP.NET team at Microsoft. For the life of me, I can't figure out why Microsoft has this site outside of the MSDN umbrella.
- Google Microsoft Search (*www.google.com/microsoft.html*)
  Although MSDN is the place to read about Microsoft technologies, its searching capabilities leave something to be desired. Fortunately, Google has a special search site that focuses only on Microsoft technologies. If you'd like to use the vaunted Google search on only the MSDN site, specify *site:msdn.microsoft.com* in your search string.
- Sysinternals (*www.sysinternals.com*)
  Mark Russinovich and Bryce Cogswell have some of the best native debugging utilities around: Regmon, Filemon, DebugView, Process Explorer, and many more. Many utilities come with full source code, and all are free! I check Mark and Bryce's site at least once a week so that I can keep my competitive edge.
- Russ Osterlund's SmidgeonSoft (*www.smidgeonsoft.com*)
  Russ has a collection of fantastic and free tools that rival those at Sysinternals. Not only is his PEBrowse Professional Interactive a native code debugger, it handles .NET debugging as well. If you want to see the insides of the operating system, Russ has you covered.
- Code Project (*www.codeproject*)
  This is a great community site for both .NET and native development.
- CodeGuru (*www.codeguru.com*)
  This is the granddaddy of Windows programming help sites. Now it does .NET, too!
- VB2TheMax (*www.vb2themax.com*)
  This is the place to learn about Microsoft Visual Basic .NET.
- Wintellect (*www.wintellect.com*)
  This is where I and all my Wintellectual friends hang out and answer (and post!) questions on our forums.

Index

Symbols & Numbers

A

B

C

D

E

F

I

J

K

L

M

N

O

P

Q

R

T

U

V

W

John Robbins

John is a cofounder of Wintellect (*www.wintellect.com*), a consulting, debugging and education company dedicated to helping companies produce better software faster. At Wintellect, John heads up the consulting and debugging services side of the business and helped debug and tune applications for companies such as eBay, Microsoft, and AutoDesk, as well as many other corporate development shops. He also travels the world teaching his "Debugging .NET Applications and Debugging Windows Applications" course so that developers everywhere can learn the techniques he uses to solve the nastiest software problems known to man. As one of the world's recognized authorities on debugging, John takes an evil delight in finding and fixing impossible bugs in other people's programs.

John is based in New Hampshire, United States, where he lives with his wife, Pam, and the world-famous debugging cat, Chloe. In addition to being the author of the books *Debugging Applications for Microsoft .NET and Microsoft Windows* (Microsoft Press, 2003) and *Debugging Applications* (Microsoft Press, 2000), John is a contributing editor for *MSDN Magazine*, in which he writes the "Bugslayer" column. He regularly speaks at conferences such as Tech-Ed, VSLive, and DevWeek.

Prior to founding Wintellect, John was one of the early engineers at NuMega Technologies (now Compuware), where he played key roles in designing, developing, and acting as project manager for BoundsChecker, True-Time, TrueCoverage, SoftICE, and TrueCoverage for Device Drivers.

Before he stumbled into software development in his late twenties, John was a paratrooper and Green Beret in the United States Army. Since he can no longer get adrenaline highs by jumping out of airplanes in the middle of the night onto unlit, postage-stamp-size drop zones carrying full combat loads, he rides motorcycles at high rates of speed—much to his wife's chagrin.

At Microsoft Press, we use tools to illustrate our books for software developers and IT professionals. Tools very simply and powerfully symbolize human inventiveness. They're a metaphor for people extending their capabilities, precision, and reach. From simple calipers and pliers to digital micrometers and lasers, these stylized illustrations give each book a visual identity, and a personality to the series. With tools and knowledge, there's no limit to creativity and innovation. Our tagline says it all: *the tools you need to put technology to work*.

The manuscript for this book was prepared and galleyed using Microsoft Word. Pages were composed by Microsoft Press using Adobe FrameMaker+SGML for Windows, with text in Garamond and display type in Helvetica Condensed. Composed pages were delivered to the printer as electronic prepress files.

Cover Designer:	Methodologie, Inc.
Interior Graphic Designer:	James D. Kramer
Principal Compositor:	Elizabeth Hansford
Interior Artist:	Rob Nance
Copy Editor:	Victoria Thulman
Proofreader:	nSight, Inc.
Indexer:	Seth Maislin

Additional .NET Courses

Programming ASP.NET

Starring Jeff Prosise & John Lam

Learn to write cutting-edge Web applications and Web Services by combining the richness of the .NET Framework with the easy-to-use programming model of ASP.NET.

Who should attend: Developers new to .NET whose primary focus is writing applications that run on the Web; ASP developers migrating to ASP.NET.

Topics: Essential Web programming concepts; C# and the Common Language Runtime; the .NET Framework Class Library; Web Forms; Web controls; user controls; custom controls; ADO.NET; XML; ASP.NET application architecture; ASP.NET security; Web Services; error handling and debugging;scalability and performance.

Prerequisites: Reading knowledge of HTML;understanding of basic object-oriented programming concepts.

Length: 5 days.

Programming Visual Basic.NET

Starring Francesco Balena

Everything new and experienced VB developers need to know to leverage the power of Visual Basic.NET and ease the transition from previous versions.

Who should attend: Visual Basic 6.0 developers migrating to Visual Basic.NET; programmers who never used Visual Basic but wish to learn Visual Basic.NET.

Topics: Langauge syntax changes; object-oriented programming; working with data; advanced language features; threading; regular expressions; assemblies; reflection; interoperability; Windows Forms; ADO.NET; Web Forms; Web Services.

Prerequisites: Working knowledge of the BASIC language and its syntax.

Length: 5 days.

Programming ADO.NET

Starring Dino Esposito

An in-depth look at data access in the world of .NET.

Who should attend: Developers new to the platform wh applications will interact with back-end databases such Microsoft SQL Server; experienced .NETdevelopers who to enrich their knowledge of ADO.NET

Topics: ADO.NET architecture; reading and viewing data managed providers; updating data; server-side data binding; advanced DataGrids; XML and DataSets; XML navigation and transformation; Web services; exposing to clients.

Prerequisites: Understanding of basic object-oriented programming concepts; familiarity with database desig fundmentals.

Length: 4 days.

Programming the .NET Framework with

Starring Jeffrey Richter

A highly detailed, no-holds-barred introduction to the platform and its programming models, with special emphasis on understanding the Common Language Run and .NET Framework Class Library — all in C#

Who should attend: Developers looking for a broad but detailed overview of .NET who wish to explore its architecture, learn about the types of applications that i supports, and get first-hand experience programming th new platform.

Topics: Platform architecture; assemblies; types and typ members; automatic memory management (garbage collection); the .NET Framework Class Library; reflection; threading; Web Forms; Windows Forms; Web services; interoperability.

Prerequisites: Understanding of basic object-oriented programming concepts.

Length: 5 days.

Expert guidance for anyone who develops with Visual Basic .NET!

Microsoft® Visual Basic® .NET Step by Step

ISBN 0-7356-1374-5

Graduate to the next generation of Visual Basic at your own pace! This primer is the fast way for any Visual Basic developer to begin creating professional applications for the Microsoft .NET platform by unleashing all the power of the .NET-ready version of Visual Basic. Learn core programming skills by selecting just the chapters you need—with code, optimization tips, advice, and samples straight from the experts. Upgrade your Visual Basic 6 applications quickly using "Upgrade Notes" sidebars, a special upgrading index, and practical advice about the Visual Basic .NET Upgrade Wizard.

Programming Microsoft Visual Basic .NET (Core reference)

ISBN 0-7356-1375-3

Accelerate your productivity with Visual Basic .NET! Building on the success of Programming Microsoft Visual Basic 6.0, this core reference equips new and veteran developers with instruction and code to get them up to speed with the Web-enabled Microsoft Visual Basic .NET environment. The book demonstrates best practices for porting and reusing existing Visual Basic code in the Microsoft .NET environment, as well as exploiting the object-oriented capabilities of the new version—complete with code samples and the book's text on CD-ROM.

Designing Enterprise Applications with Microsoft Visual Basic .NET

ISBN 0-7356-1721-X

Learn how to put the power of Visual Basic .NET to work to build enterprise applications! Most books about Microsoft Visual Basic .NET focus on the language or development environment. This book provides the detailed guidance you need to make the right design choices as you build enterprise-level applications with Visual Basic .NET. The author, who has extensive experience in designing, testing, and optimizing enterprise applications, discusses the technical and architectural tradeoffs you'll face as you develop large, multitier, distributed applications with multiple developers.

Microsoft Press has many other titles to help you put the power of Visual Basic to work. To learn more about the full line of Microsoft Press® products for developers, please visit:

microsoft.com/mspress/developer

Microsoft Press products are available worldwide wherever quality computer books are sold. For more information, contact your book or computer retailer, software reseller, or local Microsoft Sales Office, or visit our Web site at **microsoft.com/mspress.** To locate your nearest source for Microsoft Press products, or to order directly, call 1-800-MSPRESS in the U.S. (In Canada, call 1-800-268-2222).

Proof of Purchase

Use this page as proof of purchase if participating in a promotion or rebate offer on this title. Proof of purchase must be used in conjunction with other proof(s) of payment such as your dated sales receipt—see offer details.

Debugging Applications for Microsoft® .NET and Microsoft Windows®

0-7356-1536-5

CUSTOMER NAME

Microsoft Press, PO Box 97017, Redmond, WA 98073-9830

MICROSOFT LICENSE AGREEMENT

Book Companion CD

IMPORTANT—READ CAREFULLY: This Microsoft End-User License Agreement ("EULA") is a legal agreement between you (either an individual or an entity) and Microsoft Corporation for the Microsoft product identified above, which includes computer software and may include associated media, printed materials, and "online" or electronic documentation ("SOFTWARE PRODUCT"). Any component included within the SOFTWARE PRODUCT that is accompanied by a separate End-User License Agreement shall be governed by such agreement and not the terms set forth below. By installing, copying, or otherwise using the SOFTWARE PRODUCT, you agree to be bound by the terms of this EULA. If you do not agree to the terms of this EULA, you are not authorized to install, copy, or otherwise use the SOFTWARE PRODUCT; you may, however, return the SOFTWARE PRODUCT, along with all printed materials and other items that form a part of the Microsoft product that includes the SOFTWARE PRODUCT, to the place you obtained them for a full refund.

SOFTWARE PRODUCT LICENSE

The SOFTWARE PRODUCT is protected by United States copyright laws and international copyright treaties, as well as other intellectual property laws and treaties. The SOFTWARE PRODUCT is licensed, not sold.

1. **GRANT OF LICENSE.** This EULA grants you the following rights:
   - a. **Software Product.** You may install and use one copy of the SOFTWARE PRODUCT on a single computer. The primary user of the computer on which the SOFTWARE PRODUCT is installed may make a second copy for his or her exclusive use on a portable computer.
   - b. **Storage/Network Use.** You may also store or install a copy of the SOFTWARE PRODUCT on a storage device, such as a network server, used only to install or run the SOFTWARE PRODUCT on your other computers over an internal network; however, you must acquire and dedicate a license for each separate computer on which the SOFTWARE PRODUCT is installed or run from the storage device. A license for the SOFTWARE PRODUCT may not be shared or used concurrently on different computers.
   - c. **License Pak.** If you have acquired this EULA in a Microsoft License Pak, you may make the number of additional copies of the computer software portion of the SOFTWARE PRODUCT authorized on the printed copy of this EULA, and you may use each copy in the manner specified above. You are also entitled to make a corresponding number of secondary copies for portable computer use as specified above.
   - d. **Sample Code.** Solely with respect to portions, if any, of the SOFTWARE PRODUCT that are identified within the SOFTWARE PRODUCT as sample code (the "SAMPLE CODE"):
     - i. **Use and Modification.** Microsoft grants you the right to use and modify the source code version of the SAMPLE CODE, *provided* you comply with subsection (d)(iii) below. You may not distribute the SAMPLE CODE, or any modified version of the SAMPLE CODE, in source code form.
     - ii. **Redistributable Files.** Provided you comply with subsection (d)(iii) below, Microsoft grants you a nonexclusive, royalty-free right to reproduce and distribute the object code version of the SAMPLE CODE and of any modified SAMPLE CODE, other than SAMPLE CODE, or any modified version thereof, designated as not redistributable in the Readme file that forms a part of the SOFTWARE PRODUCT (the "Non-Redistributable Sample Code"). All SAMPLE CODE other than the Non-Redistributable Sample Code is collectively referred to as the "REDISTRIBUTABLES."
     - iii. **Redistribution Requirements.** If you redistribute the REDISTRIBUTABLES, you agree to: (i) distribute the REDISTRIBUTABLES in object code form only in conjunction with and as a part of your software application product; (ii) not use Microsoft's name, logo, or trademarks to market your software application product; (iii) include a valid copyright notice on your software application product; (iv) indemnify, hold harmless, and defend Microsoft from and against any claims or lawsuits, including attorney's fees, that arise or result from the use or distribution of your software application product; and (v) not permit further distribution of the REDISTRIBUTABLES by your end user. Contact Microsoft for the applicable royalties due and other licensing terms for all other uses and/or distribution of the REDISTRIBUTABLES.

2. **DESCRIPTION OF OTHER RIGHTS AND LIMITATIONS.**
   - **Limitations on Reverse Engineering, Decompilation, and Disassembly.** You may not reverse engineer, decompile, or disassemble the SOFTWARE PRODUCT, except and only to the extent that such activity is expressly permitted by applicable law notwithstanding this limitation.
   - **Separation of Components.** The SOFTWARE PRODUCT is licensed as a single product. Its component parts may not be separated for use on more than one computer.
   - **Rental.** You may not rent, lease, or lend the SOFTWARE PRODUCT.

- **Support Services.** Microsoft may, but is not obligated to, provide you with support services related to the SOFTWARE PRODUCT ("Support Services"). Use of Support Services is governed by the Microsoft policies and programs described in the user manual, in "online" documentation, and/or in other Microsoft-provided materials. Any supplemental software code provided to you as part of the Support Services shall be considered part of the SOFTWARE PRODUCT and subject to the terms and conditions of this EULA. With respect to technical information you provide to Microsoft as part of the Support Services, Microsoft may use such information for its business purposes, including for product support and development. Microsoft will not utilize such technical information in a form that personally identifies you.
- **Software Transfer.** You may permanently transfer all of your rights under this EULA, provided you retain no copies, you transfer all of the SOFTWARE PRODUCT (including all component parts, the media and printed materials, any upgrades, this EULA, and, if applicable, the Certificate of Authenticity), **and** the recipient agrees to the terms of this EULA.
- **Termination.** Without prejudice to any other rights, Microsoft may terminate this EULA if you fail to comply with the terms and conditions of this EULA. In such event, you must destroy all copies of the SOFTWARE PRODUCT and all of its component parts.

3. **COPYRIGHT.** All title and copyrights in and to the SOFTWARE PRODUCT (including but not limited to any images, photographs, animations, video, audio, music, text, SAMPLE CODE, REDISTRIBUTABLES, and "applets" incorporated into the SOFTWARE PRODUCT) and any copies of the SOFTWARE PRODUCT are owned by Microsoft or its suppliers. The SOFTWARE PRODUCT is protected by copyright laws and international treaty provisions. Therefore, you must treat the SOFTWARE PRODUCT like any other copyrighted material **except** that you may install the SOFTWARE PRODUCT on a single computer provided you keep the original solely for backup or archival purposes. You may not copy the printed materials accompanying the SOFTWARE PRODUCT.

4. **U.S. GOVERNMENT RESTRICTED RIGHTS.** The SOFTWARE PRODUCT and documentation are provided with RESTRICTED RIGHTS. Use, duplication, or disclosure by the Government is subject to restrictions as set forth in subparagraph (c)(1)(ii) of the Rights in Technical Data and Computer Software clause at DFARS 252.227-7013 or subparagraphs (c)(1) and (2) of the Commercial Computer Software—Restricted Rights at 48 CFR 52.227-19, as applicable. Manufacturer is Microsoft Corporation/One Microsoft Way/Redmond, WA 98052-6399.

5. **EXPORT RESTRICTIONS.** You agree that you will not export or re-export the SOFTWARE PRODUCT, any part thereof, or any process or service that is the direct product of the SOFTWARE PRODUCT (the foregoing collectively referred to as the "Restricted Components"), to any country, person, entity, or end user subject to U.S. export restrictions. You specifically agree not to export or re-export any of the Restricted Components (i) to any country to which the U.S. has embargoed or restricted the export of goods or services, which currently include, but are not necessarily limited to, Cuba, Iran, Iraq, Libya, North Korea, Sudan, and Syria, or to any national of any such country, wherever located, who intends to transmit or transport the Restricted Components back to such country; (ii) to any end user who you know or have reason to know will utilize the Restricted Components in the design, development, or production of nuclear, chemical, or biological weapons; or (iii) to any end user who has been prohibited from participating in U.S. export transactions by any federal agency of the U.S. government. You warrant and represent that neither the BXA nor any other U.S. federal agency has suspended, revoked, or denied your export privileges.

DISCLAIMER OF WARRANTY

NO WARRANTIES OR CONDITIONS. MICROSOFT EXPRESSLY DISCLAIMS ANY WARRANTY OR CONDITION FOR THE SOFTWARE PRODUCT. THE SOFTWARE PRODUCT AND ANY RELATED DOCUMENTATION ARE PROVIDED "AS IS" WITHOUT WARRANTY OR CONDITION OF ANY KIND, EITHER EXPRESS OR IMPLIED, INCLUDING, WITHOUT LIMITATION, THE IMPLIED WARRANTIES OF MERCHANTABILITY, FITNESS FOR A PARTICULAR PURPOSE, OR NONINFRINGEMENT. THE ENTIRE RISK ARISING OUT OF USE OR PERFORMANCE OF THE SOFTWARE PRODUCT REMAINS WITH YOU.

LIMITATION OF LIABILITY. TO THE MAXIMUM EXTENT PERMITTED BY APPLICABLE LAW, IN NO EVENT SHALL MICROSOFT OR ITS SUPPLIERS BE LIABLE FOR ANY SPECIAL, INCIDENTAL, INDIRECT, OR CONSEQUENTIAL DAMAGES WHATSOEVER (INCLUDING, WITHOUT LIMITATION, DAMAGES FOR LOSS OF BUSINESS PROFITS, BUSINESS INTERRUPTION, LOSS OF BUSINESS INFORMATION, OR ANY OTHER PECUNIARY LOSS) ARISING OUT OF THE USE OF OR INABILITY TO USE THE SOFTWARE PRODUCT OR THE PROVISION OF OR FAILURE TO PROVIDE SUPPORT SERVICES, EVEN IF MICROSOFT HAS BEEN ADVISED OF THE POSSIBILITY OF SUCH DAMAGES. IN ANY CASE, MICROSOFT'S ENTIRE LIABILITY UNDER ANY PROVISION OF THIS EULA SHALL BE LIMITED TO THE GREATER OF THE AMOUNT ACTUALLY PAID BY YOU FOR THE SOFTWARE PRODUCT OR US$5.00; PROVIDED, HOWEVER, IF YOU HAVE ENTERED INTO A MICROSOFT SUPPORT SERVICES AGREEMENT, MICROSOFT'S ENTIRE LIABILITY REGARDING SUPPORT SERVICES SHALL BE GOVERNED BY THE TERMS OF THAT AGREEMENT. BECAUSE SOME STATES AND JURISDICTIONS DO NOT ALLOW THE EXCLUSION OR LIMITATION OF LIABILITY, THE ABOVE LIMITATION MAY NOT APPLY TO YOU.

MISCELLANEOUS

This EULA is governed by the laws of the State of Washington USA, except and only to the extent that applicable law mandates governing law of a different jurisdiction.

Should you have any questions concerning this EULA, or if you desire to contact Microsoft for any reason, please contact the Microsoft subsidiary serving your country, or write: Microsoft Sales Information Center/One Microsoft Way/Redmond, WA 98052-6399.

PN 097-0002296